Entrepreneurship

In memory of
John Williamson (Jack) Legge 1917–1996
George Hindle 1917–1994

John Legge
Swinburne University of Technology

Kevin Hindle
Swinburne University of Technology

Entrepreneurship

How Innovators Create the Future

Department of
INDUSTRY,
SCIENCE
&
TOURISM

Supported by
The Commonwealth
Department of Industry,
Science and Tourism

First published 1997 by
MACMILLAN EDUCATION AUSTRALIA PTY LTD
107 Moray Street, South Melbourne 3205

Associated companies and representatives
throughout the world

National Library of Australia
cataloguing in publication data

Legge, John, 1942–
    Entrepreneurship : how innovators create the future

    Bibliography.
    Includes index.
    ISBN 0 7329 3940 2.
    ISBN 0 7329 3943 7 (pbk.).
    ISBN 0 7329 4071 0 (workbook).
    ISBN 0 7329 4072 9 (set).

    1. Marketing. 2. Entrepreneurship — Australia. I. Hindle,
    Kevin. II. Title.

658.4210994

Typeset in Adobe Garamond, Britannic and Gill Sans by
EXPO Holdings, Malaysia

Printed in Hong Kong

Edited by Elizabeth Watson
Designed by Dimitrios Frangoulis
Cover design by Jan Schmoeger
Illustrations on pages 31, 65, 129, 322, 413 by Todd Davidson

Foreword

Creating the future is an issue of fundamental importance to all Australians. The publication of this text, with its emphasis on two crucial aspects of business development — entrepreneurship and innovation — represents a significant development for Australia's future business community. I am proud that the Commonwealth government has been able to support the production of *Entrepreneurship* and I congratulate all those involved in the project for their foresight and dedication.

Peter McGauran
Minister for Science and Technology

Contents

Introduction

We wrote this book to provide practical guidance to people setting out to create a new enterprise or to initiate a new activity within an established one. For that reason our advice is, as far as we can make it, practical and relevant to anyone seeking to commercialise an innovation. We use a very general definition of innovation, including in the term every action by a commercial enterprise which creates a sustained change in market and/or social relationships. We explicitly include *pro bono* commercial enterprises with for-profit ones, and new initiatives from within established enterprises with the formation of new ventures in our definition.

We have given this edition of the book an Australian focus in the examples, and where we have discussed legal and accounting principles we have based our explanation, in general, on Australian law and practice. This does not make this a book about kangaroo entrepreneurship: the principles we set out are applicable in every market economy, and we have benchmarked our work against the best American texts on our subject. A substantial amount of the material in this book introduces the results of research that has not been published previously in a book on management or entrepreneurship. Users of this book are not being fobbed off with hand-me-down theories or a simplified version of some 'real' thing.

The book is not intended to be used purely or only as a practising entrepreneur's handbook, worthy and useful as the production of such a book would have been. Because we have taken a deliberately broad aim, covering all aspects of corporate and individual entrepreneurship, we have based our presentation on well-founded theoretical principles. Both of us have had extensive practical experience of entrepreneurship and management, and in recent years we have added the experience of researching and teaching in these areas. We have set out to write a book that can serve as a supplementary text in most post-secondary management and business programs, as the market and financial evaluation techniques that we introduce are likely to be widely applicable.

We also expect our book may be used as a prescribed text in entrepreneurship programs, since the sequence of topics is equally suited to the entrepreneur preparing a plan and to a post-secondary class of students learning, and hopefully practising, entrepreneurial plan preparation. We would be disappointed if our book's only readers were people, whether students or practitioners, with an immediate practical interest in enterprise formation. Change is the most certain thing about the real world, and very few people can put off dealing with it indefinitely. Entrepreneurship skills are change management skills, and everyone will need them at some time or other.

This book may be used as a starting point by people commencing academic research into entrepreneurship, and we think that we have the signposts in the right place and pointing in the right direction. The authors whose work we have drawn on should, for research purposes, be consulted through their original publications; researchers should treat this book as an introduction and a bibliography but not as a primary source.

The parts

We have produced this book in four parts. The first part is *about* entrepreneurship and innovation rather than how to 'do' it. We had two main reasons in putting this material into our book. First, it is the foundation for our recommendations about planning and executing a new enterprise later in the book. Starting a new enterprise is not a mechanical act, and the reader who knows why we say something will know when to ignore or modify our advice. The second is that we hope that our readers are very successful in their business enterprises and become people of influence in the community. We want them to preserve the path that they travelled on, to understand the broader social and economic factors that enabled their enterprise to be successful, and to work to preserve a society in which entrepreneurship and innovation flourish.

The second part of our book deals with the preliminaries to entrepreneurship: in Chapter 5 we discuss how to value an idea and screen it for basic financial feasibility; in Chapter 6 we discuss how a new idea or concept may be legally protected against immediate imitation; in Chapter 7 we discuss how an enterprise can be designed to exploit an idea, while in Chapter 8 we explain how to produce a planning model with which to establish the marketing and financial feasibility of the enterprise conceived in Chapter 7. This part of the book can be used as a four-stage sieve, a process which an individual can use to eliminate impossible projects before the major effort of preparing an entrepreneurial business plan commences or, still worse, an enterprise with an impossible objective is actually launched.

The third part of our book concerns the entrepreneurial business plan. The business plan has a number of uses; one of the most obvious is that it helps entrepreneurs identify serious flaws in otherwise viable projects and eliminate them while the enterprise is still on paper. The plan is also a simulation tool: different scenarios can be tested, and a chosen scenario refined, in an environment when mistakes can be deleted and history restarted. A sound plan is vital for entrepreneurs who need to raise finance, whether equity or debt, from anybody but devoted relatives. The plan tells prospective investors about the project, but also about the entrepreneurial team: who they are, what they have done before, how they will guard their investors' interests. The plan sets out objectives, so that the entrepreneurial team and their investors agree what constitutes success and what the plan's scope is: even the most successful plans eventually become history.

An entrepreneurial business plan neither describes nor creates *the* future. The plan describes a *possible* future, and sets out some of the steps towards it; it also describes certain milestones or targets that the enterprise will aim for. The plan will be based on certain assumptions, most of which will prove more or less false in the event. A major part of the planning process is the identification of the critical assumptions and setting up contingency actions to take when reality asserts itself. Not all unexpected events are bad: the market may like the product more than forecast and other unexpected opportunities may appear. Hasty action can turn success into disaster: scaling up a business too quickly can create a cash flow crisis, while chasing a new opportunity may lead to the main business failing from lack of attention. A properly maintained plan lets the entrepreneur, and successor managers of an enterprise, test the impact of a plan variation and take preventative action before a crisis occurs. The aphorism that 'banks won't lend money to anyone who actually needs it' contains a solid kernel of truth. Successful entrepreneurs and managers approach their bankers and other financiers *before* they need the money while they are in a position to explain what they propose to do with it, not simply to describe the disaster that will occur if they don't get it.

The final part of this book describes the financing and launching of an enterprise. Once the launch is complete the business will diverge further and further from any single model of business development, but more importantly from our view, the enterprise has been created and can now be managed. We set out to write a book on entrepreneurship because we did not feel that any existing book did full justice to the topic, especially from an Australian viewpoint. There are many books on management available, including some excellent Australian ones, and this book is not another 'management' book; it complements rather than replaces the existing management guides and texts.

Entrepreneurs and managers

In the simplest terms, entrepreneurs create enterprises and managers run them. Like all generalisations, this one needs handling with care. Entrepreneurs do not spend every waking minute in a whirlwind of creation, while managers have to step outside the company procedures manual sometimes. Entrepreneurship and management should be seen as the end points on a continuum, with all real people and businesses somewhere in between. It is often more useful to concentrate on the task rather than the person.

Management only makes sense as an activity when there are some things to manage and a purpose in managing them. The managed things are resources: people, assets, capital; and success consists of achieving a set of measurable objectives. Management is needed as a purposive activity to limit the effect of unexpected events, to preserve the *status quo* against forces that may tend to disrupt it. A member of staff is sick: reassigning duties so as to keep the operation functioning is a management task. An item of equipment breaks down: a management decision is required to repair or replace the unit. The bank restricts the overdraft: the debtors and other assets must be managed to release cash. Whether the enterprise is entrepreneurial or stable, for-profit or *pro bono*, government, voluntary or private sector, management is an ongoing and vital task.

Entrepreneurship is the creative application of change. The entrepreneur's objective cannot usually be achieved with the resources currently controlled by him or her; sometimes the resources don't exist at all and must be created as part of the process of creating a new enterprise. The act of entrepreneurship leads to an *innovation*, a new product, process or organisation that changes the balance of market or social forces. The most important resource in a market economy is the favourable regard of a substantial population of satisfied customers, users or clients. The favourable regard of these customers, users and clients finds an outlet in recommending the new product or organisation to others; and it is this virtuous circle of satisfaction and recommendation that enables a new commercial enterprise to offer an adequate return to the entrepreneur and the other investors in the enterprise. A similar virtuous circle enables a new social organisation to reach and involve far more people than its initiator could ever speak to personally.

Continuous improvement, often referred to by the Japanese term for it, *kaizen*, lies between conventional management and entrepreneurship. Each step of continuous improvement is a change, and therefore something more than routine management is involved, but the individual steps are usually too small to change the balance of social and market forces, and therefore cannot be properly called innovations. Japan's rise to dominance in the motor car and consumer electronics industries is the result of a series of organisational innovations that made *kaizen* possible.

Creation and creativity

The two halves of the brain, in healthy humans, tend to specialise in different types of thinking. On one side, usually their left, people calculate and analyse. On the other, people look for patterns, first in what they see and in images that they remember, but also in information that they have collected verbally and from reading. In real life people need to use both facilities: a person goes shopping, and chooses an item of clothing that fits his or her self-image, very much a 'right brain' activity, and then pays for it and counts the change accurately and analytically.

On the other side of the transaction may be an entrepreneur, who has chosen the fabric and the design in a flash of inspiration, and has then negotiated with fabric suppliers and manufacturers down to the last cent and the last stitch. One very important group of lines in a business plan is called 'marketing expenditure', and nothing is more certain than that a product which no one sells and no one promotes will fail in the market. There are even fairly general rules to estimate how much a business should spend on sales and marketing activities, given a certain set of resources. There is nothing creative and right brain about booking and paying for advertising space or paying a sales commission or a distributor discount. At the end of the day there is very little numerical analysis involved in designing a successful advertisement or recruiting an effective salesperson.

The entrepreneur has a concept which starts as a piece of imagination, but he or she, following the precepts set out in this book, will produce a plan, a plan made out of words and numbers. The written part of a plan may be stored and processed on a computer; the numerical part almost certainly will. It is important to use the computer as a tool, and not let it become a substitute for the entrepreneur's creative imagination.

Computers, with very few specialised and uncommon exceptions, are 'left brain' carried to extremes. An inexpensive personal computer can complete arithmetical operations millions of times faster than a human can. Such a computer, provided with modern software and programmed with a modicum of skill, can present its analytical, coldly logical results in a flash of brilliant colour, sound and movement, bypassing a human's analytical capability and going straight for the emotions. This false intuition can be extremely convincing, as the reaction of children (and many adults) to computer games shows, and some people come to give more credence to the synthetic reality of the computer screen than to the reality of the living, breathing world.

A young man whose imagination comes from a computer is called a nerd, but there are lots of nerds in well-cut suits presenting plans and strategies to businesses and corporations. In Chapter 8 we tell the reader to build a model. At best, the model will be an approximation to one of many possible real world outcomes. Do not become a nerd! Sooner or later the real world will make every model irrelevant. A given model is a tool and an aid, a way to produce a plan and develop pro-forma financial outcomes. It is not a substitute for the real world, and changing model parameters does not change the real world. The best models are continually updated to reflect actual experience; the worst are those that entice their users to view reality through a distorting lens.

Acknowledgements

We gratefully acknowledge the help and encouragement that we have received from our families, our friends and our colleagues while completing this book. This covers so many people that we have certainly failed to acknowledge some of our helpers by name, and for this we apologise most deeply. Our colleagues at Swinburne have offered us advice and encouragement, and many of them have read and commented on parts of the book. In this regards we thank John Batros, Barbara Cargill, Barbara Evans, Murray Gillin, Bruce Johnson, Adam Koch, Bruce McIntosh, Jim Murray, Peter Pascoe and Robert Wenban. We owe especial thanks to our collaborators, David Ch'ng, Helen Evans and Alfred Tatlock for their specialist contributions.

Many distinguished academics from other institutions provided us with encouragement and advice: we especially thank Frank Bass, Avinash Dixit, Dan Jennings, Robert Pindyck, and Peter Singer. Australian government agencies have offered us help and advice: we particularly thank Hank Spier of the Australian Competition and Consumer Commission and Judy Cunningham of the Department of Industry, Science and Tourism. Bob Beaumont of VECCI gave us valuable information about their Business Finance Support Program. Peter Roberts of the *Australian Financial Review* has been generous with his encouragement and his material.

We and our readers owe particular thanks to the organisations which provided material for our major cases including Helen Nankivell of Nexus Pty Ltd; George Littlewood, Neil Prideaux, Ian Head and Daphne Morros of the RTZ-CRA Group; and Ron Conry, Roger Richmond-Smith, Susan Mastrantonio and Peter Clyne of Multistack International Ltd. We also received help and advice from members of the staff of Ansett Airlines Ltd, ANCA Pty Ltd and many others.

The general editing of the book was carried out by John Legge. The entire text was checked for coherence by Robyn Legge before the typescript was passed to the publisher. We thank Peter Debus, Elizabeth Gibson and our editor Elizabeth Watson of Macmillan for their efforts in making this book available and presentable.

We acknowledge the generous grant we received from the Department of Industry, Science and Tourism, formerly the Department of Industry, Science and Technology, under the Innovation Awareness Scheme. The book could not have been produced without this support.

John M. Legge
Melbourne
August 1995

Registered trade marks

The following registered trade names are mentioned in the text and are the property of their respective owners:

Apple Macintosh™
Biro™
Cellophane™
Energiser™
HIsmelt®
IBM OS/2®
Microsoft Windows®
Microsoft Windows–95®

Microsoft Word®
Post-it® Notes
Ramset™
Sony Walkman™
Sun Microsystems Solaris®
Thermos™
Zincalume®

Part I

Chapter 1

Entrepreneurs in society

Entrepreneurs

Human society is made up of a large number of unique individuals. One of the many ways in which each person differs from those around them is in their ambitions, their hopes and dreams. Some people wish to become outstanding athletes, or dancers, or scientists, or politicians, or writers, or musicians. These ambitions need not be engraved in stone; as people go through their life their circumstances, and their ambitions, change. Some people, at some stages in their life, feel a powerful urge to build an organisation that will do something, or produce something, that has not been done before. When they put these urges into practice they become entrepreneurs.[1]

Who are they?

The word 'entrepreneur' was first applied to Frenchmen who 'entered and took charge' of royal contracts. Typically, the king would grant some nobleman the right to build a road or a bridge and to collect the tolls, in return for a suitable donation to the royal treasury or in return for some other favour. The nobleman would appoint an entrepreneur, who would arrange finance, supervise construction and manage the completed facility. The entrepreneur guaranteed the nobleman a fixed annual payment and kept anything that was left over. Noblemen generally wished to earn a steady income without getting their hands dirty. They could do this by engaging an entrepreneur. The entrepreneur accepted the various risks in return for the chance of earning a profit. Since these early entrepreneurs tended to be smart and closely involved with the project, and the noblemen who nominally owned the projects were usually neither, the profits were often very substantial.

The fundamental principle of entrepreneurship has not changed: entrepreneurs earn their reward by managing projects and accepting and managing the associated risk. This does not make an entrepreneur a gambler: far from it. The best entrepreneurs are not risk-takers as much as risk-managers. Entrepreneurs choose to 'enter and take charge' of projects where they have some special advantage that means the risks, as long as the entrepreneur is managing them, are less than they would be if the government, or the financier, or the customer, were doing it themselves.

Figure 1.1 shows the entrepreneur 'in between' the major stakeholders in an enterprise. There is the government, in our enlightened days representing the community rather than the king. The government sets the limits on what is acceptable, while still requiring a more or less substantial donation to the treasury in return for the needed approvals and permits. There are the financiers, because without money an entrepreneur can run no more than a cottage industry. Last, and far from least, are the customers for the new enterprise, because without customers there can be no profit.[2]

This brings us to the kernel of ethical entrepreneurship:

▲ the entrepreneur *takes charge* of some project that will deliver valuable benefits and brings it to completion

▲ the entrepreneur *manages risk*, reducing the risk that the other stakeholders bear

▲ the entrepreneur has some *advantage* that means that the personal risk that the entrepreneur carries is less than the risk any other stakeholder would have had to accept to achieve the same result.

The paper entrepreneurs

The word 'entrepreneur', literally translated, means 'someone who comes between and takes hold'. Not everyone who takes hold of a relationship between

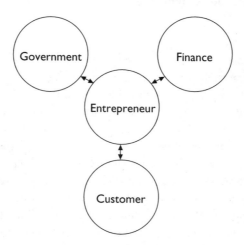

Figure 1.1 The entrepreneur — always in the middle

others does so ethically. Some people take charge of a project and deliver valuable benefits, but they take the benefits for themselves and leave the other stakeholders the dregs. They manage risk, but they put all of it onto their unsuspecting investors and employees and carry none themselves. Their advantage is not some special competence at managing an enterprise, but in concealing the true nature of their activities until it is too late for the investors to get their money back.

All paper entrepreneurs use one of two basic tricks: they sell assets and treat the returns as trading income; or they borrow money and then raise new loans to pay interest on the earlier ones. Some of them do both. Their two main skills are, first, the ability to hide what they have been doing, and second, to get favourable press coverage. In the 1980s in Australia the leading swindlers called themselves 'entrepreneurs' in the expectation that this good word would stop people looking too closely at where their large published profits were actually coming from.

Entrepreneurship

1   It is initiated by an act of human volition.

2   It occurs at the level of the individual firm.

3   It involves a change of state.

4   It involves a discontinuity.

5   It is a holistic process.

6   It is a dynamic process.

7   It is unique.

8   It involves numerous antecedent variables.

9   Its outcomes are extremely sensitive to the initial conditions of these variables.

Taken together, these characteristics create a set of parameters and criteria that will have to be met by any 'ideal' model of entrepreneurship.

Bygrave and Hofer 1991: 17

Entrepreneurs and 'intrapreneurs'

The word 'entrepreneur' reflects its history, and is usually applied to the creator of a new enterprise. Many major innovations have been introduced by new companies founded by entrepreneurs. Many others, however, have been launched by large companies. About 60 per cent of private sector output in Australia comes from large companies, and another 20 per cent comes from medium sized ones. These companies are not immune from the changes taking place in the economy: their products get less profitable and their processes less competitive as they get older. The process of corporate rejuvenation, when it occurs, is led by 'product champions' or 'intrapreneurs'.

Wealth and greed

Some entrepreneurs have become extremely wealthy, and no doubt more will become so in the future. Some people, entrepreneurs and others, have demonstrated extraordinary greed. Active entrepreneurship is not compatible with uncontrolled greed, but an entrepreneur who has created, or inherited, a major wealth-generating enterprise will have a disposable income considerably greater than is needed to sustain an extremely comfortable lifestyle. People who are driven from the start by greed seldom become ethical entrepreneurs, or entrepreneurs at all under our definition; fraud, theft and deception are far quicker routes to wealth, while outright banditry and extortion provide a quicker route still in those countries in which they are tolerated.

In most countries there are many people on the edge of society or altogether outside it, and the redistribution of wealth from those who are conspicuously dissipating it to those who have none at all is often just. Practically every civilised society confiscates the proceeds of crime: why, might it be asked, should entrepreneurially gained wealth be treated differently? There are two linked reasons: one is that the ethical entrepreneur creates new wealth, most of which passes to the new enterprise's workers, suppliers and customers, and a relatively small fraction stays with the entrepreneur, so that the entrepreneur's wealth is not gained by unjustly depriving others; the second is that prospective entrepreneurs might be discouraged by the prospect of confiscation and public obloquy, and so society would, over all, be worse off.

The former Soviet Union provides a dreadful example of what can happen to a society in which entrepreneurship is outlawed; ethical entrepreneurs are useful members of society. The conditions in which ethical entrepreneurship could develop and make such a contribution are, however, very new when the whole of human history is considered.

The paradox of progress

Many people would like to enjoy a better lifestyle than they currently do, or to be able to ensure that their children enjoy a better lifestyle than they have enjoyed, or endured. Most of the rest of us hope that things will not get worse and our children will be no worse off than we have been. We work and study, and we encourage our children to get a good education and learn social and other skills, in the hope that we and they will secure a better future.

Common experience would seem to damn such hopes: people get old, structures decay, machines wear out. The Second Law of Thermodynamics declares that the ability of a system to deliver useful work declines inexorably. Quite recent human history seems to bear this out: from the time of the Black Death in the 1300s until 1830 European living standards were steadily declining: there were prosperous periods, but they were never as good as the previous prosperous period; and there were famines, each worse than the last. When old people talked about the 'good old days' they were generally believed. Ancient Greek and Roman literature were studied intensively, and the ancient writers concurred in declaring that the Golden Age lay in the distant past. The Classical economists, such as Smith and Malthus, considered that the natural state of the mass of humanity was survival at the edge of starvation.[3]

From 1830 to the present time experience has confounded the pessimists. People still grow old and die, buildings still decay and machines still wear out, but the economy as a whole, and the lifestyle of the mass of the population in western Europe, North America and Australia has improved enormously, and it goes on improving. Some of the east Asian economies have achieved even more rapid progress: Singapore, for example, took only thirty years to change from being a coolie port to become one of the world's most affluent cities. Obviously technology has played a role, but technology on its own doesn't do anything. Before technology can improve the quality of human life it has to be put into service: people must get involved. When some people come together to put some technology to use in order to produce goods and services, and then sell the resulting products profitably, they have created an enterprise.

For reasons that will be discussed later in this book, it can be very difficult to start a new enterprise and keep it going and growing. Three things that can make it easier are:

▲ some new enterprises offer goods and services that are new: either different from, or superior to, the products that had previously been available to their likely customers

▲ some new enterprises use new methods of production or marketing, or draw on new sources of materials or components, that enable them to offer their goods and services much more cheaply or more conveniently than existing suppliers can

▲ some new enterprises are able to establish a new industry structure or exploit a new style of regulatory environment more effectively and/or more rapidly than their rivals.

All these activities involve the introduction of *innovations*, and the people who lead the teams and organisations that introduce these innovations are entrepreneurs. In many but not all cases the successful introduction of an innovation adds to the total sum of wealth in the economy. Economists have analysed the available data in order to determine how the period from 1830 to the present is different from the period from the start of recorded time to 1830. They have concluded that innovations of various kinds are four times more significant than the next most important factor.[4] Entrepreneurs, or some of them, are a major force for economic growth.

Entrepreneurs act in, and are part of, society. They all have customers, most of them have suppliers and employees, and many of them have investors and financiers. If the entrepreneur is to be successful the other party to each of these relationships must believe that 'there is something in it for them'. The fact that another person is better off by agreeing to a transaction than by refusing it does not mean that they are *absolutely* better off: the peasant who surrenders his pig at bayonet point to foragers from an invading army does so in the hope that they won't take his wife and daughter as well, but he would have rather kept the pig *and* his family.

The unique fact about the form of capitalist society that developed in Europe and North America in the years after 1830 is that many, but by no means all, enterprises succeeded by making *all* their stakeholders *absolutely* better off. When a railway took a peasant's pig to the Paris markets the peasant paid for the transport, but the higher price in Paris more than compensated for the freight charge. At the same time, householders in Paris paid less for a better quality of pork once the railway replaced the ox-cart and the drover. Peasant families spent the extra money on curtains for the windows of their cottages, shirts for the men and petticoats for the women. The price of the cloth paid the wages of workers and profits for the owners in the cotton industry, and they could now afford the occasional sausage or other meat dish.

Within a few years the higher margins generated from low-cost access to the growing markets of the towns earned the peasantry enough discretionary income to afford sties for their pigs and to send their children to village schools. The virtuous circle turned and turned: in less than twenty years from 1830 living standards for workers, smallholders and agricultural labourers in Europe and North America had passed the last peak of four hundred and fifty years earlier, and they *doubled* every twenty-five years or so from then until the present day.[5]

To use the jargon of game theory,[6] the foragers who took the peasant's pig were playing a 'win-lose' or 'zero-sum' game: their gain was the peasant's loss. The entrepreneurs who created the nineteenth century railway systems had discovered a 'win-win' scenario, a 'positive-sum' game: every participant was better off after the game than they had been before it. Even the drovers and carters who were no longer needed to take pigs to market found less arduous and better paid jobs in the cities.

Practically all positive-sum games share a common characteristic — that of restraint. In every relationship one party or the other has superiority from time to time, and is in a position to use or threaten force in order to increase their share of the rewards from the current transaction. Only when these opportunities are routinely passed over can a win-win situation develop. When Arthur Wellesley (later first Duke of Wellington) led his army into Spain in 1809 during the Peninsular War he ordered his foragers to pay, at market prices, and in gold, for everything that they requisitioned. The astounded peasants, whose expectations had been set by the behaviour of their own nobility as much as the pillaging of the French, became Wellesley's most loyal allies, passing him intelligence, bringing food to his armies, and ambushing French couriers and isolated units.

Modern businesses can pillage just as effectively as the French did in Spain, despoiling the environment, exploiting their workers, gouging their customers, and cheating their creditors. In every case the business appears to be better off when only the immediate results are considered: the money not spent on pollution control, fair wages and settling accounts, and the money gained by overcharging customers, is reported in the accounts as extra profit. This profit is not a reward for creating value: it is a trophy, value shifted from the environment, the workers, the customers and the lenders to the shareholders. Some corporate takeovers, including many that took place in the 1980s, take the form of raids. A raider pillages the value contributed to an enterprise by its employees, customers, suppliers and creditors. The typical result of such takeovers is the destruction of some value and the shifting of more. Any manager who declares that 'the only purpose of a business is to make a profit for the shareholders' is being short-sighted and potentially anti-social; as we explain in Chapter 11, he may not even be interpreting the law correctly. The medium-term consequences of such behaviour are those the French experienced in Spain: contempt, hatred, defeat and, finally, destruction.

There is a deep paradox here: firms that do not spoliate, exploit, gouge, pillage and cheat make lower profits in the short term, and may even be forced out of business by their less scrupulous competitors, but in the medium and longer term those that survive grow faster and generate much greater wealth for their shareholders. Only

Firms that do not spoliate, exploit, gouge, pillage and cheat grow faster and generate much greater wealth for their shareholders

those companies who look for win-win solutions to their problems and restrain the urge for short term profit in order to create long-term value contribute to economic growth and the general well-being. Societies whose citizens wish to enjoy the benefits of economic growth must make laws and form community attitudes that effectively limit the scope for exploitation and gouging.

Firms are one example of the way people associate to pursue certain ends, but by no means the only one. Society is built from a complex web of relationships: family, friends, colleagues, fellow supporters of sporting teams and political parties, fellow parents of children at a school, old boys, old girls, alumni, members of clubs and societies, tenants, landlords, customers, suppliers, clients, workers, supervisors, bosses ... the list goes on. These relationships have their histories and traditions, their obligations and expectations, their conflicts and their periods of harmony.

Societal relationships and exchanges involve a mixture of consent and authority. In some relationships one party commands and the other obeys: if the government wants to use some private land to build a road, there may be an offer to buy and the appearance of negotiation, but at the end of the day the government will own the land and the former occupier will have to be satisfied with the compensation offered. The government's power to tax is exercised even more directly: if a taxpayer does not pay on demand the government may send in bailiffs or the police.

Commercial relationships, both within and between firms, can rely on power or be built on consensus. A firm that uses legal, or other, tricks to prevent its customers buying alternative products may be doing the right thing by its customers and society generally, but since there is nothing to compare such a firm's performance against, no one can find out. A firm that offers a better product, while taking no steps to prevent the suppliers of older products from trading in the same market, is almost certain to be creating net social, as well as personal, value. Firms and industries that lobby or otherwise persuade governments to give them special privileges are seeking to use government power to restrict consumer choice. Such firms may be value creators or they may simply be value shifters. Every firm or industry that is given a privileged position by law is a potential, though not necessarily an actual, value shifter.

Value-shifting is often socially desirable. Society as a whole is taxed to support an education system which, among other things, ensures that entrepreneurs can find literate employees and customers. Universal education cannot be provided without taking resources from those who have earned or in other ways acquired them and spending them for the benefit of children. The major single factor contributing to increased life expectancy in the developed world is the general supply of clean water with a complementary sewage system to dispose of the waste. Typhoid and cholera do not recognise distinctions of wealth or status, and the wealthy could not gain safety from these diseases without agreeing to be taxed so as to protect the poor as well.

Some forms of business are closely regulated, when society believes that the disadvantages of open competition would outweigh the advantages. Many pharmaceutical preparations are only available on prescription: people who want them must pay a doctor as well as a chemist. The many dangers that can arise from the uncontrolled use of such powerful chemicals justifies limiting the privilege of prescribing them to appropriately qualified and registered doctors. Sometimes competition is impractical simply because of the minimum scale of enterprise needed to handle any of the demand, for example suburban water supplies, can handle all of it. Sometimes competition is self-extinguishing, or at least self-limiting, because in the relevant industry large companies have decisive advantages over small ones, and it is impossible for new firms to get established. When industries are dominated by a few large firms, individual customers or suppliers have very little market power, and look to the government to pass laws and make regulations defending the small against the threat, real or imaginary, from the large.

Nearly every country has a government of some sort, and in Australia the legitimacy of each level of government is regularly tested by elections. Government action can have one of two effects: often both, in varying balance, will follow a single action. On the one hand, governments make laws and regulations that discourage, or even prohibit, exploitative and socially destructive behaviour by firms. When these laws and regulations are effective, they even up the balance of power between enterprises with a short term and a longer term focus. On the other hand the same governments may pass laws which have the effect of limiting or even eliminating consumer choice and creating an environment in which a few value-shifting, zero-sum enterprises may flourish at the expense of the community as a whole.

During the 1980s and early 1990s most governments in English-speaking countries aggressively deregulated their economies, arguing that the costs of regulation outweighed the benefits. The possible impact on economic growth was not, apparently, considered. Many laws and regulations had tended to encourage firms that took a long-term view and discourage those that considered only their immediate interests. Australian taxation law, for example, used to tax distributed profits at rates of up to 80 per cent, while allowing shareholders to enjoy the capital gains that followed long-term investment strategies based upon retained earnings tax-free. The taxation law was 'reformed' so as to treat short-term and long-term profits equally: it is not clear that Australia as a whole is any better off.

The economists whose arguments in support of deregulation persuaded the Australian government to level the taxation playing field made certain assumptions, one of which was that all transactions in a deregulated market are bargains between equals. True equality of power and authority is almost impossible: even when the two parties to a negotiation appear to be equally strong, there are almost certain to be factors giving one or the other a temporary advantage.[7] The philosopher Thomas Hobbes considered what life might be like if every interaction between people was governed by their relative strength. His conclusion was that life would be 'nasty, mean, brutish … and short' (Hobbes 1967). In real societies there are commonly accepted rules of behaviour which govern, or at least moderate, most interactions. These rules are each society's manners and morals.

Are commercial morals different?

Some people believe that morals are prescribed by divine authority while others believe that they have evolved with the development of human society. There is little difference in practice: an evolved morality would include rules that promoted a prosperous and harmonious society (because those societies that adopted less suitable rules would have declined and vanished), while a benevolent deity would have dictated rules that produced a prosperous and harmonious society naturally.

The philosopher Jane Jacobs observed that humans don't observe a single, universal morality, but that there are two quite distinct sets of moral precepts in common use in developed societies (Jacobs 1993). She refers to them as the 'guardian' and the 'commercial' syndromes.[8]

Guarding the territory

Humans must eat to live, but we also need shelter, access to water, and materials from which to make essential tools. People in modern developed nations expect a lot more than these basics, of course, except after a disaster, when such basic life-preserving facilities will usually be acceptable enough. The simplest human societies live much closer to the basic subsistence level than most readers of this book. Like practically all animal species, the most basic human societies support themselves within a well-defined territory, hunting here and gathering there. People who rely on a territory face two major hazards: they may be invaded and lose access to the most productive areas; and they may over-exploit their territory, killing all the game or burning all the timber.

The rules that emerged from hunter-gatherer societies are familiar to modern humans, and many people would claim that they are the only true morality. Since the survival of the tribe depends on the preservation of the tribe's territory, guarding the territory is the first duty of every able-bodied member. Jacobs suggests that our earliest sets of moral rules applied to the specifically male guardians of the tribal territory. Many human females are faintly amused by the antics of men in uniform, and while they may not like the consequences of conquest much, women adapt to it much more rapidly and successfully than men. Accounts of the end of the Second World War in Europe concur in relating how German women took the lead in first protecting their families, including their husbands and adult sons, from the occupying forces, and then in securing food and accommodation for them. General Eisenhower's stern anti-fraternisation orders had to be abandoned in a matter of days; the charm offensive launched by German womanhood at the GIs was more than a match for the General. Jacobs' 'guardian' rules, which are summarised below, come with more than a hint of testosterone.

The first rule of guardianship is 'shun trading' and be suspicious of strangers: trade requires you to give something away, and it might be more valuable than that which you receive in return. Trading encourages judgement of the relative value of the various options on offer, an approach that may not be consistent with defending an outpost to the death. 'Exert prowess' both by being a skilled hunter and a brave warrior; be skilled and active, and be seen to be skilled and active, in feeding the tribe and defending its borders. 'Be obedient and disciplined' because success in the hunt and in the battle depend on obedience and self-control. 'Adhere to tradition' because our forefathers knew more than we do and their rules must be observed if we are not to put our territory at risk. 'Respect hierarchy' both in deferring to your superiors and enforcing the obedience of your subordinates. 'Be loyal' and obey orders without question. 'Take vengeance' and punish any infraction of the rules with exemplary severity. 'Deceive for the sake of the task': trick strangers and trap prey before they do the same to you. 'Make rich use of leisure' because hunting and warfare are only sporadic activities and idleness leads to trouble. 'Be ostentatious' to impress and terrify your enemies and to assert your own status in the tribe. 'Dispense largesse'; not only charity to the deserving, but rich gifts to guests and dependents: wealth is for display, not for hoarding. 'Be exclusive' and only be intimate with equal status individuals from the same tribe, because any other behaviour will subvert the hierarchy upon which the security of the tribe depends. 'Show fortitude' and bear discomfort and pain without complaining, and 'be fatalistic' because thinking too much about outcomes is subversive of military and hunting discipline. Finally, 'treasure honour', defined as rigid adherence to the standards of guardian behaviour irrespective of the consequences.

Jacobs gives plenty of examples of well-documented historical societies where these guardian standards formed the basis of the moral code. Rules such as these formed the lifeblood of the English aristocracy well into the twentieth century. Lord Palmerston, British Foreign Secretary for sixteen years between 1830 and 1851, and Prime Minister from 1855 to 1865, dispensed largesse and practised ostentation so effectively that he was frequently short of cash, an embarrassment he resolved by not paying the tradespeople who supplied his various mansions. When his butcher, desperate for payment, forced his way into Palmerston's presence the noble lord put on a pair of gloves, wrote out a cheque, and while the butcher was still trying to make a graceful exit flung the pen, and the gloves, out of the window.[9]

Different guardian qualities were illustrated by the exchange between the Duke of Wellington and Lord Uxbridge at the battle of Waterloo, immediately after a cannon ball had narrowly missed the Duke and shattered Uxbridge's knee:

> 'By gad sir, I have lost my leg.'
> 'By gad sir, so you have.'

Uxbridge was then carried to the operating table, where he discussed dancing while the surgeon removed his leg (in the days before anaesthetics) and the Duke continued directing the battle from roughly the same place with the cannon balls still whizzing past and removing various members of his staff from time to time.

Jacobs traces the guardian syndrome back to Plato (circa 428–347 BC). Plato was strongly influenced by the practice of the Spartans. All the citizens of Sparta were brought up to be soldiers or soldiers' mothers, while the Spartans maintained an underclass of Helots to do all the productive work. The guardian moral syndrome can be found at work in ancient Rome: the destruction of the Roman Republic by the strife between Caesar, Pompey and Crassus was the result of an insane rivalry to be supreme in public honour, totally separated from any considerations of personal or family advantage, and ending in the violent deaths of all three men and, in due course, the utter destruction of their families. It is not simply a western phenomenon: it was fully developed in India before the British conquest (1763) and the British ruling caste in India adopted guardian behaviour to the point of parody. The same set of values can be found in feudal Japan (before the Meiji Restoration of 1867) with echoes persisting today.

Guardian moral values have less hold on Australia than in many other countries; the larrikin tradition, the survival value of mateship, the equation of authority with the worst type of aristocratic twit, and the relatively short national history have all weakened the general respect for hierarchies of any sort. Australians are likely to meet guardian morality at its most intense if they listen to a school football coach's three-quarter time address to a losing team.

Trading up

The starting point of Jacobs' analysis of the two moral syndromes is an example of trust in the financial system: anyone can walk into a bank, practically anywhere in the world, hand money to a perfect stranger, and expect with near-total confidence that the sum, less the agreed (and generally modest) charges, will be accurately and promptly remitted to an account in a completely different bank in a completely different part of the world. Jacobs calls this an example of the 'commercial syndrome' at work. Even in the most primitive societies trade enables mutual benefits to be realised. If one tribe's territory is rich in game, while another's is rich in edible plants, each tribe will be malnourished — unless they can agree to swap surplus meat for surplus vegetables. Even this simple transaction cannot proceed without breaking three or four of the guardian moral precepts.

Jacobs suggests that trade was originally 'women's business': since women were not expected to be hunters or warriors, they were not required to adhere so rigidly to the guardian code. In modern west Africa the 'market mammas' dominate commerce while their menfolk perform various antics that serve to disguise their unemployment when they are not demonstrating their prowess by joining coups against their government or provoking riots with the men of other tribes. Jacobs lists a set of moral principles which she refers to as the 'commercial syndrome'; these are described below.

First, 'shun force': commerce is impossible under threat, and when people meet to bargain they implicitly agree to come to a voluntary agreement or to none at all. As a corollary of shunning force, merchants attempt to 'come to voluntary agreements', since otherwise their attendance at a market becomes a waste of time and trouble. 'Be honest'; effective merchants are always looking past the current transaction to the future, and deceit in one transaction will create distrust in the negotiations for further ones. 'Collaborate easily with strangers and aliens' because these are the people with whom the most mutually advantageous bargains may be struck. Jacobs points out that the ancient Roman laws governing markets were known as the 'Law of Foreigners'. 'Compete' to expand your business; do not use force or deceit to damage your competitors even when the opportunity arises. Similarly, 'respect contracts' even when circumstances change and it might be advantageous to break one: the boot may one day be on the other foot. 'Use initiative and enterprise'; whatever the traditional way of doing something, or a traditional place or manner of trading, may have been, it is worth looking for a better one. 'Be open to inventiveness and novelty' wherever or whoever it comes from. 'Be efficient' and sparing of effort and resources. 'Promote comfort and convenience' at the expense of ostentation and self-indulgence. 'Dissent for the sake of the task'; don't blindly obey orders. 'Invest for productive purposes'; the purpose of wealth is to create more wealth, not to be frittered away. 'Be industrious' and don't waste time in unproductive activities. 'Be thrifty'; when there is no good reason to spend time or resources, don't spend them. 'Be optimistic'; difficulties can be overcome and adversity can be deflected, or at least moderated, by foresight and perseverance.

A man travelling to a far country called his own servants and delivered unto them his goods.

And unto one he gave five talents, to another two, and to another one; to every man according to his ability; and straightway took his journey.

Then he that had received the five talents went and traded with the same, and made another five talents.

And likewise he that had received two, he also gained another two.

But he that had received one went and digged in the earth, and hid his lord's money.

After a long time the lord of those servants cometh and reckoneth with them.

And so he that had received five talents came and brought another five talents, saying, Lord, thou deliverest unto me five talents: behold, I have gained beside them five talents more.

His lord said unto him, Well done, good and faithful servant: thou hast been faithful over a few things, I will make thee ruler over many things: enter thou into the joy of thy lord.

He that had received two talents came and said, Lord, thou deliverest to me two talents: behold, I have gained two other talents beside them.

His lord said unto him, Well done, good and faithful servant: thou hast been faithful over a few things, I will make thee ruler over many things: enter thou into the joy of thy lord.

Then he that had received the one talent came and said, Lord, I knew thee that thou art an hard man, reaping where thou hast not sown, and gathering where thou hast not strawed:

And I was afraid, and went and hid thy talent in the earth: lo, thou hast thine.

His lord answered and said unto him, Wicked and slothful servant, thou knewest that I reap where I sowed not, and gather where I have not strawed:

Thou oughtest to have put my money to the exchangers, and at my coming I should have received mine own with usury.

Take, therefore the talent from him and give it unto him which hath ten talents …

And cast ye the unprofitable servant into outer darkness: there shall be weeping and gnashing of teeth.

Matthew 25: 14–30

It doesn't take much thought to see some glaring contradictions between the guardian and the commercial codes of behaviour. When Lord Palmerston ignored his butcher's bill he was asserting their relative places in the social hierarchy. A few hundred years earlier in England, and persisting into the nineteenth century in Russia and the southern states of the United States, the butcher would have been a serf or slave obliged to provide meat for the nobleman's table in return for permission to live on the estate. The English butcher, adhering firmly to his more modern commercial morality, defied Palmerston's social and political eminence and insisted on his fulfilling his half of their contract.

The medieval Catholic church represented the guardian morality in stone and marble, while the Protestant reformation celebrated commercial virtues. The philosopher Weber[10] went so far as to ascribe capitalism to the 'Protestant work ethic', but modified his opinion when it was pointed out that the great trading cities such as Amsterdam, Geneva, Florence, Venice and London had been commercial long before the Protestant reformation, and the cities of northern Italy remained commercial, and Catholic, after it. The Catholic church itself adapted to the reality and value of commerce in a long process beginning with the Council of Trent (1545–63) and culminating in the Second Vatican Council, called by Pope John XXIII over the years 1962–65.

Chaos and conflict

Jacobs returns to Plato for the origin of the argument that guardian and commercial moralities must coexist while remaining clearly separate. In the very first instance merchants, shunning force and in any case too busy to undertake martial training, risk falling victim to robbers of various kinds. Until 1856, as far as most of the world is concerned, international law recognised the rights of states to issue 'letters of marque' to a private individual, who could then acquire a ship and operate as a legally sanctioned pirate. Many impoverished young gentlemen did so: preying on trade was honourable, while participating in it was not. One account of the foundation of the Royal Navy suggests that the merchants of London, unwilling to arm their own vessels but equally unwilling to be helpless victims of piracy, built a fleet and gave it to the Crown so as to protect the trade routes.

Merchants and soldiers can develop mutually supportive relationships. The alliance between the Crown, protecting the territory of England and the rights of English merchants to ply the world's trade routes, and the City of London, whose merchants supported the Crown with loans and taxes, propelled London into becoming the commercial capital of the world and England the dominating military power. London held its role undefeated if not unchallenged from 1688 until the Second World War, and still has some pretensions to it. Visitors to London are often surprised that the term 'City' is not applied to the thriving heart of the town, the theatres of Piccadilly and the Haymarket, the shops of Regent Street and Oxford Street, but to the office district to the east. One of

London's main commercial streets is The Strand, so called because it was once a river bank lined with merchants' warehouses before the river was pushed away by land reclamation projects. The visitor's London is the local's 'West End'.

The alliance between the military and the merchant classes was never an easy one. The aristocracy, from which the officer caste was drawn, despised 'trade', and although impoverished English aristocrats frequently married well-dowered merchants' daughters, the ladies concerned were expected to show proper deference to those born to their titles. After the passage of the First Reform Act in 1830, the middle classes came to dominate the House of Commons, and although the rural gentry tended to follow the aristocratic line, the merchants and manufacturers of the great cities, led by Bright and Cobden, used the parliament to denounce aristocratic excess and military privilege.

When individuals pick and choose between the two moral syndromes, working from parts of each, the result is a social cancer which can threaten and even destroy the body politic. The merchant republics of Italy had to buy their defence from roving bands of warriors, the 'condottieri', but these soldiers, having sold their loyalty once, were all too ready to sell it again. When the French and Spanish monarchs decided to turn northern Italy into a cockpit for their dynastic fights, the towns, and their merchants, had no defence. In 1527 a Hapsburg army entered and sacked Rome, killing more people and destroying more buildings than the Huns, Goths and Vandals combined.

Jacobs looks at the dismal performance of America's largest companies between 1960 and 1990 and suggests that this was caused in part by syndrome confusion. Company directors and their financial advisers stopped seeing the companies that they managed as organisations of people combining to create, and share, wealth, and started treating them as feudal fiefs to be plundered. Workers lost their status as junior colleagues and stakeholders and became peasants, to be turned off at will. When products from better managed Japanese and European firms began cutting the profits of American ones the response was to call upon the United States government to use threats so as to force the successful companies to exercise 'voluntary restraint', and when that failed to buy set amounts of American products whether their home markets wanted them or not.

Entrepreneurs

Here, and in the rest of this book, the word 'entrepreneur' will be reserved for the man or woman who creates an enterprise, either as a new organisation or as an initiative from within an existing organisation.[11] Some journalists have used the word to describe anyone who buys and sells, no matter how disgracefully and no matter how much damage is caused to society in general or to the people and enterprises that fall into their hands. Australia's corporate swindlers of the 1980s were called 'entrepreneurs' by their sycophants and their acts of plunder and ostentation were praised by many politicians and business journalists as if they had earned the wealth that they dissipated.

Ethical entrepreneurs create wealth in the form of valuable enterprises, but the value of these enterprises is based in the trust of their customers and the dedication of their staff. Commercial ethics involving the sacrifice of temporary advantage and the exercise of restraint are essential to the running of a commercial society. There have been tests of people's reaction to opportunities to exercise restraint and share in the results with others who did likewise, as opposed to taking advantage of a short term opportunity. Roughly seven out of every ten people challenged will choose restraint and cooperation, while the remaining three will grab at an immediate opportunity and let the future take care of itself.[12] The balance between the value creators and the value takers is quite fine and has developed over many millennia.

Societies in which everyone acts like a Spartan warrior, or a microeconomist, cannot develop and grow because every shoot is eaten before it ripens. Societies in which everyone is trusting and commercial can prosper hugely, as did the cities of northern Italy during the Renaissance until they clashed with a society of warriors. Societies in which a balance is struck between the value creators and the value shifters may represent the best possible compromise. London was the undisputed commercial capital of the world for 228 years, commencing with the exquisitely commercial 'Glorious Revolution' of 1688 and only starting to decline during the insane slaughter of the First World War. London's supremacy commenced when the City and its friends invited William of Orange, the successful warrior leader of the eminently commercial Dutch, to become their King. Its end commenced when Britain's imperialist policies (then a word to be used with pride, not a form of political abuse) clashed with the imperial dreams of the German empire and provoked a fratricidal war. Modern warfare requires a 'military–industrial complex', a deadly combination of guardians in command and a commercial supply organisation. The escalating military capability delivered by modern industry makes a very bad marriage with the stubborn refusal to compromise inculcated into military commanders.

Entrepreneurial morality

In most contemporary societies people are permitted to follow their own commercial interests within fairly widely drawn legal guidelines. Even societies where freedom of expression is severely curtailed encourage business. As we have already shown, the pursuit of self-interest may, but does not have to, advance society's broader goals. We choose to restrict our definition of 'entrepreneurs' to people whose activities contribute to society's overall interests, and to exclude people whose businesses only thrive by reducing the welfare of others.

In mid 1990s Australia there was at least one business which regularly searched the share registries of large companies looking for small, stable share holdings. They then sent letters, on impressive letterhead, offering to buy these shares and attaching an official share transfer form. By concentrating on small, stable share holdings they hoped to include a significant number of older, less sophisticated shareholders on their mailing list, people who did not realise that they were being offered a fraction of the market value of their shares, or that any reputable stockbroker or bank would have paid them a great deal more money for their holding for very little more trouble. The activities of this business were definitely negative sum; their gain came from their victims' losses, with the additional social loss caused by the distress of their victims and the social costs of providing services for them which they would, in other circumstances, have been able to provide for themselves. This little scam was within the law: the letters were very carefully worded and all the formalities observed, and there seemed no obvious way, short of a general ban on unfair practice, to amend the law so as to stop it. In the context of this book, however, the person behind this scheme was no entrepreneur.

Entrepreneurship is a matter of choice; becoming an entrepreneur involves a conscious decision to create more value than you can capture personally, that no matter how well you do, the world at large will be even better off. Entrepreneurial behaviour, in this light, is moral behaviour, and the rules of conduct are ethical rules that set out a preferred form of behaviour for individuals who will, from time to time, have an opportunity to gain personally by behaving otherwise. There is no proof available that following these rules will produce the best personal financial outcome for every person under all circumstances, but equally there is no convincing evidence that a life devoted to selfish exploitation is either long or happy.

Ethics for entrepreneurs
Honesty
The requirement to act honestly is not an injunction to make a complete disclosure of everything to everyone. To quote Robert Townsend, commercial honesty means that if you are asked a question, you answer it if you can, but 'if you don't know, say so, and if you know but won't tell, say so' (Townsend 1970: 136). The commitment to be honest means making an active effort to avoid deceit, whether by outright lie, implicit falsehood, or concealed fact. The duty of honesty extends to customers, suppliers, employees, and competitors.

You are walking in the bush when you find an old man dying from injuries caused by a fall. He is still conscious and gives you a scrap of paper:

'It's five units on the winning quaddie', he says, 'please give this ticket to my old mate Bert Smith of Erewhon East', and lapses into unconsciousness.

You put the paper in your pocket and go for help, but when you return the man is dead. A little while later you remember the bit of paper, which really is a tote ticket, and check the newspaper. The ticket is worth over $90 000.

How hard do you look for Bert? Before you get very far you see a short note in the newspaper to the effect that one Bert Smith, late of Erewhon East, has died in a Salvation Army home for the indigent. What do you do next?

The command to be honest sounds easy, but it can lead to painful dilemmas in real life. If a new product is going to be late, or to fall short of its specification, or even to fall short of a customer's exaggerated expectations, it is all too easy to avoid revealing the painful truth until facts pre-empt discussion. If a subordinate, or still worse, a superior, carries out a task in a sub-standard way it is all too easy to mutter a few words about 'good effort' and let one lapse grow into an addiction. In either case a short, painful conversation early will pre-empt a major row later.

The command to honesty is not a call for impolite directness: the customer, or the under-performing colleague, may be a problem but they are also, potentially at least, part of the solution. If the product can never be delivered, or if delivered, will never perform as expected, the problem is as serious as it is with an irredeemably incompetent colleague. When, as is more usual, the problem is not absolute and a satisfactory compromise is possible the customer, or the colleague, has a positive interest in finding that solution. Every commercial culture will have developed ways in which problems can be raised and conflicts resolved without permanently damaging an otherwise mutually satisfactory relationship. Australia is one of the very few countries where it is sometimes possible to call a male boss a 'silly bastard' to his face and keep your job. Even in Australia, an investment in tact will often pay dividends.

People who trade in the global economy still retain their personal expectations of appropriate behaviour, and their cultural traditions must be respected if a mutually beneficial relationship is to develop. In some societies even formal contracts are often subordinated to the informal give-and-take that marks effective personal relationships. In 1995 the Chinese government decided that the laws applying a 25 per cent tariff to wool imports should be enforced, and so the Chinese importers simply deducted 20 per cent from their remittances to their Australian suppliers, even for shipments that they had been bought under their explicit instructions. The contracts to purchase, in their view, incorporated an implicit caveat against changed circumstances.

Secure voluntary agreement

Few individuals go through life without ever being in a position to compel someone, even if it is only the family cat. In commerce and enterprise management the temptation to use these moments of power can be strong, and occasionally irresistible, but every such occasion must be recognised as an aberration.

Contrast:	*'I'm the boss, and you will do it my way or be sacked',*
With:	*'Please do it my way for now, because I know that it will work, and we will talk over your idea tonight.'*
Or contrast:	*'Our price for this job is $25 000 — take it or leave it',*

With:	'For a job this difficult, and so urgent, I would normally ask $30 000 but if we go through the spec together we may find a way of getting it down to $25 000 or so.'

By aristocratic or guardian standards any attempt to secure voluntary agreement when it could have been compelled is an act of condescension at best and a display of weakness leading to a loss of status and authority at worst. History is littered with tales of generals who led, or sent, their troops to disaster rather than take the advice of a junior officer or NCO.

Truly ethical entrepreneurs take the requirement to 'secure voluntary agreement' seriously, to the point of ensuring that the other party's consent is truly voluntary, and not based upon limited or deceptive information. Firms selling to children, or marketing habit-forming drugs, need to examine their sales and marketing practices very carefully if they are to maintain their self respect and the respect of society. The type of statement that would be unexceptionable in a corporate boardroom might be out of place in a television commercial scheduled during a children's program. Many countries, including Australia, have strong and detailed regulations covering the promotion of cigarettes and drugs. Advertising and promotion directed at children was relatively unregulated in Australia as at 1996 and some less-than-ethical practices were causing some community disquiet.

People suffering from syndrome confusion sometimes think that becoming the owner of a business, or even a promotion to a position of authority inside one, gives them not just an opportunity but an obligation to order their subordinates about.[13] They may get an opportunity to indulge their power fantasies, but they are unlikely to build a successful, growing enterprise. There is sometimes a place for peremptory behaviour, such as a crisis when people's lives will be at risk unless someone takes charge and gives orders. People who provoke such crises in order to justify authoritarian conduct are as socially valuable as a pyromaniac fireman.

Trust strangers and foreigners

Modern economies run on knowledge as much as on valuable goods, and your unique knowledge is more likely to be valuable to people who do not know you than to those who do. Trade within the circle of family and friends, 'taking in each other's washing', may add some value but never very much. The broader the marketing endeavour the more likely it is that high value bargains will be struck.

The command to 'trust strangers' is not a call to be recklessly indifferent to the risk of fraud and deceit. By all means ask for the customary deposit and secure enough personal and address information to enable a credit check to be run. Having been prudent, approach the stranger as someone with whom it may be possible to create a valuable commercial relationship, not as a mark to be taken down or an intruder to be resented. If a reasonable discussion reveals no grounds for either a commercial or a personal relationship, the stranger has become an acquaintance to whom politeness, but no more, is required. The stranger, after all, may have acquaintances with whom more useful bargains can be struck.

The BBC series 'Fawlty Towers' reached a huge and devoted audience. It could not have been seen as funny by many of them unless they had been exposed, possibly in less extreme form, to the types of customer abuse depicted by John Cleese. Some of the laughter must have come from people who were uncomfortable with strangers themselves.

Australians as a group do not find the command to 'trust strangers' difficult. In the hospitality trade Australians seem to be able to provide service without servility, and their general ease with strangers makes them exceptionally effective sales people.

Don't attack or subvert competitors

Ethical competition is about satisfying customers, not destroying rivals. Those of your competitors who are better at satisfying customers than you set a standard that you must rise to, and those who are not as good must catch up with you or do less well. Some firms will be unable to keep up and will go out of business; others may be forced to retreat from the main market and to focus their efforts on niches. That, if it happens, should be the result of their bad management or their unlucky decisions and not your successful scheming.

From time to time firms get the opportunity to subvert a competitor by direct attack, such as spreading rumours about their solvency or product or by dumping look-alike products at below cost into their chief market. Other opportunities for subversion may come about with chances to control a common supplier or an important distribution channel. However it is done, effort directed to subverting a competitor represents an investment intended to be recovered from a firm's customers, through higher prices and reduced service, once the competitive threat is removed.

By and large attempts to subvert a competitor by manipulating distribution channels or suppliers are illegal in Australia, and any company that makes such attempts may face both criminal and civil penalties. Unfortunately there is no general ban on unfair competition in Australia, as when a large company launches a cheap copy of an innovator's successful product, or steals an innovative service or retail concept. Intellectual property law in Australia is generally written and interpreted to give the benefit of any available doubt to a pirate, and to leave some very large loopholes for copying products and services. Ethical entrepreneurs may not steal their competitors' concepts, but they should not assume that their competitors will display the same forbearance.

Refraining from subverting competitors is not an injunction to help them actively by giving them essential information without fair compensation. In Chapter 6 we discuss intellectual property law: there is nothing unethical about using the law of the land to defend an enterprise's intellectual assets against those who would rather steal than create.

Respect the intention of contracts

Only fools fail to respect properly drawn up, legally binding contracts. The full majesty of the law can be landed on the head of any such defaulters in most countries. Formal contracts have their place, but it is simply not practical to conduct most business and employment on the basis of written contracts. While the law can be invoked to enforce implicit contracts under some circumstances, recourse to law is expensive, and the result both uncertain and unlikely to fully compensate the injured party. Ultimately, the performance of the type of implicit contract that dominates commercial relationships depends on the good faith of the various parties.

The law cannot enforce moral or fair behaviour. One major Australian retailer, for example, has been known to commission a craftsperson to make a few hundred copies of something for 'test marketing', and when it sells well to commission the rest of their requirements in the form of near copies from a factory in some low-wage country. This infamous behaviour has been defended by both lawyers and economists, but it does not make it ethical. The retailer concerned subsequently discovered that innovative small businesses were unwilling to supply it, and had its lawyers search the Trade Practices Act looking for ways to compel them.

A related form of immoral behaviour under the sanction of the law involves reneging on implicit commitments given to junior partners or skilled employees. Partners and employees who put in work 'above and beyond the call of duty' in the early life of a new enterprise have been frozen out or fired when they requested a share of the rewards for success. Suppliers who supported a growing business with extended credit and extensive technical support find themselves discarded as soon as their advice is no longer vital and the business has less need of credit. This form of behaviour is a type of creeping systemic corruption, because it means that the trust needed to build a winning team in the early days of a new enterprise will be harder and harder to secure. The skilled worker may demand overtime, in advance, before working evenings and weekends. The junior partner may start secret negotiations with a rival, hoping to sell out before being sold out. Suppliers may demand cash in advance where previously they offered credit.

In the end, there are no winners.

Respect initiative and tolerate dissent

Entrepreneurs, particularly when their enterprise is new, are painfully aware of the urgency of getting their new products to market and expanding their distribution, and the dangers of wasting time and effort on distractions. It is extremely tempting to summon up traditional 'guardian' attitudes: 'get on with your work, don't argue with me, you're employed to do a job, not talk about it ...'

This temptation must be resisted, because the people who are doing the job are often the first to discover problems with it. Their statement of the problem may be imprecise and their proposals for resolving it implausible: a crushing remark or a few minutes of public mockery will suffice to shut them up, then and forever. The truly great entrepreneur realises that subordinates who practise initiative or express dissent have discovered a problem in the approach that they were told to implement. The problem may only exist in their imagination, but it is then real enough: if members of the team think that there is something wrong, they will not be able to stop the rest of the team, and the firm's potential customers, from catching a hint of their disquiet. Working through the problem, even if the answer was to go ahead exactly as planned, greatly increases the chances of success. More importantly, some of the concerns that will be raised will be the result of real problems, and some of the initiatives that subordinates take will be in response to real opportunities.

By listening to all concerns, and by extending the maximum possible tolerance to initiative, the entrepreneur gains the widest and earliest information about the problems and opportunities that lie ahead.

Look for the better way

People brought up in the guardian tradition believe that a practice that has remained unchanged for many years, or centuries, should be preserved on that account alone. Entrepreneurs, on the other hand, feel that the longer something has been unchanged the more likely it is to offer an opportunity for a successful series of innovations.

St Jerome (circa 345–419) was concerned that the Bible was only available in Greek, the language of the aristocracy, and Hebrew. He set out to translate it into the common (or vulgar) tongue; in those days, Latin. His translation was adopted by the Catholic church and is known as the 'Vulgate'. However, 1100 years later the scholar William Tyndale observed that Latin was no longer widely spoken, particularly in England, and so he prepared a translation into the common language of his time and place, English. The orthodox were so out-raged at this breach of tradition that they had Tyndale burned at the stake for heresy. One must hope that Tyndale and Jerome had a quiet chuckle in a better place about these matters.

Value comfort and convenience

Heroes of myth and legend prepared themselves for future ordeals by extraordi-nary feats of self-denial and privation, completed their quest in spite of fearful dangers and terrible hardships, and as soon as the celebration feast was over they set out again. The English Public Schools maintained this tradition well into the twentieth century: a British officer, liberated after four years in a Japanese POW camp, explained: 'it was nothing really, not after being a boarder at an English prep school.'

Tales of heroes, ancient and modern, are truly uplifting. The experience of being uplifted can be best enjoyed sitting in a comfortable chair in an air condi-tioned or centrally heated and generally well-furnished house reading a beauti-fully prepared book, preferably after enjoying a satisfying and well prepared dinner. Entrepreneurs are usually on the side of comfort and convenience, and have been as far back as records go. Louis XIV ruled his court in the dazzling — and often freezing — splendour of Versailles: not even the king could enjoy a hot dinner in the formal dining chambers, situated fifteen minute's brisk walk from the kitchens. The bourgeois of Paris, meanwhile, ate superb food in beauti-fully furnished, and warm, houses.

Many established companies treat comfort and convenience as a reward for holders of exalted positions: the lower orders are expected to rough it and like it. Such firms may have a travel policy under which the Chief Executive and a few of his intimates travel first class, the rest of the senior managers travel in business class, and the serfs ride in steerage. The more entrepreneurial companies have a common travel policy: if anyone rides in the back, everyone does.

Most people, given a choice, will avoid discomfort and will choose the most convenient of various options. Expecting them to suffer pain and endure inconvenience for a marginal cost saving will simply restrict the market for a new product. The companies that are working to develop oral forms of insulin to replace injected ones are not wasting their own or society's resources: a reduc-tion in the pain and inconvenience endured by diabetics is socially valuable. Successful products in today's affluent societies are those whose benefits are delivered with comfort and convenience, and an entrepreneur who sets out to supply such products should be able to appreciate the results.

Spend time and money carefully

Successful entrepreneurs will have a lot of money around, even in the relatively early stage of the marketing of their new products. If they want to go on enjoy-ing it they will have to spend a great deal of it on the needs of the business until it reaches early maturity, and then they will have to start spending money preparing their firm's next generation of products. After the early days of their first successful enterprise there will, however, be money that is not needed for sustaining the firm and intervals of time during which the entrepreneur's personal attendance at the business will not be needed.

An investigating accountant from the Commonwealth Development Bank visited a new enterprise in a country town, and after careful inspection of their accounts and plans, agreed to a substantial loan against very doubtful security. The accountant finished this task on a Friday afternoon, and, having friends in the area, spent the weekend in the country.

On his way back to the capital city, he passed the new enterprise, just in time to see the owner taking possession of a new, large, black BMW.

The loan was cancelled by midday.

This time and money can be directed to increasing the entrepreneur's, and the entrepreneur's family's, quality of life, but since the firm may make a renewed call on the entrepreneur's time or money or both the personal expenditure must be controlled as carefully as the business investment. First generation entrepreneurs should aspire to comfortable houses, but not mansions; modern appliances, but not live-in servants beyond the need for child care; charitable donations, but not foundations. Marble-faced offices may be suitable for lawyers and accountants, those upholders of guardian standards, but not for the new and growing enterprise. Heroes of romantic fiction may fling their purses to a beggar or stake the family fortune on the turn of a card: the true entrepreneur gives the beggar a well-judged gift and gambles, if at all, with no more money than would be spent on an alternative entertainment.

As soon as entrepreneurs can no longer endure modest affluence, they must sell their business to a person or firm that will go on developing it and splurge the proceeds in any and every direction that takes their fancy. As long as they remain in charge of an active firm their obligations to their staff, partners, customers and suppliers demand that their investments are ruled by prudence, not by ambition or ostentation.

Never threaten and waste no time on revenge

Threats are a waste of breath unless the threatener intends to carry them out, and punishing someone is a waste of time and effort that could better be spent gaining new customers or recruiting new associates. Revenge is a distraction from the main tasks of building a business. Every entrepreneur, every human, will feel let down by some person at some time, and often with very good cause. In many cases the most appropriate response is to withdraw cooperation from that person until they have demonstrated that they can be relied upon again. Sometimes the entrepreneur should practice a little self-examination:

did they secure an agreement with the offender in the first place by subtle threat and implicit intimidation? If so, the breakdown in their relationship is the entrepreneur's fault as much as the other party's. On many occasions the breakdown will be caused by one party or the other reverting to hunter-gatherer morality: 'It was there, and so I picked it up.' 'You would have cheated me if I hadn't got in first.' 'No one trusts [insert appropriate minority group here] like you.'

If a criminal offence has been committed, the police should be informed and then left to do their duty by their own lights. If the offence is merely a breach of morality or of more general commercial etiquette, depriving the offender of any further benefits from mutual trade is an adequate punishment. Even then, an entrepreneur should be prepared to resume a commercial relationship with a defaulter who takes the first step to a reconciliation. There is no need for the entrepreneur's firm to go without the future benefits that a renewed relationship may offer.

Be optimistic

The moral antonym of optimism is not pessimism but fatalism. Soldiers sit under an artillery barrage believing that they won't die unless the shell with their number on it is fired — and that they will die when it is. Until very recently many crew members on English fishing boats in the North Sea didn't learn to swim, because 'if the sea wants you she'll take you' or even that if you cheat her by swimming 'she'll take someone else' and the swimmer will have that death on his conscience (Gill 1994).

The entrepreneur, to paraphrase an ecological slogan, should be optimistic globally but pessimistic about details. The entrepreneur's global optimism asserts that the enterprise can succeed, and if this one fails, then valuable lessons will be learned in time for the next attempt. Every detail must be examined with a pessimist's eye: entrepreneurs should by all means hope for good luck, but they shouldn't rely on it more than absolutely necessary. Whenever risks can be reduced by judgement and planning, they must be. At the end of the day the entrepreneur expects to succeed; approaches problems believing that they can be overcome; and if everything falls in ruins, picks through the rubble gathering materials for the next attempt.

The entrepreneur travels bravely — and arrives.

Society and the entrepreneur

Entrepreneurs are a part of the society within which they operate, and are major contributors to it. Societies that wish entrepreneurship to flourish need to ensure that their institutions are compatible with it. Some of these social and legal issues are discussed below.

Regulate outcomes, not processes

Society cannot reasonably assume that everyone who calls themselves an entrepreneur will act ethically at all times. One of the longest running battles in legal history is the conflict between food adulterators and the public. As recently as 1987 many Austrian wine producers were discovered to be adding ethylene glycol to their products, a process that enhanced the taste but threatened serious damage to the internal workings of consumers. Various types of substitution and adulteration have been deployed by unethical traders since time immemorial.

Society has every right to demand that the adulteration of food and other personal products be made a serious crime and that it should be prosecuted vigorously. In setting out the details of the law there is often a temptation to prescribe a process, such as exactly how bread should be baked, and not the outcome, such as a law that bread must contain nothing harmful. There are two major problems with prescribing a process:

▲ it creates an implicit defence for someone who carelessly or recklessly causes harm to others — they can claim that they 'did it by the book' and if it went wrong it could not have been their fault

▲ it sets up a barrier to innovation, in that a newer process may have to be held up until the law can be changed, even when the product is unchanged or even unequivocally improved.

Trade practices law in Australia tends to be process rather than outcome oriented. The intention is to protect consumers from ruthless monopolists, but the effect tends to be to protect large enterprises from entrepreneurs.

Enforce contracts effectively

Every society will have people who would like to short-cut the normal processes of buying in a market, taking but not paying. Unless entrepreneurs believe that their property, and their ideas, are theirs as long as they want to hang on to them, they will be discouraged from creating anything worth stealing.

It is not sufficient to pass laws: there must be effective, and reasonably priced, ways of enforcing them.

Australian entrepreneurs are reasonably well off on a world scale in the matter of contract law, but some of them have hurt themselves by ignorance of the way it works. Contracts don't all need lawyers, and they don't even have to be written down, but the courts are reluctant to act on mere assertions, and prudent entrepreneurs will make diary entries, and have associates present, to confirm any verbal agreements. Sending a letter of confirmation, with the main points listed, is a polite and effective way of making a record. It also allows disagreements over a verbal understanding to be sorted out before too much work has been completed.

Protect intellectual property

Entrepreneurs create considerable amounts of intellectual property: novel designs, trade marks, trade dress, trade secrets, patentable and unpatentable inventions, operating manuals, promotional materials and more.

Once the entrepreneur has done this work a copyist can generally reproduce it at a considerably lower cost, and may be able to seize a share of the entrepreneur's market or, in extreme cases, take it over entirely. Unfortunately there is an entirely specious argument, popularised by a few economists, that purports to show that society will be better off if an entrepreneur's intellectual property is stolen as long as the thief sells the resulting copies at a low enough price.

This argument is irrefutable, as long as society is satisfied that it has all the innovations it will ever want. Economists are easier to satisfy on this point than the general public: the public persists in buying new and improved products, even at higher prices, rather than insisting on the old and familiar.

Recognise entrepreneurs in the tax system

In Australia the bulk of taxes are levied on net income, basically profits and wages. There is nothing seriously wrong with this as far as employees and mature businesses are concerned.

There can be a great deal wrong with the Australian approach when it is applied to a new, entrepreneurial business. Such businesses generate substantial accounting profits while they are still consuming large amounts of cash, and a tax demand can cripple them, while an unincorporated entrepreneur or partnership can be pushed into insolvency by the operation of the provisional tax system.

Verbal agreements and diary notes do not work with the Tax Office: Australian entrepreneurs need professional taxation advice quite early in the life of their enterprise, and will often be advised to incorporate, at considerable expense. The advice and incorporation will generally be less financially damaging than the Tax Office, but it would be nice to be able to start a new enterprise without either.

Praise, and rewards, where praise is due

When corporate pillagers and swindlers get called 'entrepreneurs' the respect society owes to genuine ones is reduced, and many ambitious people may be tempted to abandon the self-discipline that true entrepreneurship demands and launch a career of pillage and spoliation of their own. A similar form of corruption is at work when political appointees to the top jobs in a statutory or recently privatised monopoly award themselves salaries comparable to those earned by entrepreneurs who built an enterprise on that scale.

There should be no confusion between the praise and rewards appropriate to people who build major enterprises or make major contributions to their growth, and those appropriate to people whose position was secured by political favour or by a series of successful swindles.

End notes

1 An excellent treatment of the many ways that entrepreneurship can be — and is — theoretically perceived and explained is contained in Jennings (1994).

2 Defining entrepreneurship is no simple matter because it is a phenomenon embracing multiple perspectives and activities. In presenting their views on ethical entrepreneurship, the authors have worked in accordance with the definitions embodied in two works: Bygrave and Hofer (1991: 13–22); Stevenson, Roberts and Grousbeck (1989). Bygrave and Hofer state three definitions and a nine-point scorecard which can be used to estimate the degree to which processes are 'entrepreneurial': an *entrepreneurial event* involves the creation of a new organisation to pursue an opportunity; the *entrepreneurial process* involves all the functions, activities and actions associated with the perceiving of opportunities and the creation of organisations to pursue them; an *entrepreneur* is someone who perceives an opportunity and creates an organisation to pursue it. Stevenson and others writes of entrepreneurship as a behavioural approach to management but defines it with a greater emphasis on resource control: 'From our perspective, entrepreneurship is an approach to management that we define as follows: the pursuit of opportunity without regard to resources currently controlled.'

3 The societal roots of modern commerce are explored in depth in Braudel (1981, *Volume 1: The Structures of Everyday Life — The limits of the possible*). A good introduction to theorising about economic circumstances and the major theorisers since Malthus can be had by reading Heilbroner (1986).

4 The next most important factor is capital accumulation (saving), but this would not be possible on its current scale without the high level of discretionary income society enjoys as a result of past innovations.

5 The exact comparison of living standards is impossible. This figure is based on grain prices expressed as a number of days' work at the minimum wage.

6 The classic textbook of game theory in an economic context is Von Neuman and Morgenstern (1964).

7 See, for example, Wall (1986).

8 Jacobs borrows the word 'syndrome' from medicine, where it describes a group of manifestations that, when seen together, indicate that a particular condition is present. It does not automatically imply the presence of a disease.

9 See Ridley (1970).

10 For a well edited selection from the works of the father of sociology see Wrong (1970).

11 Thinking about entrepreneurship as 'the creation of new organisations to pursue opportunities' is the focus of much of the work of American academic, William B. Gartner. See, for instance, Gartner (1985); Gartner, Bird and Starr (1992); and Gartner (1993).

12 Practising and teaching microeconomists show a remarkably different psychological profile to other professionals, reversing the normal balance between cooperation and predation.

13 'The working class/Can kiss my a–e/I've got the foreman's job at last' (to be sung to the tune of *The Red Flag*).

Profile one

Sir John Monash KCMG
The entrepreneur as hero

Early in the morning of 8 August 1918 a lean, middle-aged Australian Lieutenant-General watched as the troops under his command moved to the attack a little to the south-east of Amiens in northern France. The First World War had been going for two days short of four years, and the Allies had launched offensive after offensive, and gained little but casualties. At the nearby Somme battlefield three years earlier 20 000 Allied soldiers had died before midday for a gain of 200 metres, and a million were to die over the following two years for a gain of 8 kilometres. By ten in the morning the offensive had ended, but this time the result was different. As the smoke drifted away 8000 German troops stumbled towards captivity, while Allied intelligence officers bustled forwards to search a captured divisional and a corps headquarters. For the first time in the war the Allies had breached the entire German defences, advancing 8 kilometres on a 6 kilometre front. The German Chief of Staff wrote in his diary that the war was lost that day.

John Monash had stepped into history.

Monash was born in 1865 in West Melbourne to a recently arrived middle-class immigrant couple from Germany. He had the upbringing of a middle class Australian boy; his family was Jewish but not aggressively so and Monash went to Scotch College. He matriculated to Melbourne University in 1882 with the Exhibition in Mathematics, giving him a free place and a £25 bursary, intending to study Arts and Engineering. He was neither the first nor the last bright student to find more to do at university than listen to boring lectures, and he became a founder of the University Union and an active member of the Melbourne University Company, a forerunner of the Melbourne University Regiment.

In 1886 he started work as an engineer before completing his degree, initially on Melbourne's Princes Bridge, where the stonework is to his design, and then on the Outer Circle Railway where his bridge over the Yarra at Fairfield is still in use, but by cars rather than trains. He was commissioned in the volunteer artillery in 1887 and finally completed his undergraduate studies in 1891. He formed a partnership with Josh Anderson and they became consulting engineers and architects, with Anderson doing the selling and Monash most of the engineering. Monash was in much demand as an arbitrator and expert witness, and while he was involved in a number of cases Anderson became one of the Australian pioneers on Monier (steel reinforced) concrete. Monash and Anderson became contractors for a number of bridges in Victoria, many of them in Monier concrete, and in 1901 they joined with David Mitchell to form the Monier Pipe Co. Pty Ltd, intending to manufacture concrete water, sewage and drainage pipes.

One of Monash and Anderson's major contracts, the Fyansford Bridge, became the subject of litigation, and although Monash and Anderson won their case, the partnership ended up nearly £3000 in debt. Monash became a popular clubman around Melbourne, won promotion to Major in the Artillery, and supported his family, but his finances were far from secure. Monash decided to correspond with German specialists in reinforced concrete and conduct experiments under the supervision of Professor Kernot of Melbourne University to broaden the Monier Concrete Company's intellectual property base. As a result of Monash's hard work the partnership's debts were slowly paid off. In 1905 Monash ejected Anderson from the partnership on the grounds that Anderson had made little contribution to the recovery from debt, and Monash formed a new firm, the Reinforced Concrete and Monier Pipe Construction Co. Pty Ltd. To cap a rough year, a promissory note was dishonoured scaring Monash's bankers and pushing him to the edge of insolvency. Monash's business attitudes became noticeably harder.

From 1906 on, the Reinforced Concrete Co. became steadily more successful, as Monash's experiments and correspondence enabled him to licence yet more patents, building a wall to keep competitors off the turf. Monash refused to take all the credit for himself, acknowledging the vital financial and management support that he had received from Mitchell and Mitchell's associate, Gibson. A relative hinted that Monash had in some sense demeaned himself in the transition from a professional engineer to a successful business person; Monash was having none of it:

... Gummow in Sydney, and I in Victoria, have simply and boldly been the pioneers of a new era in Engineering. We are the precursors of a new development in the Engineering profession, viz.

the Civil Engineer of the future will be first and foremost the commercial directing head of Engineering enterprise and industry — the scientific side of him will merely be an adjunct or subordinate function ...

The remaining years of peace saw Monash rise relentlessly in both the military sphere where he became a brigadier, and in civil society, where he was appointed to the Council of the University of Melbourne. The success of the Reinforced Concrete Co. ensured that he had ample means to support his elevated position. The comfort of his lifestyle showed in his figure; from time to time he dieted, but not too strenuously. He seemed destined to finish his days in affluent provincial obscurity when the First World War broke out.

Monash served as Brigadier of the 4th Brigade on Gallipoli, then as divisional commander with the Australian 3rd Division on the Western Front, and ended the war as Commander of the Australian Army Corps in France. None of his promotions came easily; he was felt to be too cold and calculating, to lack that 'glamour and dash' that marked the popular ideal of a soldier. He certainly lacked charisma: although he rapidly dieted away his civilian waistline and exercised to maintain the physical fitness needed to keep up with men ten years his junior, he was not a 'leader'. As an organiser, whether of exercises, displays or battles, he was without equal. The Australian soldiers obeyed him because of their confidence in his organisation and planning, not because of his glamour.

Monash believed that his civilian career had been an essential grounding for his military success. One factor was a sheer ability to work: Monash was used to the executive's twelve-hour day and the engineer's scramble across remote construction sites at a time when the British army was led by men who were gentlemen before they were officers. Monash had learned as head contractor to accept responsibility for the performance of subordinates; and as a commanding officer he did the same. He was a team builder, encouraging, reassuring, demanding without ever calling for the impossible; officers on his staff and under his direct command all but worshipped him. He never gave an order when a suggestion would do, and never suggested when a hint would have been enough. The ordinary soldiers respected him for the care with which he took to minimise casualties; but Monash was being an engineer — minimising scrap as much as being a humanitarian preserving lives.

Monash's last task of the war was organising the repatriation of the Australian forces in Europe: his creativity and meticulous planning saw the job completed in less than half the time that had been expected. In 1921 he returned to Melbourne, tired but fit, a national hero looking for something to do. There was nothing for him on the national scene; the Commonwealth government studiously and repeatedly snubbed him. The politicians of the day wanted no rivals in authority.

The state of Victoria was less grudging, and Monash was persuaded to become the foundation chairman of the State Electricity Commission. In 1921

Victoria looked like a state with a great future behind it. Melbourne was one of the last of the Australian state capitals to be founded, but by 1890 it was clearly the biggest. The initial growth had come on a flood of gold from the Ballarat and Bendigo goldfields, followed by the agricultural wealth flowing from the Western District. The economic crisis of the 1890s had brought Victoria's growth to a cruel halt, and while modest growth had resumed with the twentieth century, New South Wales had moved to a decisive lead.

In the 1920s growth required industry, and industry required power. New South Wales had huge black coal deposits around Newcastle, Lithgow and the Illawarra supporting a burgeoning steel industry. Victoria had a small and inefficient coal mine at Wonthaggi, producing enough to keep a skeleton service on the railways running, and no more. Victoria relied on black coal shipped from New South Wales for its industrial fuel and its nascent power generation system; an unreliable and expensive energy source.

Victoria had a major untapped energy asset, the vast brown coal deposits of the Latrobe Valley, but getting at it presented formidable problems. Brown coal was 60 per cent water and 5 per cent dirt; a bare third of each tonne could burn. The deposits were 175 kilometres from Melbourne, at a time when power stations were generally built in the suburbs that they served. The brown coal was, however, cheap and easy to get at, in seams 60 metres or more thick under 30 metres or less of overburden.

Monash decided that the SEC's, and Victoria's, future depended on the exploitation of brown coal. He took on a list of challenges that would have daunted a more ordinary man. The only previous use of brown coal had been in Germany, and public opinion in the aftermath of the First World War was bitterly hostile to the idea of buying plant from Germany or of allowing German technicians into Australia. Long distance power transmission had been used on a limited scale in the United States, but was wholly new to Australia. Yallourn brown coal was wetter and dirtier than any fuel that had ever been used on an industrial scale before in Australia or anywhere else. The sheer scale of the exercise and the technical difficulties faced meant that the SEC had to be granted a distribution monopoly and substantial government loans, politically dangerous steps for any government, then or now. Consumers had to be educated to use electricity and consumers and industry had to be sold on the advantages of briquettes as a solid fuel. Visiting experts regularly made damning pronouncements which were taken far more seriously than they deserved.

The government's determination wavered: Sir Robert Menzies, speaking in 1965, recalled what happened when Monash called on the Cabinet:

> *We all stood up instinctively, we all stood up, we were all in the presence of a man we knew would be a greater man than we would ever be ... He looked towards the Premier and he said 'Well Mr Premier, I gather that Cabinet has rejected my proposal.' 'Well, yes, yes, I think that's right, Sir John.' 'Well,' he said, 'that*

can only be because they've utterly failed to understand it. I will now explain it.' And he sat there, with that rock-like look, and he explained it, and one by one we shrivelled in our places, one by one we became convinced, or at any rate, felt we were convinced, of the error of our ways. And for half an hour he went on; he explained the thing step by step. And we were left silent ... And that settled it, there was no more, not another word came out and so Sir John said, looking at the Premier, 'Well, sir, I take it that your decision is reversed. Indeed, anticipating your approval of my proposal, and so that there will be no delay, I have brought with me (and he pulled it out of his breast pocket) the Order-in-Council that will be necessary for this purpose.' And he passed it around, and it was signed, and he went out.

By 1927 the SEC was running and generating a surplus over its interest and depreciation charges, and cheap power and cheap fuel helped Victoria on the way to becoming the centre of Australia's value-added manufacturing industries. The impetus Monash gave the SEC drove it on for a further sixty years. Over the decade from 1987 the politicians finally seized and destroyed the SEC, although by that time Victorian industry enjoyed the cheapest thermally generated high tension electricity tariff in the world; only the hydro systems of New Zealand and Ontario could supply cheaper power.

Monash died, relatively young, in 1931 and more than a quarter of a million people followed his cortege.

This account of Sir John Monash has drawn heavily on Serle (1982)

Chapter 2

Entrepreneurs and the economy

The Australian economy consists of eighteen million or so consumers and a little less than a million firms supplying them with goods and services. About 120 000 consumers will receive their final set of services in any one year, while birth and immigration will introduce another 350 000 or so. Some 40 000 to 80 000 of the firms now supplying them will cease to do so in the course of the next twelve months and about the same number of new firms will be started; more in years when the economy is growing strongly or slowing down sharply. As the wall poster says, 'Constant change is here to stay'.

Newspaper pundits write about the economy as if it was a single, uniform, and predictable beast, and it is to an observer who is far enough away from it. Astronomers tell us that the planet Venus is racked by furious storms stirring its hot, corrosive atmosphere, but to people on Earth it is just a bright dot in the evening or morning sky. Workers and managers in trading enterprises seldom find the economy smooth or predictable. Growth does not mean a change in some vague economic statistic; it means overtime, bonuses, and new colleagues. Economists say the economy is 'in recession' when some of the statistics run backwards, but on the shop floor recession means short-time working, pink slips, and business failures. Small changes in the economy as a whole turn into huge changes for the individuals who are directly affected by them.

Firms in a market economy are always under pressure from other firms, most directly from those other firms that make similar products or offer similar services. When a reasonably large number of firms or traders compete to sell similar products, none of them will have much influence over the market price and the only way to make a good profit is to have below-average costs. As soon as one trader is seen to be making a good profit, the others will try to cut their own costs, wiping out the first trader's advantage. The pressure to keep reducing costs is very strong.

One of the most obvious ways to reduce the costs of each product made or service delivered is to make or deliver more of them with the same number of workers, by using better machinery or by reorganising the way the work is done. Once most of the firms in an industry have found ways to cut unit costs by making larger quantities of their product, they will have to lower the price in order to encourage buyers to take the extra supply. Pretty soon they will reach the point where lowering the price does not attract any more buyers, and only those firms with the lowest costs will survive.

The sellers in one market are, however, the buyers in another. When the less efficient firms are driven to the wall their workers lose their jobs and their owners lose their profits; they can no longer afford to buy the things that they did before. This will put more pressure on the surviving firms to cut their costs and boost their share of the market, and another round of less efficient firms will go to the wall, and another bit of demand will be drained from the economy.

From the time modern capitalism started to emerge in England in the 1770s, this downward spiral started quite frequently. Until the 1890s periods when the world economy ran backwards were called 'crises'; the 1891–92 crisis was so bad that the next time the economy got stuck in reverse the powers that be called it a 'depression'. The Great Depression of 1930–33 gave that word a bad name, and so when the United States economy started going backwards again in 1937 President Franklin D. Roosevelt called it a 'recession', and that is the word that we use today for economic bad times.[1]

Explaining growth

Capitalist economies get into trouble quite regularly, but they have always got out of trouble again and returned to growth and fairly full employment. The history of capitalism has been a story of long-run growth, not crisis. From the end of the Roman Empire until 1830 a labourer in Europe had to work for between one hundred and four hundred days to earn the price of a tonne of grain. This was just enough to keep an average family at bare subsistence level. The typical labourer worked for about two hundred days a year; few of them had paid work in the winter months. Living standards only rose above bare subsistence level when the price of a tonne of grain fell to less than the wages of two hundred days of labour. Half the time half the population lived below subsistence level. In one out of every seven years people could be found starving to death in the streets of Europe's towns and cities.

A hundred and sixty years of capitalism has seen the real price of a tonne of grain, and fine wheat rather than coarse oats and millet at that, fall to the money equivalent of one to four day's labour. The average person in a modern western country lives better, and longer, than most eighteenth century aristocrats.

Capitalism creates unemployment, as machines replace workers and more efficient processes replace less efficient ones, but it also soaks it up. The displaced workers are employed in new forms of economic activity, and demand and output continue to grow.[2]

A capitalist economy grows when new products enter the market and new services are offered: while competition is driving down the cost of supplying well-known products and flooding the markets with them, new products have no direct competitors. Innovation offers firms an escape from price-based competition and an opportunity to earn substantial profits — until imitators follow the innovator and the price-competitive cycle begins in the market for the new product.[3] Two processes are at work simultaneously:

▲ in established markets, price competition is forcing costs and prices down and quantities up, squeezing profits and displacing workers

▲ at the same time innovators are creating new markets by introducing new products, both goods and services, earning substantial margins and taking on workers to satisfy growing demand.

In normal times sufficient new firms arise, and sufficient new divisions are created inside existing ones, to absorb the workers displaced by progress. This is a continuing process: the workers employed *last* year to make new products and deliver new services are displacing workers *this* year; the new jobs that these workers find will start displacing other workers *next* year. Not all of the new jobs are in new firms: some firms will grow, and employ more people, and other firms will reassign staff to new duties rather than retrench one lot and hire another.

A modern economy is perpetually changing. Old products get replaced by newer ones, old ways of doing things get replaced by better ones. Some firms are wound up and some divisions of large firms close, while new firms are formed and new divisions are opened. On a short time frame, a year or so, this does not amount to an overwhelming amount of change: most firms and divisions that were operating last year are still operating; most products that were on the market last year are still available.

Put in numbers: 4 to 8 per cent of the firms and company divisions that are operating today won't be operating in a year's time: about one person in twenty will find that their work, in the form that they have been used to performing it, is no longer required. About the same number will have to change jobs if they want to go on using their existing skills. For the level of unemployment to stand still, the work of producing new goods and delivering new services must add at least 4 per cent to the total stock of jobs each year. The truly amazing fact is that the capitalist system has managed to do this consistently, when the bad years are averaged with the good, for two centuries.

Economists study economies, and various economists have been trying to explain how a capitalist system works for well over two hundred years: the

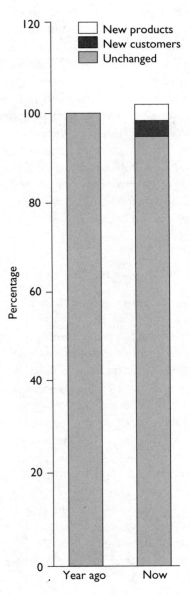

Figure 2.1 The economy changes slowly

attempt started before capitalism got properly going.[4] The standard undergraduate syllabus focuses on the 90 per cent of the economy that will not cease to operate over the course of a year, the steady state, or equilibrium, part of the economy. Even many advanced researchers in economics limit their analyses to a state of 'general equilibrium' which will occur when all innovations lie in the distant past and from which all change is impossible.

Two of the greatest names in twentieth century economics focused on the 4 per cent, the new activities that keep the economy from collapsing into an equilibrium state. The English economist John Maynard Keynes looked at ways in which demand was stimulated so as to generate employment for those displaced by the increasing efficiency of the established economy. He identified two major sources of new demand: one was entrepreneurial activity (which Keynes called the result of 'animal spirits'), because entrepreneurs place orders for new materials, buildings, machines and services in order to make or deliver their new products, pushing up demand, and employment, right through the economy; and the other was intervention by governments, whose orders for public works and defence equipment would generate immediate demand for contractors to fill these orders and provide flow-on opportunities for workers and subcontractors.[5]

Innovation

The Austrian–American economist Joseph A. Schumpeter focused on innovation rather than animal spirits as the guiding force behind entrepreneurs. Schumpeter emphasised the importance of non-price competition between differentiated products where orthodox economists, then and now, focus on price competition between perfectly interchangeable ones. Schumpeter emphasised the importance of the large firm while most teaching of economics deals with an imaginary world in which all firms are small.[6]

Two of the most famous authors on economics, Adam Smith and Alfred Marshall, are claimed by both the orthodox and the entrepreneurial schools. Smith introduced the concept of economic progress, which he saw almost entirely in terms of process and supply improvements. He did not give any serious consideration to product innovation. Smith did, however, emphasise the role of the individual entrepreneur in creating new businesses and opening up new avenues of trade. Marshall was one of the founders of the modern orthodox school, but his writing shows him to have been deeply dissatisfied with the timeless picture of the economy that emerged from mathematical models.

The majority of academic economists in Australia rely on General Equilibrium Theory, with an implicit assumption that the only interesting states of the world are those where all change has ended and the noise of all disturbances has died away. They study change by creating a new picture with the world in a different equilibrium state. Users of General Equilibrium Theory make the deep assumption that the state of an economy is determined by the economic conditions and does not depend on the way the economy developed. The equilibrium state of an economy is analogous to the steady state of a physical system. Imagine a mountainous part of the countryside just after a rainstorm: water will be cascading over every surface, splashing and falling. After a little while all the water will have gathered in the lowest places, while the higher areas are dry again. This is the equilibrium state of the water-mountain system. As long as there is no erosion and no earth movement, the water will wind up in the same place after a storm or a shower: the equilibrium state depends on the shape of the hills, not the nature of the rainfall.

If General Equilibrium Theory reflected the real world, then entrepreneurship would be quite irrelevant to the economy; market forces would be the only driver of change and individuals would have no role to play beyond assisting or retarding the economy's journey along a predefined path to a pre-determined end.

> A light aeroplane got into difficulties and the pilot warned the passengers that the plane was likely to crash. The economist on board grabbed the only parachute, slipped it on, and as he jumped called out to the people left behind: 'Don't worry, now that there is a parachute shortage market forces will satisfy your demand.'

Modern mathematics has provided conclusive proof that the state of a system as complex as an economy must reflect its history as well as its past states: individual acts do make a lasting difference. Going back to the mountain: rain does cause erosion, and the mountains are shaped by the rain just as much as the shape of the mountains determines the destiny of the water. The outcome of any attempt to change the world is never going to be entirely predictable: entrepreneurs know they are agents of change, but when they look back over their achievements they usually find out that neither the journey nor the destination was what they expected when they started.

Many, though by no means a majority, of leading economists have studied the forces behind change and development in more realistic economic models. Paul M. Romer created Endogenous Growth Theory, setting out the economic conditions necessary for sustained economic growth to become possible. Paul Krugman has applied dazzling mathematical skills to the study of differential growth. W. Brian Arthur is widely credited with being one of the first economists to make a systematic exploration of the consequences of frequent innovation.[7]

Entrepreneurs and leaders

We introduced entrepreneurs and entrepreneurship in Chapter 1, where we defined the entrepreneur as an enterprise creator and agent of change, a builder of teams and organisations. Builders of human structures need to be able to do many things, and one of them is to provide leadership. Very few projects can be completed by one person acting on their own; most rely on the extensive cooperation of suppliers and workers to anticipate problems and to expedite the work. When the project is intended to bring a new product to market the timing of the product's introduction may be crucial to its success. Equally, many modern products are complex, and a minor defect in a component can mean the failure of the whole. An entrepreneur who can create a cohesive team, one where the members anticipate problems and eliminate them before they can damage the project, has an enormous advantage over the one who must rely on bribes or threats.

> As for the best leaders, the people do not notice their existence. The next best, the people honour and praise. The next, the people fear, and the next, the people hate ...
> When the best leaders' work is done the people say: 'We did it ourselves.'
> Lao Tse (epitomised by Townsend 1970)

Corporate rejuvenation

The enterprises that exist today all have a starting point in time: there must, once, have been an entrepreneur or entrepreneurial team who turned a concept into an enterprise. Time, however, brings change, and the needs that the enterprise was created to address may become less urgent, or other enterprises may appear to address them. When established enterprises ignore these external changes, their revenues decline, their profits erode, and their shareholders see the value of their investment fall. There are three broad strategies open to medium and large firms seeking to remain profitable and valuable in a turbulent economy:

▲ They can concentrate on cutting their costs and getting better at making their products, growing their markets by cutting their prices. The price cuts will attract new consumers to their product and will force their less efficient competitors to withdraw from the market, giving them still more scope for growth.

▲ They can practice 'downsizing', abandoning their least profitable product lines and their least profitable customers, and retrenching the staff who used to service them. These firms tend to grow more slowly than their competitors, but they often report very attractive profits in the year following a major downsizing activity.

▲ They can innovate, launching new products to replace those whose sales growth is slowing down and whose profitability is threatened by competition.

The first strategy, that of flooding the market with more and more of a cheaper and cheaper product, is sometimes referred to as the 'T-model' strategy, recalling Henry Ford's success with that car and that strategy between 1908 and 1923.[8] Other textbooks may call it an 'experience curve' strategy. More recently the companies making semiconductors in Taiwan have applied this strategy to their overseas markets if not to each other, leading to their global dominance of the merchant semiconductor industry. Many companies find that their markets do not respond strongly enough to falling prices to make the experience curve strategy viable. Others have found that counter-strategies based upon product differentiation can defeat the experience curve approach.

Downsizing, de-layering, flattening and other organisational tricks became extremely popular in the late 1980s and stayed popular well into the 1990s. Many companies underwent dramatic divestment and downsizing, and in nearly every case the immediate result was a surge in profits and a lift in the share price. When the longer term results of downsizing are reviewed, the picture is less clear. Approximately two-thirds of major United States corporations that downsized were worse off two years later than they had been before the process started. In review, it appears that quite a lot of downsizing was just a repetition of one of the paper entrepreneurs' tricks — the conversion of assets into income. Before the downsizing the typical firm had enjoyed the goodwill of its customers and staff, and both sets of goodwill had a positive effect on the firm's performance. The customers trusted the firm to provide quality products and services, and so they placed orders with the firm without squeezing the last cent out of the quoted prices. The staff worked hard and loyally for rather lower wages than they might have got elsewhere in the expectation of career and job security.

Neither market share nor staff loyalty and dedication appear in the certified accounts of a public company, and so degrading them does not have to be mentioned in a firm's annual report. The combination of demotivated staff and dissatisfied customers leads to falling sales and a higher cost for each sale, so as the effects of a downsizing work through the firm and become apparent to its customers the initial profit boost is replaced by a long term decline in revenue and profit. Even when the downsized firm continues to grow, it seldom achieves its previous growth rate.

The remaining way to preserve a firm's value is to innovate, to introduce new products and processes faster than the old ones lose their market appeal. New products add most value to a firm in the first few years that they are on the market. The most innovative major corporations launch new products long before sales of their existing products have plateaued out, and sometimes while the previous product is still showing strong sales growth.

The problems and opportunities facing an innovative corporation are the reverse of those facing a downsizing one. The costs of new product development and marketing are not shown as a capital item in the accounts, and so they reduce the firm's current profit even as they guarantee its long term value. The innovative firm relies on high staff commitment to keep its product launches on track and to overcome any minor hitches in their launch or their development.

New products need enthusiastic customers who gain their enthusiasm from committed sales and other staff.

The innovative company has one problem all of its own: how to keep its highly motivated staff from 'leaping on their horses and galloping off madly in all directions'. There will always be more ideas than prototypes, and more prototypes than marketed products in an innovative company. Once marketed there will be some products that must be withdrawn in order to release resources for other ones. Deliberately or accidentally, most medium and large corporations have built organisational barriers to innovation; committees that must assess projects, tight budgetary controls, demanding performance targets based on the current product line, and even deliberate overload policies.

Whatever the particular bureaucratic procedure, and whatever the ostensible reason behind each of them, they create a set of hurdles which only a highly motivated person, with a committed team behind them, can hope to surmount. The products that do survive this obstacle course are those with a product champion, or 'intrapreneur' driving them. Relatively few products are successfully championed by their inventor or initiator: good research scientists and development engineers tend to have too high a regard for literal accuracy, and too much faith in the power of reason, to carry a project through the bureaucratic minefield. A relative outsider can also find it easier to see a new idea in the wider market context, while the developer may act as if even discussing a rival product is a criticism of their own.

Satisfying the stakeholders

An entrepreneur makes the important decisions about the initiation and the conduct of a project, and accepts the praise and the rewards for success along with the blame and punishment for failure. While the final measure of success is often financial, personal financial success for the entrepreneur is usually impossible without satisfying all the principal stakeholders. These are the customers, the financiers, and the community. In the usual case where the entrepreneur leads a team in order to bring a product to a successful conclusion, the members of the team are stakeholders to some extent, but managing and motivating them is usually treated as an aspect of leadership rather than entrepreneurship.

The customers show that the enterprise is a success by using the services it provides or buying the goods that it markets at a price that enables the entrepreneur to pay all the bills and have a fair profit left over. In most cases the customers survived before the new firm put its products on the market, and they don't have to buy them anyway. Achieving or exceeding the planned unit volumes, sales revenue and profit are good indicators that the enterprise was successful at identifying and satisfying its customers' requirements.

Some entrepreneurs become involved in public benefit enterprises, providing services to people who cannot pay the full commercial cost, if they can afford to pay anything at all. Such enterprises serve two constituencies, the people who rely on their services and the donors whose contributions pay the bills. Successful public benefit enterprises must satisfy both their clients and their donors. Their entrepreneurs must set out their success criteria and get their donors' agreement to it fairly early in the project, because if they don't they will find themselves chasing a perpetually moving target. Would-be public benefit entrepreneurs often make the mistake of thinking that, since their objectives are admirable and their motives are impeccable, donors are morally obliged to support them. Donors are likely to limit their support to enterprises with excellent objectives and realistic plans for achieving them: purity of motive is seldom enough.

The financiers often declare their measures of success before they commit any money to a project. Different financiers may enter a project at different stages of its life, and their success criteria will differ. In each case, however, the financier's success criteria come in two parts: there is the return that they expect on their funds and an associated schedule of interest, dividend and capital repayment dates; and there is the maximum level of risk that they will permit their investment to be exposed to. Many financiers control their risks by setting apparently arbitrary rules concerning the sort of projects that they will support and the security that they will require.

Would-be entrepreneurs often get a shock when they discover that their potential finance providers are interested in much more than the promised interest payments. At one end of the scale there are the major commercial banks, who charge relatively low interest and in return look for extremely strong security, such as a guarantee backed up by a cash deposit, or a first mortgage security over a valuable property. The major banks strengthen their own position even further by the rules that they impose: for example, the bank's loan agreement may allow it to demand its funds back within thirty days for any reason or none, and to seize the security if the advance is not repaid in full on the newly specified day.

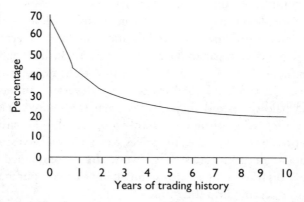

Figure 2.2 Minimum rates of return — experience in the market reduces uncertainty and the returns required by investors

Equity investors share the entrepreneur's risks; if the business fails, their money is usually lost, and so they expect higher returns than the banks do. The earlier in a project's life that equity is sought, the higher must the promised returns be. Few investors in Australia are prepared to invest in start-up enterprises, but when they do they will look to get fifteen to twenty times their initial investment back when they sell their interest in seven or so years from the date that they put up the first money. Even with this level of return such venture capitalists demand much more than promises. The new enterprise's plans will be scrutinised intensively, its marketing research tested, and its key staff interviewed and their references checked. The money will then be advanced under the terms of an agreement that may not be as onerous as the ones that the banks impose, but which will, for example, allow the venture capitalist to sack the entrepreneur and appoint a new chief executive if certain financial and other targets are not met.

The government represents the community in a democratic country, and while it does not define entrepreneurial success it has a vast number of laws and regulations. Entrepreneurs who breach these may face fines or worse personally, but more often they will be denied the permits and planning authorities that their enterprise needs. In general terms the laws and regulations are intended to protect the community from the acts of reckless, immoral or incompetent individuals. While many regulations appear ridiculous, most of them are there because, at some time, an individual caused harm to his neighbours, his employees or his customers in a way now prohibited by law.

The governments of different countries attempt to protect their citizens from harm in different ways. Sometimes there is merely a law against doing or threatening harm, such as the law against dangerous driving, but often there are prescriptive regulations, such as speed limits. Many entrepreneurs get their enterprises into serious trouble when they start to export or to do business in other countries by assuming, naively, that the regulations are the same as those with which they are familiar at home. In 1991 a United States delegation, led by the President, complained that 'unfair' Japanese regulations blocked the import of United States-made motor cars. The Japanese explained, as tactfully as possible, that their motorists drove on the left and therefore preferred right-hand drive cars: no United States manufacturer, at that time, had right-hand drive vehicles in production. Working in the other direction, many Japanese bought land in California in 1990 and 1991 expecting to develop it immediately. Only when they had paid for it did they discover that the United States has local, county, state and federal governments, all of whom need to be satisfied before a sod is turned or a brick is laid. The prices the Japanese investors paid were appropriate for development sites where work could commence immediately, but were far too high for sites where, as for many of these purchases, development was years or decades into the future.

Governments don't merely prescribe laws and regulations; they provide for remedies and punishments when these laws are broken. In most cases the law looks for a person to hold responsible for any damage an enterprise causes to its neighbours, its employees or its customers, and that person is the entrepreneur. The costs and delays caused by trials and investigations can doom an enterprise. Entrepreneurs do not want to be found innocent but broke at the end of a long and expensive trial: they want to stay out of court altogether. Like Caesar's wife, they should be above suspicion.

Staying out of court and avoiding disputes generally are signs that a new enterprise has been a good neighbour and a good local citizen.

Managing risk

'Risk' is a simple word for a very complex concept. The statistics of risk are based on 'random' events, such as tossing dice or spinning a coin. A new business venture is not really like spinning a coin: the people who will make the new enterprise a success by buying its products are mostly alive and set in their ways. There are very few totally random events in the modern world, and so when some event occurs it is usually possible to find out what caused it, what caused the causes, and so on for as long as the investigator wishes to keep looking and the people that the investigator must interview will go on answering questions.

Business risk is more a matter of uncertainty than chance: an entrepreneur might start a casino but would be unlikely to place more than a social bet in one. Business proposals are seldom set out as win/lose gambles. A proposal may require some investment in product development, and the new firm may need a certain number of customers prepared to pay at least a minimum price if it is to survive. If it starts and fails it may be because product development took too long or cost too much, or because too few customers were prepared to pay the minimum feasible price. Some projects fail absolutely, by attempting the impossible or by producing a product which generates no sales at all, but these are rare.

Uncertainty is measured by the 'standard deviation'. For planning purposes a standard deviation is the difference between the expected outcome, with a 50:50 chance of being achieved, and the one-in-six worst case. If, for example, an entrepreneur plans to sell a new venture in seven year's time for a million dollars, with a one-in-six chance that it will fail and be worth nothing before the seven years are up, the uncertainty is 100 per cent. If the one-in-six worst case is that the business will only fetch half a million dollars, the uncertainty is 50 per cent. If the one-in-six chance leaves the entrepreneur with a worthless firm and an enforceable debt of a million dollars, the uncertainty is 200 per cent.

The economist Avinash Dixit (1992) has developed a quite simple formula for converting uncertainty into hurdle rates. We reproduce Dixit's formula in Chapter 8, where we explain how to value a proposal. The hurdle rate as defined by Dixit is the expected rate of return on a project below which an investor would be better off leaving their money in government bonds. It is the minimum return a thoughtful investor would demand before supporting a proposal. This will be explained in more detail in the chapter on finance; but Dixit's work has shown that venture capitalists who demand returns of 60 per cent or more, or who will only put up $40 000 against a promise of a million dollars in seven year's time are not greedy or risk averse, just rational.

In the case of a successful new enterprise the risks often vanish entirely with hindsight; one of the facts about great enterprises is that, when they are completed, practically everybody is able to find fault with the way they were carried out, and many people are likely to comment on how obvious it all was, and how little the entrepreneur really did. Some historians, often called 'revisionists', specialise in debunking heroes: a revisionist historian recently wrote a biography of Winston Churchill that counted every bottle of brandy the man drank while barely mentioning the Second World War. When revisionist historians come to describe a really difficult decision they usually have no difficulty in showing that the entrepreneur's successful choice was only a matter of luck. In practice successful entrepreneurs create their own luck: often either of two possible courses of action will succeed if the decision is made quickly and the necessary actions put in place vigorously. Timidity, delay, and trying to 'put an each-way bet on a two horse race' may seem like caution or prudence. In fact these ways of behaving increase the risk of ultimate failure.

The degree of risk facing a new enterprise is primarily a measure of the defects in the current state of generally available knowledge about the forces in favour and against the project. At one extreme the Commonwealth government announces from time to time that it is selling ten year bonds, that the selling price is such an amount, the interest will be so much, paid according to a clearly set out schedule, and the bonds will be redeemed for their face value on such and such a date. The government usually takes considerable pains to make the terms and conditions of each issue widely known. The difference between the 'worst' outcome and the 'expected' outcome is zero. A decision to invest in Commonwealth bonds involves so little risk and uncertainty that it is often described as a 'risk-free' investment; there is little scope for entrepreneurship here.

Risk is multi-dimensional, and some of the dimensions are set out in Table 2.1. There is no single opposite to 'low risk', but practically every investment in anything other than government-backed bonds involves less certainty about the amount and timing of the investment and the size and phasing of the returns. More research will usually reduce the uncertainty in any given case, but this research takes time and costs money. The time taken by extensive pre-commitment research actually increases the risk that some other entrepreneur will pre-empt the market, while the money spent on it increases the investment and reduces the rate of return to the investor. The time and cost of this research is the cost of reducing the investment risk to some defined level.

Entrepreneurs are frequently described as risk-takers, but they don't talk about themselves that way. Psychologists describe entrepreneurs as risk tolerant,

Table 2.1   *Types of risk*

Type	Examples
Marketing	Too few customers
	Customers don't like the product
	Price doesn't cover supply costs
	Distributors and retailers demand excessive margins
	Too many competitors
	Incautious delivery or performance guarantees
Technical	Product doesn't work
	Product can't be made
	Service providers can't be trained
	Product has safety or reliability concerns
Personnel	Fraud and theft
	Incompetence
	Trained staff keep leaving
Environment	Natural catastrophe
	Government decides to have recession
	Product has environmental risk

which means that they do not act like rabbits caught in the light of headlamps when faced with uncertainty; they might not like risk, but they aren't paralysed by it. Entrepreneurs are usually very good at assessing and balancing risks in their proper context; doing nothing involves all sorts of risks in a world where other entrepreneurs may be active.

When some person takes on the risk of some enterprise without bringing any particular advantage to the task, that person is a gambler, pure and simple. The other stakeholders share the publicly available knowledge about the risks of the proposed enterprise, and are not acting rationally if they are prepared to pay an entrepreneur more than the cost (including the opportunity cost) of the research needed to reduce or eliminate these risks. Once the project is well understood the risks are low, and one or other of the stakeholders can carry out the project in person, or through a salaried employee.

The entrepreneur's advantage

If the entrepreneur has no special competence to bring to the project there is no reason to expect the costs of the project under the entrepreneur's control to be any less than the totally safe — and low return — alternative of undertaking an exhaustive study of the product and the market before actually doing anything. A successful entrepreneur must have a private view of the project risks or a personal capacity to control them which shows them to be significantly smaller than the public view.

Entrepreneurs and the economy

When Christopher Columbus set sail to 'discover' the West Indies the public view was that such a journey was impossible and that the risks were infinite. Columbus had researched the issue by reading ancient Greek authors and he knew that the world was round. By applying logic, roughly the argument that one patch of ocean was much like another, he formed the private view that the risks of the voyage were finite and manageable. The project's success made Columbus famous and extremely rich, although not, in the end, particularly happy.

Sir John Monash was Australia's greatest soldier, and the only general on either side to emerge from the Western Front of the First World War with a reputation for success unstained by one for butchery. Before the war he founded the Monier Concrete Company and after it he was the foundation chairman of the State Electricity Commission of Victoria. Monash combined the abilities to analyse, to plan, and to evaluate to an extraordinary degree, while retaining a remarkable emotional detachment. If a civil or military project was going to fail he knew it, and within the limits of his authority, stopped it, no matter whose idea it originally was. If the plan was going to succeed he knew that too, and he would not be deflected by other people's doubts, whether the doubters were the staff of the Commander in Chief (he ordered his signallers not to pass on messages) or the Victorian Cabinet (he called the Cabinet to a meeting, told them what they were about to do, and left without waiting for questions).

Part of the entrepreneur's advantage, as shown by Columbus and Monash, is the ability to form an opinion based upon the facts, disregarding unfounded prejudices and popular superstitions along the way. Part is the ability to function under pressure. These two attributes are seldom sufficient. An entrepreneur must be able to lead, and an entrepreneur must be able to contribute.

An entrepreneur's contribution will usually be based on some particular competence that sets them apart from their likely competitors. Columbus was an expert sailor, while Monash was a professional engineer and had been an officer in the volunteer artillery for many years before the war. A business entrepreneur must have a strong grasp of some key aspects of a project, whether marketing, or sales, or development, or production, or in general terms, some skill or capability that enables the entrepreneur to be personally essential to the project's success.

Leadership can be both over- and understated. Leadership divorced from any useful skill becomes a mockery and its achievements nugatory. Leadership may involve flamboyance, but integrity, competence and the ability to communicate effectively are the defining qualities of leadership. Monash became profoundly admired and respected, but he was anything but charismatic. He did not lead his troops over the parapet: he sent them, and they went willingly because of their absolute — and repeatedly justified — faith in his generalship.

Big wheels and little wheels

All entrepreneurs are not equal

Projects come in all shapes and sizes. Landing a man on the moon was a project, but so is rejuvenating a corner milk bar. No one is compelled to be an entrepreneur, but it is very difficult to run a business, or even play a significant role in a commercial or community organisation, without making entrepreneurial decisions from time to time. While the success of any project is going to be defined by its stakeholders, the success of any one person's entrepreneurial career is very likely to be defined in terms of that person's objectives.

People's objectives change as they pass through their lives, but broadly speaking a person who achieves what they set out to do is a success. An entrepreneur should not consider their life a failure if they retire without ever founding a company the size of BHP.

Creating a growth venture

Some businesses seem to grow without any apparent limit from their founding or from the entry of an outstanding individual. In 1900 BHP was a regional mining company about to hire the young Essington Lewis. In 1904 Henry Ford was a young man building motor cars as much for fun as for sale. In 1923 Alfred P. Sloan wondered whether General Motors was worth more as real estate than as a manufacturer. In 1935 R. M. Ansett was a brash young man whose Melbourne–Ballarat bus line had just been regulated out of business; he observed that Victorian state laws did not regulate the sky. In 1945 the Toyoda family owned a medium sized textile machinery factory and a small workshop assembling military trucks, neither of which was actually operating in the aftermath of Japan's defeat. In 1958 Ken Thomas and Peter Abeles decided to merge their trucking businesses under the name TNT. In 1968 Andy Groves and his friends Robert Noyce and Gordon Moore founded Intel to make 1024-bit DRAM chips. In 1980 Bill Gates's Microsoft was one of hundreds of small businesses writing software for the hobbyists and pioneers who were trying to make microprocessors do something useful, or at least interesting.

Often there is a baton change during the development of a company, when the founding entrepreneur passes control, not always willingly, to a new management team. Bill Boeing founded the Boeing Aircraft Company, but it got into difficulties, and the Boeing name is the sum of the Boeing family's interest in the present company. Ansett Airlines was taken over by TNT and News Corporation a few years before R. M. Ansett's death, and he was reduced to the role of honorary non-voting chairman.

In many cases the entrepreneur who led a company from its foundation or re-foundation to greatness did not create the opportunity that became their company's strength. The First World War and the interruption to Australia's steel supplies gave Lewis the chance to jerk BHP from being a medium-scale mining company to a large-scale industrial one. If Henry Ford had been less pig-headed, churning out Model T Fords long after General Motors had demonstrated that the market wanted variety, and colours other than black, Alfred Sloan's task would have been much harder. The Second World War and its frantic demand for aircraft maintenance services gave Ansett a tremendous boost; and the collapse of Australian National Airlines in 1957 gave him his chance to take over a functioning airline on liquidator's terms. Bill Gates actually told IBM to go and buy a product called QDOS instead of giving him the order for PC-DOS; IBM gave Gates the order anyway, and so it was Gates who bought QDOS, polished it into PC-DOS, and began the process of turning Microsoft into the world's largest software company.

What all these successful entrepreneurs have in common is that they recognised their opportunity when it came, and they pursued it single-mindedly. Another common factor is that they did not do it on their own: successful entrepreneurs build, lead and inspire teams of people to create their new enterprises. There is nothing routine about the creation of a new growth enterprise, and little chance to repeat learned behaviour. The new enterprise is seldom in a position to pay the high wages and salaries, or to make the promises and grant the perquisites that would be needed to recruit proven top performers. The new enterprise can only succeed by drawing extraordinary performances out of ordinary people.

The enterprise creator

Bill Boeing and R. M. Ansett had to be prised apart from the enterprises that they founded, but there are also people who deliberately build enterprises and sell them as soon as they have grown to the point where management begins to replace leadership. These people are less 'lifestyle entrepreneurs' than people who choose an entrepreneurial lifestyle.

Managing an established enterprise has challenges and opportunities, but these are different to those facing the creator of a new one. There are some people who find the challenges of starting a new enterprise attractive, and such people often find the task of managing an existing one boring. The archetypical entrepreneur in American textbooks founds a new business, builds it for seven years, and then sells it to a larger firm for a net personal gain of at least a million dollars. Having created and sold one enterprise, these entrepreneurs frequently start another, often investing their entire capital: having made a million dollars once, they believe that they can do it again.

Other successful entrepreneurs may hand their enterprise to managers while they involve themselves in other activities: often, in Australia at least, these activities have some public benefit in view rather than being meant to add substantially to the entrepreneur's personal wealth.

The lifestyle entrepreneur

Many people find that working for a boss is irksome, even when their managers have outstanding human resource management skills and their employer is a leader in empowerment and a provider of outstanding benefits. When, as can still happen in Australia, their boss believes that fear and insecurity are essential tools of the active manager, the delights of working for someone else diminish further. When previously loyal and hardworking employees are told that they are no longer required they frequently ask themselves whether the rewards of working for someone else are worth the pain.

People in this position may set themselves a target: in such and such a time they will be the proprietor or major shareholder in a business that will provide an adequate income without making extravagant demands on their time, or, at least, pay the bills while they are doing things that they want to do.

American books often call firms created by entrepreneurs with such closely defined ambitions as 'mom and pop' operations; they are also called 'jobs without a boss'. However the resulting businesses are described, creating such an operation involves most of the problems, though usually on a smaller scale, that face the creator of a new growth venture. Judging by the statistics on survival rates these firms are not significantly less likely to fail than new firms with less well-defined ambitions: because the scale of the problems is smaller, they may receive less attention. While the risk of a cash crisis or of a technological debacle are less, the risks that stable small- and medium-sized firms face from major changes in the market or the economy are probably greater.

Many large companies have introduced lean production and single-sourcing, following the lead set by Toyota. When firms like Ford or General Motors cut their supplier roster to a fifth of its original size, thousands of small and medium businesses are pushed to, or over, the brink of disaster. Major retailers extend their market reach by building 'category-killer' stores such as 'Toys-R-Us' and 'OfficeWorks', and as such businesses grow they draw custom away from hundreds of small and medium retailers, many of whom will be forced into drastic retrenchments, or out of business altogether.

Stable and lifestyle firms face risks that need managing because they service changing markets in turbulent economies. They will always face challenges that force the owners and managers of these firms to make decisions. Whenever the owners and managers of small and medium businesses assess risks and make decisions they are entrepreneurs, and the lessons of this book are relevant to them.

Product champions: The 'intrapreneur'

New, high-growth companies eventually become established, stable ones. One day they reach the limit to growth in their main market. Ansett went from buses to aeroplanes, but General Motors never did. Sloan decided, probably correctly, that the mass production and the segmented marketing strategies that made GM the market leader in automobiles would not transfer to aircraft. Once a company has reached half or thereabouts of its potential market its growth phase, at least with that product line, is over. From this point leadership becomes less important and management more. Independent decision-making is frowned upon; staff are expected to obey the rules and to submit their proposals for change to a committee. The committee may reject or ignore them if they are not prepared in the proper format. Worthwhile ideas can very easily become buried in such an atmosphere. In extreme cases such a firm may fall into the hands of a chief executive who sees new product development and marketing as an unnecessary expense; those who propose such a development may experience a career hiccup.

Some major corporations have made strenuous efforts to avoid such fossilisation. The American corporations 3M and Hewlett-Packard, and the Japanese firm Sony, have implemented procedures intended to encourage innovation and avoid relying on the cash flow generated by older products. While the average age of all the products on the Australian market, or all the processes used to make or deliver them, is between eight and twelve years, innovative firms strive to keep the average age of their product lines to much less than that. 3M automatically offers any product for licensing as soon as they have had it in the market for seven years, while Hewlett-Packard explicitly charges its business unit managers with keeping their product lines young: the average Hewlett-Packard product is less than three years old in the market.

Over recent years many firms have aggressively 'delayered' their management structure, cutting out middle and supervisory managers and relying on teamwork and cooperation to keep their enterprise functioning. A bureaucracy sets many barriers to change in place, but it also provides a mechanism for implementing changes once a decision is formally taken. Firms that have removed their bureaucracy have removed the barriers but they have also removed the mechanism. A sandy desert has replaced the brick wall, and it may be no easier to cross. The individual teams within a flattened organisation may have an extremely flexible and effective approach to their defined tasks, but they often become fiercely protective of them. Their interests and their commitment may be to the team goals and not to those of the overall organisation.

Some people who work for large companies cease having business-related ideas. They may become keen gardeners, or golfers; they may become pillars of their local community, or the devoted secretary of a sporting club. At work, however, they arrive punctually, greet their colleagues, managers and subordinates courteously, discharge their duties punctiliously, and switch their brains back on as they get into their car or catch their train to go home. Other people take their ideas and leave, intending to start their own businesses. A few people are, however, trapped.

People who work for large corporations are sometimes struck by ideas that cannot work anywhere else. It may be an idea for reorganising the flow of work, or an extension to the current product line, or it may need access to key people in the corporation plus lots of money. In the first two cases the project is meaningless outside the original corporation, while in the third case it is only major corporations that can mobilise major amounts of money. In all three cases the idea will lapse unless it is taken up by a product champion, an intrapreneur, who will secure corporate agreement to the project.

In a traditional bureaucracy this may involve the painstaking submission of forms and reports, every one of which carefully observes the bureaucratic rules. Alternatively, the product champion may find a way to short-circuit the process, lobbying the key decision makers of the firm, building a tower of godfathers to the top, until the innovative project becomes part of the firm's official objectives. This may seem to be an extremely wasteful process, particularly to the many product developers who believe that the superiority of their invention is so self-evident that only fools or rogues could fail to acknowledge it. It is still the only proven route to get private-sector projects with capital requirements in the hundreds of millions of dollars or more off the ground.

In a flat organisation the champion must be able to create a meta-team, a team of teams, that will accept the challenge of creating a new product and the risk that one or more of the original teams will find their own product lines superseded. Ultra-flat organisations are relatively new, and there are few documented cases of such an organisation coming together around a major initiative. More frequently, the innovations such organisations produce are limited to the capability of one or a very small number of teams.

Successful product champions cannot rely solely on their sales skills, or the cunning with which they subvert a bureaucracy. The projects that they propose must make technical and financial sense, for at least two reasons. One is that bureaucrats and other defenders of the *status quo* will seize on any technical or financial weaknesses to damn the project. The other is that the product champion is tied to the project and the corporation: there is no particular joy in being the inspiration for a monumental failure.

Many of the innovations that shaped the last quarter of the twentieth century came from corporations that committed everything that they had, and a little bit more, into a single project. Boeing Corporation did it twice, once by innovating the commercial jet airliner,[9] and subsequently by innovating the wide-bodied passenger jet. IBM created the modern information technology industry with the System/360, announced in 1964 and delivered in volume from 1966 on. In 1964 an IBM spokesman was asked whether the System/360 was important to IBM: he answered, 'You bet your company it is!'

Changing society: The public benefit enterprise

Terrible social evils often only appear so in hindsight, at least to the majority of citizens. Before 1777, the common opinion of educated men from the beginning of recorded time had favoured slavery: in that year Dr Samuel Johnson published his considered opinion on a suit to return an escaped slave from Scotland to his master, and the court, accepting Johnson's argument, set the former slave free and effectively abolished slavery in Britain. It took two further years before the right that Johnson had won for a black man was extended to coal miners in Scotland. In 1806 the young Lord Palmerston stood for the parliamentary seat of Cambridge (and lost) on a pro-slave trade platform.

By 1833 the same Lord Palmerston was enthusiastically directing the Royal Navy to enforce an international ban on the slave trade. Palmerston's biographer noted that the man was a perfect weathervane; never leading public opinion, but never far behind it. Palmerston's conversion shows that it took just fifty-six years from opposition to slavery being the preserve of a tiny minority of eccentrics to it becoming mainstream opinion.

History records that Bishop Sam Wilberforce created and inspired the anti-slavery movement in Britain, showing all the energy and leadership associated with successful entrepreneurship. Half a century after Wilberforce's triumph General William Booth inspired and led the Salvation Army, another huge entrepreneurial endeavour undertaken without the expectation or the achievement of any personal financial rewards.

The leaders of social change must employ many of the planning, organisational, and leadership skills of entrepreneurship. As Booth said to critics who complained that Salvation Army bands were playing popular tunes, 'Why should the Devil have all the best music?'

Learning entrepreneurship

Can entrepreneurship be taught, and learned? The answer is yes, and no. There are unlimited ways in which people express themselves, and becoming an entrepreneur is just one of these. People whose talents and ambitions do not include building teams of people to achieve an economic or social objective can be taught to pass exams in entrepreneurship, but this won't turn them into entrepreneurs.

The world is full of opportunities, but only those people that recognise an opportunity and create an enterprise to realise it are entrepreneurs. Many entrepreneurs fail at their first attempt; some of these are discouraged, while others learn some lessons from their experience and try again. Sometimes a new enterprise fails for reasons that could not have been foreseen, but far too often the failure can be traced to pure ignorance: the entrepreneur or product champion, in their enthusiasm, ignored some elementary rule of management, finance, accounting or marketing.

Some projects get into trouble because of a failure to integrate the skills available: such projects go through an unnecessarily long gestation and a difficult birth while various critical issues are raised, only partially resolved, and raised again. If the effect of these incessant reviews is to keep changing direction the ultimate result may be to abort the project completely.

Entrepreneurial education can spread a general recognition of the significance of innovation and entrepreneurship through the community. At the same time it can give people with entrepreneurial ambitions the skills they need to seize opportunities and avoid the most common causes of failure.

Entrepreneurial education focuses on:

▲ *Opportunity screening:* How do you sort out 'real' opportunities from mirages? How do you go looking for opportunities in the first place? We examine opportunity screening in Chapter 5 and develop the matter further in Chapter 8.

▲ *Team creation:* How do you recruit and motivate the people you will need to launch the venture with you? How do you decide what sort of team you are going to need? Chapter 12 explains the salient facts about designing new venture organisations.

▲ *Accounting:* What has to be done to keep track of the money passing through a new enterprise? How do you use your accounting data to help you manage the new business? What do you tell your accountant, and what do you expect from him or her? We explain the principles of accounting with special reference to entrepreneurial ventures in Chapter 14.

▲ *The law:* What must a business do, and what must it not do, to obey the law? What is the right structure for the new enterprise? What do directors do? We provide a brief overview of the relevant laws in Chapters 6 and 11.

▲ *Ethics:* How do you preserve your self-respect, and the respect of your community, without fudging the hard decisions? We discussed ethics in Chapter 1, because of the essential role of ethics in creating teams and building value-creating relationships.

▲ *Finance:* How do you measure the value created by a business? How do you build a financial operating plan? How do you structure an offer to potential investors? How do you find potential investors? Once you have them, how do you keep their confidence? Finance plays a significant role in every stage of venture creation: we discuss it explicitly in Chapters 8, 14 and 17.

▲ *Marketing:* How do you bring your product to the attention of potential customers? How do you estimate the time and scale of the market's response? How big should the launch and continuing marketing budgets be? What will be the effect of increasing or reducing these budgets? Marketing is crucial to the success of most new ventures: in this book we discuss it in depth in Chapters 8, 9 and 10.

▲ *Planning and integration:* How do you draw up a business plan? What goes into it? What gets left out? How do you present it to investors? How do you resolve resource conflicts? This whole book is about planning and integration, but Chapter 16 is specifically about creating a business plan.

Entrepreneurs who learn these skills before they launch their new venture are not certain to succeed, but they will be able to identify, and avoid, the most common causes of failure. Entrepreneurs who start the business first and try to learn these skills on the job need a great deal of luck if their venture is to stay afloat. People who never learn them never become successful entrepreneurs.

A well-structured entrepreneurial education program provides an opportunity for potential entrepreneurs to develop and test their skills at planning and leadership in a relatively safe environment. Such programs often involve team work and a substantial element of team assessment, and while the students' projects may lead to live enterprises, they don't have to. Where possible such programs should include exposure to practising professionals in finance, marketing and other critical areas, particularly in the plan evaluation process. This can give students a foretaste of the type of questions that they will face, and the directness of the criticism that they may be subjected to, when they set out to practice their entrepreneurial skills on a truly live project.

'Lifestyle' entrepreneurs, people who intend to start or take over a small business, cannot neglect any of these issues. One person, planning to start a new retail business, will take a day or a week to stand outside a possible site and count the number of people, and likely customers, who go past. That person is practising marketing. Another person might lease a site in a shopping centre from an agent because the rent is especially low: that person is not practising marketing. The second person's site may turn out to be one of a row of otherwise empty shops in an isolated corner; the business's failure is a marketing one, even if the word was never used.

Profit, value-added and added value

Cash and profit

One of the first lessons every budding entrepreneur must learn is the difference between cash flow and profit. The issue is obscured by the frequency with which profit is referred to as the aim of all businesses in the media and even in some popular business books. Both cash and profit are important, but their implications are different. For the entrepreneur, cash is king.

Cash provides the test of solvency of a business. As long as a business can pay its debts as they fall due it is solvent and under the control of its owners and managers. The very minute that it cannot meet a current debt it is insolvent, or bankrupt, and control passes to the business's creditors. The law does not ask whether an insolvent business is profitable, or whether the value of its assets covers its debts. The only question in bankruptcy is: Is there a properly incurred debt which is now due and upon which payment has not been made?

Profit is an accounting term that relates to a period of operations, and compares the value of the cash and other assets owned by a business at the end of that period with the value at the beginning. Every business needs a balance sheet, a statement which records the value of its assets and the extent of its liabilities, and their difference, the firm's net assets. The balance sheet serves to reconcile the cash flow and income statements as well as recording the value of its assets. A business's value takes into account fixed assets, such as buildings and machinery, current assets, such as money owed to the firm and cash in the bank, current liabilities, such as amounts owing for wages, taxes and purchased goods as well as overdrafts with the firms' bankers, and long term liabilities, such as fixed term debts. If a firm is worth more at the end of a period than it was at the beginning, after adjustments including depreciation, asset sales and capital subscriptions, it has made a legal profit and is permitted to pay a dividend.

The word 'profit' in conversational use has a much wider connotation than it does when used by accountants. Many firms have been able to declare profits and pay dividends by sticking to the letter of the law and ignoring likely future problems. If the firm uses expensive equipment which will in due course need replacing, inflation may mean that the accumulated depreciation reserves are far too small to pay for a replacement. An apparently healthy firm may be living on borrowed time. Much of the real value of a firm lies in the skill and commitment of its employees, the dominant factors in its 'core competencies'. Much of the rest is the value of its reputation and of the loyalty of its customers. These 'intangibles' are seldom recorded on balance sheets at all, and never recorded accurately.

For a stable business trading in a mature market the cash flow, adjusted for depreciation, and the profits over an accounting period will be roughly the same, but for a growth business there is no link. Consider a small or medium business that wins a large contract to supply a leading retail chain. It must buy the materials it needs, engage workers, pay its salesperson's bonus, pay any co-promotion levies, pay for transport to the retailer's warehouse, buy materials and pay wages to make up the second batch, all before the retailer pays a cent. If the small business's product is innovative the margin may well be quite high, and so the order from the major retailer looks very profitable: for each million dollars in retail sales the small business might only have to spend $400 000 on wages and materials. For each million dollars in new sales the small business might have to find up to half a million dollars in cash to finance these wages and materials, while still paying its own fixed costs.

If the new product in the example is a great success the problem can be even worse: the first order for $1 million (retail value) is delivered (say) in June (but not paid for until the middle of July) but half way through June the retailer's buyer rings up with great news: 'we want $3 million worth for July — we're taking you national!' From having little or no debt in May the small business must find $2 million before the end of June or decline the order. Profits may be pouring in, but cash is pouring out.

More generally, every firm that is growing rapidly will need increasing amounts of cash, and relatively few such firms are able to generate all the cash that they need from trading. Some firms have had to pass up golden opportunities because they could not arrange financing. Others have rushed in, only to be foreclosed by their bankers when they break their overdraft limit. There are a number of avenues which firms in this position can use to raise the necessary finance, and some of these are discussed in Chapters 15 and 17, but most of them won't work if they are not put in place until the firm is verging on bankruptcy.

Profit and value-added

A firm's value-added for a period is the difference between its revenue from sales and the amount it spends on purchased goods and services. Value-added therefore includes wages, salaries, rents, interest and income taxes as well as profits.

Broadly speaking, privately held companies everywhere and public companies in Germany, France and Japan tend to focus their planning on their value-added, while publicly held companies in England, Australia and the United States tend to focus on profits, particularly since the 1980s and the time of the 'paper entrepreneurs'. The most direct way for a firm to increase its value-added is by increasing its sales, either reaching out to more customers or by increasing the variety of the goods and services that it supplies to its existing customers. Profits, on the other hand, can be increased most rapidly, if not sustainably, by cutting wages, salaries and rents, sacking staff and closing offices and plants; even when this reduces the quality of the product offering it generally takes some time for customers to rearrange their buying patterns, and so the result of such cost cutting is nearly always a boost to profits in the short term. There is clearly a major difference between the economic impact of value maximising and profit maximising firms.

Value maximisers see profits as just one, and not the most important, measure of success, and their strategic focus is on increasing the number of their customers and the amount each customer spends with them. Profit maximisers see profits as the only objective and are prepared to sacrifice the interests of their employees and customers if this produces a profit boost. When value maximisers meet profit maximisers in the market the result is not hard to anticipate. These clashes are often portrayed as 'Japan Incorporated versus the USA', but the dramatic success of News Corporation and Wal-Mart Stores shows that the triumph of the value-adders owes nothing to nationality and everything to management orientation. Woolworths Ltd in Australia is another example of the apparently unstoppable march of a value-added corporate culture over a profit-grabbing one.

Gary Hamel[10] divides the profit maximisers from the value-added maximisers by distinguishing them as 'denominator managers' and 'numerator managers' respectively. They share a common ambition to raise, or at least maintain, the firm's return on assets (ROA).

> **ROA equals Returns divided by Assets**

One manager concentrates on reducing the assets, by divesting, or not replacing depreciated equipment, while the other tries to increase the returns, even increasing the asset base if the returns can be increased in a still greater proportion.

Added value and wealth creation

The term 'added value' (or economic value-added — EVA[11]) puts a value on the ability of some companies, even in mature industries, to earn a higher return on their assets, and to have their shares listed at a higher price relative to these assets, than other firms. Some analysts use the term 'market to book ratio' to describe these differences. Consider, as an example, Australian retailing. On 20 May 1996 Woolworths shares could be sold for $3.15 each, although the book value of assets per share was only 89 cents. By contrast, Coles Myer shares could be bought for $4.48, and each share represented assets of $2.27. The management of Woolworths added $2.54 to each dollar of assets while the management of Coles Myer added 97 cents.

The results of a comparison using market to book ratios are similar: market to book for Woolworths was 3.54 while that for Coles Myer was 1.97. (There is an obvious link between market to book ratios and added value per share.)

According to the 'value-based planning' paradigm[12] the duty of a firm's managers is to increase the market to book ratio, but unfortunately this only works if the market price is a true reflection of the firm's likely future performance. Ironically, the market price is most likely to reflect a firm's true value if the managers of the firm are not paying any particular attention to it. Once the firm's share price becomes a matter of legitimate management interest the firm's managers will be tempted to take actions that make their firm look better, whatever the real medium and long term effect of these acts may be.

An entrepreneur who intends to manage a sustainable increase in wealth must maximise the true value of the firm relative to its fixed assets. The true value is the present value of all future expected cash flows, discounted according to a correctly risk-adjusted interest rate. This is the value that the firm would have in a perfectly informed market and, for a listed company, will be the average value of the shares over a sufficiently long period of time. The subject of the valuation of a business will be dealt with at greater length in Chapters 8, 14 and 17.

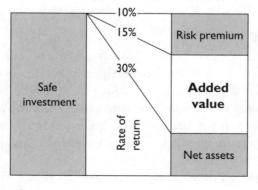

Figure 2.3 Added value

Zero sum and positive sum

The win-win enterprise

Successful business entrepreneurs are usually richer at the end of the process than they were at the beginning, and it may be wondered where the money came from. The simplest answer is that entrepreneurial firms create wealth by introducing innovations.

The entrepreneur offers a new service, or delivers a new good, that costs less to provide than people are willing to pay; in turn, the value that the average buyer receives exceeds the price that they are required to pay. In particular, the value that the buyers get, after adjusting for the price that they pay, is greater than the net value that they used to receive for their money before the innovation became available. The entrepreneur is better off, as the owner of valuable shares of a successful enterprise. The entrepreneur's employees are better off, since they are getting a more attractive package of benefits than they were before they took a job with the entrepreneur. The entrepreneur's customers are better off, receiving more value for money than before.

Clearly, now that some money is being spent on the entrepreneur's products there will be a smaller fraction of the total expenditure in the economy going on everything else. As the effects of the innovation work through the whole economy the money supply increases sufficiently to ensure that the average producer is no worse off than they were before: everybody wins; there are no losers.

When an innovation directly drives some previous product from the market some workers may lose their jobs and some shareholders may see the value of their shares fall. They may not be consoled by the thought that everyone, on average, has been made better off when they have so obviously been hurt. There are two possible answers. One is that casualties are inevitable if society is to progress, and that the social safety net is there to keep them from destitution. The other is 'Go and do likewise'.[13] Innovations may displace older products, but they seldom compete with other innovations. Firms that develop an innovative culture have little to fear from other innovators.

The money manipulator

Most of the time prices will even out across a market; a beer brewed in Brisbane will cost about the same in every Brisbane pub that sells it, and the price in Perth will be roughly the Brisbane price adjusted for freight costs. The average price of a firm's shares over a sufficient period will reflect the risk-adjusted discounted value of the firm's future cash flows quite accurately. Most of the time, in most markets, there are no super profits to be made by buying and selling the same thing.

There are, however, times when the market gets things wrong, and goods, or more often shares, are on offer at a price much lower or higher than they are

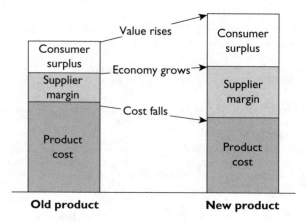

Figure 2.4 Innovation leads to economic growth

in some other place or will be in some short time. Buying when or where something is cheap, and selling where or when it is much dearer, or reversing the process by short-selling before a price fall, can produce large gains for the successful speculator. Speculation is often described as gambling, and often it is, but sometimes it is a response to superior information. In 1815, for example, Nathan Rothschild learned the result of the Battle of Waterloo several hours before the official despatch arrived, and made another large fortune by buying up government bonds cheaply. Today's market traders have the twenty-four-hour news channel CNN showing at all times.

Speculators have been known to get information by more devious means than watching television. Staff of companies — and governments — have been bribed to pass over advance information about facts that will change bond or share prices. Press releases with lucky 'errors' in them can distort a market. Companies may be managed so as to report unsustainable profit increases leading to a sharp rise in their share price, or a 'concert party' may coordinate the buying and selling of a large parcel of shares and take advantage of the price differentials this causes.

However it is obtained, a speculative profit is the clearest possible example of a win–lose combination. The people who bought before the price fell, or sold before the rise, lose exactly as much as the speculator gains. The speculator makes money without adding value. This makes speculators unpopular among the losers, who make up the majority. In what was basically a public relations driven attempt to improve the image of speculation and prevent governments trying to control it, Australia's main speculators of the 1980s called themselves 'entrepreneurs' and the Australian Stock Exchange classified their companies as 'entrepreneurial'. This was a travesty, and in the 1990s the swindlers and speculators of the 1980s are usually referred to as the 'paper entrepreneurs' when the word is used to describe them at all.

End notes

1   One of the most comprehensive analyses of business cycles was provided by Joseph Schumpeter — an economist whose work on defining the process of entrepreneurship we will encounter in subsequent pages. See Schumpeter (1939).

2   The rise of modern capitalism is well chronicled in Braudel (1981).

3   A very readable demonstration of the nature and importance of innovation and technological cycles is Foster (1987).

4   An enjoyable introduction to the history of economic ideas through the lives of their creators is Heilbronner (1986).

5   Keynes (1936) is his seminal work.

6   The economics of large firms is a branch of economics known as industrial organisation (IO) economics. Most work in IO economics, in the view of the present authors, relies on an unduly static view of the economy and understates the importance of entrepreneurship and innovation. IO economists have not (as at 1995) provided an agreed, much less a convincing, account of large, multi-product firms.

7   Arthur and Arrow give a short account of these recent developments in economics in Arthur (1994: ix–xx).

8   The T-model Ford stayed in production until 1927 but, in hindsight, this was too long.

9   As British readers may note, Boeing did not invent the commercial jetliner: the de Havilland Comet was indubitably first. Unfortunately the Comet, for technical reasons (its tendency to explode in mid-air) was not a commercial success. It showed that the product was practical and the market existed, but that was all.

10 Gary Hamel, with his colleague C. K. Prahalad, wrote an article for the *Harvard Business Review* which set a record for the number of reprints ordered (Prahalad and Hamel 1990). See also Hamel and Prahalad (1994).

11 The abbreviation EVA is a trade mark of Stern Stewart in the USA.

12 One of the first works to explore the concept of value creation was Fruhan (1979).

13 The first Duke of Wellington's response to a complaint from a number of generals whom he had passed over for Colonel of the 33rd Regiment of Foot in favour of a less senior but more efficient officer (see Longford 1972).

Profile two

Nexus Pty Ltd and Helen Nankivell

Helen Nankivell and her partner Tom Laird left Canberra in 1986 to take over and operate a woodworking business in the small town of Victor Harbour, South Australia. Helen Nankivell had, to that time, felt no need to become a professional business person, had no business — or woodworking — education or experience and spent her time as a craft potter and local citizen. Tom Laird pressed her to 'get real' and do something that would enable her to support herself in a style that he thought was appropriate.

When Helen Nankivell and Tom Laird arrived in Victor Harbour they found a business with eight employees making high quality wooden furniture for a limited group of retailers. Helen decided to learn the trade and began working in the factory, while Tom managed the business. She did not spend all her time among the sawdust: she took time out to approach a major retailer and was given a significant order. Meeting this order meant a rapid expansion of the factory and pulled Helen off the factory floor and into active management.

In 1989 Tom Laird died suddenly, and Helen had to consider her options. She could have sold her half of the business and returned to potting and pottering, and there were plenty of advisers, disinterested and otherwise, who would have supported such a decision. She decided instead to keep the business and made an offer to Tom Laird's executors for his share in it: this was accepted, and in 1990 she found herself the managing director and sole shareholder in a factory employing forty people.

The management task was complicated by the state of the back office: a small PC was used to prepare the payroll and print invoices, while every other operation was carried out manually. Helen took time off from wrestling with the organisational problems and approached another major retailer. This approach secured another significant order, and exploded her management problems into a crisis.

The back office was in a mess, but the problems in the factory threatened to be worse. In four years the business had grown fivefold: in one more it had to double. Helen decided that a large NC cutting machine was needed to speed up production. Such machines cost $500 000 and up. She had only just completed refinancing the business and thought that the bank manager might be reluctant to allow her another large sum. The bank manager told her that she would have to show him her Business Plan before the application could be processed. 'What is a business plan?' she asked.

The answer sent her to the National Industry Extension Service (NIES, now part of AusIndustry) and the South Australian Centre for Manufacturing (SACFM). NIES found her a consultant who wrote a business plan; this plan, and the business's accounts for the past few years satisfied the bank and the machine was duly ordered. Helen decided to get the SACFM to help her plan to use it; they, in turn, suggested that she should get Quality Certification. Helen realised fairly quickly that there was no point in treating quality like an examination that you pass and then forget: it had to become a normal part of business operations.

Raising quality standards is, above all, a matter of culture, since achieving high quality levels cost-effectively means that individual workers must take responsibility for their own output. Responsibility without power is paralysing, and so sufficient executive authority must also be devolved to individual operators to give effect to their responsibilities. Helen surveyed the staff to discover what the culture was at Nexus. To her pained surprise, she discovered that the outstanding feature was her own autocratic management style. Her refusal to recognise objections had served her well in securing orders, but had become a major obstacle to improving the workplace culture at Nexus. In law, employees work for a company, not the shareholders, but in many small businesses, where the owner is an active manager, the distinction can get very confused. The staff had got used to treating Helen as 'the boss' and looking to her for guidance: learning to consider the business's interests, even when this meant disagreeing with Helen, required a substantial cultural change.

One of the first actions Nexus took in the empowerment process was the formation of the 'Solver' team, a group of employees whose task was to identify the causes of waste and rejects and propose corrections. The imminent arrival of the new NC machining centre created another opportunity: a consultant from the SACFM helped the staff determine ways to improve the work flow, and by the time the NC machine arrived every other machine in the plant had been moved. Workplace discussions showed that Nexus needed a full-time manufacturing manager: the staff were involved in the recruiting and selection process, and in due course a suitable person was installed.

The early returns from the quality program were not atypical: waste in the timber preparation area was reduced from 25 per cent to 12 per cent and delivery lead times came down from between four and six weeks to a consistent three. Helen's entrepreneurial drive was not satisfied by these modest improvements and she decided to prove that her firm's products were genuinely competitive in the most direct possible way — by exporting them to Japan, the most quality sensitive market on earth.

As a preliminary step Helen persuaded the SACFM to act as marriage brokers, and with their help Nexus formed the 'Lifestyle Network' with two South Australian firms with mutually complementary product lines, South Western Manufacturing and Panda Sofas. The network could furnish 'every room in the house' and they took a stand at the Tokyo International Furniture Fair in 1994 to prove it. All three network members gained tremendously from the experience, and not only in knowledge: they received substantial orders. In Nexus's case, these were for coffee tables scaled to fit Japanese living spaces.

Early in 1995 Nexus shipped its first container load of furniture to Japan, and shortly after received a repeat order. Nexus had completed the change from being a woodworking boutique in a quiet corner of a quiet state to becoming a global competitor in the world furniture market. Helen acknowledges the help that she and Nexus received from AusIndustry and the SACFM. They were doing their job and they did it well, but Nexus created its own future.

This account is based upon a presentation by Helen Nankivell at the 9th National Quality Management Conference, Adelaide, 10–12 September 1995

Chapter 3

Entrepreneurs and planning

Plans and entrepreneurial plans

The kind of plan an entrepreneur needs differs in many ways from all other types of plan.

The word 'plan' can mean both a schematic description of something, usually a structure, and a proposed course of action. Sometimes, as in the plans for a new building, the word means both. Practically all large businesses, many medium and a few small ones use business plans. Mostly these are plans based on an extrapolation of recent history: the plan period is assumed to be like the previous period with a relatively small amount of change. Business plans can be extremely elaborate and involve large sums of money; bringing an updated model of a popular car into production can take three or more years and involve spending a billion or more dollars. The marketing assumption behind such a plan will, however, be that the new model will sell at roughly the same rate as the current one is selling. The plan may include some allowance for growth, but it will be in line with a long term trend.

An entrepreneurial business plan (EBP), on the other hand, often starts from a market with no sales history at all. When there is an existing market, an entrepreneurial plan envisages major changes in it. When Hideshiro Fujisawa and Soichiro Honda came together in 1949 to make 58 cc engines as auxiliary power for pushbikes the market was practically unlimited; their problems were very largely on the supply side.[1] The decision to make their own frames for the Honda Dream was entrepreneurial after a fashion, but it sprang from frustration with the frame supplier more than a conscious decision to pursue a market opportunity. Honda etched his name in history with the decision in 1959 to open the United States market to his bikes. Honda's motorcycles were light-weight, highly engineered, and targeted in Japan at young professional couples. American motorbikes were large, low tech, and oily, and most Americans associated motorbikes with Hell's Angels, riot and mayhem.

Honda's Executive Vice President, Kihachiro Kawashima, and Grey Advertising came up with an advertising campaign based on the slogan 'You meet the nicest people on a Honda' and, as the 'swinging sixties' started, 'The nicest things happen on a Honda'. They started a revolution that totally restructured the worldwide motorcycle industry. In due course Honda and other Japanese motorcycle manufacturers launched heavyweight machines and captured a major share of the large machine market as well. The British motorcycle industry was wiped out; the American industry nearly followed it until new managers and owners at Harley–Davidson rose to the Japanese challenge.

Honda and Fujisawa made another major entrepreneurial decision when they took Honda into motor cars. Japan's Ministry for Trade and Industry (MITI) opposed this move on roughly the same grounds that would have led to such a proposal being killed inside most western companies: the investment required was huge and immediate while the returns were distant and uncertain. Unanticipated events played a part in Honda's ultimate success: when environmental concerns in the United States led to strict motor vehicle emission laws being passed, Honda Motor's experience with super-efficient, low capacity motorcycle engines enabled it to meet the first stage United States limits without catalytic converters and without sacrificing fuel efficiency. The rise in fuel prices following the first 'oil shock' of 1972 turned fuel efficiency from an academic to an extremely practical matter, and Honda received a second major boost. The Honda Motor Company, more or less on its own, redefined the world's view of motor car engine technology.

Haig's strategy, Monash's plan

One of the lessons of military history is that a good plan can overcome a bad strategy. Lord Haig, the British commander-in-chief on the Western Front during the First World War, had a strategy of going to Berlin by the shortest possible route. A succession of army commanders adopted this strategy as a plan: large numbers of men would be assembled, given rifles with bayonets attached, and told to walk through the German lines killing any of the enemy who did not promptly surrender. Officers who had the temerity to complain about obstacles like barbed wire, machine guns and semi-liquid mud ten feet deep were told that they were 'defeatist' and 'lacked fighting spirit'.

A series of events lead to John Monash being appointed to command the Australian Army Corps, and that Corps being one of the few intact fighting units left to the British in August 1918. Monash did not criticise Haig's strategy, but insisted on his 'entrepreneurial' right to plan his own offensive, to the point of threatening to cancel the battle of 8 August if the High Command interfered.

On 8 August, as in every other battle, the strategy was Haig's of going straight to Berlin, but the plan was Monash's and the offensive reached and then stopped at the line Monash had drawn.

All Monash's plans had a number of things in common:

▲ he insisted on a clear and unambiguous definition of the immediate objective

▲ he insisted that individual initiative should be encouraged within the boundaries of the plan

▲ he insisted that the plan should be understood by those carrying it out

▲ he insisted that if circumstances changed to the point that the chief assumptions upon which the plan was based could not be treated as reliable the plan should be suspended and redeveloped for a later implementation and not attempted with inadequate resources or under conditions of remediable uncertainty

▲ but above all Monash insisted that the plan should be practical — when Monash planned, failure was exceedingly unlikely.

Monash's rules are still valid for a business developing an entrepreneurial business plan.

An ordinary, non-entrepreneurial plan will succeed unless some extraordinary events disrupt it. Until 1972 the American motor car industry had been used to building inefficient and highly polluting cars; when they were forced to make them less polluting they took the path of least resistance and made them even less efficient. Their ordinary plans assumed that their customers would go on buying them anyway. A successful innovation brought to market by an entrepreneur is the sort of extraordinary event that sends businesses relying on ordinary planners off a cliff. The American motor industry might have gone on selling its dinosaurs indefinitely if their customers had not been able to see Hondas, not merely using a quarter of the fuel, but leaving them behind at the traffic lights as well.

Three key questions
In search of two definitions and one paradigm

This chapter is about three words: *entrepreneurial business planning*. Entrepreneurial business planning is the midwife of new ventures. Without entrepreneurial business planning, and the business plan that results from it, a new venture is likely to be stillborn, unable to attract the physical and financial resources it needs to get it started and to sustain it until it reaches profitability, positive cash flow and self-sufficiency. Three key questions must be answered before we can say with any confidence that we can offer valuable guidance to an entrepreneur engaged in planning a new venture.

In every-day speech, 'planning' is a word capable of a great many meanings and is often used very loosely. So, our first question is one of definition. What do we say distinguishes planning as undertaken by entrepreneurs from all the other activities than can legitimately be called 'planning'?

The second question concerns entrepreneurship as a distinct field of human endeavour. We must relate business planning to the more general concept of entrepreneurship before we can answer the question: When should a given business planning process be called 'entrepreneurial'?

A third question remains. From the point of view of someone setting out on the path of entrepreneurship, an accurate map would be more useful than a dictionary. Practical entrepreneurs require guidelines — or better still a systematic model — that will make the task of preparing an entrepreneurial business plan easier and make the resulting plan more useful. Such systematic models of general procedures are called 'paradigms'. So, the third question becomes: Is there a paradigm of entrepreneurial business planning?

Only when we can give useful answers to all three questions are we able to set out a definitive set of prescriptions which, when applied to a specific opportunity, will guide an entrepreneur to the production of a high quality entrepreneurial business plan.[2]

Why is an EBP paradigm important?

The field of entrepreneurial business planning — sometimes called 'venture planning' — occupies a central position in the discipline of entrepreneurship. It is at the heart of all formal teaching of entrepreneurship worldwide: there is a universal emphasis on the importance of teaching a student how to create an entrepreneurial business plan. Untaught entrepreneurs learn that a business plan is important as soon as they ask a bank or a professional investor for money. Students and active entrepreneurs can go to one of a large number of books and other instructional media and find a model upon which they can base a business plan. This book also sets out a model which students and practitioners are advised to use in order to prepare an entrepreneurial business plan. Readers may fairly ask: Why is this book different from the dozens, if not hundreds, of other books which describe model business plans, most of them different from each other and from this one?

The authors of the many books, articles and learned papers setting out prescriptions for the creation of a venture's entrepreneurial business plan are almost unanimous in certain of their recommendations, and relatively few examples will be found where one author directly contradicts another one. Whatever book an aspiring entrepreneur reads, he or she will be told to address their audience, write clearly, demonstrate that there is a market for the venture's products, show that the management team is competent and experienced, and so on. The proverb says that 'In the multitude of counsellors there is wisdom' but there is also a great deal of repetition and tautology. There has been no single abstract model, or paradigm, which every writer agrees on as constituting the core of entrepreneurial planning. Academic researchers into entrepreneurship regret this because the lack of an agreed paradigm hampers the conduct of 'normal science'. The problem goes further than this. Writing and presenting an entrepreneurial business plan is important to the success of every new venture. Most new ventures will simply never achieve sufficient resources to commence operations unless the entrepreneurial business plan has been successful in convincing investors and other stakeholders that the venture's probable outcome, weighted by prudent consideration of its inherent risks, is sufficiently attractive to justify their participation (Hindle 1996: ch 3).

The field of entrepreneurial business planning needs a clearly set out, widely agreed, generic paradigm. In its absence, any entrepreneurial business plan prescription might be held to be as good as any other. We believe that the paradigm of entrepreneurial business planning presented here represents the state-of-the-art in the development of systematic ways to describe the process of entrepreneurial business planning. The recommendations here were derived in part from a content analysis of a large number of books on business planning, tested against some well documented entrepreneurial histories and finally used in a number of real life situations.

Chapter design

The rest of this chapter divides into two major sections. In the first of these we develop the entrepreneurial business planning paradigm: a set of prescriptions, including boundaries, laws, success rules and instrumentation requirements, which an entrepreneur can use as a comprehensive and systematic way of ensuring that an entrepreneurial business plan is complete and effective. We follow this with a section containing some examples and explanations, through which we set a context in which the rest of the book, and most particularly Chapters 5 to 12 inclusively, can be more easily appreciated.

What is planning?
We first discuss the concept of 'planning'. Henry Mintzberg (1994) set out a comprehensive model of planning, plans and planners in his book and we adopt and adapt his perspectives and definitions to come to our definition of what planning is and — most importantly — is not.

What is entrepreneurial business planning?
We then explore the definition of 'entrepreneurship' itself, and important related concepts. Bygrave and Hofer (1991) have given us a checklist of nine parameters which they suggest can help us to determine whether any given process should properly be called 'entrepreneurial'. By applying these parameters and drawing

on some other well-accepted definitions of entrepreneurship we will define an EBP.

What is a paradigm?

Third, we briefly examine and extract the common elements of four definitions (Hindle 1995; Barker 1992; Kuhn 1970; Chalmers 1976) of a very important concept — that of a 'paradigm'. We consider that paradigms are important to both understanding and directing all kinds of human endeavour but we think that they are particularly important to business practitioners when they step beyond the familiar and routine and implement new processes, launch new products, and start new enterprises.

What is the entrepreneurial business planning paradigm?

Finally, we present our paradigm of entrepreneurial business planning. This paradigm has been tested and shown to be useful to entrepreneurs writing a business plan for a new venture (Hindle 1996: chs 5–7).

What is planning?

Mintzberg's model of planning, plans and planners

We have adopted the definition and perspectives on planning set out by Henry Mintzberg (1994) in his book. The major part of Mintzberg's book is concerned to refute all assertions to the effect that some person, group or company has developed a systematic process for developing strategic plans for modern corporations. A strategic plan represents the highest level of a corporate planning process and sets out the markets and industries that the corporation should invest in and the amount to be spent in each, often including the choice between expansion by acquisition or by development. It is possible to use complex systems theory to show that the existence of any universal strategic planning paradigm is extremely unlikely, but Mintzberg chooses to proceed by showing the internal inconsistencies in each of the most widely praised strategic planning methodologies and recounting the awful disasters they caused to the corporations that adopted them.

Mintzberg acknowledges that once a strategy is in place, then it is not merely possible but essential to develop a series of mutually consistent sub-plans that express that strategy. A complete set of plans:

▲ describes the actions needed to give effect to the predefined corporate strategy

▲ describes the expected outcome to some level of detail

▲ shows the resource commitment, primarily but not exclusively financial, that will be needed to put these plans into effect.

Nobody, simply by studying architecture textbooks, can decide whether a corporation should put the building of a new head office into its current year strategy (and by implication pay a smaller dividend to shareholders or defer investment elsewhere), but if a corporation has decided to build a new head office it would be reckless in the extreme to start building it before a complete set of architectural plans have been prepared and reviewed. The essential defining statement of the Mintzberg perspective is: 'Organisations engage in formal planning, not to create strategies but to program the strategies they already have, that is, to elaborate and operationalize their consequences formally.'

Mintzberg and Waters had made the same point in slightly different words some years earlier:

> ... *companies plan when they have intended strategies, not in order to get them. In other words, one plans not a strategy but the consequences of it ... Planning gives order to vision, and puts form on it for the sake of formalized structure and environmental expectation. One can say that planning operationalizes strategy.* (1982)

Figure 3.1 is a schematic representation of Mintzberg's model of the elements and relationships linking planning, plans and planners. The diagram provides an illustration of the key elements of Mintzberg's planning–plans–planners process model and the integrated flow of activities which connects them. For planning and plans, the 'stone tablets' of strategy are taken as given. Planning as a process and plans as process outcomes can only commence subsequent to a

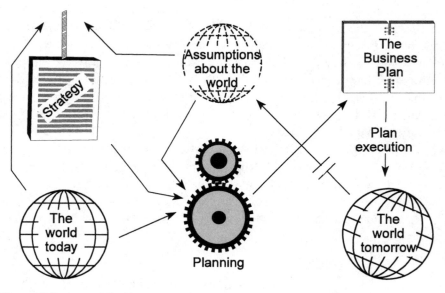

Figure 3.1 A model of planning and plans[3]

strategy having been formulated or 'found'. The roles of 'planning', 'plans' and 'planners' must then be carefully distinguished.

Planning turns a strategy into a program, converting a given set of strategic directives into a set of plans that can in due course be carried out. In Mintzberg's model planning proceeds in three ordered steps:

1 the strategy is codified, turning it from a set of aspirations to a set of objectives with magnitudes and dates

2 the codified strategy is then elaborated, taking each of the objectives and analysing it to determine the necessary antecedent actions

3 the elaborated strategy is then recorded in a hierarchy of functional area plans (such as: a marketing plan; a production plan; a human resources plan etc) which can, once approved, become the authority to carry out the actions determined in *2* above.

The completed, integrated plan, Mintzberg suggests, has three distinct roles and so can be used in three distinct ways:

▲ it is a communications medium: those charged with carrying out particular actions can refer to the plan and expect that those charged with carrying out complementary actions to be consulting the same plan

▲ it is a control device: senior management, having approved a plan, expect their subordinates to adhere to it and to report progress against the targets documented in the plan

▲ a plan can be used as a simulation device, testing the effect of different assumptions and modified strategies with a view to arriving at an improved plan or, where necessary, abandoning an unrewarding strategy entirely.

Planners have, in Mintzberg's model, three roles that go beyond their programming and simulation duties:

▲ they find the strategy, decoding the corporate mission statement and other Delphic utterances from senior management as a necessary precedent to formulating quantified objectives

▲ they analyse the found strategy as a necessary precedent to programming it

▲ they may act as catalysts in the strategy formation process, offering senior management a palette of options and data with which a realistic strategy may be formed.

The planner may or may not have been involved in strategy formation, but that is irrelevant to planning and the production of plans. Simulations (feeding alternate data into a plan's information evaluation instruments) may or may not be useful in amending strategy, but the essential feature of Mintzberg's model is his insistence that planning is conceptually distinct from, and subsequent to, strategy formulation.

A brief elaboration of the roles Mintzberg assigns to planners, plans and planning follows.

Planning has one role — achieved in three steps

Mintzberg writes:

> *Planning helps to translate intended strategies into realized ones, by taking the first step that can lead to effective implementation. We present this not as our first role for planning but as the only one. All other roles we shall discuss pertain to plans and planners but not to planning ... Planning as programming is clearly decision making, or more exactly a set of coordinated decision processes evoked by the dictates of strategy. And it clearly involves future thinking, and often controlling the future as well — specifically the enactment of desired end-points. (1994: 333–4)*

Achievement of this single role — developing the program — involves three steps.

First, Mintzberg (following Hafsi and Thomas 1985: 32–7) stresses the key codifying attributes of planning: to make all implicit assumptions explicit; to consider all major hurdles; to 'take everything relevant into account' and to uncover and eliminate all inconsistencies. He writes 'Planning thus brings order to strategy, putting it into a form suitable for articulation to others ...' (Mintzberg 1994: 337)

Second, elaboration of strategy is the decomposition of the codified strategy into a three-part hierarchy: sub-strategies; ad hoc programs and specific action plans. The result (quoting Katz 1970: 356) is ' ... a timed sequence of conditional moves in resource deployment'.

The final step — converting the elaborated strategy — involves proceeding from arrangement (of strategic hierarchies) to performance (establishing budgets and control mechanisms).

Plans have three roles

The first two roles for plans are as communications media and control devices. Mintzberg writes:

> *Plans, as communications media, inform people of intended strategy and its consequences. But as control devices they go further, specifying what behaviours are expected of particular units and individuals in order to realise strategy, and then being available to*

feed back into the strategy-making process comparisons of these expectations with actual performance. (1994: 361)

The third role of a plan is as a simulation device. Mintzberg goes on:

Plans, especially in the operational form of budgets, can be used to consider the impact of possible changes on the organisation's current operations, including the testing of new strategies ... In other words, plans can feed back into the strategy-making process and so find a third role for themselves in the organisation, namely as simulations (although this would seem to be less common than the roles of communication and control). (1994: 377)

One can almost see the evolution of Mintzberg's thought development in these two passages, separated though they are by sixteen pages. The key linking concept is 'feed back'. All control systems feature feed back. So, it is not inconceivable to regard certain simulations as part of the feed back (and hence control) process. However, a great many simulations transcend feed back and feature 'feed new' — that is, the input of new data based on an alternative strategy. His final position is to distinguish simulation as a third major role for plans. It is to be hoped that in a second edition of his book, Mintzberg might tidy his exposition by presenting the three roles of planning in an integrated rather than fragmented manner.

The several roles of planners

Finally, Mintzberg (1994: 361) argues, uncontroversially, that *planners* can have several roles, depending on the circumstances confronting the business. At one time a planner may be primarily fulfilling the role of analyst; at another time the planner may be acting as a catalyst of change. The discussions of a selection of some of the unlimited number of roles which planners might play are interesting but the empirical, logical and modelling components of Mintzberg's work are complete without them.

What is entrepreneurial business planning?

Setting some limits: The boundaries of entrepreneurship

Though it is a very ancient economic phenomenon, the study of entrepreneurship is not a 'mature science'. The American Academy of Social Sciences formally admitted entrepreneurship as a distinct discipline as recently as 1989. In many of its major sub-fields this has not been long enough for scholars to articulate and secure general acceptance for paradigms which scholars and practitioners might use as a foundation for practice and further research.

Bygrave and Hofer (1991) produced a trinity of linked definitions which culminate in a nine point list of scales which can be used to test the degree to which a given proposal or process is 'entrepreneurial'. Bygrave and Hofer's three linked definitions are:

▲ an *entrepreneur* is someone who perceives an opportunity and creates an organisation to pursue it

▲ an *entrepreneurial event* involves the creation of a new organisation to pursue an opportunity

▲ the *entrepreneurial process* involves all the functions, activities and actions associated with the perceiving of opportunities and the creation of organisations to pursue them.

Bygrave and Hofer state that their further investigations enabled them to list the nine defining parameters of entrepreneurship. They write that, 'Taken together, these characteristics create a set of parameters and criteria that will have to be met by any "ideal" model of entrepreneurship' (1991: 17): readers will have already seen their 'nine points' in Chapter 1.

Bygrave and Hofer, in concept if not in practice, suggest that these nine parameters could become scales and some function could then be developed which would produce an 'index of entrepreneurship' for any given proposal or project. They make this suggestion, not because they consider it either practical or useful, but as part of their demonstration of how difficult it will be to obtain a paradigm of entrepreneurship *in toto*.

For the would-be entrepreneurial business planner there is an important implication of Bygrave and Hofer's work. If there is to be an ideal model — a paradigm — of that subset of entrepreneurship called entrepreneurial business planning, the entrepreneurial process parameters simultaneously define its contextual boundaries and establish the level of generality at which it must operate.

Entrepreneurial business planning as a subset of entrepreneurship

In common with Bygrave and Hofer, Stevenson writes of entrepreneurship as a behavioural approach to management but defines it with a greater emphasis on resource control: '[Entrepreneurship is] ... the pursuit of opportunity without regard to resources currently controlled' (Stevenson, Roberts & Grousbeck 1994: 5).

Stevenson and his colleagues contrast an entrepreneurial or 'promoter' approach to management with the traditional or 'trustee' approach across six dimensions: strategic orientation; commitment to opportunity; commitment of resources; control of resources; management structure; and compensation/ reward structure. They built an entire text-and-cases instructional book around this approach to the creation and development of new business ventures by entrepreneurs. The significance of the Stevenson behavioural definition to the EBP field is twofold:

▲ it adds substance to Bygrave and Hofer's somewhat truncated definition of the entrepreneur as an opportunity perceiver and organisational creator by distinguishing the key managerial behavioural characteristics which make certain activities entrepreneurial as distinct from custodial

▲ it establishes the central importance of entrepreneurial business planning to the discipline and practice of entrepreneurship.

The essence of entrepreneurial behaviour is the creation of a new enterprise by employing resources that the entrepreneur does not control at the start of the endeavour to create a new set of resources. In the market sector of an economy the current holders of the necessary resources cannot be compelled to offer them to the entrepreneur; they must be convinced by the attractions of the offer and the possibilities of the new enterprise. These stakeholders include, at the start of an enterprise, key staff and critical component and service suppliers. As the enterprise develops, customers and distributors will also become stakeholders. Nearly every entrepreneurial project cannot start until it has secured finance beyond the personal capacity of the entrepreneur. All of those stakeholders who are expected to make a substantial commitment of their time and resources to the new enterprise may reasonably ask to see a plan that lets them make their own judgement about the enterprise before joining it or offering it useful support. Professional financiers, whether offering equity or debt, may refuse to consider any opportunity not described in a well-prepared business plan. The preparation of such a plan is of central importance to the entrepreneurial process.

Stevenson and his colleagues write:

> *A business plan is a document that articulates the critical aspects, basic assumptions, and financial projections regarding a business venture. It is also the basic document used to interest and attract support — financial and otherwise — for a new business concept. (Stevenson, Roberts & Grousbeck 1994: 64)*

The following three points distinguish entrepreneurial business planning from all other forms of planning:

▲ its *subject matter* — it will be a programmed strategy to create a growing enterprise, either by launching a new venture or by reinvigorating an existing organisation whose returns (essentially the sum of the current return and growth rates) are no longer adequate to justify its resources

▲ the *approach* it proposes will conform substantially to Bygrave and Hofer's nine entrepreneurial process parameters

▲ the *audiences* for whom the plan is intended — the audience can be considered as made up of two groups of people: external prospective investors and/or lenders; and stakeholders whose personal and corporate commitments are essential to the achievement of the performance projected in the plan.

Timmons (1982: 30) characterised entrepreneurial ventures as being possessed of four key ingredients (Timmons 1990: 30):

▲ a talented lead entrepreneur with a balanced and compatible team

▲ a technically sound and marketable idea for a product or service

▲ a thorough venture analysis leading to a complete business plan

▲ appropriate equity and debt financing.

The emphasis on financing in the definition is most important and is a theme which will recur in later chapters of this book. All reader-users of entrepreneurial business plans have one crucial thing in common: they use the information the plan contains to help them make decisions about committing themselves and the resources that they control to the venture. The target audience for an entrepreneurial business plan consists of 'resource providers'. In economic theory, if not always in practice, all resources in a market economy can be represented by dollar values and evaluated using discounted cash flow techniques. In theory, the whole audience for an entrepreneurial business plan can be treated as investors.

In practice, while there are some people who can be excited by a 'beautiful set of numbers', there are many who cannot. There are people who, on hearing the term 'good figures', do not think about balance sheets and cash flow statements at all. All entrepreneurial business plans must deal with certain key issues in essentially the same way, although individual examples may be very different depending on who (as an individual or as a member of a well defined group) controls the key resources a new enterprise needs. Everyone who is asked to go beyond the normal conventions of trade to support a new enterprise is making an investment in it, sacrificing the current use of some asset in the expectation of an adequate future return. Labourers paid hourly wages, and business service providers paid on their monthly invoice, are not investors. Experts who are asked to sacrifice the security of a public service or corporate career (such as it now is) and the opportunity of selling their skills elsewhere are investors. Suppliers who are asked for long credit terms are investors, as are bankers. The entrepreneur should consider anyone who takes any sort of risk to support the new venture as an investor. People who subscribe equity capital are, though vitally important, still just one class of investor.

Summary: Two core definitions

Entrepreneurship is a managerial process of opportunity realisation through a creative approach to resource control. The entrepreneurial business plan is the entrepreneur's major device for defining and gaining control of the resources a new venture needs. Now that we have established the nature of the entrepreneurial process and described the investor audience, we are in a position to provide formal definitions of entrepreneurial business planning and the entrepreneurial business plan. The definitions make use of the categories of the entrepreneurial process defined by Bygrave and Hofer; the emphases supplied by Stevenson; the boundaries defined by Timmons and the concepts of planning employed by Mintzberg.

▲ *Entrepreneurial business planning* is the process of convincing the owners and controllers of certain resources of the feasibility and desirability of participating in a new venture. The process takes a predefined strategy and determines the set of resources that will be needed to implement it and how they must be deployed. It leads to a forecast of the economic outcome to be expected, a determination of the sensitivity of this forecast to the value of various antecedent factors and an assurance that the proposed plan represents at least a locally optimum outcome.

▲ An *entrepreneurial business plan* is a formal document that sets out the expected results of the entrepreneurial business planning process, including, *inter alia*, the assumptions that the planner relied on and the confidence that can reasonably be placed in each of them, the resources that will be used and how they will be combined, the key managers and their qualifications and experience, detailed financial forecasts covering revenue, expenditure, investment and returns, and in general all the facts and arguments needed to obtain, with the consent of their current owners and controllers, the resources needed to carry through an entrepreneurial venture.[4]

What is a paradigm?

Four definitions

We define a paradigm as a 'model of models'.

> *It consists of the irreducible minimum set of combined principles — theoretical and practical — upon which scholars and practitioners in a discipline both agree and rely. It is a framework, both for the conduct of research capable of furthering the knowledge of a discipline, and for an implementation capable of producing a desired outcome in the practical world.*

This definition is a synthesis of the work of Kuhn (1970) (who first established the importance of paradigms to the practice of science), Barker (1992) (who recommended paradigm-based thinking to business planners as a means to

Entrepreneurs and planning

anticipate the future) and Chalmers (1984) (a philosopher of science). We briefly review their definitions below.

Thomas Kuhn set out what he saw as the two critical attributes of a significant scientific discovery. One was a paradigmatic approach (which Kuhn calls an 'achievement') which had to be 'sufficiently unprecedented to attract an enduring group of adherents away from competing modes of scientific activity'. At the same time '... it was sufficiently open-ended to leave all sorts of problems for the redefined group of practitioners to resolve' (Kuhn 1970: 10). His definition of a paradigm (or achievement) was:

> *Achievements that share these two characteristics I shall hence-forth refer to as 'paradigms' a term that relates closely to 'normal science'. By choosing it, I mean to suggest that some accepted examples of scientific practice — examples which include law, theory, application, and instrumentation together — provide models from which spring particular coherent traditions of scientific research. (Kuhn 1970: 10)*

In a book focused on enhancing businesses' ability to anticipate and plan for the future, Barker (1992) — deriving his insights very substantially from Kuhn (1970) — provides an extremely succinct and useful definition of a paradigm:

> *A paradigm is a set of rules and regulations (written and unwritten) that does two things: (1) it establishes or defines boundaries; and (2) it tells you how to behave inside the boundaries in order to be successful. (Barker 1992: 32)*

In a book dedicated to answering the question: 'What is this thing called science?' Chalmers provides a short but comprehensive definition:

> *A paradigm is made up of the general theoretical assumptions and laws and techniques for their application that members of a particular scientific community adopt. (Chalmers 1984: 90)*

A synthesis

A comprehensive statement of any paradigm can be organised and described under five classification areas:

▲ boundaries

▲ laws

▲ success rules

▲ instrumentation

▲ theory.

We need to distinguish between 'law' and 'success rule'. This is fundamentally a distinction between the mandatory and the optional. A law is a rule recognised by a community as binding. Laws circumscribe. They are closely related to boundaries because non-conformity with the law puts one outside the community. On the other hand, success rules, as the name implies, are indicative rather than prescriptive. Not being successful does not place one outside the community. Success rules are principles intended to increase the probability of solving the types of problems which fall within the purview of a particular paradigm. Laws (together with boundaries) define what that purview is.

An illustration may be useful. The boundaries of a tennis court are clearly marked. One of the many laws of tennis is that the server gets only two chances to land the ball in the designated landing area. One of the success rules of tennis is to 'get a high percentage of first serves in play'. Someone who cannot achieve a high percentage of first serves (or fails to implement any other success rule) does not cease to be a tennis player. However, anyone who breaks the law of 'two serves are all you are allowed on any given point' or any other law, or continues to play after a shot lands outside the appropriate boundaries, has left the community of tennis players and is playing some other game.

What is the entrepreneurial business planning paradigm?

An analytical framework

Our analytical framework for investigating any planning paradigm is presented in Figure 3.2. It is a matrix whose columns are four of the core elements of a paradigm — boundaries, laws, success rules and instrumentation requirements — and whose rows are the three roles of a plan set out in Mintzberg's model — communications medium, control device and simulation mechanism.

Together, paradigm boundaries and laws provide a clear statement of what elements comprise the paradigm. Together, paradigm success rules and instrumentation requirements describe methods of achievement: an approach that gives their user the best chance of success. Overall, the paradigm should possess a clearly set out theoretical justification: a statement of why the paradigm consists of the mandated boundaries, laws, success rules and instrumentation requirements. This analytical framework for paradigms in general can be specifically focused upon entrepreneurial business planning by defining appropriate boundaries, and that is what we have done here.

Where does it apply?	What must be done?
Paradigm boundaries	**Paradigm laws**

	Paradigm boundaries	Paradigm laws
Communications	**Receivers in general (total audience)** • Investors — defined as potential providers of the funds or resources not currently controlled but needed to achieve identified plan objectives **Receivers in particular (sub-audiences)** • A tailored version of the plan should be targeted to each sub-audience distinct enough to warrant a separate investment offer **Definition of the sender (business plan writer)** • An entrepreneurial individual or team seeking resources required to overcome the factors impeding growth • Sophisticated, having both depth and breadth of generic business skills as well as all required venture-specific skills	**Encoding laws** 1 Codify the selected strategy as a multi-disciplinary continuum 2 Integrate the codified strategy as a 'base case' scenario (Note: Obeying this law is intimately linked with the simulation success rule) **Message content laws** 3 Nominate the intended audience 4 Identify all major plan objectives, primarily as financial targets 5 Define the investment offer(s) as an expected ROI 6 Distinguish the venture's business concept, distinctive competencies and sustainable competitive advantages 7 Provide comprehensive statements of opportunities and risks **Feedback law** 8 Seek and respond to feedback (Note: Obeying this law is intimately linked with the simulation success rule)
Control	**The fundamental defining circumstance** • Impeded growth **Entrepreneurship process boundaries** • The nine entrepreneurial process parameters (identified by Bygrave and Hofer) must apply **Defined limits of planning as a process** • Planning is strategic programming — not strategy formulation (Mintzberg's definition)	**Elaboration law** 9 Elaborate the selected strategy as a set of sub-plans **Conversion laws** 10 Convert the selected strategy into a differentiated suite of financial budgets 11 Re-combine the differentiated budgets into an integrated suite of financial projections
Simulation	**(Simulation possibilities are unbounded)**	**Adaptive capacity law** 12 Be able to answer the audience's 'what if' questions in financial terms (Note: Obeying this law is intimately linked with the simulation success rule)
	Why is it so? Theory based on Mintzberg's planning model; Lasswell's communication	

Figure 3.2 The enhanced entrepreneurial business planning paradigm: This box summarises the original research completed by Kevin Hindle and described in detail in his PhD thesis (1996) and certain articles

How is it done?		
	Paradigm success rules	**Instrumentation requirements**
Communications	**Fundamental communications success rules** 1 Adapt plan length and depth of detail to the interest level and stage of involvement of the target audience 2 Empower the plan reader 3 Create investor confidence by providing flexible credibility	**Fundamental communications instrument** • A unique, purpose-designed document — embodying high standards of literacy and numeracy — of the minimum length appropriate to the subject matter and the target audience's information needs
Control	**Fundamental control success rules** 4 Anticipate and address the target audience's due diligence requirements 5 Create a value-adding deal structure	**Fundamental coordinating and control instrument** • A comprehensive financial projection model capable of enumerating the financial implications of alternative scenarios
Simulation	**Fundamental simulation success rule** 6 Employ simulation techniques to obtain a realistic 'base case' scenario which can then survive rigorous 'due diligence' examination	**Fundamental simulation instrument** • The same financial projection model
model; discovery and logical critique of a prevailing paradigm, and grounded theory		

Figure 3.2 *Continued*

From guidelines to implementation

Communications

The plan is a means of communicating with investors (in the economic sense); people who are being asked to sacrifice the opportunity to use certain resources in other, undefined ways in order to dedicate them to this particular project. While in general, all members of the target audience are investors, in particular they will have different motives for examining the plan:

▲ equity investors will wish to see that the risk-weighted return on their investment is better than any of the alternatives that they are currently considering or consider themselves likely to be offered in the near future

▲ debt financiers will wish to see that their loan is backed by good security and the business will generate cash flows sufficient to cover the agreed interest and principal repayments

▲ owners of proprietary companies will wish to see that their key personal objectives are not placed at undue risk — these may be non-financial objectives; one accountant discovered that a promise of 'golf every Wednesday afternoon and all day Saturday' meant far more to the small business owners that she dealt with than concepts such as return on investment

▲ managers of public companies will wish to see that the new venture will support, rather than cannibalise, their existing sources of revenue and shareholder value

▲ the finance directors of public companies will seek assurance that the costs of the venture are fully declared and the commitments being sought are all that will be sought

▲ licensors of patents and other providers of intellectual property will seek to maximise their revenue consistent with preserving their reputation and the security of their intellectual property

▲ key employees will want to see that their skills are being complemented by the venture and that the rewards that they are promised are both adequate to the risks that they are being asked to take and likely to eventuate.

Entrepreneurs may find it necessary to prepare variants of the plan, or at least of the executive summary, tailored to each of these audiences. In each of these versions, while the core data, research results and arguments are retained, the presentation will be adjusted to the interest and capabilities of the particular audience. It is not ethical to prepare different plans incorporating different data for different audiences, and quite apart from the possibility of criminal proceedings for fraud, an entrepreneur should allow for the probability that the recipients of different versions will compare notes.

The writer of the plan is setting out certain promises and declarations on behalf of an entrepreneur or an entrepreneurial team. Ideally, the writer will be the lead entrepreneur, and in many cases he or she will be, but excellence at entrepreneurship is not always associated with excellence in written expression. When a specialist writer is engaged, it must be on the basis that the writer will set out the entrepreneur's plan, not merely prepare a document to bemuse the local bank manager.

By far the most important of the messages conveyed by a plan is that the entrepreneurial team are capable of carrying out their promises, that they have the right combination of skills and experience to complete the tasks that they set themselves and to recruit employees and partners to complete the rest. The second most important message is that the team are committed to the project, that they are not trying to pass the risk to an investor or lender and keep the profits, or still worse, the subscribed capital, for themselves.

The technical excellence of the project is a relatively minor consideration as far as most of the people being approached to contribute resources to the venture are concerned. Such relative outsiders will know less about the industry and the markets the venture will address than the entrepreneur and the entrepreneurial team. By describing the project in the business plan, the entrepreneur and the entrepreneurial team should set out to convey confidence in their judgement and ability rather than to make a technologist or marketer out of a bank manager. A serious potential investor will, nevertheless, have the technical sections of the plan reviewed by an expert in the appropriate field: errors or omissions are likely to be detected.

Plan boundaries

The fundamental assumption of every entrepreneurial business planner is that there is a significant obstacle to overcome and something valuable to be gained by overcoming it. If there is no obstacle there is no call for entrepreneurial skills; if there is nothing valuable to be gained, there is no point in deploying them.

The process boundaries described by Bygrave and Hofer were set out above. First, entrepreneurship is a deliberate act, not purely driven by a change in circumstances, and one is closely associated with a single economic entity. Second, the result of a successful entrepreneurial process will be a change that extends beyond the original entity's boundaries, and one where the 'before' and 'after' circumstances are clearly different. Third, each entrepreneurial process is unique; it attempts something that has not been done before; and even if it fails it establishes a new knowledge base from which further attempts will begin. Fourth, the entrepreneurial process starts from a state of significant uncertainty, in that small flaws in the assumptions, or apparently minor incidents, can have major effects on the direction and outcome of the process.

The major exclusion we make from our definition of the entrepreneurial process is the strategic choice of industry and market, and decisions such as the minimum and maximum scale of any single initiative. These are strategic decisions and establish a prior framework upon which an entrepreneurial process can be built. This distinction is not very important to an entrepreneur creating a new, freestanding enterprise, but it can be critical to the chances of an internal venture launched within a major corporation. When Coles Myer Ltd decided to enter the 'category killer' field, this was a strategic decision; but when they decided to launch 'World 4 Kids' instead of forming a partnership with the United States chain 'Toys R Us' they were making an entrepreneurial choice.

A proposal that a firm should seek certification to the appropriate world quality standard in the ISO 9000 series is not entrepreneurial; success will not be a unique event except on the most pedantic definition, and will not in any case result in a significant change to the external economic environment. By contrast, a proposal to establish a firm that will assist, through consultancy and training services, many other firms to achieve ISO 9000 series certification may be entrepreneurial because it opens a new market or introduces new techniques, and if the firm succeeds it will change the external environment by increasing the number of firms with ISO 9000 series certification and the flow on effects from that.

An article in a Sydney newspaper in the mid 1970s disclosed that the Sydney Harbour Bridge had been designed to withstand a wind of 110 miles per hour. A minor panic ensued: 'What', wrote the editorials, 'would happen if a 115 mile per hour wind blew in Sydney?'

The last survivor of the Bridge design team neatly punctured the hysteria with a letter pointing out that, if a wind of 100 miles per hour should blow in Sydney, the Harbour Bridge would be the only structure left standing.

A proposal to buy a twentieth HaulPak truck for a mine in order to meet rising demand is not entrepreneurial, because it is an incremental decision without any implied discontinuity; but a proposal to replace all the HaulPak delivery trucks at a mine site with a conveyor system running to the wharf or rail loader may well be entrepreneurial, since it will involve a radical change in the economics of the mine operation with consequences that may go well beyond the original firm. A firm that rebuilds a warehouse after a fire is not being entrepreneurial, since it is merely responding to external events, but a firm that builds a new warehouse in order to establish a new warehousing and distribution business may, if its technology, organisation, or marketing is sufficiently innovative, be carrying through a genuine entrepreneurial process.

Simulation limits

The only limits to the simulation process are the laws of humanity and nature.

An entrepreneurial planning process explores the effect of what can happen, not just what might happen. Statistics show us that, when a large number of variables are present, it is practically certain that one or more of them will take 'unlikely' values. Murphy's Law — whatever can go wrong, will go wrong — is soundly based in theory and in experience.[5] The simulation model is constructed to answer the type of 'what if' questions that potential stakeholders may ask. An inability to answer them, or to provide a qualitative answer, must reflect badly on the entrepreneur.

The practice of working with numbers can obscure the essential asymmetry of many outcomes. If an engineer orders too much concrete and steel for a new bridge, it will end up costing more than it had to; but if he orders too little the structure will fail at great cost in money and possibly in lives as well. When in doubt, a civil engineer adds strength. Likewise a new enterprise: a cautiously phased entry into a new market, or a contingency on the product development plan, may lead to lower profits; but the consequences of seeking to maximise the expected profits from an enterprise is that risks are also maximised, and the consequence of failure is not lower profits, but bankruptcy, the loss of the equity capital invested in the firm, and often the loss of the founding entrepreneurs' personal assets as well.

In general, entrepreneurs set out to create enterprises with an indefinite life, and events that are unlikely in any single period become almost certain when enough consecutive periods are considered. Entrepreneurs contemplating entry to rural businesses in Australia may base their plans on the average rainfall, and yet in any seven year period an Australian farmer can expect to experience at least one drought or flood. It might be considered bad luck to start a new rural business just as a drought starts, but it would definitely be bad planning if a business that had been running for two or three years failed because of the onset of a drought.

Making a plan successful

A plan is successful when it secures the commitment of the owners and controllers of the resources that the plan requires to the project described in the plan. The fact that a plan is successful doesn't guarantee that the implementation of the plan will be a success, but if the plan fails the implementation must, either because the project will be aborted or because the project will start without vital resources. When Compass Airlines Ltd started operations in Australia in 1991, the business plan as described in the prospectus showed that it would need $110 million in equity capital to succeed. The public offering only raised $65 million, but instead of either handing back the money or preparing a new plan, Compass Airlines followed the original plan, went broke, and the investors lost all their money.

The plan and its readers

A good plan does more than communicate with its target readers; it opens up a dialogue with them. The dialogue can be wordless on the other side: it is conceivable, but unlikely, that a professional investor will read a plan and then silently reach for a cheque book. Success rule 2 from Figure 3.2 says 'Empower the plan reader'. This is necessary because the typical reader starts from a position of technical inferiority, knowing substantially less about the industry, the markets, and the product than the entrepreneur. By the time readers reach the end of a plan they should feel that they understand the key facts about the industry and the project. They do not aspire to an equality of knowledge with the entrepreneurial team, but to a level of understanding that makes them feel competent to assess the risks and benefits of participation.

Plan design and writing and presentation skills can be critical: the plan readers do not wish to feel patronised, condescended to, or lectured at. Equally, different readers will have hugely different tolerance levels for detail. For instance, in the part of a plan describing a new product a professional engineer or industrial chemist will look for a level of detail that would have a bank manager or venture capitalist reeling in confusion. The best way of satisfying such a disparate audience requires a soundly structured approach to the plan's development and presentation. This is not to say that there is a single structure which every plan can fit: the entrepreneur must develop a structure that is appropriate to both the project and the audience.

Figure 3.3 shows some of the elements of such a business plan:

▲ a *title page*, with sufficient clarity and design to ensure that everyone who picks up the plan will at least read the title, and that the target readers will actually look inside the plan

▲ an *executive summary* of one or two pages, which makes it clear from the first line who should be reading the plan, what they are being asked to contribute and what they can expect to get out of it

▲ an *overview* of the proposed enterprise, written, audio-visual, or multimedia; not a home shopping program hard sell, but dispassionate and informative

▲ the *business plan* itself (described in much more detail in Chapter 16 of this book), containing the minimum amount of material that every target reader needs to be presented with

▲ a series of *appendices* or *supplements* containing information that some, but not all, of the target readers will wish to review.

Executive summary

This plan has been prepared under the direction of the General Manager of the Steel Division for presentation to the Finance Committee of the Board. It seeks authority to invest US$110 million in a joint venture to build and operate a minimill in California. The expected return on this investment will be between 22 and 27 per cent, which comfortably exceeds the current corporate hurdle rate ...

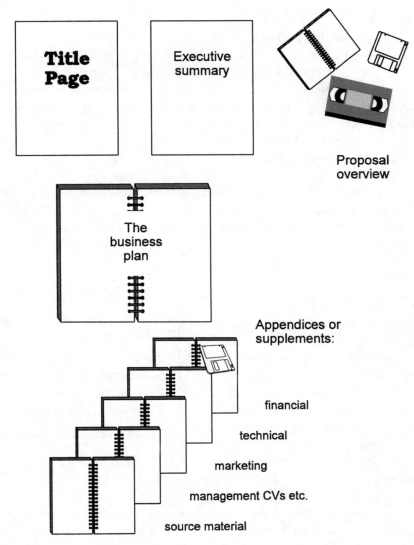

Figure 3.3 A structured business plan

It may be advisable to prepare more than one executive summary when the expected readership is diverse: the risk of a target reader failing to read the body of the plan because the executive summary makes it seem irrelevant is high, while the cost in time and effort of preparing multiple summaries is relatively low. In general terms the appendices and/or the supplements should not be bound with the main plan, for fear of making the combined document hard to carry and terrifying to contemplate, but they should be available and delivered promptly if they are requested.

Flexibility and credibility

Almost anyone who is offered a proposal on a 'take it or leave it' basis feels an immediate urge to 'leave it'. This includes both the proposition and the plan itself; even if the proposal looks attractive and the plan seems convincing, the prospective stakeholders will wish to feel that they are active participants. One reason is that they do not wish to see their own knowledge and experience slighted; another is that their questions test the entrepreneur's ability to cope with the unexpected during the evolution of the plan.

Questions can be probing and uncomfortable: 'Have you thought of ...'; 'What if you don't get ...'; but enthusiasm can be even harder for the unprepared to cope with: 'Gee, that's great, but you're rollout is so slow that you'll lose half the market. Let me put up double [treble, ten times ...] what you asked for and we'll really give the competition a run for its money ...'

Good answers raise the credibility of the plan, but often good suggestions raise the value of it even further.

Think of the audience

Many people, preparing their first business plans, fail to give much or any weight to the interests of their readers. Broadly, every reader will have two key interests: one, 'due diligence' strictly speaking applies to the officers of a corporate investor or stakeholder, and the way that they take proper account of their own shareholders'

> *The investor will not be offered a board seat and there will be no dividend distribution during the currency of this plan ... (From a student's business plan)*

interests; the other, the return or harvest, enables them to compare the proposed investment with the alternatives that may be available to them.

The plan must address both these interests. The 'due diligence' requirement is satisfied by making the plan complete and intelligible: whatever the actual outcome of a given stakeholder's participation, they should be fully informed, or as fully informed as is reasonably possible, at the time that they enter. The plan should not include any false statements, and neither should it omit any relevant true ones. The proposed return must be set out clearly, and in general terms the deal offered to any prospective participant should represent a proposal laid on the table for discussion. Most professional investors will feel professionally obliged to restructure any deal that they are offered, and so the entrepreneur should concentrate on showing them the size of the needed investment and the practicality of making a return on it.

It is not sufficient to show that a new enterprise will be profitable: it must either, come harvest time, be generating large amounts of cash such that the venture's investors can receive a capital return, or it must be a saleable enterprise such that the venture's investors can sell their interest, either to a larger company or by way of a public float.

A quality project

Not only are there an effectively infinite number of possible innovations, the number of ways in which one concept can be commercialised is also effectively infinite. There is a much smaller number of 'locally optimum' projects, and although there may be no way of finding the best possible project design, it is possible, in general terms, to develop a proposal that is better than any of the alternatives that result from making minor changes. Put slightly differently, the 'first guess' proposal for implementing a new concept is, for all practical purposes, capable of significant improvement with relatively little effort. The base-case scenario described in an entrepreneurial business plan must have been refined to the point that there are no easy ways to improve it, which means that it should not be a 'first guess' but a thoroughly refined proposal.

The entrepreneurial team's experience should provide prospective participants with an assurance that the starting assumptions were well-chosen, but no amount of experience leads to a perfect first attempt. Every project proposal involves some controllable and some uncontrollable variables. Two sets of simulations are needed, and they need to be kept clearly separate during the planning process: one tests the effect of changes in the uncontrollable variables on the plan outcome, systematically analysing the intrinsic risk of the proposal; the other tests the effect of changes in the controllable variables, systematically searching for an optimal plan.

Factors such as the timing of the entry of the first major competitor are uncontrollable variables; some plans may only offer attractive returns if competitive entry can be deferred for some minimum period. The planners should determine, using sensitivity analysis, what this minimum period is and explain why they believe that competitors will not, in fact, enter before this critical period is over. Factors such as the distribution channels, pricing, and marketing expenditure are controllable variables, and the planners should use simulation to find the best values for these variables.

We describe model building in Chapter 8, and we consider that computer-based models are an essential tool for all but the most trivial planning exercises. Having a good model does not guarantee that the two sensitivity analyses will be carried out completely, and the computer certainly can't do the job on its own, but it does increase the planner's, and the readers', confidence in the quality of the entire plan.

In summary, the entrepreneurial business plan is an active model of the proposed venture. It is used to produce a 'base case scenario', which is the entrepreneur's view of the most likely outcome if all the resources noted as required in the plan are obtained and deployed according to the plan. The same model can and normally will be used to explore a variety of different scenarios, both different environmental constraints and different resource sets. The world is constantly changing: it will certainly be different on the day the plan is completed from its state when the plan was commenced; and will change further between the completion of the plan and the start of its implementation. The mark of an excellent entrepreneurial business plan is that it can be brought up to date rapidly: there should never be an excuse for launching a venture based on a plan incorporating assumptions that are known to be false.

End notes

1 For an approachable account of the rise of the Honda Motor Company see Sakiya (1982).
2 The concepts presented in this chapter are substantially based on Hindle (1996).
3 This figure originally appeared in Mintzberg (1994: 392, fig 6–7)
4 Well based systems theory can be used to demonstrate that no finite process can be guaranteed to produce a globally optimum outcome to any non-trivial problem: technique, including entrepreneurial business planning, is limited to refining a given concept, not to creating an ideal one.
5 Consider also O'Toole's corollary: 'If nothing can go wrong, it will.'

4
Chapter

Entrepreneurs and time

Product, market and technology life cycles

Humans are all too aware of the cycle of birth, growth, maturity, decline and death. It is tempting to use this sequence as an archetype of much that we observe in society. Like all analogies, it is easy to get carried away. Some facts should always be kept in mind when the term 'life cycle' is applied to anything more dynamic than an insect or plant species.

First, a *cycle* goes around and eventually returns to the place it started from. Neither the sequence of human life nor of social and technical development ever gets back to exactly the same place: 'no man can step in the same river twice'. Human and economic development is not cyclical; it is chaotic. This does not mean that near-cyclical repetition will not occur, just that every sequence of apparently similar events will eventually get broken, usually when almost nobody expects it. Even biological evolution seems to show this pattern; species that appear to have stayed unchanged through tens of millions of years evolve rapidly over a period of a few hundred thousand years and then settle down again in a new form until the next burst of change.

Second, there is no single cycle or sequence that can adequately describe either history or contemporary society completely. Humans are organised into nations, tribes, clans, families, companies and associations: each of these has its own pattern of development which interacts in various ways, many of them unanticipated, with all the rest. Humans are only part of the biosphere and rely on it for air, water and food while fearing the emergence of diseases and famines. The biosphere itself is affected by the state of the atmosphere and the earth's crust, both of which are affected by human activity.

Finally, humans are not perfectly 'rational' in the sense of doing the objectively reasonable thing under all circumstances. This is partly because the objectively reasonable thing to do can only be determined in hindsight in most interesting situations; but also because humans have hormones as well as brains. They are living organisms, subject to emotions that can, on occasion, quite overwhelm reason. Humans are not instinctual like insects either, doomed by their genes to repeat a certain pattern of behaviour until they die, whether it works or not. Most of the higher animals can learn from experience, a few can learn from watching others, and humans can learn by hearing or reading about other people's experience as well. The result of learning is often a change in behaviour. When the change spreads through a community and affects the way people behave, the sort of things they buy, the way things are made, sold or delivered, markets, technologies and products move through their so-called life cycles.

The balance of this chapter describes the patterns of technological and market development and change that have been observed in the past. We know that the future will be different, but we don't know just how different it will be. Every entrepreneur sets out to reshape the future so as to include his or her enterprise as a successful part of it, but many entrepreneurs make the mistake of thinking that the changes that they are planning are the only ones that are going to take place. For those aspects of the future that are totally unknown the assumption that the future will be like the present is false, but may still be the best possible guess. Some aspects of the future are relatively predictable, and in these cases the cautious entrepreneur will assume that the indicated changes will actually occur.

Nobody can tell what the most fashionable colours will be in four years time, but all the children who will start school within the next four years are already born. An entrepreneur whose business is likely to be critically dependent on the use of fashionable colours should put off making any irreversible decisions for as long as possible, but an entrepreneur whose business is related to the number of children in Australian schools can find out the most probable numbers, by year of schooling, for nearly twenty years ahead with relatively little effort and with a high degree of confidence.

Some definitions

Unfortunately, it is not possible to provide perfect and exclusive definitions of products, markets and technology, much less of their life cycles. When someone buys a product they simultaneously grow a market and help to spread some technology. Products, markets and technology can only make sense as concepts if it is remembered that every definition is only partial. Practically every product on the market today is the output of a complex system, and each of these production systems is linked to many others. People who ignore these underlying linkages and try to deal with a single aspect of an economy, an industry or even a business in isolation are generally incapable of explaining or predicting the actual result of any action in the real, interlinked world.

Technology

Technology, broadly speaking, represents a set of techniques and capabilities that can be used to create a consumer product, or an industrial precursor to a consumer product, rather than a consumer product itself. Many consumer products involve a range of technologies in their implementation, and still more in their preparation and delivery.

A household CD player, for example, relies on advanced materials technology to produce its semiconductor laser and detector and other electronic components. The purity of the materials used and the precision with which they are deposited in a current-model CD player were both unimaginable sixty years ago and available only in sophisticated research laboratories as recently as ten years ago. Another range of technologies are needed to produce its variable-speed drive, and some sophisticated software is required to recreate an analogue audio signal from the digital recording. The housing involves more sophisticated materials technology; even the corrugated cardboard box the player was delivered in is the end product of some complex ways of rearranging trees.

Many different technologies are embodied in the CD player; many more were used to produce it. Further technology was used to deliver it: some of its components may have been airfreighted: heavier-than-air flight was first demonstrated in 1903; jet engines were not put into service until 1944; and the triple-shaft 'jumbo' engine that makes long-haul airfreight economic was not introduced until 1974. Practically every good produced on earth spends some time in a diesel-powered truck: the truck, its electrical system and its pneumatic tyres are all twentieth century technologies.

The marketing of the CD player involved still more technology: the owner may have read about it in a newspaper (printed on a high speed multi-colour web-offset press, first available in the 1980s) or seen it on television (not seen in Australia until 1956), or talked about it on the telephone (dating back over a century). It may have been bought in a shop, but more likely a speciality supermarket (first seen in the United States in the 1930s); and taken home on foot, but more likely in a mass-produced motor car (1908). The store was stocked under the control of a sophisticated computer (first demonstrated in 1950, delivered in industrial quantities for commercial use from 1961, and not mass-produced until 1981).

Technology is ubiquitous, even when the product that is bought and consumed looks absolutely natural. If some nineteenth century Rip van Winkle was woken today he might be at least as surprised at the sight of ordinary Europeans eating fresh fruit and vegetables in the depths of winter as at any of the gadgets on display in the shops. Although the fruit and vegetables themselves have not changed much, the technology used to grow, order and deliver them has changed radically over the last century.

Products

A product is some thing or some effect deliberately produced by one person or firm with the intention of exchanging it for some different thing or effect. Usually the term means a good or a service that is intended to be sold for money or the equivalent. Life is quite possible without 'products' in this sense: feudal lords lived off their estates and, in theory at least, saw merchants as either the providers of decadent luxuries or as parasites who added to the price of what they sold without adding to the product itself.

Modern managers and marketing executives start their definition of a product with the prospective buyer. The consideration to be offered in exchange is assumed to be money. Medieval merchants added nothing physical to the products that they sold, but they performed many services on behalf of their customers: among other things they selected suitable products from the range on offer in distant markets, they undertook the journey, often a long and hazardous one, from the source to the destination market, they provided essential advice on the use of novel products, and they financed their stock. Today's consumers and industrial buyers need these services as well, and so looking at a product as if it is nothing more than some physical object is a mistake. Every product is a package of goods and services; the goods are optional, but the services are not.

From the earliest recorded time many products have consisted entirely of services: physicians, surgeons, advocates and teachers offered their services for a fee in classical Greece, five centuries before Christ. Military officers from classical times onwards would contract to a city or to a tyrant to raise and command soldiers in any number from a company to an army on a fee and incentive basis. This army would then fight who, when, and where their customer directed — until their commander received a better offer from someone else.

Trying to distinguish between 'products' and 'services' tempts people to forget that all products include a substantial service element. Buyers spend their money to resolve a problem and will select the option which they believe best matches their needs (including the need to have some money left over to spend on other things). Often the same effect may be achieved with a good or a service: a man needing a shave can visit a barber or buy a razor. The same man may make different choices at different times.

Fee-for-service warfare in renaissance Italy

Fee-for-service warriors in the Italian Renaissance were called *condottieri*. These men often dispensed with fighting altogether: the commanding officers would meet, discuss the size, morale, and disposition of their respective forces and from this decide who would win a battle. Having decided, no battle was needed: the 'defeated' army would abandon its customer and go and look for another one while the 'victor' would conduct an auction in which its original employer and the city whose army it had just defeated could buy victory.

Using a customer-focused definition of product means that a significant change in the delivery or sales method represents the introduction of a new product. Biscuits sold by weight from a tin by a traditional grocer are a different product from identical biscuits sold pre-packaged in a supermarket, just as they are different from speciality biscuits sold in a patisserie.

The brand

Once a consumer has decided to buy the resolution of some need or desire (as distinct from doing it themselves or going without) they are 'in the market'. In most cases their problem, unless defined extremely tightly, will have several solutions, all of which are reasonably likely to succeed. Once the choice has narrowed to a small selection a prudent consumer will recall that purchased solutions can be disappointing or even hazardous. Packaged food may look appetising in the picture on the box, but once the contents are on a plate the box itself might taste better or be more nutritious. The holiday hotel at the beach resort that looked so delightful in a brochure may turn out to be designed and run along the lines of a prisoner-of-war camp, while a few square metres of polluted sand may be visible from a corner of the roof, if a sufficiently powerful telescope is used during a break in the rain.

A Japanese consumer seeking a culinary delight may order a dish of fugu, or blowfish. If the meal is not prepared meticulously it may well be the last one that that particular consumer eats.

Consumers and industrial buyers often want to minimise the risk of disappointment or hazard when they are about to use an unfamiliar product for the first time. One way that they do so is to look for a well known and well-reputed brand. The brand may be marked on the product, or it may be the name of the supplier. If the product worked as expected and the anticipated benefits were realised two things follow: first, the buyer may prefer that brand the next time a related need requires satisfaction; and second, the buyer may tell others about the satisfaction obtained, enhancing the reputation of the brand and making other people more likely to rely on it.

As always, brands must be evaluated from the point of view of the customer, not the supplier. Sometimes a customer chooses a familiar brand because he or she recalls a favourable association between that brand and that product. On other occasions a customer enters a familiar and trusted store, or engages a familiar contractor, and relies on the store's or contractor's choice of product supplier. The two forms of brand association are often complementary, in that a highly reputed store may make a point of stocking highly regarded brands.

Marks and Spencer, the British clothing and fresh food chain, have an international reputation for the quality of their products; so much so that products marked with their house brand 'St Michael' are often sold at premium prices in countries where Marks and Spencer do not operate. There are no supplier brands available at all in Marks and Spencer's British stores; the only supplier identification is that of Marks and Spencer themselves. Even product categories dominated by strong consumer brands, such as chocolate and alcoholic drinks, are packed and labelled to Marks and Spencer's requirements before being put on sale.

An Australian was visiting London for the first time, and felt the need for a change from English pub food. He was passing a steak house at the time, and so he went in. In the event the steak was small, tough and overcooked, the salad limp and skimpy, and the service slow and surly.

Two years later the same person was visiting London again and the same urge arose. He saw a steak house that seemed vaguely familiar, and it wasn't until a slow and surly waiter delivered a small, overcooked steak accompanied by a limp lettuce leaf that he remembered why.

The British grocery chain Sainsbury also has a premium reputation, and is also a strong user of house brands, though not to the same extent as Marks and Spencer. Over 60 per cent of the product lines carried in a typical Sainsbury supermarket will be house branded. The major Australian grocery chains tend to follow American rather than British practice, and about 30 per cent of their lines will be house brands, usually matching each house-branded line with one or two supplier-branded ones. American studies suggest that a choice between three product lines is sufficient to maintain a store's reputation among consumers, while stores that carry house brands only, or only one outside brand, may, in the United States, acquire a down-market image and must charge below-average prices to maintain their volumes. Discussions with Australian packaged goods producers and observations in Australian supermarkets suggest that the Australian situation is similar to the American one.[1]

There have been a number of American retail chains that developed an international reputation in the period since the end of the nineteenth century but at the present time none of them appears to have created and maintained the brand strength of Sainsbury or Marks and Spencer. One factor in this may be the Robinson–Patman Act, an American law that prevents supermarket chains making full use of their buying power. In Australia in 1994 Coles Supermarkets announced its intention to raise the proportion of house-branded merchandise in its stores significantly, but the proposal met strong supplier resistance and was dropped, or at least, ceased to be talked about publicly.

Markets

The most obvious sign that a market has emerged is when people start paying an independent supplier to satisfy a need that had previously been neglected or satisfied within the firm or the household. Equally, a market can contract when people draw an activity back into the household or firm, having previously bought services, or when some new market develops that eliminates the original need altogether.

Until the 1950s in Australia, most households had a wash boiler and mangle with which to do their household laundry. The work was heavy, unpleasant, and moderately hazardous, and so many families, even those of very limited means, were prepared to pay for a washerwoman to visit and either do the washing or take the dirty laundry and return it washed and dried. With the widespread availability of washing machines and the introduction of widow's pensions the cost of engaging a washerwoman went up and the inconvenience of doing the household laundry within the household fell: the market for washerperson services contracted drastically, while the demand for washing machines rose.

The underlying need, for clean clothing and household linen, was more-or-less constant by the 1950s. It had risen steadily since the 1830s, when cleanliness began to become a middle class virtue from having been a sinful luxury indulged in by a few foppish aristocrats. Before 1830 there was no market for either washing machines or laundry services; the aristocracy and upper middle classes had servants who did their washing while everyone else stayed dirty.

It could be claimed that, since 1830, there has been one growing market in 'the means to achieve socially acceptable levels of personal and domestic hygiene', or that there have been two markets, one for contracted washing services and one for household washing machines, or even that there has been a succession of markets as each generation of washing machines replaced the previous one.

This semantic minefield simply illustrates that markets are best defined by reference to the customers who use them. On this basis the novelty of a market should be assessed in terms of the changes (if any) in the pattern of user behaviour involved. An industrial laundry whose salespeople collect and return washing involves little if any behavioural change, as far as the customer is concerned, from giving the wash to a local washerwoman; such a laundry might be said to be competing against the washerwomen in the laundry services market. By contrast, buying a washing machine and using it personally involves a significant behavioural change and so the introduction of domestic washing machines could be described as creating a new market. A newer model of washing machine incorporating a spin drier to replace the wringer did not require a behavioural change and could be seen as a new product entering an established market.

By starting from the buyers' habits the entrepreneur can learn some useful clues about their likely response to a new product, whether it is a novel good, a new service, or even a new sales or distribution method applied to a familiar product. Habits tend to change slowly, and the sales of a new product which requires its buyers to make such a change will start slowly, no matter what the apparent advantages of the invention. By contrast, a new product that carries out, or helps its user carry out, a familiar task in a faster, cheaper or better way may face few barriers to adoption. Business travellers showed no reluctance to be flown in Boeing 747 'jumbo' aircraft when they were first introduced, since the main change from narrow-bodied jets was (in those happy days) that there were lots of empty seats in economy. The capacity of the aircraft had doubled, but the number of passengers had not.

It took ten or so years from the introduction of wide-bodied international jet aircraft for the market in long-distance tourism to develop to the point that all the seats were regularly sold and the airlines could start working on ways to jam more in. Taking an international instead of a local holiday represented a major change in behaviour, and so the habit of taking such holidays spread relatively slowly through the population of potential users.

Industry life cycles

Many industries have shown a consistent pattern of development as the technologies that they relied on matured:

▲ When an industry is very new individual firms tend to be vertically integrated, not only performing practically all the tasks involved in transforming raw materials to finished goods, but even making their own machinery. At one stage Henry Ford not only owned iron ore mines, he even owned a cattle ranch so as to have guaranteed supplies of leather for his cars' seats.

▲ The success of the earliest firms leads to the entry of many competitors, most of whom will also be vertically integrated to some extent. The growing market for the final product also involves increased demand for intermediate products, offering a chance for industry-wide scale economies. One of the earliest opportunities to be exploited often involves the formation or spinning out of specialist firms to produce the industry's machinery.

▲ The industry's structure undergoes a 90 degree rotation, as firms merge or drop out at the final product end and the survivors disaggregate, transferring much of their common production to specialist firms.

▲ The disaggregation process continues, with firms outsourcing services such as transport, cleaning and plant maintenance to specialists. Even apparently core activities such as design and procurement may be contracted out (Langlois & Robertson 1994).

In the years leading up to 1994 Ford Australia's plastics division was an active centre of innovation, pioneering, for example, a plastic petrol tank for the Falcon range. In 1994 the plastics division was sold, and now operates independently of Ford. In the opinion of Ford's Australian managers, the division could not remain competitively viable as long as its market was limited to Ford's Australian operations, while as an independent operation it could grow by servicing other Australian manufacturers and by exporting. The fact that the division's innovative technology would be available to Ford's competitors was less of a threat than the possibility that Ford would lose access to it altogether.

The trend to disaggregation is one of the drivers of Australia's move towards a 'service' economy. When breweries owned their own delivery trucks and employed their drivers, the costs of delivery were counted as part of the brewing industry. Now that the breweries have contracted out their transport to specialists such as Linfox, the delivery operations are counted with the service fraction of the economy.

Vertical integration is superficially attractive. The more vertically integrated a firm is, the more control the firm's management has over every part of the production and distribution chain. The downside is the commitment of time and capital to activities that have nothing to do with the entrepreneur's particular advantages. There is, of course, a risk that an entrepreneur who outsources some critical component or service to a specialist firm may find that the specialist captures too much of the total value added. This risk can be exaggerated: the specialist usually needs the innovator's business too. If an entrepreneur encounters a specialist supplier whose margins are wholly out of line with its contribution, the entrepreneur might consider suspending work on the original innovation and going into direct competition with the excessively greedy supplier. Trying to compete with the established intermediate supplier and launch an innovation at the same time may be an unduly risky option.

Entrepreneurs should be very wary of being drawn into activities where they have no distinct advantages. Many parts of the production and delivery process will be needed by their business but will have nothing to do with their innovation. The more of these that they can contract out the greater the leverage that their own particular advantages will provide. The need to concentrate on those parts of their business where unique value is created is driving many large firms to move towards 'lean production' where every activity that does not contribute to the firm's *unique* operating advantages is a candidate for buying in or outsourcing. This is, in turn, creating numerous new markets which provide opportunities for new and growing firms.

When a firm spins off a technologically proficient unit that has historically contributed to the firm's competitive advantages, as with Ford Australia's plastics unit, the firm has clearly lost control of something valuable. This will be offset in two ways: first, the selling company will be paid, in cash, shares, and other valuable considerations for the unit; and second, the newly-independent unit will incorporate market, product and technological innovations inspired by the original owners' competitors in the products that the original owner can now buy. Firms that share a common supplier can use their supplier relationship to build a mutually beneficial communications channel through which technological and market intelligence can be exchanged.

The tendency to vertical disaggregation and horizontal aggregation is not a particularly recent one, and can be demonstrated in the history of the nineteenth century railway industries. The very earliest railway companies did their own

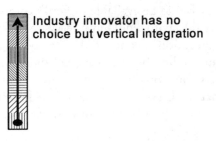

Industry innovator has no choice but vertical integration

New entrants copy innovator and vertically integrate

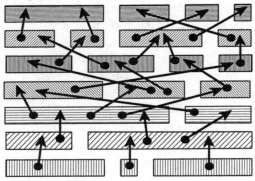

Mergers and failures reduce horizontal competition

Mature industry marked by horizontal concentration, vertical disaggregation

Figure 4.1 The pattern of industry development

surveying, designed and built their own structures, laid their own permanent way, and designed and built engines, as well as carrying people and goods. By the end of the nineteenth century specialist firms were carrying out most of the civil and engineering works and the railway companies generally restricted themselves to track maintenance and train operation. The 1994 restructuring of the British rail system separated the maintenance of the track and operation of the signalling systems from the running of trains, carrying disaggregation even further.

The development of the United States and British textile industries offers another example. The medieval textile industry in England was almost totally disaggregated. Different specialists scoured, carded, spun, wove and dyed the fabric. This pattern was maintained as the industry moved from cottages to factories during the industrial revolution of the eighteenth and nineteenth centuries. The United States textile industry was established in New England in the early nineteenth century in direct opposition to the British industry and in the teeth of considerable hostility from it.[2] Early American textile factories were almost totally vertically integrated, with mill owners making their own machinery and processing raw cotton into fabric. By the beginning of the twentieth century the United States industry had disaggregated almost as completely as the English one.

There is a long and consistent pattern of industries moving from vertically integrated monopolies to oligopolies to vertically disaggregated 'monopolistic competitors' selling unique but mutually substitutable products. This strongly suggests that the move adds to the aggregate value of the industries concerned, and so is likely to continue into the future.

The adoption process

Every technology, market, product and brand has a starting point in historic time: once no one used it, and at some later time it was used by at least one person. Every successful technology, market, product and brand was, at some time, used by many people, and there must have been a time when it was used by some intermediate number. The thought precedes the deed, and the idea of using a new product must have preceded the decision to use it in most buyer's minds.

At the individual level there is a need to learn at least some elementary facts about a novel technology, market, product or brand before making a decision to become a user. Prospective users of the Sony Walkman needed to learn that it was light, portable, and could entertain them as they moved around. They did not have to learn the principles of transistor operation nor understand how Sony had designed and built the tape drive system. The facts that buyers needed could be learned by trying the product in a shop, by talking with their friends, or by reading a Sony advertisement.

Sometimes the knowledge needed is much greater. Steel, in every sense, provides the foundation for modern industrialised societies. It is produced in huge quantities in huge plants; even a 'mini-mill' dwarfs most factories. A decision to change technology represents a massive investment commitment and may involve a huge write-down of the value of previous investments, forcing the steel-making company to declare a reduced profit or even a loss. Decisions with these implications are not going to be undertaken in a hurry.

The hard decisions

Until around 1970 the dominant steel-making technology was the Siemens-Marten 'open hearth' furnace, a huge brick frying pan in which a charge of pig-iron and scrap steel was slowly cooked until it reached the right composition.

The *basic oxygen converter* was developed in Austria in the 1950s, and began to be adopted by the world's steel industry from 1960. The basic oxygen converter was smaller, faster, and much less labour-intensive then the open hearth. The major United States steel companies delayed adopting the new technology because of the profit impact of writing off their open hearth furnaces.

Japanese, Korean, Brazilian — and Australian — steel makers were not so dilatory, and in just ten years the United States steel industry plunged from market dominance to a minor player in the global steel market.

Australian families face at least three sets of decisions that are proportionately, if not absolutely, comparable to a choice between major industrial technologies. They buy houses to live in, they buy motor cars, and many of them buy secondary education for their children. All these decisions involve a major up-front investment, the full results of which may not be known for many years. Often a decision in these areas will be preceded by months or even years of anxious discussion and eager information-gathering.

Entrepreneurs promoting a new technology, or trying to create a new market by proposing the outsourcing of some internal process, are often frustrated and upset by the apparent stupidity of the people that they are trying to sell the idea to: something that seems blindingly obvious to them is met with suspicion and even hostility from the people that it is intended to benefit. Many decisions are irreversible, or only reversed at great cost, and even a small chance of disaster will make most people hesitate as long as the alternative is not equally unpleasant. Rather than fret about the stupidity of those who do not rush to embrace their new concept, entrepreneurs should imagine themselves choosing a school for their only child: if the match between child and school proves to be a bad one, they cannot wipe the slate clean, reset the child's age, and start him or her at an alternative establishment.

Of course, for some people their child's schooling presents no problems at all: 'I went to St Y's, and that is where my son is going.' Quite.

The diffusion of innovation

Most entrepreneurs will not realise their ambitions by securing one customer; they need lots of them. When the focus 'zooms out' from the individual to the group the correct approach is to use statistics rather than case studies or the sales manual. Fortunately the progressive adoption of a new concept by a population is relatively easy to handle statistically.

There are two processes at work behind the progressive adoption of an idea:

1   There may be a deliberate attempt, or series of attempts, made to convince people that the new idea is valid and should be adopted. If the idea is a religious one, the process is described as 'proselytising' and the people who carry it out are called missionaries; if it is political, it will be called 'education' by its proponents and 'sedition' by its enemies; if it is a new scientific concept, it will be announced by a letter to *Nature* followed up by a series of learned articles; while if it is concerned with the sales of a new product it should be called 'promotion'.

2   Prospective users will progressively learn by observation, direct or reported, of the successful experiences of others who have adopted the new concept. This may lead them to accept the validity of the idea themselves. This form of adoption can be split into two sub-groups:

a   decisions which are regarded as complex and important to the person making them may be preceded by a process of conscious or partly conscious research, seeking the opinions of others and taking opportunities to observe the actions and learn about the experiences of prior adopters

b   the adoption by a trusted surrogate may be sufficient when the level of trust placed in the surrogate outweighs the risks inherent in a decision — a Ford buyer trading up to the latest model without visiting any other manufacturer's dealers, or someone buying a new frozen desert from their Woolworths or Coles store, is acting in this way.

Method *2b* usually follows a successful application of method *1* or method *2a*: the first visit to a Woolworths store, or purchase of a Ford car, may have been a response to a promotion by the supplier or the result of a search by the user — the trust needed to make the supplier a surrogate will have been built up over repeated visits to stores in the Woolworths chain or the continued satisfactory use of the Ford car.

The known statistics about method *2a* show a remarkable consistency between products and across cultures.[3] For every two people who have adopted an idea and found it satisfactory, one more is likely to adopt the idea as a result of their influence in any given year. There are two provisos: one is that only a limited number of people will adopt two mutually exclusive ideas; and the other is that, as the adoption of an idea spreads, much of the influence of prior adopters will have the effect of reinforcing each others' beliefs rather than persuading members of the uncommitted group to adopt the idea. While a new idea begins to spread with a growth rate of up to 50 per cent per year, this tails off sooner or later.

The interaction between adopters and the previously uncommitted members of a population generates the characteristic 'logistic' curve shown in

Figure 4.2.[4] The exact shape of the curve depends critically on the number of adopters in the population at the time of the first introduction of the new idea, and on the fraction of the adopters who are sufficiently satisfied to influence others. Growth patterns similar to that generated by this curve have been found in the history of early Christianity, the sales of powered lawn mowers in California, the number of citations of learned articles; in fact, practically everywhere the spread of new ideas has been measured.[5]

A simple diffusion model fails to explain how the first few adopters enter the population. It cannot, without assuming unrealistically high levels of satisfaction and/or influence, explain the actual pattern of diffusion observed in many markets or the relatively short time such markets take to develop. These deficiencies are made up, for commercial markets at least, by assuming that a certain amount of adoption is induced by deliberate promotion: type *1* processes from the list above.

While the rate of idea diffusion resulting from interpersonal interaction is known fairly accurately, attempts to find some single number, or even range of numbers, to describe the effect of deliberate promotion have failed to determine it to within six orders of magnitude. This suggests that human response to the unsolicited offer of a new product is not a constant; at the very least, the degree of response seems to vary with the degree of effort put into promoting it. This idea will be developed in the section on market life cycles below.

Technological cycles

The idea of 'technological cycles' comes from economics, and in particular the work of Schumpeter, Kondratieff and others, who identified what they believed were 'long cycles' in economic development.[6] Such cycles started with the intro-

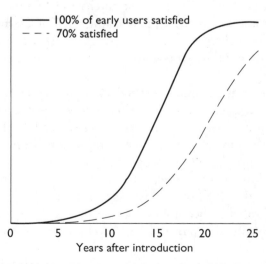

Figure 4.2 The basic logistic or 'S' curve illustrating diffusion: Population of 500 with one initial adopter

duction of a new technology, resulting in a spurt in economic growth. Growth then continued for many years as the new technology was applied in more and more areas, but it finally petered out as the technology approached its physical and commercial limits. Technology cycles may be more relevant to students of the macroeconomy than to entrepreneurs, but understanding the nature of technological development may assist many entrepreneurs to recognise that there are more and less propitious times to launch a new technology.[7]

The development of military technology has been thoroughly documented[8] and the process can provide many analogies to the application of technology to commercial purposes. Some highlights of the development of military technology in Europe include:

▲ the Spartan hoplite, a heavy-armed infantryman trained to fight in line, could defeat peasant levies even when outnumbered five or more to one

▲ the Macedonian phalanx, pikemen trained to use the long sarissa in a deep formation, could defeat sword-carrying heavy-armed infantry

▲ the Roman legion,[9] a combination of heavy-armed and light-armed infantry trained to manoeuvre and fight in ranks and columns and supported by light cavalry, could defeat a phalanx

▲ the invention of the stirrup and girth enabled the Gothic tribes to create armies of heavy cavalry whose long spears and even better manoeuvrability could defeat a legion

▲ the invention of armour-piercing projectile weapons, the long-bow and the arquebus, enabled infantry supported by pikemen to defeat heavy cavalry

▲ and so on to today's cruise missiles and stealth aircraft.

One of history's most profound lessons is that major military innovations seldom if ever came from the nations that had raised themselves to dominance by an earlier military innovation. The Romans introduced the legion four centuries before Christ, and for the next seven hundred years progressively refined the weapons, the command structure and the training of the legions as they expanded their empire. Only after the Goths captured Rome did the Roman army take the development of heavy cavalry seriously. The Goth's heavy cavalry enabled them to hold Rome and found the Holy Roman Empire. Our word 'knight' comes from the Gothic word for an armoured cavalryman. Knights ruled the battlefield — and the countryside — for a thousand years until the Welsh longbowmen at Agincourt demonstrated that the heavy cavalry era was over.

There are good examples of something similar happening with national technical capabilities. Britain led the industrial revolution, and the two technologies that the British became pre-eminent in were the application of steam power, and the smelting, casting and machining of iron. British steam engines powered most of the railways of the world until the world's railways switched to diesel in the 1960s. Australia imported British railway engines into the 1950s. British researchers and innovators worked in other fields as well; Faraday laid the groundwork for the practical application of electricity while Perkin founded the world's first synthetic chemical industry. Germany, rather than Britain, became the home of the world's leading electrical (Siemens) and chemical (I. G. Farben) firms. British managers and investors were too comfortable with the technology that they knew to put sufficient effort into alternatives. Even the apparent British dominance of railway technology was lost to the Japanese and French as high speed trains were developed: the British became locked into the view that the speed limit for steam-hauled trains was a limitation of the system rather than of the engine.

This lesson is often repeated in the history of individual firms, at least in the English-speaking countries: product-based companies that have been built on one innovation are seldom successful in the successor markets. IBM did not invent the computer, but they did take it from being a laboratory toy to an essential tool of commerce. IBM's archetypical product was the 'mainframe', a powerful computer that needed a special environment and a team of specialist operators, analysts and programmers to make it useful. The mainframe was a sort of central power station, where all the computing work of a major organisation would be carried out. At one stage IBM held 80 per cent of the mainframe computer market, and only fear of the United States anti-trust laws stopped it taking over the rest.

The mini-computer, less powerful but much more environmentally tolerant than the mainframe, and cheap enough to be used for one task rather than having to be managed as a central utility, was innovated by Digital Equipment Corporation. Digital in turn saw their market shrink as their customers abandoned them for the interactive workstation, innovated by Sun Microsystems. IBM launched the personal computer, taking it away from hobbyists and putting it on to the corporate desk, but failed to secure control over either the hardware architecture, embodied in the microprocessor, or the software environment. The dominant innovators in the history of the personal computer market to the time of writing are Intel and Microsoft; the rest of the players, IBM included, are essentially their distributors.

An example of overcoming technical limits: The development of the computer

The computer industry did not spring from nothing. Calculating machines go back to the eighteenth century, and Babbage designed and started building his 'analytical engine' in the mid-nineteenth century. Tabulating machinery was in widespread use for commercial calculating applications before the Second World War. 'Colossus', the British code-breaking machine built and commissioned at

Bletchley Park during the Second World War, incorporated most of the essential features of a modern computer.

The computer could not become the basis of an industry while two major technological barriers remained. Computers need components to implement logic, and they need to be able to store and modify data. As Babbage discovered, mechanical logic could be used to build an adding machine, but it was not technically possible to put enough of it together to make a working computer. More components meant that each component had to be smaller and therefore more fragile, but more components meant more friction and therefore more force needed to drive the machine. The lines 'more force' and 'more fragile' crossed before a working machine could be built.

Hollerith invented the tabulating machine and built it out of mechanical components only, but the cost, complexity and fragility was such that the machines Hollerith built stayed where he built them — in the United States Bureau of Census. Hollerith's machines stored data on punched cards, and modified it by punching new ones. The electromagnetic relay could be used to implement logical functions, which seemed to solve the problem that had stopped Babbage and restricted Hollerith, and electromechanical tabulators entered the commercial market and were used for account keeping and other purposes. The first machines used at Bletchley Park, the 'bombes', got their name because of the audible ticking that came from their electromechanical components.

Electromechanical technology could be used to carry out quite complicated tasks, whether in Bletchley Park's bombes, IBM's tabulators, or in automatic telephone exchanges, but it was 'hard-wired logic': the components were joined with soldered wire, and if the logic had to change then the wire had to be cut and rejoined in a different way. As the British genius, Alan Turing pointed out, a true computer had to be able to change its own logic, and this was impractical, to say the least, with soldered connections.[10] IBM tabulating equipment cut down on the soldering problem by bringing some of the connections onto a plugboard where the functions could be controlled by inserting little wire links. The people, invariably female, who plugged up these boards were referred to as 'programmers'. While changing plugs on a board was quicker than soldering, it fell far short of the flexibility a true computer needed, and in any case most of the logic connections in a tabulator were still soldered and could not be modified on the plugboard.

Colossus, ENIAC, Mark 1, MANIAC and the other early computers used electronics to give them the flexibility they needed to implement programmable logic, but the only active electronic components available to the people building these machines were thermionic 'valves'. A thermionic valve consisted of a cathode, which had to be at red heat for the device to function, an optional number of grids and screens which could be used to control the current flow, and an anode that had to be maintained at a high enough voltage to attract electrons from the cathode. All these components had to be enclosed in an airtight, evacuated container; the most compact thermionic valves were about the size of an acorn, while the standard size was similar to a man's thumb.

Force and friction had defeated Babbage: heat and statistics fought the early developers of computers. Each logic element or 'latch' needed active elements (one or two valves) as well as several other components, which meant two cathodes, two heaters, and a power demand of four to six watts. The most basic computer needed 10 000 thermionic valves which gave out 40 to 60 kilowatts of heat: enough to keep ten suburban homes comfortably warm in the middle of winter. Getting rid of all this heat was one problem, and the effect of it on the components was another. The internal heat ensured that thermionic valves drifted off their specification or failed altogether fairly quickly. The expected life before failure of each thermionic valve was about 1000 hours, but the time before one of the 10 000 failed was a matter of a few hours only. The first computers were slow, hot, and very unreliable.

Computers became generally practical once William Shockley of Bell Laboratories had invented the transistor, a solid state electronic device that did not need a heater and which had an indefinite service life. Even before the development of the integrated circuit it had become possible to build reasonably reliable — and cool-running — computers. IBM's 1401, introduced in 1961, and wholly transistorised, became the first commercially successful computer range.

One of the lessons of this, and many other, examples of industrial history is the sheer magnitude of the time lags: it took over a hundred years from the time the concept of a computing machine was formulated to the development of a commercially successful product. Turing published a formal proof of the logical feasibility of computing machines in 1938, twenty-three years before computers reached commercial success. Mark I and MANIAC were both demonstrated in the laboratory by 1951, ten years before computers achieved commercial success. The key enabling technology, the transistor, was demonstrated in the laboratory fourteen years before the IBM 1401 system was launched.

The growth phase of the mainframe computer market did not really start until 1966, and the market's growth phase did not end until 1984. If any of the key inventions had been patented, only Shockley's transistor (which Bell Labs did not patent, for United States anti-trust reasons) would have earned any royalties from licensing, and then the amount would have been minuscule by comparison with the ultimate size of the computer and communications industries.

History teaches us that technical inventions and scientific discoveries are neither a necessary nor a sufficient condition for the development of a new enterprise. One of the most successful enterprises of the twentieth century was IBM, yet not only was IBM not the inventor of the computer, but from 1956 on IBM was legally obliged to license any and all of its patents at no charge to any United States corporation that wished to make use of them. Entrepreneurs in control of a secret or patented invention would be silly to give their rights away, but they should not imagine that the invention on its own will bring success to their enterprise.

Technology development: The ecological model

While the term 'cycle' may not, as we suggested above, be an appropriate way to describe the history of any particular technology, there is certainly a fairly well-established general pattern:

▲ *inventors* and *researchers*, in or out of laboratories, discover physical phenomena or logical relationships that are intriguing to specialists, but which have only a limited, if any, immediate practical application

▲ an *entrepreneur* links several of these ideas to create a product which addresses a sufficiently wide market at a sufficiently profitable price to become commercially successful

▲ *success* in the first market leads to increased volumes, falling costs and prices, and the use of the innovation in other applications, extending the original market and creating new ones

▲ *other entrepreneurs* see that the functional elements of the new product, combined with apparently unrelated inventions (not necessarily their own), can be used to create a newer product again, further extending the original market and/or creating more of them

▲ *still further entrepreneurs* see that certain components of the original or of one or more of the derived products can be replaced with an enhanced version, improving the final product's performance and/or reducing its cost

▲ eventually various *physical limits* will be reached, and no further progress can be made with products based on the original core technology.

The elaboration of the original innovation does not trace a straight line from a primitive device to a modern one. One quite good analogy is that of the growing bush: the original innovation resembles the trunk, while each subsequent innovation represents a new branch. At each stage the branches get smaller, while there are many more of them. Finally an innovation, like a bush, reaches the limits to its growth. The outer boundary is fixed by physical limits, the zone of superiority of other products, or by the end of market demand, while inside the bush the spaces that remain are too small to allow leaves to develop. Renewed growth may be triggered by cross-fertilisation with a new technology, or the technology may cease to develop, and its market space may be invaded by products relying on new technologies.

Until the fifth step in the list above is reached the new technology is unquestionably driving economic growth. As each new market segment is opened up, or as superior products displace older ones, both consumers and producers gain. At the fifth step some of the innovative drive turns on the technology itself, cutting its cost rather than widening its application. These internal improvements will lead to lower prices, and in the early stages, actual market growth as the rise in the number of users overcomes the lower average prices that they are paying. Eventually the point is reached where further price cuts do not widen the market sufficiently for revenue to grow, and the technology ceases to contribute to economic growth; rather, it starts to subtract from it.

The first great technological thrust of the modern era came from the steam railway: the era is generally dated from the opening of either the Liverpool to Manchester railway or the Baltimore and Ohio Railroad in 1830.[11] Human civilisation had previously been limited to thin strips around natural harbours and along the banks of navigable rivers; the railway turned this one-dimensional pattern into a two-dimensional one. The effective completion of the United States railway system in the 1890s coincided with a great, worldwide economic crisis. The slackening pace of railway building may not have caused the crisis, but it removed an underlying force for growth.

The second great technological thrust came with the development of the mass-market motor car, generally dated from the introduction of the T-model Ford in 1908. The motor car industry had not developed sufficiently to hold off the Great Depression of 1930–33, but it did underpin the long boom following the Second World War. In the 1970s the United States car market slowed down markedly, and so did the economy of many western nations.

By the mid 1990s no single technology or industry had appeared to take over economic leadership from the motor car. The computing and communications industries, although huge, did not seem to have the scope for further growth that would award either of them the title of 'most significant industry'. The term 'information superhighway' was introduced in 1993 to promote the development of computer networks offering near-universal access. Its proponents clearly hoped that the information superhighway would boost the development of information service industries as successfully as the United States interstate highway program of the 1950s and 1960s had boosted the development of the motor industry. If they are right, the growth of information and entertainment industries will drive economic growth in the first part of the twenty-first century.

It is also possible that no single industry will replace the motor car as the primary engine of economic growth, that nothing will dominate the economies of the twenty-first century the way that the railway dominated the nineteenth and the car, the twentieth. There are certainly people who will argue that the industrial era is ending with the twentieth century. Whether this means that economic growth is also ending, or that future growth will be driven by forces that are different in impact and organisation, as well as technology, from those of the past, is for the future to discover.

The market life cycle

A market comes into existence when an identifiable group of people begin to satisfy a need by purchase when they had previously left that need unsatisfied or dealt with it within the household or the firm. Using the definitions set out above, a market may also emerge when a new way of satisfying a previously purchased need becomes available: 'new' in this case means that the users will be required to do new things to acquire and use the new product, and says nothing about the technology it embodies.

Clearly there must be someone who is prepared to supply the new good or service, or to deliver an established good or service in a new way before a new market can appear. The person who first offers the new product is an entrepreneur or an innovative firm, hoping to create or expand a business by satisfying the future demand for the new product. Once the market is established, demand is self-sustaining as satisfied current users make repeat purchases and influence other potential users to try the product. At the point where the entrepreneur or the innovative firm is first ready to supply the new product, however, it has no current users, satisfied or not: the demand is wholly potential. Before the new product can have a lot of users it must have a few of them, and it is worth considering the relationship between the entrepreneur and the first few users.

A potential user of a new product is in the same position as an experimental subject: the entrepreneur, like the experimenter, promises the subject that nothing but good can come of trying the new product out. The potential user, like the experimental subject, will see that the entrepreneur, or the experimenter, is bound to get some good out of the trial, but the user benefits are by no means so certain. Experimental subjects are often paid for their time, with cash or other benefits, and indemnified against risk. Early users of new products expect no less.

Ways in which early users obtain benefits that offset the risks that they are being subjected to include the following:

▲ Extensive personal attention from a sales person backed up by a team of support staff during the period of installation and early use. This is common practice in the marketing of major industrial products. The early user does not merely get the benefits of risk control: suppliers of new products to key users will carry out many of the commissioning and early operating tasks that later users will have to perform for themselves.

▲ Extensive advertising of a new product may offer potential early users the assurance that the supplier is even more exposed to the success of the product than they are, giving an implied promise of performance.

▲ Celebrity endorsement of a new product may encourage new users to give it a trial, particularly when the persuasiveness of the advertising is sufficient to convey the impression that the celebrity is already a user,[12] and therefore further buyers are less subject to first-user risks.

▲ Samples of a new product may be given away, or sold on an extended free trial basis, relieving the early buyers of any financial exposure in the event of the product failing to perform.

▲ Early users may be offered inducements greatly exceeding their apparent exposure. Party plan and similar sales schemes promise early users a commission on those future sales that they will arrange.

Harmless cigarettes

A world-famous operatic tenor of the 1930s allowed his photograph to be used in a cigarette advertisement over the words 'Brand X cigarettes don't affect my singing voice'.

A personal friend of the tenor remonstrated that the tenor was a life-long non-smoker.

'Right,' said the tenor, 'that's why they don't affect my voice.'

All these approaches require the supplier to offer a substantial, and expensive, inducement to the early buyers of a new product. A new customer will spend a certain amount with a supplier in the course of the first year of their relationship, while the supplier will spend money on promotion and selling. As a general rule, the promotion and selling costs needed to secure a typical new, unreferred customer will be no less than the gross margin on one year's business from such a customer. This is not really a matter of one-on-one accounting, with so many dollars spent on each new customer. Rather, it represents the likely return, measured in customers, to an investment spread across a large population. This is most obvious with media advertising; for many products a TV or newspaper advertisement will be seen by large numbers of people lacking either the means or the desire to buy the advertised product. The great majority of the people with a need which the new product addresses and the means to pay for it will not buy as a result of seeing one advertisement either. The value generated by sales to a small fraction of the exposed population must be sufficient to compensate for the cost of advertising to all of it.

Since every customer introduced to a new product involves a large accounting loss, and often a cash loss as well, the prospects for a supplier with a new product look dim. Dim they are if the 'three Rs' of product marketing cannot be brought into service. These are recommendation, repurchase and replacement.

Recommendation is the dominant engine of market growth for durable goods and high value, infrequently purchased services. The recommendation can be tacit, as when very early motorists aroused public interest merely by driving their cars around, but it is often volunteered or sought. It would probably be possible to construct a chain of common directors linking every listed company in Australia, for example, such that a few telephone calls would be sufficient for a company director to get a personal recommendation about practically anything or anyone.

Some ideas are spread with very little paid-for promotion. The concept of mass overseas travel was effectively diffused through Australia by a series of slide nights. The comedian Barry Humphries satirised the Australian slide night hilariously, but at the same time spread the concept of overseas tourist travel even further. Home video became popular in much the same way. Any concept where early users gain an increased benefit by bringing others into the market is likely to diffuse very rapidly: building trades people were the first occupational group to become major users of mobile telephones in Australia. One of the major applications was coordinating trades at a site; clearly, if the plasterer wanted to know if the plumber had finished the pipework it was easier to telephone than visit, but this was only possible if both were on the mobile network. There wasn't much for the early mobile telephone sales people to do apart from collect the money, because the early users did the real selling work.

Repurchase beyond the familiarisation period generates cash for the suppliers of frequently purchased products, cash which can either be harvested or invested in gaining new customers. Often the repurchase decision is triggered by the purchase of a durable product: the Gillette Company sells a package containing a handle and some blades at or below cost, counting on future sales of razor blades to generate profits. Some prescription drugs need to be taken for the balance of the patient's life: the profits on these future sales provide a return on the investment in persuading doctors to prescribe the drug as well as on the cost of developing and proving it.

Replacement sales offer a useful chance of future cash flow to the marketers of durable goods, since durable goods purchasers tend to return to their original supplier when they need an upgraded product. The tendency to return erodes over time, but when users are particularly satisfied with their current product their loyalty erodes quite slowly. A United States study in 1989 revealed that 90 per cent of buyers of Toyotas and other Japanese cars in the United States would trade their car for another model from the same maker after owning the original car for three years, while only 70 per cent of owners of the major American marques would buy from the same maker three years later. The difference is enough to explain the whole of Toyota's superior profit and growth performance over the 1980s as against that of General Motors.

A new market often starts slowly, as one or a small number of innovative suppliers attempt to generate customer interest within the constraints of a tiny or non-existent advertising and general marketing budget. The onset of rapid growth may coincide with the entry of a major company, as when IBM entered the personal computer market in 1981, or when one of the early entrants gets access to an adequate source of capital, as when Sun Microsystems formed an alliance with AT&T. The additional capital allows the early products to be refined to marketable standards and a properly organised sales and marketing effort to be initiated; this will build a pool of early users whose influence and repurchasing will cause rapid growth in industry revenues.

Eventually, which usually means within seven or so years of the professional stage of marketing commencing, more than half of the potential customers will have joined the market and revenue growth will slow quite sharply, eventually stabilising as the flow of new users becomes limited to those people whose changing economic or demographic circumstances bring them into the market. Looking back to the standard diffusion curve (Figure 4.2) the onset of maturity can be seen as the point of inflection, the centre of the 'S'. Until this point sales have been accelerating; after it, they are still growing but decelerating.

Markets show birth, growth and maturity, and lovers of analogy would look for periods called decline and a time of death as well. These may be rare: since markets grow when people decide to satisfy a need by purchase, their decline and death would require that people should cease to have certain needs, or cease to purchase their solution, or that some alternative market should arise that completely eliminates the original one by satisfying the relevant needs in a significantly different way.

There are many examples of markets stabilising at some level, possibly below their peak, and then declining relatively slowly, if at all. The market for men's hairdressing services declined sharply with the growth in the market for safety razors as the product — a clean-shaven appearance — was drawn back into the household. The men's hairdressing market suffered a second shock when the 'short back and sides' appearance ceased to be mandatory for all working men and schoolboys. A residual market remains.

Product life cycles

Markets may have an open-ended life cycle, but products, taken as precisely defined packages of goods and services offered to customers, do not.[13] Products are introduced, modified, and eventually withdrawn following executive decisions made by specific suppliers. Some suppliers are obstinate, some are timid, and some are unlucky; this means that the exact length of time between a product's launch and withdrawal, its price trajectory, and its sales volumes can be estimated but cannot be determined precisely in advance.

It is possible to suggest an idealised product life cycle, the sequence which would have been followed if every decision had been perfect. Real product histories cannot be any better than this, and they may be significantly worse. In general terms products follow the following sequence:

▲ There is an *introduction* — or *launch* — phase, during which the product will be new to the majority of people who notice it. Some of them will give it a trial; those who give it a trial, being human, will have differing reactions, ranging from great satisfaction to utter disgust; and if too large a fraction of the early trials generate a lukewarm or worse response, there will be few repurchases and recommendations, and sales will fall sharply. The supplier may withdraw the product or the distributors refuse to carry it. Either way, the life cycle ends at this point.

▲ Products enter a *growth* phase when a significant fraction of the early users of a product are sufficiently satisfied by it to repurchase it and/or recommend it. Sales will begin to rise, encouraging the supplier to increase production and the distributors to give it greater prominence; and the success of the product will generate more recommendations, more repurchasing, and more sales, giving the supplier rapidly rising revenue and encouraging other suppliers to offer directly comparable products.

▲ The entry of more suppliers will reduce the apparent value of any unique features of the original product and consumers, believing that the various products are largely interchangeable, will become increasingly price sensitive. This will force prices and margins down. Such competitive pressure is typical of the *mature* phase of the product life cycle.

▲ Eventually the *decline* phase commences and the revenue earned by the original product is no longer sufficient to provide an adequate return on the capital tied up in producing it, and the product will be progressively withdrawn, possibly shortly after a new, improved variant is introduced.

One of the most common management mistakes is to delay the fourth step, keeping a product in the market for too long. At the point where the margins earned by a product can no longer justify the capital resources needed to support it, they are still positive, and some managers may argue that a product should be kept available as long as it is earning any money at all. Such managers need their aim redirected: businesses do not succeed simply by making a profit, but by adding the greatest possible value to a given stock of capital. Maintaining an ageing product line may appear to maximise current profits, but it depresses

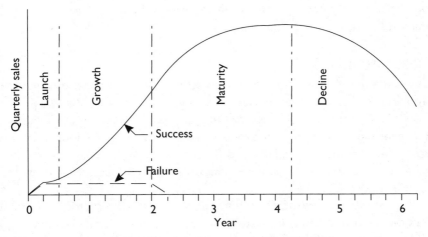

Figure 4.3 Stylised product life cycle model — note that this figure represents a consumer product rather than a market, which would generally be much longer-lived. A replacement product is assumed to be launched at the start of year 4

future ones. The value of a company reflects both its current and its prospective future profits.

Intel gets cunning

The first microprocessors made by Intel for the PC market were known as the 8088 (in the original PC), the 8086 (in the PC/XT) and the 80286 (in the PC/AT and the first generation of clones). Each of these stayed in the market, more or less unchanged, for four or five years with a certain amount of overlap.

By the time the 80286 had been in the market for a year or so the value and growth rate of the PC market attracted other chip suppliers, whose products were near-perfect substitutes for the Intel one, and prices began to fall precipitously.

When Intel launched the 80386 they followed it with a few variants with different speeds and power consumption, and regained control of the market. The 80486 launch was followed by a variant of some sort every two or three months, ensuring that Intel always had some high margin chips in the market. Intel's revenue, profits and share price all boomed.

Another mistake that many managers make, particularly those in high technology industries, is to exaggerate the degree of change needed to make a product sufficiently new to restart the product life cycle at the first step. With some packaged consumer products little more is needed than new packaging, new advertising, and some new varieties, but even with quite sophisticated products a product can be new to the market without being new from the ground up. New products must be sufficiently novel to bring about an increase in perceived value that will, in turn, justify a profitable price. Often a series of relatively minor product changes will achieve this: 'All-singing, all-dancing new' products are the necessary exception, at least outside the theatre, not the general rule.

Whose product?

Many marketing text books refer to the 'four Ps' (the four factors making up the 'marketing mix': *product, promotion, place* and *price*) in their discussion of the factors affecting the success of a new product. Clearly, when all other things are equal, consumers will prefer the product that is available in the most convenient place. When products are clearly differentiated people will seek the better product even at some inconvenience. For any single product one factor will tend to dominate the other.

Most packaged consumer products are offered in supermarkets of one sort or another, and consumers make the decision to go to a particular supermarket and then select the products that they need from the range available. The choice of supermarket determines the selection from which the choice of product will be made. The fraction of the consumer population inside one supermarket will tend to divide their choices of product within a category to reflect the amount of shelf space each product occupies.

Things are never quite what they seem — two distinct processes underlie the decision to display a product in a supermarket and the allocation of shelf space between those products selected:

▲ Supermarkets want to be attractive to customers, which means that they must stock popular brands. In addition, they know that customers who visit a supermarket to buy an advertised branded product will usually buy most of their other requirements as well on that trip, and may increase their tendency to patronise supermarkets in that chain.

▲ The managers of a supermarket will tend to increase the space allocated to a rapidly-moving product, while that of slower-moving products will be contracted. Since the rate of sales is affected by the amount of space allocated, success builds on success.

Suppliers of branded consumer goods advertise, in the first instance, to justify and maintain their place in retail outlets, and second, to ensure that the space which they are allocated pays its way and is maintained and extended. Rather more than half of the sales of packaged consumer goods come from people who enter the store intending to buy from a category (like toilet soap) and only decide on a brand (like Palmolive) once they have seen the selection on display. Only a minority of supermarket sales are to people who decide to buy a specific product before they enter the store. If a successful consumer product advertising campaign draws people into supermarkets looking for the advertised product, the attracted customers will buy many other products as well. This generates a certain amount of tension between branded goods suppliers and the major retailers, since the retailers are clearly beneficiaries of the packaged goods suppliers' advertising; even more so when people whose interest in a category is aroused by the branded goods supplier's advertising buy the retailer's own brand product instead.

In the United States, but not yet in Australia, there are firms which specialise in producing imitations of new branded goods, copying the package design, the colours, and even the typefaces on the label, and selling these copies as own-brands to supermarket chains. In Australia, but not in the United States, an original package design can be protected by registration. In both countries the common law on 'passing off' has failed, on occasion, to protect branded goods suppliers from what they saw as unfair copying of their products.

In 1995 Pacific Dunlop Ltd disposed of its food division, citing poor returns on the capital employed as the immediate reason, and blaming the pressure the two major retailers put on the division's margins as the cause. The retailers insist on keen wholesale prices, but this does not seem to upset branded goods suppliers as much as the retailers' demands for 'cooperative' advertising and promotion. Many branded goods suppliers find that the costs of cooperative advertising and promotion can reach 10 per cent of the wholesale price.

There is a clear lesson to anyone whose products are to be sold through major retailers: either such suppliers must be so fantastically efficient that they can earn decent profits while selling at wholesale prices too low for any competitors to undercut them, or they must have such strong brands and such distinctive products that the retailers' house brands cannot get a free ride on the supplier's advertising. Packaged goods suppliers are often offered quite tempting deals for supplying retailers with their products in house-brand packaging. On a narrow accounting view, these deals are bound to look attractive, taking up spare capacity with guaranteed orders and no co-promotion or other levies. When the broader picture is considered things are not so simple, and some leading packaged goods suppliers, such as Nestlé, refuse to manufacture for house brands on any terms.

Large companies, either supplying or planning to supply packaged goods to major retailers, must plan on vigorous and continuing new product programs in order to keep their products distinctive, and must be prepared to support each new product introduction with a major advertising and promotional campaign in order to boost sales while the margins are still reasonable and before imitators and house brands are positioned to take a free ride on the original supplier's advertising.

Small companies and entrepreneurs should look very carefully at their distribution plans before relying on major retailers to sell their products. Many small businesses have found that party plan or other forms of direct marketing can be used to build their business without the commitment of capital to manufacturing and promotion that the large retailers demand. Once a product has proved itself through direct marketing channels it will be much easier to attract investors who will fund further market development, if the original entrepreneurs' wishes run that way. Some small businesses that grew large through direct marketing, like Amway, Avon and Nutrimetics, have chosen to stick with the methods that they know. Others, including many heath care brands, started with direct selling and moved their products into supermarkets once their market success was established.[14]

Cycles and the entrepreneur

An entrepreneur must consider the state of the technology, market and product life cycles when preparing to launch a new product. In extreme cases a careful review of these issues will lead to a proposal being abandoned, but in nearly every case they can be used to refine the product introduction plan.

Technology

Technology must be taken into account in at least two dimensions: the technology in the new product, and the technology that will be used to *make* and/or to *deliver* the new product. There is a third direction, one that is not easily taken into account: the possibility of someone else introducing a new technology that will radically reshape the market for the entrepreneur's product.

The world is full of inventors, but relatively few inventors turn into successful entrepreneurs, or get adopted by one. Very few inventions reach the market, and even fewer become the foundation of a successful enterprise. Many inventions that do reach the market enjoy a brief flash of market interest before dropping into the museums and the history books. When the impossible and the fraudulent are weeded out two of the common reasons why an innovation does not succeed in entering and holding a significant market are *mismatch with the market cycle* and *wrong state of technology cycle*.

The ideal point to launch a technological innovation is at the stage when the existing technologies are at or are approaching their physical limits, while demand for the products enabled by these existing technologies is rising strongly. The jet engine was first developed as a power plant for fighter aircraft at a time when the demands of the Second World War were encouraging the rapid development of piston engine technology, and it wasn't until the very last months of the war that jet aircraft were put into service. With the onset of the cold war, however, it became apparent that the speed of sound represented an absolute performance limit for propeller driven aircraft, and the jet engine (and its close relative, the gas turbine) became the dominant technology for aircraft power. It took approximately forty years from the first laboratory demonstrations of jet engines to the maturity of the technology with the triple-shaft turbofan engines as used on modern wide-bodied passenger aircraft. The companies (General Electric, Pratt and Whitney, and Rolls-Royce) that were prepared to invest at a sufficient rate to grow their capabilities in line with the growth of the technology, prospered, though not without some anxious moments.

The penalty for attacking at the wrong point in the technological cycle can be seen in the relative failure of a series of attempts made by Sun Microsystems in 1990–93 to get their Solaris software technology out of the technical niche which it (very profitably) occupied and into the general personal computer market. Purists might have had some reservations about Solaris, but the comparable technology on personal computers, MS-DOS, was dramatically inferior.

The MS-DOS world was not, however, standing still. User software suppliers, such as WordPerfect Corporation, Lotus Developments and others, worked tirelessly to improve the products they sold to MS-DOS customers, overcoming the limitations of the technology. Microsoft Corporation relaunched their Windows software, a step which improved the useability of MS-DOS dramatically, and finally overhauled Solaris with Windows-95, launched in 1995. Those MS-DOS users approached by Solaris salespersons did not, in general, simply compare that product with Solaris, but they estimated the time and effort required to convert their work to Solaris and compared it to the state that the MS-DOS world might have reached by the time their conversion was finished. The general conclusion seemed to be that MS-DOS users would get all the benefits of Solaris, in the same time and for much less effort, if they waited for Microsoft to get around to providing them. Sun Microsystems launched at the wrong point in the technology cycle, long before the technology that they were attempting to displace had reached any serious barriers to its own development.

The market

A product can only succeed in the market if sufficient people want, or can be persuaded to want, to buy it. The ideal point to launch a new product is at the beginning of the market life cycle, when there are a large number of potential users, none of whom have developed any form of loyalty to any other supplier. There is a risk involved in basing a strategy around being first into a new market, and that is the possibility that the market does not, in fact, exist; that whatever people said to market researchers or when shown samples, the net benefits of the new product were not sufficient to justify an adequate, or any, price. Some large companies make a point of being 'fast followers' for this reason; they wait until a pioneer has shown that the new market is real before launching their own product.

Companies that do pioneer a market must expect the entry of major competitors if their product is successful, and they should assume that the entering competitors will invest generously in promotion, selling, and product development in order to overcome the first mover's advantages. The English company EMI invented the first CAT scanner (computerised axial tomography: a technique using computers and new-generation sensors to build up a cross-sectional picture of the body rather than the simple shadow seen in a conventional X-ray) and launched it in 1972. Early technologies for non-invasive medical imaging had reached a series of physical limits while demographic, economic and other technological factors had precipitated an explosive growth in demand for medical services. The demand for scanners was enormous, yet the scanner proved a financial disaster for EMI. EMI began building production capacity and ordering components to meet the huge demand their sales staff reported, but the first of their competitors had a superior machine on the market just fifteen months after the first EMI scanner was delivered; EMI's order backlog evaporated and their technological triumph turned into an inventory nightmare.

EMI's strategy did not allow for the entry of competitors.

The fast follower's window may be open for up to four years, depending on the type of market, the technology involved, the speed with which the first mover has updated the original product, and the effort that the first mover has put into promotion. If the first mover and other early entrants have produced excellent products which are strongly recommended by their users, the fast follower's window shuts long before the onset of market maturity. Maturity is generally seen to set in when 50 per cent of the potential users have become actual ones, and from this point until the market reaches a post-mature stage new firm entry is very difficult. Because each satisfied current user casts a 'future shadow' of potential users who will follow that user's recommendations, effective maturity may occur as much as two years before apparent maturity.

IBM and Digital Equipment Corporation both chose to adopt a 'fast follower' strategy in the market for engineering workstations that Sun Microsystems and others pioneered in the early 1980s. By the time that they were ready to enter, mid 1988, Sun Microsystems had an impregnable position, and while both IBM and Digital Equipment enjoyed modest success, neither went close to challenging Sun Microsystems' dominance. This relative failure in the workstation market led to an equally disappointing performance in the market for office server systems, where Hewlett-Packard converted an early entry into market dominance; while Hewlett-Packard was a slightly smaller company than Digital Equipment in 1985, by 1995 Hewlett-Packard was twice Digital Equipment's size. Sun Microsystems and Hewlett-Packard had been in the market, earning a strong reputation, for nearly six years when IBM and Digital Equipment tried to enter it. This reputation, far more than any technical details about their products, ensured that Hewlett-Packard and Sun Microsystems would continue to prosper in the teeth of attempts to enter their markets.

For some time after a market has reached maturity, entry is extremely difficult. The firms who entered during the early growth phase of the market will have secured a huge 'share of mind' among both the actual and potential user population, and their mutual competition will have ensured that they have left very few technological or market niches unexplored. The prize that the established firms are fighting for, the last half of the market, is sufficiently attractive to make sure that interlopers will be seen off.

Many markets enter a post-mature phase, as the established suppliers find that there are few rewards left for technical innovation or marketing effort, and turn inwards, looking to cut their own costs rather than to increase their sales. During this post-mature period there is often a substantial concentration of ownership followed by rationalisation of product ranges and distribution channels. Such rationalisation can lead to growing numbers of dissatisfied customers, people who are in the market but are actively dissatisfied with all of the suppliers that they have been able to try. This can create an opportunity for an entrant, or a rejuvenated competitor, to seize a substantial and valuable share of the market.

In 1987 Australia's retail grocery industry was dominated by three firms: Coles Supermarkets, Woolworths (trading as Safeway in Victoria), and Franklins. Franklins was doing well with its 'no frills' discount image, Coles Supermarkets was also doing well, more because of the excellent sites that the Coles Myer real estate arm had acquired than for any particular retailing excellence, while Woolworths was not doing well at all. A couple of years before, Woolworths had purchased Safeway's Australian operations from RJR-Nabisco in the aftermath of the 'Barbarians at the Gate' takeover.[15] Safeway's up-market reputation had enabled it to earn better margins than Woolworths, but in a fit of misplaced corporate pride Woolworths' managers had renamed the Safeway stores in NSW as

'Woolworths'. The effect had been a major loss of market share in NSW, near-zero profits, and a collapsing firm value.

Woolworths was taken over, and Paul Simons recruited to the position of executive chairman. Simons observed that no Australian supermarket chain was doing a particularly good job of fresh food marketing. The margins on fresh produce are good, and the customer appeal considerable, but all the Australian retailers had become used to handling packaged goods with a shelf life of weeks or months and tended to treat the produce section in much the same way. Simons relaunched Woolworths as 'the fresh food people'; he appears to have decided that the various issues were so urgent that he did not wait until the computer systems had been modified to cope with the demands of fresh food but trusted the staff to clear away any stock that was less than perfectly fresh. Neither of Woolworths' main competitors had a strong reputation for their fresh produce at the time that Woolworths relaunched itself: Franklins had problems with selling space; and Coles were suffering from serious management problems which led to their stores paying premium prices for compost-grade produce.

At the time Simons was appointed at Woolworths their market share was 21 per cent and falling, and their shares were worth little more than the paper that they were printed on. When Simons stood down as chief executive seven years later, Woolworths' market share had passed 29 per cent, the company had been successfully floated for a billion dollars, and the new shareholders were sitting on a substantial capital gain. Woolworths' market share continued to grow, passing 31 per cent in 1995. Simons demonstrated that entrepreneurial success is still possible in a very mature market.

Checkpoint

An entrepreneurial concept can only succeed in a window of opportunity, or more properly, when a series of windows coincide. The entrepreneur must be able to access an appropriate level of technology, and the market must be capable of absorbing a sufficient quantity of product. These two factors are not entirely independent: the market's capacity to absorb product will be affected by the price, which will in turn be affected by the state of the available technology.

There are many historical examples of ventures failing because the market was not ready for their product; there are many other examples of the market willingly accepting a new product only to reject it when the technological limitations became apparent. Even when the technology works and the market wants it, there may be social or physical barriers to its widespread adoption. Excellent technology may fail in the market if the older technology it must compete with has sufficient remaining development potential and a well-established position in the market.

Above all, *invention is not innovation*. Just because something can be made does not mean that people are prepared to pay for it.

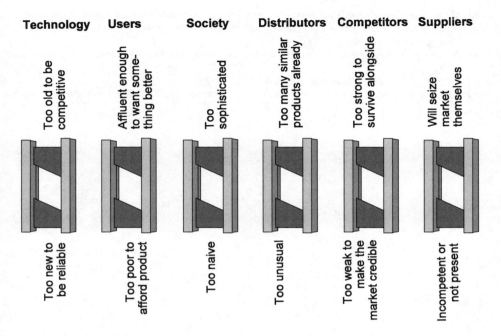

Technology   Users   Society   Distributors   Competitors   Suppliers

Top labels: Too old to be competitive; Affluent enough to want something better; Too sophisticated; Too many similar products already; Too strong to survive alongside; Will seize market themselves

Bottom labels: Too new to be reliable; Too poor to afford product; Too naïve; Too unusual; Too weak to make the market credible; Incompetent or not present

Figure 4.4 Some of the windows an entrepreneur must thread

End notes

1 The trade magazine, *Retail World* (published monthly), is very informative about all aspects of the Australian supermarket milieu.

2 Contemporary economists argued that the US was making a terrible mistake by establishing manufacturing industries: the 'law' of comparative advantage (invented by the English economist Ricardo) stated that manufacturing should be done in Britain while foreigners concentrated on raw material production. The British government took a strongly pro-south view during the American Civil War: the south grew cotton to supply English factories, while the north was home to a protected textile industry that competed with the British.

3 For a comprehensive survey of market life cycle models and the evidence supporting their use see Mahajan, Muller and Bass (1990). For the results of a study showing the consistency of certain model parameters see Sultan, Farley and Lehmann (1990).

4 Most books concerned with mathematics in business applications find space for a description of the basic logistic or 'S' curve which has the general form $f(x) = \dfrac{M}{1 + ae^{bx}}$ where a>0, M>0, b>0 are real numbers.

5 An entertaining book devoted to the predictive power of 'S' curves is Modis (1992).

6 See Schumpeter (1939).

7 The nature and importance of innovation and technological cycles — focused on the practical utility of 'S' curves — is described in Foster (1987).

8 See Ropp (1959); or Jones (1987); or any of the many other specialist books on this subject.

9 The phalanx and the legions clashed for the first time when Pyrrhus invaded Italy in the third century BC. Pyrrhus won both his battles, but his losses were so great that he lost the war and gave his name to the term 'Pyrrhic victory'.

10 For an excellent account of Turing and his achievements see Hodges (1983).

11 George Stevenson's Stockton and Darlington line of 1826 is generally discounted because only some of the haulage was by steam: passengers travelled in horse-drawn rail coaches. The B&O started revenue generating steam-hauled passenger traffic some months after the L&M, but the American system was developed independently and incorporated some unique inventions.

12 Under Australian law (see Chapter 11) it is an offence to claim an endorsement that has not been actually provided. The trick with the tenor (see box page 116) might well be caught under the laws banning misleading conduct if tried today.

13 An early positive view of the utility of the product life cycle as a useful marketing concept is found in Levitt (1965).

14 An entrepreneurship focused marketing text is Legge (1992).

15 For an entertaining account of the takeover of RJR-Nabisco by KKR see Burroughs and Helyar (1990).

Profile three

Sir Reginald Myles Ansett KBE
Seizing the time

R. M. Ansett was born in 1909 in northern Victoria. His father ran a small bicycle repair business until he enlisted in the First AIF for service in France. On his return from the war, Ansett's father used his resettlement bonus to buy a small knitting mill in Melbourne, and R. M. Ansett left school at 14 and became an apprentice mechanic in the factory. The factory was relocated to Seymour, where it was to continue to trade as Ansett Knitting Mills until 1992, but the young R. M. Ansett decided to do some relocating of his own, and spent some years working in the Northern Territory as an axeman and general labourer. The approach of the Great Depression of 1929 reduced opportunities in the Northern Territory, and R. M. Ansett returned to Victoria, to Hamilton rather than Seymour; close to his family, but not too close. Ansett liked machinery at least as well as he liked people, and had a particular fascination with aircraft and flying. Money that other young men might have spent in other ways went towards flying lessons, and in 1929 he gained a civil pilot's licence.

Victoria, in 1930, had one of the most extensive railway systems, whether measured per head or per hectare, in the developed world. The system had largely been built, and was wholly owned and operated, by the state government. Successive Victorian governments had seen the railways as a tool of government policy, opening up the country to agriculture and the country towns to decentralised industry. The network was, accordingly, designed to bring freight to the ports of Melbourne and Geelong efficiently; it provided a reasonably frequent, if not very fast, passenger service between the main centres, and an infrequent and very slow passenger service to most of the minor towns. Most of Victoria's rural population, whether small 'cockatoo' farmers or rural labourers, were poor, and even a weekly slow train was a better way to travel than walking. Western Victoria includes some of the world's best sheep raising country, and the graziers, or 'squatters', were often men of very great wealth and by no means contented with their passenger transport arrangements.

Ansett had some money in his pocket from his work in the Northern Territory, and laid out £50 to buy a secondhand Studebaker car. He then offered a hybrid taxi/bus service, based on Hamilton, taking graziers and other affluent men and their families between their homes and the main railway centres of Hamilton and Ballarat. The Victorian government, in which R. G. (later Sir Robert) Menzies was Attorney-General, gave itself extensive powers to regulate road transport in 1931, but held back from using them for a while. Ansett's business grew, and he bought more vehicles, engaged more drivers, and opened a maintenance workshop in Hamilton.

In 1935 Ansett extended his services through Ballarat to Melbourne, paralleling one of the railway system's busiest and most lucrative passenger routes, and the government acted to preserve this revenue, effectively banning the operation of private buses or taxis between Melbourne and Ballarat.

The government may have hoped that Ansett would be forced back into running rural feeder services to the main railway junctions; even in the 1930s the government was looking for ways to reduce the losses on branch line passenger services without antagonising electors by cutting off their public transport services entirely. Ansett did continue to develop his bus routes, and his Pioneer coach lines eventually became Australia's largest long-distance road operator. He also dusted off his pilot's licence, spent most of his business's cash on an aeroplane, paying £1000 for the aircraft and £250 for a spare engine, and began an air service between Hamilton and Essendon, a northern suburb of Melbourne.

Ansett's airline network could, by the expedient of incorporating interstate towns, enjoy constitutional protection against state regulation, and the government probably did not see a single-engine six-seater aeroplane as a threat to the railways in any case. Ansett's network expanded, after a successful stock market float in 1936 enabled him to buy three twin-engine, ten-passenger Lockheed 10B aircraft, and by the outbreak of the Second World War Ansett services were linking Narrandera, Mildura and Broken Hill to Sydney, Melbourne and Adelaide.

The war forced a sudden change of direction; Ansett's routes were either closed or transferred to other operators to conserve fuel and manpower, and his facilities at Essendon were pressed into service to maintain and repair military aircraft. When the war ended, Ansett owned world-class airframe, engine, and instrument maintenance and testing facilities, but no aircraft and no route licences. The first post-war Prime Minister was Ben Chifley, a former engine driver on the NSW government railways, and no admirer of *laissez faire*.

The Chifley government bought out the private shareholders in Qantas, Australia's overseas airline, and when the Holyman family refused to sell Australian National Airways (ANA), Australia's major domestic airline, the government started Trans Australia Airways (TAA, later AA, and now part of Qantas) in competition with ANA. Ansett was refused any licences to operate direct inter-capital services, and began rebuilding his pre-war network, flying Melbourne–Albury–Sydney and Sydney–Broken Hill–Adelaide, for example. Ansett imported a Convair 240 aircraft, the first pressurised aircraft to enter passenger service in Australia.

After the 1949 elections the Menzies Liberal (conservative) government replaced Chifley, and Ansett approached Menzies, offering to buy TAA and free the government from the taint of socialism. Menzies did not take the offer seriously, but did allow Ansett to operate non-stop Melbourne–Sydney flights. The government passed a Two Airlines Act, with Ansett tolerated rather than encouraged, and used their import licensing power to make sure that no intruder should upset the balance. The balance was upset, nevertheless, by two major purchasing errors by ANA's management. When TAA and ANA had to upgrade their fleets in the early 1950s, TAA went for pressurised Convair 340 aircraft while ANA chose un-pressurised Douglas DC4 'Skymaster' aircraft. ANA compounded this error in the mid 1950s by buying Douglas DC6 aircraft while TAA bought the smaller, but faster and more comfortable, Vickers Viscounts. ANA suffered a steady loss of market share on the main east coast routes, and by 1957 was insolvent.

Ansett remarked to his friend F. W. Haig that he would like to replace ANA as the official non-government carrier under the two-airline policy, but that raising the capital needed looked like a problem.

Haig worked at that time for Vacuum Oil Co., which was a major unsecured creditor of ANA's. He persuaded his management to put up £500 000 in cash and the same amount in fuel credit, and then persuaded Shell Oil Co. to do the same. Haig then rang Ansett and told him that he had £1 000 000 available in cash and some breathing space. Ansett promptly bid for ANA, offering the whole £1 000 000 as a down-payment, and eventually agreeing to two further payments of £1 250 000 and £1 050 000 over the next two years. Ansett's next call was on Menzies, who was facing the unpalatable prospect of becoming a free enterprise Prime Minister presiding over the final socialisation of the Australian air transport industry. A change of ownership would not save ANA; a change of aircraft was needed, too.

Menzies agreed to revise the two-airlines agreement and Act, and ordered TAA to agree to lease three of their precious Viscounts to ANA, soon to become Ansett-ANA, and to lease two of ANA's unwanted DC6s in return. The two airlines were, from then forward, legally bound to consult each other on fleet selection, an arrangement that was formalised into a common fleet purchasing policy between 1960 and 1977. The two-airlines agreement also prescribed a common fare schedule and capacity limits; for the entire life of the two-airline policy successive Ministers for Aviation fretted about their inability to stop the two 'competitors' operating the same schedules on all the major routes.

In the years following his capture of ANA, Ansett moved vigorously to prevent any other regional operators from following his example, buying Butler Airlines (now Ansett NSW) in a fiercely contested takeover in 1958, and mopping up most of the rest in the following few years. When the government decided to make additional TV channels available in 1964 Ansett secured two licences and later purchased a third: this may have reflected a sudden interest in entertainment, but the fact that, as a TV licensee, ownership of Ansett shares was subject to sharp limits may have also interested Ansett.

In 1969 Mr R. M. Ansett became Sir Reginald. He continued to buy up regional airlines.

Ansett himself was ambushed in 1979, when a joint bid from TNT and News Limited succeeded in a contested takeover. He was promoted to non-voting Chairman, and allowed to retain 0.5 per cent of the common shares (but not to vote them) during his lifetime. He died in 1982, an essentially private man, but Ansett Airlines continued to thrive; in 1995 TNT's half share in the airline was sold to Air New Zealand for $450 million. Ansett's original £50 had grown at an average annual rate of over 28 per cent, through good times and bad, war and peace, for over sixty years.

This account of R. M. Ansett is based on Brogden (1986) and other material supplied by Ansett Australia Ltd

Part II

Chapter 5

Screening and valuing an opportunity

The new venture process

Figure 5.1 contains a stylised map of the enterprise creation process. The starting point of every new enterprise is a problem, and an idea for solving it. We do not consider that either the identification of problems or the generation of ideas needs to be dealt with at length in this book, because while the availability of an idea is a precondition for entrepreneurship it is not part of the entrepreneurship process. Many successful enterprises are based upon an association of an entrepreneur or entrepreneurial team and an 'ideas person'.

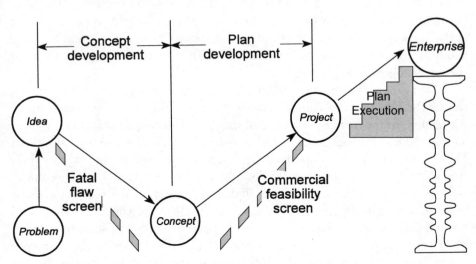

Figure 5.1 Screening, planning and execution

135

Every idea is the product of a human's imagination, and some ideas are bound to stay there. Ideas must be tested for fatal flaws before they can be set out as a concept. Concepts are a combination of an idea for resolving a problem and a practical proposal, in outline form at least, for delivering that solution. Many nascent concepts suffer from fatal flaws, as we discuss below.

A concept may address a real problem and be technically feasible, and yet it may be commercially infeasible: the total cost of turning the concept into a marketed product, and then supplying the product to customers, may be too high in relation to the revenue that the new product would generate. The development of a business plan, the topic that takes up Chapters 6 to 16 of this book, is fundamentally about turning a concept into a commercially feasible proposal. Developing a complete business plan takes time and effort, and it is disappointing, to say the least, to get to the end of the process and discover that the concept cannot be turned into a commercial proposition.

In this chapter we describe the process of turning an idea into a concept, and then applying a fairly simple commercial feasibility test that will screen out commercially hopeless concepts before the full effort of developing a business plan commences. Entrepreneurs and students may wish to use a systematic guide to opportunity screening: we provide such a guide in our separately published *Workbook*.

Ideas

Good ideas are legion. Some people like to talk about their ideas, while others keep their own counsel, but it is hard to spend more than a few minutes awake without coming across some inconvenience or irritation. Many people, confronted by a nuisance, will grin (or not) and bear it; some will repeat the everlasting cry of the English lower middle classes: '"They" ought to do something about it.' Lots of people will wonder whether anything really could be done about it, and if they have the habit of letting their imagination work, many of them will come up with an idea.

Every innovation starts with an idea, but only a few ideas become innovations. There is no certain link between the idea and the innovator: Hero of Alexandria, in the first century AD, had the idea of steam power and made a few gadgets, like self-opening doors and moving altars, but no industry arose and Hero's ideas were largely forgotten. They were revived by Newcomen, who built steam driven pumps for mines, the first in 1712. A few copies of Newcomen's engine were made, but demand was slight, and several of the few engines that were built were used infrequently, if at all. In 1769 the engineer James Watt secured the first of his many patents for improvements to the steam engine. In 1776 James Watt and his partner Matthew Boulton put steam engines incorporating Watt's improvements into serial production (and Jefferson wrote the

United States Declaration of Independence); the Power and the American revolutions started in the same year.

Watt and his partner Boulton became extremely rich as Watt and his colleagues added a series of innovations to the basic idea, improving the flexibility, efficiency and applicability of Boulton and Watt engines. Watt did not invent steam power, but he and Boulton were the entrepreneurs who turned steam power from an idea to a commercial reality. Watt is justly credited with responsibility for the innovation 'steam power'. If a contemporary entrepreneur had considered commercialising either Hero's or Newcomen's work, they would have discovered that, given the markets, technology and business environment of the day, it would have been impossible. A proposal to commercialise steam power at any date significantly earlier than 1776 would have encountered one or more 'fatal flaws'.

Fatal flaws

Fatal flaws are facts about an opportunity that make it impossible for a new enterprise based upon it to succeed. They should not be confused with fatal stumbles, operating or management errors which destroy a product or a business but which, in the glare of 20–20 hindsight, could have been avoided. The following list of potential fatal flaws is not exhaustive, and we accept no responsibility for ventures that find a new way to attempt the impossible. Nonetheless, if this list was routinely consulted before people put their time and money into a new venture a lot of heartache and disappointment might be avoided:

▲ **Scientific feasibility:** Does the product depend on the suspension of any of the laws of nature, such as the Special or General Theories of Relativity, the Second Law of Thermodynamics, the Laws of Conservation of Energy and Momentum?

▲ **Economic feasibility:** Does the product involve an economic absurdity, such as a selling price lower than the minimum cost of its components, or a service provider's income insufficient to support life?

▲ **Technical feasibility:** Can the product be made, or if a service, delivered, using currently available, or at least feasible, technology?

▲ **Marketing feasibility:** Does anyone want it? Has the product any features that would persuade someone to choose it ahead of currently available products?

▲ **Fundamental legality:** Is it legal?

The laws of nature

The laws of nature serve humanity well; if they were only slightly different, we would not be here. This may be some compensation for the repeated disappointments nature's laws inflict on inventors and the occasional gullible investor. Elaborate urban myths have circulated in Australia about the water-powered motor car and the supposed conspiracy of the oil companies to suppress it. The oil companies, in this matter at least, are innocent. Water represents the most stable, and therefore the lowest energy, combination of hydrogen and oxygen. It cannot be used a source of energy, and the inventors who demonstrate water-powered motor cars to the popular press and to populist politicians every few years may possibly be fools, but it is more likely that they are rogues. All real-world processes are dissipative; they require a source of energy to keep them going. Perpetual motion machines do not exist and cannot be produced, which does not stop people trying to invent them and persuading investors to back them.

The silent and irrevocable operation of the laws of nature should not be confused with the squawking of assorted pessimists and congenital knockers. The difficult and the unusual should not be confused with the impossible. There are large published collections of quotations from people who should have known better saying that something was impossible, or would never happen. Investors and entrepreneurs who do not understand the Second Law, or the work of Newton, Einstein, Maxwell, Heisenberg and others should consult a physicist or engineer before putting money into an amazing invention. When briefing their consultant they should make sure that the report distinguishes 'improbable' from 'impossible'. In the latter case they should get out at once; in the former, they may consider investing a little more money in a full technical report — if the inventor will let a consulting engineer anywhere near their product.

Some inventors are profoundly reluctant to allow their concept or proto-types to be examined in detail by experts. As a broad generalisation, an entrepreneur or investor who backs a product so secret that a reputable consulting engineer cannot be trusted to examine it and prepare a confidential report is putting their money at high risk.

Economic absurdity

The standard form of economic absurdity is the system for winning at gambling (not to be confused with a proposal to operate a casino or a totalisator, or with schemes involving rigged bets or unequal contests). One of the most common gambling schemes is known as the 'martingale'. Many of these schemes appear quite logical, and some fairly subtle argument is needed to show why they must eventually fail. There is a famous statistical proof known as 'gambler's ruin' which demonstrates that a gambler with a finite purse playing a fair game against a strong house must, eventually, be ruined. 'Ruin is certain, but the time it takes is indefinite.'

The martingale

There are various forms of martingale, but the principle is always the same. At roulette the martingale player puts a unit bet on one colour (say black). If it wins (and the croupier returns the original stake and the same again as winnings), the gambler pockets the winnings and repeats the original bet. Otherwise the gambler doubles the stake and repeats the process. When black turns up again (as it statistically must) the gambler will make a profit of one unit. The fatal flaw in the martingale is the existence of house limits on the one hand and finite resources for the gambler on the other. If the wheel is a fair one, it is certain that there will eventually be a losing streak so long that the gambler will no longer be able to afford a doubled bet, or the house will refuse to accept it.

The system is called a martingale after the piece of harness that can be used to stop an unruly horse turning its head; once a gambler starts on a martingale he cannot stop or turn aside until he is ruined.

Other forms of absurdity can be shown to be the logical equivalent of proposals for selling hundred-dollar bills at a discount. One of the hero-entrepreneurs in Ayn Rand's novel *Atlas Shrugged* (1985) invents a new alloy of iron and copper with all sorts of marvellous properties, including being cheaper than steel. Since copper is vastly more expensive than iron, this imaginary product is economically absurd. J. R. R. Tolkein imagined an equally impressive material, mithril, in his *Lord of the Rings* (1966), but he had the economic good sense to make mithril rare and expensive.

Some entrepreneurs have been known to make dramatic mistakes in their estimate of the likely competitive response to their initiative. Among the many flaws that eventually grounded Compass Airlines Mk I[1] was a confusion of average and variable costs: because the *average* cost per passenger experienced by the established airlines on the Melbourne–Sydney corridor was $180, the management of Compass assumed that it could set a fare of $160 and capture all the traffic. The *variable* cost per passenger was, however, less than $25 and the established airlines were better off flying passengers at $160 (and as the price war developed, for fares as low as $79 and even $69 for one week) than not carrying them. Both the established airlines and Compass lost money during the price war; Compass, as the newest and smallest airline, ran out of money first.

Product feasibility

A product can be scientifically and economically feasible without being practical given the current state of technology. Newcomen's engine was dreadfully inefficient, not only because it lacked an external condenser, but because the fit between the piston and the cylinder was so poor. In the early 1700s there were no precision metal working machines available capable of boring large cylinders or turning large pistons, and so Newcomen's cylinder was a ring of rough castings bolted together and the piston a rough framework built up with leather and cloth stuffing. Boulton and Watt were able to buy large scale lathes and boring machines; with the better fit and the external condenser, a Boulton and Watt engine did ten times more work per tonne of coal than a Newcomen engine had been capable of.

More recently, the Danish architect Joern Utzon's original design for the Sydney Opera House was based on ellipsoidal shells, reflecting the shape of the sails on the yachts in Sydney Harbour. The design of such shells cannot be completed using readily soluble equations, and if one of the computers available in 1960 had been set to the task it might still be running without having found a feasible design. Utzon and the consulting engineers, Ove Arup, redesigned the roof with spherical segments which could, with difficulty, be designed using the mathematical and computing tools available, and construction of the Opera House proceeded.

If an innovation involves manufacturing something, and if unusual shapes or materials, or extremes of performance are required, then the project should proceed cautiously until there is some confidence that the product can actually be produced and have the appropriate performance. If the product is to be used in mission-critical or life-critical applications, then it must be possible to manufacture it at a guaranteed quality level. Often, as with Utzon's Sydney Opera House, the concept will stay but the prototype will need significant modification before it can be put into production.

Lack of manufacturability is only a fatal flaw when there is some aspect of the plan that eliminates the time needed to work through potential manufacturing problems. Rolls-Royce set out to design and build the RB211 triple-shaft, high-bypass engine on the timescales demanded by the Lockheed L1011 'Tristar' project. Their original concept involved carbon fibre composite blades on the first stage fan; when these could not be made to work to the demanding specification set for them (a number ten chicken arriving at 120 km/h while the fan was spinning at its rated speed) the cost of rushing alternatives into production sent Rolls-Royce bankrupt in 1972.

Innovations involving service products can fail for similar reasons: if the prototype works because of the unique talent of one or a small group of individuals, it must be possible to train ordinary people to deliver the service at a similar standard in order to grow the enterprise. One of the keys to the continuing success of the McDonald's organisation is their refusal to offer any products that they cannot reproduce using semi-skilled staff, and another is the ingenuity with which they have standardised some difficult tasks. Making good French fries consistently is quite difficult, in general, but McDonald's, by standardising the size of each chip and the breed of potato it was made from, and controlling the heat of the cooking oil by thermostat and the cooking time by a timer have made chip-making a routine task.

Does anyone want it?

Specialists and experts often fall into the trap of doing something because they can, and assuming that other people will want the result. Other specialists and experts don't want it, because they would prefer to do it themselves, while prospective users can't see the point at all. The Newton hand-held computer launched by Apple in 1994 seems to have been close to this category: Apple had made some technical advances in handwriting recognition, and rushed a product into the market to allow customers to admire their cleverness. The Newton achieved a certain distinction as the first electronic device to be ridiculed in an internationally syndicated comic strip, but not as one of the world's great marketing success stories.

Marketing legends tell the tale of a pet food company in England, whose technicians discovered a new way to process dog food. The product seemed to be a certain winner, and the company invested in substantial advertising and negotiated extensive distribution. For the first few days sales were fantastic: the product 'walked off the shelves'. The company stepped up production and waited for the repeat orders, but none ever came. Dogs loathed the stuff.

Is it legal?

Visitors to Ireland report an extensive demand for the services of fertility control clinics, and those who do not study the sociopolitical background may wonder why until very recently there weren't any. Visitors to Thailand may be surprised to see that there are no T-shirts on sale bearing caricatures of the King. No one in Singapore publishes a popular newspaper or magazine critical of Senior Minister Lee. Many citizens of the United States get extremely irate at any disrespectful use of the Stars and Stripes. Some Americans are surprised at the bureaucratic hurdles in the way of anyone wishing to sell handguns in Australia. There are many products that are freely available in some countries and strictly banned in others.

There are also many products whose sale is only conditionally legal. In most developed countries pharmaceutical preparations may only be sold once regulatory approval has been obtained. Many types of business may only be conducted in premises that have been approved, either specifically or in general terms, by one or more levels of government. Entry into certain trades and professions may be regulated. Very strict standards, backed up by severe penalties, apply in Australia and in many other countries to facilities where food is prepared or stored. Appliances that are intended to be connected to the water, gas, or electricity supplies, or to the telecommunications network, must meet strictly enforced standards.

The existence of rules and regulations often creates the illusion that a business opportunity is available by breaking them, and in countries where exemptions from the laws are traded in an informal market the opportunities may be very real and very profitable. If a country embarks on a program of deregulation, permitting a more general right of entry to various forms of economic activity, then rather too many entrants may try to seize the opportunity: the United States deregulated its airline system in 1978, and there was a rush into the market, which peaked with twenty-eight competing carriers. As of mid 1995 there were five major and a few large regional carriers left, and at least one of the major carriers was reported to be looking for a merger.

If an opportunity is blocked by laws and regulations, the entrepreneur can plan to secure an exemption, or lobby to have the regulations amended. In the absence of an exemption or deregulation such a proposal is fatally flawed.

Valuing the opportunity

Business is not all about profit, but without profit there is no business. Once a proposal has survived screening for fatal flaws, the entrepreneur should find out whether it forms the basis of a profitable enterprise. Six main factors determine whether there is going to be a profit at the end of the day:

▲ What is the selling price to the final consumer?

▲ How many units will be sold at that price?

▲ What is the variable unit cost, including all materials and subcontract labour on the inward side, and all commissions, allowances and discounts on the outward?

▲ What are the fixed costs of operating a business, including staff salaries, utility charges, site value taxes and the like?

▲ How much capital is needed to operate the business?

▲ What is the minimum risk-weighted rate of return to be applied to the capital?

The economic profit, if any, is given by the formula:[2]

Profit = units × (selling price − variable unit cost) − fixed costs − rate of return × capital

A business is not profitable just because the selling price is greater than the unit cost; a successful business must also represent a valuable use of the capital tied up in equipment, stock, work in progress and debtors. The five factors are not independent variables: Figure 5.1 shows some of the interactions involved. The true situation is, of course, much more complex than this simple diagram, and many of the relationships between management decisions and profit, or firm value, will be discussed at some length in later chapters of this book.

This chapter will concentrate on the problem of estimating the selling price and the units. The first step is to estimate the value in use of the product; roughly, how much would you have to pay a user to persuade them to sell the product back to you.[3]

Value to the user

Entrepreneurs need some form of advantage that will enable their new venture to make headway in their selected market. They must be able to attract some new customers into the market and to persuade some customers of their firm's rivals to change to a new (to them) supplier. Consumers and industrial purchasers make their decision on the basis of the apparent value of the products on offer, and select the one that appears to offer them the greatest net value (that is, value in service less the price and any specific costs of ownership). Most economics text books work on the assumption that the highest value product is the one which is available at the lowest price, an assumption which implies that every product is identical.

Users ...

▲ A *user* of a product is the person or firm that gets the financial or other advantage from its use.

▲ An *end user* is the person or firm who actually interacts with a product.

A radiologist is the user of an X-ray machine; the radiographer and the patients are end-users.

Of course, a buyer offered two products identical in all respects except the price would be silly not to choose the cheapest, but in practice no two suppliers offer identical products: even if everything else was the same, different suppliers trade from physically different premises, and one will be more convenient than the other as far as any one customer is concerned. In real life there is much more variation between products than the addresses of the various competing suppliers. Most suppliers offer a range of different products, several of which might satisfy the requirements of any single customer, but differing in significant, but not critical, ways. Often there is a necessary tradeoff between the features offered and the price demanded. Users also differ: 'little old ladies' who only drive to church on Sunday and young sales representatives working western New South Wales both need cars, but they are unlikely to choose the same model.

There is a further complication facing most prospective purchasers: they must make their decision and commit their money before they start getting any benefit from their purchase. The benefits themselves may be affected by unexpected events: the little old lady might get an illness that makes driving impossible, even on Sunday, and discovers, too late, that she would have preferred to spend the money on a world tour; while the sales person might have chosen a different car entirely if she had known that she was about to be promoted to an area manager working from a city office. Even when a buyer is confident about the future, the time spent searching for a perfect match to the buyer's requirements comes off the time that the buyer can enjoy the benefits of owning and

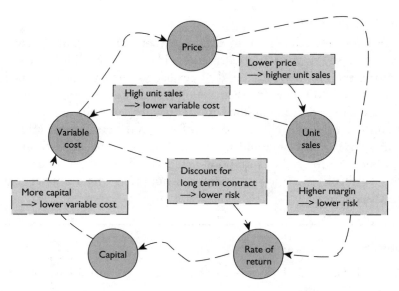

Figure 5.2 Some relationships between the pricing variables

using the new product. A supplier may have the perfect match for a particular buyer's requirements, but if that buyer does not find out about it before they settle for an alternative, there will be no sale.

When a new product is put on the market it generally has a marked price, and for most products a higher price will mean a lower net value, making it harder to sell.[4] Lowering the price may make it easier to sell a new product, but it also means that the entrepreneur will earn less from each sale after direct costs are covered. The entrepreneur needs the difference between the price and the direct cost to pay for promotion so as to generate further sales, to cover the administrative costs of the business, and to earn a return on the capital invested. Pricing decisions can be crucial to business success, and the correct price is often anything but obvious, except in hindsight. Most new firms have some room to move their prices after their product is launched, although putting prices up is often harder than cutting them, but a major pricing error can destroy a product. Such errors can run either way: a product that is launched at a much lower price than established similar products may be regarded as being of inferior quality; while a product launched at too high a price may be ignored as irrelevant by its most likely buyers.

The entrepreneur faces a further complication, in that no two buyers are identical. Factors that may cause one person to value a product highly might be

> *Factors that may cause one person to value a product highly might be regarded as unimportant, or even unpleasant, by another …*

regarded as unimportant, or even unpleasant, by another. In working out the value of a new product, the entrepreneur must create an imaginary typical buyer and then avoid double-counting benefits. Most products will have several value-enhancing features, but very few buyers will see the total value of the features as cumulative. The value a typical buyer will assign to a product will often be less than the sum of values that they will assign to each of the features. Some features may be expensive to provide but will only be noticed if they are left out: few people would agree that clean linen was a value-adding feature of a resort hotel, because if clean linen was not provided they would not consider the place a 'resort' at all.

The implicit contract between the buyer and the seller includes the buyer's obligation to pay the agreed price, but it also includes the expectation that the buyer will consider that supplier for their additional and related requirements, and that the buyer will inform other people of the high satisfaction obtained by owning and using the supplier's products. The seller also provides an implicit, unenforceable warranty that the buyer is paying the best current price; that similar buyers are not receiving better terms. The penalty applied to a seller who discriminates, unfairly, between buyers is that some, or all, of the buyers affected will refuse to buy future products from that supplier, or fail to recommend it, or both.

The difference in the value to a supplier of a satisfied and an unsatisfied customer varies with the industry, the nature of the product, and the phase of the market life cycle, among other factors. It is clearly very high with a new product in a new or rapidly growing market, but it can be quite significant even in a relatively mature industry. During the first few years following the launch of a new product the cost, in terms of the present value of lost future sales, of dissatisfying one customer can amount to three or more times the contribution earned on the original sale. The importance of recommendations by satisfied customers rises with the contribution margin. In industries like software, entertainment, leisure resorts, golf courses, air travel and the like with very high fixed costs and relatively low variable costs each dissatisfied customer can cost a supplier up to four times the purchase price in lost future business.

The new industrial product

Perceived value is seldom an absolute number; it tends to be thought of as a preference, given the known price. When two products are known to be identical in all respects, the more valuable will be the cheaper, and when they differ, it will be the differences that justify, or fail to justify, the difference in price.

Example: Value and price in industry

> ## What's it worth?
>
> A certain type of sulphuric acid plant needs flexible 'O-rings' to seal the joints around valves. A traditional O-ring costs $2.50 and lasts about three months before it has to be replaced in a task that takes two fitters about half an hour.
>
> A new O-ring has been invented using a superior elastomer, less subject to degradation by sulphuric acid. The service life of the new ring will be at least nine months, and so the sales manager proposes to set the price at $7.50

It is conceptually easier to look at value in an industrial context, where the output is well-defined, than in consumer products, where the major benefits may be less tangible. The O-ring case (see box) has no great claims to originality, but the results of discussing it in various forums have produced a few surprises. The sales manager, in suggesting $7.50, is protecting her revenue targets, but she may also be revealing a genuine insight into the customers' buying process.

The naive version of the value-based approach suggests that the value of the new, corrosion-resistant O-ring is far in excess of $7.50. Fitters are paid $15 or more per hour before overheads, and so the customer is going to save $40 a year in fitters' wages for every valve by adopting the new rings. While the fitters are working the plant is not, and so an hour's contribution from one section of the plant could be added to the delivered value. One popular text book finishes its analysis of the O-ring case by suggesting that the value of the new O-rings is at least $90, and that the fair price is at least $50.

When the case was discussed in Australia with a group that included an engineer with responsibility for the maintenance of a sulphuric acid plant as well as several accountants the conclusion was less dramatic. The following points were made:

▲ real plants have budgets for consumables, and O-rings, bought in thousands, were a significant part of this — at any price above $7.50 each the budget would have to be renegotiated, a process that would take months or years

▲ the auditor regularly checked the prices paid for consumables and would start a witch-hunt if the price went to $2.51, much less $7.50 — the order clerk might refuse to process an order for the new rings

▲ the plant needed fitters anyway, employed for 37.5 hours per week, and they did many other things apart from changing O-rings — if they didn't have to change the rings they would be drinking cups of company tea on full pay

▲ the plant produced to order, with an average utilisation of 75 per cent — cutting down on the number of O-ring changes would increase plant idle time, not revenue.

A business in the situation of this O-ring maker must also consider the effect on potential market entrants of setting a price in the stratosphere. Since it is extremely unlikely that either the materials used or the additional manufacturing complexity will push the cost of the new O-rings much above the cost of the old ones, a high price will become an incentive to enter the market.

Finally, the firm must consider its customer relationships. At any price over $7.50 there will be a substantial transfer of money to the supplier. Even at $7.50 the supplier will get a substantially increased margin while the direct benefits to the buyer look negligible. When everything is taken into proper account, the most appropriate price for the new O-rings may be about $5.00: the supplier does better, the customer does better, and no debatable imputed benefits enter the equation. In this case the reference price for an O-ring was $2.50, and an acceptable price for an improved form of O-ring had to be related to this figure.

Example: The price of efficiency

Who is looking?

A 100 watt incandescent lamp lasts about 1000 hours and sells for about $1.50. A 15 watt compact fluorescent give the same amount of light, lasts for 8000 hours, and sells for about $30.

The householder says that one compact fluorescent lamp replaces eight incandescent ones, and so should sell for eight times as much, or $12.

The lamp companies say:

Incandescent cost	
8 lamps @ $1.50	$12
800 kW/h @ 12¢	$96
Total	$108
Compact fluorescent cost	
1 lamp @ $30	$30
120 kW/h @ 12¢	$14
Total	$44
Saving	*$64*

A related situation has been created by the invention of various kinds of long-life lamps, both the compact fluorescent globes that can replace incandescent lamps and superior designs of standard fluorescent and other types of industrial lamp. The development of these newer lamp types and building production facilities for them represents a major investment. Unless the long-life lamps can be sold at a significantly higher price than those that they replace the manufacturers of the newer types cannot earn a return on their development and tooling costs. The manufacturers of 8000-hour compact fluorescent lamps want a retail price of about $30 to justify their investment and cover their variable costs, while householders, who only pay $1.50 or so for 1000-hour incandescent lamps, don't want to pay any more than $12 to $15. Promotions, in Australia and the United States, where the retail price of compact fluorescent globes were subsidised down to this level produced a strong buyer response, but sales are slow at the standard price in spite of the apparent total benefit.

The various classes of long-life lamp meet their best response from organisations in a position to capture the benefits directly. An electrical contractor might, for example, have a contract with a retail store obliging the contractor to replace any failed lamps promptly, including lamps in hard-to-access locations. Such a contractor might happily pay more for long-life lamps, since the full savings in replacement effort come back to the contractor as lamp buyer.

A similar arrangement might have made a major difference to the O-ring manufacturer discussed earlier. If the sulphuric acid plant was being maintained by a contractor instead of by employees, the contractor would have had a very direct interest in using the superior product. Such a contractor would be much less reluctant to share the value created by using long-life O-rings with their manufacturer.

Value in consumer products

As the previous section showed, suppliers often have trouble persuading industrial purchasers to recognise all of the superior value embodied in an improved product, even though cost accountants are available to analyse production processes in minute detail and calculate the value of the benefits a new product in greater and greater depth until they reach entirely specious levels of accuracy. Households do not generally employ cost accountants, and so there is no precise way of expressing the value of a consumer product as a sum of money except by offering it for sale and finding out who buys it.

The ultimate aim of all production is to supply goods and services to consumers and their governments: such 'final consumption' expenditure is the major driver of the economy. Even capital goods purchases, recorded as investment rather than as consumption in the national accounts, only makes sense if there are going to be consumers in the future to buy the goods and services whose production such capital equipment is intended to support. For this reason the buying behaviour of consumers is intensively researched, both by academic institutions and by private sector consultancies.

Some of the lessons that have been learned are discussed below.

Thank you, I don't want any ...

The modern world offers such a profusion of products that no one consumer will ever use more than a tiny fraction of those on offer. A typical supermarket will stock over 10 000 lines while a large one might carry 25 000 lines or more. Every motor car manufacturer offers several models, each of which is available in several different factory variants, each of which comes in several colours. Cars can be tailored further with dealer-fitted options. Buyers, even in a relatively restricted price range, must choose from hundreds of possibilities. Queensland alone offers four major holiday destinations, each of which offers the visitor a choice of resorts, resort hotels, motels of various degrees of comfort and facility, caravan parks and camp sites. The entertainment pages of a metropolitan newspaper offer forty or more different movies and shows on any given day, with the list changing rapidly. A person could take a Queensland holiday and buy a new car every year, go to the pictures every week, and still die at a ripe old age having bought only a fraction of the models of car, taken only a small selection of the available holidays, and having missed most of the pictures.

> *Your main competitors are other ways people can spend their money, not just people selling products like yours ...*

Every time a consumer fills a shopping trolley, buys a car, books a holiday or goes to a show they are saying 'yes' to one offer and 'no' to tens or hundreds of alternatives. Consumers have a finite amount of money, and buying a product in one market, such as a new house, will often leave them in a position where they must withdraw from other markets for a while, such as those for expensive cars or holidays. Some consumer decisions cast a long shadow: the decision to buy a house in a particular suburb also implies a series of decisions to limit the household's choice of supermarkets, specialty and department stores, professional service providers, home maintenance services and many other decisions to those available within easy travelling distance of the new home.

> *Most offers to sell will be rejected, even when these offers are closely targeted at potential buyers who would receive a genuine benefit from using the product offered ...*

Even when the number of potential buyers is very large, as with packaged supermarket goods, it is possible for a product to fail in spite of offering definite benefits, simply because its value proposition does not raise it to the top position in an adequate number of buyers' minds. Buyer preferences are not 'transitive': people may prefer product 'A' to product 'B' and product 'B' to product 'C' but then choose product 'C' ahead of product 'A'. People who show such apparently perverse preferences are neither stupid nor irrational. They are responding

> *Successful products are those that offer a definite reason to buy ...*

to the fact that preferences reflect a multiplicity of factors and cannot be reduced to simple linear relationships.

Successful products are those that offer a 'definite reason to buy', some point on which, for an adequate number of buyers, this product is the best option. The definite reason to buy may be a gimmick or it may be a seriously useful feature, but it only gets the product considered, it doesn't clinch a sale. Consumers will compare a new product to two or three familiar ones, and will only switch if they are convinced that the new product offers them better overall value.

That's nice, but do I need it?

It is extremely easy to confuse technical excellence with user-orientation. It is also very easy to generate confusion by using percentages. Consider a new domestic washing machine that is 50 per cent faster than the models that it competes with: is it worth 50 per cent more than its rivals? In many households, the answer will be, no. When an automatic washing machine is started the operator can get on with other tasks, or go to work, or shop, or be entertained. The only time a faster machine would be more valuable would be when the washing is wanted in a hurry, but since it is going to be wet and will need drying when it comes out of the machine, just speeding up the washing cycle won't make that much difference to the time before the clothes are available.

All Australian states have speed limits which the police enforce with devious tricks such as radar, lasers, and cameras. While some drivers in the Northern Territory, and reckless drivers elsewhere, might like a car than can travel at 200 kilometres per hour, a high top speed will only have a limited appeal to other drivers. The Ford Edsel (launched in the United States in 1952 and withdrawn three years later) has entered marketing folklore for the number of mistakes made in its development and marketing. One of these poor marketing decisions was to fit the car with the most powerful engine in its class: this greatly appealed to irresponsible drivers, and as a result most normal drivers formed the view that owning and driving an Edsel was an anti-social act.

The various airline business clubs, such as Golden Wing or Qantas Club, have proved extremely popular and very effective at building customer loyalty. While they are not directly associated with the flying process they do make delays more palatable and waiting less uncomfortable. Because they have a relatively steep subscription charge, relatively few passengers enrol in more than one of them. To a member of the Qantas Club, membership adds considerable value to Qantas flights, while Golden Wing members will fly Ansett unless there is a strong reason not to. The clubs are not particularly effective at inducing new customers to use an airline, since both major Australian airlines have them, but they are very effective at generating preferential repeat business from the customers that an airline has already attracted.

Is it really worth the trouble?

Buying something often involves much more than simply paying for it. Car buyers have to travel to a dealer, negotiate an option and feature package and agree a price, and then arrange insurance. Holiday buyers may have to endure a long drive or flight to their destination, and an equally debilitating return journey. The owner of a new domestic appliance may need to spend a lot of time spent learning how to use it before its features are worth having: video recorders have entered folklore for this reason.

Most people value what economists call leisure, or what other people see as unpaid activity. Females, and males over the age of 25, generally rate driving a car in traffic as a low-value activity, so much so that they are prepared to sacrifice cost-saving opportunities to avoid it. Commuters and business travellers will pay (or sacrifice) between $25 and $100 per hour to reduce uncharged travelling time, while people on routine journeys act as if their time was worth as much as $11 per hour. The act of choosing goods and services may be seen as valuable, or at least, value neutral, but queuing and waiting time will be seen as a cost.

These figures can be related quite directly to prices and to market catchments. Given that average urban travel speeds in Australia don't go much over 40 kilometres per hour, consumers' apparent cost of purchase will rise by between 50 cents and $5 per kilometre. If a consumer must choose between competing service providers, one of whom will repair a breakdown rapidly, while the other generally takes at least an hour longer, the faster provider may find a price differential of up to $10 is acceptable. Suppliers of emergency repair services to businesses will find that time is very much the essence of their product. The distance buyers can be reasonably expected to travel to complete a purchase will tend to grow with the size of the probable purchase: a major corporation planning a multi-million dollar plant investment may make several international trips before selecting a supplier, while a neighbourhood mixed business could charge 20 cents more per carton of milk than a supermarket a kilometre away without losing much business.

Anyone who uses an Australian domestic airline for both business and leisure will be struck by the size of the fare differentials. In mid 1995 a full fare return trip between Melbourne and Sydney cost almost $500, while discount tickets were available for as little as $149. The anti-delay features of the full fare ticket, basically the ability to make a booking, or change a booking, up to twenty minutes before the scheduled flight departure time and the ability to miss a flight without penalty, are worth about $350.

How many?

One of the key questions is: 'How many potential customers are there for this product?' Only when this is answered can the next two questions be answered: 'How many will buy it from us?' and 'When will they buy it?' Some methods for finding answers to the last two questions will be answered later in this book, and the first question will be dealt with in this chapter.

To be a potential customer the following statements must be true:

▲ the buyer must be able to gain substantial value from owning and/or using the product

▲ the buyer has a reasonable opportunity to find out about it

▲ the buyer must have free resources to pay the purchase price and all the other costs of acquisition and ownership

▲ the product must be physically available to the buyer.

The first point must be answered from the buyer's point of view, not the seller's. Someone might wish to market a line of attractive and comfortable tropical clothing in Thailand, and observe that there are a lot of men in that country who wear plain saffron robes and could be dressed a lot more fashionably. Buddhist monks are not, however, a good target market for western casual wear. A great many marketing initiatives have failed because the product was something that the seller thought would be good for the buyers, but not something that buyers actually wanted for themselves.

Many marketing initiatives have failed because the seller thought that the product would be good for the buyers, but it wasn't something the buyers wanted for themselves ...

The second point can be addressed, to some extent, by marketing effort, but practical business plans have to be limited in space and time. A new consumer product, proposed to be launched in Australia, might appeal to a million Russians, but since very few of them read Australian newspapers or magazines, watch Australian television, or are likely to interact with Australian users of that particular product, very few of them will find out about it; not knowing about it, they won't buy it. Other products might become known in Russia and other countries quite rapidly: a number of Australian companies specialising in laboratory instruments and medical devices see the world as one market, because all their likely customers read the same specialist journals and meet each other at international conferences.

The third point is often neglected in marketing at all levels: people who have trouble paying for an adequate amount of food will be extremely sparing in the amount of money that they will be prepared to spend on anything else. Most Australians are now prepared to pay for conservative dental treatment, yet well into the 1950s it was common for young people to have all their teeth extracted so

Unless using the new product means that there is something users no longer have to do at all, the extra work needed to make use of it may be seen as a heavy cost ...

as to avoid future treatment costs. Crooked teeth and squints are now routinely treated in Australia where they were once neglected, and are still neglected in many less affluent countries.

Entrepreneurs often underestimate the costs of owning their new product, with the result that they set a price which the users see as unreasonably high. Computer people are particularly liable to this error, seeing only the benefits that their new equipment can deliver and being blind to the costs in training and effort that using it will inflict. Most new products require their users or end users to do various things that they did not do before; unless using the new product means that there is something that they no longer have to do at all, this extra work may be seen as a heavy extra cost. EFTPOS has been a great success in Australia, partly because end users can draw cash while paying for their super-market or petrol purchases, and they don't have to make a special visit to a bank or an automatic teller.

Physical availability seems too obvious to neglect, but it often is when entrepreneurs are writing business plans. Often delivering the physical part of the product, if there is one, presents few problems: Australia Post can deliver a small parcel to practically any person living in Australia, and commercial carriers will take larger consignments anywhere at all, for a price. Service products, and the necessary services associated with a physical product, are a different matter. A software product may be launched with an 'on site warranty', which is not much of a problem if the customers are all in the same suburb, but will be one if single customers demanding service turn up in North Queensland and the Pilbara.

People who ignore the natural environment may find that it has ways of reminding them of its importance: physical products sold into tropical places, including northern Australia, must be capable of withstanding high ambient temperatures, concurrent high humidity, and fungal attack. The telephone manufacturer Exicom Ltd failed to ensure that this was so in its products shipped in 1993 and 1994 and a large number of faulty handsets had to be replaced, and other costs endured. Exicom staggered on for a while, finally going into liquidation in 1996. Working in the other direction, a certain Swedish motor manufacturer, famous in Australia as the supplier of vehicles for anxious mothers to shuffle their attention-grabbing darlings around in, took a long while indeed to realise that Australians expect their motor car air-conditioning to work when the outside temperature exceeds 25 degrees Celsius.

Electrical equipment shipped to North America must work off a 110 volt, 60 hertz supply and must obtain Underwriters Laboratory approval. Equipment imported into Australia must work off 240 volt, 50 hertz supplies and be certified to IEC standards. Power plugs on domestic and office equipment sold in Australia must (in general) be moulded on to the cable, while for equipment sold in Britain the cable ends are left bare for customers to fit their own plug. There have been plenty of importers and exporters who have neglected basic facts such as these, to their considerable cost.

Setting out the facts

Having developed a product concept, the entrepreneur should record certain facts and inferences so as to build up a picture of the likely customer profile for a product. We discuss some of the most important of these below. We have not set out all the questions that a prudent entrepreneur might ask before actually launching a new product, but it could be a serious waste of time for an entrepreneur to go very far into the planning process without collecting and considering this information.

The product description

The essential facts about the product should be set out on about half a page, or 250 or so words. Very few inventors will feel that a space as small as this will do justice to their product, but it is a good idea to make the effort: it should concentrate the mind on getting the most important points across rather than attempting a complete description. Pictures and extended descriptions may be useful in a sales brochure or even in a prospectus, but they would merely cause information overload if used here.

Basic method of distribution

Product producers seldom see the distribution system as forming part of the product, but buyers certainly do, and so it must be mentioned quite early in the plan. Mail order involves a relatively low advertising outlay and, assuming production is well-organised, relatively little stock and low debtors. By contrast, once distribution through major retailers starts (if it ever does) there will have to be a major marketing outlay to obtain a listing and then a shelf space allocation, and either a stock inventory or a very slick manufacturing system indeed to meet the large retailers' demands for same- or next-day restocking.

Frequency of use/purchase

Something that is used regularly can acquire a high value in use even though the value contributed on each occasion is small. By contrast, something that is used infrequently, or only once, must make a significant impact on the user on that occasion if it is to command a non-trivial price. As at 1995, extraordinarily accurate position indicators based on the GPS satellites[5] operated by the United States Department of Defense are becoming generally available, and are fitted to some luxury cars. People who only use their car for commuting and an annual holiday to the same location every year will not see a GPS receiver as anything more than an interesting gadget, while people whose business regularly takes them long distances across unfamiliar terrain are likely to think that a GPS receiver is essential. Many brides spend large sums on a wedding dress to be worn on one occasion only, but very few people will spend more than a few dollars on a pair of pantihose which likewise may be worn once only.

Frequency of purchase is a vital factor in determining the economics of a business supplying a given product. This is partly a matter of relative volumes: for each time someone buys a car, they are likely to buy petrol a hundred or more times. The frequency of purchase statistic has a major effect on the variability of a supplier's income: when consumer confidence is low, people may delay replacing their car, but as long as they have a car at all they are likely to go on using it and buying petrol for it. This variability in expected revenue means that the average returns, and margins, must be higher for the infrequently purchased product to make investing in its suppliers worthwhile. Imagine a country where a well-defined group of people replaced their cars every three years: the motor car manufacturers would seem to have a nice, steady business building thirty-three cars per year per hundred new car owners. Imagine that some event damages consumer confidence, and everyone decides to keep their car for six months longer. When things settle down, the motor car manufacturers will find that they are only making twenty-nine cars per year per hundred owners, but for the six months immediately following the universal decision to keep cars an extra six months, no new cars are sold at all. Annual sales levels per hundred owners go from thirty-three to fourteen to twenty-nine. When confidence returns and everyone with a car over three years old decides to replace it immediately, sales in that happy year leap to fifty units before dropping back to thirty-three.

Across a whole country, mood swings aren't synchronised quite as well as this imaginary tale requires, but in a given sales area they may well be: a new car dealership in Dandenong, Victoria had been selling sixteen cars per week before the recession of 1990–91; with the onset of the recession, sales dropped to four per week and after struggling for a few months the dealership was forced to close. Before the recession about half the new cars sold by the dealership had been fitted with tow bars, and a small business in Dandenong had achieved modest prosperity making and fitting them. With the onset of the recession only a quarter of the buyers wanted optional extras such as tow bars, and with sales dropping from eight to one per week the small business was bankrupted.

The Dandenong area was hit quite hard by the recession, with unemployment rising rapidly, but most of the people living there kept their jobs and their cars: petrol sales drifted slightly downwards as the unemployed cut back on their driving, but by nothing like the 75 per cent and higher falls in activity suffered by new car businesses.

Significance

The entrepreneur should attempt to establish the importance of the product to users, since this will be reflected in a number of key business variables. When a product is regarded as critical to a consumer's life or to a business's viability, sales will not be seriously affected by the economic cycle, customers will be reluctant to experiment with alternative suppliers, and the price, within reason, will not be a major issue. IBM's fabulous profits in the years 1955–85 came largely from their position as suppliers of centralised computing facilities to 70 per cent of the world's major corporations and government departments, and in particular, the almost universal use of these computers for billing applications and the debtors' ledger. Total and permanent loss of the data that underpinned these applications led inevitably to the collapse of a corporation, and so most of IBM's major customers neither took alternative suppliers seriously nor objected strenuously to the prices IBM charged.

> Queen Victoria visited India in her capacity of Empress at the end of the nineteenth century, and let it be known that she expected all the comforts of home. Royal flush lavatories were installed the length and breadth of India, each fitted with Mr Crapper's ingenious flush mechanism. In Nepal, however, there was no running water and no plumber, but they ensured Her Majesty's convenience was respected. A young Nepalese lad was positioned on the floor above the toilet with his eye glued to small hole in the floor. As soon as Her Majesty pulled the chain, the young man tipped a bucket of water into a funnel that led to a pipe that flushed the toilet.

Prestige is very important to people, and only slightly less so to corporations. Perfumes and cosmetics, and designer clothing, are examples of categories where individual consumers may be very loyal to their favoured supplier or suppliers and in consequence these suppliers earn high margins and relatively stable cash flows. Adult gifts always carry a heavy load of implication: beaux who boast of the low price they paid for the flowers they present or the engagement rings that they proffer seldom prosper in their suits!

Buyers tend to resent any expenditure that merely preserves the status quo ...

The preserve/enhance dichotomy can also moderate consumer and business response to an offer. Preservation merely maintains the *status quo*, and buyers tend to resent any expenditure that doesn't make them any better off: householders know that their exterior woodwork must be painted fairly regularly to prevent rot, but the money spent on such maintenance will be grudged. Many companies under-spend on preventative maintenance, even when the coldest of calculations show that 'an ounce of prevention is worth a pound of cure'. During the early 1990s the Mt Isa mine practically abandoned preventative maintenance as a 'cost saving measure', with the predictable result that by 1995 time lost due to missing or broken equipment almost wiped out the operating profit from the mine. The mine management then called upon the miners to accept cuts in pay and conditions in order to restore profitability, and claimed to be pained and upset by the response.

By contrast, a painter who explains how the use of appropriate colours can enhance the value of a house, and who spends some time with the householder working out an ideal colour scheme, will not find the payment for a well-finished job grudged. The increased value of the house is a fair return for the payment to the painter. Equally, someone who approaches a corporation offering ways to increase their revenues is bound to get a hearing. While the Mt Isa mine was skimping on preventative maintenance, it was spending freely on ore body modelling software and the supercomputer time needed to run it. Making sure that new mines were put in the right place, and that new drives and shafts for the existing mine hit ore rather than rock, could provide a major boost to the value of the company, and so expenditure under the relevant headings was regarded as a rewarding investment, not a grudged expense.

Perceived value caps the price

The value of a product to a user can be estimated by a thought experiment: if they had the product already, and they couldn't go straight to a shop and replace it with a perfect copy, how much would you have to pay to get it back from them? If the product was a life-saving drug with the unique ability to cure the buyer's (or the buyer's child's) life-threatening medical condition, the value could be very high. If the product was 'Big M, strawberry flavour' the value might be no higher than the price of 'Big M, chocolate flavour' if that was still on sale, or possibly the cost of fresh milk and a separate bottle of strawberry flavouring.

An industrial buyer will limit the range of options to functional substitutes: the value of a new machining centre will not exceed the cost of the various machines it replaced and the present value of the wages of the workers needed to operate the old equipment. Consumers are much less limited in their approach, particularly for purchases that are driven by pleasure and convenience rather than necessity. If Big M is not available, a child might buy a fizzy drink or a sweet, or even save the money and spend it on a toy.

> *How much would you have to pay to get it back from them?*

The more similar a product is to its nearest substitute, the more closely the value of the one will be determined by the price of the other. In the extreme case, when users do not believe that there are any significant differences between two products the price of one determines the value of the other and both products are commodities. In every case the apparent value is the limit price: at prices above this level no one will buy the product.

Cost of acquisition and ownership

When computers first entered business use they were not very reliable: completing an eight-hour shift without a hardware failure was unusual. Buyers were offered, and generally accepted, maintenance contracts for an annual charge roughly equal to 10 per cent of the purchase price. As manufacturing technology improved, and integrated circuits enabled single, highly reliable, chips to replace whole assemblies, breakdowns became less frequent and systems began to operate for weeks and even months between major equipment failures. Maintenance charges stayed at about 10 per cent of the purchase price, and computer equipment maintenance became extremely profitable.

It became so profitable that IBM's customers were approached by independent contractors who offered to maintain installations for as little as 5 per cent of the purchase price. IBM initially did nothing about this, apart from uttering a number of very pointed remarks about the pretensions of people who claimed to service IBM machines as well as IBM themselves did. Quite suddenly in the late 1970s IBM decided that this tolerant approach wasn't working, and they dropped their maintenance to 3 per cent of the purchase price, a level at which maintenance was still modestly profitable to IBM but far less attractive to outsiders.

The English computer company ICL had been quite comfortable about charging 10 per cent for maintenance, and went on doing it for some years after IBM cut their maintenance charges. ICL's sales staff noticed that, if they wanted to keep their customers, they had to offer them discounts of up to 35 per cent off the purchase price of a new computer. The customers' argument was simple: IBM had demonstrated that the value of maintenance was 3 per cent of the list price, 7 per cent less than the smaller company charged; the customers evaluated decisions over five years; and the extra maintenance charges had to come off the purchase price or there would be no deal. For two years a heated battle raged inside ICL, as the maintenance department fought off demands from the sales staff that the maintenance charges be brought into line with the perceived value of the service: 'We make all the profit in this company', said the maintenance managers, 'you don't make any profit at all, what with those great big discounts you keep giving away.'

Customers, whether as consumers or industrial buyers, are not stupid. 'Hidden extras' don't stay hidden for long, and in many industries those companies that, for a limited time only, offer their goods or services for sale at a single, inclusive price generally make a major promotional feature of this behaviour. The limiting price is the perceived value less any of these not-so-secret extras.

Alternatives

It is nice to have a product which delivers unique benefits, but in practice this is rare. Going without is always an option, and one that is widely adopted, even with very successful products. For planning purposes the alternatives tested should assume that potential customers are prepared to pay for the benefits that the new product will deliver, and use this section of the research documentation to explore some of the more probable alternatives. Even when these alternatives are relatively unlikely to be adopted by a serious prospective user of the new product, they tend to set the value of it. The ICL customers who objected to paying three times as much as IBM customers did for maintenance services were very unlikely to ask IBM to maintain ICL equipment, but they did see IBM as setting the benchmark for service charges. As it happened, ICL charged half IBM's rates for software but no customers offered to pay the difference.

Points of superiority

Having drawn up some possible alternatives, the planner must make sure that potential users have a real reason to buy the new product. The points listed here should be based on the argument that would be used to sell the new product to a wavering potential customer: 'Brand X is a good product, of course, but if you buy ours you will get ...' If there is a product against which the proposed innovation has no advantages at all, or where the only advantage is a small reduction in price or running costs, the would-be entrepreneur must ask: 'Is this really a product worth launching?'

> *A small advantage in product terms may be very significant for users ... and the opposite may also be the case ...*

A small advantage in product terms may, of course, deliver a large value to its users: a new jumbo jet engine that is 1 per cent more fuel-efficient than its rivals delivers major user benefits, not so much in the cost of the fuel as in the payload freed for revenue-earning cargo and passengers. Saving 1.5 tonnes of fuel on a long-haul international flight sector is worth $250 or so to an airline, but selling an extra 1.5 tonnes of freight can be worth three times that. Over a year a 1 per cent fuel cost saving could be worth $3 million or more per aeroplane to an international airline. By contrast, a 1 per cent fuel efficiency gain would not be noticed by a domestic motor car user.

Estimated value premium

The entrepreneur should record what he or she thinks the user will value the product at in a reverse auction, for example, as a differential value: 'If I offered you $10 and this alternative, would you let me take "X" away?' Using a differential value reduces the tendency to value the proposed product in an extreme situation: obviously a powerful light would be much more highly valued on a dark, wet night in the suburbs than in a comfortable, well-lit shop, but it is in the shop or some equally comfortable environment that consumers usually exercise their choice.

Estimated sustainable price

This is the most important single number in a plan, and often the one arrived at most casually. The entrepreneur must set out his or her opinion as to the highest price at which the proposed product will be regarded as a 'good buy' by a solid

> *When the value premium is not instantly obvious it may not be possible to turn it into a price premium ...*

majority of its prospective purchasers. Quite clearly, it must be less than the sum of the price of the closest alternative and the value premium. When the value premium is a little 'woolly' and it is hard to fit definite numbers to it, the price of a new product can be set at exactly the price of its closest alternative: the sales message becomes 'for the same amount of money you get all this extra value'. When Apple launched their first graphics user interface (GUI) computer, the Lisa, they tried to get a price premium sufficient to cover their high manufacturing cost, but few buyers would pay it and the Lisa flopped. The Apple Macintosh, launched shortly after the Lisa, matched the IBM PC in price and rapidly achieved volume sales. The Xerox Star was a high-quality GUI system launched well before either the Lisa or the Macintosh. The Star was offered at a price that made the treasurers of major corporations gulp: it vanished from the market so completely that Xerox Corporation was refused standing in a lawsuit between Apple and Microsoft concerning the invention of GUI computing.

> *'Cheaper' and 'better' are contradictory messages ...*

The Star and the Lisa show that technically better products may not succeed if offered at a higher price than the market expects to pay. Launching a better product at a lower price than its most direct alternative is not always a good idea either, since 'cheaper' and 'better' are contradictory messages. If a new product is launched at a slightly lower price than a close alternative, the competitor may see this as the opening shot in a price war. Entrepreneurs with new products and a very small market share are seldom in a position to win price wars.

The dangers of price cutting should only be ignored when a new product can be sold profitably at a price too low for its closest competitors to match while covering their variable costs. No one can survive for very long if their variable costs aren't covered, and they will be forced to withdraw from the affected market.

How many consumers?

Knowing the price a new product can command does not establish what revenue it can earn. We must find out the number of people who are prepared, or can be persuaded, to by the product.

There are some basic questions whose answers will let us estimate the number of possible sales for a consumer product. This is (usually) a much larger number than the number of sales that our new firm will achieve in any given period, and some ways of estimating per-period sales are discussed in later chapters. We should be fairly sure that the number of sales won't be any greater than this number. Users of any demographic estimator should not hesitate to use several different sheets when a number of different market segments may find the new product attractive. It is very easy, on a spreadsheet, to add up three rows to give a total. It is much harder for someone evaluating a plan to disentangle a single, composite number, or to find out how to adjust the plan after the product is launched if the response from some segments is outside expectations.

Sex and relationship

Most people are either male or female, and no matter how liberated women are and how equal their opportunities, there will remain subjects upon which most women will have different opinions to most men. Sex is so important that if males and females are equally likely to want the new product the plan should say so explicitly.

People's relationship status affects some aspects of their behaviour and not others. People in relationships are not good customers for introduction services; people without children are not good prospects for child care centres.

Age range

Knowing the age of people in a target market can help to modify the entrepreneur's promotional and sales plans as discussed in later chapters, but it also enables an estimate to be made of the rate at which new customers enter the market. As discussed in Chapter 4, re-purchases and recommendations by satisfied customers are very important factors in the growth of markets, while the success of a new enterprise is often determined by the number of people in the market without a prior attachment to a competing supplier.

The shorter the age range the faster the buying population turns over: a firm specialising in 21st birthday parties will have a 100 per cent change in its target population every year, while a product that appeals equally to people of every age will (in Australia) enjoy a 1.5 per cent entry rate and an 0.3 per cent rate of exit.

Income range

The income of the members of a target market raises both affordability and cohort size issues.[6] People below a certain minimum income simply won't be able to afford some products even though they could have made good use of them if they were free. In some markets there is a maximum income level as well: people above this level address the problem that the new product solves in quite a different way. Dish washing machines don't sell well in countries where servants are readily available for low wages. Gadgets that make international travel in economy class more comfortable don't sell well to people who always travel first class, or who use their corporate jets.

Other distinguishing features

There will often be something to say about a new product's most likely customers after their sex, age and income is determined. This will be particularly true when the product is one for which age, sex and relationship status are irrelevant. When a product is likely to appeal to a number of different consumer segments this section can become of a short segment description.

Geographic range

A large scale marketing campaign may cover many countries, while a small one may only affect a few suburbs. In the first case 'the world' is too diverse to be treated as a single market segment and the demographic estimates should be broken down into tolerably homogeneous regions. Regions are homogeneous when the people in them can be reached by a single set of distribution and promotion channels, and when there will be no marked difference in the response to the product and its promotional messages across the region. Metropolitan Australia is one region for some products but must be broken into multiple regions for others. The United States is usually treated as at least five regions for marketing purposes while some products must be marketed to much more closely defined segments.

> *Marketing plans that treat 'Australia' as a single segment will be treated with suspicion; those that refer to 'Europe' or 'the United States' may be regarded as a joke.*

Cohort size

The planner must estimate, coldly and cautiously, the total size of the actual and potential user population. Every preceding step has redefined the market so as to exclude large numbers of people. We are left, at this point, with those who might reasonably be expected to buy the new product at some time in the indefinite future.

> *Naive or enthusiastic inventors frequently decide that their market is 'everyone' or 'every car owner' or 'every parent' ...*

Instead of declaring that the market for our product embraces all six million car owners in Australia, we might see a product as reaching a maximum of 130 000. Naive or enthusiastic inventors frequently decide that their market is 'everyone' or 'every car owner' or 'every parent', and project huge revenues and profits for any financier who is brave enough to back them up. They very rarely get their projects to market at all, and usually then only after calling on their family and friends to stand in for the unwilling professional investors or fund managers. Forty-fold errors in market estimates are not unusual when the discipline of examining the market dispassionately is neglected. Entrepreneurs should be optimistic, but not foolhardy: launching a product without making a serious effort to estimate the size of its potential market is like giving money away.

Entry and exit rates

People enter a market when they grow into the appropriate age group, move into the appropriate region, acquire an appropriate income or participate in some defining event, such as marriage, house purchase, or the arrival of a child. A similar set of criteria and events define people's exit from a market.

The rates of entry and exit should be recorded in the demographics section of the planner's research record, although their principal importance comes later, when they play a large part in determining the volatility of a market, the rate at which an entrant's market share can grow — or decline.

Information sources

Recording the sources of information used to estimate the number of potential customers in a market is a lot more than academic pedantry. For one thing, it shows that some sources have been consulted, and the credibility of the plan will be limited by the credibility of the sources. Australian Bureau of Statistics data will generally be regarded as quite accurate, as will the published reports of similar organisations in other countries. The main problem with such bureau data is that it never quite answers the questions which an entrepreneur, and the entrepreneur's financial backers, want answers to.

Trade associations often produce useful reports, while the scanning systems at supermarkets collect vast amounts of data on packaged goods sales, much of which is available in reduced form, for a price, from market research organisations. Informal surveys, if documented, can produce quite valuable results from a very small sample. If the only people who can be found to say a nice thing about the proposal are the entrepreneur's adoring parents, a dispassionate observer might not give the product much of a chance in the market. By contrast, if twenty relative strangers are shown a prototype, and nineteen offer to place a deposit, the omens are rather better. Products can often be successful if only a very small proportion of the total population buys them, but they will fail if nobody at all buys them, and an enterprise may fail if consumer response is vastly overestimated. It is much easier to raise finance to expand production of a successful product than to support the stockholding costs of a near-failure.

Proper test marketing and formal marketing research can add great credibility to a plan, but both processes are very expensive and many entrepreneurs will feel that there are more urgent demands on their limited financial resources. Marketing research often produces deceptive results with very new products, possibly because it is hard for respondents to work out how badly they would want something that they had never seen.

Example: Post-it Notes

Among the many active projects in the 3M Corporation in the early 1980s was one developing easy-parting adhesives for the plastics moulding industry. One of the compounds that was tested and rejected by the project attracted the attention of Art Fry. Fry was a keen member of his local church choir, and discovered that paper coated with this adhesive made an ideal bookmark in the hymnals, not falling out as the pages were turned, yet leaving no mark when it was removed. He became convinced that paper coated with this adhesive could command a wide market, as, under the name Post-it Notes, it eventually did.

Both marketing research and a test marketing exercise appeared to show that Post-it Notes would be a failure: it was only when the returns from the test marketing failure were mailed out as Xmas novelties and potential users experimented with them that Post-it Notes became indispensable. One major advantage of Post-it Notes was that when documents were circulated around a corporate or government bureaucracy for comment each respondent could put their comments on Post-it Notes and not on the original. When the master document was eventually filed, all the notes would be discarded, leaving no evidence for future inquisitors to find if the file were to be retrieved at a later date. Even with perfect hindsight it is not easy to see how a marketing researcher could have discovered the value of Post-it Notes in this application.

How many business users?

Planners whose product will be used in the course of business rather than by final consumers must use a different approach to estimating the size of the potential market. These are 'intermediate' products, also referred to as 'industrial' or 'business' products. Their value is not intrinsic, but arises either from their potential to leverage the efforts of their users into creating higher consumer value or from the new product's ability to reduce its users' operating costs.

Some products are very highly targeted: nobody other than an integrated steel producer is likely to be very interested in accessories for Basic Oxygen Converters. This would seem to make the task of counting potential users quite straightforward, and for steel producers, with reservations, it is. What about a new pressure valve or torch for oxy-acetylene equipment? Even the major gas supply companies aren't quite sure how many of their cylinders are out there, and the data that they have got is not available to an upstart competitor. While the targeting is quite precise, counting the potential users, even those in one city or suburb, is not going to be an easy task.

Broadly targeted products present even greater problems in user identification. In the mid 1950s the IBM Corporation believed that the total United States market for computers might be saturated after 100 systems were sold, and the ferocity with which they fought for every possible sale eventually led to their being prosecuted for anti-competitive behaviour and shackled with anti-trust orders. By 1980, just before the PC was launched, there were about 90 000 IBM computers in service with their customers. The experience of underestimating the original computer market led IBM to be broadly optimistic about the PC business, and in 1981 they predicted the market contained more than a million potential customers. Fifteen years later the best estimates suggested that at least 130 million PCs were in service around the world.

Not all errors are underestimates: there are plenty of examples of firms launching products into markets where there were no more than a tenth of the customers that they expected; there are a few where false optimism led a planner to overestimate the potential market by a hundredfold. By far the best form of market testing is to launch a product into a small subset of the anticipated total market and see what happens. The results of such a market test enable the plan estimates to be corrected before there is any major commitment of resources to production or to marketing. For many products such a test will be prohibitively expensive: it is then all the more important to make the best possible paper estimates before committing to a product launch.

Careful prior estimates are still needed even when a market trial is planned. Running a trial without a prior attempt to estimate the size of the potential market means that there is no basis upon which to evaluate the results. Running a trial at all is likely to alert a firm's competitors to the existence of a market opportunity, and so a decision to run a trial only makes sense if there is a prior commitment of all the resources needed to follow it up with a full launch.

Geographic range

The corresponding paragraph for consumer products emphasised the need to avoid unreal aggregation. This is crucial with industrial products. Similar industries in different countries will speak different languages, observe different conventions, obey (or ignore) different regulations, and follow different decision-making processes. Even when these differences are insufficient to make firms in different countries buy different products, they are likely to be profound enough to require different marketing approaches and to be separable for planning purposes.

> *A common language does not turn two countries into a common market ...*

Australians may gain a certain amount of amusement from the occasional failure of a British or American product to succeed when marketed in Australia; but they should also be aware of the number of times Australian companies, both large and small, have gone to America full of optimism only to find that a common language does not turn two countries into a common market. Any plan where disparate markets are lumped together for planning purposes will have a credibility problem when it is reviewed and is likely to present quite unnecessary problems in execution.

Cohort size

This first number for cohort size is the statistical count of firms in the selected geographic range meeting the earlier criteria. In many cases it will be possible to base this number on published statistics with a minimum of personal interpretation added. In countries where bad planners get sued, getting this number wrong would be almost an admission of guilt. It takes a pretty determined optimist to believe that every firm in a statistical cohort is a potential customer for a new product, and so a probable penetration level should also be recorded.

This subsection lets the planner eliminate the impossible from the statistician's defined cohort and come up with a realistic target market size.

The entry rate and exit rate should be quantified and recorded at the same time as the cohort size is estimated; they will be used later in the planning process to estimate the likely volatility of market shares and the speed of response a new entrant may expect.

Information sources

The credibility of any plan will be limited by the credibility of the information sources used to prepare the market size estimates contained in it. If there are no sources there will be no credibility.

The available annual gross margin

Once a reasonably full set of statistics have been collected about the market for a new product, they can be 'boiled down' into a single financial number, which we call the available annual gross margin, or AAGM. This is the amount of money that would be spent if every potential user bought the product at their average annual rate, less the direct costs of producing and delivering the amount of product needed to supply them all. The AAGM must be sufficient to cover the fixed expenses, development cost recovery, and reasonable profit for, not only the venture, but the venture's likely competitors.

The AAGM is an hypothetical annual amount, and the actual revenue that a new venture can earn is bound to be substantially less than this:

▲ by no means all the potential customers for a product will buy it in the first few years it is on the market, and so part of the AAGM represents future revenue, which is, of course, less valuable than current revenue

▲ if the new product is a success it will attract imitators, who will appropriate some of the AAGM to themselves

Table 5.1 *First stage financial screening*

Product security	Launch day value (fraction of AAGM)
The product is an unbreakable, unavoidable and indefinite monopoly	14%
Competitive entry will not occur for at least four years from the full launch (that is, after market testing completed)	7%
Otherwise	4%

▲ because of the way cohorts change, some of the people or firms that are now seen as potential customers will leave the market without ever buying the product, and others may never get around to buying it.

It is possible to make a reasonable estimate of the revenue and gross margin a new enterprise can earn in its first few years of trading. This can be reduced to a present value by applying an appropriate discount rate.[7] We have undertaken extensive simulation using appropriate market development parameters and risk-weighted discount rates to relate the present value of a proposal to its AAGM. We present a summary of the results in Table 5.1. This table provides a quick way of estimating the launch day value of a new product, once the AAGM is determined.

If the present value of a concept is not greater than all expenses before the launch day and all the fixed expenses other than product supply and marketing for a year or two afterwards, the project is unlikely to prove a wise use of the funds needed to bring it to a launch.

Example: A modest proposal declined

An entrepreneur considers preparing a superior study guide for students taking the Victorian VCE. She determines that there are 15 000 students who are used to paying $25 or so for a text book; she finds that the variable costs of book production are about $18 including the reseller margin. She computes the AAGM: 15 000 × ($25 − $18) = $105 000. She notes that the market is an easy one to enter and so the last line from Table 5.1 is appropriate: the launch day present value is $105 000 × 4% = $4200. She decides not to resign from her job to write and publish the book.

Reality check

At this point an entrepreneur should be able to make a quick market feasibility check on the new idea, and decide whether it is worth the effort of taking the plans any further.

This boils down to three questions:

▲ Is it possible to launch this product without actually losing money?

▲ (Very roughly), how much up-front capital is required or must be committed?

▲ Is it possible to gain a reasonable return on the necessary investment?

The answer to the last two questions lets the entrepreneur ask a fourth question:

▲ Can I get access to sufficient resources?

You may need to work through the whole of this book, and a certain amount of reality too, before you can say 'yes!' to the second and fourth questions, but there are some very early signs when the answer will be 'no'.

The first question is the quickest to answer: we know, at this point, how many people are potential customers for the new product and how much they are prepared to pay. Can we make or procure the product, in these volumes, for a unit variable cost of no more than half the end user price? If we can, the product may be worth investigating further. If we can't, we are unlikely to be able to generate enough cash flow to launch a new enterprise. Mass market products may have slightly higher variable cost ratios: Toyota, the world leaders in lean production, have unit variable costs of around 60 per cent of the end user price. Established retailers do better still: Myer department stores run with unit variable costs of about 75 per cent, as do United States supermarkets; Australia's Coles and Woolworths supermarkets run at about 66 per cent. In the United States most supermarkets rely on jobbers or manufacturers to restock the shelves, while Australian supermarkets use centralised warehouses and employ their own shelf stackers.

Mass market retailers and manufacturers can run on relatively slight margins because they do not have the bootstrap problems facing new enterprises: they start with a substantial market share, and so their marketing expenditure only needs to be enough to maintain it, or, if they are truly aggressive, to expand it at the edges. They don't need to find the cash to create a market, or to build market share, from zero. When mass market companies do launch innovations, like Toyota's Lexus luxury range, they look for substantially higher margins than their established products earn.

The second question may take pages to answer in a full-dress business plan, but at this stage a quick answer can be put together by counting all the money that must be spent or irrevocably promised before the product is launched; and adding all the money required to keep the business operating for one year, excepting only the variable product supply and marketing costs needed for the first year sales target. Pessimists might like to add a second year's business expenses when computing this sum.

To answer the third question:

▲ estimate the AAGM

▲ estimate the degree to which competitors can be inhibited from entering the market

▲ use Table 5.1 to compute a present value for the project and compare this to the answer to the second question.

The third question has now been answered: if the fraction of the AAGM that must be committed before the launch and to the launch budget is too high, the project should not be expected to make an appropriate financial return.

Established products

These rules cannot be applied directly to a proposal for a new version of a product with an established market share, because the majority of the marketing investment has, in such cases, already been made. The rule should still be true for the incremental margin that the new feature or the replacement product is targeted at. A decision to replace an existing product with a new model, or to extend an established product line must be based on an estimate of the difference that the new product will make. If the same number of sales, at the same margin, could have been gained without launching a new product, then the investment required by a new product would be impossible to justify. If, on the other hand, the established product was on the point of sinking without a trace, all of the expected sales post launch date can reasonably be credited to the new product. In every case it is going to come down to a matter of judgement supported by research.

Successful firms are those that judge correctly most of the time; some of the most successful, such as Hewlett–Packard and 3M, deliberately bias their judgement in favour of the new products and against the old ones. The majority of large publicly-held corporations in the English-speaking countries over the period since 1970 tended to overestimate the sales potential of their established product lines. For this and other reasons they under-invested in new products. When their optimistic expectations were dashed and their old product lines suffered serious losses of market share, many, perhaps a majority, of the major corporations simply abandoned the relevant market rather than investing sufficiently to stay in it. This improved their apparent returns on investment, but by reducing the investment rather than by increasing the return. The end result of the wide adoption of such policies of indefinite retrenchment are all too predictable. There was vast social disruption as large corporations reduced their staff in line with their narrowing ambitions. The Anglophone countries developed huge trade deficits as their high added value industries declined and their markets were taken over by imports. International currency markets were destabilised as vast amounts of cash, no longer productively invested by major corporations, were applied to speculation.

Corporate entrepreneurs will find, later in this book, some suggestions on preparing business cases that may persuade corporate managers to increase their level of new product investment, or at least to support some of the readers' favourite projects. The short-sighted behaviour of major corporations in the Anglophone countries in the 1980s and the early 1990s was only rarely the result of a deliberate decision to cause social chaos or to reduce the long term viability of their business. More often it was that they could neither see, nor were they told of, any worthwhile opportunities.

The people who get appointed to senior management positions in major public companies have usually been out of the front line for a considerable period, and to the extent that they have any vision of where the corporation should be heading, it is framed by their experiences of fifteen or twenty years before. Most of them can remember having their own good ideas suppressed or distorted, and though they suppress and distort the ideas that float up to them in their new, exalted positions they don't do so deliberately. Clear, well presented business cases supported by properly presented numbers will usually get a very favourable hearing.

End notes

1 Compass Airlines Ltd started operations in Australia in late 1991, following deregulation, and failed after approximately a year.

2 'Economic profit' is the money left after the normal return on the assets of the firm are deducted and so is the reward for entrepreneurship. In conventional accounting (and economics) the return on capital (that is, rent, interest and dividends) is taken as part of the fixed cost, but this assumes that the capital structure is known, which at the concept stage it isn't. Chapters 14 and 17 deal with this issue in greater depth.

3 The economist most noted for his contribution to the concepts of value-in-use as against value-in-exchange is J. R. Hicks.

4 Price and value sometimes rise together, as with an exclusive object bought by a wealthy individual. The buyer expects the benefits of owning the object as well as the esteem owing to one who can afford such an object.

5 Global positioning system, a military targeting system based on satellites, now available for civilian use as a location and direction-finding aid.

6 'Cohort' originally described a Roman military unit comparable to a modern battalion. The term is used correctly when it describes any well-defined statistical group.

7 The appropriate discount rate under uncertain conditions can be calculated using the equations of Dixit and Pindyck, described in more detail in Chapter 8.

Intellectual property

Property

Property is a social construct with a long history of development. The oldest form of property is personal property: the money in our purses, the clothes on our backs, and our essential tools of trade are all forms of personal property. Personal property is very largely ours to do what we want with; to use it, lose it, or give it away. The concept of personal property rights go back into the mists of ancient history: even Roman slaves, whose person could be bought and sold, could own personal property; when they saved enough money Roman law recognised their right to buy themselves from their owners. Personal property rights are recognised, if not always respected, in virtually every human culture.

'Real' (probably from the word 'royal') property, personal ownership of land, is a relatively recent invention. Before real property was invented, land was the common property of members of a community, tribe or clan, and managed according to traditional laws. Each member of the community would enjoy certain rights and some members enjoyed much more extensive rights than others, but few of these rights were exclusive, and there were many things that no one could do, including fence or sell part of the common land. When white settlers from England arrived in Australia they found that there was no one from whom they could buy land, and so they assumed, under the legal doctrine *terra nullius*, that no one owned it.

The origins of real property lie in the Norman conquest of north-western Europe in the tenth and eleventh centuries. When William the Norman killed Harald the Dane at the Battle of Hastings, the prize was England, and William had no intention of letting Harald's many relatives take any of it back. William

This chapter was prepared by Mr A. Tatlock, Bsc LLB MEI, Solicitor and Patent and Trade Mark Attorney of Melbourne, and was edited into its final form by the principal authors

could not afford to maintain a standing army to stop a Danish reconquest either, and so he instituted the feudal (as in 'fealty') system: William's main officers were made barons and given personal grants of land, which were then theirs and their heirs' to manage in return for promises of loyalty to William and his family and an obligation to raise an agreed number of soldiers to serve the king whenever the king should summon them. The barons could not manage their entire holdings on their own, so they made sub-grants to knights, some of whom made yet more sub-grants to squires.

All these grants, and the modern day real estate titles that descended from them, were and are conditional: title was always given subject to continuing conditions and can be revoked or modified if the holder breaches the conditions. When someone refers to 'my land' or erects a sign saying 'trespassers prosecuted' they are making statements that may not, legally, be nearly as forthright as they sound: real property is a legal creation, not a natural right. 'Ownership' of real property is by no means as clear cut a matter as ownership of clothes or hand tools. Libertarians and others might like to fantasise about a society where property rights are absolute, but modern Australia is not such a society and is unlikely to become one. Intellectual property rights are somewhat newer than rights in land, and they are hedged with many more conditions, but they arise from the same cause. A private right is granted because to do so is believed to advance the public good.

Intellectual property

From the fourteenth century or earlier the English monarch granted monopolies, often of staple commodities, such as salt, but also of luxuries, such as playing cards, in return for a capital payment. These monopolies caused popular discontent, both because they raised prices and because of the unpleasant people and methods the monopolists employed to suppress competitors. During the reign of Elizabeth, in the mid sixteenth century, Lord Cecil introduced the Monopoly System to limit abuse, but there was still discontent and, in 1628, parliament passed the Statute of Monopolies. This statute restricted the right of the crown to grant oppressive monopolies, while permitting it to grant monopolies for 'new manners of manufacture'. These monopolies were called 'Letters Patent' (or open letters) as they could be viewed on a public register. These Letters Patent were not, as now, for inventions made personally by the owner of the patent or the inventor from whom he obtained rights, but rather for the first person to bring the manufactures into England for use by the English. Two of the first patents granted were for methods of glass blowing and weaving, inventions imported from Belgium.

The traditional way in which authors, painters and musicians had been supported was by gifts from noble patrons, whose benevolence tended to be recognised in the flowery and elaborate dedications associated with the works.

TO THE RIGHT HONOURABLE THE EARL OF CHESTERFIELD

My Lord,

I have been lately informed, by the proprietor of the World, that two papers, in which my Dictionary is recommended to the public, were written by your Lordship. To be so distinguished is an honour, which, being very little accustomed to favours from the great, I know not well how to receive, or in what terms to acknowledge.

When, upon some slight encouragement, I first visited your Lordship, I was overpowered, like the rest of mankind, by the enchantment of your address, and could not forbear to wish that I might boast myself *Le vainqueur du vainqueur de la terre*; – that I might obtain that regard for which I saw the world contending; but I found my attendance so little encouraged that neither pride nor modesty would suffer me to continue it. When I had once addressed your Lordship in public I had exhausted all the art of pleasing which a retired and uncourtly scholar can possess. I had done all that I could, and no man is well pleased to have his all neglected, be it ever so little.

Seven years, my Lord, have now passed since I waited in your outward rooms, or was repulsed from your door; during which time I have been pushing on my work through difficulties, of which it is useless to complain, and have brought it at last to the verge of publication, without one act of assistance, one word of encouragement, or one smile of favour. Such treatment I did not expect, for I never had a Patron before.

'The shepherd in Virgil grew at last acquainted with Love, and found him a native of the rocks.'

Is not a Patron, my Lord, one who looks with unconcern on one struggling for life in the water, and when he has reached ground, encumbers him with help? The notice which you have been pleased to take of my labours, had it been early, had been kind; but it has been delayed until I am indifferent, and cannot enjoy it; till I am solitary, and cannot impart it; till I am known, and do no want it. I hope it is no very cynical asperity not to confess obligations where no benefit has been received, or to be unwilling that the public should consider me as owing that to a Patron, which Providence has enabled me to do for myself.

Having carried on my work thus far with so little obligation to any favourer of learning, I shall not be disappointed though I should conclude it, if less be possible, with less; for I have been awakened from that dream of hope, in which I once boasted myself with so much exaltation, my Lord,

Your Lordship's most humble, most obedient servant,

SAM. JOHNSON

Figure 6.1 Samuel Johnson's observations about patronage led to the reform of the copyright law

Inventors had been encouraged by gifts and prizes. The patronage system began to break down when literary works became useful rather than purely entertaining, and Dr Johnson, whose attempts to gain patronage for his dictionary led to a humiliating rebuff, was awarded a special pension, paid for out of taxes, instead. Johnson's grant did not inaugurate a universal system of literary pensions, but it did increase the pressure for reform of the copyright laws.

Copyright, as is now generally accepted, can be considered to be first recognised in the Statute of Anne in 1709. Prior to this there were various forms of protection, but the protection applied more to the printers of books than to authors and the measures were intended to give effect to the crown power of censorship. Prior to the introduction of printing, in the late fifteenth century, books were copied more or less at will, but when printing was introduced this was seen by the crown to be a most important development and, very soon thereafter, a king's printer was appointed.

The Company of Stationers, which was originally the guild covering copiers of books and related material, became the guild of printers as well, and therefore asserted a degree of control over printing, and who printed what. As the guild represented printers and publishers it tended to be very sensitive to its members' rights and rather less so to the rights of authors. At the same time the crown granted patent monopolies to certain printers giving them the exclusive right to produce particular books and particular classes of book. These patents were left intact by the Statute of Monopolies. It was only the Statute of Anne and a codifying statute of 1790 which led to vesting copyright in the author and allowed authors an alternative to the tyranny of patronage.

The United Kingdom Copyright Act of 1911 finally codified copyright law and this Act was introduced in Australia as an attachment to the Australian Copyright Act of 1911. The first British Patents Act, which can be considered modern and on which the present British and Australian Acts are based, was passed in 1883. The Australian colonies all had Patents Acts and in 1906 the first Commonwealth Patents Act was passed as the states had given up the constitutional power to legislate for industrial property.

Whenever legislation for the protection of intellectual property is proposed, many economists argue that such laws would raise the cost of knowledge and slow down the adoption of inventions. A number of modern economists still argue for a system of cash grants to replace copyright and patents. History since 1770 suggests that any damage the copyright and patent systems do to an economy are easily overcome, and many economists are prepared to argue that the patent and copyright systems, on balance, are forces for economic growth rather than against it.

Over the last one and a half centuries, copyrights and patents have been joined by a series of other forms of intellectual property, each created by law with the deliberate purpose of encouraging some activity by giving certain people potentially valuable rights, but no claims on the taxpayer. Most entrepreneurs rely, to a greater or lesser extent, on the legal protection of their intellectual property. There are many examples where a slipshod approach to intellectual property protection has cost an entrepreneur very dearly.

The entrepreneur's property

Traditional property rights are fully exclusive: each baron was allowed to grind the faces of the poor within his own domain, but not in any one else's. The money in my purse or wallet is mine, and you can't spend it. In modern economic jargon, traditional property rights are 'rival', if one person has control of the property, then no one else can use it without that person's permission. Property rights are valuable because they may be used to generate an income, as when a landlord permits a tenant to occupy certain property in return for the regular payment of rent.

Some entrepreneurial property is exclusive, but much of it is not. The design of a new piece of equipment, or the plan for a new service, is not changed by being copied, but the value of these plans and designs to the entrepreneur can be drastically reduced if they become available to others. The law is a very uncertain shield for an entrepreneur, particularly an entrepreneur who neglects certain precautions. In England a hacker dialled in to a computer system and copied a firm's confidential client list, which was then published. The offender was charged with stealing a few milliwatt hours of electricity, since nothing else could be proved to be missing. The victim might have been able to sue the hacker for breach of confidential information but the success of such a suit might depend on the way the material was held in the computer; and in any case, the hacker lacked the means to pay significant damages and/or costs.

From the start of an entrepreneurial venture, information starts building up, information which is only valuable as long as it is private to the entrepreneur. An entrepreneur has an idea and gathers elementary marketing information about it. Even if the information is unfavourable, suggesting that the resulting product would appeal to very few people and only then at a derisively low price, this is valuable information to the extent that other entrepreneurs could use it to avoid the same blind alley. In cases where the research information reveals that the market is enormous and the value huge, the value to the entrepreneur, as long as the information stays a secret, is also very large.

Once an enterprise launches a new product the details of the manufacturing or delivery processes, and particularly the records of problems encountered and their solutions, are valuable as long as they are exclusive. The names of early customers, the prices that they paid and the special terms that they may have been offered, and the names of active prospects should be protected by an entrepreneur because they would be useful to a rival. Commercial details, such as internal costings, supplier and distributor agreements, promotional plans, customer complaint histories and the like are also more valuable when they are exclusive.

Sometimes information must be published and yet an entrepreneur wants to retain certain rights over it. Patents are granted on condition that a full specification is lodged on the public record, for example, while new entertainment, user manuals, innovative designs and the like can't earn anything without being made widely available, and it is seldom easy to separate potential rivals from paying customers.

Entrepreneurs' rights over these kinds of information are conditional, not absolute, where they exist at all. Lawmakers attempt to balance the interests of entrepreneurs against those of society as a whole and so, for example, ex-employees cannot be bound to a lifetime vow of silence.[1] Information may have some legal protection, but, by and large, ideas do not. No one is allowed to assert any rights over the idea of publishing romantic novels, for example, but Mills & Boon Ltd are allowed to protect their trade marks and the contents of the works they publish.

A sound business plan should take account of the intellectual property that both the planning and execution processes will generate, and include appropriate measures for protecting the entrepreneur's rights in this property.

Forms of intellectual property

Table 6.1 lists the types of intellectual property recognised by Australian law.

In the rest of this chapter each type of intellectual property will be explained with information that an entrepreneur should find helpful when deciding which of the various options for protecting intellectual property to use.

Copyright

How do you get copyright?

Copyright is created automatically by creating an original literary or artistic work, including a new technical manual or computer program. When publishing such a work it is advisable to ensure that its copyright is respected by including the following line close to the title:

© *Copyright [Name of person(s) or firm(s) who own copyright] [year of first publication], [year of a revised publication]*

What is protected?

Copyright protects the results of creative endeavour, meaning the sequence of words or notes or the form of a literary work, musical composition or work of art. The ideas expressed in the work are specifically excluded from protection, and so someone who independently produces a new work expressing the same ideas but in substantially different words, note sequences or form is free to publish it.

It must be stressed that copyright is what it says it is, it is not a monopoly protection, it is a protection against copying. Thus, unless the work has been

Table 6.1

Property type	Protects ...	Rights obtained	Duration
Copyright	Original literary or artistic works, including diagrams and technical manuals	Copying for commercial purpose prohibited except under licence from copyright owner	Author's life plus fifty years
Patent	Inventions: new products and processes including chemical and biochemical compounds and new micro-organisms	Manufacturing and/or use prohibited except under licence from patent holder	Twenty years from filing complete application
Petty patent	As for Patent	As for Patent	Six years from filing
Registered design	The appearance of a manufactured product	Monopoly protection for the same or similar shape except under licence from the owner	Sixteen years from filing date
Trade mark	Manufacturers' marks of origin	Injunctive relief against infringers and damages, if confusion and damage proved	Perpetual
Registered trade mark	Manufacturers' marks of origin	Use of same or similar marks by other manufacturers prohibited; import and sale of imitations prohibited; violators may be sued for injunction and damages	Previously seven years, renewable for fourteen year periods, now ten years continuously renewable
Plant breeder's right	New plants	Protects against commercial exploitation, private use is not breach, purchasers can use seeds for own use	Twenty-five years trees and vines; twenty years other
Circuit layout	Physical design of electronic circuit for use on printed circuit board or integrated circuit	Owner can reproduce drawings, produce integrated circuits and exploit design	Ten years
Trade Practices Act	Visible product attributes	Deceptive sale of similar products may lead to prosecution; right to damages for losses caused by such deception	Perpetual
Common Law 'passing off'	Tangible product attributes commonly associated with a manufacturer or service provider	Right to injunctive relief and damages in respect of deceptive use of similar attributes on other manufacturers' products	Perpetual
Common Law 'trade secrets'	Information communicated in confidence to employee, supplier or customer	Right to injunctive relief and damages from both recipient and communicator	As long as the secret has not become generally available.

available to the alleged copyist, there can be no breach of copyright. For example, two persons with cameras can stand side by side and take effectively identical pictures and each will have copyright in his or her own picture. If a third person copies one of these pictures, he or she infringes the copyright in the picture concerned but not the other and so, for infringement to be proved, it is necessary to show which picture was copied.

If a court believes that the new work has been developed from the old, even if they are superficially very different, infringement can be found. Some courts, particularly in the United States, have found, where the alleged infringer has had an opportunity to see, or more often to hear, a copyright work, there can be 'unconscious' copying. In general terms translation into another language is not considered sufficiently creative to overturn the original copyright; this, when applied to computer software, has created a lawyers' bonanza.

When assigning copyright great care is needed: such assignments must be done in writing.[2] A contract to produce material which is the subject of copyright is not, in itself, sufficient to transfer the copyright to the purchaser, it will simply give an implied licence to use the material. To protect against subsequent disputes it is essential that, where an entrepreneur makes an agreement with an unrelated party to develop copyright material, such as a user manual or a computer program, there should be, as part of the agreement, an obligation on the contractor to execute an assignment when asked to do so.

> *The purchase of a copyrighted work does not transfer copyright to the buyer*

It is important to realise that the purchase of a work which is the subject of copyright does not transfer copyright. If you buy a painting, this does not give you the right to use it on Christmas cards; such use is an infringement of copyright. There can also be an infringement if a video or film is made in an area where copyright works are displayed, if the works are placed on film more than incidentally. A clip for television which shows copyright material could infringe copyright.

Although there is no registration system for copyright material in Australia, there has been very little dispute about copyright ownership, although any person alleging infringement must be prepared to prove ownership if this is challenged. This is particularly important in the light of the way devolution of title of copyright material works.

Patents

What are patents for and what is an invention?

Patents are granted for inventions, and are basically industrial in application.

As we mentioned above, the definition of an invention in the Statute of Monopolies included 'any manner of new manufacture' and this is still the definition in the current Patents Act. This actually has three elements which are considered, and some persons say there are four.

Manufacture

This can be a product itself, the method of making a product or any other part of the manufacturing process. To a degree the definition of a manufacture can be a matter of statute law (for example, dealing with human bodies — both alive and dead) and otherwise is decided by the courts. The Australian courts have been liberal in their definition and, on occasions, have made decisions which, *de facto*, changed what the Patent Office treats as an invention, although some such decisions are overturned by higher courts. One such recent case was an application by IBM to do with a computer program to draw curves. This would normally not be considered to be inventive since there was no end result other than a curve on a screen; but it was held by Mr Justice Burchett of the Federal Court that it was not clear there was no invention and he directed the Patent Office to accept the application. This has lead to a general easing in the concept of invention but this easing may be limited if a case goes to appeal.

Newness

This is critical for the entrepreneur. An invention must not be disclosed before a patent application is filed. Too often, in their initial enthusiasm, inventors publish their invention and then find that they cannot get a valid patent. As we mentioned above, part of the contract with the crown at the time of the Statute of Monopolies was that something new had to be brought to the kingdom. If the invention has been published, there is no reason to give monopoly protection to it in return for publication.

Newness has a second head: the invention must not have been published by anyone else. This is international newness. Searches can be done to find out whether an invention is new but these can be very expensive and it is impossible to be certain that such a search has not missed an obscure but relevant example. Provided reasonable steps have been taken, it is often best in practice to assume newness.

Invention

This is usually established after considering whether the invention is 'obvious' in the light of what has been known and used before and to the use which can be made of the prior art base by a person 'skilled in the art'. This is a most difficult matter when patents are contested and the courts consider each case on its merits. Patent attorneys can usually give a good indication as to whether the Patent Office will permit an application to proceed to grant but this does not mean that a court would find invention. Indeed the Patent Office is obliged, if there is any doubt, to accept an application and to grant a patent as it is always open to the courts to determine whether there is an invention. If the Patent

Office refuses an application, then the rights of the applicant may have been destroyed without the opportunity of full consideration.

Utility (or usefulness)

Lack of utility is a ground for revocation of a patent and is regarded as more significant by barristers in contested cases than by patent attorneys. In patents, utility has a rather special definition and relates to whether the invention does what it says it does rather than whether it is indeed useful from a commercial point of view.

Other considerations

If there is any doubt, we suggest that an entrepreneur should lodge a patent application. It is conceivable that more money has been made from applications which are not able to be granted or patents which would be held by the courts to be invalid than from valid patents. An applicant can licence an application which never goes to grant and can keep the application alive for a number of years, possibly equal to the commercial life of the invention.

Further, the existence of a patent application can act as a deterrent to possible copiers or infringers. There are three types of these:

▲ The first are the cautious or over-cautious. These people take positive steps to make sure that they do not infringe. If they see a patent application number, they will immediately abandon plans to produce a potentially infringing product.

▲ The second are the prudent who would rather not infringe. These people would take advice before entering on a course which may be infringing and, as patent applications are not published for eighteen months from initial filing, would often take some time to decide whether or not to copy an invention. This time can be most valuable to an applicant who markets the new product vigorously.

▲ The third are the cowboys who will copy and be damned. There is little you can do about these, but they are by far the smallest group, at least in Australia. (Politicians and law enforcement agencies in lesser-developed and developing countries often regard patents and other intellectual property as tools of neocolonial oppression, 'more honoured in the breach'. The United States has, in recent years, been a strident advocate of intellectual property rights in international forums, but through the nineteenth and well into the twentieth centuries the United States treated free access to foreigners' intellectual property as the birthright of every American. Even in modern times, the United States courts have, in deciding between competing claims by foreigners and Americans, left the foreign claimant feeling severely aggrieved in many instances.)

How do you get a patent?

Patents are granted by the Australian Intellectual Property Organisation (AIPO) (of which the Patent Office is a part) and corresponding offices throughout the world. Australian patent law provides for two types of patents, *standard patents* and *petty patents*. Generally petty patents are considered to be of little use, except in specific circumstances which will be described below. Our discussion of petty patents follows the subsection on standard patents.

Standard patents

In Australia, an inventor or a person having rights from the inventor, may file an application with either a provisional or a complete specification with the AIPO and, if with a provisional specification, must lodge an application with a complete specification within twelve months. In most countries other than Australia it is not possible to file provisional applications although the concept was introduced in the United States in 1995 and *de facto* applications (which are complete specifications without claims) can be filed in the United Kingdom.

There are two international conventions which are important in this area. The first, the International Convention for the Protection of Industrial Property, permits applicants to maintain the priority of their home application provided applications are filed within twelve months of the home application. The second is the Patent Cooperation Treaty (PCT) which enables a single filing to give notional protection in most countries of the world (with the exception of some Asian countries, notably Taiwan, and some South American countries) for a further period of eighteen months before it is necessary to file in individual countries (or 'enter the National phase', in the language of the Treaty). The PCT can be used in association with the International Convention which means a PCT application can be lodged up to twelve months after the first home application.

The PCT allows an inventor to avoid the cost of overseas patent applications until a firm decision has been made to exploit the invention commercially in foreign as well as domestic markets.

The steps leading to the grant of patents vary widely: some countries carry out substantial searches and carry out a stringent examination; others effectively rubber stamp each application and leave it to the courts to adjudicate on its validity. Australia is in an intermediate situation: patent applications are examined but the examiners normally search only the Australian records; although if the same invention has been filed elsewhere they will examine the search reports of the other countries; or if an application was based on a PCT application, they will make use of the extensive PCT search.

Examination does not commence until requested by the applicant, either on his or her own initiative or after recept of a Direction to Seek Examination from the Patent Office. Such directions are usually issued about two years after the lodgement of the complete application and must be responded to within six

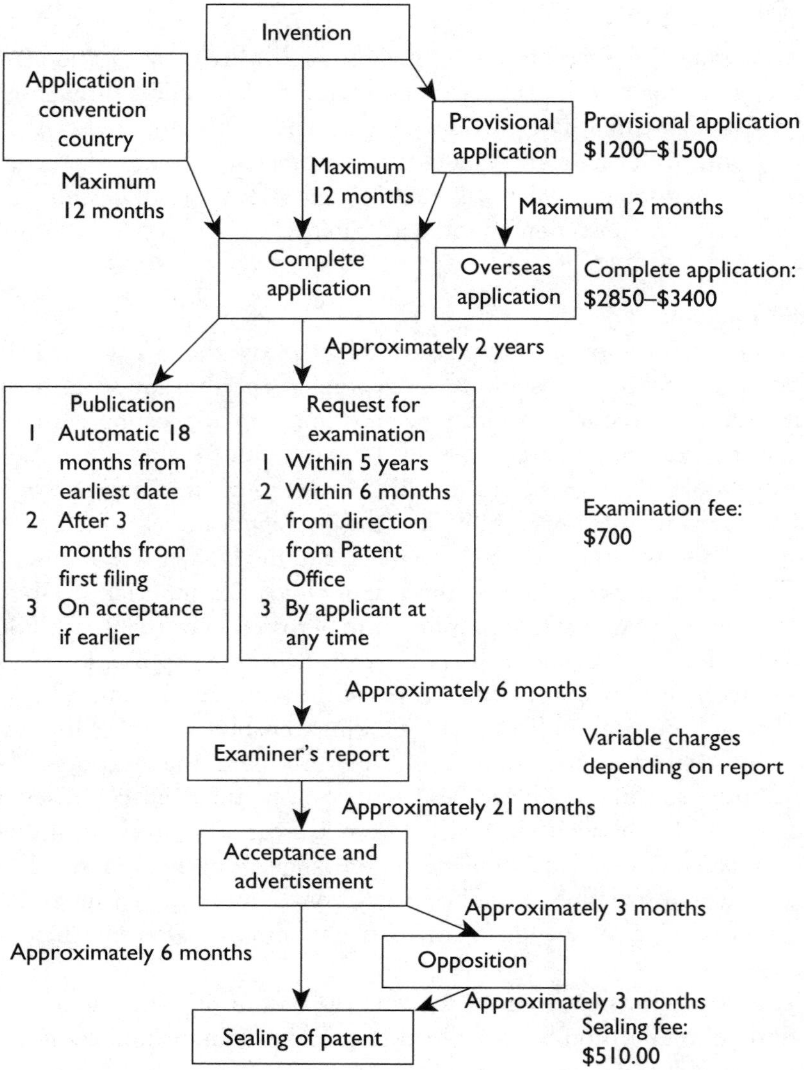
Invention
Application in convention country
Maximum 12 months
Maximum 12 months
Provisional application
Provisional application $1200–$1500
Maximum 12 months
Complete application
Overseas application
Complete application: $2850–$3400
Approximately 2 years
Publication
1 Automatic 18 months from earliest date
2 After 3 months from first filing
3 On acceptance if earlier
Request for examination
1 Within 5 years
2 Within 6 months from direction from Patent Office
3 By applicant at any time
Examination fee: $700
Approximately 6 months
Examiner's report
Variable charges depending on report
Approximately 21 months
Acceptance and advertisement
Approximately 3 months
Approximately 6 months
Opposition
Approximately 3 months
Sealing of patent
Sealing fee: $510.00

These estimates are indicative and the actual charges can vary substantially from case to case

Continuation/renewal fees are payable from the third year and annually thereafter — the fees start at $215 at the end of the third year and rise to $1020 at the end of the ninteenth year

© Copyright A. Tatlock & Associates, January 1996 — reproduced by permission

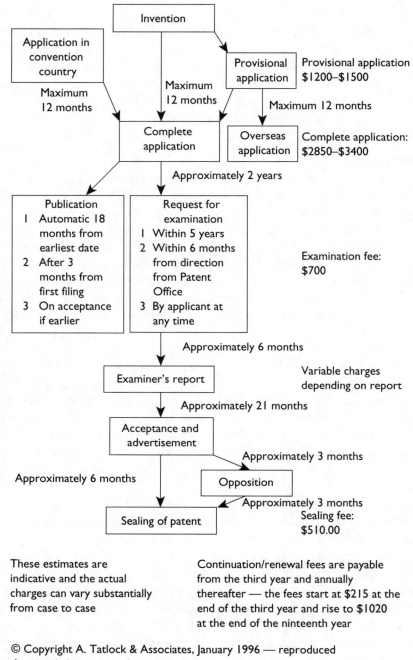

Figure 6.2 Patent application flow chart

months. After receipt of the examiner's report, the applicant has a maximum period of twenty-one months within which to obtain acceptance of the application, although after twelve months extension fees are payable.

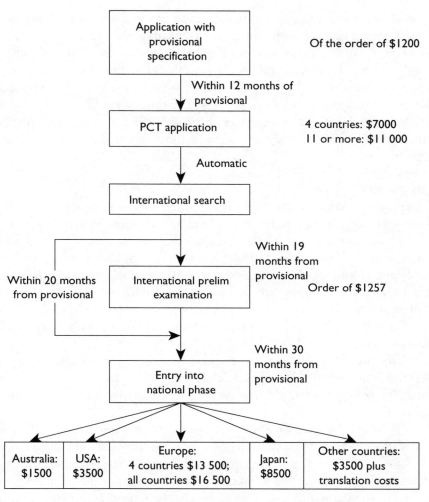

| | | Application with provisional specification | Of the order of $1200 |

Within 12 months of provisional

PCT application — 4 countries: $7000 / 11 or more: $11 000

Automatic

International search

Within 20 months from provisional — International prelim examination — Within 19 months from provisional / Order of $1257

Within 30 months from provisional

Entry into national phase

| Australia: $1500 | USA: $3500 | Europe: 4 countries $13 500; all countries $16 500 | Japan: $8500 | Other countries: $3500 plus translation costs |

Figure 6.3 The stages of a PCT application

Examination is in respect of both form and function. The examiner asks whether the specification meets the requirements of the Act:

▲ *form* — has the application been made in accordance with the requirements of the Act?

▲ *novelty* — is the subject matter new?

▲ *inventiveness* — is the subject matter obvious or not?

Examiners are restricted in the way they take objections as to obviousness and generally this aspect is left to the courts. Once the application has the

Intellectual property

approval of the Patent Office the application is accepted and this is advertised so that any person interested can oppose the grant of the patent.

The maximum life of a patent is twenty years from the date of filing the complete application and annuities are payable before the end of the third year from the lodgement of the complete application until the end of the nineteenth year. If these annuities are not paid, the application/patent lapses. Most patents are allowed to lapse after about eight years, either because they have not been commercially successful or the invention that they describe has been superseded in the market.

Petty patents

Petty patents were introduced with the intention of having protection for lesser forms of inventions than standard patents but the requirements for novelty and inventiveness are identical to those for standard patents so the basic concept was not realised. Petty patents cannot be lodged with provisional specifications and the requirements for a petty patent specification are the same as for a complete specification but with a limitation that there can only be three claims. The cost of lodging a petty patent application can be greater than for lodging an application for a standard patent with a provisional specification.

Petty patent applications are examined relatively shortly after lodgement and there is no need for the applicant to request examination. Searching is done but this is generally relatively shallow and the petty patent is granted without opposition.

The original period of a petty patent is twelve months from the date of grant with one extension to the end of six years from the date of lodgement.

The main value of a petty patent can be where there is a standard patent application and an infringement occurs before the grant of the standard patent. Under these circumstances, a petty patent can be lodged as a divisional of the standard patent application with the claims of the petty patent directed at the infringer. The petty patent can be granted quickly and, if necessary, legal proceedings commenced. Effectively in all other circumstances it is better to lodge an application with a provisional specification and to follow this with a standard complete application.

Do I need help?

Yes.

Patent law is complex and securing a patent is quite expensive. Figure 6.2 shows the steps needed to gain a patent, the approximate time each step takes, and the approximate cost if the work is undertaken by an Australian patent attorney.

It is relatively easy for a novice to prepare a provisional specification which, under the Act 'must describe the invention'. There are often, however, substantial changes made to an invention between the time when the concept is first set out and the time when the novel product reaches the market; and there are often substantial differences between the description of an invention at the time the provisional specification is lodged, and its description at the time when the complete specification must be submitted. A patent attorney will attempt to draft a provisional specification in such a way that even if there are changes to the invention, the complete specification will be 'fairly based' on the provisional specification, and will retain the same priority date. If the complete specification cannot be shown to be properly based on the provisional specification, the complete specification may be forced to take the date on which it was filed. If there was any publication of the invention by the applicant or any other person between the date of the provisional application and the new date on the complete application, such publication may be used to destroy the patent.

Some patent attorneys have little difficulty in taking over the management of patent applications where the inventor has filed a provisional without their help while others may not wish to act for such an applicant when a complete specification and application are to be prepared. Of course, no patent attorney would ever take responsibility if an application failed because of a fault in a provisional specification prepared by an applicant.

An applicant who prepares his or her own complete specification is most unwise. The Act states that a 'complete specification must describe the invention fully, including the best method known to the applicant of performing the invention; and ... end with a claim or claims defining the invention.' There are two completely separate aspects here:

▲ The description must be full. This is so that an interested skilled party can duplicate the invention without having to make an invention. This goes to the historical basis of granting patents: the patentee must put into the public knowledge details of the invention for which he or she is granted monopoly protection.

▲ The invention must be defined by the claims which are part of the specification. These are single sentence statements and for the patent to be infringed, the infringement must lie clearly within the wording of at least one of the claims. It is thus critically important that the claims be in the best possible form as they may well have to be scrutinised and interpreted by a court.

A standard patent may have a large number of claims and, if well drafted, these will cover all the practical ways of applying the invention. A set of well-drafted claims minimises the possibility that an imitator could avoid infringement by making relatively minor changes to the patented product or process. It is also important that all aspects of the invention be claimed as the claims are not interrelated, as far as the courts are concerned. Should some, or even most of the claims are held to be invalid or irrelevant in a particular case, infringement of a remaining claim or claims can still be found.

How much does it cost?

The costs of obtaining a patent or a petty patent can vary widely as, to a major extent, the charges made by an Australian patent attorney are time based.

The cost of an application with a provisional specification is shown in Figure 6.2 as between $1200 and $1500. Figure 6.2 describes a relatively simple case and the costs shown are based on the fees charged by one patent attorney. Some patent attorneys charge substantially more and would normally quote as much as $2000. The charge includes the preparation of the specification, and drawings if any, any amendments as a result of comments from the applicant and the filing fee. It also ensures that the application is on the attorney's records and reminders will be forwarded near the end of the twelve months life of the application, often at nine and eleven months.

The preparation and filing of the complete application is the most expensive single step of an Australian application, being of the order of $3500. This will almost invariably have drawings and takes substantially more time than the preparation of the provisional specification. The specification must be full and drafting a good set of claims can often require substantial time and effort. The filing fee is also substantially higher than the fee for a provisional application.

If overseas applications are to be lodged at this time, a decision must be made as to whether to go on a country by country basis, or by way of the PCT. The PCT is, at best, a delaying step. It does not limit overall costs but defers the date by which they must be paid. This gives time for income to flow from the invention or for a decision to be made that the invention is not commercially viable.

The costs of overseas application can vary widely but as a rule of thumb the costs will be of the order of $3500 to $4000 per country plus the costs of translation. Costs in Japan have been increasing rapidly, quite apart from exchange rate movements, and tend to be substantially higher than the average, as are costs in Scandinavian countries. Protection in Europe can be by way of the European Patent Convention under which examination is done centrally and identical patents granted in all designated countries. As an indication, filing in Europe designating four countries is of the order of $14 000 and designating all the members of the convention about $16 500.

Entrepreneurs should remember that the cost of filing is usually about half the total cost of being granted a patent and there will, in all cases, be substantial further costs over the following two to three years.

In Australia, there are three further costs:

▲ lodging a Request for Examination, which is normally about two years after the lodgement of the complete application, at 1996 prices will cost about $700

▲ the cost of satisfying the Patent Office that the invention is good subject matter for a patent and of meeting various formalities, which run from about $300 to substantial amounts if there are difficulties

▲ the sealing fee of $510.

There are, in Australia and most overseas countries, ongoing renewal fees. In Australia these start at the end of the third year after the complete application and are paid annually. The first renewal costs $215 and the one at the end of the nineteenth year $1020 (at 1996 rates). Most other countries have annual renewals, although the year of first payment can vary widely and can be based on the filing date or grant. The United States and New Zealand have fees which are paid at greater intervals.

Australian petty patents have fewer fees and filing will cost in the order of $2200 for a normal case. There is no examination fee but there is an examiner's report and in straightforward cases the cost of the response to this could be as low as $300, but this could be substantially more if the objections are serious. There is no sealing fee and only one renewal (extension of term) and the fee for this is paid within twelve months of grant and is $625 (1996 rate). The petty patent expires six years after the date of the application.

When does protection start?

The protection of a patent before sealing is a complex matter. Newness is a precondition for the grant of a patent so any publication of the invention before an application is filed destroys the validity of the application on the grounds that it is no longer new. However, once the application is filed publication will not retrospectively damage newness, and so it is quite reasonable to publish the invention and license it or get it on the market as soon as the application is filed.

However, immediately after filing there is no recourse against infringers. Only once the application has been published (normally for a standard patent in eighteen months from the earliest date; or, if requested, three months after the complete application has been put on file; and for a petty patent, on grant), and an infringer is made aware of the existence of the application, then damages or account of profits can accrue.

An action for infringement cannot be commenced until a patent is granted. It is here that the petty patent comes into its own. Because a petty patent can be granted quickly, where there is an infringement it is often worth while preparing a petty patent as a divisional of a standard patent application. Such an application can have claims directed particularly at the infringement without the need to consider the broader aspects since these will be protected by the standard patent when it is eventually granted. There is little or no benefit in lodging a petty patent application before an infringement occurs as one does not know the best form of claim until an infringer markets a patented product or uses a patented process.

What happens if someone infringes a patent?

Infringement only occurs when an imitator's product or process can be shown to be properly described by at least one of a patent's claims. If you believe that someone is making a product or using a process for which you hold patent rights you should consult a patent attorney or a solicitor.

Patent attorneys can consider the alleged infringement in the light of your claim, as can some solicitors, but most will recommend that the matter be put to counsel. If it is agreed that there appears to be infringement, it is usual to write to the infringer bringing the infringement to their attention, requesting that it cease and often stating that action will be taken without further notice.

Such a letter of demand serves three purposes. It may lead to settlement of the dispute but, if not, it ensures a positive date for damages or an account of profits. Also, if it is necessary to start litigation then this can be done without further notice. Courts do not like litigation to be commenced without the infringer being given an opportunity to cease infringement.

If proceedings are to be commenced, these can normally be taken in the Federal Court or the state Supreme Court although, with cross vesting, more junior courts can be used. *Prima facie*, these would be cheaper but because the judges (and even in extreme cases the magistrates) are likely to have little experience in the area, we do not recommend it. Court proceedings are expensive. To get to the first Directions Hearing in the Federal Court is likely to cost, in a simple case, at least $5000 and if the case is run through a single Justice and then to Appeal of the order of at least $80 000 and possibly much more than this. Litigation should be avoided if at all possible.

If the proceedings are outside Australia, not only does one have to bear the additional costs of travel and local attorney's fees, there can often be a feeling that the local party will enjoy a 'home ground advantage'.[3] This risk is not sufficient to automatically prevent the defence of a patent overseas, but the expenses are likely to be very high and such a case should only be launched after a very careful consideration of the value of a successful outcome.

In Australia and in many common law countries, but generally not the United States, the successful party can expect to receive costs, but these are often only a third to a half of the money that is actually spent and, since they are often discretionary there is no guarantee of even this partial compensation. Even winners may find that the damages and/or the account of profits that they actually receive are often very much less than the money that they have spent. No one should assume that the gains that they may achieve from litigation are in any way equivalent to the profit which they could have earned by marketing the invention.

In general terms, unless there is a good legal reason, such as a condition in a license agreement, for having to take an action, it is often far better to try and reach an agreement with the infringer.

Other values of patents

Quite apart from the value of having one's own patents, patents can be of great value to entrepreneurs. Why re-invent the wheel?

A search of the patent records will reveal substantial information about what has been done before. Quite apart from informing the entrepreneur what he or she can't do, because there is a subsisting patent or application, the complete specification of a patent or patent application must include 'the best method known to the applicant of performing the invention'. This means, first, if one can find a good invention that has not been commercialised, and in respect of which the patent or patent application has lapsed, one is well on the way to getting a product without the work needed to start from scratch. Second, it means that entrepreneurs can find out what their competitors are doing and this can lead to 'spring boarding', rapid development of superior products and processes to the benefit of the public and the entrepreneur.

Registered design

What can be registered?

In law, a design refers to the appearance of an article and can relate to one or more of the shape, pattern, configuration or ornamentation of the article. It does not protect the principles of manufacture or operation of an artefact: if these are to be protected at all, they must be protected by patents. A design does not extend to two dimensional impressions which are covered by copyright.

How do you get one?

A design is registered by lodging representations of the design, normally drawings or photographs, with the Designs Office (part of the AIPO) or the equivalent offices overseas. The actual forms are usually simple, although in the United States a specification similar to a patent specification (although simpler) must be filed. In the United States, the protection granted is, in fact, a design patent; this may give some functional protection in certain cases.

Patent attorneys are available to help with the lodgement of designs for registration, but many designers have found it convenient to lodge their designs with the Design Office directly. As with any form of statutory protection, there are aspects where knowledge can be useful.

How much does it cost?

Figure 6.4 sets out the steps, time scales and costs of design registration for a straightforward submission by a patent attorney. If the application is prepared by a patent attorney the cost will be of the order of $575, which includes the filing fee of $90, plus the costs of the representations necessary. If filing is urgent, the application can, in many cases, be filed with informal representations, such as Polaroid photographs.

The only other costs before registration are those incurred in responding to any objections taken by the examiner. The total life of a design can be sixteen years with renewal being due within twelve months of registration ($230) at the end of six years from filing ($390) and at the end of eleven years from filing ($450) — all based on 1996 fee scales. Each of these estimates includes patent attorney's fees.

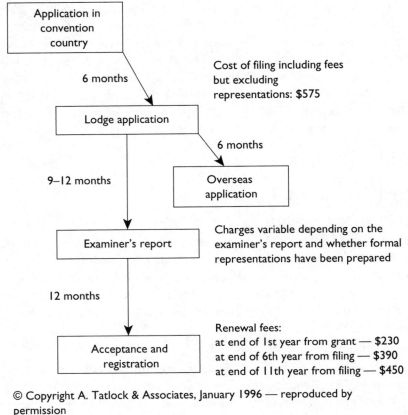

© Copyright A. Tatlock & Associates, January 1996 — reproduced by permission

Figure 6.4 The stages in applying for design registration

What happens if someone infringes a registered design?

A design is infringed if the design or a fraudulent or obvious imitation is applied in Australia to an article; by importation of an article which, if made in Australia, would be an infringement; or if articles under the above categories are sold or offered for sale or hired or offered for hire.

Whether or not there is an infringing use of a registered design is, today, considered by a person with a instructed eye, normally the judge trying the action. Previously other tests, the 'man on the Clapham omnibus' or the 'person with a skilled eye' were used, but both had difficulties. The ordinary man could find it hard to differentiate between quite different articles, the skilled man could differentiate between almost identical articles. It will be appreciated that the test as to whether or not there is infringement is subjective and is largely based, not only on the differences between the two articles but also the relative similarity of the prior art. In a crowded area the difference must be much less then in an area where there is little other material.

If you believe that a registered design has been infringed you should consult a patent attorney or a solicitor, who will probably recommend writing to the infringer and demanding that infringement cease. The demand will also often request several further actions, such as the destruction of infringing articles, and the payment of damages and costs. This notification also acts as a starting date for damages if the infringer can show he or she was an innocent infringer (under the Act, the onus is placed on infringers to have taken all reasonable steps to ascertain whether a monopoly in the design existed).

If writing to the infringer does not produce the desired result, it is open for the proprietor to institute proceedings for infringement. As with the other areas of intellectual property, actions are often taken in the Federal Court but can be taken in state Supreme Courts and even lower courts, if required. Normally, an owner of an infringed design seeks an injunction and either damages or an account of profits made by the infringer.

Trade marks and registered trade marks
What is a trade mark and how do I get one?

A trade mark is any sign used to distinguish the goods and services of a trader from those of other traders. Simply by adopting a particular word or device (or even a sound or a scent, as described below) as a symbol to distinguish goods or services, it becomes a trade mark. Of course, it may not be a very 'good' trade mark and may not be able to be protected.

In the common law countries, Australia, the United States, the United Kingdom and New Zealand, as well as in most countries whose legal systems are based on the British tradition, the first user of the trade mark has unassailable rights although a concurrent user may also develop rights. In the civil code countries, generally Europe and Japan, rights go to the first applicant for registration although the first user will normally be entitled to continue to use the mark.

Historically, a trade mark was a word, a number of words or a device, or a combination of word(s) and a device; but under the recently proclaimed (1 January 1996) Trade Marks Act 1995, the definition can relate to anything which can be set down in writing, including as well as the more historical forms of trade marks, such things as sounds and scents (although it is difficult to imagine a verbal description of a scent that could enable anyone other than a highly skilled person to recognise the scent, even if the scent itself was distinctive to an unskilled nose).

A good trade mark should be distinctive and preferably should be inherently distinctive at the time of adoption, but on use, even inherently non-distinctive marks can develop a secondary meaning and become distinctive. Most people would have little difficulty in associating Great Western with champagne or IBM with computers. Under the common law, and under the new Trade Marks Act, acceptance by the market place is most important to marks, while under the older Trade Marks Acts, a registrable trade mark had to meet somewhat artificial requirements.

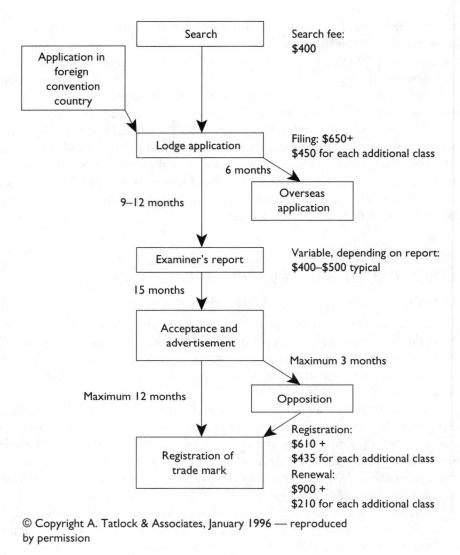

© Copyright A. Tatlock & Associates, January 1996 — reproduced
by permission

Figure 6.5 Stages in registering a trade mark

Historically, the statutory protection of trade marks developed from the common law action for passing off. Tradesmen and merchants with a good reputation marked their products to identify their origin, and customers, relying on the trader's reputation, sought such products out. A common law rule developed giving traders certain rights over the marks they placed on their products, and marks generally used in association with a particular trader's products. Traders who could show that their particular marks were recognised and respected in the market place could take action to obtain an injunction against someone who copied or imitated these marks, gaining a 'free ride' on the original trader's reputation. A passing off action succeeded when the aggrieved trader could show that purchasers were deceived as to the source or provenance of the product; and that the aggrieved trader was damaged by loss of profits and/or reputation. Passing off, as an action, is still alive and well and, on some occasions, is the only way by which legal recourse against copying can be obtained. The usual remedies are the grant of an injunction and damages or an account of profits.

The first Merchandising Marks Act, an endeavour to codify the law of passing off, was passed in England in 1862. In 1875, the Trade Marks Registration Act was passed. These Acts introduced a definition of a trade mark — broadly, that such that the mark must be capable of distinguishing the goods of the owner — and they set out specific classes of words which could be registered as trade marks. Some classes of words and marks outside these definitions could not be registered regardless of the amount of use and acquired distinctiveness (for example Oxford for dictionaries). Others could only be registered if the mark had acquired distinctiveness through use (generally descriptive marks). The Trade Marks Registration Act introduced the trade marks register, which is still used.

In Australia, the various states had their own Trade Marks Acts, some of which established registers of trade marks earlier than the register set up in Britain under the Trade Marks Registration Act. These Acts ceased shortly after federation as the states lost constitutional power to legislate for industrial property and the Commonwealth Trade Marks Act 1905 was passed. The legislation was updated by the Trade Marks Act 1955–1958 and this, in turn has been superseded by the Trade Marks Act 1995.

Under the new Trade Marks Act, where a mark is inherently non-distinctive but the owner can show that the mark has been used widely over a long period and at a substantial level, the mark can be registered. There has been an indication that the use of a mark for ten years on goods valued at over $1 million per year will lead to acceptance of almost any trade mark by the Trade Marks Office; but it is believed that in many cases, very much less use than this will suffice for registration. The boundaries as to what is and is not acceptable will emerge over time; there may be some words and phrases that will not get registered irrespective of the amount of use.

A major advantage of the registration of a trade mark lies in the protection of the mark. Registration gives rise to a monopoly right to the use of the mark, and prohibits the use of deceptively similar marks in respect of the goods for which the mark is registered. Under the Act, if the same or a deceptively similar mark is used on goods which are of the same description as the goods for which the mark is registered, provided that there is a likelihood of deception or confusion, then there is infringement. The Act goes further in that if a mark is a well known mark, there can be infringement by the use of the same or a deceptively similar mark on unrelated goods if there is likelihood that the infringing mark would be taken to be connected to the registered mark.

These provisions substantially broaden the protection given by registration. They have been introduced to bring the Australian trade mark law into conformity with the harmonised laws in other countries as agreed in the Trade-Related Intellectual Property Schedule (TRIPS) of the recently amended General Agreement on Tariffs and Trade (GATT).

Trade marks are also protected in Australia under the Trade Practices Act (Cwlth) and the State Fair Trading Acts. (These are parallel and have been introduced because of constitutional difficulties; in broad terms the Commonwealth Act related to corporations and the state Acts to individuals, although there is an overlap.) These Acts, in the relevant sections, are basically designed for consumer protection and proscribe, in trade and commerce, actions which are likely to deceive or mislead purchasers. These are, however, widely used by traders as they have an advantage over the passing off action in that only the likelihood of deception and confusion has to be proved; not reputation *per se*.

A trade mark must distinguish the goods or services of the application and so a word which is completely descriptive of a class of goods or services has not been able to be registered as a trade mark, no matter how distinctive it has become. For example the Oxford University Press was not permitted to register 'Oxford' in respect of publications, although it could show about 400 years use. This situation may have changed under the new Act. If a word used as a trade mark passes into common use by other traders, that mark may be removed from the Register. The Univac Corporation first applied the word 'computer' to a programmable calculating machine and registered it as a trade mark, but they were unable to prevent the term 'computer' passing into general use and so they retain no particular rights over the use of the term. However, 'Biro', 'Cellophane' and 'Thermos' all remain on the register in Australia; although they are used generically by the public they are not so used by other traders.

It is desirable for a user of a trade mark to assert that the word is a trade mark whenever it is used. The 'TM' symbol, as in '… to use Splodge™, first prepare …' can be used to assert the rights of the proprietor in the word 'Splodge' and counters the contextual implication that it is a general term for products used in the manner described.

Registration

In Australia, a trade mark must be registered in respect of goods or services in a particular class of the International Classification of Trade Marks and under the new Act, goods or services in more than one class can be included in a single application, although on payment of increased fees.

The application is examined, usually within eight to ten months of filing, by an examiner of trade marks who must be satisfied that the application is in the proper form as well as describing a mark that is capable of being registered under the Act. The examiner must be satisfied that the mark must be capable of distinguishing the goods or services of the applicant from the goods or services of another person. Until the introduction of the 1995 Act, the Trade Marks Office had acted more to prevent the registration of trade marks than to assist it, the rationale being the standard economists' assertion that all restraints on competition are guilty until proved innocent, and probably still guilty then. Under the new Act, the Trade Marks Office has indicated that they will generally let the market decide whether a mark should be registered or not. It is too early to decide how far this attitude will prevail in practice.

The applicant is given the opportunity to answer any objections taken by the examiner and, if not satisfied, can ask to be heard by a Delegate of the Registrar of Trade Marks and can take an appeal to the Administrative Appeals Tribunal. The acceptance of an application is advertised so any interested person can oppose the application and, in the absence of opposition or after the dismissal of the opposition, the mark is registered. The mark will remain in force for a period of ten years from the date of filing and can be renewed indefinitely for further periods of ten years.

While the '®' symbol is not specifically recognised in Australian law, it may be desirable to use it in association with the mark after registration to assist in maintaining the rights in the trade mark. Marks cannot be hoarded; they can lapse if they are not used. There are provisions in the Act to have a mark struck from the register if a period of three years elapses after the mark has been registered (and registration actually dates back to application) during which the mark is not used.

Costs of registration

Figure 6.5 shows the stages, time scales and costs involved in registering a trade mark. Before registration is sought, unless the mark has already been used for some years, it is most desirable to search the Trade Marks Register to ascertain whether there are any other marks which are the same or deceptively similar to the proposed mark in respect of the same or similar goods or services for which it is to be used.

Such a search can be carried out at the AIPO, or one of the state sub-offices, but not by staff members of the AIPO or through the AIPO computer. In most cases it is desirable that the search be carried out professionally, and patent attorneys generally have the greatest skills in carrying trade mark registration applications, although there are some solicitors who practice in the area. A solicitor without experience should not be used. The cost of a search for a single mark will be of the order of $400 with additional searches at the same time being of the order of $300, although some patent attorneys may charge on time for additional searches.

An application for registration is deceptively simple and in many cases an applicant can successfully lodge his or her own application, and obtain registration. However, if the Trade Marks Office objects to some aspect of an application, the applicant would be foolish not to seek professional help. As a general rule patent attorneys are the best people to consult in this area, but there are some skilled solicitors. If a patent attorney is engaged to lodge an application for a mark in a single class the cost should be of the order of $750, including the filing fee of $200 (1996 rates).

The costs to overcome any objection raised by an examiner can vary widely, depending on the seriousness of the objection and in normal cases could be of the order of between $200 and $400. After the application is accepted, the registration fee, including the patent attorney's charges, will cost about $600. Renewal fees payable every ten years are, at 1996 levels, $900, including patent attorney's charges.

Protecting trade marks

Owners of valuable trade marks should be active in discouraging their use as generic terms, particularly in relation to their application to similar products by other traders. Descriptive use by others is not in itself damaging; but it is important to guard against the use of a trade mark as a noun: the IBM Corporation was not seriously troubled by the frequent (and anachronistic) references to 'IBM Machines' in Joseph Heller's *Catch 22*, but if Heller's book had referred to 'IBMs' his publisher could have expected a visit from IBM Corporation's lawyers. The sole proprietor of the 'Big Blue' Laundromat in suburban New York was astounded by the arrival of three partners in one of America's largest legal firms, accusing him of damaging IBM's reputation and demanding that he adopt a different name. One edition of the Merriam-Webster International Dictionary decided not to identify trade marks and was withdrawn after very substantial complaints by trade mark owners.

Defending trade marks

If you suspect that one of your trade marks has been infringed you should consult a patent attorney or solicitor. They will probably recommend an initial demand on the infringer requesting that the use of the mark cease. The demand may also include a request for other remedies. If this does not produce a satisfactory result, then infringement actions can be commenced, normally in the Federal Court, but such actions can also be commenced in state Supreme Courts and even in lower courts, although actions in lower courts are unusual. As we mentioned above, trade mark infringement actions are almost invariably joined with actions for breach of the Trade Practices (or Fair Trading) Acts and actions for passing off.

Plant breeder's rights

It is possible to obtain protection for new varieties of plants under the Plant Variety Rights Act but it is also possible in some cases to obtain normal patent protection.

Under the Patents Act, a new plant is deemed to be a manner of new manufacture and to get protection it is necessary for the plant to meet the other requirements of invention, it must be new and it must be inventive, or nonobvious. Because the newness requirement of the Plant Variety Rights Act are less stringent than the Patents Act, there may be occasions where protection can be sought under the former Act where they could not be sought under the latter.

The specific requirements of the Plant Variety Rights Act is that the variety was originated by a person (that is, natural variation cannot be claimed); it must be homogeneous and stable; it must be distinguished from other varieties by one or more important characteristics; it must not be a species or genus which is excluded from protection; it must not have been offered for sale in Australia more than one year or overseas countries more than six years for trees and vines or four years for other varieties, prior to the filing date.

The period of protection is twenty-five years for trees and vines and twenty years for other varieties. It is not an offence to grow the variety provided that this is for private and non-commercial use; nor is it an offence to grow the variety for experimental purposes. If protected plants or seeds are properly purchased by farmers, it is not an infringement for them to save and use seed derived from them for their own purposes.

The costs of protection under the Plant Varieties Act can be relatively expensive as it may be necessary for the plants to be test grown. The cost of the actual application can be of the order of $3000.

Circuit layouts

The Circuit Layouts Act 1989 is intended to protect the owners' copyright in the layout of integrated circuits.

Basically, like copyrights generally, it is not necessary that the copyright be registered but there is a necessity to obtain a written assignment if the author is not the owner, or is not employed by the owner. The protection of the Act is that it gives the owner the right to copy the layout, the right to produce integrated circuits in accordance with the layout and the right to exploit the layout. These rights are infringed by copying the layout, whether directly or in a material form (that is, by the manufacture of integrated circuits in accordance with the layout). There is protection against innocent infringement: if the infringer did not know and could not have been expected to know there was infringement no liability accrues.

In order to prove infringement for an integrated circuit, it would normally be necessary to section and polish the chip and then take micro-photographs of the etched circuit. A chip or circuit designer might feel that demonstrating that a competing chip or circuit board performed to exactly the same specification and used an identical pattern of terminations ('plug compatibility') was sufficient to prove infringement, however, a number of plug compatible chips have survived challenges by proving that they were different in design.

Because of the esoteric nature of the Act there will probably only ever be a few cases of infringement, but the Act does give positive protection to designers of integrated circuits.

Trade Practices Act

The Trade Practices Act and the various state Fair Trading Acts[4] were briefly discussed above. Section 52 and the following sections of the Trade Practices Act are the relevant ones here; these are basically consumer protection sections. When the Trade Practices Act was initially introduced it was believed that the Trade Practices Commission (now the Australian Competition and Consumer Commission) would, acting in the public interest, be the primary user of these sections. However, relatively early in the life of the legislation, corporations found the Act was a strong weapon against unfair competitors and it is much more widely used in inter-party matters than by the Commission; although the Commission has had notable successes under the sections.

The sections basically proscribe a corporation (and we shall refer to corporations meaning corporations under the Trade Practices Act as well as individuals under the relevant Fair Trading Act) from acting in trade or commerce in a manner which is misleading or deceptive. Later sections expand on specific conduct which lies within the definition and the most important of these in this context is that a corporation cannot act to indicate a connection with another organisation which it does not have.

The Federal Court, which is the most used court under the Act, is seen as an applicant's court under these sections and appears ready to find that there is a likelihood of people being misled or deceived. It is rare for a trade mark infringement action, or an action for passing off to be commenced without including a claim under the Trade Practices Act. As we mentioned above, it is not essential to prove either substantial reputation or specific damage[5] to succeed under the Act making it, on many occasions, less difficult to succeed in a trade practices claim than under passing off.

Common law

Passing off

The action for passing off has been mentioned both under trade marks and under the Trade Practices Act. The action is still widely used, usually in association with the actions for infringement of registered trade marks and breaches of the Trade Practices Act. Historically the action was triable in the Supreme Courts of the states, as the federal government has no constitutional power to control the common law. With cross vesting of jurisdictions, the Federal Court can now hear passing off actions whether or not they are tied to an action under the Trade Practices or other Commonwealth Act.

Trade secrets

Firms often have confidential information which, if it was taken and wrongly given to some other party, perhaps by a disaffected staff member leaving the firm's employ, could cause great damage to the company. Generally, if this information is treated by the company as being confidential, it will be regarded by the courts as being so.[6] Information about a firm which is readily available through publication in a catalogue or an annual or other report cannot be confidential.

> *No signed agreement can make public information confidential ...*

If there is a breach of confidentiality, it is possible to obtain an injunction to prevent further breaches, but this may be like unscrambling an egg and the only practical action is to seek recompense for the damage which has occurred.

Inventors or entrepreneurs may wish to disclose their invention or a concept, perhaps to a manufacturer, a prospective investor or a potential lead customer. If, prior to the disclosure, the material is stated to be confidential and the person receiving the material accepts this as a fact, then a relationship of confidentiality has been established between the two parties. This does not have to be more than a verbal agreement but for the purposes of proof, it is desirable to have some form of written statement in which the person to whom the material is disclosed agrees to respect confidentiality. If the material is not confidential, that is, it is already available to the person to whom it is disclosed, it does not matter what documents are signed, this does not give the material any status which it did not have before.

Some companies, particularly American ones, to whom material is to be disclosed, have their own form of confidentiality agreement which must be signed by the discloser before the company is prepared to consider material given to it. These agreements are to protect the company against being informed of something of which they are already aware, but which has not been published. For example, the company may have been carrying out research in an area to which a disclosure made to it relates and may have already made a development which is the same or very similar to the material disclosed to it. The company, of course, wants to ensure that the value of its own knowledge is not affected by the disclosure. A disclosing company achieves protection by limiting what is accepted as being confidential to what the discloser can obtain a valid United States patent for. Because of a peculiarity of the United States patent law, where there are two inventors of the 'same' invention, the Patent Office can decide who was the first inventor and the first inventor can be granted that patent even though his or her application was the later filed one. The non-American inventor is at a disadvantage as the earliest date he or she can claim, if they are working outside America, is the date of their earliest application.

One substantial advantage of seeking confidentiality is to bring the situation to the attention of the person disclosing information. Most breaches in this area are inadvertent rather than deliberate and if people are told that certain information is confidential, they are generally likely to respect its confidentiality.

Intellectual property

There are other old common law actions which are still available, although seldom used. The most relevant one is Trade Libel or alternatively known as Slander on Title or Injurious Falsehoods. This action is not *per se* an unfair trading action but it can be used to deter people from uttering falsehoods which would be damaging to another firm's trade and to punish and obtain damages from offenders.

Conclusion

Many, possibly the majority, of innovators rely on intellectual property to give their firm a competitive advantage in the market. There are a number of legal ways in which the entrepreneur can protect this advantage. Some of these are only effective after a product or service is placed on the market and has developed some reputation, while others can be useful very early in the life of a product. Some, such as patents and designs must be initiated before a product is displayed, used or sold. For this reason it is essential that every entrepreneur takes positive steps to ensure that all reasonable protection for the new or growing firm's intellectual property is in place.

Since about 1980 many law schools have included intellectual property in their undergraduate curriculum, but seldom as a compulsory subject and so many solicitors are woefully ignorant in the area. Large city firms generally have specialist intellectual property sections but the staff in these sections are generally more experienced in technology transfer and litigation than in obtaining intellectual property protection. Patent attorneys are skilled in obtaining protection but are often weak in general business or legal advice. It is essential for an entrepreneur to be careful in selecting his or her intellectual property advisers as it is in every other area.

End notes

1   They can, however, be bound in respect of information which is confidential, for as long as it remains confidential.
2   This is advisable but may not be always necessary when changing the ownership of other forms of intellectual property.
3   In the USA patent infringement cases are tried by a jury and, in any case, a tweak in the law favours the home side.
4   The overlap of the Commonwealth and state legislation is because, constitutionally, the Commonwealth cannot legislate about dealings by individuals in a single state. In general terms, the Trade Practices Act controls the actions of corporations while the Fair Trading Acts control individuals.
5   As it would be under the common law or when defending an unregistered trade mark.
6   The subject of 'whistle blowing' has opened up a complete new field in this area: criminal activity cannot be concealed under the rubric of confidentiality, but what about disgraceful conduct?

Chapter 7

Strategy, organisation, process and assets: SOPA

Practical planning

A business plan is a model of a world the entrepreneur hopes to make real, and in particular, a world including the entrepreneur's new enterprise. The fully developed plan will have an organisational design set out as described in Chapter 12, a set of pro-forma accounts as described in Chapter 14, and a number of other sections as described in Chapter 16. These describe the complete plan, but there are a number of important decisions to be made before the final plan can be drafted.

We suggest the acronym SOPA to embrace one of these sets of decisions.

▲ the new enterprise will need a strategy, a word picture of where the enterprise, and the entrepreneurs want to be in the future

▲ the new enterprise will need an organisation, a number of people sharing the tasks in some systematic way

▲ the new enterprise will create value by some process, the core activity of the new business

▲ the new enterprise will need some assets in order to commence operations and, as the business develops, it will create and acquire more of them.

This chapter deals with the design of the value-adding process and the creation of valuable products that we defined and then valued in Chapter 5 and protected in Chapter 6. We also discuss in this chapter the organisation to make the process work. The decisions that we make here will be elaborated into an organisational plan in Chapter 12 and will provide the information needed to complete the costing sections of Chapter 14.

Life's unlimited variety

No two firms are identical, if for no other reason than the legal requirement to have different names for different firms. New entrepreneurial ventures go further than this; they should be essentially different from any existing firm for the reason that, if they were too close a copy of an existing firm, they would be permanently second to market, doomed to low growth or prompt failure. Sometimes there is one clear difference between the new firm and existing ones, while every other aspect is as close as possible to an established model. Franchising succeeds when each new franchise preserves the successful features of existing ones while opening up a new local market segment. At the other extreme, radical innovations may involve processes, organisational structures and distribution methods never previously used.

A new venture starts with an opportunity. In Chapter 5 we discussed how to screen and value opportunities. If the resulting product is easily and cheaply copied, the opportunity may be of little value unless it can be, to some degree, exclusive. In Chapter 6 we discussed the ways in which an entrepreneur can delay or deter imitators. In this chapter we will assume that the opportunity exists, is valuable, and can be protected to a sufficient extent. This chapter will discuss the type of organisation implied by the nature of the opportunity, and set out, in necessarily general terms, the success factors specific to that class of organisation.

There are four broad classes of economic activity. Primary industries harvest Nature's bounty by mining, forestry, agriculture, hunting or fishing. Modern horticulture and plantation forestry are classified statistically as primary industries, but, given the high degree of science involved in their operation, and the relatively large proportion of farm or plantation gate revenue spent on inputs such as fuel, pesticides and fertilisers, they have more in common with manufacturing industry than traditional peasant farming. Secondary, or manufacturing, industries take primary and partly manufactured components and materials and transform them into higher value products; there are many more manufacturing firms that buy in processed materials and components than firms that work directly on raw materials.

Tertiary industries take fully manufactured and directly useable primary products and make them available to consumers, in some cases repacking or performing final customising operations on them but in many cases providing a transport, storage and display service only. The fourth class of activity is the provision of pure services, industries where there is no physical product delivered, but users have their person or their property transformed in a way that they either cannot or choose not to do for themselves. Service industries span an enormous variety of activities: cardiac surgeons and stockbrokers perform services, as do street-sweepers and prostitutes. Building and construction is often categorised as a service, although the modern builder, like the modern farmer, operates rather like a manufacturer, using elaborate equipment to transform materials and components.

All businesses face the threat of competition, either from current rivals chasing the same customers with similar products, or from entrants to their market seeking to displace them. When a small number of very large companies supply a market they are described as an oligopoly. Oligopolists take each other's likely reactions into account in their pricing and marketing strategies in the knowledge that a price war would damage all of them and, unless suspended, eventually destroy all but one of them. In a market supplied by small and medium sized firms, few of them will refuse an attractive order if it can be gained by a modest discount, and as one firm after another offers such a discount the general price level will drop to the point that many firms will be forced out of business. The process of forced exit will continue until an oligopoly develops or some form of price regulation is introduced: in Australia, such regulation requires either direct government intervention or an authorisation from the Australian Competition and Consumer Commission.

Firms that are not large enough to be part of an oligopoly, and not self-confident enough to believe that providence will ensure that they are among the few tenths of a per cent of companies that can survive an extended period of price competition, will take steps to avoid getting embroiled in it. Staying out of price competition requires a sustainable competitive advantage. Such competitive advantages come in a number of forms:

▲ A firm may have exclusive control over some scarce resource, such as a rich mineral deposit or a particularly favoured area of land.

▲ A firm may have a patent or other legal monopoly over the production of some widely demanded product or over the use of a process that significantly improves the manufacture of such a product.

▲ A firm may have exploited a 'first mover advantage', getting into a particular market before its potential rivals and then establishing a reputation and securing a market share that protects its margins from competitive pressure.

▲ A firm may exhibit consistently superior product development performance such that it is 'first to market' more often than its market share would suggest, with an unusually high proportion of its product portfolio in the high margin growth phase of its product life cycle.

▲ A firm might have earned a reputation for consistently superior delivery and/or product performance such that its products command a price premium.

Strategy, organisation, process and assets: SOPA

The essence of strategy: Sustaining a competitive advantage

A firm, by setting out a strategy, establishes some objectives with dates at various times in the future, but no firm can survive without some form of competitive advantage. The essence of an entrepreneurial plan is the creation, protection and development of the firm's sustainable competitive advantages.[1]

The fact that a competitive advantage is sustainable is no guarantee that it will, in fact, be sustained. Mineral deposits get worked out, patents expire, newer innovations let rivals break into previously secure markets. Firms that achieve superior performance will find their techniques imitated. At the same time, firms may acquire competitive disadvantages that, if allowed to flourish, will offset the benefits of their advantages. New firms, in particular, suffer from a number of inevitable disadvantages: they are small, they have no credit history, they have no market recognition; entrepreneurship would not be challenging if there were no problems such as these to overcome.

Entrepreneurs planning new businesses around innovations have two clear advantages over all their possible rivals: the entrepreneurs have their innovation, and the rivals do not; and the entrepreneurs can design an organisation to maximise the competitive advantage their innovation offers, while their rivals are more or less saddled with their current organisation. The decisions an entrepreneur makes at this time about the firm structure and its place in the final value chain cast long shadows; they are strategic, and while strategic freedom offers opportunities it also involves hazards.

Planning, as we made clear in Chapter 3, focuses on one opportunity; it implements a strategy, it does not establish one. The strategic context, however, constrains the plan: obviously, the strategic approach chosen must be compatible with the current opportunity, but pursuit of the current opportunity should not be allowed to close off too many future possibilities.

The null strategy

An entrepreneur may decide not to consider future possibilities in the current round of planning. A plan developed under this strategy may involve winding up the business and selling whatever assets the firm has at some point in the future. Entrepreneurs adopting this version of the null strategy may find it difficult to motivate staff, and so only enterprises where the great bulk of the intellectual and management contribution will be coming from the entrepreneur and the entrepreneur's partners are suitable for this approach. This is still the only reasonable strategy to use when the opportunity is strictly a one-shot opportunity, like an Olympic Games, a Bicentenary, or other singular event.

A decision to concentrate on the present opportunity with a view to moving from an entrepreneurial to a managed business as the firm's markets enter maturity is also a null strategy, in that no future beyond the current oppor-

Competitive advantage	Product	Process
Unique features	VESDA fire protection systems provide better protection for expensive assets than any alternatives. Other products with valuable unique features are in this group.	A leading barrister or surgeon who provides a high assurance of best possible outcome in critical situation. Entertainment and leisure products may often be found in this group.
Value for money	Toyota Motor's product range consists of reliable, well-made, competitively priced motor cars. Most mass market consumer products are in this quadrant — it is a 'ticket to play' rather than an advantage in many cases.	Woolworths/Safeway stores: Good product selection, well presented, competitively priced. Convenience stores and nightspots, fast food chains, economy air travel and packaged holidays also in this quadrant.

Figure 7.1 Some examples of competitive advantage

tunity is taken into account. A business managed in this way will cease to grow a few years after it is launched, but if its competitive advantages are reasonably secure, possibly with a combination of intellectual property and a strong position as a specialist supplier in a closely defined market, this strategy can lead to a comfortable lifestyle support system.

The 'million bucks and out' approach

One stylised model of the entrepreneurship process is cited frequently. In this model the entrepreneurs who create a business sell it as a going concern, either by a stock market flotation or to an older business, after about seven years. At this time the growth phase of the product life cycle, at least in the original market, is over and with it the entrepreneurial value creation process. The new owners will get a return on their investment, and may realise some further value growth by imposing cost disciplines or through synergies with their existing operation, but the entrepreneurial task of venture creation will have been finished.

The strategy, such as it is, adopted by such entrepreneurs is to keep the business as a tightly saleable entity, with none of the loose ends or commitments that a growth strategy requires, so as to make the business's sale as expeditious and remunerative as possible.

There certainly are people in many countries who seek the challenge and excitement of creating a new venture, and find the tasks of managing a continuing business, even an actively growing one, boring or irritating. These people are entrepreneurs by any measure, and yet they are not the only ones. People who manage growth businesses, people who champion innovations from inside corporations, even people who create and grow voluntary and *pro bono* organisations are entrepreneurs too.

Growth business strategies

An entrepreneur who intends to create a lasting business, like the manager of a major corporation which has decided to base its growth strategy on innovation, needs to make some strategic choices before getting down to writing a business plan. We quoted Mintzberg in Chapter 3, showing that no one has yet produced a mechanical system for generating corporate strategies, and we hinted that modern systems theory suggests that such systems may be impossible to produce. One reason is that their publication is self-defeating. Imagine a national lottery (like Tattslotto) in which the winner nominates a set of numbers; imagine further that an infallible system for predicting the winning numbers has been published. Every ticket buyer would insist on the winning numbers, everyone would share the first division prize pool, and everyone would get about 60 per cent of their money back — what everyone knows has no commercial value.

Since there is no proven system for generating a strategy, entrepreneurs must develop a strategy without relying on one. Every entrepreneur should accept two facts:

▲ their chosen strategy will almost certainly conceal some problems, and as these reveal themselves the strategy will need to be modified

▲ their chosen strategy will be selected from such a large number of possibilities that it is impossible to prove in advance that it is the best possible one; at some stage the entrepreneur or corporation must settle on a strategy because otherwise consideration of the subject would never end.

Entrepreneurs who wish to have a place in history should note a further fact: whatever they did, and no matter how successful they were, someone is going to come along after the fact and point out real or imaginary instances where they could have done even better.

Strategic theories and advice

An entrepreneur or manager wanting to read a book about strategy will have no trouble finding one,[2] and entrepreneurs without the time to read a complete book will find plenty of interesting articles in the popular business press. An academic wishing to conduct research in the strategic management area will find that there are several learned journals which accept and publish articles of great interest. There is a common thread running through these books, articles and learned papers, and that is that they nearly all deal with particular examples of successful and unsuccessful strategy formulation; what passes for theory is an abstraction from a selection of cases.

The limits of military analogy

A lot of popular writing about strategy uses military examples, and since wars and battles are often intensively researched it is possible to make some very interesting observations and to draw very plausible analogies with business. We do so in this book. There are, however, some major differences between military activity and business. War is a 'negative sum game'. Winners and losers are both generally worse off at the end of a war than at the beginning; although one side may suffer more than the other, everyone loses. Some businesses are conducted on negative or zero sum principles, but many are managed to build value, and do not waste time or resources on irrelevancies like damaging potential rivals. The study of the history of wars and battles can be extremely useful in explaining and testing problem solving principles, but an appeal to the glamour, heroism, courage and triumphs offered by warfare is misplaced.

Many historians rate the Russian Marshal Georgi Zhukov the outstanding general of the Second World War. He is recalled for his strategic brilliance, but also for his way of phrasing orders.

'Capture the objective by 10 o'clock or be shot at midday', he advised one officer.

His subordinate and admirer, Marshal Rokossovsky, wrote that Zhukov sometimes 'displayed unjustified sharpness'.

Zhukov's account of his 'unjustified sharpness' on 30 November 1941 can be found in his memoirs Zhukov (1969).

There is a second crucial difference between war and business: private soldiers have historically been conscripts, forced by law and custom to fight and to submit to military discipline. Even soldiers in volunteer armies surrender many of their civil rights for the period of their enlistment: refusing to obey a lawful order is a military crime, and officers are generally empowered to compel battlefield obedience on pain of death. Businesses cannot compel obedience by any threat more violent than dismissal, and in many cases the special talents or unique knowledge of the refractory staff make even that threat a hollow one. 'I can call up spirits from the vasty deep', said Glendower. 'Aye, so can I or so can any man,' responded Hotspur, 'but will they come when you do call them?'

The greatest military leaders were as remarkable for their ability to secure the willing cooperation of their allies and their subordinates as they were for their military insights. That is a lesson that every entrepreneur should take to heart.

Personal and strategic objectives

Someone who decides to build a growing business must recognise that they will, themselves, be intimately bound up with the business for many years; an entrepreneur's personal and business strategies are closely linked. There is no point in entrepreneurs condemning themselves to lifetimes of torment, and so they should devise strategies that will reward them when they are successful, not the reverse.

In general terms people perform better when they enjoy the work, and entrepreneurs are no different. Most good opportunities involve the deployment of multiple skills in a variety of tasks, all of which contribute to the development of a competitive advantage. It is hard to imagine a new enterprise being totally self-contained while remaining part of a modern economy and society, and in practice the boundaries of the enterprise, the point at which outsourcing starts, are readily changed.

The core parts of an enterprise are those that are, by definition, not eligible for contracting out. If the strategy defines the core so as to include those activities that the founding entrepreneurs are happiest doing, there is little reason to challenge this choice, and the entrepreneurs will at least know that the success of their enterprise will not mean the failure of their personal ambitions.

Business expansion: Wider or deeper?

In Chapter 4 we discussed the progressive transformation of industries from vertically to horizontally aggregated. It may help to consider the delivery of a consumer product, whether a good or a service, as the final step in a series of transformations and combinations. Some of the operations and components will be unique to a single product, particularly when an industry is new; while others will be part of the history of many products. McDonald's provide a fairly elementary series of products, and their business is built on the reliability and consistency with which they deliver them. Part of most children's McDonald's experience is a serve of French fries; but in Australia McDonald's don't grow the potatoes, clean or slice them, freeze them or deliver them; neither do they make the fryers or the thermostats or the timers that their staff use.

When McDonald's opened a Moscow store in the last months of the communist regime few of the goods and services which they use in Australia were available. One of their first activities was to find farmers willing to grow appropriate breeds of potato, explain to them how the job should be done, and arrange transport, cutting and freezing services. As the Russian move to a market economy continues, McDonald's will shed these peripheral activities and concentrate on their core business.

The core strategy of every business should include activities that protect its key sources of competitive advantages, but such precautionary actions do not produce growth. A firm's current competitive advantages, its core competencies, can be leveraged into growth in one of two ways: deeper, with the firm undertaking more of the transforming activities itself; or wider, as when the firm finds new markets for its products. Going deeper, the move towards more vertical integration can be either forward, as when an iron ore mining company builds a reduction plant; or backwards, as when a steel mill acquires an iron ore mine.

Vertical integration

Backwards integration is essentially self-limiting: if McDonald's were to move to extensive backwards integration they would become a much larger and more complex company, but they would have no more revenue. McDonald's have, in fact, been becoming even thinner vertically over their history, outsourcing much of the final operations of their business through franchising. Even the core element of the original McDonald's product, the hamburger patty, is produced by a partner company.

Forwards integration often looks much more attractive as part of a growth strategy: each step forwards will offer a substantial growth in revenue and in value added. It is so attractive that it may be wondered why it is so rare. Most Australian dairy farmers sell their produce through a cooperative. At leat one of these, Murray–Goulburn, has developed a major business exporting milk-based manufactured products, to the great profit of its farmer members. Australians are also aware of the failure of any substantial wool-processing industry to develop in Australia. Attempts at forward integration are certain to face a number of hurdles:

▲ a company that decides to integrate forward may find itself competing with its customers who may in turn take pre-emptive action such as switching their own purchasing

▲ whether the traditional customers of a company planning downstream integration retaliate or not, the new downstream operations represent a new venture into an established market; such operations are usually cash negative for one or more years, and the firm may find this drain on its liquidity hard to support

▲ the management and operating techniques appropriate to the new operations may be quite different to those familiar to the managers of the existing company and the resulting cultural clashes may make synergy impossible.

BHP's move into coated steels, and CRA's move into direct smelting, were possible because at least some of these hurdles could be circumvented. BHP's coated steels are sold for structural use, largely as cladding and roofing, and the traditional suppliers to these markets, the brick and tile industries, the timber industry and the fibrous cement industries are not large steel users. BHP, as a major structural steel supplier, had an established sales channel into the construction industry, and the Zincalume process produced a product with different, and in some cases superior, characteristics to the traditional roofing and cladding materials. The production and finishing of coated steels uses processes broadly similar to those already familiar to BHP, and so there were few cultural problems.

CRA's expectations for the product of the HIsmelt direct smelting process are based in part on the fact that it will not be competing directly with its iron ore customers. Iron ore is consumed by integrated steel mills such as the BHP plant at Port Kembla, while direct reduced iron will be consumed by mini-mills such as BHP's Rooty Hill plant in NSW and the ARC mill in Footscray, Victoria. CRA's established competitors for direct reduced iron are scrap merchants, and CRA's product will be a suitable feed for mini-mills producing higher-quality steel products, while much of the available scrap steel is only suitable for producing relatively low-grade reinforcing bar and light structural members.

The economists' perspective

Some economists describe vertical integration as a symptom of defects in the economy: there may not be a market in which the intermediate product can be bought and sold, or the transaction costs of using the market are such that they outweigh the possible efficiency gains. Such economic analyses usually exclude certain considerations such as firm-specific competencies and the value of reducing uncertainty. The standard economic assumptions include the assertion that people only work for the money, and would immediately change jobs for a dollar a week raise; conversely, they assume that firms only employ individuals, any one of whom could be immediately and costlessly replaced if they left. Such factors as people's enjoyment of work or the company of their workmates are excluded from a standard economic analysis, as is the possibility that a long-established team of people may perform better than a group of newly recruited individuals with the same qualifications.

Economic analyses of industry structure are only conditionally valid. The proper way to use the standard treatment of vertical integration in economics text books is to recognise that *unless* there is some useful synergy between two operations that could be run at arms length, integration may produce only minor if any benefits. One benefit of vertical integration, or at least long term supplier relationships, is that it, by stabilising demand, makes it easier for the upstream division or supplier to invest in cost saving and quality enhancing equipment and processes. We discuss hurdle rates in Chapter 8; it will be clear from that discussion that the level of demand uncertainty is critically important in making investment decisions.

Some economists are fond of an *ex post* style of arguing: if an upstream division or supplier has made a special investment in order to service a particular customer, the threat of switching the business or outsourcing it may force the upstream supplier to reduce its prices, demonstrating greater economic efficiency.[3] We consider this practice morally dubious and, over the long term, detrimental to the firms that practice it as well as to society as a whole.

Horizontal extension

Vertical integration involves developing new assets to increase a firm's value added while supplying the same final users with essentially the same product. Horizontal extension policies attempt to use the existing assets more intensively. These assets include the technology and core competencies of the firm, but they also include the favourable view of the firm taken by its satisfied users, its goodwill and brand equity.

The Adelaide-based firm Britax–Rainsfords makes outside mirrors for motor cars. In 1960 it began supplying mirrors to some Australian manufacturers. The firm developed this business until by 1991 it supplied all the external mirrors used on Australian-built cars and had a substantial business in the United States; so substantial, in fact, that the firm built a factory in the United States and as United States-based production built up from 1990 the Adelaide plant had some unused capacity.

Britax–Rainsfords had an excellent relationship with Ford, and this secured them introductions to Ford's Japanese ally Mazda. As it happened, some of the mirrors that Britax–Rainsfords were making for Ford were a Mazda design, and negotiating a contract to supply Mazda with the same mirrors was (relatively) easy. Having one Japanese customer did not seem to be enough, and so Britax–Rainsfords decided to build their share of the Japanese market and began negotiating with Suzuki. As at 1995, Britax–Rainsfords had a solid business supplying Suzuki and was looking for further Japanese orders.

One common form of horizontal extension is by increasing the geographic range over which the product is offered; from local to regional, regional to national, national to world trade. At each stage the knowledge gained from serving the existing customer base can be used to improve the product and the marketing strategies in order to secure a foothold in the next group of markets rapidly and economically. There are a number of ways in which such market broadening may be carried out. Franchising and licensing are commonly used for service products and for fast moving packaged consumer goods. Industrial goods and services can be offered through agencies, licensees, partnerships, branches or subsidiaries. The markets can be served by exports or by local manufacture or by an appropriate combination of the two. BHP's Zincalume products are available in many markets; some supplied directly from Australia, some supplied with coiled sheet from Australia for local forming, and in some markets the sheet itself is manufactured in local mini-mills.

The resort hotel

The Hyatt Coolum resort hotel has a beautiful setting, but no action that they can take will stop other resorts being opened in beautiful settings. It is run very efficiently, but efficient hotel management is even easier to replicate. Its pricing is not dictated by its competitors, but it will have to stay in the same ball-park. It can, however, set out to provide a unique experience to a clearly defined market segment, levering the benefits of its site with the selection and training of its staff.

The hotel's marketing, along with collecting as many conventions and meetings as it can, sets out to attract families in which at least one member wants to play golf on a championship-standard course while the rest of the family enjoys gentle leisure pursuits; the food, accommodation and service are appropriate for an upper-middle income clientele.

Hotels like the Hyatt Coolum will be successful as long as 100 000 families from Australia and the region fit its target profile and take, on average, at least one holiday there every two years. This is a small number given that there are six million families in Australia alone, and at least another six million families in the right income bracket in the region.

Horizontal extension can be by brand leveraging. This involves offering a wider product range, with the intention of increasing the revenue per customer or per geographic market segment. The chief asset used to support this form of horizontal growth is the goodwill of the established customer base, which predisposes the people in it to consider the supplier as a suitable source for their additional requirements of related products, and prompts them to influence other potential users to give the supplier's products a trial. Since the cost of developing a customer base is often the largest of the investments needed by a successful innovation, development of the customer base itself should always be considered carefully as a first option. McDonald's now offer chicken McNuggets and even (in some markets) McVegieburgers as a result of successful efforts to broaden their customer base to include those who do not wish to eat beef. Attempts at horizontal extension do not always succeed; McDonald's, in Australia and the United States, has been trying for years to build up their evening patronage without any dramatic signs of success.

At least two factors must be present before a firm can successfully leverage its brands:

▲ the chosen extension must relate, in the customers' perceptions, to those aspects of the supplier's product that attracted them in the first instance

▲ the chosen extension must represent an extension of the supplier's established business strengths.

The other major basis for horizontal growth is by *capability leveraging*. While brand leveraging builds on a firm's superior market position, capability

Table 7.1 *Setting out a strategy*

	At launch	After 3 years	After 10 years
Key competitive advantage (there must be one on the top of the list)	New product/early mover OR new pricing point/low cost producer OR new level of delivered value OR fast follower/superior marketing OR something else?	More new products OR superior customer relationships OR what?	Well?
Annual revenue	Ambitious but not ridiculous		
Value of assets controlled	The minimum viable set		

leveraging starts from inside the firm. Firms planning this form of growth look for opportunities to use the established organisational knowledge and facilities to create new products directed to new or extended markets. Honda Motor started with tiny auxiliary engines for push bikes and its products can now be found practically anywhere petrol engines are in service, from lawn mowers and portable electric generators to Formula One motor cars. 3M will tackle any product where their surface technology skills can be brought into play. BHP's move into coated steels is an example of capability leveraging: they had existing capabilities to make strip and roll-form sheets; they had well-established distribution channels, including export channels; and so setting up the Zincalume process was just one extra step in a smoothly working chain.

The design of the firm
Success factors

A number of issues should be resolved before the structure of a new venture is finally determined:

▲ What is the competitive advantage the firm will have at venture launch, and what will be the main advantage three and ten years later?

▲ How will these competitive advantages be protected from competitive imitation and emulation and, as they are eroded, how will new advantages be developed to replace them?

▲ How will the value implicit in this competitive advantage be captured, immediately following the launch and three years later?

▲ What are the critical success factors for the venture, immediately following the launch and three years later?

When a new venture succeeds it makes profits, typically much larger profits, relative to its capital base, than established firms are accustomed to. Before the venture succeeded, these high returns were needed to justify the implicit risks, but once the venture has succeeded the risks vanish in the full glare of perfect hindsight and other firms will want a share of the new market. In most cases the entry of direct competitors can be delayed but not halted by measures such as patents. Major firms tend to watch each other, and generally plan on the assumption that a new product will not be alone in the market for more than fifteen months. Unless there are special reasons to the contrary, it should be assumed that any worthwhile innovation will be matched on the market within three years.

Imitation is, of course, the most sincere form of flattery, and entrants to a new market generally want to share in it, not destroy it. If the original product was sound and its launch well managed, competitors who don't enter within two years will not challenge the entrepreneur's leading position, and competitors who don't enter within four years will not, without a genuine innovation of their own, make a successful entry at all. Those determined competitors who followed the innovator into the market rapidly will have launched their own development projects; if they were fifteen months behind the innovator, they will require no more than another fifteen months to bring their own innovation to market. In a keenly contested market, products superior to the original one are to be expected within thirty months of the first product's launch.

People factors

Success factors are relatively abstract concepts, which become practical when they are used to guide the planner in designing an effective organisation. The practical value of success factors continues once the venture is running, because they help the people in the organisation get their priorities right. For the entrepreneur and his or her senior associates, one critical success factor will be the morale and commitment of the new venture's staff.

Entrepreneurs planning to create growth enterprises should start work on their product's successor, or a major enhancement of their product, at or before the time of the original product's launch. At the same time they should avoid giving their prospective competitors any more help than necessary. Few things can be as helpful to a competitor as the arrival on their doorstep of disgruntled ex-partners or former senior employees of their main rival. When an innovation has been sponsored from within a major corporation, few events are so disconcerting as the appearance of a group of former colleagues launching a directly competitive entrepreneurial venture.

Having a competitive advantage and capturing value from it are not the same thing. Of Professor Porter's (1980) five competitive forces, the threats from entrants and substitutes are latent at the time a new venture is launched. The threats from suppliers and buyers are, however, magnified. The new firm may need credit; it will certainly need a reliable source of supplies (whether of components, consumables or services doesn't matter at this level of abstraction).

Unless the venture is dealing directly with final consumers it will need orders from major customers or listings with distributors, wholesalers or retailers; all of these are in a position to strike a tough bargain with a new firm offering them an untried product.

If the product must be sold through established distribution channels, the firm will need a sales manager with experience in the relevant area or the profits will vanish into a series of wholesale price rebates. If particular components, services or supplies will be needed, and there is only one or a very few suitable suppliers, then the new venture must consider recruiting an experienced purchasing executive, or special charges will eat up whatever profit the wholesale rebates leave. As an alternative, a firm in this position could try to form alliances with the critical suppliers, offering them exclusivity or even equity in the venture to secure their fullest cooperation.

McDonald's is only one of many retail service concepts created by successful entrepreneurs. *Establishing* a retail venture is relatively easy, although earning a fair return on the effort put into running it is harder; *growing* a retail venture usually means more outlets, and the most common form of expansion is by franchising. The franchiser preserves its capital, and the additional direct cost of each new outlet is relatively small. McDonald's typify the crucial skills needed for successful franchising: the type of systems analysis that enables the complete task to be broken into easily learned and easily repeated steps, and the training and supervision system that ensures that franchisees earn a fair return on their investment while preserving the integrity and reputation of the brand.

Organisation designs for success

Critical success factors should not be confused with the causes of sudden death. If a relatively young person dies of a heart attack the immediate cause of death is usually obvious in the form of a clot in or obstruction of the coronary arteries. Health professionals do not go around telling people to avoid clots and to keep their coronary arteries clear: they tell them to adjust their lifestyle long before the symptoms of heart disease appear. Firms all fail the same way: they are wound up when they can no longer pay their bills or when such a situation is imminent. Telling a business on the point of failure that 'it mustn't run out of cash' is like telling a man in the middle of an acute heart attack that he mustn't obstruct the flow of blood though his coronary arteries.

Those little hints ...

An Australian coal mining company with spare capacity received a fax from a Polish steel works asking for a quotation to supply a large annual volume of low-sulphur coking coal. They ignored it, as they ignored another four messages over the next six months; finally the Polish mill placed an order with a mine in another country at a price considerably higher than the Australian miner was used to receiving.

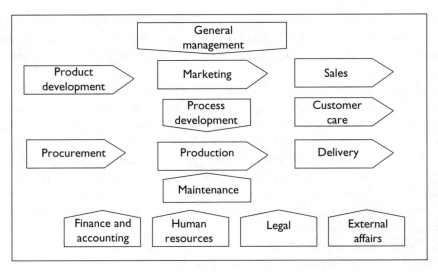

Figure 7.2 The organisation's tasks: Some organisations will have more; few will have less — the tasks need people to do them, and the people need objective setting and reporting lines

The critical success factors are those indicators that can tell a firm that things are going wrong long before the receivers are called in. For a growth business, capturing the small hints that, when acted on lead to new markets and new products, are also critical success factors. The critical success factors differ dramatically from one firm to another even when they are in similar industries. They also change as a firm develops and as its products move through their life cycles.

The critical success factors for some firms are mainly financial; all firms must watch their cash flow and their available financing capacity. Firms that have overdrafts, fixed interest debt, or venture finance agreements will find that these all have conditions which must be observed. Measures like average debtor days can show important trends, including an early warning of sales staff padding the order book to boost their bonuses. When a firm's performance depends on the fast turnover of low-margin products, purchasing prices and terms are critical. Firms where a small change in a financial statistic can have a rapid effect on its viability need to ensure that they have staff with the right skills, and the right access to the entrepreneur, to spot a deviation and recommend an effective corrective action.

The viability of firms serving consumer markets directly is critically dependent upon the level of customer satisfaction, as represented by the rate of conversion of trial to regular use, and in the case of consumer durable products, use to positive recommendation. Such firms must be able to collect, analyse and take action on measures of customer satisfaction. Bad publicity following a product failure or a major customer relations error can be fatal: failure to respond promptly and effectively to one customer complaint can be the stone that starts an avalanche of them. All firms serving the consumer market must have an effective complaint response mechanism in place; if there are health or safety implications in the product there should be a PR emergency plan prepared as well.

Firms serving business markets inevitably have fewer customers per million dollars of turnover than firms serving consumers, and they are also likely to find that a very few customers account for the majority of their sales, their revenue and their profit. This presents a double challenge: the firm must be able to prevent the loss of any of its major customers; at the same time it must be able to either control the service cost or build the revenue it gains from its smaller ones. Keeping the large customers allows the firm to survive; improving the handling of smaller ones allows it to grow. In contrast to consumer products, components and services sold to businesses generally earn quite large margins; short term at least, financial data will be less useful as an indicator of the firm's progress than indexes such as the number of customers and the average revenue per customer.

Firms that provide professional services have traditionally been invited to do so on a fee per service basis, in which case an accounting and billing system that captures a record of every service performed is essential. There is a trend for fee-for-service to be replaced by price-for-job, as, for example, when corporations put their audit requirements to tender, or when health insurance funds start paying on a case mix basis. Success under such circumstances depends on tight project control rather than on good accounting, and in many cases good task analysis skills will also prove vital. Such changes in the contractual relationships expected in a market may put established firms, and their suppliers, at a significant disadvantage, offering a corresponding opportunity to an entrepreneurial entrant.

The process model

Firms earn revenue by performing services and delivering goods that customers want keenly enough to pay for. If the firm is to earn a profit, the price must exceed the firm's costs, while at the same time being less than the cost to the customer of doing without, doing it themselves or getting an equivalent benefit from an alternative supplier.

Every firm buys some inputs, performs some transformation processes, and produces some valuable products. The process and organisation design must be built around the factors that enables a firm to gain and keep customers while still making a satisfactory profit. Each of a firm's operations can be replicated by a firm's rivals and its customers: the firm survives because it creates more value for its customers than its rivals or the customers themselves could provide for the same cost. Remember that customers face search costs and risks (which can be expressed as the cost of an appropriate insurance premium) if they change suppliers, and so a

Input	Process	Product
List of purchased inputs to the value creation process (include all direct and semi-direct cost items)	Statement of transformation effected on inputs (if a service, state of the customer before service is delivered)	Definition of final product including service delivery arrangements (if a service, state of the customer after service delivered)

Figure 7.3 The process model

supplier with a good reputation and a record of consistently high quality performance does not necessarily have to match the lowest price rival.

The value can be relatively high because the firm performs an ordinary task extraordinarily well; or it may be because the firm's product is truly unique and customers who have the relevant need will not believe that there are any comparable products available. When the Channel Tunnel installed VESDA fire detection systems it was because they believed that the performance of VESDA systems was essential to protect their $12 billion asset and the two or more thousand people who can be in the tunnel at any one time. By contrast, Woolworths/Safeway sell the same types of food and groceries as competing retailers at similar prices: they attract and keep their customers by the selection of products that they offer, the layout of their stores, the courtesy of their staff, the freshness of their products and all the other factors that distinguish a good retailer from an ordinary one.

The entrepreneur must answer questions about the firm's competitive advantage before starting the process design:

▲ Is the competitive advantage based upon the product or the process? Will the firm attract and keep customers because of what it provides them or how it delivers it?

▲ Is the competitive advantage based in unique features or unique value-for-money? Can competitors remain in the market in the short and medium term by cutting their prices or must they replace their current product range?

Figure 7.1 shows some examples of enterprises classified by their major source of competitive advantage. In the two 'value-for-money' quadrants there is no 'magic bullet' to drive competitors away; rather, the total product offered is sufficiently good to hold a sufficient number of customers after they have given it a trial. Such trials take place as the result of an almost random process. Success with this type of advantage is often a matter of being lucky with one's competitors: Toyota enjoyed great success in the American market in the 1980s while Ford and Chrysler were struggling with financial problems and General Motors was dissipating its vast resources on a series of management fantasies; Woolworths' dream run in Australia from 1987 to 1995 came while its major rival, Coles Supermarkets, was afflicted with management problems at all levels; Wal-Mart's rise in the United States, and News Corporation's global growth, might not have been possible had the families of the chief executive also not been major shareholders. They could invest their cash flow in growth while their competitors were being bled dry by corporate predators.

Entrepreneurs with good concepts may look at Figure 7.1 and feel that it is a little too easy: their competitive advantage will fit in all four quadrants. The point of planning is to decide which of the quadrants must not be surrendered to competitors while the business survives, and therefore which of the quadrants their organisation will be built around. In three of the quadrants industry standards will be good enough, but in one, at least in the eyes and hearts of the firm's customers and targeted prospects, the firm must be unique. The industry standards may be extremely stringent: airlines whose planes crash and hotels whose guests get poisoned don't stay in business long, but these are not matters on which competitive advantages are built.

The firm's assets

Every firm is involved in a minimum of two quite separate groups of activities: the firm must maintain and develop its asset base; and the firm must carry out some value-adding processes that attract customers and generate sales revenue. The assets and the cash flow from operations can be separately valued, and a firm only creates value when the value of the cash flow is greater than the value of the assets. The subject of firm value is dealt with at greater length in Chapter 8.

A firm's assets can be grouped into four categories:

▲ there are tangible assets, such as buildings, land, plant and equipment (referred to as 'hardware' in computer industry jargon)

▲ there are intangible assets, such as intellectual property ('software') and customer goodwill

▲ there is the firm's human capital ('liveware') made up of the firm-specific skills of its principals and employees and the various team competencies that they have developed

▲ there are the firm's financial assets, such as cash, bank deposits and the debtors ledger, net of financial obligations such as creditors and loans.

Management of the financial assets has a chapter of this book to itself, but it is important to note that, strategically, something is an asset as long as the firm can use it in its operations; the question of legal ownership is quite separate. Most firms need premises to operate from, and so the business plan must show these, but new firms usually need to be very careful with their money, and so they often choose to rent or lease their premises and major items of equipment. A decision between renting and buying is essentially a financial one, but one way or another the firm will pay.

Tangible assets

The entrepreneur must develop a list of all the tangible assets that the new firm will need to control in order to operate. For each item there will be a cost of acquiring it and a separate cost of maintaining it; there will also be an implicit throughput limit. When a firm's growth leads to equipment or premises becoming redundant, there will be a salvage value or disposal cost. Some items of equipment and the premises needed to house them may not be needed until the business has grown to a certain size, with the relevant operations being carried out on a service basis beforehand.

Preparing a good estimate of the fixed assets required is worth the effort, both for the confidence that it will give the plan evaluators and the fact that these assets are potential security for debt or lease finance. There is no need to be obsessive, listing individual office chairs, but if there is no line at all for office furniture, or the amount provided is not commensurate with the number of professional staff that will be employed, the plan will be considerably less credible than it could have been.

Particular care is needed to define the scale dependencies of each asset, showing at what revenue level the asset will need to be augmented, what the augmentation will cost, and how the augmented asset will perform. Sometimes the relationship between revenue and asset is obvious, as when a growing supermarket comes to need more checkout lanes, but sometimes it is not obvious at all, at least to an outsider, as when a manual batch manufacturing process might get replaced by an assembly line operation, or when parts of an assembly line are replaced by robots.

Intangible assets

Intangible assets can readily be divided into goodwill and brand equity on the one hand, representing the value to the firm of its reputation among current and potential customers; and intellectual property, the value of its unique corporate knowledge, on the other. In practice these are two effects of the one cause: the firm's corporate knowledge leads to the delivery of unique products with an appropriate reputation.

These assets are referred to as 'intangible' because, with limited exceptions, they are of no value to the firm's creditors in the event of bankruptcy. Plant and equipment can be seized by the bailiffs or receivers and auctioned, but by that stage the firm's goodwill and brand equity will not be worth much even if they could be crated up and offered for sale. Intangible does not mean unimportant or immortal, however.

Intellectual property is only valuable as long as it is unique, and yet product innovations will be imitated in as little as fifteen months, while process and management innovations can only remain confidential for a few years. A firm can only maintain the value of its intellectual property by ongoing research. This does not necessarily mean a formal R&D or marketing research department. It could be as simple as a regular tour of the appropriate trade shows and a press clipping service, but simple or elaborate, the business plan and proposed organisational model must show how the firm's intellectual property will be maintained and developed.

Goodwill and brand equity need looking after if they are to maintain their value. Australian firms are notorious for not returning telephone calls, for leaving people hanging on a line, and for tricks like putting coupons marked 'return this for more information' in their advertisements and trade show brochures and not sending anything to the people who do. In an established company this sort of behaviour leads to a slow erosion of customer confidence, but in a new one a few serious errors in dealing with customers and prospects can spell doom. An entrepreneur looking for a market with quick growth possibilities could do worse than look for one dominated by a firm that combines an essential product with a poor reputation. People will flock to an alternative even if there are few tangible differences between the incumbent's and the entrant's products. Being polite can be an innovation in some circumstances.

Human capital

There is no business without people. A firm can only grow and be profitable if it secures a good reputation among its actual and potential users. Two of the critical factors in establishing and maintaining a reputation are the quality and consistency of the product and the quality of the customer contacts with the firm's staff. With a very new business the *esprit de corps* is likely to be sufficient to ensure that customers are properly attended to, that bad products aren't shipped, and that service standards stay high.

Once a business expands to the point that new staff need to be employed there will be employees with less commitment and less understanding of what the firm is about. Many firms have found that the telephonist/receptionist can be the most important single member of staff when customer satisfaction is measured, but in these communications-intense times any member of staff may find themselves answering the telephone to a customer or prospect. Devices like orientation programs and company handbooks may seem dreadfully pretentious to a business with half a dozen people, but they may be an essential insurance policy: the person who gets a crass response from the storeman, or who won't leave a contact number because the telephonist said 'we don't do that' might be the one who was going to give that critical order.

Training programs serve the direct purpose of transferring and enhancing skills, but they also serve a secondary role in bonding employees to the organisation and to each other. Well managed firms spend a lot more on training than less well managed ones, not just because their managers want to be nice to their staff, but also because reducing staff turnover rates can have a dramatic effect on the profitability of a business. Staff with four year's experience (the average for Japanese manufacturing firms) can be 30 per cent more productive than staff with eighteen month's experience (the average for United States manufacturing firms). Working faster plays a role, but so does working smarter: experienced workers make fewer mistakes, meaning that less rework is needed, and they don't stop to ask advice as often.

There is a marketing reason for taking some care of the ordinary staff of the business, and that is that these are the people who get to learn about customer and process problems first. One of the reasons for the success of Japanese manufacturing industries since the mid 1970s is their success at involving all the staff in product and process development. Some Japanese firms have staff suggestion programs that yield a workable suggestion per employee per year: these Japanese employees know what their company is trying to do and want to be part of doing it.

Counter staff, process workers and delivery personnel are part of the human capital of a firm: they can, with good management, become part of the product and market development process as well.

The asset model

The process only exists to capture value from the firm's assets: Figure 7.4 presents this graphically. The financial assets are on top, because they are part of the rules of the game: the firm is legally obliged to maintain certain financial standards and an entrepreneur may be committing an offence if a firm continues to trade with negative net assets. The intellectual property of the firm is placed, in Figure 7.4, second only to the firm's financial assets. Entrepreneurship and innovation are fundamentally about ideas, not things. The firm's reputation, or goodwill, is treated here as part of the intellectual property portfolio, because marketing (securing trial) and product development (ensuring that trial is satisfactory) must be treated as a combined activity. Readers familiar with Harvard's Professor Porter (1985) will know that he puts marketing and sales together as part of the process line. We disagree: sales is part of the delivery process, realising the value embodied in currently available products and existing customer relationships. Marketing is about building future value, new customers and new products.

We put the firm's human capital below its intellectual assets because people form the link between the idea and the real process. It is a two-way flow: people, often the same people, contribute to the intellectual property of the organisation

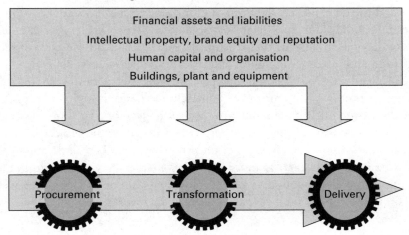

Figure 7.4 The asset registers

as well as carrying out the various tasks implicit in the process. Entrepreneurial firms are often exciting and satisfying places to work, but excitement and satisfaction should be the result of the proper implementation of an entrepreneurial value creation process, not the chief object of it. Buildings, plant and equipment are properly placed at the lowest level of the asset hierarchy. These are transient incidents in the life of an entrepreneurial firm.

From organisation and process to market and profit

In Chapter 8 we explain how to develop a marketing and financial model from which the financial viability of a proposed venture can be established. The integrity of the financial model depends on the integrity of its assumptions, and most particularly the assumptions about the recurrent and equipment costs that will be required at each level of revenue as the firm and its markets grow. The most critical are those that occur soonest: the minimum viable organisation and asset base that can create and deliver its product at and immediately after the product launch.

The design of the organisation and the process will interact with the financial model and constrain it: in real life, there may be several iterations of the organisation and process design needed to find a viable one, and some more to look for the best possible launch structure. Firms launching new products must walk a narrow path between not making their project viable because of too much excess baggage, staff, inventory, equipment, and launching and failing because the organisation is simply too anaemic to deliver its promises.

A more subtle error comes from launching with an ultra-thin organisation structure and asset base, and then failing to build sufficient muscle as the market grows and the demands on the firm's staff multiply. Such firms appear to make a successful launch, but fail, or at best stall, one or two years after the launch because they fail to support their customers and this cuts off the cycle of recommendation and repurchasing upon which all long term success depends.

To avoid this the organisation, process and asset planning should reflect two market states: at the time of the launch, uncertainty is high and capital precious; after two years for a durable product, rather less for a consumable one, the market response is in. If the market response is negative, the project is over, but if the market response is favourable, uncertainty is far lower and capital, while still to be used with care, is more readily available. Having an 'exploitation' structure complete, if only on paper, avoids the waste of precious time when a decision to move from market trial to major launch is made.

Checkpoint

Entrepreneurial business planning is not an 'efficient' process, as we emphasised in Chapter 3. For all practical purposes each successful proposal emerges from the debris of many failed ones. There is no dishonour in declaring at any stage that the concept cannot be successfully elaborated along the lines that are currently being pursued. The concept may or may not survive, but the doomed route must not.

Look at the SOPA factors: Do they make sense? Can the people they need be recruited, and if they can, will they work in this structure? If they don't, they can't, or they won't, **stop now**, rework the organisation or the process or the asset base, or even go back and redevelop the concept, but don't go on to complete a plan for certain failure.

End notes

1   A widely quoted work on sustainable competitive advantage as the essence of strategy is Porter (1980).

2   An excellent work for on the relationship between strategy and planning is Mintzberg (1994).

3   The economists' argument is more easily appreciated once one accepts the assumptions of perfect knowledge and perfect foresight. Where these assumptions hold, the only reason for forming a vertical alliance is to capture some value that would otherwise flow through to consumers, and betraying an alliance partner is justified by the ultimate consumer benefit.

Chapter 8

Marketing and financial modelling

Planning spreadsheets

The development and elaboration of the concept of 'management by objectives' represented one of the twentieth century's major landmarks, relieving entrepreneurs and chief executives of the God-like responsibility for ordering every aspect of an operation and allowing them to delegate without threatening the integrity of the organisation. There is still the problem of developing the objectives. For the continuing operations of an established organisation this is relatively simple: the chief executive, with or without the help of a planning unit, examines the historic data and sets objectives based upon some projection of it. Monitoring is then a matter of comparing actuals with the projections and taking action to control any variances. Those chief executives who earn their salaries do so by resolving the conflicts that arise when various objectives become incompatible: when manufacturing can't meet the increased volume projections, reduce variable costs, and avoid any capital expenditure; or when the sales manager cannot meet the revenue forecast without allowing reps to overspend their petrol allowance; or when the service manager can't increase customer satisfaction and halve the number of service representatives in the same period.

Entrepreneurial businesses must be managed, often much more carefully than established ones, since there is so little room for error. There are, however, no historical records from which objectives can be derived. A planning spreadsheet generates, among other things, 'pro-forma' sales and cost projections which serve two major purposes:

▲ they provide a pseudo-historic base upon which objectives can be set and the performance of the organisation in its early months monitored

▲ they provide a tool which can be used to test the financial feasibility of a proposal, and to refine the marketing and organisation plans of a feasible one, without going to the trouble of developing a full set of operating financial projections (which we describe in Chapter 14) or actually launching the venture (Chapter 18).

Financial modellers have used spreadsheets for centuries; but until the 1980s these were usually paper and pencil efforts. Marketing models can be developed systematically and automated by using a spreadsheet, and we describe one way of doing so in this chapter. Putting a marketing model onto a spreadsheet is something of an innovation, but the methods that we recommend here are based on over twenty-five years of published research on marketing, economics and sociology.[1]

Fear, facts and fantasies

Models were once made of balsa wood, and a few still are, but the models that entrepreneurs use to help them plan and run their businesses are made out of numbers, and stored and calculated on a computer. Stored program computers are relatively new, dating from about 1950, and personal computers cheap enough for most people to own and powerful enough for most people to find useful have only been available since 1985 or thereabouts. Most white collar workers in Australia, by 1995, regularly used a computer at work, but quite a few did not, and for many people the computer remains something of a mystery.

In one very real sense, computers do not 'do' anything: a computer is a machine which obeys a detailed program, such that if the same computer is given the same data and made to execute the same program it will produce the same result. Programs often have 'bugs' in them, meaning that, for at least some data values, the result may be different from the one that the people who programmed the computer intended. This is not a 'computer error'; it is a person error. If the data given to a computer is not a good reflection of the real world, the results may be equally unrealistic: one of the earliest computer acronyms was GIGO, meaning, 'Garbage in, garbage out'. Erroneous computer output generated from bad input is not a computer error either; it too is a person error.

There is a sense in which computers do more than simply carry out their instructions; the sheer calculating speed of a modern computer means that calculations which would take a human a lifetime to complete are finished in a matter of minutes on a computer. Such results can't be checked by hand, and so they can be said to be 'computer generated'. Computer-generated results can be in error even if the program used has no bugs. This can be because of subtle (or not so subtle) errors in the data, or because the program used is not a perfect model of the real world, or because the problem does not have a calculable solution.

Computers are tools, just as hammers are. A hammer can drive in nails or crush a thumb. A computer can be a useful tool or a way of accelerating disaster. We don't blame the hammer for a broken thumb, and we should not blame a computer for a rotten outcome to a venture. We would laugh at a carpenter who tried to drive in nails with his bare hands for fear of hitting his thumb with a hammer. An entrepreneur who refuses to use a computer for fear of making a mistake with it is just as foolish.

Perfection

The world that people live in is messy, full of unexpected events, some pleasant but many downright nasty. The ancient Greek philosopher Plato suggested that people felt this way about the world because they did not understand it. Plato used the analogy of people sitting in a cave, with their backs to the entrance, watching the shadows made by people and events happening on the outside.[2] Humans, Plato suggested, are trapped in their illusions; the messiness of the world that we perceive and the apparently randomness of the events that batter us is an artefact of the limitations of our senses. The real world, the world outside the cave, is perfect, obeying immutable laws and moving in a perfectly predictable way. If we want to understand the real reality, said Plato, we should disregard the flawed evidence of our senses and look for the underlying truth in mathematics and logic.

Theoretical physicists and so-called economic rationalists still follow Plato's advice. Economic rationalists talk in formulas and equations; they refer to perfect markets and general equilibrium. When anyone confronts economic rationalists with evidence from the real world they dismiss it as 'anecdotal'. Theoretical physicists concern themselves with the first billionth of a second after the 'big bang'. Nobody is going to go back and take a look, and so the problem of contrary evidence does not arise. Theoretical physicists are 'often in error but never in doubt'; the same has been said of economic rationalists.

The words 'perfect' and 'ideal', when used by theoretical physicists and economic rationalists, mean 'explained by our equations'. The opposite to 'perfect', in this sense, is not 'imperfect' but 'real'. The opposite to 'rational' is not 'irrational', but 'practical'. An entrepreneur does not require nor expect perfection nor certainty. He or she is not afraid of 'perhaps': perhaps it won't work out this way, but I'm here to maximise the chances that it will. This is how entrepreneurial market and financial models are intended to be used: they help the entrepreneur eliminate the impossible and the very unlikely; and they help the entrepreneur improve the route to his or her objective; but they don't replace the real world or try to deny its richness and complexity.

Chaos and complexity

The Platonists based their stand on mathematics, so much so that the entrance to Plato's Academy in ancient Athens had the sign 'No Entry Without

Geometry' engraved over the entrance. From the 1890s on a series of discoveries in mathematics have shattered this foundation. These can be summarised under the headings 'chaos' and 'complexity'.[3]

Work on chaos, or more properly, 'deterministic chaos' goes back to the French mathematician Poincaré. He was the first to observe that, even when 'perfect' equations are available, it can be impossible to produce an accurate prediction. Technically, as soon as the equations that describe a perfect system have non-linear terms, the implicit error may grow without limit. All predictions about the future state of such a system are strictly less accurate than the data about the present state, and the possible error grows exponentially with time.

There is nothing special about 'non-linear' behaviour. A perfectly straight horizontal beam made of perfectly uniform material and balanced on perfectly frictionless hinges is mathematically linear, but the same beam stuck in the ground to make a column is not. Even the stars in the heavens are affected by chaos. Astronomers know the position of the moon to a precision of about one second in a thousand years, and so a prediction of an eclipse in a thousand years from now would be good to the nearest second. A prediction for ten thousand years into the future, ten times as long, would not be good to the nearest 10 seconds, but could be out by as many as 1000 seconds. A prediction for a million years into the future would be no better than a random guess.

Related work on complexity theory has shown that the behaviour of complex systems cannot be predicted from a knowledge, no matter how perfect, of their pairwise interactions. The equations governing such a system do not have 'perfect' analytical solutions, and the best numerical solution processes are 'NP-complete', meaning that the time needed to compute a solution grows exponentially (or worse) faster than the number of components in the system. We don't need to search the heavens for an example; one shopper in one supermarket could spend the lifetime of the universe (or longer) trying out all the ways to fill a simple shopping list.

Commercial lottery games such as Tattslotto demonstrate how even a very small number of choices can lead to a huge number of outcomes. Only one choice of numbers will win the first division prize in any draw; finding the optimum, the best possible, state for a real system is just about as hard as picking the winning Tattslotto numbers.

Reality

The real world is built on compromises, most of them quite satisfactory. A table of eclipses that is good for ten thousand years satisfies most practical requirements. Most people who enter supermarkets emerge eventually with their immediate needs satisfied. Architects and engineers are quite good at specifying columns that won't buckle. Even when we do not have exact information about the future it is often possible to make a very accurate guess of the limits to the range of possibilities: the next Melbourne Cup will almost certainly be won by a horse.

An entrepreneur planning a venture can make guesses about the future, and as long as the guesses are based upon a reasonable base of research and experience they can be used in a business plan. The planning process should recognise two sources of variance:

▲ the initial guesses will have an explicit or implicit margin of error — these errors compound with time, so the longer the forecast, the less reliable the numbers will be at the end of it

▲ the plan, like every human endeavour, is subject to systemic upheaval, or catastrophe; factors that no one was taking any account of may interact in ways that no one would have imagined, leading to an outcome that nobody ever forecast.

The entire point of the plan is to anticipate the first type of errors and either counter them or build on them as the plan evolves. If early sales are slower than planned, actions can be taken that will bring them back on track. If they are better than anticipated, the plan will help the entrepreneur avoid a cash flow crisis as the new venture takes advantage of the favourable turn of events.

The word 'catastrophe' has a mathematical and a colloquial meaning. To a mathematician, a catastrophe is a sudden, discontinuous change in a system. A Melbourne cool change, when storms from the south-west break up a hot spell, is a catastrophe in the mathematical sense. Colloquially, a catastrophe is a disaster, but in retrospect, most systemic shocks have been turned into disasters by human action. All too often, the human action has consisted of following a plan even after its major premises are shown to be wrong.

A myopic entrepreneur may not be able to see the difference between a variation from the plan arising from the inevitable imprecision of forecasting and the effects of a catastrophe. A small scale entrepreneur might open an ice cream stall, and find that sales on the opening day are 50 per cent down on budget. The marketing text books explain that sales can be boosted by more promotion and so the entrepreneur might erect a bigger and more colourful sign. This might be an unnecessary expense if the weather had been unseasonably cool on the opening day: the weather fluctuates, and ice cream sales fluctuate with it. One day may be too short a time in which to decide that a trend has been established. On the other hand, if the Environment Protection Authority has just erected a huge sign banning swimming and setting out a list of vile pollutants contaminating the nearby beach, every day the entrepreneur stays on that site is one more step on the road from catastrophe to disaster.

Building a marketing model

In the following section we take some of the concepts described in Chapter 4 and show how to use them to make numerical predictions.

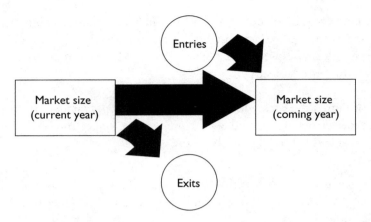

Figure 8.1 A basic population model

The population sub-model

Every model should quantify the market that the new venture intends to satisfy. This market must consist of a certain number of people or firms, with an expected entry and exit rate. If the plan covers an entry into more than one market, there can be more than one population sub-model, but common sense should limit the complexity of this part of the business model. Proposals can be viable over a wide range of possible market sizes, and the population sub-model serves to chop off wildly over-optimistic forecasts and to set out certain assumptions, including the exit and entry rates.

Models that are intended to be used to produce pro-forma accounts or presentation charts should normally include rounding functions to stop such models predicting sales to fractional customers. If a model is to be used for simulation, rounding can make it unstable, but if rounding is not used the accounting rule of exact amounts will be broken. In general, separate but related models should be used for mathematical simulations and for the preparation of pro-forma accounts.

External influence

The first step in every successful marketing campaign is to persuade someone to buy the product, in the hope that they will continue to buy it and that they will recommend it to other likely customers. For the top level of an entrepreneurial business plan, all forms of marketing expense are equal, and a good simulation starting point is to assume that the marketing expense required to secure one new, unrelated and uninfluenced customer equals the total gross margin to be earned from an average customer over the course of a year. This is the difference between the user price and the variable cost of production or delivery, and includes retailer and distributor margins as well as the salaries and commissions paid to sales staff and money spent on promotion.

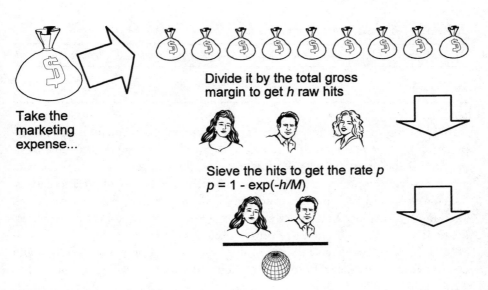

Take the marketing expense...

Divide it by the total gross margin to get *h* raw hits

**Sieve the hits to get the rate *p*
p = 1 - exp(-*h/M*)**

Figure 8.2 Externally generated sales rate

If the model is programmed to follow the concept in Figure 8.2 the result will be a rate rather than a number of sales, because the final adjustment has not yet been made. The sieve function shown produces an 'adjusted hit rate', a gadget to stop the model implying that sufficient advertising can force sales to more than 100 per cent of the market. The adjustment forces a diminishing returns effect into the rate calculation. The adjustment in the form shown is mathematically appropriate, in that it eliminates customers who are influenced more than once but still only buy once. In practice, very few companies can afford a marketing expense so high as to reach anything like the ultimate population in the first few months of a marketing campaign, and leaving out the adjustment won't make very much difference to the outcome — until someone experiments with a 'what-if' simulation that involves doubling the marketing budget. Figure 8.2 and Table 8.2 (see page 236) include the assumption that the new firm's advertising and promotion is pretty effective. Cautious modellers might include an 'advertising effectiveness coefficient' to test the effects of gaps or errors in the promotional plan.

Repurchases and recommendation

A good starting estimate for an estimate of the fraction of users who will recommend a product is to carry out (or simulate) a customer survey, where respondents rank the product from 'awful' through 'dislike it', 'don't care', 'like it', to 'excellent'. People who rate it 'good' or 'excellent' are likely to repurchase it, if nothing better comes along before they need to replace it.

If the real or simulated customer survey produced results like those in Table 8.1, some 70 per cent of the people induced to buy the product once

Table 8.1 *A possible survey result*

Strong approval	Moderate approval	Neutral	Moderate disapproval	Strong disapproval
28%	42%	24%	6%	1%

would be predisposed to buy it again, and presumably recommend it. The interpretation of such results must take into account the existing and probable competition: if the proposed new product has close substitutes, many of those who give it moderate approval may have a strong preference for one of the alternatives. When a new product is being considered for introduction to a crowded market, anything less than a 70 to 80 per cent 'strong approval' rating may prove inadequate. The quality movement recommends 'six sigma' quality, meaning that if 1000 users were asked their opinions of the product, approximately 978 would describe it as an 'excellent' fit to their requirements with 22 calling it a 'good' fit.

The core adoption model

Initial purchase is treated in this model as a response to one of two stimuli: there are the externally influenced adopters, responding to advertising, promotion and sales effort, and there are those who join as the result of influence from earlier adopters. Figure 8.3 shows how this model works. When implementing this model in a spreadsheet there are a few points that must be watched carefully. One is that people who have been induced, by external influence, to give the product a trial and who like it will begin exerting internal influence after they acquire or use the product, not at the start of the relevant planning period. They will, on average, only exert half as much influence as those who were adopters

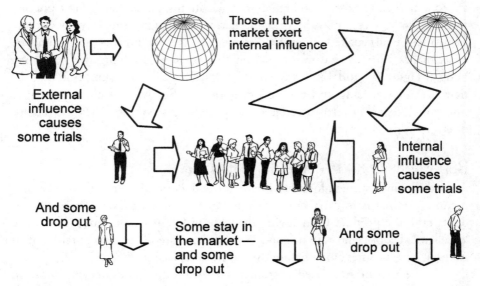

External influence causes some trials

Those in the market exert internal influence

Internal influence causes some trials

And some drop out

Some stay in the market — and some drop out

And some drop out

Figure 8.3 The basic adoption model

when a period started. This effect can probably be ignored if the model time interval is very short, but it is important when each model period is a year. You should also note that not everyone who tries a product will become a user, and that over time, users drop out. The minimum dropout rate will be the rate of exit from the eligible population illustrated in Figure 8.1.

Everybody who is influenced to make a trial constitutes a sale, but only those who like the product are candidates for repurchase and stay in the influence group. When implementing the model shown in Figure 8.3 the influence rates must be discounted as the number of people 'in the market' grows. The easiest discount formula to use is:

$$discounted\ influence = influence \times \left(1 - \frac{in\ the\ market}{total\ market}\right)$$

If you don't remember to adjust the influence effects as the market develops, the projections take off, promising far more users than there are people or firms in the market.

The model can be extended to allow for competitors, but it then becomes more of a simulation model than a planning one; a business can plan its own product launches and marketing expenditures, and reality often still turns out to be different. Assumptions about competitors' future launches and marketing plans can be little better than guesses and to the extent that they are used to build a forecast they detract as much from its credibility as they add to its apparent precision.

Turning adoption into sales

The fact that a number of people have given a new product a trial and decided that it is good may give an entrepreneur warm feelings, but it won't satisfy the bank manager. What is needed is continuing revenue from sales of the product and any associated, separately sold, services. For some products adoption leads automatically to a continuing revenue stream, as with a cable TV subscription: an adopter of such a service becomes a subscriber, and makes a payment every month until they fail to renew at some time in the future. Sales of frequently consumed products can also be modelled in this way; since there is no minimum contract period, the short term revenue is rather more uncertain than for a product with an annual or longer contract period, but the difference does not matter much in practice: factors outside the model are considerably more important. One thing that modellers must be careful with is to count no more than half the revenue from new adopters in the period of their adoption; an effect that is small when the periods are very short, but important for longer model intervals. Failure to make this adjustment has the effect of bringing cash collections forward, and since cash is so important to a new venture it is not an area where optimistic estimating should be encouraged.

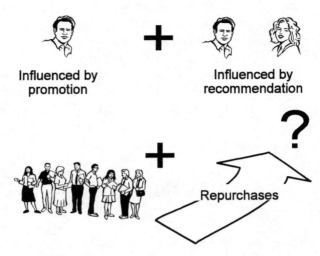

Trial purchases

Influenced by promotion

Influenced by recommendation

Repurchases

Figure 8.4 Turning adoptions into a sales forecast

When the product is purchased infrequently the problem of developing a sales forecast is, as suggested by Figure 8.4, not altogether simple. The obvious approach, simply taking the non-dropouts from the appropriate number of periods before, discounting the number for market exit, and recording them as sales in the current period, puts a suspicious kink into the sales figures, and a large corresponding bump in the sales growth curve, at the point where repurchases are presumed to start. If this is undesirable, and particularly if the model is to be used to simulate the effect of increasing or decreasing the interval between repurchases, some rather complex programming involving statistical distribution and/or smoothing functions and possibly some matrix arithmetic will be needed. Attempting this programming and getting it wrong is almost certainly worse than using the short cut. If you do use the short cut, remember that the kink is a model artefact and not a prediction with which to skewer the sales manager in five years time.

Seasonality

Some products are sold more easily at certain times of the year. If the model uses annual periods in which to forecast, this doesn't matter, but if the model is used to forecast months or quarters a seasonal adjustment should be applied. Seasonality comes in at least two guises: there are seasonal events and conditions, such as Christmas or winter, and there is the fact that different months have different numbers of working and non-working days. As long as the model is being used for venture planning, the pattern of the weeks is not critically important, but if it is retained as a management tool after the venture is launched a good understanding of seasonal factors is essential.

Small populations and prediction errors

When the expected number of sales per period is small, the model may 'fail to start' since there is never enough influence in one period to bring in the first customer. To avoid this, add rows to the spreadsheet to carry unused influence forward into the next period. This will avoid the model showing a permanent zero, and may lead to results with a remarkably realistic feel to them, with early sales proceeding in a series of fits and starts. When this happens it is a good indication that real-world sales will proceed in a pattern of fits and starts, at least until the product is well established, but the pattern in the model is extremely unlikely to be the same as the pattern in real life.

Predictions are subject to error, no matter how soundly they are based, and the probable error will usually be no more than the square root of the number of units expected. If the plan, or even a forecast based on a series of successful periods of selling, predicts 10 000 sales in a period, the probable error range is ± 100, or about 1 per cent. Quite small changes from the forecast, assuming that it has been seasonally adjusted correctly, are a matter of concern. By contrast, if the number of sales per period is expected to be 1, the error range is ± 1, and an actual sales achievement of 0, 1, or 2 units should not cause any great surprise. If the sales per period are expected to be about 1, then only about 37 per cent of periods would be expected to see exactly one sale; about the same number of periods would see no sales at all, and in around a quarter of the periods there would be more than one sale.

Given an expectation of one sale per period, every eight months or so you should expect consecutive periods with no sales at all. Panic in such situations is understandable, if statistically unjustifiable. It is possible to make a computer model simulate vile tricks such as this, and this is useful for simulation purposes when very large amounts of money are at stake. It is, however, rather dangerous to include random or pseudo-random numbers in a forecast that is going to be used to build financial projections.

The adjusted sales forecast

Clever or simple, if the model has been completed to this point you have a sales forecast built on logical premises. It will not be perfect, and it may not even be as good as the intuitive forecast produced by a sales manager with enormous experience in the type of market involved. It will help an entrepreneur to avoid making ridiculous assumptions, such as achieving the entire market forecast sales rate for a new, complex product on the opening day, or selling more product than there are people in the world to buy it.

We have included a simple market model as Table 8.2 in order to show that the spreadsheet programming required is not very complex. There is nothing seriously wrong with students or entrepreneurs copying out the formulas from Table 8.2 and trying the model out with their own numbers, **as long as** they make a serious effort to understand how the model works and move fairly rapidly to the point that they can build their own.

Table 8.2 *A simple market model*

	A	B	C	D
1	Base population	100 000		
2	Gross margin	50		
3	Internal influence	0.45		
4	Year	0	1	2
5	Total market	100 000	102 000	104 040
6	Marketing spend		100 000	50 000
7	Raw hit rate		=C6/($B$2*B5)	=D6/($B$2*C5)
8	Adjusted hit rate		=1−EXP(−C7)	=1−EXP(−D7)
9	External sales	0	=C8*B12*C5	=D8*C12*D5
10	Internal sales	0	=$B$3*B12*(B11+C9/2)	=$B$3*C12*(C11+D9/2)
11	User population	0	=B11+C9+C10	=C11+D9+D10
12	Fraction left	=1−B11/B15	=1−C11/C5	=1−D11/D5
13				
14	New user sales	=B9+B10	=C9+C10	=D9+D10
15	Consumable sales	0	=B11+C14/2	=C11+D14/2

The spreadsheet formulas are shown above, and the same formulas with the more usual presentation below. Sales are in units, not dollars. For consumable sales, the number is the count of full year equivalent sales (someone who becomes a user late in the year counts less than someone who became a user earlier).

	A	B	C	D	E	F	G
1	Base population	100 000					
2	Gross margin	$50					
3	Internal influence	45%					
4	Year	0	1	2	3	4	5
5	Total market	100 000	102 000	104 040	106 121	108 243	110 408
6	Marketing spend		100 000	50 000	100 000	100 000	100 000
7	Raw hit rate		0.0200	0.0098	0.0192	0.0188	0.0185
8	Adjusted hit rate		0.0198	0.0098	0.0190	0.0187	0.0183
9	External sales	0	2020	990	1928	1847	1738
10	Internal sales	0	454	1304	2461	4145	6199
11	User population	0	2474	4768	9158	15 149	23 087
12	Fraction left	100%	98%	95%	91%	86%	79%
13							
14	New user sales	0	2474	2294	4389	5991	7938
15	Consumable sales	0	1237	3621	6963	12 153	19 118

This is, as new product models go, a very simple one. More sophisticated models may allow for dropout rates, different trial to repurchase figures, advertising effectiveness less than one, repurchases and replacements and the like. Model builders should be careful not to create models that cost more than the last bit of refinement is worth; they should be even more careful not to start confusing models with reality.

The financial planning model

Accountants and financial information

All sorts of people become accountants, but they all have one thing in common: they like numbers, and if they see a column of them they add it up. If the number at the bottom purporting to be the sum is not, an accountant fidgets and writhes. In most people addition is a 'left-brain' or analytical skill, but in many accountants it is a 'right-brain' or imaginative one. Even when they don't know what the correct answer is, they can point unerringly at a wrong one.

Over the centuries, accountants have devised a number of cunning tricks to keep errors out of the accounts and to make the columns add up. One is a rounding rule: credits and debits are always an exact number, either of cents or dollars. No matter what the calculator says, 12.5 per cent of $99.50 is $12.44. Another is that accountants are never happy with one way of getting an answer; they always want at least two. Three separate charts are needed to describe a company's accounts: a cash flow statement; a profit and loss account; and a balance sheet.

The cash flow statement is basically the story of the cheque butts: this much money was deposited in the account, and this much was paid out. The money in can be sales receipts, equity subscriptions, or drawn-down loans. Sales receipts can be 'ordinary' as in the normal course of trading in goods or services, or 'extraordinary', basically the sale of an asset. The profit and loss account goes further than the cash flow statement, looking at creditors and debtors as well as cash, but leaving out capital items such as the sale or purchase of assets. The balance sheet links the two together: the profit (or loss) is the difference between the opening and closing value of the firm's net assets after the appropriate adjustments for dividends, asset sales and purchases, equity subscriptions and returns, and additions and reductions to loans.

If the balance sheet does not balance, the accounts have a mistake in them. Even if the discrepancy is only 1 cent, there must be a flaw somewhere. Bitter experience has proved time after time that a tiny discrepancy in the accounts of an enterprise is as harmless as a smouldering cigarette butt in an oil refinery. Once the integrity of the accounting process has been breached, anything can get through.

Young programmers are particularly prone to the view that getting the program to work is the important thing, and the results will look after themselves. Sometimes it is only after they have made spectacular fools of themselves that they learn to put self-checks into their work. When generating sets of accounts, whether pro-forma or actual, the balance sheet should be calculated properly and checked within the spreadsheet or program.

We describe the financial operating model an entrepreneurial business will need in Chapter 14, and the complete set of interrelated spreadsheets and schedules as described in that chapter must be prepared before the business is ready to seek and obtain investment and loan finance and begin operations. An abbreviated form of the accounts can be put together rather earlier in the business planning process in order to test the feasibility of the project and to search for the best possible financing and marketing strategies. The creation of these financial models is not an option but a necessity for the committed entrepreneur.

The preliminary model

The financial planning model takes as its input the sales forecast and marketing expenditure projections produced by the market model, together with any other available planning data, and produces a present value estimate using the appropriate risk-weighted rate of return. The project is only feasible when this calculated value is positive, and the optimum financing and marketing strategy will be that which maximises the present value. The preliminary model differs from the final, operating model in three major ways:

▲ the final model includes, in its primary or subordinate schedules, lines for every possible item of revenue and expense, while the preliminary model uses separate lines only for major items and groups many of the minor ones into aggregates

▲ the final model is designed to allow estimated figures to be progressively replaced by actual ones, and so it is constructed from a hierarchy of schedules designed to produce accurate aggregates, while the preliminary model generates most of its cost rows by applying standard ratios

▲ the final model produces exact results in cents and units, while the preliminary model will accept fractions of either.

It is often useful to prepare two, closely related, preliminary models. In one, intended for the planner's use, there is no rounding and truncation. In the second there is rounding and truncation in order to generate graphs and tables for a business case or an early iteration of a business plan. Figure 8.5 shows a treated and an untreated forecast. Use of two models is particularly appropriate for plans for slow selling, high value items. If a plan includes a graph showing 0.52 units sold, or 3.7 customers signed up, for a particular period there will almost inevitably be questions about the missing 0.48 units or 0.3 customers.[4] In some audiences there may even be someone capable of making a witty joke about it. Tidying up the presentation avoids such embarrassments, but the 'tidy' model is very hard to use with any optimising software and can easily 'lock in' to a seriously sub-optimal result even when hand-optimised.

The sales forecast and associated customer base forecast triggers several revenue and cost predictions:

▲ sales revenue per period is the number of sales times the forecast average price in that period

- ▲ service revenue is the *average* number of customers in each period times the average service charge times the proportion of customers who are expected to use the supplier for their service requirements

- ▲ supplies and consumables revenue is related to the customer base in a similar manner to service revenue

- ▲ goods supply cost will be related to the number of sales

- ▲ manufacturing investment and inventory will be related to the change in the forecast number of sales from the preceding period

- ▲ manufacturing head count will be related to the forecast number of sales

- ▲ warranty and customer relations expenditure will be related to the average number of customers in each period

- ▲ distribution costs and reseller commissions will be related to the number of sales

- ▲ the number of customer representatives and service staff will be related to the average number of customers in each period

- ▲ administration and general management costs will be related to the total number of staff.

The market model is driven by a forecast of promotional expense by period: this is an additional line in the financial model, quite separate from any other marketing and sales cost lines.

The individual lines may need some massaging for different businesses: a service business may not sell its new customers any physical good in the first transaction, but the first transaction may involve a different charge and/or a different cost structure to subsequent service deliveries to a typical customer. When the service is delivered on the supplier's premises, the size of the premises and therefore the rent and utility charges will depend to some extent on the number of customers. All businesses must provide some excess capacity if they are not to force their customers to wait an indefinite time for service; exactly how much depends on the pattern to service requests over time and the fraction of customers the supplier is prepared to force to wait for an excessive period.

For most businesses at least some of the sales will be on credit terms, and so a separate schedule will be needed showing cash flow projections: the average debtor and creditor days must be used as parameters to this section of the model. The cash flow projections will, in general, be negative for the early periods of a project, and the cumulative sum of the cash flows shows how much capital the business will require. A financing schedule will show how this capital is to be raised, and the associated financing charges will be included in the cash flow projection. To avoid making the model circular, finance charges are usually calculated on the basis of the closing balance of the preceding period; to avoid

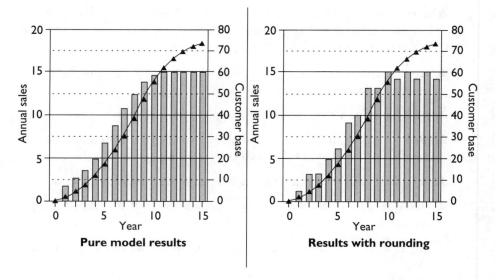

Figure 8.5 Model results with and without truncation: The truncated (right hand) model *looks* more realistic but is *less* accurate

making the cash flow model optimistic, the periods should be kept to months as long as the cash flow is negative.

The cash flows and the financing transactions generate the data needed for a balance sheet, which must be shown to balance: shareholder's equity plus total liabilities must *exactly* equal total assets.

The difference between the sales and the direct costs is the gross margin; the gross margin less fixed costs (including leasing charges but excluding interest) gives the earnings before interest and tax (EBIT); the EBIT less net interest costs gives the earnings before tax (EBT); and as soon as the cumulative EBT turns positive, tax must be paid, leaving profit (or earnings). The profit per period, discounted by the appropriate risk-weighted rate of return (see the next section for a discussion of risk weighting) gives the net present value (NPV) of the project.

A project is only commercially feasible if the risk-weighted NPV is positive, and the optimum financing and marketing plan is that which results in the highest possible risk-weighted NPV.

It is good practice to display as many as possible of the model-builder's assumptions in a 'hot box' so that they can be adjusted during the plan building and review period without rewriting the model every time someone asks a question. Some of the parameters that should be presented in the hot box rather than being included as model constants are:

▲ material costs as a percentage of revenue for each revenue class

▲ sales commission rates as a percentage of revenue for each revenue class

▲ reseller commission rates as a percentage of revenue for each revenue class (including co-promotion levies, slotting and listing fees as applicable)

- ▲ heads per unit of revenue for each revenue class

- ▲ wage rates for each class of employee

- ▲ oncost ratios for each class of employee

- ▲ administration and management staff ratio

- ▲ value of capital equipment value needed per unit of output per period

- ▲ value of capital equipment value needed per unit of service per period

- ▲ equipment leasing rate as a per period percentage

- ▲ average interest rates on long term loans

- ▲ average interest rates on overdrafts and other short term loans

- ▲ average interest rates on deposited funds

- ▲ corporate income tax rate.

Risk weighting

The complete market model produces three critical numbers for the financial projection: the marketing expense, the unit sales, and the size of the user population. The financial model will in due course turn this into a set of forecasts covering profit and loss, asset values, and cash flow. The main reason for a planner to produce these financial forecasts is to get the answer: yes or no. The most basic question the financial model sets out to address is: Do the prospective returns from this investment justify the associated risks?

There are two slightly different ways in which this question may be put into financial terms:

- ▲ Does the risk-weighted net present value of the projected returns from this investment exceed the cost of it?

- ▲ Does the prospective internal rate of return exceed the hurdle rate appropriate for this class of investment?

Each method has its advantages, and taken to the limit the two methods converge in any case. The theory of investment under uncertain conditions is very new, and the leading workers are Avinash Dixit and Robert Pindyck, whose papers and books on this subject have been appearing since 1989.[5] At the time of writing this book, they have not paid very much attention to innovation, but this omission will no doubt be filled in due course. An extremely simplified version of their argument is as follows:

- ▲ The level of demand in any given market tends to follow a 'random walk' such that each period's demand can be analysed into three components: a base level, a trend (up, down or flat) and a random component, again up or down. If demand takes a large fall (purely by chance) it may take some time before it ever comes back to its previous level or trend; similarly, if it takes a large jump up, it may remain above its average or trend level for some time. At any given time no one knows whether the next move in demand will be up or down.

▲ If an investment is made just before demand drops, it is relatively unlikely that the project will achieve the level of returns that had been planned for on the assumption of constant, or at least definite, future returns. If the investment had been a borderline case, and demand did drop, the investor would be worse off than if the money had been left in a perfectly safe non-entrepreneurial collection of government bonds.

▲ If there were ways to buy insurance against the risk of markets turning down (as there are, in the form of traded options, commodity futures, currency hedges, and derivatives plain and fancy in financial markets) a prudent investor would have paid an insurance premium to guard against loss, and the cost of the investment should be considered to be the sum of the cash required by the project and the cost of the insurance premium (or the price of an appropriate portfolio of derivatives, futures and options). Since this is larger than the cost of the investment alone, the true expected returns are lower than the apparent ones.

▲ A prudent investor will therefore only invest in projects where the expected return is sufficiently high to justify both the cost of the investment and an appropriate insurance premium.

To take an example more or less directly from Dixit and Pindyck's book, a company considering opening up a new copper mine at a cost of $10 million could put the money instead into Commonwealth Bonds at 8 per cent. If, at the current copper price, the mine could make a profit of $1 million per year into the indefinite future, this looks better than the bonds, but Dixit shows that, in practice, the miner would be unwise to invest until the prospective profits were at least $1.47 million per year. The 14.7 per cent return is the *hurdle rate* which investments of this class should be expected to exceed.

A second Dixit and Pindyck result allows a planner to adjust the risk-adjusted hurdle rate when the profit stream is expected to run dry after some number of periods. If the ore body in the mine above had an expected life of ten years, the expectation of failure is one failure per ten years or 10 per cent per year and this should be added to the hurdle rate: In this case, the mine should not proceed until the prospective profits were $2.47 million. Again, uncertainty demands a higher return: if the mine was known to have reserves that would last *exactly* ten years the appropriate risk-adjusted rate of return would be rather lower and the profit stream would be acceptable at $1.71 million per year. The effect of discounting over time means that the risk of the mine running out early has greater weight than the possibility of the profit stream continuing past the expected life of the mine.

The Pindyck–Dixit equations

Anyone for whom all forms of mathematics are black and obscure should skip this subsection, but they should make sure that whoever is setting up their spreadsheet reads and understands it.

Concepts and variables

ρ (rho) is the *riskless* rate of return per period, the return to an investor in gilt-edged government guaranteed stock: obviously, no one would wish to put their money into anything that earned less than this.

ρ' (rho prime) is the *risk-adjusted* rate of return per period, the lowest return acceptable to a rational investor with access to riskless investments returning ρ when offered an opportunity whose (perpetual) profit stream has a variance of σ^2 in a market with a long term growth expectation of μ.

μ (mu) is the trend growth rate per period, either of the general economy or of some other indicator that will result in an effortless increase in the profit stream.

σ^2 (sigma squared) is the normalised variance of the de-trended expected profit stream per period. (Note: the variance is the square of the standard deviation.)

β (beta) is a Dixit and Pindyck parameter that must on no account be confused with beta in the capital asset pricing model.

Equations (2) and (3) show how ρ' can be derived from the other parameters.

$$\beta = \frac{\sigma^2 - 2\mu + \sqrt{(\sigma^2 - 2\mu)^2 + 8\rho\sigma^2}}{2\sigma^2} \qquad (2)$$

$$\rho' = (\rho - \mu)\frac{\beta}{\beta - 1} + \mu \qquad (3)$$

ρ' is the minimum acceptable rate for a perpetual but variable income stream; if:

λ (lambda) is the expected length of time the income stream will flow

ρ'' (rho double prime) is a discount rate that can then be used as if the revenue stream was actually perpetual

(4) allows the discount rate ρ' to be adjusted when the revenue stream has an expected (not a certain) time before the profit flow will cease:

$$\rho'' = \rho' + \frac{1}{\lambda} \qquad (4)$$

Table 8.3

Source of variation	1:6 worst case (std deviation)	Variance (square of std dev)
Economy may go into recession	–5%	0.25%
Fashion trade liable to significant swings	–25%	6.25%
Range of outcomes for marketing campaign	–10%	1.00%
	Total variance	7.5%

Example 1

An entrepreneur is considering a new retail concept in fashion clothing. Riskless investments offer 7 per cent and economic growth is expected to be 2 per cent. No profit is expected in the first year, a profit of $500 000 per year is then expected until competitors imitate the format, and thereafter a profit of $200 000 per year until the concept is buried by a superior one. The entrepreneur estimates that competitors will enter at the end of year three and a superior concept will appear at the end of year ten.

The variance is estimated as shown in Table 8.3 above.

The expected profits can be divided into two:

a from year two for about two years: $300 000

b from year two for about nine years: $200 000.

From (2) and (3) β can be calculated as 1.62 and ρ' as 15.1 per cent. From (4) ρ'' is calculated to be 65.1 per cent for the high return element *a* and 26.2 per cent for the medium return element *b*. At the start of year two, therefore, element *a* will have a then-present value of $460 800 and element *b* will have a then-present value of $763 400. When these are discounted back to the start of year one at the same rates, element *a* has a present value of $279 100 and element *b* has a present value of $604 900.

The present value of the revenue stream is the sum of these, or $884 000, which is the maximum day one amount that a rational investor would subscribe for 100 per cent of the equity in the business, even though the business is expected to return $2.4 million over the ten years that it is expected to operate. The safe alternative investment, a term certain annuity for ten years at 7 per cent, would pay just over half this amount.

Example 2

An entrepreneur has developed a concept for a novel consumer durable and has borne all the costs of getting it ready for the market. She has completed a business plan showing that the product will be profitable from the second year on the market and the project will achieve a positive cash balance early in the third year, while profits will rise to a steady $2 million per year from year four until her patent expires in twelve years, after which competition will reduce the profit stream to $1 million per year. She asks a venture capitalist for $1 million to finance initial production and advertising.

The venture capitalist assumes that the rate of return on riskless investments and prospective economic growth is the same as in the previous example, 7 per cent and 2 per cent respectively. He recalls that new ventures such as this have a one-in-six expectation of total failure, and the standard deviation and the variance are therefore 100 per cent. β is 1.09, ρ' is 63.5 per cent and the present value of the promised profit stream is only $571 000. The venture capitalist shows the entrepreneur to the door.

On the Robert the Bruce principle, the entrepreneur raises a small sum of money from her friends and relatives, postpones her nationwide rollout, and markets her product through a regional network marketing group, where sales exceed expectations. After two years she returns to the venture capitalist, shows him the results of this market trial, and asks once more for $1 million for a national rollout through Target. The venture capitalist believes that the one-in-six worst case result for a venture with two years of trading history is a 60 per cent shortfall against expectations, the variance is therefore 36 per cent, β is 1.21, ρ' is about 31 per cent and the profit stream is worth $2.4 million. After some haggling, the venture capitalist offers the $1 million in return for 41 per cent of the equity in the business.

Asset classes

Risk is only appropriate for an investment that will be lost if a business fails. Marketing and product development expenses create intangible assets that are only valuable as part of a continuing business, and therefore money under these headings is wholly at risk. Buildings and land, on the other hand, will usually have a continuing value, although a sale by the receivers may not get back all the money spent on them. Plant and machinery will also have some value in bankruptcy, but if it is industry-specific, not very much: if a business failed because of low demand and prices for its product, no rational investor will want to pay very much money for plant and equipment that is only useful for someone wanting to enter that industry and experience low demand and inadequate prices.

To be super-logical, an entrepreneurial business plan should analyse all the expense items in asset classes: those that are lost with the business, those that will have only a low value on disposal, and those that may have a substantial value on disposal, and use a separate risk weighting calculation and discount rate for each. In practice, firms and investors use a single discount rate to evaluate the cash flow from a proposed project, implicitly placing a very low salvage value on any assets. From the view of an investor in new enterprise, this is quite reasonable: very few firms are wound up at the point where all creditors can still be paid from liquid assets and so the hard assets will be sold to satisfy the creditors. It is possible that a firm that was so well managed that it could anticipate failure in this way would not actually fail.

New entrepreneurial businesses are wise to lease as many of their assets as possible, even though this means sharing the eventual profits with lease

Marketing and financial modelling

financiers. By leasing these assets the business minimises its up-front cash requirements and improves the risk-weighted return for the investors: the returns can be higher even though the profits are lower.

Corporations are not usually in the position of investors in a new venture, in that the assets can, in general, be put to use elsewhere in the corporation even if the venture itself is terminated. Those that are not required can be disposed of in an orderly manner, and even the marketing and product development expense may not prove to have been totally wasted. The Apple Lisa was, by any measure, a failure as a product, but its software technology was re-used for the Apple Macintosh and the marketing and sales effort devoted to it built public awareness of Apple as an exciting company, an effect which may have had a positive effect on early Apple Macintosh sales.

Even assets like cars and computers, which receivers struggle to give away when winding up a bankrupt firm, retain most of their value inside a corporation. Economists describe the difficulties experienced by receivers as a 'lemons problem': once the firm has ceased to trade there is no one who knows which of the cars or computers were properly looked after and which weren't, and they are sold at prices that assume that they are all no better than the worst of them.

Corporations which do not intend to put up artificial barriers to innovation should be careful not to lump in the purchase of reuseable assets with the sunk marketing, development and tooling costs when evaluating proposals, since this would involve an exaggerated risk-weighting. Either the corporation should set up a notional leasing arrangement for the reuseable assets or it should use a separate asset class for them.

Example 3

A financial services company decides to offer a new service after a successful pilot. The major cash outlays and the relevant salvage value will be as shown in Table 8.4.

Their planners estimate that there will be a zero net profit in year one, $1 million in year two, $3 million in year three, and $5 million in year four and subsequent years. The estimated variance is 40 per cent, based upon 20 per cent observed variation in demand for similar services over the economic cycle and

Table 8.4

Outlay	Cash	Salvage
Working capital including launch promotion	$2.5 million	nil
Computer programming	$3.0 million	nil
Computing equipment	$1.5 million	$800 000
Premises	$2.0 million	$1.5 million
Total	$9.0 million	$2.3 million

20 per cent specific project risk based upon analysis of the pilot project results. They can earn 7.5 per cent on the Commonwealth Bond portfolio, and anticipate 2.5 per cent economic growth. For these parameters β is 1.19 and ρ' is 34 per cent.

The present value of the $9 million cash investment into the project is $7.9 million, which seems to be inadequate, but the at-risk expenditure is $6.7 million, and on that basis the project should proceed: its risk-weighted present value *exceeds* the required at-risk investment.

Variance

The variance of an estimate is the measure of our ignorance about the future. The square root of the variance, or standard deviation, can be thought of as defining a comfort zone: the outcome of an 'experiment' will, most of the time, be no further away from the expected value than one standard deviation. Roughly, four times out of six the result will be no more than one standard deviation away from the expected value, once in every six tries it will be less than the expectation minus the standard deviation, and one in every six tries it will be greater than the expectation plus the standard deviation. For example, if we observed sixteen consecutive spins of a roulette wheel we would expect black to appear eight times and red to appear eight times; but since the standard deviation in this case is two, we should not be surprised to see as many as ten reds or ten blacks to appear. The longer that we observed the wheel, the tighter, relatively, we should expect the balance to be. In sixty-four consecutive spins we could have no reasonable doubts about the wheel if the number of reds was between 28 and 36, we should view fewer than 24 reds or blacks with surprise and fewer than 20 with suspicion.

A business that puts a product on the market makes certain assumptions about the size of the potential market, the fraction of the potential users who will give the product a trial after a certain amount of advertising and at a particular price, and the fraction of those who give the product a trial who will become regular users and/or recommenders of it. Each period the product is on the market can be considered a statistical test of these assumptions. The standard deviation of these test results declines with the square root of the number of trials: if the number of sales in the first period was ten and the standard deviation was 80 per cent this means that the plan should not be treated as faulty if it had projected anywhere from two to eighteen sales in the first period. After four periods the standard deviation is down to 40 per cent, and if the cumulative sales forecast was within plus or minus 40 per cent of the actual, the plan should not be considered discredited.

If:

n is the total number of sales reported over a number of consecutive periods and

M is the total number of potential sales in the market then (5) produces the standard deviation of n where n is the best estimator of the 'true' or 'share of mind' sales the supplier gained.

$$\sigma_n = \frac{\sqrt{(n+1)\left(1 - \dfrac{n}{M}\right)}}{n} \qquad (5)$$

For example, the product manager of a firm selling a new, infrequently purchased product estimated the total market size at 10 000 users and in its first six months the product achieves 100 sales; σ_n equals 10.0 per cent and as long as the plan predicted something between 90 and 110 sales at this stage there is no reason to doubt the validity of the original plan forecasts. If, as happens all too often during the launch of a new product, the actual result is well outside the implicit range predicted by the forecast sales and their standard deviation, the marketing model should be adjusted until it produces a result that fits the data: there should be no attempt made to fit the world to the model!

At the planning stage, there are no real sales at all from which to estimate σ. The planner must rely on his or her experience, supplemented by such advice as they can get and such research and interviewing that they can carry out. In principle, a quite small sample of the population can produce useful results; in practice, it is very hard to estimate the repurchasing and recommendation behaviour of potential users from interviews and experiments. Advertising response can be estimated, and is, routinely, by major advertisers and their agencies, but good advertising, of itself, does not guarantee the success of a new product.

It is possible to estimate σ_0 (the standard deviation at time zero) with great precision, if with rather less realism, by setting each of the key parameters in the market model to their one-in-six worst case, observing the shortfall in the predicted sales revenue, expressing each shortfall as a percentage, and finally taking the square root of the sum of the squares of the percentage shortfalls. A simpler, and generally satisfactory estimate of σ_0 is 100 per cent (or for true pessimists, 150 per cent). In real life, each month's sales returns provide information that reduces σ and, as long as the sales themselves are meeting expectations, justifies a continued investment in product marketing.

The plan should anticipate real life, and in particular, allow for review points at which the plan can be revised or abandoned if reality is not coming up to expectations. The critical marketing parameters are:

▲ the advertising response rate, expressed as the value of new sales per dollar of advertising and promotional expenditure (we suggest that this may be as much as the reciprocal of the gross margin, but it can be less than this)

- ▲ the trial to user conversion rate (40 per cent would be considered acceptable in packaged goods marketing)
- ▲ the churn rate, the fraction of users in one period who revert to non-users in the next (10 per cent per year would be considered good in packaged goods marketing)
- ▲ the repurchase frequency and
- ▲ the effective recommendation rate (generally less than 50 per cent per year).

The uncertainty about the planner's estimate for each of these parameters will be reduced with actual marketing experience, but not all the 'real' parameters emerge together. The advertising response rate can be determined almost as soon as the first buying cycle is complete. The rate at which the other parameters emerge depends on the expected repurchase frequency. For a frequently repurchased product, the conversion rate and the repurchase frequency will become apparent within a couple of months of the product's introduction, and the churn rate, if it is going to be significant, will emerge within six months. For an infrequently repurchased, durable-type product, the most critical market parameter is the effective recommendation rate, and this is hard to estimate without two years of sales history.

Launch strategy

The launch of a new product takes place under circumstances of considerable uncertainty, and the appropriate planning discount rate is high; this in turn limits the amount a prudent planner will commit to the launch of a new product. After the product has been on the market for a reasonable length of time the uncertainty will be greatly reduced and the appropriate discount rate will be much lower. If the market has responded more or less as expected, this suggests that the planner's estimate of the key market parameters was close to their actual values, and a much more vigorous promotional effort may be appropriate.

Figure 8.6 sets out an illustrative flowchart: the planner assumes, of course, that both the decision diamonds will produce a 'yes' exit, but the plan must allow for one or both of them to lead to a different outcome. One way to do this is to compute two optimum launch plans: one for the original launch, using a discount rate of 70 plus per cent, as appropriate for an untried product: and plan for the development of a major launch once the repurchase/recommendation parameters and their confidence levels can be estimated from real data, using a more appropriate discount rate — say 30 per cent or so, after two years of trading experience.

Note that for a sound product, with a reasonable rate of trial to conversion, a low churn rate and a reasonable level of recommendations, marketing

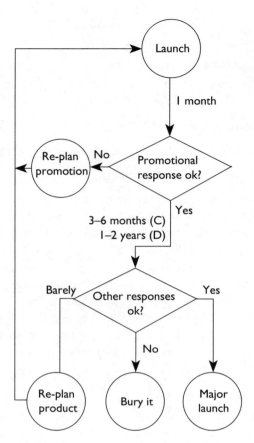

Figure 8.6 Launch decisions

operations become cash-positive very rapidly and are profitable almost from the launch. Even when a high discount rate is applied, the optimal strategy when marketing costs alone are considered may involve a very heavy launch expenditure, sometimes even pre-empting the 'major' launch. The best strategy for any particular product will depend on the non-marketing, scale-related fixed costs.

When scale-related fixed costs, such as leasing equipment and premises and recruiting and training production, delivery and service staff are substantial, the best strategy may involve a very low-key pilot launch followed by a very major one once the market response parameters have been determined to a reasonable level of accuracy and the market has shown its readiness to accept the new product. The time needed to gain confidence in the market response parameters can be as little as three months for a frequently repurchased consumer product to as much as two years for a durable one. Every plan is unique, and so we cannot set down any immutable rules, but a plan that involved a test-marketing expenditure of less than a tenth of a per cent of the annual available gross margin (see Chapter 5), to be followed, if the test was successful, by a major launch spending 5 per cent or more of the AAGM, would not seem unreasonable to us.

When scale-related fixed costs are very low the plan tends to become a pure marketing one, and the best strategy may involve a single launch with a budget of 5 or more per cent of the total available gross margin. For instance, magazine publishers can subcontract their printing and distribution, and so once they have covered their scale-independent editorial and composing costs they have few other fixed commitments: the single launch strategy is appropriate in their circumstances.

Amstrad Ltd became a major PC supplier in Australia and the United Kingdom over the years 1986–92; its product supply strategy was to subcontract manufacturing, transport and distribution, eliminating scale-related fixed costs. Amstrad launched each new package with an advertising blitz and promptly abandoned any that disappointed. Amstrad's PC business was eventually eclipsed by pressure from two directions: rival marketing companies and retail concepts eroded its market share, and its suppliers, firms such as Acer and Samsung, began to develop their own distribution channels and to promote their own brands and became less ready to concede large margins to a pure distributor.

Firms that, for one reason or another, can't or won't pursue the Amstrad route and intend to develop more than a marketing shell, may find themselves in a stalemate: once the market acceptability of their product is proved, it appears likely to be extremely profitable, but the cost of the capital equipment needed to make test-marketing quantities of their product is such that they can't justify a market trial to prove market acceptability.

Checkpoint

At this point in the planning process the planner should have a good estimate of:

▲ the most probable sales and revenue per period

▲ a reasonable estimate of the gross margin and the directly related marketing expense per period

▲ a good estimate of the fixed and variable costs that will be incurred in supplying the goods and delivering the services that make up the sales and revenue forecast and hence

▲ a good estimate of the per period profit or loss.

When the per period profit and loss row is turned into a net present value, using an appropriately risk-weighted discount rate, the value will be sensitive to several of the model assumptions. If the product is viable there must be some valid combination of parameters under which the risk-weighted present value is positive. If there is no such combination, it is extremely tempting to revisit the assumptions: raise the effectiveness of promotion to 110 per cent, or increase the trial to user conversion rate to 60 per cent for example. Such games might make the plan look better but they will certainly not improve the outcome of the eventual project.

The best of planners will overlook more possible problems than opportunities; 'cooking' the parameters to make a doubtful project look viable increases the risk of ultimate failure by relaxing the search for a truly viable way of bringing the product to market. There should be no shame attached to the planner who, after a conscientious effort to develop a viable plan, aborts a project. Very great blame should fall on a planner who bends the data to make an unviable project look attractive, and encourages people to commit time and money to a probable failure.

If one concept won't fly, find one that will; don't just stand there huffing and puffing.

End notes

1 Some of the papers consulted in developing the marketing models used here are: Bass (1969); Dodson and Muller (1978); Foxall (1988); Dockner and Jorgenson (1988); Mahajan, Muller and Bass (1990); and Bass and Krishnan (1992).

2 The most cited English translation of Plato's Republic is Cornford, (1966).

3 See, for example, Waldrop (1992) or Coveney and Highfield (1995). Both these works provide a reasonable, accessible overview of recent developments in the field.

4 Untreated model results are a statistical expectation, not a prediction. A sales forecast of 0.52 suggests a 60 per cent chance of gaining no sales in the relevant period, a 31 per cent chance of gaining exactly one sale, and a 9 per cent chance of gaining two or more sales.

5 The definitive text at this stage in the development of the theory of investment under uncertainty is Dixit and Pindyck (1994).

Part III

Chapter 9

Marketing decisions

Marketing: What is it?[1]

Marketing, in a law-abiding market economy, is the collected theory and practice of customer satisfaction. Marketers satisfy people by providing them with the information that they need to select goods and services that, in their users' possession, are worth more than the price. In the absence of this information, people would not be aware of the possibility of improving their businesses or their lives by the use of the marketed products and would be, to that extent, worse off.[2]

Many people are uneasy with the idea of 'marketing'. To people with strong concerns for those less well off than themselves, marketing may mean persuading people to buy things that they don't really need. To people who have just invented a new device, marketing may seem like an egregious waste of money: many inventors feel that their product is so outstanding that its mere existence will bring customers rushing.

Marketing can certainly be abused, as can most skills. To be good at marketing is to be good at organising the persuasion of people to buy a product or to adopt an opinion. If the product is dangerous to its users or the opinions lead to anti-social behaviour, then it is quite proper to condemn the messenger as well as the producer. Clever people are not always good. On the other hand, when marketing is directed towards the promotion of superior products and socially beneficial opinions, the marketers deserve to share the social approval and rewards consequent upon success.

Both the critics and advocates of marketing tend to exaggerate its power. In fact, people are very reluctant to change their opinions on any subject, including their opinions about the type and brand of goods that they buy and the nature and providers of the services that they consume. Running a saturation advertising campaign or unleashing a team of high-pressure sales people may secure a lot of sales, but if the product does not stand up there will be no repurchases, no recommendations, and no continuing business.

No one should confuse an act undertaken or a statement made under psychological stress with a genuine change of opinion. Most people can be persuaded to act in a way that is inconsistent with their opinions, once sufficient pressure is applied. Experiments conducted by psychologists have shown that university students can be made to doubt their own ability to add up if they are surrounded by sufficient people who insist that a wrong answer is 'correct'. Other experiments have shown that apparently normal people can be persuaded to inflict what looks like serious torture on others. The Colonels' Junta in Greece (1967–74) diverted an apparently arbitrarily chosen fraction of army conscripts to torture school, where most of them became quite efficient at torture and brutality.

When the pressure is released, people will rapidly revert to their previous opinions unless they are convinced that there is a good reason not to. Accounting students recover their ability to add up as soon as the door of the psychology lab closes behind them. As soon as the Colonels' Junta collapsed, the conscripted torturers turned, quite genuinely, into ordinary democratic Greeks.

Exact and extensible

The Australian firm Multistack International has become a major force in the supply of chillers, an essential part of commercial and industrial air-conditioning systems. The traditional suppliers of chillers build their systems to order as a single unit sized to each customer's specification. If a building is enlarged, or its use, and the load on the chiller, changes, increasing the chiller capacity is an expensive and messy job.

With the worldwide ban on the production of CFC refrigerants now in force, chillers that can't operate on the newer refrigerants have to be replaced. Getting the old chiller out means cutting it up into lift-sized pieces; replacing it with another single unit system requires major surgery to the building.

Multistack make modular chillers, which can be batch produced in their factory and then assembled on site. Their installations are competitive with traditional chiller suppliers for any level of specification for new buildings, and infinitely superior when old, CFC-dependent, chillers must be replaced in an existing building.

A marketing campaign involves a form of pressure, but legal, economic and political limits on the activity of marketers ensures that the pressure is far short of that generated in a psychology lab or a military conscripts' training camp. In most cases marketing aims to secure no more than a trial, and then from a small fraction of the target population, relying on repurchases and recommendations to build and hold market share. Repurchases and recommendations occur well after any promotional pressure has been withdrawn, and it is therefore the quality of the product that determines its long term success, not the power of the advertising.

Without advertising and other forms of marketing activity, of course, there may have been no trial and the people who would have come to value the product and freely choose and recommend it will not have had the chance. As long as regulations keep dangerous and addictive products off the market, marketing, even of unwanted and un-needed products, can do little harm. As suggested in an earlier chapter, the sales a business gains from marketing endeavour (as distinct from those by recommendation and repurchase) are, at best, cash neutral and, since there is no contribution to fixed costs, seriously unprofitable.

As long as an entrepreneur is confident that a new product is good for its users, will satisfy them and will be repurchased and recommended by them, there should be no moral problems with a marketing campaign aimed at securing trial purchase and use.

Whether a marketing campaign is going to be effective in securing an adequate number of trials without breaking the bank is another matter altogether.

Elementary marketing: The four Ps[3]

Marketing, at least at the elementary level, is usually discussed as a function of the 'four Ps' — product, price, promotion and place. Reality is never that simple, but most marketing activity can be put under one or other of these 'marketing mix' headings.

Product

The product, sometimes called the offer, is what the buyers and users see, and this can go far beyond the contents of the box — if there is a box. Every product has a primary function, but it is quite uncommon for this function to be the main reason for a particular purchasing decision. Someone who wants personalised road transport may well decide to buy a motor car, but this underlying need will not lead the buyer to a particular dealer to buy a particular model with a particular set of options. An object that cannot provide personalised road transport will not be selected by someone trying to buy a motor car, but in a market with many different ways of satisfying the primary functional requirement the ability to provide personalised road transport does not confer any particular advantage: you won't sell if you haven't got it and you mightn't sell even if you have.

Some secondary aspects of a successful offer are described below.

Precision fit

Other things being equal, a product that looks like a close fit to someone's requirements is more likely to be chosen than one which has excess performance or unwanted features, or one that involves the user in gap-filling. Someone wanting a holiday on Australia's Gold Coast might prefer to book a flight direct to Coolangatta rather than a flight which terminated in Brisbane with the journey completed on a road coach.

Features that a potential purchaser sees no need for can detract, rather than add, to the value of an offer, particularly when the buyer is not the ultimate user. Equally, excess capacity may not be seen as a benefit, even when, on a cost per unit of potential output basis, it makes the product seem to be extremely economical. A commuter airline moving a hundred or so passengers a day on its routes would not be attracted by the offer of a Boeing 747, even at a steep discount; the ability to carry 500 passengers is of no use to an airline that seldom picks up more than fifty.

Future constraints

The act of buying one product deprives the buyer of the cash to spend on an alternative, but many purchase decisions have effects that last longer than this. A single person may buy a two-bedroom flat or house, keeping open the option of inviting a friend to stay. It was mentioned above that excess capacity may detract from value; equally, a perceived inability to expand or adjust may be seen as a problem.

Product offers which lock a buyer into future decisions, such as having to buy compatible equipment in the future, or having to rely on a particular maintenance service, or having to use a single provider of consumable supplies or raw materials may be seen as relatively unattractive in some circumstances.

Persistence

A trotting horse flings material from the road backwards and upwards, and when a road is frequently used by horses this material can be particularly offensive. Horse-drawn carriages had dashboards fitted to prevent this thrown material hitting the driver or the passengers.

Horse-drawn transport is all but gone, but every modern car still has a dashboard.

Of course, if the lock can be promoted as a benefit, value can be added to an offer. Instead of 'you will have to buy supplies from …' it may be possible to argue 'we can guarantee the availability of essential supplies because …'

Uncertainty and risk

The future is inherently uncertain, and reasonable people are unwilling to load the downside any more than they have to. Entrepreneurs market innovations,

innovations involve novelty, and novelty detracts from product value. There is nothing much that can be done about this when the innovation is the core of the offer, but products that incorporate a major innovation may lose value in many people's eyes if there are 'changes for change's sake' involved.

Identification and esteem

Buyers and users of a product may become associated with it in the minds of their friends and colleagues. This is obvious with clothes, cosmetics and gifts. It is an important factor in a choice of house or car. It can be important in decisions about quite prosaic industrial equipment. AWA Ltd had, for many years, supplied electronic control equipment in plain steel boxes, finished in grey hammertone paint. This was regarded as normal in the Australian market. When they started exporting to Asia and the United States, AWA discovered that equipment packaged this way was all but unsaleable. American and Asian users expected to see equipment of this type in attractively styled housings, usually involving injection-moulded plastic. These housings added significantly to the cost and the price of some low-volume products, but the products were unsaleable without them.

Price[4]

The price, in marketing, is more than the number on the sticker. It includes all the direct charges that the buyer is expected to meet. Most non-government buyers now realise this, and treat the price as the starting point of their cost/benefit calculations when selecting a supplier. Government buyers tend to go for the lowest quoted price, and businesses selling to governments have made 'get well' measures into an art form. 'Get well' items are essential to the application of the product to the customer's problem but do not appear in the quoted price; technology companies selling to Australian governments have frequently earned two or more times as much revenue from 'get well' additions as they did from the original contract.

Private and corporate buyers are less bound by red tape and more directly affected by the cost of 'get well' items; they try to get quotations on a solution basis rather than trying to force different suppliers into making identical offers which can be discriminated on price alone. Such buyers look for 'inclusive' prices, allowing suppliers to package their offer to the closest possible fit to the user's functional requirements. Packages can often create a win–win situation: the buyer is spared the considerable cost and risk of developing a comprehensive package, while the seller is able to target a unique and potentially profitable product to a customer segment without the formidable expense of ensuring that every component element is unique.

Economists talk about the 'law of supply and demand', and in general terms, raising the price of a product will lead to fewer people buying it, or to people buying it less often. There are some limitations on the applicability of the law of supply and demand to innovations. For many products there will be a critical price above which sales fall off dramatically but below which they increase only slowly. Many retailers and packaged goods suppliers are convinced that in many markets these 'price points' are just below certain rounded numbers, and so only prices at these points will be tested. Price points are believed to exist at $10, $15, $20, $25, $30, $40, $50, $80, $100, $150, $200 and $500; there may be more. If a product is not selling at $79.90 the price may be set to $49.90 in the belief that all intermediate prices will still be seen as 'over $50' and if $79.90 is too high, so is every price between $50 and $79.90. Equally, if a product is selling so well at $99.50 that the supplier decides to change the packaging and raise the price, the new price may be $149 rather than anything in between.

Skimming and penetration prices

When a product is very new to the market there may be quite a wide spread of views as to its exact value. Most people, as we have seen, would not buy an innovative product in the year of its launch even if it was offered at a price well below its cost. Of those who have been persuaded, by promotion or by the recommendation of a satisfied user, to give the new product a trial there will still be a wide variation in the price that they would see as fair and reasonable. At this stage of a product's life cycle the entrepreneur has a clear choice: the price can be set high at the launch, so that a quarter or less of the potential adopters can afford it, and gradually lowered, or it can be set close to its ultimate level, drawing the largest possible number of potential adopters into the market and growing market share as rapidly as possible. Early in a product's life, when a few people may be prepared to pay quite a lot for it, setting the price to a point where only these people will buy it generates the highest possible revenue and profit. As the product gets more widely known, and its properties are better understood by potential buyers, there may be much less variation in buyers' opinions, and a high price strategy then ceases to make commercial sense.

Setting the price high and then lowering it is referred to as a 'skimming' strategy, while going for market share at once is called a 'penetration' strategy. In practice firms use a mixture of both strategies: when a product is new the supplier may be faced by heavy fixed costs and high loan repayments, and such a firm is forced to keep the price relatively high to generate cash flow, while as the market develops and volumes grow variable costs will fall and fixed costs will be spread over higher volumes; the price can then be allowed to follow the costs down.

Skimming strategies work best when firms have a unique product, secure from direct imitation. This can be a breakthrough drug, protected by strong patents. It can be a copyrighted literary work, first published in an expensive hardcover edition, then as a paperback at a lower price, then through book clubs at a still lower price, and finally set out as a remainder at less than the cost of the paper it is printed on. It can be a range of high fashion clothing with a registered designer label, sold at boutique prices at the start of the season, at '60 per cent off' clearance sales at the end of it, and at flea markets a few months after that.

Penetration pricing is most likely to be used when there are few formal barriers to market entry and where experience effects are likely to drive variable costs down rapidly (or when they are already negligible). Microsoft used penetration pricing with its Windows software: the near dominance of the PC software market that followed the success of this strategy locked rivals like IBM's OS/2 and Sun Microsystems' Solaris out of the PC market. There were few technical features in Windows that could not have legally been imitated, and so Microsoft's market position had to be established before it could be defended.

Many entrepreneurs have used a skimming strategy quite unwittingly: they have added up their costs, put a margin on top, and sat back to enjoy the profits. Since they did not investigate the market they did not realise that there was a great deal of latent demand that would appear if the price could be lowered. Until 1912 the world's motor car industry had been in this position, with each manufacturer selling a few thousand cars a year as rich men's toys. Ford spoilt this party with his T–model, launched at less than half the price that the established manufacturers were charging for their cheapest models. Although rich men did not buy T–model Fords, the high visibility of the T–model in the market changed their view of what was a reasonable price, and their demands for better value forced a drastic reduction in the number of firms building cars. Many firms vanished altogether, while others only survive as brand-names used by the remaining manufacturers.

Promotion

'Promotion', when used in a marketing context, has a strictly defined technical meaning: it is the deliberate communication of information about a product and its supplier to potential users. The primary purpose of promotion is to persuade potential users to give a product a trial, in the expectation that enough of them will be sufficiently impressed to become regular users and to recommend it to other possible users. Promotion is also used to support products at an above-average price point by emphasising their particular special properties; promotion may, with some products, serve to reinforce user loyalty by presenting a favourable image of the product's users which in turn may increase their attachment to the product and reinforce the effect of their recommendations and their example.

Promotion is primarily about communication, but there are a number of ways in which information can be delivered. These split naturally into two groups: there can be person-to-person communication, as with a direct sales force or with network marketing; and there can be media-delivered messages, basically advertising and public relations.

Sales persons

Properly trained, managed and equipped sales staff are by far the most efficient method of persuasion when it is measured as a ratio of prospects exposed to the messages to prospects adopting the product. Sales staff are the method of choice

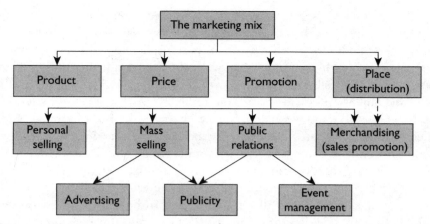

Figure 9.1 The marketing mix — with particular reference to promotion

for high value products and high value supply and service contracts whose potential customers can be identified accurately. There are, for example, two steel manufacturers in Australia, four car manufacturers, three major supermarket chains and three grocery wholesalers, one maker of external mirrors for cars, one maker of float glass and a similarly small number of buyers in many other industries. Industry-specific products are often best promoted by sales people.

Factors such as the number of hours in the day and the minimum salary or commission a sales person needs mean that other forms of promotion must be resorted to when the use of sales staff becomes uneconomic. A business-to-business sales person can make a maximum of 400 calls per year and will cost $70 000 or more in wages, commission, and overheads including a car and accommodation. Top line sales staff can cost three or more times this. Since each call costs $200 or more, a product so attractive that one was sold at every call would need a selling price of at least $400 to make sense. In practice, personal selling in a business environment makes little sense unless the average sales person can achieve $3 million or more in gross sales value per year.

Door-to-door selling now represents a tiny proportion of retail sales in countries like Australia; even though the walking or van-driving sales person can make more calls per week than the industry sales person the minimum value order is still relatively high and the selling costs are a major fraction of the final price.

Direct marketing

The term direct marketing is used to describe selling carried out primarily by mail (either by posting an offer or by having a product included in a regularly mailed catalogue), telephone, and future electronic communication media. Direct marketing can work well for medium and low price consumer durable products, and at least one company operating in Australia targets its direct marketing efforts at the consumable product requirements of small and medium businesses.

The cost per contact is much lower for direct marketing than for personal selling, and so the economics of direct marketing depend a great deal on the accuracy of the mailing lists used or the distribution of the selected catalogues. Mailing lists can be rented from list brokers; or an offer can be carried as an insert or outsert with a regularly published journal whose subscribers are expected to like the new product; or the major credit card operators can arrange mailing to a selected sample of their cardholders. Once a business can build up a mailing list of its own from which all hopeless cases have been purged, direct marketing can be a very efficient form of promotion and selling. For a new business, one of the great attractions of direct marketing is that the up-front capital cost can be so small: the number of prospects mailed can be limited by the size of the available budget.

The growth of cable television networks, and even the technology that allows broadcast stations to operate around the clock at little extra cost, has opened the opportunity for TV shopping. Most cable TV networks in the United States carried a home shopping channel by 1995; such services will almost certainly be offered in Australia. By 1996 Australian insomniacs could watch shopping programs in the early morning, and 'send no money — we bill you!' direct TV selling has entered Australian folklore.

Emerging networking technologies may give direct marketing a significant boost; the cost of a 'virtual shop' on the Internet is a small fraction of the cost of a real one, and potential purchasers pay the cost of finding virtual shops where their needs may be satisfied, reversing the economics of direct mail. The software technology needed for supporting Internet-based marketing may provide numerous opportunities for entrepreneurs.

Media advertising

Advertising, defined as 'a paid communication in a published medium associated with an identified supplier, product or service', whether through the print or electronic media, gives by far the lowest cost per person for a promotional message. Whether the use of advertising is economically sensible or not depends upon the fraction of potential buyers in the audience. Common consumer products can be advertised efficiently on national television and in popular newspapers, because practically every viewer and reader is a potential user and a large fraction are potential buyers.

More specialised products can often be advertised effectively through industry or specialist newspapers and magazines.

Free samples

Distributing free samples of a new product to likely users, or arranging for a no-obligation trail with new industrial equipment, provides a strong incentive for trial; the user can then form an unbiased opinion in private. Free sampling programs can even be used with some consumer durables, as long as the sampling program is tightly controlled.

Dr Dan Cohen of Minnesota, United States, invented the 'Breath Right' nasal strip to decrease nasal resistance and increase airflow through the nose. His firm had little money for advertising or selling, and so he sent a box of strips free to the chief trainer of every team in the United States National Football League. One player tried it, others saw him and tried it too, and by the time of the 1995 Super Bowl eight out of ten touchdowns were scored by players wearing the strips. Paid advertising during the Super Bowl costs US$1. 2 million for a 30 second spot. Cohen's firm now has no trouble with paying the bills and it now uses a professional advertising agency.

Marketing News 1995

Editorial and advertorial

A description of a new product in the daily press or on television will tell a large number of potential buyers about the product at very little cost to the supplier. Editorial comment need not be wholly favourable to have a good effect; descriptions of products can be 'too good to be true'. Good press stories include challenges faced and problems overcome, as long as there is a suitably happy ending. Suburban newspapers and most trade publications employ very few journalists, and are often willing to run pre-packaged stories. Sometimes stories passed on from regular advertisers get selected more readily than their literary quality or news content would suggest: such pieces are called advertorial. Advertorial is better than nothing, but it will have very little effect if it is too easily spotted by readers. Breathless puffery is one giveaway; running a contributed story on the same page as the contributor's advertisement is another.

Place

'Place' is the somewhat forced term used to bring the distribution network into the four Ps. In abstract theory, 'place' is a variable corresponding to the breadth of distribution, on the basis that something that is sold in more places will gain more sales than a similar product available in fewer. In practice, distribution is such a complex matter and varies so much between products that abstract theory has not yet demonstrated much relevance to the real world in the 'place' area.

When a product is marketed through sales persons or by direct marketing, the mechanism for promotion and selling is the same; physical distribution can then be contracted out if needed. In some other forms of distribution, the promotion and selling functions are quite separate.

Wholesalers, distributors and agents

A supplier can outsource the entire sales and distribution operation by contracting with a wholesaler, distributor or agent. In all three cases the original supplier ships the goods as directed and has little or no contact with the final purchasers and end users. Wholesalers buy the product outright (in theory at least), while distributors and agents return unsold stock for credit and don't pay the original supplier until they themselves have been paid. In economic theory distributors and agents take smaller commissions than wholesalers, compensating for the longer credit period they require; many small manufacturers and other producers doubt whether the theory applies to their particular circumstances.

The clear advantages of distributing a product through third parties is that the supplier's organisation can be more compact, with the added benefit when dealing with wholesalers of a shorter credit cycle than with most other forms of distribution. One disadvantage is the loss of contact between the supplier and the user: the flow of ideas that often leads to further innovations is blocked. Another problem with third party distribution is that the sales information channel is long and error prone: if sales slow down the first time that the supplier might hear of the problem is when a wholesaler fails to place an order or a distributor returns most of a shipment.

Subcontracting in service industries is conceptually similar to the wholesaling of consumer goods. A head contractor finds clients and negotiates a schedule of requirements, a price, and a time scale. The head contractor then engages subcontractors to do practically all the work. If a job is completed in a particularly satisfactory way this is very likely due to the efforts of one or more of the subcontractors; the head contractor will, however, get the bulk of the credit and a corresponding boost to its reputation.

Private-label supply

The private-label referred to is the retailer's: the supplier makes and packs a product as directed and delivers it to nominated retail outlets or warehouses. Marks and Spencer, the British retailer, is the world leader in this form of retailing, but practically all major retailers have private labels on some fraction of their stock.

The advantage of supplying private labels, as with supplying a wholesaler, include a compact organisation and prompt payment. If the retailer follows Marks and Spencer's example, the orders will be regular and the relationship will be treated as valuable. Whether the retailer is paternal or otherwise, a firm supplying private label business has little contact with its final purchasers and little opportunity to build a valuable brand of its own. The greater part of the value of its innovations, whether in products or processes, are likely to be captured by the retailer.

Firms that make components for inclusion in other people's products can fall into the position of private label suppliers if they are unable to maintain a unique set of competencies beyond the ability to manufacture other people's designs to order. Without any direct appeal to the final consumer or the ability to contribute unique value to their immediate customer's product they will be unable to hang on to much of the value of any of their innovations. Leading manufacturers do not encourage their suppliers to degenerate to this extent and when prices are comparable will prefer a supplier whose innovations add value to the final product over one whose sole contribution is their ability to follow instructions accurately.

Branded goods retailing

The marketing of branded goods involves so many twists and inversions that expert practitioners often have trouble explaining it to an outsider.

The formal sequence is:

▲ A branded goods manufacturer or assembler develops a new good of some kind.

▲ A promotional plan is worked out.

▲ One of the manufacturer's sales representatives calls on the buyers of the appropriate retail chains and describes the new product, its wholesale and recommended retail price, and the promotional plan.

▲ The buyers declare that the product lacks appeal, the wholesale price is too high, the promotional plan is hopelessly inadequate, and their time has seldom been so thoroughly wasted. Return to the third step several times.

▲ The buyer finally concedes that the product might sell a pallet or two, and agrees to the product being entered onto the retailer's computer system, a process known as 'listing'. Some retailers raise an invoice for the expense involved; such charges are known as 'listing fees'. More subtle retailers expect a gratuitous shipment or two when a product is first listed; they vehemently deny charging listing fees.

▲ The advertising campaign starts.

▲ Depending on the sophistication of the retailer's control systems, two paths can be followed from here:

▶ the buyer may arrange for the product to be ordered by certain classes of store

▶ the manufacturer's sales representatives visit the managers of stores in the chain seeking orders.

▲ Some retailers may expect to be paid, in money or in more uncharged merchandise, for allocating shelf space to a product; such charges are referred to as 'slotting fees'.

▲ The goods are delivered to the retailer's stores or warehouses and find their way onto the shelves where customers may see them and buy them.

▲ The manufacturer's merchandisers visit the stores to make sure that the products are properly displayed and that damaged stock is removed; merchandisers are always alert to the possibility that other firms' merchandisers may have invaded their space.

▲ From time to time the retailer may honour the manufacturer by including the manufacturer's products in a list of specials or in a series of
advertisements. The cost of such activities will be debited to the manufacturer as 'co-promotion levies'.

▲ If the new line sells really well retailers may flatter the manufacturer
by placing orders with the manufacturer or one of the manufacturer's competitors for a similar product to be supplied with a private
label.

Naive people have gone into branded goods supply, seduced by the apparently large difference between what they think the product will cost to supply
and the retail price. When they add the cost of the initial promotion, the listing
fees, the slotting fees, the co-promotion levies and other incidental charges they
may discover that the actual margins that branded goods manufacturers can earn
are not as large as they appear.

The actual dynamics of branded goods retailing are even more complex,
because purchasers must make a double decision before they buy a product; they
must choose the store first, and then select the product from the lines displayed
in that store. Purchasers are, of course, all different, and the attitude that one
purchaser takes to different categories is also different. It is clear, however, that
the space given to a manufacturer's products has an important effect on the sales.
Since some of the people entering a store will intend to buy a particular branded
product, while others will be looking for a 'best buy' from a range of possibilities, the retailer's private label brands get a free ride on the advertising expenditure on branded goods.

The retailers do not hold all the aces, particularly when dealing with suppliers who have strong brands and support them through constant innovation.
Australian and United States retailers certainly have no interest in crippling their
branded goods suppliers, since very few of them have the sort of brand strength
that would enable them to get good margins out of private label only stores. In
the United Kingdom things are slightly different; Marks and Spencer have a
sufficiently strong brand franchise in their own right to support private label
only trading, while Sainsbury's allocate over 60 per cent of the shelf space in
their stores to private label goods.

New enterprises with new products may be able to sell them through the
major retail chains, but they will have to deal with some exceptionally knowl-
edgeable and tough-minded people on the way.

Dealers

Dealers are retailers, but they differ from the mass-market retail chains in being
more fragmented and having much less power than their suppliers while being
closely identified with them. Because of the relatively great involvement of

dealers with the product range that they sell, they will devote much more effort to promoting their supplier's products and providing skilled advice and service to purchasers and users.

Motor cars have been sold through dealers almost since the industry started, but from the early 1990s entrepreneurs in the United States began building 'auto malls'; essentially, motor car supermarkets. At the same time the service functions of dealers are either becoming less important or facing competition. Since the 1950s the distance a car can travel between services has risen by a factor of six or more, while specialist single-category chains compete with dealers for tyre and battery replacement and exhaust repairs. The predominant role of dealers in motor car retailing may be ending; it is certainly changing.

Dealers are often an important distribution channel in the early life of complex products; motor cars have been traditionally sold through dealers and until the early 1990s practically all personal computers were sold through dealers. As products become more reliable and their users better informed, mass-market retailers start supplying the market. Many computers are now sold through retail outlets such as Harvey Norman or OfficeWorks; in the United States there are now 'auto malls', essentially motor car supermarkets with many competing brands offered under a single roof. Since major retail firms can use their buying clout and their channel control to get substantial discounts off the wholesale price, they are able to undercut the smaller dealers just as super-markets all but eliminated corner grocers.

Network marketing

Network marketing, also known as party plan selling or direct selling, is based on a network of part time distributors and sub-distributors, basically selling within their 'chatter group' of 100 to 130 friends and close acquaintances. The major nodes in the network represent keen distributors, who take their selling tasks seri-ously, and who earn commissions on what they and their sub-distributors sell. Secondary nodes are held by less committed distributors, who join the network and sell in it to support their friend, the major node holder and to offset the cost of the goods they use themselves from commissions. The terminal nodes repre-sent users, pure and simple, who trial the products offered by distributors out of friendship and continue to buy them if they are satisfied with the offer.

Network marketing can degenerate into pyramid selling; if distributors are paid for recruiting sub-distributors out of the money the sub-distributors pay for trading stock (as distinct from being given a commission on sales actually made by sub-distributors) the plan has become an illegal pyramid. Paying a commis-sion on the initial trading stock delivered to sub-distributors also turns a legal network into an illegal pyramid.

Network marketing is only practical when the goods sold have a fairly high contribution margin and moderate unit variable cost, because there are a lot of commissions to be paid out of the retail price, and the stock does not always move very quickly. When these conditions are met network marketing can be a good way for a new product range to secure distribution. New suppliers do not always have to establish their own network; established network organisations such as Tupperware, Amway and Nutrimetics are always on the lookout for complementary products to extend their product range.

Catalogues and direct mail

Catalogue selling used to be the major distribution vehicle for consumer durables and made up clothing into rural Australia, but urbanisation and the growth in car use seemed to make the catalogue obsolete. At the end of the twentieth century catalogues are enjoying a resurgence and many major retailing firms have launched catalogues, for example Myer Direct, and achieved considerable success.

On the cost side, a catalogue selling operation does not need a retail outlet with its associated high rent, and physical distribution can be through one of the many competing courier firms, keeping that cost under control. On the value side, a catalogue can be browsed at a time and place convenient to the buyer, at home or in the office, and so the buyer is spared the time and expense of a shopping trip. Families with a single resident parent or with two parents working may use catalogue shopping, consulting the catalogues at night and maximising the time that they can spend with their children. Small and medium businesses, and even large ones who have downsized their stationary clerk, find that buying from a catalogue, such as OfficeWorks or Viking, does not disrupt their normal operations.

Catalogues are usually operated by specialist companies, like Viking, or by specialist divisions of established retailers, such as Myer Direct. Getting a new product listed in such a catalogue will usually require some negotiation, possibly including payment for the space used on top of the catalogue operator's commission.

Direct mail, as mentioned above, can be a suitable way for a firm with very limited cash resources to promote and distribute a new product. The use of direct mail requires that there is an effective mechanism for responding to customer orders in place. Very small scale trials can rely on a single telephone, as long as arrangements are in place to keep it continuously attended; but it will often be advisable to contract a telephone response organisation to capture orders. Asking people to respond by mail cuts out the expense of a telephone answering service, but it also may cost the supplier lost orders: a buying impulse that may have been strong enough to prompt a telephone call may dissipate before a form is filled in and a letter posted. If mail responses are being asked for, the brochure should include a reply-paid return mailer: few mail order respondents will be happy paying for their own stamp.

Segmentation[5]

No two people or firms are identical, and every supplier hoping to win the business of more than one customer will be aware of differences as well as similarities. From the supplier's viewpoint, the major element of similarity will be that all the customers for a given product can get some use out of it. There can be three major areas of difference:

▲ How do they gain value from the use of the product? Even with simple products, different users can have differing objectives: a spade can be used by a domestic gardener, by a commercial gardener, by a builder, by persons digging ditches and by Russian soldiers engaging in political debates; there may be yet other uses.

▲ How does the supplier tell prospective users about the new product? Do large groups of potential users watch the same television programs, or read the same newspapers, or subscribe to the same magazines and journals?

▲ How does word-of-mouth information about the product spread? Over back fences, at the coffee machine at work, at the club or pub, at conferences, via Internet user groups?

Any or all of these questions can be used to subdivide the population of potential users into market segments. 'All' should be taken with a grain of salt; when more than one approach is taken the subdivisions must be multiplied: the spade market can be subdivided into at least 120 segments using the categories mentioned above. The main point of segmentation is that it allows promotional strategies to be optimised, using techniques ranging from rewriting advertising copy into the right language to selecting appropriate people to give testimonials.

A secondary use of segmentation, appropriate for a business with a very limited launch budget, is to identify those segments with the highest density of potential customers and target them first. There is some evidence to the effect that promotion and selling is subject to threshold effects: if a sales person calls on 200 prospects once only she may close fewer orders than she would have by calling on twenty prospects ten times each. If 'fewer' means zero and 'more' works out to one, segmentation brings the first customer onto the order book quicker. The first customer will recommend the product to more, and the growth phase of the product life cycle is ready to begin.

Experienced sales staff segment their territory without much formal analysis; given a list of 200 prospects (more properly, 'suspects') the skilled sales person will canvass the list until he or she gets a 'nibble'. The call sheets may show that eighteen customers were visited once, one was visited or called eighty times and another a hundred; the sales person ends the year with two orders, asks about the arrangements for the 100 Per Cent Club, and makes suggestions about the appropriate level of high-performance bonus.

A firm using segmentation to phase a product's introduction may try to use the orders flowing from one segment as a way to justify the injection of debt or equity capital to fund the penetration of more of them. Entrepreneurs who imagine that the cash flow from the early segments will fund marketing efforts in later ones are usually mistaken; markets, and market segments, drain cash during their growth phase and pulling cash out of a segment in which product sales have started to grow in order to start marketing into an untouched segment is a plan to fail in both.

Marketing decisions[6]

The first decision about marketing is to determine a phased marketing budget covering at least the new product launch and the first few periods of trading. For ephemeral products like new board games the planning period is probably a week and the planning horizon six months.[7] For products with a longer life cycle planning periods can be months or quarters, and a fairly detailed plan can be constructed for the first couple of years. For subsequent years an appropriate item should appear in the pro-forma accounts, but the world is unlikely to slow down to the point that a detailed marketing plan drawn up three years in advance will prove to be valid in the event.

The planning model described in Chapter 8 can be used to develop a marketing budget and a sales forecast simultaneously. If the product is a line extension this budget and forecast can be reviewed in the light of historical experience with the product's antecedents, and if the product is a new entrant in an established market an experienced sales or marketing manager should be asked to review the budget and forecast. If the product is a genuine innovation the planning model will produce a good estimate of the 'average' outcome, but every innovation is unique and averages, at least before the product is launched, may not seem to count. When exceptional successes are looked at closely, entrepreneurs who have succeeded in making a major impact on a tiny budget are often found to have conjured up 'ghost dollars' with an innovative marketing approach. They have secured exposure for their product, either in the media or to a key group of users, at a fraction of the cost that a professional public relations firm or advertising agency would have charged.

Some firms are able to add ghost dollars to their marketing budget by gaining general interest editorial exposure in the press or on television. This can be a matter of luck, in which case the marketing and business plans can be revised when it happens, or the extra publicity may be the payoff from public relations expenditure, in which case it is a budget item after all. The traditional and current behaviour of the suppliers of competitive products can also be a source of ghost dollars: if their marketing has lost part of its relevance, or their promotion neglects some significant market segments, your promotion may be unusually effective.

Serendipity is not to be sneered at, but it is not a good idea to write it into a business plan. The future will have some nasty shocks in store, and the lucky breaks will go some way to offsetting them.

Distribution

The distribution decision will affect all the other marketing decisions, and so it has to be made early in the planning process. If the product is a line extension, then there is little point in attempting to set up a new distribution channel, and so the decision will take little time to make. If it is a new product from an established multi-product company, then the question of distribution must be addressed very seriously. Toyota decided that its Lexus marque needed to be thoroughly differentiated from its existing range of cars, and while it decided to use dealers it set up a new dealer network, dedicated to Lexus. General Motors' Saturn is the first new marque created by a United States auto company in a generation; GM decided to follow Toyota and set up a new dealership chain.

Figure 9.2 shows some of the distribution options available to the marketer of a new product. There may be more; many successful innovations have involved developing new distribution methods. Other innovators have succeeded by making an original match of distribution methods and product. There are no algorithms which will generate the ideal distribution method for a new product, but there are some signposts.

Channel competition and confusion

Many channel choices are either/or; while one or the other would probably work, both together will create confusion among buyers and hostility between the channel operators. A direct sales force does not mix well, at least in the same country, with any other form of distribution. Network marketing is generally incompatible with distribution through the major retail chains because the network gets its value from there being something exclusive about the products distributed through it.

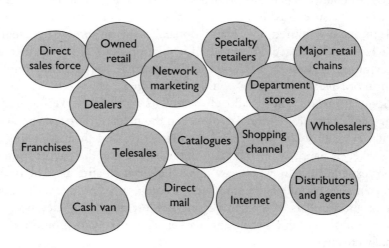

Figure 9.2 Some distribution options

Entrepreneurship

It may seem to be a clever idea to have two or more channels competing to sell your product, but the channel operators may not see it the same way. The result of such competition may be a lack of enthusiasm for your product in both channels, or it can lead to one or both of them declining to carry it. Buyers are also likely to be confused: products take on some of the attributes of their channel, and a product that is sold through two contradictory channels may do poorly in both.

Small companies with new products should consider carefully whether they will offer an exclusive deal to one operator in their chosen channel: Woolworths but not Coles or Franklins; or Target but not Big W or Kmart. The Trade Practices Act and similar laws in other countries may prohibit retailers insisting on exclusive dealing contracts, but under most circumstances suppliers are allowed to deal with whomever they like. If one retailer makes a realistic promise of a special promotional effort this can be rewarded by a short period of exclusivity, but the value of the additional sales produced by the special promotion must be set against the loss of sales caused by the narrowing of the distribution. In the very early life of a new product a supplier may be simply unable to meet the stocking requirements of more than one retail chain. This situation should not be frozen in place with a formal agreement: if the product does well the other retail chains may get sufficiently enthusiastic as to offer significant help to the supplier, such as cash with order or a special promotion of their own.

In the early 1980s the major computer companies identified a market in medium and scattered enterprises for computers with the sophisticated data processing capabilities of a mainframe but at a fraction of the cost. One way of reducing the support costs was to make the hardware more reliable and the software more automatic, but this meant that when faults did occur no one on the customer site would have the experience to correct them. This problem was solved by implementing telediagnosis; faults could be diagnosed and corrected from a support centre anywhere on earth.

The Australian firm ANCA uses the same solution to the support problems of its computerised tool-grinding machines. Such tools provide, quite literally, the cutting edge of modern manufacturing machinery and any defects will lead to poor quality output while failures will shut down production. When a customer, anywhere in the world, has a problem with operating or setting up an ANCA machine, ANCA dial up the machine by telephone and diagnose and correct the problem without leaving Melbourne.

On the rare occasions when the problem is in the machine rather than the operator, ANCA's remote diagnostic facilities allow them to distinguish between faults that user staff can rectify and problems that must be resolved by flying a specialist from Australia.

ANCA Pty Ltd was founded in 1975 and began exporting in 1985. In 1994–95 ANCA's sales were close to $30 million and growing at 50 per cent per year. ANCA's machines are exported to every major industrial country; 95 per cent of their output is exported. ANCA, as at mid 1995, employed 170 people.

When the new product is being sold by a new firm the risk of fatally dispersing management effort will be greatly increased if more than one channel is used. Understanding the full complexity of one channel can stretch the capacity of an excellent marketing executive. Trying to drive two or more can lead to bad decision making and lost opportunities.

Complex products

Products where potential customers will need substantial assistance in selecting the precise mix of components from the supplier's catalogue or where after-sales service may be complex and require well trained staff to deliver will usually have to be sold through dealers or by an employed sales force. Ordinary retailers are not organised to provide specialised selling and support services. Where the sales and service task is more demanding than average, but can be taught by limited supervised training supplemented by a good manual and a comprehensive set of diagnostic tools, a franchise approach may work.

The choice between employed sales staff and dealers tends to be a function of geographic customer density and unit price. High-priced items can be sold by either; low priced items can be sold by dealers as long as there are a sufficient number of prospective customers within each dealer's catchment area.

There are strategic arguments for using an employed sales force for high value items: dealers can legally sell a competitor's products,[8] but employed sales staff cannot. Given the ties that may emerge between sales staff and their customers when managing long, complex projects the use of sales staff may strengthen a supplier's market position. Good sales management is required to ensure that the ties run through the sales person to the supplier: if the relationship between customers and sales staff is purely personal the sales team is more of a Trojan horse than a barrier to entry.

Medium value complex products with a low density of potential customers may be extremely hard to sell at all. An entrepreneur contemplating such a product may look to innovating new distribution methods, or of sparing users from the complexity inherent in the product by innovations in the way products of its class are used or maintained.

Success on a small budget

Products without any special selling or support complications can be marketed through a number of channels. The deciding factor may be the capital available to the entrepreneur. The major retail chains want assurances of continued supply before they will stock a new product; often they will demand a significant promotional investment as a condition of listing. While the exact sums demanded by any chain depend on the product and are in any case confidential, an entrepreneur should not be surprised to hear demands that several hundred thousand dollars must be committed to media advertising before the new product will be listed.

Direct mail and network marketing are, by comparison, low cost channels with the additional advantage that the supplier is in control of the volume. A first mailout can be limited to a few postcodes, while the first distributor in a new network can be the entrepreneur or a member of the entrepreneur's family.

The degree to which potential competitors will be alerted to the market value of a new product may also influence the choice of distribution method. The product gets very limited public exposure when sold through a network or by direct marketing; likely rivals are relatively unlikely to see the product at all, and if they do see it they will get little hard data on its market acceptance. By contrast, if a product is sold through Woolworths or Coles a rival needs no more than a tape measure to get a quite precise estimate of sales. The supermarket chains treat sales per square metre per year as a key performance index, and so a product that fills a metre-wide bin in a supermarket with aisles every four metres must sell $20 000 or more in that supermarket per year.

Physical distribution

Goods may need to be warehoused and in most circumstances delivered; an established firm will have delivery arrangements in place, but a new firm must set them up. Several firms operating in Australia and elsewhere offer contract warehousing and distribution services, and unless the distribution requirements are extremely simple, or extraordinarily specialised, contracting this activity out should be given careful consideration. There is a strong and continuing trend for retailers to cut down on their storage space and the number of identical items on display in the interests of increasing their selling area and the variety of their offerings. Modern retailers, like major manufacturers, rely on just-in-time delivery to avoid stockouts in the store or holdups on the production line.

Most retailers and manufacturers would rather deal with reliable suppliers of moderately attractive products and components than erratic suppliers of excellent ones; they would, of course, prefer reliable suppliers of outstanding products.

Promotion

Once the distribution method has been selected, the promotional plan can be prepared. The promotional plan covers much more than media advertising; at least the following activities must be considered and if required, planned and budgeted for:

▲ sales training (or in firms with only one or two sales persons, an in-depth product and market briefing)

▲ the preparation of sales presentation aids, which can range from a presentation folder to a multimedia experience

▲ the production and printing of catalogue sheets and brochures; for technology-based products there may need to be at least two brochures prepared, one to impress the technicians and the other to persuade the users

▲ the design and commissioning of packaging and of point-of-sale material, as relevant

▲ preparation of detailed sales instructions including 'ideal' scripts for telesales people, network distributors, counter staff and anyone else who may come into contact with customers

▲ securing exposure for the product at conferences and exhibitions, as relevant

▲ public relations, both of the warm and fuzzy kind and a prepared strategy for handling the unexpected, including both opportunities and disasters

▲ the booking of advertising space and the preparation of suitable copy, artwork and shooting scripts

▲ setting up and running a system for sales lead generation and management.

The launch

Except in the rare case of a product totally immune from imitation, the faster the potential market is turned into an actual one the better. There are limits: one is that money spent on launching a flop is money lost and a point can be reached where the risk involved in the increased cash exposure starts to reduce the value of the enterprise; another, and rather earlier, point is reached when the firm, whatever its size, refuses to spend any more on the product launch.

Actually getting a product into the market is a matter for congratulation, and so the entrepreneurial team is entitled to a small celebration. This is not, however, an excuse to blow a gigantic launch budget on a party. Journalists who are offered a river of free booze at a launch party may be too hung over to describe the product at all the following day. Journalists, like nearly everyone else, respond better to individual attention, and journalists take a particular pride in securing exclusive stories. Instead of the river of booze, the entrepreneur should consider a series of one-on-one meetings, in suitably congenial surroundings, between interested journalists and key people on the entrepreneurial team. It can't cost any more than a party, and it may secure a great deal more relevant publicity.

A launch offers a chance to present the new product to the largest possible number of people before any of them have had any exposure to actual or potential competitors trying to play it down. Equally, no money will be wasted advertising to people who have already bought the product apart from a few pre-launch test users.

Launches need planning: for industrial products, dealers and lead prospects need to be invited to an appropriate event; while for consumer products the advertising needs to be synchronised with the appearance of the new product on the shelves. If the product needs any explanation, then all staff should be properly briefed about how it works, who should be using it, and what to say when people, whether prospective customers or friends and acquaintances ask about it. Don't assume that anything is obvious: new computer software needs explaining;

but so does a new range of clothing. Don't assume that prospects will only talk to sales people: the switchboard operator, delivery staff, staff maintaining previous products, and everyone else involved with the enterprise is likely to be asked questions, and not only out of idle curiosity.

Every deprecating remark made by a member of staff, every shopper who rushes to the supermarket to find the shelves empty, every matron who thinks that a new style, intended for teenyboppers, is meant for her; every launch error causes a black shadow spreading into the future. It does not take too many mistakes to doom a product; the same cycle of recommendation and resulting trial that marks a successful new product can turn into an accelerating spread of damaging rumours started by mistakes in a launch program.

Research and feedback[9]

Money should never be spent on marketing research unless the information gained exceeds the cost of gaining it. Before spending time or money on marketing research, the entrepreneur must make two internal decisions by answering these questions:

▲ What decisions are going to depend on the results of the research, and how important, in money terms, will these decisions be?

▲ What is the least amount of data, and precision in each data element, that will be sufficient to make the decisions adequately informed?

Marketing research before a product is launched can be very useful for a line extension, but it seldom produces worthwhile results when a product is completely new. New magazines are normally put straight on the market: the cost of preparing convincing mockups in order to get consumer reaction is so close to the cost of making a real magazine and printing it that any effort spent on prior research would be a waste. Sony spend very little on formal pre-launch research: the Sony Walkman was market-tested by putting a million of them into the shops and seeing what happened.

After the launch research can be extremely valuable. The response to advertisements, in terms of unprompted recall and attitude to the product, can be measured for a small fraction of the cost of creating and placing the advertising. If an advertisement isn't working, there is no point in spending more money repeating it. If a dealership is not performing, then its problems must be identified and corrected or it must be deleted. Most stores now have scanners: scan data is available, at a price, and when products are sold through retailers, suppliers should make it their business to spot trends before the stores themselves do.

Firms that currently supply retailers with branded goods know all this and act on it: they would not still be trading if they didn't. New firms, and established firms putting their first product into a retail channel, often learn that these things are necessary after a disaster.

The marketing section in the business plan

Launching a new product without a marketing plan is rather like sailing off into the ocean without a map or a compass. The voyage may end at El Dorado, but that is not the most likely outcome. People who read a business plan will want to know that there is a marketing plan, that it has costs and objectives, and that it makes some kind of sense. They do not need to see the whole marketing plan; the marketing section of the business plan should be an overview (not a summary) of the marketing plan.

The key elements of the marketing plan to be shown in the business plan include:

▲ a description of the product concentrating on the user benefits that it provides

▲ a phased expenditure budget, monthly for the first one or two years and quarterly or annually thereafter

▲ a phased sales target using the same periods as the expenditure plan showing planned sales per period and planned cumulative sales at each period end

▲ a brief explanation of the segmentation strategy and the launch phasing

▲ a short description of the proposed distribution strategy

▲ a short description of the proposed promotional strategy

▲ the CVs or job descriptions for the sales and the marketing managers, if the firm is a new one

▲ basic details about the sales staff.

A good plan has more than a sales target and marketing budget. There should be a cumulative sales forecast containing a running total of all the sales predicted to be achieved by the end of the indicated period. Once the enterprise is launched, it is this column that should be used to estimate progress against the plan. The individual monthly sales forecasts may be good guesses, and they are needed to develop pro-forma accounts, but they are too uncertain, and real monthly sales figures are too variable, to be a good planning and control measure. The cumulative totals smooth out the monthly variation and uncertainty and are better indicators of actual progress against plan. As the business develops it may become appropriate to use still more sophisticated statistical forecasting techniques, but these are irrelevant at the planning stage.

The plan should forecast the marketing expense ratio, that is, the total cost of marketing as a proportion of retail or final purchaser sales revenue. The marketing expense ratio should be shown by period and as a ratio of the cumulative sales and expenses, also to smooth out per period variations. The plan should show this ratio falling steadily as the product passes into its growth stage. If the ratio does not fall, either in the plan or in real life, the product is not getting a sufficient number of repurchases and recommendations and the enterprise is unlikely to produce an attractive return on its investment. The best marketing plans bring sales to book at the retail or final purchaser price; the margin allowed to distributors and resellers is then included in this price and treated as part of the marketing and distribution expenditure. If the distributor and reseller margins are not shown it is not possible to demonstrate that the distribution strategy chosen is, in fact, the most appropriate.

The marketing summary should have sections covering segmentation, distribution, promotion and sales staff. Sales representatives, or at least the good ones, have a nice sense of their own value and they will expect that their on-target earnings will place them firmly in the top 1 or 2 per cent of salary earners. This has been known to cause great distress among senior managers of large businesses and owners of small and medium ones: the thought of a sales person taking home two or three times their own earnings upsets them to the point that they will veto the appointment of any high-fliers. There have been definite examples of small firms going broke and large ones losing major contracts rather than employ a first-rate sales person at the going rate, or countenance a reasonable high-performance bonus.

End notes

1   This chapter is intended to provide an overview of the marketing function and the ways in which an entrepreneur should apply marketing principles in the development of an integrated business plan. This chapter is not a replacement for the far more detailed examination of the very broad and complex field of marketing to be found in a well-written marketing text. There are many basic and advanced marketing text books available from the major business and academic publishers, and nearly all are of a high standard. We believe that a student of entrepreneurship should also undertake a course in marketing as an essential part of their program. Their course convenor will specify the marketing text to be used in the course. Most such texts have one thing in common: they tend to draw their examples from research into firms operating in mature market places. One marketing text has a focus upon the innovative enterprise: Legge (1992).

2   Elementary economics is usually taught with the assumption of 'perfect knowledge' to simplify the development of the theory. Some economists graduate and even become professors while holding the belief that this assumption is justified by the facts: such economists tend to use the term 'marketing' as a form of abuse, with the implication that it only serves to confuse users whose information, in the absence of marketing, would be perfect and complete.

3   The notion of the 'marketing mix' dates back to the teaching and research interests of Professor Neil Borden of Harvard University in the early 1950s. Classifying marketing mix elements under the now ubiquitous '4 Ps' headings is an invention of Professor E. Jerome McCarthy whose marketing text books (with various co-authors) compete with those of Professor Philip Kotler (also with various co-authors) for market leadership in number of copies sold, worldwide. Every marketing text book will feature extended treatment of the marketing mix.

4   Pricing is, of the elements of the marketing mix, by far the least discussed in the academic marketing literature and is often treated superficially in otherwise comprehensive text books. A discussion of price is more common in economics texts and journals, but very few of the treatments of pricing

decisions in the economics literature are of any practical use, because the degree of abstraction needed to make a pricing decision mathematically tractable generally makes it too unreal for a practising manager to relate to. A useful, if somewhat dated, bibliography is Lund, Monroe and Choudhury (1982). One of us has attempted to produce a practical approach to the topic: Legge (1993).

5 There is literally an unlimited number of segmenting variables — from hair colour to shoe size — and selecting which segmenting variables to use combines art and science in one of the most important judgement calls a marketer will ever have to make. See Dowling and Midgley (1988).

6 Most marketing text books tend to combine their exposition of marketing principles with advice on their application, that is, marketing management. A text devoted exclusively to application — on the assumption that readers are already familiar with marketing principles — is Haas and Wotruba (1983).

7 Successful marketing of a board game is at the heart of 'The R&R Case', one of the most instructive cases ever written about the entrepreneurial process. It is found in Stevenson, Roberts and Grousbeck (1989), pp. 71–88.

8 Dealership agreements that prohibit the sale of a competitor's products are potentially illegal under the Trade Practices Act in Australia; this is discussed further in Chapter 11. See a lawyer before including such clauses in an agreement; you may be advised to gain protection for the contract by the process of notification.

9 There are many excellent books concerned with marketing research techniques. A good one is Peterson (1982).

10

Entering Asian markets

For the first time in 500 years, the centre of global economic gravity is set to return to East Asia. (Gareth Evans, former Foreign Minister, Australia)

A model for marketing in Asia

With some reservations, which we will explore through this chapter, marketing in Asia is like marketing anywhere else: suppliers secure trial by promotion, and secure further trial and eventual profits from recommendations, and from replacement and replenishment purchasing. The specific difficulties involved in entering Asian markets may be no greater than the difficulties a supplier might experience in entering a European or an American market, but they are different, and it is on these differences that many attempts have come to grief.

Successful entry to Asian markets requires an in-depth understanding of the Asian environment prior to commencing operations, and one of the first markers on the route to developing this understanding is the achievement of an appropriate mindset. Once a firm has initiated an offshore venture, its managers must not forget what they learned during the planning phase, building on it as opportunities arise for local innovations. These four essential steps for marketing in Asia are summarised in Figure 10.1. Marketing operations are a major component of the Asian marketing model, but they enter fairly late into the picture after a lot of pre-market entry work has been completed.

A proper mindset

In the *Art of War*, the ancient Chinese military strategist, Sun Tze, says:

> *The act of war is vital to the state. The battlefield which really counts is in the mind of men. This is where wars are won and lost.*

This chapter is an edited version of a paper by David Ch'ng, Senior Lecturer in International Marketing at Swinburne University of Technology

A proper mindset

Pre-entry environmental scanning
(PEST analysis)

Key determinants of success
(the strategic diamond)

Post-entry marketing strategy
(the four Ps)

[Implementation and control]

Figure 10.1 Steps for successful marketing in Asia

Marketing in Asia should be approached with seriousness and determination, and each task should be tackled with an open mind and a readiness to innovate. The final outcome of many marketing ventures in Asia has been decided before the first of the firm's representatives sets foot in the target market. It will have been determined by the firm's mindset: its attitude to Asian customers; its preparation for the difficulties it will encounter; and how well its executives have been mentally prepared for the challenges awaiting them.

A walker passing through unfamiliar country is often delayed by tangled undergrowth. An entrepreneur planning to enter an Asian market for the first time is like a walker trying to follow a neglected mountain track. The walker must get past bushes, fallen trees, and washaways; the entrepreneur must overcome mental blocks, the 'mental walls that block the problem-solver from correctly perceiving a problem or conceiving its solution' (Adams 1986). Successful entrepreneurs clear their personal mental blocks before trying to remove those embedded in their firm's culture.

Many western companies have been prevented from exploiting attractive opportunities in the Asian region by preconceptions. These preconceptions have become part of the 'received wisdom' of western management; over time, they have become deeply entrenched in the minds of a generation of executives. Many older people, who grew up with an obsolete conception of the relationship between the east and the west, have become firmly attached to their prejudices. The younger executives in western international companies may be better prepared to lead forays into Asian markets.

The three major mental barriers which have inhibited western executives, either consciously or unconsciously, from seeking a greater penetration of Asian markets have been erected on three erroneous beliefs:

▲ *mental block 1:* Asia is too difficult

▲ *mental block 2:* Asia is one homogeneous market

▲ *mental block 3:* western marketing principles do not apply in Asia.

Mental block 1: Asia is too difficult

An experienced western executive summed up his feelings about the difficulty of doing business in Asia in the aphorism: 'Bloody hard to get in; bloody hard if you do get in!' (Booz, Allen & Hamilton 1993). It reflects the prevailing western

> *Bloody hard to get in; bloody hard if you do get in!*

sentiment. In 1993 Booz, Allen and Hamilton suggested that dissimilarity is the greatest obstacle to increased Australian investment in Asia. The conventional wisdom among Australian business leaders is to seek cultural affinity and avoid the Asian markets because they are seen to be significantly different from the west. Asia is seen by some Australian firms to be a market where incompatibility is an additional risk factor. Some Australian firms have mentally positioned themselves closer to North America and northern Europe than to their northern neighbours. In their 1992 report to the Australian Manufacturing Council, Yetton, David and Swan (1992) pointed out that the combination of the 'neighbour' issue and the 'one risk at a time' issue provides an explanation for the observed behaviour of Australian manufacturers in choosing the United States, United Kingdom and New Zealand, as 'neighbours' for their offshore expansion. This has occurred in spite of the well publicised advantages proximity and size confer on Asian markets. A continuing alignment of Australia with North America and Europe may not be in the nation's long term interest. Both the North American and European markets are important to Australia and should not be ignored, but they should not be pursued at the cost of neglecting Asian markets. Australia and New Zealand are committed to Asia by geography. In 1993, Australia sold more than two-and-a-half times as much to Asia as it did to North America and Europe combined.

Some of the most pressing problems facing western companies in Asia stem from a lack of understanding. Michael Dobbs-Higginson, the former Chairman of Merrill Lynch Asia Pacific, says that to understand Asia Pacific's economic and political dynamism requires knowledge of the region's discipline and focus, its culture and philosophy, and '... it is the lack of understanding of these characteristics ... that has created the barriers which still exist between the East and the West' (Dobbs-Higginson 1993). Asia poses a cultural enigma. It can be seen as exotic, mysterious, chaotic, unfathomable, or simply bizarre. The Asian business culture is significantly different from that of the west, in part because it has to cope with an inadequate legal system. Laws and regulations are still relatively underdeveloped in many Asian countries. Where business laws exist, law enforcement is often uncertain. Investors may find the framework for investment and currency exchange unsettled. Under these circumstances, business trust is built on personal relationship rather than contracts drawn up by lawyers.[1] Personal networking is the essence of business anywhere, and particularly where companies are still largely family owned, as they are in most of Asia. The Chinese word *guanxi* or 'personal connections' is entering the western business vocabulary, often with somewhat pejorative undertones. Western business culture operates within a sophisticated legal environment and, to a limited extent, personal trust can be replaced by formal, binding contracts. Relationship building takes time and effort, and not only from the parties; disagreements or conflicts may arise during the relationship building process and a mediator may be needed.

Mental block 2: Asia is one homogeneous market

Asia is enormous, both in terms of its geographical spread and the number of people who live there. Over 50 per cent of the world's population live in the Asia Pacific region and the Indian subcontinent. The region is no less complex than the diverse group of national and regional markets that Australians, misleadingly, call 'Europe'. It can be a fatal mistake to enter this huge market by treating it as uniform, not taking proper account of its complexity and variation. Asia comprises not only many geo-political units at different stage of economic progress, but a multitude of ethnic groups, religions, historical backgrounds, life-styles, values, usage patterns and preferences.

The term 'Asia' may be an important concept in international politics. It may even be used by the head office for the purpose of regional control and accountability. For example, an international company[2] may appoint a marketing director for the Asia Pacific region. But this would backfire if the Asia Pacific marketing director took the title literally and attempted to standardise all the firms' marketing efforts across the region. To the practising marketer, Asia is an abstraction: Asia is not a uniform market. Organisations such as ASEAN (Association of the South-east Asian nations) or APEC (Asia-Pacific Economic Cooperation) have been created for regional security and trade liberalisation purposes respectively, but they represent aspirations rather than current reality. A successful marketer needs to understand the myriad cultures within Asia and the diverse consumer preferences that result from them. Marketing strategies will often need to be formulated for specific target segments, many of which will cross national boundaries.

Mental block number two traps an international marketer into treating Asia as a uniform market. The victim is unable to see the rich diversity in the region, and is blind to the possibility of exploiting cross-national market segmentation. Mental block number two may in fact be the most dangerous from a marketing point of view. It lays the foundation for potentially disastrous marketing mistakes.

Market segmentation

When defining market segments in Asia, a geo-political division should precede an ethnic one. East Asia can be divided into North-east Asia (Table 10.1) and South-east Asia (Table 10.2). When developing a market entry strategy, who the customers are (their values, attitudes, aspirations and motivation) is more important than where they are. The countries in North-east Asia — Japan, China, Korea, Taiwan and Hong Kong — are ethnically homogeneous. For instance, the population in Japan is 99.4 per cent Japanese; South Korea's population is 99.96 per cent Koreans, while ethnic Chinese comprises 98 per cent of Taiwan's population. With the exception of the Philippines, the nations in South-east Asia tend to be multicultural and multi-ethnic. Thailand's population is 75 per cent Thai, 14 per cent ethnic Chinese and 11 per cent 'other'. Singapore's multilingual population is 76 per cent ethnic Chinese, 15 per cent Malay and 6 per cent Indian. Malaysia's population is also ethnically mixed with 59 per cent of Malay and other indigenous people, 32 per cent ethnic Chinese and 9 per cent ethnic Indian. Indonesia has perhaps the highest diversity with 336 ethnic groups spread over 17 508 islands.

According to Rod Wright (1993), Ogilvy and Mather's Asia Pacific Chairman, Asia can be culturally divided into three main market segments, each one containing a number of sub-groups. The three main market segments are:

▲ the mainland Chinese, Taiwanese, overseas Chinese, Japanese and Koreans who have been shaped by centuries of Confucian influence

▲ the Indochinese whose culture has a strong Buddhist-Hindu base

Table 10.1 *Ethnic composition in North-east Asia, 1995*

	Hong Kong	Taiwan	Japan	South Korea	China
Population (million)	6	21	125	45	1190
GDP (US$billion)	141	252	4304	384	670
GDP per capita (US$)	22 527	11 709	24 299	8436	557
Ethnic composition					
Chinese (%)	95	98	†	0.04	91*
Japanese (%)	–	–	99.4	–	–
Korean (%)	–	–	–	99.96	
Other (%)	5	2	0.6	–	9
Literacy rate (%)	77	86	99	96	78

† Included in 'other'
* Han Chinese

Table 10.2 *Ethnic composition in South-east Asia, 1995*

	Singapore	Malaysia	Philippines	Indonesia	Thailand
Population (million)	3	20	70	200	60
GDP (US$billion)	62	80	59	153	123
GDP per capita (US$)	21 361	3914	829	752	2037
Ethnic composition					
Malay (%)	15	59	95.5	7.5	†
Javanese (%)	–	–	–	45.0	–
Sudanese (%)	–	–	–	14.0	–
Madurese (%)	–	–	–	7.5	–
Thai (%)	–	–	–	–	75
Chinese (%)	76	32	1.5	4.0	14
Indian (%)	6	9	–	–	–
Other (%)	3	–	3.0	22.0	11
Literacy rate (%)	88	78	90	77	93

† Included in 'other'

▲ the Malays who are the ethnic majority in Indonesia, Malaysia and the Philippines.

Market segmentation by ethnic composition implicitly separates the religious sub-groups such as Muslims, Christians, Taoist-Buddhists, Theravada Buddhists, Hindu and others. Religion is one of the prime determinants of culture and religious observance influences consumption behaviour. For instance, the consumption of pork and alcoholic beverages are forbidden in Islam and only meat prepared in a strictly prescribed manner is *halal* and acceptable to Muslims. The Malaysian Code of Advertising Practice stipulates that 'Advertisements should not contain statements or suggestions which may offend the religious or racial susceptibilities of any community'. Television and radio advertisements for products or services specifically concerned with pork and pork products, liquor and alcoholic beverages are prohibited because they have a specific religious significance to the Muslims.

A third segment boundary in Asia divides the urban and the rural population. The rural population is primarily engaged in agriculture and generally has the lower income level. In Bangkok, for instance, the average gross domestic product per capita of the ten million urban dwellers is more than US$2500. This is two-and-a-half times the US$1000 for the rest of the country. In the north-east rural region of Thailand the per capita income is as low as US$400. The same is true in Vietnam where 75 per cent of overseas investment is currently directed to Ho Chi Minh City. The demographic definition of 'urban' and 'rural' differs from nation to nation, and this complicates the task of conducting multi-country marketing research. Marketing research in Asia has, however, verified that there is a substantial difference in the usage pattern and consumption characteristics of urban and rural households. A large part of rural Asia is still without essential public services such as running water and electricity, in spite of the recent economic 'miracles'. The penetration of household electrical appliances such as refrigerators, microwave ovens and washing machines is generally low in rural areas, particularly those where no electrification scheme has reached the villages.

Mental block 3: Western marketing principles do not apply in Asia

The principles and theories of marketing, which originated in the western, developed economies, have been shown to be applicable in the marketing environment of developing economies, provided they are adapted to the local requirements and conditions.[3] Western marketing text books, especially the standard North American texts, are used in tertiary institutions throughout Asia. Future Asian marketers are being taught western marketing principles, methodologies, and case studies under the justified assumption that these are adaptable to the Asian environment.

Western multinationals such as Unilever, Colgate-Palmolive, Glaxo, Beecham and Ford have been operating for decades in Asia and certainly share this basic assumption. Marketing campaigns which have been proven winners in North America and Europe have been equally successful in selected markets in Asia, provided they have been carefully edited to eliminate content offensive to local sensitivities, and to adapt the marketing mechanics to the host country circumstances. Innovative distribution methods, such as direct marketing and party-plan selling, have been well received.

Kracmar (1971) wrote that:

The principles and methods of marketing are inherently universal in the free markets and so is its research. Thus, marketing research in the developing countries is the same as in the developed ones; only the application of certain methods is different.

The experience of major marketing research agencies in Asia, such as Research International, Frank Small and Associates and the Survey Research Group, has substantiated this claim. Kaynak (1984) wrote that success in using the various basic research techniques in Kuwait, Thailand, Malaysia and Indonesia has been as high as it is in the west. Even relatively sophisticated marketing research techniques such as perceptual mapping, retail audit, Assessor or its modified version, the sales wave experiment, have been used successfully. Whatever is possible (and desirable) in the developed world in terms of research is possible in developing countries.[4]

Environmental scanning

The host environment in which the international company has chosen to commence offshore operation can be subdivided into four sectors:

▲ *political-legal* environment

▲ *economic* environment

▲ *sociocultural* environment

▲ *technological* environment.

A macro-environmental analysis on these four sectors is known as PEST analysis. PEST (or STEP) analysis examines the environmental influences on the firm. It focuses on environmental trends and is therefore a forecasting tool. It is an essential part of strategic management. The use of PEST analysis enables us to examine the environmental influences on the firms systematically (Bowman 1990).

Political-legal environment

The host government plays a central role in each nation's political environment. Porter (1990) writes that government can influence each of the four determinants (the factor conditions; demand conditions; firm strategy, structure and rivalry; and supporting industries) which jointly shape a nation's competitive advantage. It is therefore important for the international company to understand the host country's political-legal environment in terms of its political structure, national interests, pressure groups, and government controls on foreign businesses. Political risk assessment involves an estimation of the level of political stability; the risk of expropriation; and the likelihood of political and market liberalisation. A political risk assessment should be conducted prior to market entry. Appropriate risk control strategies can then be devised and implemented.

A company venturing into a new offshore market needs the answers to a number of questions. How politically stable is the host government? What is the current attitude of the host government towards foreign private enterprises, and is this attitude likely to change in the near future? Are there any entry restrictions that would need to be overcome? These questions prepare the entrepreneur for the overriding question 'How safe will my investment be?' The activities of pressure groups, official statements on the national interests and the degree of legal transparency are all useful indicators.

Overall, political-legal environment analysis should address three areas:

▲ market accessibility

▲ profit repatriation

▲ product viability.

The political-legal environment in the host country directly affects market accessibility as can be seen across Asia where the difficulty of doing business varies considerably from country to country. Some countries, such as China and South Korea, remain relatively closed and are very protective of their domestic markets. In India, the domestic market is closed to the import of many consumer goods by home industry protection, but it is relatively open to the import of capital goods by local industries. Among South-east Asian nations, Singapore and Malaysia are very open markets. They are politically stable, with a transparent legal system based on the British judicial model. Their major commercial language is English and these economies are supported by world-class facilities in transportation and telecommunication.

Host country legal requirements

Siddons Ramset Ltd is a wholly-owned Australian firm within the listed Siddons Group of companies. Manufacturing light industrial automotive, electrical and construction components. Siddons Ramset specialises in industrial and DIY fasteners under the 'Ramset' brand. Siddons Ramset Ltd is an international company and has operations, including reseller divisions, in New Zealand, South-east Asia (Singapore, Malaysia and Hong Kong), the United Kingdom and Canada.

Siddons Ramset does not manufacture in Malaysia but maintains a reseller division with its head office in Kuala Lumpur. This division distributes industrial fastening equipment and hardware products. The Malaysian operation is controlled from the Singapore regional office which was established in 1973.

The main product exported by the Ramset Group from Australia is the Powder Actuated Fastening System, commonly called the Ramset Gun, or more formally known as the Ramset D90 Low Velocity Fastening Tool. A suitable fastening accessory is placed at the front of the tool and an explosion forces the accessory into a solid surface. The explosive technology has led to the tool being classified a 'firearm' in Malaysia, and subject to the very strict law for firearms in the country. Part of the anti-communist strategy in Malaysia during the post-Second World War insurgency was to stop the supply of ammunition, of any form, to the communists.

Under the strict Malaysian gun control laws, potential users of Ramset D90 must acquire a firearm licence. The 'gun' uses a number of accessories such as disc adaptors, small guards, drive pins, thread studs, eye pins etc. These consumables are sold in packages of 2000. The Malaysian laws stipulate that repeat purchases of these consumables are only permitted if the users can produce empty packets to the stockists as proof of usage. The stockists in turn may be held accountable for the quantity of 'ammunition' sold. The law has virtually made wide acceptance of the Ramset D90 impossible. In this case, a product innovation which has succeeded in the home country is not viable in the host country.

An important area to be investigated in pre-entry market assessment is the ease with which resources and profits can be moved in and out of the host country. A market may possess great potential but if profit repatriation is impossible, the market might have to be avoided unless an appropriate post-entry strategy can be developed. Some international companies operating under capital and profit restrictions have established their credentials through local reinvestment. By proving that they are good corporate citizens and are willing to participate in the growth and development of the host country, they have forged strong relationships with the host government which ensures that their remittance requests receive a sympathetic hearing.

Each potential host country should also be assessed and monitored for economic and financial risk such as the risk of adverse currency and/or labour cost movements. Some firms, particularly in the clothing industry, control these risks by organising themselves into 'caravans', ready to up stakes and move as soon as a different potential host offers a better combination of political stability and low labour costs. Other firms anticipate rising labour costs and install relatively advanced equipment, reducing the impact of labour cost movements on their profitability. In some countries (by no means only in Asia) bureaucracy and even corruption may add to the cost of doing business.

Some potential host countries have legal requirements that render some products non-viable. Unique laws, which may have been enacted under particular historical circumstances, may apply in the host country. It is generally easier to adapt a product or avoid a market than to persuade a potential host county to revise its legal code. As described on page 289, Siddons Ramset cannot market its innovative powder-powered fastening system in Malaysia.

Economic environment

The international company must investigate the nature of the economic environment of the host country, and contrast it with the conditions it is familiar with. The two may be fairly similar or drastically different. In the latter case, marketing in a different economic environment may compel the international company to acquire new knowledge and expertise. A pre-entry market analysis provides data on the stage of economic development, the economic trends affecting the country, possible changes such as market liberalisation and deregulation, and the potential demand for various products at the country's current stage of economic development.

Data on the local economy, for example, GDP growth rate, GDP per capita, rate of inflation, rate of savings, demographic profiles, income (both personal and household) of the urban and rural population, wage rates and like data are vital in assessing the potential market for a firm's products and services. One important source of information is the host country's national economic plan. Beside serving as a blueprint for economic development, this government document is often the source of data on national interests, national sovereignty, national prestige and national vision.[5]

Table 10.3 *Growth in annual real GDP per capita 1965–90 (% pa)*

	1965–73	1973–80	1980–90
East Asia	5.3	4.9	6.2
South Asia	1.2	1.7	3.0
Latin America	3.8	2.5	−0.4
Sub-Sahara Africa	2.1	0.4	−1.2
Developing countries	3.9	2.5	1.6
Industrial countries	3.7	2.3	2.3

Source: The World Bank 1991

The economies of Asia

Ten of the eleven major economies in Asia are in East Asia and only one in South Asia. The ten major East Asian economies are Japan, China, South Korea, Hong Kong, Taiwan, Singapore, Thailand, Malaysia, Indonesia, and the Philippines. The only economy of global significance in South Asia is India. The East Asian economies have attracted worldwide attention because of their phenomenal growth. East Asia's share of world GNP was barely 10 per cent in 1960. It had risen to 15 per cent in 1970, 20 per cent in 1980, and 30 per cent by 1990 on a purchasing power parity basis. Between 1965 and 1989, East Asia continually registered a higher growth rate in real GDP per capita than any other region in the world (see Table 10.3).

During the late 1980s and early 1990s, while the annual growth rate of advanced industrial countries were decreasing from 3 to 4 per cent to a virtual standstill, that of East Asia surged ahead at 6 to 8 per cent (see Table 10.4). At this high rate of growth, some of these economies — albeit starting from a

Table 10.4 *Growth rate of GDP in East Asia (% pa)*

	(Actual)					(Forecast)	
	1989	1990	1991	1992	1994	1995	1996
North-east Asia:							
Hong Kong	2.8	3.2	4.2	5.0	5.4	5.3	5.8
South Korea	6.2	9.2	8.4	4.5	8.4	9.0	7.5
Taiwan	7.6	4.9	7.2	6.6	6.5	6.6	5.9
China	4.4	3.9	7.5	6.6	11.8	9.9	10.5
Japan	4.3	5.3	3.6	0.4	0.6	1.0	3.9
South-east Asia:							
Singapore	9.2	8.3	6.7	5.8	10.1	7.3	7.0
Malaysia	9.2	9.7	8.7	8.0	8.7	9.2	8.3
Thailand	12.0	10.0	8.2	7.5	8.5	8.8	8.5
Indonesia	7.5	7.1	6.6	5.9	7.3	7.2	7.0
Philippines	6.1	2.7	−0.7	0.0	4.3	5.6	6.2

Source: Asian Development Bank 1994

Entering Asian markets

Table 10.5 *Years to double GDP*

	GDP 1995 (US$)	Years
China	557	9
Indonesia	752	18
Thailand	2 037	12
Malaysia	3 914	24
South Korea	8 436	8
Hong Kong	22 527	13
Singapore	21 361	14
Australia	16 943	58
Canada	19 473	33
USA	26 025	33
Japan	34 299	19

Source: Partly based on Shell Australia 1993

relatively low base — will double their size in ten to fifteen years (see Table 10.5). In the mid 1990s, East Asia contained markets with a total turnover estimated at US$3 trillion a year and growing by US$3 billion a week.

While North-east and South-east Asia share a common commitment to rapid economic development and enjoy ever strengthening commercial ties, these two regions are quite different in one important aspect: North-east Asia is a giant in both economic and geo-political terms. Two North-east Asian nations, China (population 1190 million) and Japan (population 125.1 million), are major players on the world stage. Indonesia (population 200 million) as the most populous nation in South-east Asia, is certainly important in the sub-region. But overall, South-east Asia's total GDP is only one-eighth that of North-east Asia. In 1989 Garnaut wrote that 'Growth has proceeded faster for longer in Northeast Asia over the past four decades than had previously been known in human history' (1990). By the 1990s, North-east Asia had emerged as one of the three main centres of world production, trade and savings. The economic dynamism of North-east Asia has induced accelerated growth in South-east Asia.

The East Asian nations have become each other's own best customers. Over the past twenty years, through the adoption of export-oriented economic policies, the East Asian nations have implemented significant domestic economic readjustment. These measures have enabled them to move away from over-reliance on the western advanced nations and, at the same time, foster subregional economic linkages and cooperation. East Asia was partly shielded from the 1990–91 global recession, indicating that it has achieved a critical mass in trade capable of sustaining a virtuous circle of mutual prosperity. The proportion of East Asia exports absorbed within the region rose from 19 to 30 per cent in the two decades from 1975. However, the momentum of economic development in East Asia cannot be sustained in isolation — it needs to be integrated with the world economy. The United States is still East Asia's most important export market.

East Asia's share of world exports rose from about 14 per cent in 1960 to about 25 per cent in 1990. At the same time, it became a significant importer. East Asia accounted for 25 per cent of total world imports in 1995 compared with only 16 per cent in 1960. The emergence of East Asia as a major centre of world economic activity has had two major outcomes: First, partly as a result of the East Asian challenge, member-countries in the European Union (EU) have been motivated to accelerate internal integration. The East Asian ascendancy has directly contributed to the formation of NAFTA (the North American Free Trade Agreement). Second, the phenomenon of sustained, rapid, internationally oriented economic growth in East Asia has greatly ameliorated Australia's and New Zealand's relative isolation.

Keith Mackrell, the regional coordinator for the Royal Dutch Shell Group of Companies, released the following scenario analysis conducted by his company on the characteristics which Shell believes have been advantageous and perhaps crucial to the economies of the Asia Pacific region:

▲ no old infrastructure

▲ pronounced modernisation talents (no sentimental attachment to the past)

▲ very disciplined in parts, positively individualistic in others

▲ altogether more entrepreneurial than anywhere else

▲ remarkable high savings rates (social benefits spending relatively low)

▲ relatively small proportion of government participation in GDP

▲ easy access to most economical form of transport, that is, seaborne trade

▲ existence of advanced trading and financial centres.

Sociocultural environment

The sociocultural environment constrains business activities in any given country. It is determined by physical, demographic and behavioural parameters. When the home and host countries do not share many common cultural traits, there are ample grounds for interpersonal misunderstanding. Smooth running of an international operation is impossible unless home country personnel appreciate the key dimensions of the culture of each host country; these include the language, education, social structures, morals and values, and religion. Training of expatriate executives can take the form of pre-departure briefings and in-country training programs. Host country personnel can be exposed to the home country culture through executive exchange programs and training secondments.

The enormous impact sociocultural factors have on international marketing is frequently overlooked. Inexperienced expatriate executives in a host country tend to misread local consumer behaviour, because of an unconscious reliance on their own cultural values and traits. In 1966 Lee described this phenomenon as the self reference criterion (SRC) and suggested that the SRC underpins most of the mistakes made in international business. While the SRC describes the personal blinkers on an unenlightened executive, a measure known as 'sociocultural distance' is a good predictor of the frequency with which an organisation will exhibit blindness to its customers' needs and show a lack of empathy with them. Excessive sociocultural distance is one of the strongest barriers to internationalisation and is greatest in those international companies whose executives are quite unfamiliar with the sociocultural environment of the host country.

The SRC can do a lot of damage when it leads to the misinterpretation of foreign marketing research results. There is a saying in marketing research circles that bad research is worst than no research. Wrong conclusions drawn from valid research can be worse still, leading to the misallocation of resources and to a costly misdirection of promotional efforts. Only people familiar with the foreign culture concerned are competent to analyse and interpret foreign marketing research. The meaning of words, attitudes, consumer usage habits and interviewing situations can all distort research findings and analysis, so those involved in their interpretation must possess a high degree of cultural understanding and empathy. In fact, local inputs during analysis and interpretation are essential so that explanation of reasons does not accidentally become western.[6] A brief introduction to Confucianism, one of the most important driving forces behind the East Asian economic miracles, is given in the box below. The Confucian emphasis on proper order and vertical relationships within a society have shaped a distinct business culture in East Asia.

Confucianism

While western ethics is the ethics of reason, the ethics of the individual, Confucian ethics on the contrary is characteristically the ethics of relationships, the ethics of community. (Bum-Yun Sung 1977)

The mentality of modern Japanese, Koreans, mainland Chinese, Taiwanese and overseas Chinese are shaped largely by the teachings of Confucius, who lived in China more than 2500 years ago. In his autobiography, Dr An Wang, the founder of Wang Laboratories, wrote:

A Chinese can never outgrow his roots. Ancient ideas such as Confucianism are as relevant today as they were twenty-five hundred years ago. There is also a practical genius to Chinese culture that allows it to assimilate new ideas without destroying old ones.

Confucianism probably has more influence on the Japanese than any other traditional religions or philosophies. Any discussion of Japanese religions that overlooks this point would be seriously misleading. Strong Confucian traits are revealed in the Japanese emphasis on interpersonal relations and loyalties, faith in education and hard work, and belief in the moral basis of government.

The Confucianist ethics of thrift, diligence, respect for educational achievement, avoidance of overt conflict in social relations, loyalty to hierarchy and authority, stress on order and harmony have been the foundation on which the East Asian economic miracles were built. These cultural elements had effectively complimented other supporting political and economic conditions.

Some of the common characteristics shared by the North-east Asian Confucian communities include:

▲ an emphasis on obligation within society rather than rights

▲ an emphasis on rule by man, or virtue, rather than the law

▲ a high emphasis on rigorous, even ruthless competitive education

▲ an acute sense of the linkages between past and present

▲ placing a higher value on human community and order than on material possessions

▲ a high regard for logic and rationality

▲ an acute awareness of the changing nature of reality.

The culture of host countries is not static but is constantly changing in response to new influences. Some of the changes are brought into the host country by international companies marketing new products to local consumers; international marketers are change agents introducing new elements of culture and lifestyle. This is sometimes seen as a serious threat to the local culture, values and tradition. During the 1960s and early 1970s, the multinationals came under repeated attacks by western academia and the Third World intelligentsia as the destroyers of native tradition and culture. In the 1990s, reactions to the presence of international companies are less severe, but nevertheless, they are well advised to behave like good corporate citizens, participating in community projects including those that help to preserve the indigenous culture. Marketing campaigns mounted by international companies should respect local values and cultural idiosyncrasies. Advertisements should be pre-tested to avoid offending local sensitivities. The Indonesian government, for example, imposed a TV advertisement ban in 1981 which lasted eight years. They were concerned that the continual portrayal of a 'western' affluent lifestyle in television advertising might develop unrealistic expectations among the general population of their country.

Technological environment

The Asian technological environment has been developing rapidly and this continues to create marketing opportunities for international companies. However, the lack of supporting services and infrastructure may adversely affect their market entry if the host country is not ready to absorb their technology. A technology-rich international company can find:

▲ the host country's desire for technology transfer provides an entry to the domestic market

▲ Asia's vision of a developed economy permits the international company to align its corporate objectives with the national vision but

▲ a lack of technological capability in the host country may render the product or service non-viable.

Asian governments generally recognise that technology is pivotal to a nation's economic progress. Modern technology helps to expand a country's industrial base and enhances its international competitiveness. Consequently, many countries have made the acquisition and transfer of technology a high priority national goal. Technology-poor countries seek access to more advanced technology either through generous investment incentives or the use of government mandated counter-trade, such as offset programs.[7] The governments of several Asian countries use counter-trade measures to secure technology transfer; some examples are:

▲ in 1989, Garuda (Indonesia) ordered twelve passenger aircraft from Boeing and McDonnell Douglas in a deal estimated at US$2 billion — the contract stipulated 35 per cent offsets

▲ the Malaysian government decided to emphasise the offset program in April 1991; subsequently Malaysia signed a contract with a western company to build a power station, with offsets requiring technology transfer, sales of Malaysian manufactured goods amounting to 30 per cent of the value of the contract, a soft credit, and an aid component.

The senior management of technology-rich firms should align their firm's offshore objectives with the national vision of the host governments that they will encounter. This is often the key to a company's effort to become a good corporate citizen in the host country. Hewlett-Packard, for example, mounted Malaysia's biggest R&D symposium in 1992, announcing Hewlett-Packard's intention of working towards the objectives set out in Vision 2020. Transfer of technology, however, is not without its difficulties and problems, one of which being that rhetoric may not suffice: the host government may demand evidence of transfer.

Malaysia's Vision 2020

Vision 2020 was unveiled by the Malaysian government in January 1991. The year 2020 AD is when Malaysia will achieve the status of an industrialised and developed country. Prime Minister Dr Mahathir B. Mohamad outlined nine objectives for Vision 2020. These are:

▲ establish a united Malaysian nation

▲ create a psychologically liberated, secure, and developed Malaysian society

▲ foster and develop a mature democratic society

- ▲ establish a fully moral and ethical society
- ▲ establish a mature liberal and tolerant society
- ▲ establish a scientific and progressive society
- ▲ establish a caring society
- ▲ ensure an economically just society
- ▲ establish a prosperous society.

The level of technology to be transferred has to be appropriate for the host country. A developing country may not have the supporting services and the necessary infrastructure to make sophisticated technology workable. Some Australian marketing research firms are excellent at analysing and interpreting scanner data, but this would not have helped them enter Vietnam in 1995: the distribution system in Vietnam had not, at that date, reached the stage of retail industry development where computers replaced human effort in warehouse management.

Technology transfer: Critical success factors

The Japanese Chamber of Commerce and Industry of Malaysia (JACTIM) conducts an annual survey among its corporate manufacturing members on technology transfer. The results from JACTIM's 1991 Survey attempt to evaluate the rate of success among its members in Malaysia.

Numerous methods for transferring technology from advanced industrial countries to developing countries are available. Private Malaysian companies may pay a fee to acquire specific technology through technology licensing agreements. Japanese government officials may transfer technology by training Malaysian engineers as a result of an agreement between the two governments. Further, when state-run or private companies in Malaysia purchase machines and equipment, they may acquire the technology through operating this equipment. Finally, technology transfer occurs through foreign direct investment. This is the most important method in Malaysia.

The sharp appreciation of the yen since September 1985 has prompted a large-scale relocation of production facilities outside Japan. The shift of electrical and electronic companies into South-east Asia is particularly visible. Small and medium-scale Japanese companies supporting these industries have also been compelled to follow suit. The move has only been made recently and it is JACTIM's aim to find out, at this early stage, the situation with regard to technology transfer between Japanese manufacturers and their counterparts in Malaysia. The survey covers eleven technology transfer categories:

- ▲ relatively simple manufacturing technology
- ▲ labour management technology
- ▲ production control technology
- ▲ advanced manufacturing technology

▲ financial management technology

▲ quality control technology

▲ purchasing management technology

▲ production technology

▲ sales management technology

▲ business management technology

▲ R&D technology.

According to the results, a rate of success of 65 per cent or above has been achieved for simple manufacturing technology, labour management technology, production control technology, and advanced manufacturing technology. As for financial management technology, quality control technology, and purchasing management technology, 55 per cent or above have been completed. On the other hand, technology transfer in the last four categories is below 45 per cent. In particular, transfer in R&D technology is as low as 16 per cent.

Factors which hindered technology transfer have been found to be:

▲ difficulty in securing personnel with basic education

▲ period of service of employees is short due to job hopping

▲ undeveloped supporting industries

▲ long period of time required for technology transfer (43 per cent of companies in this survey are less than three years old)

▲ restrictions on work permits

▲ language barriers.

Extracts from a paper by Yokio Shohtoku, Group Managing Director, Matsushita Airconditioning Group of Companies in Malaysia, presented at the National Conference on Industrialisation in Malaysia, June 16–17, 1992

A PEST analysis provides a comprehensive framework to be used in the selection of potential offshore markets for foreign direct investment. It is a standardised environmental scanning tool used by the Industrial Development and Investment Centre (IDIC) in Taiwan. Taiwan has, in the last decade, become the largest foreign direct investor in South-east Asia. The data in Table 10.6 show how the IDIC rates four developing nations in ASEAN as possible destinations for the relocation of labour-intensive industries from Taiwan. The criteria included not only the prevailing government incentives and the political and economic situation, but also the attitude of the host government towards its ethnic Chinese residents. Anti-Chinese sentiment might have a negative impact on Taiwan's direct investment. Thailand and Malaysia were far more favourably rated than either Indonesia or the Philippines, for the following reasons:

▲ The political environments in both Thailand and Malaysia are more favoured. They are more stable politically and have fewer bureaucratic hurdles to cross.

Table 10.6 *Investment climate in South-east Asia (for labour-intensive industries)*

	Thailand	Malaysia	Philippines	Indonesia
Geographical				
Natural resources	2	4	1	5
Infrastructure	4	5	1	2
Political				
Political stability	5	5	1	3
Bureaucracy	4	5	2	1
Legal				
Law and regulations	3	5	2	1
Tax incentives	4	3	5	1
Cultural				
Comparable facilities	3	5	2	1
Ethnic policy	5	3	5	1
Religion	4	3	5	1
Wages	3	1	5	5
Worker level of education	3	3	5	1
Labour-management relations	5	3	1	4
Economic				
Exchange rate	5	5	2	1
International credit	4	5	1	2
GSP privileges	5	3	5	5
Customs tax obstacles	2	1	3	5
National income	4	5	2	1
Inflation	4	5	1	1
Total scores	*69*	*69*	*49*	*41*

1 = least favourable
5 = most favourable
Source: Industrial Development and Investment Centre, Taiwan.

▲ The economic environments in both Thailand and Malaysia are more favourably regarded after considering exchange rates, credit facilities, rates of inflation and national income levels.

▲ The sociocultural environment in the Philippines is the most favoured while that of Indonesia is least favoured.

▲ Technological environments, although not specifically rated in this example, are considered to be better in Thailand and Malaysia because of their better technology infrastructure.

Key success factors in Asia

All of today's industry leaders, without exception, began by bold deployment of strategies based on the key factors for success.
Kenichi Ohmae, The Mind of the Strategist

The key success factors (KSFs) of a company are those attributes or functions which must be carried out particularly well for the organisation to out perform its competitors. Firms which have strengths matching their industries' KSFs tend to perform better than those which do not (Sa & Hambrick 1989). KSFs must be relatively few in number and restricted to factors which are important to the overall corporate goals and objectives (Freund 1988). Once identified, they should be applicable to all the companies with similar objectives and strategies in an industry. KSFs are hierarchical in nature with some of them crucial to the overall company while others are focused on one functional area. The KSFs discussed in this chapter are not industry-specific but are relevant to all firms operating in the international environment. They are the common attributes of high performing international companies.

A domestic company becoming international for the first time needs to adjust to a fundamentally different working environment. It will be catering to the demands of foreign customers and working under a new set of operating constraints and competitive forces. Its domestic success came from concentrating on one set of key success factors, but it must add new ones to succeed internationally. The domestic KSFs are industry-specific and home country-specific. A company venturing offshore for the first time needs to recognise that its foreign venture has international KSFs. Failure to take these into account will prevent the new venture achieving the depth and quality of relationships with its new customers, agents, partners and host governments that are needed to build a defensible and profitable market position.

Four key success factors apply to every international company hoping to succeed in the Pacific region (McLean 1986). These are:

▲ long term commitment

▲ awareness of market needs and trends

▲ investment in appropriate skills and technology

▲ the ability to deal with host governments.

A study of the causes of poor export performance among British companies showed that, as a group, British exporters in the early 1980s exhibited significant export and cultural myopia (Hooley & Newcomb 1988). Other factors included a lack of commitment to export marketing by top management, a failure to adapt their product offerings and marketing mix to the foreign market place, and a tendency to dissipate their efforts over too many different markets and countries. (The issue of limiting one's international involvement to a few markets is a point of contention. Piercy (1988) challenged the validity of concentrating on five or six 'best markets' instead of penetrating a large number of countries. He asserts that such a recommendation may introduce a self-imposed barrier to improving export performance.)

Among small and medium United States exporters, the factors inhibiting export during the 1980s were: a lack of information on prospects and markets overseas; a lack of knowledge on how to market overseas and of foreign business practices; an inability to minimise foreign exchange risk; fear of competition from foreign and United States firms abroad; unfamiliarity with export procedures; problems with pricing for foreign markets; and unsuccessful communication with overseas clients (Kedia & Chhokar 1986). A similar study, conducted by the Australian Trade Commission during the 1980s, reported the inhibiting factors among the Australian exporters as: delays experienced at the domestic waterfront; cost of raw materials; overseas import restrictions; lack of finance for export activities; and inability to strike a competitive price or to match the more favourable credit terms offered by overseas competitors. Conversely, the factors contributing to export marketing success, as found by Butler (1987) in his sample of 240 Australian exporters, were:

1   personal visits to the market

2   drive and persistence of particular executives or other employees

3   development of export marketing strategy

4   attention to customer relations

5   change of product to meet overseas customer requirements

6   devaluation of the Australian dollar

7   contribution of agents

8   distribution arrangements

9   use of market research

10   participation in trade displays

11   information or advice from Austrade

12   use of advertising

13   bringing customers/clients to Australia

14   special financial or credit arrangements.

In 1992 the Jackson Report called on Australian companies venturing into Asia to recognise the diversity and fragmentation of the region. International firms must understand the way business is conducted in Asia so as to assess and contain risks. They must strive to become 'insiders' in regional markets. They must involve their senior management, especially their chief executive, in the overseas undertaking. The firm needs to select people with qualities which are likely to enhance their success in Asia, and allocate resources to developing managers for future Asian operations.

In 1993 McKinsey and Company reported to the Australian Manufacturing Council that the most significant difference between exporting firms and non-exporting firms and between low and high export growth firms is the leadership and commitment of the firms' top management to exporting. Other characteristics shared by successful export companies included competition on value, particularly in quality, technology, and product design. These firms have a strong customer orientation and tailored their products to meet overseas customer requirement. Emerging exporting firms have a rich diversity of skills in their organisations, and have developed the ability to innovate both in terms of product and process. Successful firms think strategically about their external environment. They develop linkages with financial institutions and R&D providers. Finally, they attempt to become 'insiders' in overseas markets by locating some functions abroad, but ensuring integration with functions back home.

A survey among 126 Australian businesses dealing in and with Asia, conducted in 1992 by the East Asia Analytical Unit of the Department of Foreign Affairs and Trade, reported that issues which are crucial in South-east Asian markets are: choosing the right local partners; understanding the local business culture; a long term commitment to the export or investment project and to the commercial relationship; finding and keeping good local staff; obtaining Australian staff who have been trained to deal with that market; and the capability and readiness to modify products for a particular market.

In an analysis of Australian business opportunities in Asia, McIntosh Baring (1993) suggested that the four cornerstones of success in Asia are:

▲ the identification of a business opportunity in Asia

▲ matching the opportunity with the transferable corporate strengths of the Australian company

▲ selection of an entry vehicle that will deliver 'insider status'

▲ a high level of commitment to the region.

In 1993 a BIS Shrapnel report ranked the following KSFs in their order of importance:

1   quality of service

2   long term commitment

3   ability to work with local companies

4   ability to select the right local staff

5   negotiation skills, cost effectiveness

6   the understanding of overseas language and culture.

Table 10.7 *Characteristics of successful Australian companies in Asia*

CEO and board leadership	Management is prepared to invest substantial financial resources and to plan long term
	Senior managers devote time to building personal relationships with Asian partners and long term relationships with Asian customers
	The management structure of the company complements the needs of the Asian operation
	Everyone in the company understands the importance of the Asian market to the company
Thorough knowledge of the market	Thorough research verified by frequent visits to Asia
	Familiarity with the international funding available in the region
	Complete familiarity with Asian customer requirements resulting in products or services targeted at those specific requirements
Selection of highly skilled personnel	Staff with high skill levels, thorough knowledge of the business and an ability to get on with Asians
	Local staff are appointed right through to general manager level and are integrated into the company's personnel management system
	Long term staffing of the Asian operation

Source: CEDA 1993

A comparative study between the performance of small to medium Canadian and British exporters (Beamish, Craig & McLellan 1993) concluded that the common key determinants for successful exporting are a commitment to international involvement, frequent contact with foreign representatives, an ongoing distribution arrangement, clear targets for the firm's markets, product uniqueness, and a wide geographical focus. Some of the key determinants reported are similar to the Austrade study conducted among Australian exporters.

The Strategic Forum 1993 (CEDA 1993), organised by the Committee for the Economic Development of Australia (CEDA) identified three major characteristics of Australian companies which have been successful in Asia. These were chief executive and board leadership, knowledge of the market, and selection of highly skilled personnel. Their detailed analysis is shown as Table 10.7.

The international strategic diamond

The preceding section described a range of studies carried out in the United States, Britain, Canada and Australia, on factors which are crucial to success in international expansion. Although the studies were in most cases conducted independently, the results were very similar. It is possible to group the key determinants for international business success under four major headings, namely:

▲ the company's commitment

▲ the counterpart

▲ competitors

▲ the customer.

We refer to these four key success factors as the *international strategic diamond*. Together they provide an essential operating framework for an international company, irrespective of its mode of market entry.

Colonial Mutual group

In 1989 the Colonial Mutual board decided to evaluate the opportunities for life insurance business in Asia seriously. Alan Beanland was made Regional General Manager — Asia Pacific, and he and a small project team drove the initiative. He had worked in Hong Kong earlier and had seen many large American and European companies stumble. He thought that they had failed to recognise that Asia was different. These companies undertook inadequate research on the region and therefore failed to adapt their products, operating policies and prices to local conditions. Nor did they see the need to build strong long term relationships. Beanland decided to avoid these errors while fast-tracking Colonial Mutual into the region.

Beanland's team started their research in late 1989. The team put in the equivalent of two man-years of research in Australia and Asia. In one particular month they visited eighty different companies in the region with many repeat visits. Two factors contributed to Colonial Mutual's success: a significant budget for research and travel, and the involvement of high level, experienced staff. Beanland's opinion is: 'If you can't afford the research, you can't afford to operate in Asia.' Management invited some Colonial Mutual top people to participate in their Asian initiative. In their view, Asia is definitely not a testing ground for novices. 'It takes more skill to achieve a goal in a foreign country, often on your own, and without support infrastructure, than it does in your home base,' observed Beanland. Before starting, the team was given a fundamental knowledge of the targeted country, its language, and its culture.

The Colonial Mutual team used the Department of Foreign Affairs and Trade, Austrade, local embassies, bilateral business councils, local accounting and legal firms, banks, Asian government departments, Australian Clubs and Sundowner Clubs as information sources. They also spoke to the people who understood their particular market. They found that even their potential competitors were flattered to be asked their opinion.

By mid 1990 Colonial Mutual had a cohesive strategy involving a joint venture with Jardine Matheson, a Hong Kong-based conglomerate with a long history of trading and finance in Asia. The joint venture was to establish a life business in Hong Kong, Manila and Jakarta. Jardine had 150 years of experience in Asia to steer Colonial Mutual through the cultural and regulatory minefields, and could provide ongoing support processes quickly and effectively. Colonial Mutual's Hong Kong Life Insurance office is now the fourth largest in the territory and has been growing at 50 to 60 per cent per year.

Beanland believes you must establish the basis on which you will operate before making an agreement. He defined business objectives, management control, boards, fees, profit expectations, dividend policy and the use of expatriates. The agreement should also include a termination clause and a method to resolve problems. Successful business entry, Beanland says, is to do with 'partner, partner, and partner'. Beanland recognised that the way Colonial Mutual would be perceived in Asia would depend upon the partner with which it was associated. 'Not only do you need to research your partner's background, but they yours, as you may well be totally unknown.'

Beanland's advice is: 'Expect it to be different. Search for those cultural, market and economic differences as they affect your business and tailor your solutions to them before you start.' Knowing about the diversity of Asia is important for targeting your product and strategy. As Beanland pointed out:

> *You can't, for example, have the same strategy for Thailand as for the Philippines or Taiwan. Even within countries it is different. Peninsula and East Malaysia, for example, are very different in a business sense; Penang is predominantly Chinese, while Johore has a Malay approach. To be part of this complex region takes time and emotional commitment. You can't be a fair-weather friend or take a short-term view if you want to succeed.*

The reasons for the Colonial Mutual group's success are:
▲ commitment at chief executive and board level
▲ appointment of high calibre, experienced staff
▲ thorough research involving face-to-face discussions in Asia
▲ focus on finding a reputable joint venture partner
▲ willingness to adapt the product, pricing and operating procedures to the reality of the Asian market
▲ sensitivity to cultural differences.

CEDA 1993

The company's commitment

The most important factor in the success of a company's international ventures is commitment. The firm's commitment must extend beyond the need to utilise excess production capacity; management must become dedicated to a long term goal. This commitment will be shown by a willingness to put an international strategic plan into action; and as the company's involvement in the foreign market deepens, the firm's management will accept and encourage changes in the domestic corporate culture as well. A company's commitment to international marketing eventually brings about a transformation of its vision, mission and operating philosophy. The head office gradually loses its domestic focus and develops into the headquarters of a regio-centric or a global company.

The counterpart

Overseas counterparts are local agents and joint venture partners. They can make a major contribution to the success of the international company in the host country; if they fail, so will the venture. They help the firm forge linkages with respected local political, military or business elites; always a useful, and sometimes an essential, step towards becoming accepted in a foreign market. International executives must build an extensive network of personal relationships with current and potential counterparts and allies. The home office needs to select the sort of people it sends overseas carefully: they should not be culturally myopic, but rather should possess the capacity to understand the business customs and practices in the host nation. As a company becomes more involved internationally the competence with which it recruits and works with local staff should increase to the point that they become an integral part of the new corporate culture. The bilateral communication channel between the corporation and the counterpart must be established and supported by strong personal relationships fostered by frequent contacts.

The selection of an appropriate counterpart is especially important during the early stages of internationalisation. A mismatch will usually lead to a setback to the company's offshore venture, with a consequent drop in enthusiasm and loss of commitment. At the very least such a setback will cost the company time and financial resources as it taps into new networks and cultivates new relationships.

A good counterpart can open many doors to an outsider which would otherwise be closed. As a local person, he or she can help the foreign partner find a satisfactory way of resolving unique local problems. Local counterparts often act as mediators between the international company and the host government. They are particularly useful in sensitive situations where 'face' is a major concern. CSR Ltd is one of the largest companies in Australia. In Asia, CSR's preferred method of expansion is through joint ventures with local partners; either in greenfields projects or in existing operations that can be upgraded and expanded as necessary. Their managing director was quoted as saying that 'While joint-venture partners can make life complicated, we depend on them for local knowledge about sales, marketing, government policies and regulations' (Richardson 1995).

A good local counterpart is someone who has a good 'strategic fit' with the exporting company. The partners should be reasonably well matched in terms of size, operational history, stage of development, and corporate needs. Other important considerations may include product complementarity and current strategic position in the market place. (A company's 'strategic position' in its industry is defined by the role it plays in the target market (Kotler 1994).) Both the strengths and the weaknesses of any potential partner should be evaluated and considered during the selection process.

Competitors

A new venture into Asia will bring a company into contact with new competitors. These may be other international companies operating in the host country or local firms, or, in the more sought-after markets, both. Competitor analysis is an essential part of your marketing audit in the new environment. It is important to conduct a SWOT analysis on each competitor. A SWOT — strengths, weaknesses, opportunities and threats — analysis is an essential step in the international marketing planning process. Knowing the major competitors' strengths and weaknesses in offshore markets permits an international company to refine its overseas strategy so as to take advantage of its competitors' limitations, while avoiding contests where competitors are strong. Information on competitors' strengths and weaknesses can be collected from published reports, government statistics and trade publications; this can be supplemented by data collected during personal interviews with customers, dealers, suppliers and government officials; and, where justified, the firm may commission specific marketing research reports and studies.

Northern Iron and Brass Foundry

Northern Iron and Brass Foundry is a market leader in the Australian market for industrial castings for water equipment and the sugar, mining and timber industries. The Schmidt family, who started the company in the 1930s, operated it until the mid 1980s when it was sold to a United Kingdom-based engineering company. In 1990, its general manager, Herb Foxlee, and Bob Macalister, general manager of the company's sales division, acquired the business in a management buy-out.

'The market for our products in Australia has shrunk, and we were faced with excess production capacity. We've had to look at expanding markets overseas,' Foxlee said. And that's exactly what the company is doing. One of its tactics is to make sure staff understand the cultural aspects of overseas dealings:

Companies targeting export markets must ensure that they have consistently good quality, competitively priced products, and that their supply is reliable. They must build up a rapport with their clients. It has been vital that we behave appropriately with our clients, and be sensitive to their social, business and cultural norms.

Marketing tools used by the company include foreign language brochures and instruction booklets and product videos dubbed into Asian languages. But Foxlee warns that developing brochures for Asian markets requires expert advice in choosing appropriate colours and languages. Product packages and presentation also play an important role in establishing a corporate image for quality.

'You must always be aware of what your international competitors are doing,' he said. He travels regularly to the United States to monitor developments in technology, methodology and training in the heavy engineering industry. He also emphasises the importance of careful selection when choosing agents in target markets.

'Export market development is tough and there is a lot of outlay before you see any return, but if you don't make that first step you will never get that significant sale.'

NIES Magazine 1993–94

The customer

Customer focus takes on a whole new meaning when a company is operating in a foreign market. In most cases, the international company is working with counterparts and customers from a different sociocultural background, with a different first language and having significantly different value and belief systems. An international company would find it virtually impossible to understand the needs of the foreign customers, let alone trying to fulfil them, if it did not have people on its staff who are sensitive to local attitudes and conventions. Maintaining this level of sensitivity requires frequent visits by key executives, possibly supplemented by the services of local marketing research agencies.

The impressive economic growth that has taken place in East Asia, and the corresponding expansion of the Asian middle class, has brought about a very significant change in consumption patterns. Higher income levels have created new demands for more sophisticated products and services. Singapore was a coolie port emerging from colonialism in the 1960s. By 1992, its 3.7 million people had a per capita income of about A$23 700 (US$18 000). It has been estimated that the new middle class in East Asia may total 150 million people (Monash Asia Institute 1993). Even China, one of the last bastions of centrally planned economics, has developed a sizeable middle class since the 'open door' policy was unveiled in 1979. The Survey Research Group estimated that about 20 per cent of the urban population in China can be considered middle class.[8] The total number of middle class families in the country is probably between 30 and 40 million (Nielsen 1995). In 1993, it was estimated that 55 000 Chinese customers a day visited the newly opened McDonald's restaurant in Beijing; each hamburger cost more than most Chinese earned in a week. Official attitudes to wealth and wealth creation in China have taken a 180 degree turn since 1980. While personal wealth was frowned upon in the early 1980s, by 1995 official Chinese slogans included 'don't be afraid to be rich' and 'let a few get rich first and then the rest will follow suit'. Expatriate executives need to understand the psychographic changes in the foreign market environment. How does the pressure of economic liberalisation influence the traditional social values such as respect for the old, filial piety, family cohesiveness, marriage arrangement, gender relationships, quality of life, work, frugality and leisure? How does the new global village affect styles and trends, ecological awareness and health consciousness?

The international strategic diamond represents the four key success factors for international involvement — the 4Cs (commitment, counterpart, customer and competition) — represent the four parties who are the main players in each international venture. The venture's strategies must be implemented so as to ensure that all four parties are winners in the relationship. Some strategies are directed at the international company itself. These strategies require introspection followed by explicit actions to create an international corporate culture. These strategies have been used successfully by many international companies in Asia.

Information given in the boxed material on pages 304–5 and 307 illustrate the workings of the key determinants within an international strategic diamond.

The firms differ in the way that they set about internationalisation, with one directly exporting from a home base and the other forming an international joint venture. The story of Northern Iron and Brass Foundry shows how the 4Cs underpin export marketing success. The other box describes the successful entry of the Colonial Mutual Group into the Asian market. Although Colonial Mutual has been an international company since it was founded in 1873, with branches in Fiji, New Zealand and the United Kingdom, it had made no further attempts to develop internationally until 1989 when the initiative described commenced.

Marketing mix
Product
An international company must create a viable product line for each country in which it operates in order to attain long term success. A firm should not assume that a product which is successful in the home country will automatically be viable in a foreign market. It should also realise that a product may need more than consumer acceptance to be viable (see boxed information on Siddons Ramset, page 289).

An international company can often gain a competitive advantage by offering new products and new solutions to customers' problems. This may mean adapting some products and developing some new ones. A commitment to quality in both the product and in after-sales services are essential in winning customer loyalty in Asia.

Branding
For a consumer product manufacturer to be independently successful in Asia, sustaining a significant and profitable market share over the long term, its product range needs to be branded. More is required than putting brands on its products: the manufacturer needs to invest substantially, both at home and abroad, to create a popular, internationally recognised brand name (see boxed information below). Unbranded products can only be successful for goods of low perceived value or low user involvement.

International consumer brands in Taiwan

With a rise in the nation's per capita income, consumers in Taiwan are expecting more value and quality for their money. Darlene Lee, a director of marketing research consultants Frank Small & Associates, says that Taiwan's new affluents are going for brand name products with little regard to cost. This is a marked departure from the market situation in the 1980s. Lee adds that brand name items were foreign to Taiwan's consumer market five years ago. Says Lee:

You couldn't get anything. They've gone from nothing to being flooded with hundreds and hundreds of brands from every part of the world. So what you put on your product packaging is often critical to acceptance, depending on how you market and display it. What people want to know is very tangible and product-specific: 'Tell me what this product is and what it does for me; tell me what it costs and what it costs in relation to similar products'.

'Don't tell me that it looks European, or American, or something unrelated to my needs.' To a certain extent the price then becomes the indicator of quality. When you take away the brand(name) and you take away the price, you totally lose the consumer. Many find it difficult to decide on taste alone.

While Taiwanese consumers are brand conscious, they have not shown a strong tendency to be brand loyal. There has so far been very little research conducted on the various factors which influence consumer choice. According to Lee, product labelling plays an important part in the consumer decision making process. 'If it's an imported product then the package has to be clearly identified as a foreign product, so there has to be more foreign language than local language on the label, but it has to have some Chinese as well.' The average purchaser of mass merchandising consumer items in Taiwan appears to demand a fine balance between the amount of foreign versus Chinese writing on the label. If the label shows too much English and not enough Chinese, then the consumers may think the manufacturer is being colonial and treating the local consumer with disrespect. On the other hand, if the label is totally Chinese they may think that the product is packaged in Taiwan and is somehow inferior in quality.

Based on *Overseas Trading* 1993

There is a widely held fallacy to the effect that Asian manufacturers are good in production but poor in marketing, lacking the expertise to build strong brands. This is certainly not true of Japan, whose companies have built many globally recognised brands. The four 'Asian Tiger' economies started their industrialisation program by relying on original equipment manufacturer (OEM) contracts from the advanced nations, and many manufacturers in these countries still tend to concentrate on production at the expense of marketing. The move from an exclusive product focus to a balanced marketing strategy was already well under way by 1995. Marketers from South Korea and Taiwan are narrowing the capability gap with strong Asian brands such as Samsung, Lucky Gold Star, Daewoo, Acer, Evergreen and Giant. Colgate-Palmolive's acquisition of two leading local brands of toothpaste — Zaitun in Malaysia and Darkie in Hong Kong — shows that some local brands have begun to challenge the market position of global brands. The information in the box opposite contains a case study of a Taiwan bicycle manufacturer which progressed successfully from being an OEM producer, supplying bicycles on which foreign firms applied their own brands, to become a global marketer with its own well-recognised brand.

Giant bicycle company

Among the ten brands of bicycles exported by Taiwan, namely Dahon, Fairarrow, Fisher, Giant, Kenstar, Merida, Pacific, Scott, Suzico and Wheeler, Giant is the most popular. Giant Manufacturing Co. Ltd, one of the largest private companies in Taiwan, was started in 1972 by a group of friends who saw an opportunity in the expanding domestic market for bicycles in Taiwan. Giant's corporate mission in 1976 was to 'offer customers high quality products at reasonable prices'. The original intention of the company was to be an OEM supplier to major brands in western economies. Based on its manufacturing philosophy of continual quality improvement, coupled with an aggressive entrepreneurial drive, Giant became the largest bicycle manufacturer in Taiwan by 1980. Measured by value, it is now the world's biggest bicycle exporter. The entire business operation was computerised in 1982; CPM wheel truing robots were introduced in 1987; and an automated warehousing facility was added in the same year. It now has an annual output of 1.5 million bicycles.

From its inception to 1980, Giant produced 'unbranded' bicycles for export. These products were re-branded by the contractors in their respective markets. International contractors such as Specialised Bicycles, Nishiki, Raleigh and Schwinn Bicycle Co., imparted to Giant new product design concepts and technical expertise. In 1981, the management decided to combine its OEM strategy with an OBM (Own Brand Manufacturing) production and sales strategy. It proceeded to market its own brand 'Giant' first in the domestic market, followed by a similar attempt at the export markets. The company's distribution policy is to secure a wide distribution network, working totally through dealers without any direct sales. Giant began its international sales network by establishing Giant Europe BV in the Netherlands in 1986, then expanded into Germany, England, France, and Italy. It entered the North American market as Giant Bicycles Inc. in the United States in 1987. Giant Company Ltd was established in Japan a year later and Australia in 1990 with Giant Bicycle Co Pty Ltd.

Giant in the 1990s is the market leader in Taiwan with approximately 30 per cent domestic market share. It competes with at least fifty other local manufacturers of 'complete bikes' and has maintained a distribution network comprising 230 dealers who collectively sell about 10 per cent of Giant's total production.

Giant has now achieved its vision of an export-oriented company with 90 per cent of its production destined for twenty overseas markets. Its OEM business takes only 25 per cent of Giant's annual production. The remaining 75 per cent is sold under the Giant brand name. Major export markets are North America, Japan, Europe and Australia.

Giant is currently manufacturing four product lines, which are:

▲ road and racing series

▲ mountain series

▲ hybrid of all-terrain/fitness/sport

▲ exercise bikes.

It produces 250 models in total, each one is available in six sizes with a choice of up to three colours. The company's sustainable competitive advantage is its quality and innovative features. Giant is no longer a low cost producer and has consciously moved to the medium and premium price segments of the market. By 1990 Giant had become the world's largest manufacturer of bikes with carbon-fibre frames. Its best-selling range retail for US$400 to US$600. The company invests substantially on R&D in Taiwan as well as in North America. It maintains a design facility in the United States with a strong product development team. In order that it does not totally abandon the lower end of the market, Giant has built two factories in mainland China of which one is a joint venture with a Chinese partner.

Tanzer (1993) and Taiwan Products: Bicycles, January 1989

Price

Pricing is a complex issue for an international company. An international company may have a policy of charging the same price in all markets.[9] This practice is often found to be unworkable because it assumes that all markets share the same cost structure, and experience the same supply and demand conditions.

International companies from developed economies have traditionally competed in Asia with a non-price strategy. As long as their products were perceived to be of higher quality, prices could be set to reflect this perception. More recently many western companies have been forced into price competition by the loss of their foreign mystique and the rise of strong local brands.

Asian economies were traditionally sharply divided on class lines, with a small, extremely wealthy upper class ruling a large, mainly rural and extremely poor underclass. The economic development of East Asia is beginning to add a substantial middle class to this picture, while enough 'trickles down' to give many of the urban, and some of the rural, poor a modest discretionary spending capability. With this spread of incomes, price segmentation has become an important tool for Asian marketers. Products within the same line can be clearly positioned in the premium, standard, and lower (value-for-money) ranges.

Asian consumers are generally more price aware than are consumers in the west, and any trading price agreed with an Asian partner should take this into consideration. A partner will probably wish to employ a penetration pricing policy, keeping prices low until demand for the product has been established. A western-based international supplier might wish to profit from the higher quality perception of its products and choose a skimming price policy instead. Many western partners have agreed to go with a lower price initially on the basis of an assurance from the local counterpart that a price rise can be implemented later. This is a fertile ground for future conflict. Raising a price in Asia is not a simple manoeuvre, since the firm's Asian partner company and its business contacts are linked through personal relationships. Any proposal for a sudden and/or substantial price increase would be rejected for fear of disrupting these relationships.

If a price rise is ever implemented it may well be a small one, and delayed for an extended period at that.

Countertrade
Countertrade is an unconventional form of financing where goods or services are supplied in the place of cash or a banker's letter to settle part or all of the price of an import contract. It exists because developing economies and some other countries have limited or no foreign exchange reserves, and place strict restrictions on the type of items for which importers are allowed to settle in hard currency. An international company which insists on letter-of-credit terms will lock itself out of many markets. The rapid expansion of countertrade in the past decade presents an international company with new challenges and opportunities. In 1982 roughly twenty countries around the world were engaging in countertrade. The number had increased to more than a hundred by 1987. Countertrade's share of world trade has grown rapidly.

With the exception of Brunei and Hong Kong, all of the countries in Asia utilise countertrade to some extent. Almost all of the countries in South-east Asia require countertrade for public sector purchases. Trade with east European countries, the former Soviet Union, China, and many countries in Africa and South America is largely based on countertrade. It would be wrong to assume that countertrade is only used in trading with truly impoverished nations and with members of the former communist bloc. Countertrade transactions undertaken by the Malaysian government with developed countries have been increasing since their introduction in 1983. In 1985, Malaysia signed nineteen countertrade agreements valued at M$319.79 million, and in 1989 there were 102 agreements valued at M$1.618 billion (*Star* 1991). Examples of countertrade transactions entered into by the Malaysian government included the supply of offshore patrol vessels from Samsung, South Korea; rail fastening from France, muriate of potash and rail fastenings from Germany, and special wear-resistant rail from Poland.

Place
The sophistication of the distribution system in a country is closely related to that nation's level of economic development. Distribution is the least developed in less developed countries, where the retailing system involves a large number of people each selling a very small quantity of goods. As a country develops, there is an increasing concentration in the retailing sector. Advanced industrial countries have far larger retail outlets and a relatively smaller number of retail institutions than the developing countries do.

Not all industrialised nations have an efficient, modern distribution system. A notable example is Japan. Although a developed economy, Japan has a complex distribution system with many small retail outlets and several intermediaries between each manufacturer and its final consumers. Some international companies have blamed the Japanese distribution system for their failure to secure a profitable market share in that country. Broadly speaking, the Japanese prefer to deal with suppliers who deal with them as they are, as distinct from demanding that Japanese society be reorganised for the importers' convenience. The Japanese distribution system is evolving under economic pressure at least as much as under political pressure, but there is not much point in expecting it to favour any one company.

Distribution systems are undergoing a revolution across most of Asia and the most visible evidence of the retailing revolution is the spread of supermarkets and shopping malls in major urban centres throughout East Asia. Part of the driving force behind the current retail sector modernisation is provided by the internationalisation of United States, European and Japanese retailers.

Retail revolution in Asia

The spread of supermarkets is the most visible evidence of the retailing revolution sweeping through East Asia.

Indonesia

In 1985, the 7.9 million people of Jakarta were served by eighty-five supermarkets. In 1993 there were more than 240. One in five adults in Jakarta visit a supermarket at least once a week. In the AB socioeconomic group, the proportion rises to one in three. Between 1990–92, the number of large supermarkets (five or more checkouts) in nine principal Indonesian cities — Jakarta, Bandung, Surabaya, Yogya, Semarang, Solo, Medan, Palembang and Padang — increased from eighty-one to 112. The number of medium-sized outlets (three to four checkouts) increased from seventy-two to ninety-one, while the number of mini-markets rose from 250 to 293.

According to SRI Retail Audit conducted by Survey Research Indonesia, 69 per cent of all baby talc is now bought at supermarkets. Supermarkets similarly account for 62 per cent of milk powder and 53 per cent of shampoo, and even 50 per cent of savoury snack sales.

Taiwan

Between 1990–92, Taiwan registered a 13 per cent increase in large supermarkets. The market leader is the Wellcome Group which opened its fiftieth store in October 1992. Wellcome's aim is 100 supermarkets in Taiwan within two years. Growing even more rapidly than large supermarkets are convenience stores, mostly under the banner of international franchises such as 7 Eleven, Circle K and AM/PM. At the lower end of the retailing market, the number of small provision stores in Taiwan have dropped by a quarter over the past two years. In order to survive the onslaught of supermarkets and convenience stores, traditional small retailers have positioned themselves as the 'Cut-Price' stores, equipped with modern shelving and price marking. These stores concentrate on low-price, often multi-pack product ranges, with a focus on household commodity items such as toilet tissue and laundry detergent.

China

Since the open door economic policy took effect in 1979, retail sales have grown at a compound rate of 15 per cent a year. In 1980, there were two million retail outlets throughout the country. In 1993 the number had increased to more than twelve million. Mass media advertising expenditure rose from RMB370 million to RMB3500 million between 1984–91. Yaohan, the Japanese retail giant, announced that it will open 1000 supermarkets in China over the next eighteen years.

Malaysia

Nearly 90 per cent of Malaysia's retail outlets are in the capital, Kuala Lumpur. New shopping plazas are springing up all over the city and the influx of Japanese and Hong Kong department stores has altered the retail landscape. The foreign luxury goods shops and international chain stores are pursuing the middle class into new suburbs beyond the capital. A Malaysian government report predicts that the nation's retail sector will have a minimum growth rate of 30 per cent per annum for the next thirty years.

SRG News 1993; the *Australian* 1995

Promotion

The promotional practices of an international company tend to reflect its policies and practices in its home country. The growth of international travel means that it is hard to sustain conflicting messages even in different countries. As a firm moves from being an exporter, becoming an international company, its promotional messages and strategies will also have to become international ones. There will always be a need to avoid practices in one market that damage a firm's products in a different one, but particular local circumstances and the development of local product variants may require the development of localised promotion strategies.

Do-it-yourself advertising is seldom used by international companies operating in host countries because the risk of failure is just too large. This does not mean that a firm must start its promotional planning from scratch in a new country: international advertising agencies normally follow their clients overseas:

> *The advance of the multinationals can be likened to that of an army with a large band of camp followers. When the company settles in a new market it likes to have familiar faces around it, and to seek advice from the local subsidiaries of the same firms who provide it at home. (Tugendhat 1973)*

Forming a promotion strategy for an Asian country requires knowledge of the current advertising expenditure patterns. Only those international companies that have attained a sound understanding of their target market segments

Table 10.8 *Advertising expenditure by medium, 1993*

	Total (A$m)	TV (%)	Newspaper (%)	Magazine (%)	Cinema (%)	Radio (%)	Other (%)
Japan	30 960	49	34	11	–	6	–
Hong Kong	1 485	43	36	11	1	6	3
Taiwan	1 403	59	30	10	–	n/a	–
Thailand	1 032	48	27	9	–	11	5
Indonesia	772	56	36	8	–	–	–
Singapore	526	32	53	7	1	4	3
Malaysia	521	34	55	6	–	2	2
South Korea	345	32	58	6	–	4	–

Sources: *Ad News*, 22 April 1994 and Asian Advertising & Marketing, April 1992

and their prospective customers' media choices are in a position to develop effective promotion strategies. Gaining maximum advertising returns requires that the advertising budget spent is correctly divided between the appropriate media. The professional services of advertising agencies based in the country are needed to complete an effective promotional plan. Table 10.8 contains the advertising expenditure by medium for eight countries in East and South-east Asia as it stood in 1993.

Noticeable differences in media split can be seen among the eight countries in Asia. Japan, being an advanced industrialised nation, has the highest advertising expenditure in the region. Television advertising receives the largest promotional allocation in Japan, Hong Kong, Taiwan, Thailand, and Indonesia; while newspaper is the most popular medium in Singapore, Malaysia, and South Korea. The growing sophistication of the local markets has enticed many foreign magazines to develop Chinese editions in Taiwan, including *People*, *Cosmopolitan*, and *PC World*. These new magazines have given advertisers new avenues for targeting specific market segments. It is interesting to note that advertising expenditure on cinema and outdoor media is relatively insignificant in all of the countries listed.

China, one of the last unexploited marketing and advertising frontiers of the world, is rapidly attracting the attention of international companies and foreign advertising agencies. The explosive rise in demand for advertising space has resulted in a seller's market. The relatively young advertising industry in China is yet to nurture a strong body of local creative talent and consequently much of the creative and production work has been farmed out to Hong Kong firms. The most important task for creatives is to integrate mainland Chinese sensitivities into ideas conceived in Hong Kong. Foreign advertising agencies operating in China are hampered by a lack of true understanding of the market. Reliable audience data or media rating figures are not available. In addition, marketers are discovering that Chinese consumers exhibit unique purchasing and consumption behaviour; perhaps it is due to their long isolation and decades of making do with very few consumer items. Chinese consumers, as at the time of writing, generally do not have strongly formed brand loyalties. A well known brand name perceived to be an 'old' brand in the west may attain a new lease of life in a country which has just been exposed to the brand for the first time. The Chinese are also eager to try new brands and new product features. Foreign advertising executives are learning much about this huge market through trial and error.

Ten tips for marketing and advertising in China

1 **Research products thoroughly:** Ensure any consumer research uses a realistic cross section of the population. Significant regional differences may be experienced in how a product is received.

2 **Beware of geographical limitations:** Unless a good distribution system or service network has been established, the nationwide launch of a product will be largely ineffective. A better strategy would be to concentrate on key cities and gradually fan out.

3 **Create a trustworthy brand and protect it:** Chinese consumers tend to stay with brands they have tried and can trust. It helps them to avoid bad experiences; anything from fake and sub-standard products to those making exaggerated claims. Having established a reliable brand, take steps to protect it from imitations and lookalikes.

4 **Convey a quality message:** Quality products that are reliable and long lasting are at the top of Chinese shopping lists so cost-effectiveness and quality should be prominent messages in advertising.

5 **Respect China's sensitivities:** Never use the Chinese national flag or anthem in advertising: never refer to Hong Kong or Taiwan as a country; and never omit Taiwan and the South China Sea islands from a map of China.

6 **Know the people you deal with:** Become more effective in business by getting to know distributors, wholesalers, sales people, merchandisers and even truck drivers. They can give advice on problems and generally help make things happen.

7 **Think outside traditional media advertising:** Treat packaging, for example, as part of advertising; it may be the only 'sales person' talking to customers. Assume the customer knows nothing about the product. Explain it, say why it is good, give directions for its use.

8 **Be innovative and creative with media:** A little imagination can take sales a long way. Locally developed advertising, by contrast, is usually no more than a list of product facts accompanied by a product photograph.

9 **Understand the media rate structure:** Reliable statistics to support media rates hardly exist. Besides the frustration, there is a three-tier rate structure: for imported goods, for goods made by joint ventures, and a third for local products.

10 Consider Taiwan and Hong Kong as part of Greater China: It makes sense to use the same Chinese brand name, packaging and advertising across China, Taiwan and Hong Kong. There has to be a good reason to do otherwise.

Ad News, 22 April 1994

Although the boxed text above specifically refers to China, much of the information is applicable to all markets in Asia. In the final analysis, successful marketing in Asia requires:

▲ thorough market research

▲ building trust between yourself and your local counterparts

▲ building trust between your products and your consumers

▲ respecting local sensitivities and, *above all*

▲ being innovative!

End notes

1   Trust is extremely important in western business culture too, but this is obscured by the rhetoric of competition.

2   A business organisation whose business activities cross national borders. The term refers to both global and multinational companies.

3   Many articles cover this topic. See, for example: Drucker (1958); Carman (1973); Aydin and Terpstra (1981); Dholakia (1981); Kinsey (1982); Varadarajan (1984); Akaah and Riordan (1988).

4   See, for example: Assael (1985); James (1983); Aldridge (1987); Tuncalp (1985); Goodyear (1982).

5   See, for example, *The Strategic Economic Plan: Towards a Developed Nation*, published by the Economic Planning Committee, Ministry of Trade and Industry, Republic of Singapore, 1991. This report outlines Singapore's plans for the twenty-first century. Part 1 provides an overview of the economic landscape over the next twenty to thirty years. Part 2 consists of nineteen programs, each of which contains specific measures to support the objectives of the eight strategic thrusts.

6   For a discussion of this topic see, for example: Kushner (1982); Goodyear (1982); Stanton, Chandran and Hernandez (1982); Aldridge (1987); Cateora (1993).

7   Offsets usually apply to government purchases of aerospace, defence, telecommunications, and major projects. The offsets requirement can vary from 20 per cent to over 100 per cent, and can include technology transfer, investment and educational projects.

8   Middle class in the sense of having some discretionary purchasing power after paying for the necessities of life; and probably in the sense of not performing manual work for hourly wages. Their cash incomes are not, as at 1995, comparable to those of middle income earners in the developed countries.

9   Those that don't may be accused of the economic sin of *international price discrimination* if they are too blatant about it.

Case study one

Multistack: Establishment
Background
Refrigeration

Refrigerators are a form of heat engine, but instead of energy flowing from a hot source to a cold sink, as in boiler to condenser, the energy flows from a cold source (like the inside of a refrigerator) to a hot sink (the warmer room-temperature air). Instead of energy flowing out of the system, as with electricity from a power station, energy must be supplied to a refrigerator. Nature has a pleasant surprise available to refrigerator builders: the Second Law of Thermodynamics says that a power station must use much more energy than it delivers, but that a refrigerator can pump much more heat than it needs to drive it.

Mechanical refrigeration was invented in the second half of the nineteenth century, eighty or so years after the condensing steam engine, but the principles are now extremely well known. A refrigerator has four main components: an evaporator, in which a boiling fluid absorbs heat; a pump, to reduce the pressure in the evaporator, dropping the boiling point of the working fluid; a condenser, to disperse the heat absorbed by the evaporator into the environment and turn the gas back into fluid; and a pressure reducing valve to limit the flow of cool fluid to the evaporator.

The choice of working fluid, or refrigerant, has an important bearing on both the efficiency of the refrigeration system and its potential environmental impact. Water can be used, but its normal boiling temperature is relatively high and so a refrigerator based upon water would have to maintain a very high vacuum in the evaporator. Carbon dioxide has the opposite problem: its normal boiling point is so low that the system would have to operate at very high pressure, making its mechanical design difficult. Ammonia and carbon disulphide both have normal boiling points which are convenient for use in refrigerators, but they are both quite poisonous which makes maintaining refrigeration systems using them hazardous and has caused real problems to emergency crews in the event of a fire or other accident; ammonia can also form an explosive mixture with air.

Butane and propane have the right boiling point and aren't poisonous, but they are very inflammable and undesirable on that account; their thermodynamic and physical properties are also less than ideal.

Freon

In the 1930s the American chemical company Dupont discovered the 'Freon' group of compounds; ethane, butane and propane modified by having the hydrogen atoms along their carbon backbone replaced by a mixture of fluorine and chlorine (hence CFCs, for chlorinated fluorocarbons). Freons have some amazing properties. They are non-flammable and non-poisonous, they can be tailored to nearly any boiling point/pressure combination, and they can even act as lubricants.

The invention of Freon made the 'sealed unit' refrigerator practical, with the moving parts of the motor and the compressor in a single, hermetically sealed casing. This combined motor-compressor had fewer moving parts than a separate motor and did not need a seal through which the drive shaft had to enter the compressor. Seals and around rotating shafts are always a source of trouble, being subject to wear and leakage, and systems relying on them need regular maintenance. The sealed unit rapidly became the unit of choice for domestic refrigerators, with the result that most domestic refrigerators complete their entire life without every experiencing a mechanical failure or requiring a service call.

Air conditioning

The American, Robert Carrier, is generally credited with the invention of air conditioning in the early years of this century. Carrier noted that simply cooling the air in a building was not satisfactory: unless the hot air was extraordinarily dry, the cooled air would be super-saturated with water and the inside of the building would be filled with fog. Carrier developed a practical dehumidifier to go with a refrigeration plant, enabling the air to be 'conditioned', not just cooled.

Carrier's original market was the supply of air conditioning plant to cotton mills and tobacco factories, where the maintenance of a constant temperature and humidity was essential if the quality of the output was to be maintained. Manchester, England enjoys year-round cool, humid weather and was, until the middle of the twentieth century, the major centre for cotton textile production in the world. Air conditioning allowed mills in the southern United States and elsewhere to operate year-round, depriving Manchester of its advantage and eventually of its cotton industry. Manchester also became the centre of an engineering industry supplying the cotton mills: the engineering industry has largely survived the departure of the cotton industry, illustrating once again that advantages based upon human skills are more sustainable than advantages based upon natural resources and conditions.

Carrier's innovation was applied to the comfort of people fairly rapidly, with the United States Congress getting air conditioning in the 1920s and therefore being able to legislate year-round instead of being forced to take a four month summer vacation. More recently the development of the American south and south-west, and countries such as Singapore and Malaysia, has been enormously facilitated by the use of air conditioning, both because of the industrial benefits and because the middle classes are not obliged to flee in search of comfort.

Commercial and industrial air conditioning operates on a completely different scale to the domestic refrigerator and air conditioner: 1 to 2 kilowatts of cooling is more than adequate for a domestic refrigerator-freezer, but a commercial building might require well over 1000 kilowatts. Commercial buildings are less common and less standardised than domestic refrigerators, and so there was no economic case for designing and mass producing sealed unit compressors: the typical building air conditioning plant involves a very large motor driving a very large compressor. Freon is too expensive to pump all around a building, and so a building air conditioning plant chills a flow of water which is then pumped around the building to secondary coolers in the ventilation system. The hot heat sink is often a water-tower on the building roof, with a second water system carrying heat from the chiller to the water tower.

In a commercial air conditioning system the evaporator and condenser are each incorporated into heat exchangers.

The ozone layer

The sun can be thought of as a huge, continuously exploding hydrogen bomb, and so it is just as well that the earth is 150 million kilometres or so away from it. Even at this distance quite a lot of what leaves the sun is not wanted on earth, and most of these unwelcome visitors are trapped long before they reach the ground. Among them is a torrent of high energy ultra violet rays, capable of causing sunburn, cataracts, and melanomas. Most of these are absorbed by a thin layer of ozone, a special form of oxygen, in the top of the atmosphere. In the mid 1980s a team of scientists from the British Antarctic Survey reviewed certain data that they had been collecting and showed that the ozone layer above Antarctica was getting thinner every year.

Scientists suggested, and satellite observations and laboratory experiments confirmed, that the ozone was being catalysed back to ordinary oxygen by free chlorine atoms. The source of these extra chlorine atoms could be traced to the widespread use of Freons. The properties of the various Freons were so malleable that CFCs had become very widely used, not only in refrigerators but in aerosol cans and for blowing insulating foams.

In 1987 an agreement known as the Montreal Protocol was drawn up, under which the production of CFCs would be stopped in the developed countries by 1995 and their use progressively eliminated. Subsequent agreements declared that a group of near-Freons with some hydrogen atoms left, the HCFCs, could be used in air conditioning until 2030, after which the production of all forms of ozone-depleting gases had to stop. HCFCs can be used as direct substitutes for Freon in some, but not all, refrigeration equipment. The best HCFC refrigerant, R22, is only one ten-thousandth as hazardous to the ozone layer as the common Freons R11 and R12, but even this level of hazard caused political problems and most developed countries have decided to bring forward the cutoff date for R22 production to 2005.

There are, as at mid 1996, three candidates for use as a refrigerator working fluid over the long term. Greenpeace favours butane, in spite of its poor physical and thermodynamic properties: the fact that the use of butane would make air conditioning more expensive to operate is not a 'green' issue. Authorities in the European Union are leaning towards ammonia: it is cheap, it has appropriate thermodynamic properties, and there is no explosion hazard as long as commercial air conditioning plant is located on roofs or other well-ventilated areas. The United States favours R134a, which is not cheap but it is neither explosive nor poisonous.

Butane, ammonia and R134a do not have ideal chemical properties; in particular, they lack the self-lubricating ability of R11, R12 and R22.

Ron Conry

Ron Conry decided, shortly after completing his apprenticeship as a refrigeration mechanic, that he did not like working for other people and so he founded his own air conditioning maintenance business in 1975 at the age of 23, starting with a great deal of enthusiasm and very little capital.

Conry specialised in the maintenance and repair of commercial and industrial air conditioning systems, and fairly rapidly saw an entrepreneurial opportunity: the manufacturers of commercial air conditioning plant and equipment marked up their spare parts and sub-assemblies to levels that had little connection with the cost. A component that a skilled fitter could reproduce in a well-equipped workshop in a matter of hours might be sold for $1000 as a spare part. A set of gears which a number of Melbourne firms were prepared to cut, heat treat and finish to order for $4000 to $6000 could cost $30 000 when bought from the original equipment manufacturer (OEM) as a spare.

Conry built and staffed a small workshop, and offered his customers locally sourced and manufactured spares at a substantial discount to the OEM's list price, usually 50 per cent off. The gears for which he paid $6000 would appear on his customers' bills at $15 000, a saving of $15 000 to the customer and a means of keeping the wolves a substantial distance from Conry's own door. Conry's business prospered, and by 1983 he employed twelve servicemen and four fitters, and serviced many of Melbourne's most prestigious buildings.

The substantial cash flow Conry's firm earned from remanufacturing spare parts suggested an even larger business opportunity. The reliability and maintenance expense of commercial air conditioning plant contrasted very poorly with the performance of domestic refrigeration equipment. As Conry saw it, the commercial air conditioning chillers available at the start of the 1980s had at least the following defects:

▲ Each chiller consisted of a few large, heavy and complex items of plant, so large and heavy that they were frequently installed with the foundations of a new building and then 'built in' such that major structural work was needed to get them out again.

▲ A single component failure could deprive a whole building of air conditioning unless the owners had gone to the great expense of installing duplicate plants.

▲ As mentioned above, conventional chillers had a separate motor and compressor, meaning that there had to be a gland through which some refrigerant would inevitably leak around the drive shaft, therefore requiring regular service and recharging.

▲ The refrigerant compressor in a conventional commercial chiller was usually a centrifugal model with a very high efficiency at its rated capacity but a quite poor part-load efficiency, meaning that in places like Melbourne the plant would only operate efficiently on a few very hot days in a year while wasting energy the rest of the time.

Conry believed that it would be possible to build a modular system, incorporating a compressor and two heat exchangers, such that the compressor could be hermetically sealed, offering the same high reliability and freedom from maintenance associated with domestic refrigerators. When (as was usual) the cooling requirements of a particular project were such that one of Conry's units were inadequate to the load, two or more could be bolted together in a stack. Conry predicted that a stack system would have the following advantages:

▲ The individual units of a stack would be very reliable and require little if any maintenance, but if a unit did fail the rest of the stack would continue to operate, and except at times of exceptional load, the building's cooling system would continue to operate within its normal parameters.

▲ The units would be light enough for one man to manage with a trolley, and would fit into a standard lift, meaning that installation could be postponed until a building was nearly ready for occupancy, and replacement, if ever needed, would not involve any structural work.

▲ Conry envisaged equipping each stack with a computer-based controller, so that at times of part load some units would be switched off, leaving the remaining units operating at close to their peak efficiency and offering users substantial energy savings.

Conry was referred to a reliable patent attorney, and in 1984 was granted Australian (and subsequently worldwide) patents on the 'modular commercial chiller'. He registered the name Multistack for his new enterprise.

The launch

Patents, as Conry already knew, do not pay the rent; rather the reverse. He decided to commercialise his invention, and developed a plan which, assuming that he did most of the work himself in his own workshop after hours, would cost $250 000 and take three years to develop a prototype. Conry knocked on many doors and waxed extremely eloquent, but no one offered him $250 000 on any terms. One financier showed some slight interest, and told Conry that the proposal looked more like half a million than a quarter. Conry, full of enthusiasm, reworked his plan over the next fortnight to cost $500 000 and took it back.

'How much were we talking about?' said the financier. 'Half a million,' replied Conry. 'It looks like a million dollar plan to me,' said the financier, and Conry went back to his office and did the numbers again. At a million dollars the plan aroused wide interest, and Conry signed up with APR Ltd (not the helpful financier), and began work on the prototype.

Conry wasn't (and still isn't), a Freemason, but he had the service contract for Dallas Brookes Hall in Melbourne, a major entertainment venue as well as being the headquarters of the Masonic Lodges in Victoria. In 1984 the Head of the Lodge was John Connell, a partner in the engineering consulting firm Connell-Wagner, and Conry had to give him the sad news that the hall's air conditioning plant was worn beyond repair. Conry offered to supervise the purchase and installation of a replacement plant, or, as an alternative, to install his prototype modular chiller at the Hall. Connell's interest was aroused, and after looking over Conry's plans he agreed to accept the first modular chiller for installation in Dallas Brookes Hall, where installation was duly completed in December 1985.

Connell went further: his firm was consulting engineers to the State Bank Centre project, a fifty-storey office building, banking chamber, and retail complex in the centre of Melbourne. When the Dallas Brookes Hall installation proved successful, Connell recommended Conry's Multistack plant for the State Bank Centre, and the recommendation was accepted.

The brazed plate heat exchanger

One technical problem needed to be solved before Multistack's modular heat exchangers could be genuinely compact: heat had to be exchanged between the refrigerant and the building's cold and hot water circuits. Heat exchangers had been invented by James Watt in 1776, and refined by Robert Stevenson in 1830, and their basic design, although often on a larger scale and usually using more modern materials, was still in use: a large tank held one fluid, and the other flowed through immersed pipes running through the tank. Such heat exchangers were large, heavy, and took a lot of working fluid to charge.

The Swiss engineering firm Alfa-Laval had invented a much more compact heat exchanger, made by pressing a suitable pattern into plates of bronze or stainless steel and then brazing a stack of plates together so that two fluids could be kept in close thermal contact while being securely separated physically. The unit making these compact heat exchangers was spun out by a group of Swiss venture capitalists as the firm SWEP, but neither Alfa-Laval nor SWEP saw any great business opportunities in supplying a small chiller manufacturer in Melbourne. Multistack bought a press and a furnace and developed their own heat exchanger production line, protecting themselves from SWEP's uncertain deliveries and onerous commercial terms.

The State Bank Centre installation, completed in September 1986, used Multistack-built heat exchangers. Other components, including the compressors, were sourced commercially.

Responding to Montreal

When the 1987 Montreal Convention set a schedule for the cessation of production of Freons, and in particular the common refrigerants R11 and R12, Multistack was able to switch to R22 almost immediately.

There was a major opportunity for Multistack created by the switch: R22 required substantially higher working pressures than the commonly used R11, and many existing installations would need to replace their compressors and their heat exchangers at their next major overhaul after R11 ceased to be available. This presented a formidable problem for many users: some of them had the plant on the roof, where it had been lifted by the construction crane; others had it in basement plant rooms, sometimes installed before the next floor had been cast. Getting the old plant out presented no problems to anyone equipped with a cutting torch, but getting a replacement in was rather more difficult.

Multistack modules could be moved by one man using a trolley and fitted into standard building lifts, and so once the cutting torch had finished its job, a Multistack system could be wheeled in to replace the old discrete system, one unit at a time. Multistack started a subsidiary in the United States to sell replacement systems to users whose R11 plant needed to be scrapped and where Multistack modules offered a clear installation advantage. The United States business enjoyed (and as of mid 1996, enjoys) modest success. Its main competition comes, not from United States plant manufacturers, but from an apparently endless supply of R11 smuggled into the United States. By 1995, R11 and R12 may have displaced cocaine as the highest value contraband item arriving at Miami.

The awakened giant

In 1981 China's 'Gang of Four' were arrested, tried and imprisoned, and the Chinese government embarked on the path from rigid state control of the economy to a more liberal system, in which private enterprise was tolerated and foreign capital cautiously accepted. By the mid 1980s liberalisation was general in China's coastal provinces, and a huge program of construction was in full swing. The new offices and factories needed air conditioning, and Chinese demand seemed to be inexhaustible. Between 1985 and 1995 there were more office buildings of forty or more stories completed in the single province of Guangdong than there are in Australia. In the capital of Guangdong, Guangzhou, there were over 1000 cranes visible on the skyline in 1992: by contrast, at the height of the building boom of the 1980s in Melbourne there were eighty.

The Hong Kong based entrepreneurs, S. W. Yan and S. Leung, recognised the opportunities in China, and their firm Super Link Ltd sought agencies from a number of western suppliers, including Multistack. The Chinese authorities encouraged local manufacture of the plant needed for their country's industrialisation, and Super Link built a plant in Panyu as a joint venture with the local government. Multistack licensed the Super Link plant in Panyu to assemble its modular chillers.

By the end of 1989 Multistack had shipped a total of about 1200 modules, equal to about 150 complete systems, with approximately 1000 in Australia and the rest in China, Taiwan and the United States.

Chapter *11*

Legal options and obligations

This chapter discusses some legal issues in general terms; but if you have any doubt about your legal rights and obligations, *consult a lawyer*, preferably one who has experience in the area of concern. Good faith and good intentions are not always enough.

> *The man who advises himself has a fool for a lawyer.*

    As far back as recorded history goes, merchants traded personally, and if a merchant had partners, they were all entitled to share in the profits of a venture and all obliged to discharge any outstanding debts in the event of a loss. The law contented itself with enforcing contracts, and if a customer was unhappy with a deal the law could only say, *caveat emptor* — 'let the buyer beware'. What we now call employees were termed 'servants', and their employers, or 'masters', had few obligations towards them. From the 1830s on, the law in most countries began to develop alongside the industrial revolution. The two major developments were the emergence of the limited liability company, and the development of consumer rights. From the 1950s onwards, at least in most developed countries, the law developed to recognise workers' rights as well.

Limited liability

The historic forms of business structure, the sole trader and the partnership, are still permitted, and are obligatory in some professions. There are no complications involved in setting up a business using these historic structures: a person can become a sole trader merely by starting to trade, and two or more people can form a partnership by opening a joint account at a bank. We strongly recommend that partners set out their agreement in writing and sign it, to avoid, at the least, future arguments. When sole traders or partnerships do not wish to trade under their personal names they are obliged to register their business name with the appropriate authority, but this is usually a simple counter transaction with a low fee.

From the sole trader's or the partners' viewpoint, there are two obvious potential problems with the traditional organisation:

▲ the Commissioner of Taxation (or equivalent) will treat their business and personal affairs as one for the purposes of assessing their tax liability, which may result in more tax being paid, or it being paid sooner, than under an alternative arrangement

▲ if the business gets into difficulties, creditors will be allowed to seize the trader's or the partners' personal assets to discharge their debts, and likewise, if one of the partners or the sole trader gets into financial strife, the creditors may seize the assets of the business in settlement.

These problems bring on another one: if the business requires cash to grow or to survive a transient downturn, this can only come from the entrepreneur and the entrepreneur's partners; if the needed money is borrowed, it will be on their personal security. There may be affluent outsiders who think the business attractive, but the only way such outsiders can invest in the business is by becoming partners: investment is an all-or-nothing affair.

From the societal viewpoint these may not always be disadvantages. If one group of people is able to minimise their tax liabilities, other groups will have to pay more. If someone running a business knows that their personal assets are at risk, they may be more careful than otherwise about letting the business run up debts of a size to stretch its ability to repay. Managers will be required for companies with many shareholders, and some of them may be running private agendas. Much corporate fraud takes the form of diverting company funds to private accounts or spending them on private benefits. Sometimes it is hard to distinguish between a fair reward to managers for their successful efforts to advance a company's interests and fraudulent diversion of the company's assets. The subject of 'corporate governance' has been actively debated for twenty years or more without any definitive conclusions being reached.[1]

From 1830 to the present a series of companies and other Acts in Britain and their equivalents in every developed country have tried to preserve the socially valuable features of the limited liability company while battling the share price manipulators and the asset thieves. In Australia and Britain, the law has tended to prohibit certain acts and rely on self-regulation and disclosure rules to limit the rest: the amount paid to directors of a public company, and parties related to them, must be shown in the annual report, but it is left to market forces to determine whether these transactions were in the true interests of the firm. In the United States there are much broader and more general laws on disclosure, and there is also a Securities and Exchange Commission, with extremely broad powers to investigate and prosecute.

The company

A company is a legal person, separate from its directors and shareholders. It is capable of entering into contracts and incurring debts, but the actions of a company are, in fact, the actions of people. There are several classes of people who may be identified with any company:

▲ there are *shareholders*, essentially passive investors, who economists describe as the *residual claimants*, entitled to any of the company's assets not already pledged to someone else

▲ there are *directors*, who are elected by the shareholders but whose primary duty is to act in good faith in the company's interest — they are ultimately responsible for the company

▲ there are *senior executives*, who are appointed by the directors (and in some cases may be directors) and who enjoy the delegated authority of the directors between board meetings

▲ there are other *employees*, who (at least in theory) do what the senior executives tell them to do.

Ethical entrepreneurs will usually operate through companies, both because of the possibility of receiving more appropriate treatment by the Tax Office and the possible need to be able to raise capital by the sale of shares, if not immediately, then in the reasonably near future. Taxation law is complex and frequently changed, and an entrepreneur should consult an accountant and/or a lawyer, both to advise on the most appropriate company structure, and for assistance in drawing up and registering the necessary documents.

The company form will allow the entrepreneurs to keep their private affairs separate from those of the business, and their investors will be protected from risks beyond the possible loss of their investment. Ethical entrepreneurs will not treat the company as a device for diverting investors' money to their own pocket or for swindling the firm's creditors or employees.

Directors

The directors of a company are elected by the shareholders but they are responsible to the company: if shareholders wish to limit the directors' freedom of action they can pass a resolution amending the company's articles at the company's general meeting, but they can't, or at least shouldn't, treat the directors as their employees or their delegates.

The duties of directors of Australian company law include:[2]

▲ to act in good faith

▲ to act in the best interests of the company

▲ to avoid conflict between the company's interests and the director's interests

▲ to act honestly

▲ to exercise care and diligence

▲ to prevent the company trading while it is unable to pay its debts

▲ if the company is being wound up — to report to the liquidator on the affairs of the company

▲ if the company is being wound up — to help the liquidator (by, for example, giving the liquidator any records of the company that the director has).

Company directors who fail to perform their duties may be guilty of a criminal offence with a penalty of a fine of up to $200 000 or jail for up to five years or both. They may also be personally liable to the company and to others for any loss or damage that the directors' actions or omissions cause. They can also be prohibited from serving as a director of their current or any other company. A director's obligations may continue even after the company has been dissolved.

There is extensive law dealing with the relationship between the directors and the public, as potential investors, customers and creditors of a company. In current Australian law, company directors who allow a company to continue to trade when it is unable to pay its debts as they fall due may be sued personally to make up any losses suffered by creditors. Uninformed ignorance is no longer an excuse in Australia: directors who could, by reasonable inquiry, have discovered that their company was insolvent can still be liable for its debts even if they made no such inquiries and remained blissfully unaware of the firm's problems.

A company, as a legal person, can commit crimes and be punished for them if tried and found guilty. If a penalty is applied, a company can be fined, but not put in gaol; if it is a crime for which the penalty may include gaol, the directors may, under certain circumstances, be prosecuted. Companies and their directors can usually avoid punishment by showing that the crime was committed by a junior employee acting against the policies of the company and the instructions the employee was given, unless the crime was one for which 'strict' or 'absolute' liability applies, in which case the company can be found guilty. The offences constituting false and misleading conduct (s. 53 of the Trade Practices Act

(Cwlth)) are examples of strict liability crimes, and the illegal conduct of directors, servants or agents within the scope of their actual or apparent authority is deemed to be the conduct of the company. If a sales person, on the way to visit a customer, commits a traffic offence, that will normally be the sales person's problem; but if, after arriving, the sales person makes false and misleading statements in the process of gaining or even of attempting to gain a sale, the company may be prosecuted and/or sued.

In most public companies, and practically all private (proprietary) ones, some of the directors are full-time salaried staff, generally described as executives, or 'executive directors'. The ACCC (the Australian Competition and Consumer Commission, formerly the Trade Practices Commission) has made a practice of prosecuting executives as well as companies when pursuing apparent breaches of the law, arguing, on several occasions successfully, that the executives were committing crimes when they tolerated, even if they did not actually order, illegal behaviour.

Australian company law allows, in some circumstances, for people who give advice to boards of directors, either as consultants or as senior executives, to be treated as if they were directors in matters of insolvency or malfeasance.

Other employees

Most company employees are neither directors nor senior executives, and will generally be assumed to be following their company's policy in their actions. Except where statute law has intervened, companies inherit the common law rights of 'masters' and employees owe the duties of servants. These duties include the diligent discharge of any assigned duties and the careful protection of their employer's property and commercial interests. Employees cannot use the instructions that they are given or the policies within which they are required to operate as a defence against criminal charges, but they are generally indemnified by the company for the civil consequences of actions they take in the pursuit of the instructions that they have been given and in accordance with the firm's policies as explained to them.

In small firms generally, and in most entrepreneurial ones irrespective of size, the relationship between ordinary employees and senior executives does not follow the master and servant model. Employees have wide responsibilities and a corresponding amount of discretion. Under the *kanban* system innovated by Toyota and now used by most of the world's car makers in Australia and elsewhere, ordinary production employees are responsible for ordering parts worth millions of dollars annually.

Efficient and entrepreneurial companies want their employees to operate under the most general instructions and do not expect them to be perpetually referring to a policy manual. As long as both sides act in good faith, empowered employees using their devolved authority are unlikely to get themselves or the company into serious trouble, but entrepreneurs (and progressive managers) need to be clear in defining how far the empowerment extends. If junior employees are in an environment where a mistake could lead to an offence being committed, they should be given appropriate training. Most managers are well aware of this where safety issues are concerned; training in matters of contract and trade practices law may also be very important.

Investors

Australian law attempts to protect investors in two ways: they are protected from invitations to subscribe capital to a firm where the invitations contain misleading information or exaggerated forecasts of the prospective returns; and when trading in shares in publicly traded companies, investors are protected, to some extent, from losing money by buying or selling shares where the other party has access to information that the investor does not have.

Prospectuses

Companies that raise capital from investors are legally obliged to prepare a 'prospectus', a document that contains 'all' the material information an intelligent investor would need to make an informed judgement. This will generally include financial information going back for several years as well as directors' forecasts (if such forecasts can reasonably be made) for the future of the firm and their statement of the purpose for which the capital is being raised. In principle (and in the United States, in common practice) the directors and advisers to a company can be sued by aggrieved investors if the firm fails to perform as forecast in the prospectus; in the United States (but not yet elsewhere) the writs may fly if the share price of a new company falls below the issue price, even if no defect can be demonstrated in the prospectus.

In Australia and many other countries the law is deliberately vague about the contents of a prospectus, but the fear of the civil and criminal consequences of publishing a misleading prospectus leads firms to draw up elaborate documents and to have them certified by senior partners in leading accounting and law firms. The cost of such a prospectus can run into hundreds of thousands or even millions of dollars.

In Australia, no prospectus is required in certain circumstances. These include:

▲ where the minimum amount to be raised from any one investor exceeds $500 000 (that is, only 'professional' investors are involved); *or*

▲ when only certain classes of investor (such as stockbroking or venture capital firms) are the only ones approached; *or*

▲ where a maximum of twenty persons are *approached* in a twelve month period for equity subscriptions.

Since the average person has 110 friends, relatives, and close acquaintances, it could be very easy for an Australian entrepreneur to breach the second clause without any law-breaking intent, just by talking about a proposal socially.[3]

Continuous disclosure

The stock exchange rules of many countries, including Australia, require that all circumstances that may affect the share price of a firm should be notified to the stock exchange as soon as the directors of the firm learn about them. This rule is intended to make insider trading impossible by ensuring that the general public is as well-informed as any director, adviser or employee of the company, as well as preventing a false market developing in the shares. Since 1994 a similar rule has been incorporated into Australian company law: the Australian Securities Commission must be notified on a continuous basis so as to keep the public informed of the information needed to make an up to date assessment of the prospects of the company and the rights that attach to its securities.[4] Companies in which members of the public *invest* are covered by the law; this is not necessarily the same thing as a stock exchange listing.

This rule leads to a more or less continuous flood of information reaching the stock exchange and the financial information services, much of it along the lines of 'Trickel and Drydup Oil NL reported that their Mordor 3 well had reached 1000 metres without any hydrocarbons detected'. Innovations only seem to count when they go wrong: no reports such as 'Joanna Ximenes of dispatch at Grunge and Grunt Ltd has made a suggestion which, if Fred Antifem doesn't stuff it up, will increase profits by $250 000 per year'; but if Screw, Wring and Squeeze, Attorneys at Law of Texas, USA, file a writ alleging that their clients didn't like the new menu on their flight to Australia and accordingly they are suing Qantas for $100 million, the press will be full of it.

Australia is only catching up on the United States in the matter of disclosure: North American firms routinely disclose far more operating information than Australian firms do, and willingly answer analysts' questions about their product and marketing initiatives in considerable detail. Major United States corporations regularly report their progress with major new products, but generally only once they are nearly ready for launching or actually on the market. The general failure to report early-stage innovations, in the United States as well as Australia, may be based on the assumption that the share markets are so myopic that a change in the state of an innovation that would not, in any case, have affected the current year's profits would have had no effect on the share price if disclosed.

Employment

A growing enterprise will need to expand the number of people doing the work, and while some of this extra effort may be provided by new partners or by contractors, some of it, and in general, most of it, will be supplied by employees. Employees may be described as 'staff' employed at an annual salary, or 'workers' or some equivalent term, and paid an hourly wage rate, but they are, as far as the law in concerned, employees, and the relationship between employer and employee is governed by a number of laws and regulations. From time to time a few firms try to evade their responsibilities to their employees by describing them as subcontractors, but the courts generally assume that anyone who performs tasks as directed by a single person is an employee, whatever the position is called.

Taxation and statutory payments

Employers are directly liable for some taxes, such as Payroll Tax and Fringe Benefits Tax, and are also required to collect personal income tax from their employees under the PAYE scheme and from their subcontractors under the Prescribed Payments System. The Commonwealth taxes are collected by the Australian Taxation Office, a statutory body with very wide powers to investigate suspected breaches of the law, to enter premises and to seize documents. State taxes are collected by the various state Taxation Offices.

PAYE collections have brought many firms to grief: the money, once it is recorded as part of an employee's gross pay, ceases to be available to the employer and must be forwarded promptly to the Taxation Office. Employers who apply any of their PAYE collections to any purposes of their firm, and consequently fail to forward them to the Tax Office on time, are not simply being slow at paying a bill: they are defaulting on their statutory obligations and may be subject to criminal prosecution.

Employers are required to contribute a certain amount of money to each employee's superannuation account in an appropriate fund. They are also obliged to keep their employees insured against workplace accidents; in Australia, each state operates its own workers' compensation scheme.

Conditions of employment

Employees may come under a relevant state or Commonwealth award, in which minimum standards of employment are set out, covering matters such as hours of work, overtime and shift rates, annual, long service and special leave as well as the actual rates of pay for employees carrying out the duties described in the award or a related enterprise flexibility agreement.

Other people may be employed under personal or collective employment contracts, in general imposed by the employer on a 'take it or leave' basis; such contracts are also subject, in Australia, to statutory minimum conditions. Employment law is complex, and large firms generally employ specialists to draw up and maintain employment contracts or to conduct award negotiations. Small firms should either engage an appropriately qualified consultant to draw up contracts or should rely on the award.

Dismissal

Employment may, in general, be terminated because the duties of the position have been superseded by a reorganisation or the introduction of new technology; this is termed 'redundancy'. Employment may also be terminated because the employer's trading performance has declined and the employee can no longer be profitably employed. This is termed 'retrenchment'. Employees who are retrenched or made redundant are usually entitled to a payment based upon their period of service, but they are not, under normal conditions, entitled to dispute their termination.

Under other circumstances dismissal may be deemed 'unfair', and the employee may be entitled to compensation and/or reinstatement, or a dismissal may even be illegal, in which case the employee may be entitled to compensation and possible reinstatement, and the employer may be fined as well. It is, for example, illegal to dismiss an employee because they have become pregnant or because they are summoned for jury service.

There is a grey area, involving dismissal for incompetence, misbehaviour or dishonesty. If any of these are proved, dismissal without compensation is legal, but there is a significant difference between allegations and proof. Someone who is not told what their duties are, or what the required standard of performance is, cannot be dismissed out of hand for failing to perform them or to achieve an acceptable standard. Even someone who has been so informed should be given an opportunity to improve their performance.

Proven acts of misbehaviour or dishonesty may be grounds for lawful dismissal, but the ground may shift if the behaviour had previously been tolerated or even encouraged. If the storemen have been in the habit of running drag races with the fork lift trucks during the lunch break while the boss acts as timekeeper, the boss may have no grounds for dismissing an employee who damaged one of the fork lifts while mucking around. Similarly, if the boss or the foremen are in the habit of swearing at employees, it might be considered unfair to dismiss an employee for swearing back.

Employers who take their cue from North American movies, and fire someone without giving an explanation, may be risking considerable trouble.

Health and safety

Until quite recently, certain occupations were regarded as naturally hazardous and dangerous to health, and if a worker suffered death, injury or illness this was considered that worker's bad luck, but the risk 'came with the territory'. Employers could only be sued or prosecuted if their deliberate acts had caused an accident. Lion-taming, for example, was considered hazardous, and a lion-tamer who got mauled by a deaf lion would have to write it down to experience; only if the employer had provoked the accident by, for example, stuffing cotton wool into the lion's ears or poking it with a sharp stick before its entry could the lion-tamer sue.

More prosaically, workers were often routinely exposed to noisy or hazardous machinery or dangerous chemicals, and if they became deaf or contracted cancer or liver disease, this was unfortunate, but no blame attached to the employer. If an unguarded guillotine removed a few fingers the worker received a settlement from the workers' compensation insurer as set out in the Table of Maims from the relevant Act.

The law still recognises the possibility of accidents and the concept that certain activities are naturally hazardous, but there is now a strong obligation placed upon employers to make the workplace safe, both in respect of accidents and the employees' long term health. Hazardous chemicals must be contained in enclosed vessels, and employees whose tasks require them to be exposed must be equipped with respirators and protective clothing. Guillotines and presses must be intrinsically safe and rotating machinery must be enclosed.

Employers are obliged to provide a healthy, safe workplace. This requires them to take all the steps necessary to eliminate all the hazards of which they are, or could reasonably become, aware. There are some very limited exceptions for tasks which cannot be completed without a degree of hazard, such as fire fighting (or lion-taming), but even in these cases the employer is obliged to take all practical steps, in terms of both training and the provision of protective equipment, to limit the hazard while permitting the task to be completed.

Equal opportunity and sexual harassment

Employers are obliged, when recruiting, assigning duties, providing training, offering promotion, selecting staff for retrenchment or redundancy, and, in general terms, in all the ways in which they conduct their business, to refrain from discriminating between employees on the grounds of their race or national origin, sex, age, union membership, or political or religious beliefs. This list is not exhaustive and may be extended in the future.

Employees who are discriminated against may seek redress.

Sexual harassment can be active — from occasional touching or lewd suggestions to the explicit or implicit offer of promotion or job security in return for sexual favours — or it can be passive — where the working atmosphere is one in which a 'reasonable woman' would feel threatened or uncomfortable. Employers are obliged to actively prevent one group of their employees acting in threatening, harassing or intimidating ways towards other employees.

Products

Firms, whether incorporated or not, that offer goods and services to the public must meet certain minimum standards of conduct. The following list is not exhaustive:

▲ suppliers owe a qualified *duty of care* to those who may use their products or be affected by the use of their products

▲ suppliers offer certain *statutory warranties* when they sell goods and
services

▲ suppliers must not engage in *deceitful conduct.*

The Trade Practices Act (Cwlth) was amended in 1994 to add Part VA,
which is intended to provide for the compensation of people who suffer loss
caused by defective goods without having to prove that the supplier was
negligent.

The duty of care

The concept of a 'duty of care' is an ancient one, but was originally limited to
a supplier's obligation to direct customers and could be qualified by the supplier's understanding of the purchaser's competence. This worked well enough
when most commercial dealings were direct, but tends to leave aggrieved users
without a remedy in a modern economy with its multi-stage manufacturing
and distribution processes. When, in the 1920s, an English lady was distressed
to find a snail in a bottle of soft drink the English High Court extended the
duty of care past the retailer and distributor to the bottler, who was found to
have injured the plaintiff by negligence and was obliged to pay an amount of
damages.

Statute law and case law have progressively extended the duty of care to the
point that a supplier, filling an order from a manufacturer exactly as specified,
might still be found negligent if the component was unsuitable for its intended
purpose and harm to persons occurred as a result. The courts may look beyond
such issues as whether the product was being used as directed, or even used
legally, and ask whether the supplier could have reasonably anticipated harm
coming to third parties. If a motor car accident was caused by brake failure,
itself caused by the fracture of an under-engineered component, and bystanders
were hurt, the bystanders might have a case against the brake manufacturer even
if the car had been speeding and under the control of an unlicensed driver before
the accident.

United States case law has gone further than that of most other countries in
extending the duty of care to remoter and remoter parties, and firms planning to
export goods to the United States, or offer services to United States citizens,
should endeavour to ensure that their product will not cause unexpected harm
in any circumstances in which it may reasonably be expected to be used. A manufacturer of hammers would probably not be liable to the estate of someone
murdered with one of their products, but might well be liable to someone
blinded by a chip flying from the head, even if the placard under which the
hammer had been sold had phrases like 'Use eye protection' and 'Not for use
with hardened nails' in bold print.

United States law does not, in general, recognise territorial boundaries
where United States citizens or businesses are involved. Since it is generally
impossible to ensure that a manufactured product is never sold in the United

States, or that a service is never provided to a United States citizen, prudent entrepreneurs will operate as if the United States standard of care applies universally.

Statutory liability

Under the 1992 amendments to the Trade Practices Act (Cwlth) goods are regarded as defective if their safety is not such as persons generally are entitled to expect. The Act instructs the courts that all relevant circumstances are to be considered, including: the manner and purpose for which they had been marketed; their packaging; the use of any marks in relation to them; any instructions for, or warnings with respect of their use or misuse; what might reasonably be expected to be done with them; and the time when they were supplied by the manufacturer.

The law protects suppliers who improve the safety of their products from the inference that previous versions of them were unsafe, and provides a 'state of the art' defence if the manufacturer can prove that the defect could not have been discovered, given the state of scientific and technical knowledge at the time of manufacture. Manufacturers who can prove that the goods complied with a mandatory standard, or that they only became defective because they were incorporated into finished goods, or that they became defective after shipping, are also protected.

Statutory conditions and warranties

Consumer-type products manufactured and sold:

- ▲ must be fit for a specified purpose
- ▲ must correspond with the description given to them
- ▲ must be of merchantable quality
- ▲ must conform to sample
- ▲ must be able to be repaired for a reasonable time period
- ▲ must comply with an express warranty given.

Australian consumers also enjoy non-voidable statutory obligations with respect to services:

- ▲ the service must be delivered with due care and skill
- ▲ any goods supplied with the service must be fit for their purpose
- ▲ where the purpose is made known, the services and any goods supplied with the service must be fit for that purpose.

Under Australian law, when the goods are sold or services provided to a final consumer a contract which purports to negate these conditions will be void.

Fitness for purpose

Whenever a purchaser expressly or implicitly makes known the use to which a proposed good is to be put, the supplier may be legally obliged to make good any loss incurred by the purchaser if the goods were not, when supplied, capable of satisfactory use in the manner expected. Under Australian law a supplier can defend a claim, including claims from final consumers, under this heading by proving that the purchaser did not rely, and could not have been reasonably expected to rely, on the supplier's recommendations.

Correspondence to description

It is an offence for a supplier to supply goods that do not conform to a description used in advertising, or marked on the goods or their packaging, when the goods are supplied to final consumers. Industrial buyers are legally entitled to refuse to accept or pay for shipments of goods that do not conform to their advertised or marked description, and to sue for the recovery of any damages caused by such goods, but the supplier will not be prosecuted under the consumer protection sections of the Trade Practices Act for making such a shipment.

Merchantable quality

Merchantable quality is a delightfully vague legal term that generally protects purchasers from unpleasant surprises caused by hidden defects or faulty workmanship. It does not imply perfection (unless the normal standard for that class of product is zero-defect). Goods explicitly sold for repair, or as damaged, or for scrap will not generally be required to meet the merchantable quality standard.

Conformance to sample

If a purchaser is provided with a sample of some goods, and refers to that sample in placing an order, then the main order must be filled with goods of the same specification, standard and performance.

Repairable

Under Australian law, consumers have an unavoidable right to reasonable repair services, but commercial purchasers do not. Prudent commercial purchasers will ensure that any purchase contract includes a statement of a minimum maintenance period.

Express warranty

Australian consumers enjoy an unavoidable right to the performance of any claims made by a supplier or the supplier's representative that induce them to make a purchase. Commercial purchasers will usually be offered a contract limiting the warranties to a limited number of documents and excluding other representations or material. Under normal circumstances, the courts would be expected to uphold such a contract.

Promotional practice

In Australia the Trade Practices Act (Cwlth) and the various state fair trading Acts, forbid 'misleading and deceptive conduct'. Since this is a somewhat vague and general term, some classes of misleading or deceptive conduct are singled out and specifically outlawed. The courts have refined the definitions by their decisions in a number of cases, and an entrepreneur who sets out to skirt the edge of the law may be able to do so if he or she can secure the help of an equally unethical lawyer.

Endorsements

It is an offence, in Australia, to claim an endorsement or approval that a product does not, in fact, have, or to say that some person or firm is a user if they are not. It is an offence to make a false claim about a product, whether or not any one is actually deceived and whether or not any person or company suffers harm by believing the claim. It is also an offence to assert, falsely, that the use of a particular product or class of products is mandatory or essential when it in fact is not. An exception is made for commercial hyperbole, or 'puffery', covering claims that are so outrageous that no reasonable person would take them seriously.

In general terms, a company may compare its products to those of its competitors, but it is prohibited from making false statements about its competitors' products on matters of objective fact such as the normal trading price or measurable aspects of performance. Firms have got into trouble by quoting their competitor's list prices in markets where the normal trading practice involved substantial discounts, for example. Equally, firms should avoid claiming or implying that their product is the same as that of one of their competitors. Such assertions do not have to be explicit to be caught by the law; a firm that uses packaging that is deceptively similar to that of one of its competitors may be committing an offence and may also be the target of legal action by the affected competitor.

Spurious claims

Australian firms may not advertise a product at an especially attractive price and then claim to have 'sold out' the special offer with a view to switch-selling consumers onto a higher-priced product. Neither may they use terms like 'limited quantity' when supplies of a product are, for practical purposes, not limited. The word 'new' must be used with care, and firms have been successfully prosecuted for using the word 'new' to describe reconditioned goods sold with an as-new warranty; other firms have been prosecuted for selling unused goods as 'new' when they were not from current production.

Games and contests

Promotions offering prizes in return for coupons may be treated like illegal lotteries in some states in Australia and jurisdictions elsewhere. The law on illegal lotteries is complex and changes from place to place. Putting a card into a package and promising that 'those who return a completed card will be entered into a draw for a prize' may constitute a crime in some places, or require a special permit in others. Many entrepreneurs and small business operators flout these laws almost routinely, and as long as no one complains, they will continue to do so. The gaming police generally have bigger fish to fry. Breaking the law gives, however, a hostage to fortune, and the prudent entrepreneur will consult a lawyer before starting a promotional game.

Trading stamps

It was once a common practice to attach or print a coupon to the packaging of some commonly purchased good, and promise buyers a gift if they collected a sufficient number of them. In the United Kingdom, New South Wales and elsewhere certain companies ran merchant schemes, where buyers would receive stamps in proportion to their purchases which could then be redeemed from a catalogue. These practices are now subject to regulation or even bans in some jurisdictions, and the prudent entrepreneur will avoid them or consult a lawyer before doing something similar.

Gifts and free samples

Gifts as such, like a free brush with each large can of paint, or a glass with a bottle of drink, are unlikely to run foul of the law. Things may be more tricky when the buyer does not know the value or nature of the gift until after the purchase is concluded, as with prizes for finding certain symbols on the inside of the packet; if the prizes are valuable enough the promotion may constitute a lottery requiring an appropriate permit. Free samples are also generally safe, although there may be state regulations limiting such offers in particular cases. If the product could cause damage in the wrong hands, like razor blades that might fall into the hands of young children if left in letterboxes, the firm responsible for the promotion could find itself in considerable trouble.

Summary

Entrepreneurs should be honest about their own products. They should not make any claims about third parties, whether competitors, customers, or standards and testing authorities, unless these claims can be backed up by sound, documentary evidence.

Competition

Australian law, and similar law in the United States, New Zealand and the United Kingdom, contains a strong presumption in favour of competition in the sense used in economics text books. An early judgment of the Trade Practices

Tribunal implied that, should it be demonstrated that a firm had the ability to administer its prices and control the volume of its production, there was an inference that such a firm was indulging in monopolistic behaviour.

Entrepreneurs generally set out to introduce innovations which have some unique advantage such that the entrepreneur's firm can administer production and control the volume of its production. An offence only exists when market power is abused, and while a product is new and its supplier small it is unlikely, within the meaning of the Act, to even have any market power, much less be abusing it.

> For over sixty years Australian farmers have kept the sheep from the wheat with wire fences threaded through steel fence posts with a 'Y' cross-section. The posts have been made by BHP for most of this time in a two stage process, first rolling Y-bar stock, and then cutting and punching it. In 1989, Queensland Wire Industries decided that it would like to make its own fence posts, but didn't want the bother of building a rolling mill or negotiating a contract for the supply of Y-bar stock. They obtained a court order under the Trade Practices Act, upheld in the High Court, forcing BHP to supply them with Y-bar stock, a product never previously traded, at an administered price.

Innovators are not routinely prosecuted, at least on the grounds of their misuse of market power, but there are other clauses that can catch them if they are careless. Large companies may, however, find themselves forced to help their rivals enter competition with them even when there are no legal barriers to entry such as patents, trade marks or registered designs. Being larger or owning expensive equipment can be deemed an unfair barrier to the entry of competitors into a market. A firm is not permitted to use its rights under a legally granted and current patent in contravention of sections 46 or 48 of the Trade Practices Act (Cwlth). (See Table 11.1, pages 344–5.)

The competition code should not be taken lightly: companies can be fined up to $10 million for each offence under the code, and individuals up to $500 000. Note especially that the bans on resale price maintenance and price fixing are absolute; unless and until a firm holds a specific authorisation these practices constitute an offence irrespective of their effect on competition or the harm if any to purchasers. There is no such thing as innocent price fixing in Australia.

Resale price maintenance

Resale price maintenance gets one line in the Competition Code[5] and four explanatory sections (ss. 96—99) later in the Act. The breadth of these sections is such that they are most lawyers' first port of call in a dispute between a supplier and distributor, retailer or dealer. Firms can get into trouble with the resale price maintenance clauses in two ways: their deliberate acts in pursuit of a reasoned business strategy may be found to be illegal; and acts which a firm may have considered to be normal business practice can be found to constitute resale price maintenance. Both are discussed below.

Ambushes

From time to time a firm may wish to discontinue supplying a distributor or dealer or to refuse to supply a prospective distributor or dealer, or to apply particular conditions to business with a particular distributor or dealer. The ostensible reason may be that the distributor or dealer concerned may not have appropriate display or service facilities, or that they have not been paying their bills, or that they are not credit worthy, or that their conduct has been devaluing the supplier's brands and trade marks, or that their service provision has been defective.

Any or all of these reasons could be justified under the circumstances of a particular case, and yet the courts could still find that the main, or a significant, reason for the supplier's action was the maintenance of resale prices. If the courts so determine, the supplier may be fined heavily, may face large damages claims, and may become the subject of orders which make the carrying on of the supplier's business more difficult.

Actions that have the effect of making a distributor or dealer feel that they might suffer any adverse consequences, should they discount below the recommended resale price or advertise prices below the recommended resale price, are an offence: a supplier does not have to be caught using a bludgeon to be found guilty. The only circumstances where a dealer or distributor can be legitimately terminated for discounting is if they 'loss leader' a supplier's products, selling them below the net cost of acquisition in order to increase store traffic. This defence can only be used in extremely restricted circumstances.

Business practice

The most common business reason for an entrepreneur wishing to maintain resale prices is to support a vertical differentiation strategy. Vertical differentiation is often achieved by unique designs and finishes, matters which raise the fixed costs of supply much more than they affect the variable ones. Recovering these costs requires relatively high prices; disproportionately high because of the reduced demand at higher price levels. Resellers will not wish to carry these premium lines except at premium margins, while retailers will need premium facilities in which to sell these high value products. The whole structure can be placed under threat by discounters, who may target standard quality buyers with the premium product at the standard product's price.

Table 11.2 sets out a (hypothetical) manufacturer's dilemma (in this example, a shirt manufacturer's). The manufacturing firm wishes to add a premium line and so must engage a designer, raising its annual fixed expense by $75 000; for the sake of simplicity it is assumed that the unit fixed and variable costs are unchanged. (In practice the variable costs for the premium line would

Table 11.1 *Layman's view of the Competition Code in the Trade Practices Act*

Section	Behaviour described	Safe behaviour
45	Contracts purporting to exclude others or to restrict, or with the effect of restricting, competition are void and the parties may be prosecuted	Secure an authorisation from the ACCC on public benefit grounds; avoid agreements that 'substantially' lessen competition
45A	Contracts, agreements, understandings, broad hints, or any other behaviour leading to the fixing of prices between nominal competitors are void and the parties may be prosecuted	Secure an authorisation from the ACCC on public benefit grounds; otherwise, avoid proscribed behaviour
45B	Covenants (conditions attached to the sale or purchase of goods and services) are void where they may lead to a substantial lessening of competition and the person responsible for creating the covenant may be prosecuted	Some covenants are protected by specific exclusions; avoid covenants that 'substantially' lessen competition; secure an authorisation from the ACCC on public benefit grounds
45C	Covenants are void if they have the effect or intention of fixing or maintaining prices, whatever the state of competition and the person responsible for creating the covenant may be prosecuted	Secure an authorisation from the ACCC on public benefit grounds; otherwise, avoid proscribed behaviour
45D	Boycotts: arrangements, agreements, hints or whatever may have the effect of persuading a third person not to supply or buy from a fourth person are void and the organisers and participants may be prosecuted	Secure an authorisation from the ACCC on public benefit grounds; only participate in consumer or end-user boycotts
46	Misuse of market power: where a person having a substantial degree of market power takes or omits to take an action such that a competitor is damaged or eliminated, or deters or prevents a competitor from entering a market, or affects the behaviour of competitors in some other market; the firm with such market power can be prosecuted or ordered to behave differently or both	Don't be successful; don't compete vigorously; don't grow large; be prepared to argue that the ACCC or private complainant has defined the relevant market too narrowly

Table 11.1 Continued

Section	Behaviour described	Safe behaviour
47 (2), (3), (4), (5), (8) (a) or (b), (9) (a) or (b) or (c)	Exclusive dealing: includes exclusive distribution and supply agreements, exclusive geographic distribution rights, resupply restrictions and the like that substantially reduce competition; the agreement may be void and the parties may be prosecuted	Notify the ACCC and continue the arrangements until and unless the ACCC issues a notice of revocation; avoid substantially reducing competition; use certain prescribed exceptions
47 (6), (7), (8) (c), (9) (d)	Third line forcing: terms express or implied in a contract that require one party to buy from, or sell to, a nominated third party; the relevant terms are void and the parties may be prosecuted	Notify the ACCC and the arrangement will be protected after the prescribed period elapses until and unless the ACCC issues a notice of revocation; use certain prescribed exceptions
48	Resale price maintenance: any acts, omissions or hints that threaten, persuade or encourage resellers to adhere to a fixed price list and/or discount schedule are illegal and the person or firm responsible may be prosecuted	Only recommend prices; avoid all acts, omissions, hints &c. that are primarily concerned with resale prices; show that the reseller had engaged in 'loss-leading' without the supplier's explicit or implicit consent; secure an authorisation from the ACCC on public interest grounds
[49 repealed in the 1995 amendments]	Price discrimination: charging different customers different prices for similar goods, thereby substantially lessening competition [In the USA a similar law has been used against a packaged goods manufacturer who supplied branded and private-label lines at different prices]	No longer an offence in Australia (but see Section 46), but a very live issue in the USA (the Robinson-Patman Act); companies with branches in the USA or exporting to multiple outlets should take care to comply
50	Mergers and acquisitions that substantially lessen competition: these are illegal unless authorised	Secure an authorisation from the ACCC on public benefit grounds; avoid mergers and acquisitions involving current or potential competitors

Legal options and obligations

Table 11.2 *The business economics of vertical differentiation*

	Standard line		Premium line
Manufacturer			
Design expense		$0	$75 000
Variable manufacturing cost/unit	$18.00		$18.00
Manufacturing overhead allocation/unit	$9.00		$9.00
Wholesale price	$30.00		$42.00
Manufacturing revenue		$3 000 000	$1 050 000
Manufacturing profit		$300 000	$300 000
Units		100 000	25 000
Retailer			
Recommended retail price	$39.00		$78.00
Retail revenue		$3 900 000	$1 950 000
Contribution		$900 000	$900 000

be a little higher, but with the increased throughput the fixed costs per unit would drop a little. The assumptions behind Table 11.2 are a reasonable approximation.) The design expense must be recovered from a higher wholesale price, and in order for retailers to justify a new, lower volume line the retail price must go even higher. We have assumed here that if the retail price of the premium line is double that of the standard the unit sales of the premium line will be a quarter; this again is a reasonable guess but not the only possible outcome.

The manufacturer is happy: by increasing fixed costs 33 per cent she is able to raise her annual profits 100 per cent. The retailer is happy: the new line is 'earning its keep', returning the standard margin per unit of floor space. The customers for the premium line are happy, as they prove by buying it at double the price of the standard one. The community is happy, with increased employment and higher dividends.

The fly in the ointment is a barrow trader who the manufacturer uses to dispose of seconds and returns. The trader, armed with a copy of the Trade Practices Act (price $14.95 from the Government Bookshop) demands a supply of premium shirts at $42 each from the manufacturer. He then wheels his barrow to the front door of the retail shop and starts offering the premium shirts for $60, an $18 saving off the recommended retail price. The retailer can no longer afford to stock the premium shirts, since at any price below $78 she should allocate the display space to another line. Premium shirt buyers won't pay $78 inside the shop for a shirt when the same thing is on display on a barrow for $60 outside, and most of them won't buy from the barrow either.

Premium shirt sales don't have to drop very far before the line stops looking like such a good idea, and if premium lines can't get stocked in the right outlets they won't sell anywhere else. If the manufacturer can't maintain the retail price, she can't afford to start the new line and can't employ a designer or additional machinists. The retailers import their premium lines directly or through a retailer's buying cooperative, insisting on an exclusivity agreement with the overseas manufacturer, and the barrow trader looks for an easier target.

Authorisations (s. 88)

Since 1995 the ACCC has had the power to authorise resale price maintenance on the grounds of public benefit, including the authorisation of restrictive covenants that have the probable effect of maintaining resale prices. A supplier might seek to appoint distributors or dealers in particular territories, and require a covenant that they will not trade outside their franchise area nor supply any other person or firm that does so. An appropriately authorised contract or covenant between a supplier and one reseller can be extended to other resellers as long as a list of such extensions is maintained and provided to the ACCC on request.

Authorisations are 'loaded guns' in economic terms, and the ACCC does not hand them out freely. An authorisation does not merely protect the holder against prosecution by the ACCC and the very high penalties that can be imposed upon conviction; it also blocks private suits for damages. Substantial documentation must be provided in support of a claim, much of which will be placed upon a public register; the ACCC may require private and public hearings, and a substantial fee must be paid with each application. The ACCC may call for further documentation while examining a claim, and the time taken to provide such documents is added to the time the ACCC is allowed to spend deliberating.

Except in the case of mergers and acquisitions, the Trade Practices Act (Cwlth) does not define public interest, and the ACCC's view of the public interest is not always the same as that of an applicant for an authorisation. A determined student could visit the Commission and review the public register to gain the flavour of the type of authorisations that are granted; someone actually running a business should consult a specialist lawyer, both to advise whether an application has a reasonable chance of succeeding, and to prepare the application if the firm decides to make one. In very general terms, applications should show that they will allow investments to take place that will increase the efficiency and/or the rate of progress of the Australian economy. The welfare of individual firms or of their employees does not rate very highly against such criteria.

The public interest

The ACCC has issued the following list of public benefits that have been successfully used to justify authorisations for exemption from sections of the Competition Code:

▲ promotion of competition in an industry
▲ economic development through encouragement of exploration, research and investment

- ▲ fostering business efficiency, especially where this results in improved international competitiveness
- ▲ industry rationalisation resulting in more efficient allocation of resources and in lower or contained unit costs
- ▲ expansion of employment or prevention of unemployment in efficient industries
- ▲ industrial harmony
- ▲ assistance to small business, such as guidance on costing and pricing or marketing initiatives which promote competitiveness
- ▲ improvements in the quality and safety of goods and services and expansion of consumer choice
- ▲ supply of better information to consumers and business to permit informed choices in their dealings
- ▲ promotion of equitable dealings in the market
- ▲ promotion of industry cost savings resulting in contained or lower prices at all levels of the supply chain
- ▲ development of import replacements
- ▲ growth in export markets
- ▲ steps to protect the environment.

Authorisations are not pardons, and subsequent authorisation does not legalise conduct that took place before the authorisation was granted.

Notifications (s. 93)

Firms wishing to engage in exclusive dealing, and not having previously been refused an authorisation for such dealing, can protect themselves from being prosecuted or sued under section 47 simply by giving notice in the prescribed form to the ACCC. For most forms of franchise and dealership agreements immunity starts with the lodgement of the notice, and continues indefinitely unless the ACCC gives notice that it objects. Where 'third line forcing' is involved, the relevant agreement is not immune until the ACCC has had a prescribed period to consider it.

'Third line forcing' means coming to an agreement requiring that a third party is nominated as a supplier or purchaser of specified goods and services. If, in the example above, the manufacturer appointed a particular shop as its exclusive distributor for some suburb, and added a condition that the shop should also buy trousers from a particular (unrelated) firm, the trousers would be the 'third line' and the more elaborate procedures would apply. There is no 'lessening of competition' test when third line forcing is involved; unless such an agreement is authorised or protected by notification it is a crime. If the agreement was limited strictly to the supply and reselling of the manufacturer's shirts, the barrow boy could be refused supply, or supplied on condition that he stayed away from the retailer, immediately the notice was lodged with the ACCC. Even if there was no notice lodged, the manufacturer would have an arguable defence if there were other suppliers willing and able to supply the barrow boy with standard grade shirts; if the courts accepted that there was a single shirt market, in which many suppliers competed, refusing to supply one line to one potential reseller would not constitute conduct with the effect of 'substantially lessening competition'.

Notifications, like authorisations, need to be professionally prepared, but they involve a lower fee and less preparation, and unless the ACCC decides to query a notification, no need to attend and be represented at public hearings. The ACCC's practice is to review notifications in an informal atmosphere, and to provide pre-notification guidance with a view to dispensing with the notification, and the fee, if the proposed conduct is exempt under section 47 subsection (10). The critical issue, where third line forcing is not involved, is the definition of the relevant market and the likely effect of the proposed practice on competition.

In Australia, for example, the ACCC tended, in 1995, to the view[6] that there was no 'McDonald's' market. As long as the ACCC holds this view, McDonald's could include clauses in their standard franchise agreement prohibiting the sale of non-McDonald's products in franchised stores, and refuse to supply McDonald's goods to people without franchises, without fear of prosecution under section 47. In a different market, the ACCC's predecessor, the Trade Practices Commission (TPC), successfully forced Massey-Ferguson to drop an exclusivity clause from its dealer agreements. The TPC argued that, in many country towns and regions, the market was too small to support more than one agricultural machinery dealer, and if these dealers were linked to a single manufacturer by an exclusive dealing agreement, buyers' choice, and therefore competition in these markets, would be substantially reduced.

The North American equivalents to the ACCC, the Federal Trade Commission (FTC) and the Anti-Trust Section of the Attorney-General's department, take a more closely focused definition of 'market'. They have argued, for example, that there is a 'Coca Cola' market and an 'IBM' market. Readers will come across books and articles written for a primarily North American audience in which these subjects are discussed, but they should not automatically assume that United States practice will be followed in Australia.

Notifications only apply to section 47: all the other potential offences under the Act are still lurking; in particular, an aggrieved distributor or dealer still has section 48, resale price maintenance, as a weapon to wield if a supplier discontinues or refuses to renew an agreement. This suggests that a dealership or distribution agreement needs to be very carefully drawn up to make it quite clear that the reseller is perfectly free to set prices below the recommended resale price (not necessarily above it), and the conditions for continuing in the arrangement are based upon the provision of specific facilities, the discharge of agreed duties and the like.

Returning to the shirt manufacturer and retailer: a distribution agreement could probably be terminated or not renewed without giving grounds for prosecution or civil suit if the retailer, in defiance of specific terms in the agreement:

- ▲ did not display the new line in the manner agreed upon
- ▲ did not advertise the new line with the prominence agreed upon
- ▲ did not deal with customer returns in the manner agreed upon
- ▲ did not maintain the outlet to an appropriate standard
- ▲ ceased trading at the location mentioned in the agreement
- ▲ supplied a barrow boy with stock to sell outside some other franchisee's shop.

It is still a good idea to speak to a lawyer before ceasing to supply someone: careless words can cost more dollars than any lawyer.

The courts and the ACCC are likely to give a supplier or franchiser considerable latitude in the matter of agreed standards. It is said of the late Ray Kroc, founding entrepreneur of McDonald's, that if he visited a franchise and saw a single fly in the kitchen or a single member of staff smoking in uniform, he would tear up the franchise agreement on the spot. Australian courts might (or then again, they might not) consider this behaviour extreme, but they would certainly sympathise with a franchiser concerned to maintain health, safety and service standards. If, on the other hand, the basis of a dispute was the reseller's pricing practices, a supplier or franchiser would be on extremely dangerous legal ground if they attempted to terminate an agreement because of it.

> *If you are planning anything that causes a competition concern, come and see the Commission. We frequently give people guidance (we cannot give legal advice) and we suggest that this is done before an application for authorisation is actually lodged ... (From a letter to the authors from the General Manager of the ACCC)*

Exports

By and large, the resale price maintenance sections of the Trade Practices Act do not apply to export contracts, but agreements involving the maintenance of resale prices in export contracts must be notified to the ACCC.

General precautions

▲ Don't start up a business without consulting a lawyer.

▲ Don't approach anybody but a close family member, a bank or a professional investor to put money into a proprietary company before consulting your lawyer.

▲ Don't take risks with the health or safety of your customers, users, employees, or anyone else who might come into contact with your business or your product.

▲ Don't mislead or deceive anyone, and don't let your employees or agents do it either.

▲ Never discuss prices with your competitors and don't let your employees or agents do it either.

▲ Never discuss marketing territories with your competitors and don't let your employees or agents do it either.

▲ Consult your lawyer before concluding any franchising, distribution or dealership agreement.

▲ Consult your lawyer and the ACCC before concluding agreements involving exclusive dealing, and submit a notification unless you and your lawyer are confident that your proposed agreements cannot lead to a substantial lessening of competition.

▲ If you are planning a major project involving a joint venture or any form of non-compete or price-setting agreement, consult your lawyer and the ACCC and if necessary get an authorisation before spending any significant amounts of money.

End notes

1 See http://www.wp.com/CORPGOV/cgbibliography.html for an on line bibliography on the subject of corporate governance. See also Kay and Silberston (1995) for an alternative view of the subject.

2 From the 'Small business guide', part of the Corporate Law Simplification Bill 1994.

3 At the time of writing these conditions were under review, but whatever the result of the review, the law is certain to take a close interest in all offers to sell shares in a company.

4 Corporate Law Reform Act 1994 (Cwlth).

5 Part IV of the Principal Act; Schedule 1 to the Competition Policy Reform Act 1995.

6 Based upon informal discussions with the authors: if a formal complaint were to be made the ACCC would have to come to a formal view which might differ from this.

Legal options and obligations

12

Designing the new venture organisation

People

This chapter focuses on the way in which the new venture is organised and structured. We will emphasise the relationship between structure and strategy — from the smallest venture to the largest enterprise — and we will emphasise the need for the venture to be highly adaptable and flexible, ready to ride out the shocks and seize the opportunities that it will encounter.

The creation of a new venture starts with a concept, which passes through successive stages of screening and elaboration on the way to becoming the central focus of an active enterprise. This book has followed the process from Chapter 5. We have reached the point where we are concerned with the human structures the new enterprise needs so as to realise its core concept. This chapter is about the relationships between the functions and the processes of the business, the strategies and structures required to run these processes and the people who will implement and manage both the structure and the processes of the organisation.

The founding entrepreneur of an enterprise will determine the initial design and structure of the organisation. The entrepreneur's approach to this task will be heavily conditioned by his or her previous experience in work, family, educational and social settings. Experience gives us all various skills and attitudes, but it is important not to let history become a constraint on the new organisation. Successful entrepreneurs are capable of examining problems from many perspectives, and shaping solutions that can work in their current, and often novel, circumstances. The most successful entrepreneurs grow with their organisation, changing as the needs of the venture change.

Changes in attitude do not come easily, and major paradigm shifts are required before some people can think and act entrepreneurially. Because each new venture is different the best structure for every new venture will also be

This chapter was prepared by Helen Evans, Lecturer in the School of Management at Swinburne University of Technology, and edited into its final form by the principal authors

new. The wheels will still, however, be round, and it is this sort of fundamental organisational design principle and the equivalent human factors that we address in this chapter.

Organisations are made of people, and the people in organisations are the link between the concept and the result. Without people the concept remains just a sterile idea and the process stays nothing but an empty form. The 'received wisdom' about management has a long history, stretching back to Julius Caesar's legions and the Imperial Civil Service in China. Caesar, like Alexander three centuries earlier, welded armies tens of thousand strong into integrated fighting units. Alexander was the warrior king of a militaristic nation, but Caesar invented the professional army. The Chinese Civil Service gave that country the longest period of continuous civilisation in human history.

Caesar's example, like the Imperial Procedure Scrolls, belong to history, not to current management practice. Today's best entrepreneurial management practice is less reliant on rigid structures and pre-ordained procedures and takes a more human-oriented approach. Today's managers recognise the essential contribution of individuals to the development of a business. They allow their organisation and the individuals in it to adapt and respond to the actual situations that they encounter. Entrepreneurial organisation design is about creating an adaptable structure, built of people with the competence and confidence to respond to developing situations in innovative ways.[1]

An entrepreneurial organisation must be adaptable, flexible and responsive to changes in the external and internal environment, the markets in which it buys and sells, and the capabilities of, and relationships between, the people in it. These issues often seem to lack urgency while the entrepreneur or the entrepreneurial team are elaborating their concept and even in the first few months of an operating business, but the more successful a venture is, the more urgent the organisational issues become, and the greater the risk that mishandling them presents to the continued success of the venture.

The shrinking spear point of the evolving organisation

Julius Caesar's strategic unit was the legion of 4000 men, and his tactical unit the cohort of 500 men. At the start of the First World War the strategic unit had become a division of 20 000 men, while the tactical unit, the battalion, was the same size as Caesar's cohort.

John Monash broke the organisation down further for his offensives in 1918, using the battalion as a strategic unit and the company, nominally of 100 men but actually of sixty or so, as the tactical unit. The Australians went into the Second World War with Monash's organisation, but the tactical unit rapidly shrunk to the platoon and then, in the jungle, the section.

In mechanised and aerial warfare the tactical unit shrinks further, to the one or two person crew of a modern warplane. Independent thought was the last thing expected of Caesar's legionaries, but is close to the top of the list when the modern RAAF chooses pilots for its aircraft.

As a successful new venture grows and matures it will move away from being a 'happy band of brothers' (and sisters), and become a more formal organisation where people have specific functional responsibilities and a defined place within a structure. The nature of the management styles, the type of skill and qualification required and the number of employees needed will change. No single design will carry a venture from birth to maturity.

Human capital

In Chapter 7 we introduced the concept of 'human capital', the human element of the new venture. We wrote, 'buildings, plant and equipment are placed at the lowest level of the asset hierarchy because they are transient incidents in the life of the entrepreneurial firm'. Firms only exist because they add value to the assets that they control: the difference between a schedule of buildings, plant and equipment and a successful, operating business is people.

Many companies claim that 'our people are our best asset' and it is often emblazoned on their mission statement, but when you talk to the employees you find that very few of them believe that their employer actually follows this through in practice. The most successful entrepreneurs recognise that it is the skills and talents of other individuals that enable them to make their new venture a success. Entrepreneurs who recognise, acknowledge and reward their employees appropriately will probably avoid the cliché but treat their staff as their firm's best asset anyway. These are the entrepreneurs who will be successful in the longer term. First rate people hire first rate associates and share in the general success. Second rate people hire third rate associates so that they themselves can shine against this pallid background.

Trust and ethics

Competence and togetherness are not enough to make an organisation effective and successful. Most entrepreneurs find matters of trust and ethics difficult to manage both in the initial stages of the venture and as the venture grows. Even with the best organisational design, the best employees, and the best systems and processes in place, if these two elements are not addressed adequately, the venture will fail.

We started this book with a chapter on ethics and morality, and the theme of cooperation and self-restraint leading to mutual trust and mutual benefit runs right through it. Trust and ethics must be addressed at every level of the venture and at every stage in its development, or the business will fail to earn a reputation for ethical behaviour and trustworthy conduct, and failure to earn such a reputation leads rapidly to absolute failure. A business is only as good as its people, its customers and its suppliers make it, and the trust and ethics embedded in the business will affect all of these people. The leading entrepreneurs' personal codes of ethics become the yardstick from which all employees take their cue, and their behaviour sets the example from which their employees will model their own behaviour. All the employees of any venture are ambassadors for that venture, and as they model their behaviour on the entrepreneur, their, and the venture's, success will be a measure of the individual entrepreneur's ethical and professional behaviour, or lack of it.

The entrepreneur needs to be consistent and ethical in all actions and at all levels. These factors in turn become a measure of a person's effectiveness as a leader, and value as a mentor during the transition and succession phases of the venture in due course.

Functional demands on the new enterprise

Each different functional aspect of a new venture must be designed in a way that enhances the day to day operations of the venture. A venture's goals, size, industry and ambition all affect the functional design of an organisation. There are, however, generic functional demands that all ventures encounter, and they are all 'equally important except when they are not'. The trick is knowing when they are not. There are strong interdependencies between functional areas, and there is a need for all of them to communicate on both a regular and an exception basis. Good communication channels link the strengths of each area, creating synergies in and between functional areas. As this is achieved the organisation moves forward and grows as an effective, fluid and entrepreneurial 'whole', rather than as a fractured, departmentalised and factionalised wandering brawl.

When you talk to a manager in a poorly structured organisation you are likely to hear something like: 'If the other managers ran their part of the business as well as I run this one the whole place would be far more successful.' It doesn't matter which manager you talk to: they all say the same thing. Making the whole organisation successful often involves compromises in each of its parts, because no single functional area can operate in isolation from the rest. There must be systematic, two-way communication mechanisms that bind the various

Table 12.1 *The mathematics of communications in groups*

The number of relationships and therefore possible conversations and alliances grows rapidly as a group or team gets larger.

People	Sub-groups
2	1
3	3
4	7
5	15
6	31
7	63
8	127
9	255

functions into a cohesive organisation. The traditional approach goes back to Julius Caesar, with the managers of the interacting units having regular, formal meetings. Such meetings are an anachronism in the modern, team-oriented workplace, where all staff are involved in the decision making processes, but the fundamental need for coordination remains.

A firm can't simply abolish the managers' meeting and bring everyone together: firms are divided into functional areas largely because of the communications problems created by large groups. Many successful firms use regular meetings involving all the staff of each functional area at which recent corporate and divisional decisions and current problems are discussed. The task of attending inter-unit meetings can be shared around, rather than making it a managerial prerogative. The structure, and the operating and reporting procedures in each functional area must be designed so as to complement and enhance the other functional areas within the organisation.

Whether an organisation is based on teams or on command-and-control, the people within a single functional unit will always tend to relate more strongly to the other people in the unit and to the unit itself than to the other people and units making up the organisation. The entrepreneur must have a vision and the ability to communicate it, both in meetings with key staff and when addressing or communicating with wider groups. It is this shared vision that builds cooperation across unit boundaries, that fosters a spirit of constructive emulation rather than destructive competition. People are very quick to recognise hypocrisy and self-aggrandisement: if their experience of the organisation and its practices contradicts the golden words of the entrepreneur's vision, experience wins.

Technical and procedural means can facilitate communication, but they don't determine its content. Technical systems, particularly computer systems, can, if badly conceived and implemented, become a constraint on organisational development; they optimise the present at the expense of the future. Good system design must proceed in parallel with good organisation design: the organisation will have to adapt to unknown and unknowable future circumstances, and the systems must be able to adapt with it. The entrepreneur must guard against tacit assumptions becoming constraints.

We will, in this chapter, discuss some of the functional areas needed by most new ventures. Any given venture may need more functional areas than we examine in this chapter, and equally, some of the functional areas described here won't be needed in the initial stages of some ventures. The order in which we describe functional areas should not be taken as our indication of their relative importance.

Growth is the essence of an entrepreneurial venture, and measures to facilitate growth and development must be present in the organisation design from the beginning. One of the threats to a growing venture arises because different functional units will be 'most critical' at different times. In the middle of a real crisis it is all too easy to confuse the urgent tactical need to bolster the performance of a critical unit with the strategic needs of the organisation as a whole. If the ongoing business plan, and the organisation development plan that should form a key part of it, are neglected, the business's structure will become a fossilised record of past crises and it will progressively lose the ability to respond to new challenges.

An effective structure must, as a minimum, be able to ensure that the following tasks are carried out effectively:

▲ the production of any goods created by the venture

▲ the delivery of the services expected by the customers of the venture

▲ the effective marketing of the venture

▲ the administration of the venture

▲ the acquisition, creation and operation of the information systems needed by the venture and

▲ the ongoing development of the people in the venture.

The production function

Whether the key value-creating activities of a business involve service delivery or manufacturing goods, the production, or value-creating, function must lie at the heart of the organisation design. It is crucial to set out the steps and mechanism of value creation, and recognise that they might not all be in the factory or service centre. Design, product development, and marketing may add far more value to the business than manufacturing or service operations do. Nevertheless, before anything can be sold it must be produced and the production function will often provide the most obvious influence on an organisation's structure.

An entrepreneur who wants to focus on the 'big picture' may be tempted to neglect manufacturing and service delivery and treat them as the least entrepreneurial activities of all. They are linear, sequential and detailed, attributes that may lead to them being treated as boring and uncreative. These are areas that will quickly bring a company down if they are badly set up or managed. There are several main steps in the organisation of production and service delivery. They are discussed below.

Sequence the operations

How will the raw materials or components of sub-assemblies be put together to form a manufactured product? What operations are involved in preparing to deliver a service and then in actually delivering it? How can the company conserve capital, avoiding excess stock holding and idle service facilities, without incurring disproportionate risks in the process? Are just-in-time production techniques appropriate? Do customers demand just-in-time deliveries, and if so, how can the venture be organised to satisfy these demands? Can tools such as Gantt or PERT[2] charts be used to expedite the process design or to manage the actual service delivery?

At the end of the day, does the production plan make sense, or has it been captured by its technology? The organising committee for the 1984 Olympic games commissioned a very sophisticated PERT system, but its 'earliest finish date' was months after the closing ceremony. The PERT system was discarded and simpler manual techniques were used to create a construction plan that met the required deadlines.

Build in quality procedures

Quality cannot be added to goods after they are manufactured or to services after they are delivered. Post-production QA (quality assurance) is an expensive and uncertain way of keeping defective goods off the market, and is irrelevant to service industries anyway: a surgeon who cuts off the wrong leg can't wind the clock back and start again, any more than a chef who poisons a patron or a pilot who crashes an aeroplane can. When a disaster occurs, there is always a person whose mistake triggered the disaster, and once that person is identified and punished many people are satisfied. A more careful analysis almost invariably reveals that the person who 'caused' the tragedy is as much a victim of a bad process and organisation design as any of the others: the system made a tragedy inevitable, and the nominal villain was just in the wrong place at the wrong time.

The time spent in designing quality into an organisation and its processes, and even the apparent additional costs involved in establishing intrinsic quality, are bound to be repaid many times over, not just in reduced rework and scrap costs, but in product reputations enhanced and disasters avoided.

Just too late

The Nissan Pulsar had a very patchy production record in Australia, and too many cars were shipped with defects, or broke down early in their life. This earned the car a poor reputation.

The Nissan Motor Manufacturing Company undertook a radical overhaul of the quality system, removing the quality inspectors and forming production workers into teams responsible for their own quality checks.

The Pulsar went on to win the Car of the Year award, but Nissan's Australian sales did not rise to a level that justified continued local manufacturing. The Australian manufacturing operations were closed in 1991.

Designing for quality means deciding what measures and indicators can be used to measure quality.[3] Having decided what to measure, and what the units are, targets must be set. 'Zero defect' is an excellent target, as long as everyone is clear as to exactly what a defect is. A hospital might decide to allow zero wrong organs to be removed or wrong limbs to be cut off, but it would be silly to set a target of zero deaths; people go to hospital because they are ill, and it is statistically certain that some will not recover. Japanese car factories have been producing zero per cent of cars incomplete off the production line for over twenty years, but even Japanese cars break down or wear out eventually.

Benchmarking is one way to set appropriate targets, and this has become increasingly important as more firms become involved in international trade. Benchmarking means discovering who the world leader at performing some common business task is, and their performance becomes the benchmark against which all the others are measured.

Many firms now seek ISO 9000 series accreditation,[4] making them eligible for government contracts in Australia and elsewhere, and ensuring that their products will be accepted internationally. TQM (total quality management) is a philosophy and set of techniques that can assist in obtaining, and deserving, ISO accreditation. Few firms can achieve 'quality' in isolation; most need to involve their suppliers and their customers, both in defining appropriate quality standards and in devising processes that ensure that they will be achieved.[5]

The need for quality sometimes has a decisive effect on the overall strategy of a new venture. Often contract manufacture will seem to be cheaper, and it will always require less precious capital than setting up an in-house facility; but no contractor will be as concerned for quality and the firm's reputation as much as the firm itself, and this may become a reason to develop a firm's own manufacturing facility.

Most McDonald's outlets are franchises, but McDonald's has a policy of keeping a number of company-owned stores operating in which it can test new products and experiment with modified procedures without jeopardising its franchisees. The company-owned stores also strengthen McDonald's position in any argument with franchisees about service standards or operating procedures: no franchisee is asked to do anything that McDonald's have not done themselves.

Process 'design for quality' is almost entirely about keeping mistakes out of the product in the first place, not about correcting them afterwards. Traditional factories used to employ grimy workers and white-coated 'quality police' who would measure a worker's output and reject batches which failed the tests. If the machinery had drifted out of specification the worker would stand aside until a skilled fitter was available to adjust it. The modern factory trusts the worker to maintain quality by checking his or her own output, and if a machine needs adjusting, by doing that, too. The old style worker was trained as Caesar's legionaries had been: 'Do this, then that, then this, then the other thing, then start again.' Workers were expected to leave their brains in the locker with their street clothes.[6] The modern worker needs skills training but also education in key quality concepts, including elementary statistics. The training itself is expensive, and when it is complete each worker represents a considerable investment.

The cost of staff turnover

The NRMA, the NSW motorists' organisation, used to experience a staff turnover of about 35 per cent per year, typical of similarly sized organisations in Australia. In the late 1980s they measured the costs of this turnover, and were shocked. Recruiting and training a middle level manager cost them $55 000, an IT employee cost $44 000, and even a typical member of the counter staff cost $38 000.

The NRMA surveyed its current and departing staff, and discovered that redesigning its training, personnel, and promotion policies would enable it to keep many of the staff who would otherwise have left.

In 1996, when the redesign was complete, they measured the savings and discovered that they were $2 million, or $400 per employee per year, better off in training costs alone.

Roberts (1996)

Continuous improvement

The defining fact about innovation is the break with the past: a clear change has been brought about and society is clearly different, with different products available, or different industrial structures, or even changes in the way society itself is organised. For every major change there are very many minor ones, product changes that don't send a firm's competitors' reeling from the market, process changes that don't revolutionise the economics of production, but changes which, cumulatively, can have these effects. Managing this steady flow of improvement is often known by the Japanese term *kaizen*.

Kaizen involves many small changes to products and processes. Neither the need for, nor the possibility of, these changes will be apparent to anyone except people intimately involved with the product and its production. Firms achieve *kaizen* by ensuring that shop floor workers, service deliverers, point of sale staff, and all the other people at the sharp end of the business are encouraged to look for improvements, and taken seriously when they propose them. Product improvements will be more common when the products themselves are new while process innovation becomes relatively more important as the product and its markets mature.

The introduction of *kaizen* may have been made simpler in Japan because of the social pressures to avoid overt conflict and the long tradition of being polite. Most Japanese managers are able to listen to a totally ridiculous proposal with a straight face and thank the person who made it with every appearance of sincerity. Many Japanese managers have achieved a degree of detachment from particular instances of their firm's product concept that helps them suppress any 'fight' reactions when the product is criticised or a defect in it is pointed out. Junior employees in Japanese firms are freed, by these traditions, from the fear of personal humiliation if they make a suggestion, and while many of their suggestions will not be implemented, many will. Japanese manufacturing companies implement roughly one suggestion per employee per year.

> For some reason the [NEC Corporation's Kumamoto semiconductor] plant turned out a good many more defective chips than any other NEC facility. The factory manager and employees met daily to try to fix the problem. They took corrective action and tried novel solutions without success: they could not reduce the rejection rate below a certain point. Everyone was puzzled why only Kumamoto could not meet company-wide norms.
>
> One day the heroine of this story was walking to work and stopped at the railroad crossing in front of the factory while a very long freight train passed. She felt the ground vibrating as the heavy cars rumbled by and suddenly it occurred to her that this shaking might be the culprit. Later, on the job, she felt no vibration. Nevertheless, thinking that perhaps the precision machinery might be affected, she told the foreman. Shortly after the [factory was protected by a vibration barrier] and the defect rate dropped sharply. The woman was only eighteen years old, but she took pride in her job and in NEC …
>
> Ishihara (1991), p. 40

Australians, or at least male Australians, have been brought up in a tradition where robust or even exaggerated personal comments are tolerated, and victims are expected to grin and bear it, or to respond in kind. This does not create an atmosphere where junior employees feel free to make suggestions for improving the products that they deal with or the processes that they operate. Australian firms can only expect to implement continuous improvement if they are prepared to invest substantially in training supervisors and middle managers in the arts of listening and of moderating group discussions.

Many attempts at workplace improvement in Australia have been obstructed or derailed entirely by lower-level managers and foremen using their God-given right to control their subordinates by a cocktail of bluster, sarcasm, threat and profanity.

Plan ahead

Every innovation will eventually cease to be a source of new value to either its supplier or its customers. It may be superseded or made unnecessary by a later innovation, or it may saturate its market or be swamped by imitators or both. Well before an innovation finally loses its market momentum, it will cease to generate the high margins that were possible when it was new and unique.

Designing the new venture organisation

361

A good organisation design will be capable of continuous adaptation in three dimensions: the processes that lead to the delivery of the current product line must be continually refined, shaving costs in order to maintain net margins; at the same time the current product line must be continually reviewed and updated, to preserve its unique value as long as possible; and, still at the same time, new products, new innovations must be under development ready for launching as soon as, or even before, the original products start losing market momentum.

When the new products and innovations are ready for market, the old organisation must be able to produce and deliver them, or the huge costs of demolishing one structure before building a new one may lead to progressive paralysis and ultimate corporate extinction.

Involve suppliers and customers[7]

One way to design production strategies for a new venture and find ways of improving them in an established one is spend time with suppliers and customers. They will often have clear views as to how the process should best be managed so as to satisfy their particular needs and wants. What do they want changed or improved? Is it possible to reorganise the production process easily to incorporate such changes, or would it require a restructuring of the whole business?

Such consultations will enable the entrepreneur to make decisions that minimise scrap and rework, while retaining the production flexibility that customers demand. Whenever manufacturing will play a significant role in a new venture a good manufacturing manager should be an early key appointment to the entrepreneurial team. This person needs to keep up to date with changes in technology and changes in management techniques. The manufacturing manager should be someone with a combination of practical experience in manufacturing management and the capacity to learn new concepts and implement new ideas.

Get the technology right

Modern businesses have technology options that were the stuff of science fiction a few years ago. Manufacturers can use technology tools such as computer aided design (CAD) and computer integrated manufacturing (CIM). In many parts of the production process robots can be used to supplement or replace people. There is an impressive range of software tools to help managers plan, schedule and control the manufacturing process. Goods in and finished work handling have been revolutionised by automated warehouses, just-in-time ordering, and electronic document interchange (EDI). The range of technological solutions to the problems facing service businesses is, if anything, larger.

The most successful firms steer a middle course between an obstinate refusal to leave tried-and-true methods behind and a wide-eyed adoption of every nostrum peddled by a hi-tech sales person or futurologist. Behind all the hype, a person is more flexible and adaptable than any piece of machinery; the smarter the machines and computer systems, the less flexible the production processes are likely to become. General Motors Corporation spent a fabulous amount of money on factory automation during the 1980s, but in 1995 their Fremont plant in California produced the most cars per employee, shipped the fewest defects per vehicle, and was the least automated of all GM's United States plants.

Service delivery

Some firms manufacture products, many do not, but every successful firm sells services. Even the most dedicated manufacturing firm will have less than half of its employees wielding tools or operating machines. Finished goods are of no value unless they do something for their users; it is the service, not the object, that creates value.

Entrepreneurs planning service delivery must balance three factors: people; technology; and organisation. Customers, suppliers, technology and the business structure are all closely related. If one changes, the rest must change as well. The answers to three questions guide the design of a service organisation:

▲ Who are the customers and what will we do for them?

▲ What technology is available to help me in this industry and how does it affect the way I structure my venture?

▲ Who are the people who will create and deliver my service products, what are their skill levels and what are their aspirations?

A firm can be thought of as a socio-technological system.[8] Its organisational designers should attempt to implement the best practical blend of human and technical resources.[9]

Services can be divided into three broad categories:

▲ *incidental,* such as are provided by the attendant and cashier when we buy petrol

▲ *convenience,* when the service provider does something that we could, if necessary, do without or do for ourselves

▲ *critical,* when the service makes a substantial difference to our enjoyment of life by doing something that we could not do for ourselves.

The same division can be applied to commercial services: an equipment manufacturer who supplies installation advice is offering an incidental service; a firm offering cleaning or security services are primarily selling convenience;

Designing the new venture organisation

while legal, auditing, financial, opinion research, and specialist technical services may mean the difference between a firm's success of failure, and so are fairly described as critical.

The key success factors for each class of service are different. Incidental services are best delivered unobtrusively and economically; they are an essential part of the offered product, normally only remarked on if they are missing. Success for a convenience service depends on the 'moment of truth' as the user decides whether the experience is one that they want to repeat and recommend.[10] Critical service providers live and die by their reputation for competence, diligence, and success.

The design of incidental services is relatively straightforward, and the design objective is to eliminate any service defects that might reflect badly on the underlying product. Critical services are not good subjects for design by outsiders: good cardiac surgeons make and keep their reputation in the operating theatre, not at the bedside or in the consulting room. Convenience services are most critically affected by organisation and process design, and successful convenience service providers research and refine the customer experience to the point of obsession.

Firms offering convenience services are permanently confronted by two threats: that of becoming boring, and consequently being deserted by their customers, and being imitated, and seeing the market growth captured by someone else, or even seeing the market diluted to the point that their fixed investments are 'stranded', neither saleable nor earning an acceptable return. Australians hungry for a hamburger from a national, branded chain can chose between Hungry Jack's and McDonald's. McDonald's in North America faces half a dozen competitors, fighting over an essentially static market. Australian domestic air travellers choose between two airlines on most routes; North Americans choose from up to eight. Over twenty United States air carriers vanished by merger or bankruptcy between deregulation in 1978 and 1995, including famous names like Pan American; when markets become over-serviced casualties are inevitable, and the differences between success and failure can be small.

Many service industries operate seven days a week, twenty-four hours a day, and merely ensuring that the right number of competent staff are present at all times is a challenge. The business will experience both cyclical and random peaks and troughs; if there are too few staff on board at a peak, service quality will suffer and disgruntled customers don't return; but if there are too many staff in a trough the business suffers a cash haemorrhage. This is one of those complex problems with a lot of simple solutions — all wrong. Casual and part time staff are often part of the final answer, but keeping them motivated and properly trained is anything but easy. Casual staff in particular can only provide high quality service when the service routines themselves have been standardised and mistake-proofed.

We provide a discussion of some of the particular organisation attributes of four classes of service business below. This is not really intended to tell people who are about to enter one of these industries how to plan their service delivery process and organisation, but to help entrepreneurs who are considering totally new classes of service business by showing them some of the lessons learned by those who have gone before them.[11]

Example: Prepared food

The *raison d'etre* of a prepared food business is convenience. Few people will die for the want of a single meal, and in modern urban Australia there are plenty of alternative ways of satisfying hunger. The prepared food industry is not hard to enter, but it is a hard one in which to prosper and grow. Success comes from following a threefold rule:

▲ define a product and market, clearly identifying who you are going to serve, what they are going to receive, and how they are going to receive it

▲ define a consistent promotional message, one that will arouse the interest of people in your defined market segment

▲ design and implement an organisation which will consistently meet or exceed the expectations aroused by your promotion.

The world provides plenty of examples of successful food preparation businesses, from corner pizza makers to restaurants with three stars in the *Guide Michelin*, but to be successful a new business must differ from all of them. The difference may be merely spatial, as when a successful concept from one country is introduced to another, but it will often affect the product and the target market as well.

In some businesses consistency is crucial: the McDonald's 'Big Mac' is so standardised across the world that it serves as a quick measure of the purchasing power of different currencies. By contrast, the chef in a top Paris restaurant would be upset to be told that one meal was exactly like a previous one, and infuriated if told that a meal, no matter how appreciated, was exactly like the meals served in some rival's restaurant. This does not mean that Paris chefs do not swap, or steal, ideas; but it does mean that they add their own touches to anything that they do. A meal in a top restaurant is intended to be a unique experience, one that will be remembered even by frequent patrons.

Every member of the staff of a McDonald's outlet is easily and quickly replaced, in large part because the training is so comprehensive and the operating procedures so standardised. By contrast, every person except the dishwasher in a gourmet restaurant's kitchen has a unique set of tasks, learned over a long period of apprenticeship and experience. You can't inflict the McDonald's procedure manual on the staff of a gourmet kitchen, and you can't expect gourmet food from a McDonald's restaurant.

Example: Health and beauty, sport and recreation

Very few people think themselves too healthy or too fit or too beautiful, and a very large number of people are prepared to pay, and pay well, to have their health, fitness and beauty enhanced. In an era of ageing populations and smaller family sizes, many people have time on their hands, and are prepared to pay to have it filled with activity.

The key success factors for businesses servicing these demands are similar to those that govern the prepared food industries: define the market and define a product to suit it; define the experience users will enjoy and promote it; and design an organisation that will consistently meet or exceed the expectations aroused by that promotion. Successful members of this industry will be firms with a tight market focus and a precisely controlled delivery system to match it.

The entrepreneur must not only define the market and product, but also the daily, weekly and seasonal pattern of demand. The product decisions don't merely define the user's experience, but the queuing and booking time delays. On-demand services can generally command a price premium, but they imply idle resources. Some of the variation in demand can be covered by casual and part time employees, in which case ensuring the quality and consistency of the service may be a problem. Some can be covered by multi-skilling, giving the service providers useful 'background', and interruptible, duties to fill the time between clients. Tennis coaches who can restring racquets, or golf instructors who can repair greens, are still available to drop-in clients.

The organisation design will end up as a series of compromises and balances: increased training and recruiting costs for casual and part time employees must be traded off against increased idle time for permanent ones. The key to success is not letting the product or the user experience be compromised. People are prepared to pay a little over the odds for perfect service, but they are unwilling to pay at all for poorly handled or rudely delivered services.

Example: Ancillary health care services

Many diseases that were once fatal can be cured, and with many more the symptoms can be alleviated and the end deferred for an extended period. At the same time people of procreative age are having fewer children, meaning that the average person in the population is steadily growing older, and the fraction of the population who need some form of care through reason of age or infirmity is steadily rising.

The broad market is predefined, but individual service providers will need to focus closely on the segment that they intend to address. In most cases they will need to segment vertically as well as horizontally. At the bottom will be people who are wholly dependent on government support, and the successful businesses will be those that can win price-based tenders for care provision, and then deliver the service for which they are contracted without either bankrupting themselves or breaching their minimum contracted standards. There will be intermediate quality services, offered to people who can afford to supplement the basic government provision; and there will be services to those with sufficient personal means to choose their own provider.

At every level providers must achieve 'quality care' and meet 'quality standards', which implies a documented quality system that ensures both consistency and reliability of the services provided. Adequate training of staff, and appropriate backup and emergency arrangements will also be needed.

Businesses servicing the upper market segments will be perpetually struggling to control their costs while clearly differentiating their product from the standard, government-mandated providers. One of the key factors may be achieving a low staff turnover and establishing regular rosters so that the clients see the same staff regularly; personal attention is likely to be more valued by the clients and their relatives than dazzling technology, and in particular, the substitution of technology for personal contact may be bitterly resented.

Example: Business services

The growth in business services is partly driven by fashion: through the first half of the 1990s, the stock market automatically rewarded managers who 'downsized' by bidding the share price of their companies up. There is a more valid underlying reason: the natural tendency to disaggregation in maturing industries that we discussed in Chapter 4. Large, specialist firms have clear advantages over divisions of more general ones, including various economies of scale in management and purchasing, and the greater efficiency that broader and deeper experience can deliver.

Lindsay Fox gained some early momentum on the way to creating a major transport and warehousing business because, as a truck driver himself, he was able to communicate with other drivers much more easily than the typical young manager. Truck drivers tend to be anarchic in their attitudes and direct in their expression, and some of Linfox's early customers would have paid extra just to have Fox's reassuring bulk between them and their drivers. The fact that Linfox could do the job more reliably at less cost turned out to be a bonus for his early users, and built a reputation that gained his business many more.[12]

There does not seem to be any function of large scale business that has not been considered as a candidate for contracting out, and so there is a wide range of opportunities for entrepreneurs prepared to build organisations that will take over particular functions. Outsourcing has not created a boom for small and medium businesses, as has often been predicted, because many of the specialist business service providers rapidly grow out of the small and medium enterprise classification to become seriously large ones themselves.

Fewer entrepreneurs seem to have built large businesses out of supplying small and medium enterprises (SMEs), even though SMEs represent 40 per cent of the private sector of the economy. This may be because most SMEs are too strapped for cash to make them a good business target. It may also be because most SMEs use outside accountants, lawyers, and software developers; many of them are customers of firms that, like Linfox, have grown on the outsourcing of

Designing the new venture organisation

large firms, but since most small firms never had a transport department, when they use Linfox or another large carrier it isn't called outsourcing.

The key attributes of a successful growth business built on business services include:

▲ a clear ability to use economies of scale and experience to offer lower costs than their prospective customers' in-house services

▲ a service quality that is significantly better than that provided by the in-house service

▲ a service focus that treats all the internal clients of the former in-house service as valued customers, or they may outsource away from the outsourcer.

Marketing organisation[13]

The marketing department

An innovation consists of a concept and a way of persuading people to buy it: marketing is half the battle. While preparing to launch a new venture or a new product key members of the entrepreneurial team will plan and execute the selected marketing strategy, but as the venture succeeds and the market begins to accelerate the development of strategy must be supplemented by a great deal of painstaking planning, liaison and analysis. Marketing is not a part time activity.

A specific marketing function staffed by at least one person without other responsibilities is desirable from a time three to six months before the product is actually launched; it is essential as soon as the marketing moves beyond the product trial stage and the product life cycle enters its growth phase. Exactly how many people are needed cannot be determined without a careful consideration of the number of product lines, the distribution strategy adopted and the gross margin. Immediately after a new product is launched the marketing budget and the gross margin are roughly equal; as the market matures the marketing budget might slip to as little at 20 per cent of the gross margin, but it may stay as high as 50 per cent.

The marketing budget may not all be spent inside a defined marketing department; much of it will be spent on advertising and other forms of promotion, while a substantial fraction of it may be spent in a separate sales organisation. Good marketing people tend to be somewhat introspective, careful about details, and have a tendency to worry about the longer term consequences of their actions. Good sales staff share none of these characteristics, and putting a sales department under a marketing one will produce either incessant conflict or an ineffective sales unit.

Marketing is often treated as a staff function, reporting to the chief executive, while sales is treated as a line function with its own reporting lines. The resulting conflicts will put the chief executive under considerable pressure, and many weak chief executives have avoided this conflict by putting the marketing unit under the sales director. Such an organisation is incapable of developing or following a strategy, as the people with the strongest strategic focus in it are devoted to short term sales promotion activity.

Product development

The decline of a product's viability starts with its launch, and a series of enhancements are needed to keep it alive until the market matures, and more to turn it into a long term cash generator. Death, however long postponed, is inevitable, and so a business that intends to be around indefinitely will start developing supplementary and replacement product lines almost from the moment the venture starts operating.

Product development, as an activity, is closely aligned with marketing, and the two departments must be encouraged to work together extremely closely. In general, subordinating one to the other doesn't work, because at times of stress one side or the other will be tempted to substitute authority for argument. Product developers and marketers will argue with each other, but close ranks against outsiders. The net effect is that senior managers are likely to be presented with a choice of one new product strategy or none if they call for a review; the cross-functional teams that develop such strategies are, however, usually so committed to them that they will make them work in spite of great obstacles.

Distribution

Establishing and maintaining good distribution channels is critical to the success of any venture. For major capital equipment items the whole of the distribution of a product may be handled by a shipping and installation department, but more commonly a physical product will be delivered to its final purchasers by retailers or dealers who may, themselves, be supplied by wholesalers or agents. Service products may be delivered by employees, but often by contractors, licensees or franchisees.

Once distribution meant a man in a grey dustcoat wrapping a product in brown paper or nailing it into a crate and giving it to a carter to take to the railway station or post office. These days are long gone. Successful enterprises establish close, ongoing relationships with their distributors. Time, patience, and consistency are needed to establish a relationship where trust is the key element. The firm must trust its distributors, and they must trust the firm.

Trust, while noble, should not be blind. Firms working through retailers must maintain a team of merchandisers who will visit the retail outlets, advise on stocking and display, and organise instore promotions. Licensors and franchisers need service representatives who will visit their outlets, proffering discreet advice. The merchandisers and service representatives are a vital source of marketing intelligence; in particular, in identifying under-performing outlets, catching early signs of consumer resistance to the products, and reporting on competitors' initiatives.

Sales

Introspective marketers, visionary developers, horny-handed warehousemen, and discreet service representatives all have their assigned tasks, but there is one thing that none of them do, which is to look a prospect in the eye and say, 'May I have your order?'

Good sales staff are different from the average person in the street: while they don't like being knocked back, the anticipated joys of success are such that they will regularly expose their egos to the risk of a failure.

The legendary United States baseball player, Babe Ruth, set a new record for home runs in 1926, becoming, in that year, the tenth-highest scorer in the history of the American game. At the celebratory press conference, a journalist attempted a curve ball:

Mr Ruth, you not only top the league for home runs, you're on top for strikeouts as well. How do you explain this?
It should be obvious. You can't hit home runs without taking a swing at the ball.

An entrepreneur may have to be both marketer and sales person at the time the first product is launched on to the market, but as the venture develops and evolves into a larger organisation, one of the first appointments should be a professional sales manager. As the venture develops further, budget must be found to expand the sales department. Firms should be prepared to spend half or more of the annual gross margin from a 'new name' sale in the selling costs of gaining it, and between 5 and 20 per cent of the annual gross margin on maintaining contact through regular calls by a sales person, merchandisers or service representatives.

While sales is logically part of marketing, we explained above why the emotional gap between marketers and sales staff makes co-locating them very unwise. Top flight sales staff are unhappy if they are not treated as a line function with the head of sales reporting directly to the chief executive. It is generally worth the aggravation to let them have their way.

Administration

Every firm needs an administration of some sort, but what sort and how big it should be are matters of debate.

A business administration has a number of functions:

1   it contains the essential defining elements of the business, including corporate accounting, the company secretariat, and the chief executive and chief financial officer and their staff

2   it is a location for specialists whose services are required frequently by the other departments, but not full time by any of them

3   it represents the business to the outside world of regulatory and fiscal authorities, the press, and the investment community

4   it provides an operating base for the chief executive's enforcers, checking and reporting on the functions nominally carried out by other line and staff departments.

Function *4* is often regarded as the corporate Gestapo. It is distinctly unfashionable to have such a unit in an era of teams and empowerment, in part because such departments have an almost inevitable tendency to move from reporting to interfering, but there must be some form of feedback and some degree of cross checking. There is always a risk of financial fraud, but a good chief financial officer will design checks and provide sufficient supervision to nip most attempts in the bud and catch most of the rest before they threaten the firm's existence. Most of the fraud that occurs on a sufficiently large scale to destroy companies starts with the chief executive and/or the chief financial officer. Brave employees who stumble on an indication of such a fraud may go to the Australian Securities Commission or the Police; those whose head rules their hearts find another job.

The great corporate risk, particularly to the new and rapidly growing firm, is the 'short-cut' taken by an enthusiastic employee. Environment and trade practices offences are often 'strict liability' as we discussed in Chapter 11. If an employee empties toxic waste into the sewer because the disposal contractor didn't turn up and the alternative was to suspend production; or a sales person 'gilds the lily' rather too much to get an important order; or a marketing person launches an ill-conceived promotion, the firm may be prosecuted and sued, and may be faced with heavy fines and large damages.

Training and education helps, both to avoid clashes with the law and as a defence, or at least a plea in mitigation, if an offence is alleged. Some sales people frequently make extravagant claims to get orders. If these people are not reprimanded and retrained, but encouraged by large bonuses, when a claim against the firm goes to court it may be held that the sales person enjoyed the tacit support of the firm in the misbehaviour. If a foreman regularly discharges toxic waste to the sewer, and instead of a reprimand receives praise for cutting disposal costs, the response of the Environment Protection Agency when the source of the illegal dumping is finally traced may be equally toxic.

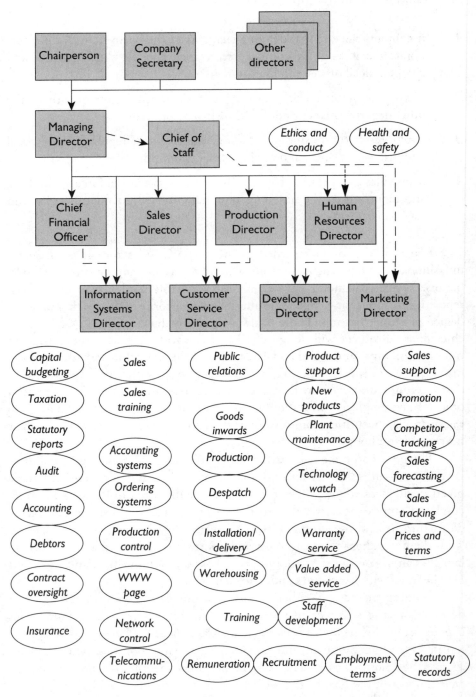

Figure 12.1 The organisation chart: The chart shows functions and their management relationships — some of the relationships may run along alternative paths, some will have to be determined to match a particular venture's circumstances, and there may need to be more or fewer functions than are shown here

Sexual harassment is illegal in Australia and most civilised countries, and firing, ignoring, or simply shifting complainants is a very dangerous practice. Women, or in some circumstances men, who are victimised by their workmates can sue the employer and gain substantial damages, while the bad publicity associated with such cases may affect sales and will certainly deter top-quality women from joining the firm as employees. Both training and a well-promulgated Code of Conduct may be needed to eliminate sexual harassment: many men have no idea of where to find the threshold between good humour and threatening or unpleasantly suggestive behaviour.

Feedback is a standard principle of system design. A Gestapo may be unnecessary, but a firm must do more than simply set out a list of good intentions in its mission statement. At the very least, there must be codes of corporate practice promulgated, and employees must be asked for a positive confirmation that they have understood and applied the code, not just once in a lifetime, but regularly. Employees must be given a fair chance to raise concerns about any internal or external events, actions or instructions which conflict with the code as they understand it, and such concerns should not be trivialised nor automatically treated as malicious.

A corporate conduct office, reporting directly to the chief executive, should be created quite early in the life of any growing organisation. The office may consist of a single person, perhaps not even full time in the early days of the organisation, who will be the secretary to an appropriate steering committee involving both the administrative and line departments; but the office must be identified to all the staff and the officer must have the clear authority of the chief executive to promulgate codes of conduct and to review known or suspected breaches.

The other administrative functions are less difficult to describe.

Finance and accounting

Every business has certain legal obligations, one of the foremost of which is the prohibition against incurring debts that are unlikely to be repaid. This obligation cannot be discharged by firms that do not know the current state of their assets and liabilities. The finance and accounting unit(s) of a firm are responsible for collecting and assessing information about the firm's assets and liabilities, taking steps to correct any deviant tendencies, and preparing statutory reports to the authorities such as the Taxation Office and the Australian Securities Commission.

Some very small and very new enterprises get away with a book keeper and an external accountant, but rapidly growing firms need to pay constant attention to their cash balances and their financing needs, and this generally requires a properly qualified and experienced accountant to be the chief financial officer.

One of a growing firm's major assets is likely to be its debtors' ledger, and its major liabilities are often to its current creditors. Until a firm has grown so seriously large that departments and divisions can afford their own financial officers, the collection of debts and the payment of accounts may well be centralised under the chief financial officer. Since the chief financial officer is responsible for settling accounts, it is a short step to putting him or her in charge of incurring liabilities in the first place. Orders over a certain, trivial size may need to be counter-signed by the chief financial officer. If this is done it is sowing the seeds of a serious conflict between the chief financial officer and the operating units, and so it must be treated as a temporary measure and the procedures for getting clearance must be expeditious.

Where possible, the chief financial officer should allocate operating budgets to the line units and monitor them, but should then stay away from routine purchasing decisions. Capital expenditure decisions are different; while the chief financial officer should not be allowed a veto, he or she should certainly be allowed to comment on all capital expenditure proposals and to determine the financing arrangements.

Legal

A new firm will probably rely on a practising solicitor for legal advice on matters such as contracts and advice on minor disputes, and in some industries this will be sufficient for all but the largest businesses. Other firms may need an in-house lawyer quite early in their development, particularly if they are heavily involved in competitive tendering or the supply of complex industrial equipment or services under individually negotiated contracts.

Firms that undertake a substantial amount of research and development (multiple millions of dollars per year) may wish to engage in-house intellectual property specialists.

Human resource management

Human resource management (HRM) goes into and out of fashion. Townsend's (1971) proposal, in *Up the Organisation*, was 'fire the Personnel Department'. Few people with any experience of working in large companies would disagree with the sentiment.[14] Nevertheless, a growing business will, sooner rather than later, have to establish an HRM function. We recommend that the entrepreneurial team make the following points to prospective human resource managers:

▲ The human resources function exists to provide a service to the rest of the organisation. It may offer advice and make recommendations but it has *no executive authority* over any employee or manager of the firm outside the human resource department.

▲ The management of the firm is concerned that all its employees shall be treated justly and fairly from the time of their first appointment until their eventual separation. This does not mean that they are to be treated equally: or that employees enjoying good luck or showing exceptional talent should be handicapped; or that employees should be compensated for bad luck or a congenital lack of talent.

Justice is vital to successful management, but justice requires that exceptional results should be rewarded, not just exceptional effort. The judges of an individual's contribution and the fairness of the rewards for that contribution must be his or her colleagues and managers, not the human resource department's. Empire-building human resource managers can paralyse an organisation: the best way to stop them is not to appoint them in the first place.

Statutory records and obligations
Firms are legally obliged to keep certain records about their employees, including their dates of appointment and termination, their dates on leave, workplace injuries and the like. Such record keeping can be done in a human resource department, who probably won't neglect it, rather than being left to line managers, who will treat it as a low priority chore.

Firms also have a number of statutory obligations towards their employees and may have further obligations as a result of industrial awards or workplace agreements. The human resource department can be entrusted with the task of monitoring these obligations and warning other managers when action needs to be taken so as to comply with them.

Recruitment
An average Australian firm turns over 35 per cent of its staff each year; world best practice is probably represented by Japan, where the turnover is around 14 per cent, or one in seven. A growing firm will need to replace departing employees as well as to hire new ones, and it is appropriate for the human resource department to manage the advertising and preliminary screening of candidates. Australian human resource departments have a reputation for automatically screening out all applicants over 40 or 45 years old; managers who want an experienced addition to their team should make sure that the human resource department lets at least some experienced people through to an interview.

The human resource department should not be allowed to make the final selection or to sign the letters of offer to successful applicants, other than new human resource staff. Appointments are the responsibility of the appropriate manager, and this responsibility should not be assumed by anyone else, even when the responsible managers want to give the task away.

Remuneration advice
Employees must be paid, and in many cases there will be a legal minimum rate. Above that level, a firm will wish to ensure that remuneration reflects contribution, and that there are no significant disparities between people doing similar jobs at similar levels of effectiveness. Operating managers will generally welcome advice from a human resource professional about the rates paid by

other departments in the firm and by other firms in the industry, and the offer of assistance in determining staff pay levels.

Industrial relations law in Australia entered a period of flux in the 1990s, and further changes are likely. Industry-level awards are being progressively replaced by enterprise or individual agreements, and the 'rate for the job' is becoming a much more flexible concept. At the same time, employers are being given much greater power to coerce employees and to eliminate or neutralise trade unions.

Blue collar workers in Australia are likely to be covered by an industrial award or a workplace (or enterprise) agreement, while other employees may be subject to an award, an agreement, or an individual contract. The definition and negotiation of such agreements is usually (and properly) treated as a line function, but appropriately skilled human resource staff can be effective facilitators in the negotiation process.

The human resource department is the logical place to maintain copies of such agreements and human resource people will generally be able to assist other managers in interpreting them.

Unfair dismissal

Employers do not have an unrestricted right to 'hire and fire' in Australia, and an employee who is terminated improperly may have a right to reinstatement and/or damages. The risk in this area can be controlled if all employees understand the nature of their duties and the measures of success in them, as well as what is required of them in terms of appropriate workplace conduct and behaviour. There must also be proper procedures for handling grievances. The human resource department can provide effective support to the operating managers in developing and operating appropriate policies.

Training

The development of technology and the speed of change in the market place means that much applied knowledge becomes obsolete rapidly. Some firms choose to make employees whose skills are no longer needed redundant and hire new ones, but in general terms this practice is bad management as well as contemptible behaviour: the experience of the older employees is lost to the firm, while the first lesson the new ones learn is that they should not commit themselves to the firm or do any more than their assigned duties.

Progressive firms spend an amount of between 2 and 8 per cent of their total payroll on employee education and training, representing one to four weeks of training per employee per year, to build and maintain a world class workforce. Planning staff training, developing individual training plans, and investigating and negotiating with outside service providers involves a substantial number of demanding tasks, and the job of managing training cannot be taken lightly or delegated to a junior employee, and except in the very largest corporations, it cannot be devolved to department or divisional level.

Some firms maintain training as an independent department, while others place it in human resource management. If it is put into the human resource department, there needs to be a strong committee of operating people overseeing it to make sure that training programs directly relevant to the business share the billing with personal development and other worthy and useful training opportunities. The worst human resource managers are scheming and manipulative, and will seek to curry favour with their bosses by suppressing vital training programs or cutting the time allocated to them, but some of the nicest and the best human resource managers will let their concern for the human aspects of their job obscure the fact that they are part of an operating business.

Information systems[15]

The motor vehicle and the related petroleum industries are the largest industry group in the world, earning most of their money from consumers either directly or from selling new vehicles to be used as part of a salary package. The computer and communications systems are the second largest industry group, and the largest single category of business expenditure. A business being run today without some assistance from computers is (almost) inconceivable; there are many industries where routine operations are simply not possible without the use of computers.[16] Electronic communication systems are, if anything, more deeply embedded in business practice, and with the development of the World Wide Web on the Internet the process will continue.

Information systems have been Janus-like since their inception, looking backward (or inward) at their owning organisations with one head, and outward into the world of entrepreneurial possibilities with the other. The very first user of automatic data processing was the United States Census, speeding up the processing of the returns, and the first commercial users of automatic data processing were the accounts receivable departments of large organisations, notably utilities. The first electronic data processing machine to be put into commercial service was the LEO (an acronym for Lyons Electronic Office: the computer industry's love affair with acronyms and three letter abbreviations goes back to its foundation), built by the Lyon's Tea Company Ltd in England[17] where it processed salesmen's orders and updated customer accounts.

The first large scale entrepreneurial use of computer systems to change markets and build competitive advantages probably took place in the United States airline industry with the development of computerised reservation systems, but there have been many instances of firms using computer and communication systems to create new marketing strategies and to reinforce their alliances with their suppliers and distributors.

An entrepreneur designing a new venture organisation needs to decide whether the information systems the new venture will use are to be solely directed to improving the internal operations of the new business, or whether they form part of the interface that the business will have with its suppliers and customers. In the former case, the information technology function is properly located within the administration of the firm, probably under the control of the chief financial officer. In the latter, information systems should be a separate unit, reporting directly to the chief executive.

Team building

Time spent actively directing staff or workers is doubly wasted, since the manager is telling people something that they ought to have known already, and the staff or workers being directed will have switched their own brains off while they listen.

In the very earliest days of many new enterprises, the firm may have consisted of a single person working on his or her own, but by the time the launch approaches most new ventures involve an entrepreneurial team, a number of people working closely together in pursuit of a common goal, helping each other through problems, cheering each other's successes, and feeling absolutely marvellous in spite of long hours, endless problems, and rapidly vanishing finances.

Many studies have confirmed that teams solve problems faster than the same number of isolated individuals can, make fewer errors, and produce higher quality output. Many new businesses will wish to carry the enthusiasm of the entrepreneurial team through the whole organisation, and so will want to ensure that tasks are entrusted to teams rather than individuals, and teams rather than individuals receive acknowledgment for outstanding performances.

The team spirit can easily be lost by a growing enterprise, or it can turn destructive, as when existing teams may conspire to obstruct a new senior appointment or a significant change of direction. The book *Odyssey: From Pepsi to Apple* (Sculley & Burne 1988) contains an excellent account of the extraordinary spirit that pervaded Apple Corporation in its early years, and of the obstacles Sculley, as a professional manager with a marketing background, faced in trying to turn his nominal authority into action. Helen Nankivell of Nexus Pty Ltd headed off this problem when her firm needed an experienced manufacturing manager by involving the shop floor staff in recruiting one.[18]

The exact time at which a formal process of team formation needs to replace the informal association which founded the new venture is uncertain, but Nankivell found it necessary well before the total employment at Nexus reached fifty. There will also have to be a choice between relying on contracted consultants as facilitators and negotiators in the early stages of team development or taking on a permanent staff member with suitable qualifications and experience.

Several techniques can be used to build a cohesive team. Personality tests can be used to obtain an overall profile of the employees. This can then be used to try to match different employees to appropriate lines of work and to build teams of individual employees with complementary skill sets. Other successful team building exercises include activities like orienteering, in which employees practice cooperation outside the work environment, in a social context that is often less personally threatening than the workplace. People often relax enough to enable an atmosphere of trust and friendship to develop, and this can have significant benefits when employees return to their normal duties.

Some sensitivity is needed in the design of team building activities when female staff are involved, particularly if the females make up a relatively small fraction of the group. Men whose only previous experience with teams has been their college rugby or football club may find that some modification to their own behaviour and expectations is required. Male sporting teams often have bonding rituals involving consuming large quantities of beer and spirits, singing obscene songs, and securing the services of workers in the sex industry for visual and more intimate entertainment. Relatively few modern females take delight in getting paralytically drunk or singing 'The Good Ship Venus'; almost none wish to be mistaken for sex workers. Firms and organisations which do not take these considerations seriously risk prosecution and public contempt; at the very least, misconceived bonding exercises will have a seriously negative effect on the morale and commitment of the female members of staff.

There is no one way to build a cohesive team, it takes time and effort on everyone's part. However, once you have a good team, don't break it up.

Rewards and remuneration

Pay, particularly senior executive pay, is sometimes referred to as 'compensation', with the clear implication that the work is so horrible that a large sum of money is required to overcome the reluctance of reasonable people to undertake it. A better view of normal people says that work is an important part of their self perception, that they want to take part in creative, value-adding activity. On this second view pay is a 'hygiene' factor; something that will upset people if it is inadequate, but will not create enthusiasm and commitment if other critical motivating factors are missing.[19]

One of the critical motivating factors is participation: in contemporary Australia every person working for a wage or salary knows that they could get considerably more as a consultant or subcontractor. Employees enjoy a degree of security in both their employment and the personal relationships that go with it that makes the gap between wages and subcontract rates acceptable; employees are also capable of contributing to the future development of a firm, while contractors are only concerned with their assigned tasks.

In general terms, employment at fair wages is a better bet for firms than contract labour, except where there is a single, defined task to complete. Contractors might build the new factory and even install the equipment, but employees should operate the plant and design and market the products.

Remuneration management is a matter of maintaining hygiene, not providing the primary means of rewarding effort. Primary considerations include:

▲ genuine compensation, as for dirty, disgusting or dangerous work, or work undertaken in remote locations or in unsocial hours

▲ horizontal equity, or 'equal pay for work of equal value'

▲ social equity, or similar pay to that earned by employees of similar age and experience doing similar work with other employers in the region

▲ vertical equity, with the rewards for success being seen to be distributed fairly.

A good employer develops remuneration packages for employees with as much care as it devotes to developing value-creating products for its customers.

Outstanding performance needs to be recognised and rewarded, and simply throwing cash at outstanding employees is an insufficient incentive, in most cases, to encourage them to go back to their jobs and to be outstanding again. At an absolute minimum the chief executive should host a function where exceptional performance is recognised, praise the people whose achievements are being recognised in front of a representative sample of peers and managers, and personally hand over some commemorative item as well as a cheque. People whose performance is outstanding but falls short of the level required to justify a chief executive level function should be recognised and praised in front of their colleagues and receive, at a minimum, a signed letter from the chief executive acknowledging their contribution.

One of the authors was asked to solve a critical problem threatening a very prestigious multi-million dollar contract. He assembled an informal team, and the problem was duly solved with some hours to spare after eight days of extraordinary effort by the team members. The author received a telephone call from a grateful chief executive, who had the unusual decency to ask if anyone else deserved praise. The author named the other members of the team.

Two days later the author was present when one of the team members, a maintenance supervisor with seventeen years of service, received a letter from the chief executive. The veteran burst into tears: this was the first time in his career that he had ever been thanked for his efforts.

Rewards may include travel and participation at conferences; in general, even when a reward conference is held in an exotic location the recipients will be enthusiastic about the material they learned and the opportunities they had to interact with colleagues and to make the acquaintance of people with similar interests and ambitions. The other attractions of the location will be appreciated, but they will not be the only, and may not be the major, component of the reward as appreciated by the recipients.

We are not sure how large a firm needs to be before there is any formal recognition of outstanding contributions, but even if there is only one employee, an effort should be made to ensure that good work is properly acknowledged.

Checkpoint

This chapter has discussed the organisation of a new venture to pursue an opportunity. By this stage in the venture planning process the entrepreneur or venture planner should be able to prepare a staffing plan and lay out an organisation design.

Figure 12.1 shows a skeleton organisation chart: such charts can be associated with bureaucracy and inflexible organisation design, which is not our intention, and even as an excuse to dodge responsibility; 'That's not my department', which is even further from our recommendations. Anyone who knows a better way of ensuring that all necessary operating, planning, and administrative tasks have somebody assigned to do them, and a functioning reporting structure, is welcome to use it. Other enterprise planners need to draw up an organisation chart and fill in names and reporting lines. Use a pencil and keep an eraser handy.

The staffing plan should set out, on a month-by-month basis until the first product has been in the market for a year, and for four years thereafter:

▲ How many front line employees, and at what cost of employment, will be needed to produce sufficient goods and deliver sufficient services to meet the market forecast produced by the model we described in Chapter 8?

▲ How many people will be needed to manage and develop the business, and at what cost?

These answers can be compared against the assumptions used to develop the financial planning model we described in Chapter 8, in order to derive the variable and fixed costs of operating the business. They will be needed to complete the subsidiary schedules of the complete financial model we describe in Chapter 14. If these refined predictions are the same as, or lower than, the planning assumptions used in the preliminary financial model, well and good; but if a detailed design of the organisation produces a significantly higher answer for one or both of these numbers, we must go back to the planning model, enter the revised figures, and re-check the project viability.

End notes

1   The 'human relations' school of management theory is very much a twentieth century phenomenon. Key figures are Roethlisberger and Dixon (1949), whose account of the 'Hawthorne Experiment'

'opened up management thinking to recognise the motivational importance of communicating concern for the employee's interests' (Ginn 1995). Another important author was Barnard (1947) who '... viewed organisations as cooperative systems ...' (Ginn 1995). Also noteworthy is McGregor (1960), who introduced the extremely influential terms Theory 'X' and Theory 'Y' to distinguish authoritarian management from human-oriented leadership.

2 Gantt was an engineer who developed a planning methodology for the US Navy during the First World War. PERT (Program Evaluation and Review Technique) was developed by the US Navy in the 1950s to control their nuclear submarine program. PERT has been extensively developed since the 1950s and several computer systems are available to help planners make use of it.

3 W. Edwards Deming, a statistically literate engineer and dominating personality, was sent to post Second World War Japan by the American occupation authorities to reorganise that country's shattered industries. Many of the practises labelled 'Japanese management techniques' today owe far less to fine traditions of Samurai ritual and national respect for authority than to the statistically-based principles expounded by Deming and his colleagues. The post war success of Japan is their justification. The relative decline of American manufacturing industry in the same period is their warning. 'A prophet is not without honour, save in his own country, and in his own house' (Matthew 13: 57). Statistical process control was first set out in Shewhart (1931). Taguchi is a widely admired recent contributor to the development of quality theory. Serious students should look at Taguchi (1985); and Taguchi (1986).

4 ISO is the International Standards Organisation. There are five standards in the ISO 9000 series: ISO 9000 and ISO 9004 are general, while the other three are specific to particular types of enterprise.

5 TQM may be broadly defined as a customer-oriented management system focused on delivering customer satisfaction through the production of quality products. Readers of this book should be aware — as many managers seeking panaceas have not been — that TQM principles are sound, desirable and useful but they are merely part of the framework for a total organisational design. There are many excellent introductions to TQM. The present authors used: Flood (1993).

6 The classical economist Adam Smith remarked on the efficiency gains associated with specialisation and the division of labour. Smith's criticism of the stunting effect of this upon the workers involved was taken up by Marx and is a fundamental part of the Marxist critique of capitalism. The use of the division of labour as a management tool reached its apogee with the early twentieth century theory and practice of Frederick W. Taylor. It was challenged by the famous Hawthorne experiments conducted under the auspices of the Australian born Harvard professor, Elton Mayo. See note 1, above.

7 The deliberate involving of customers and suppliers in the production process lies at the heart of the TQM approach to organisation and management.

8 Socio-technical systems theory, developed and developing since the early 1950s, originated with scholars associated with England's Tavistock Institute. The most famous names are Trist and Bamford, authors of the paper which pioneered the field.

9 One of the authors has written a text presenting a comprehensive analytical method for solving case studies and real-world analytical problems: Hindle (1992).

10 The 'moment of truth' concept was first presented in Carlzon (1989). Jan Carlzon was a CEO who turned an airline from near insolvency to profit by focusing upon customer service.

11 The general principles of service delivery are presented in Berry, Parasuramen and Zeithami (1990).

12 A description of Fox's early career can be found in Gleeson (1987).

13 The interface between the disciplines of marketing and organisational behaviour when it comes to designing the marketing department of an organisation are well presented in the early chapters of Haas and Wotruba (1983).

14 People without the experience of working for a large English firm can scarcely comprehend the trauma that an HRM department can inflict.

15 There are many (perhaps too many) books about information systems development and management. We have found Ward, Griffiths and Whitmore (1990) useful.

16 Fans of Sir John Harvey-Jones should search out the BBC video describing his visit to Morgan Cars, for the exception that proves this rule.

17 Lyons split out the LEO company and sold it, providing another instance of vertical disaggregation as a technology matures, and the LEO company, after many changes of name and ownership, became part of Fujitsu, a major Japanese firm.

18 See 'Profile two' in this book.

19 Hygiene factors were first described in Herzberg, Mausner and Snyderman (1959).

Chapter 13

The corporate entrepreneur

Large companies

Great trading corporations dominate the climax state of a capitalist economy, comparable to the great trees that dominate a mature forest. Like the great trees, they were once a seed and then a sapling, and like the great trees, they will fall one day. Some will last longer than others, and when their time is up, some will crash while others will rot in place. Some will seem to be on the point of collapse and yet gain a new lease of life; others will be cut down while they were still strong and turned into sawn timber, or even firewood.

There are huge differences between corporations: their industries, their ambitions, their public image, and the respect with which their stock is treated in the market all differ. The one thing that they all have in common is their sheer size: their financial resources, their expenditure level, and the number of people who work for and deal with each of them.

Entrepreneurs creating a new enterprise face all sorts of conflicting problems, but not recognising their colleagues is seldom one of them. One person is enough to start a new enterprise; four or five founding partners may be something of an upper limit. As the enterprise grows employees and subcontractors will be needed, but there will be no organisation charts, no staff development programs, possibly not even a telephone list. Companies are officially described as 'small' until they have more than ninety-nine employees in manufacturing firms or nineteen in other cases.

The passage from small to medium (up to 499 employees) is often traumatic, both for the enterprise and its staff. People start having specific duties and responsibilities on which they concentrate, resenting interference from others

383

and not interfering themselves. This can lead to dramatic disasters, when some critical task, like updating the insurance policies, is omitted altogether, but equally it can lead to a gradual hardening of the arteries, with the amount of effort devoted to internal communication rising and the proportion of the firm's efforts devoted to its markets and other external factors declining as a proportion of the total effort expended.

If these early problems do not stop the new enterprise, it will eventually pass the 499 employee mark and become, officially, a large business. One mark of becoming large is that the firm starts having middle managers, people whose jobs carry neither responsibility for making critical decisions nor the responsibility for carrying them out. Even medium-size firms need some staff people, a pay officer, a personnel person, someone to chase debtors and fend off creditors. Large firms have staff departments headed by senior executives, directors of information technology and of human resources. Employees get job descriptions and personal training plans.

Why do firms get large?

Some people wonder why firms get large. The subject provides economists with many opportunities to produce learned papers and to present them at conferences. The most probable answers focus on the efficiency gains produced by specialisation. A full time debtors clerk will be far more effective at controlling the amount of working capital the debtors ledger represents than someone for whom overdue accounts are an irritant and a distraction. A firm with 500 employees growing at 10 per cent per year and with an average Australian staff turnover rate must recruit three or four new employees every week. Placing advertisements, interviewing and selecting these new employees is a full-time job, and the bureaucracy of job descriptions and organisation charts is essential if anyone except the chief executive is to carry it out.

Whatever people are doing, they get better at it the more often that they do it. In numbers, someone who has been concentrating on one task for four years will be at least 60 per cent more productive[1] than someone who has had to deal with three other equally complex and time-consuming tasks over the same period. The employees inside a large firm are usually far more effective at their particular tasks than small firm employees or sole traders are, both because they get the chance to perfect their approach and because they enjoy a degree of freedom from distractions. People efficiency is only part of the story. Many expensive modern machines are only available in relatively high-capacity versions, and a large firm is better able to keep such expensive equipment busy than a small one is.

Service firms may need supplies; all firms need supporting services. Large firms are able to secure better bargains with suppliers and supporting service providers, not just by bullying, but by spreading the marketing and sales costs their suppliers must defray over larger and more consistent orders.

The original entrepreneurs in the United States computer industry founded the UNIVAC division of the Remington Rand company, but they were joined relatively rapidly by IBM, at that stage a relatively small company specialising in office equipment. In early 1954, UNIVAC led IBM convincingly in installed systems and even more convincingly on technical merit. IBM had one devastating advantage, a large team of excellent sales staff, and while UNIVAC concentrated on the technology, IBM secured the orders. By the time the mainframe computer market matured in 1983, IBM had grown from a $250 million a year company to a $60 billion a year one, ten times UNIVAC's size.

The efficiency advantages enjoyed by large firms are, to a significant extent, cumulative. If an industry is at some point in time dominated by small, competing firms, and chance, or some apparently irrelevant factor favours some of them, the lucky ones will become a little larger than the rest. This will make them more efficient, and able to keep their prices down while paying more for marketing effort, reinforcing their initial advantage. In a matter of a few years the more successful firms can become several times larger than their competitors.

Dynamic performance

There is a dynamic reason for the success of large firms, and that is that they are capable of applying large resources to pursue an opportunity. Some assets cannot be purchased in small pieces: Toyota spent $500 million building and equipping a new assembly plant at Altona, near Melbourne, and this was only a fraction of the total cost of getting a new model Camry motor car into production. Sums that an ordinary person would find terrifyingly large can be spent by large firms without undue angst: a corporation as large as Microsoft could spend $50 million on a new version of one of its lines of software, scrap it, and start again without causing a flutter in its share price.

Schumpeter (1942) suggested, and recent research has confirmed, that large firms are the major source of innovation in a developed economy, simply because they can afford to be. Bringing a new passenger aeroplane, or a new model of a motor car, to market can involve the investment of several billion dollars. Pharmaceutical companies regularly tie up hundreds of millions of dollars in the development and testing of a new product. Financial institutions spend tens of millions of dollars developing and implementing new service packages. A new holiday resort can cost tens or even hundreds of millions of dollars. Much of this money is borrowed, of course, but, in general, financiers prefer to lend to people who have a track record. An established leisure company will find it relatively easy to raise finance for a bland development while an individual with a genuinely innovative idea but no record in the industry will find it hard to get interviews with bankers, much less money from them.

Why aren't all firms large?

Schumpeter (1942), having correctly identified large firms as the major source of innovation, went on to predict the virtual extinction of small ones. It hasn't happened in the fifty years since Schumpeter's death, and it does not look like happening at all. The basic reason is that efficiency comes at a price: the loss of adaptability. Large firms are very efficient at producing and marketing a limited range of products, and surprisingly bad at most other things. The Boeing Commercial Aircraft Company is deservedly famous for its passenger aeroplanes, but some of its forays into ground transport systems have generated problems at least as rapidly as profits.

Much as there is a rich and flourishing undergrowth under the canopy of a climax forest, these implicit limitations on large firms give living room to smaller ones. Switching analogies, ants and elephants coexist, although those ants who find themselves directly under an elephant's foot may not do so well. Rarely, but often enough to be significant, the patch of ground ignored by the corporate elephants turns out to be extraordinarily productive, and an ant grows to elephant proportions.

Most ants stay ants, and most small firms stay small. There are a number of necessary functions in a market economy where larger firms, at least after a certain stage of growth, have no particular advantages over smaller ones. Taxi cab and messenger services can gain very little from being highly centralised, since the main activity involves reacting to essentially random customer demands. Large firms were needed to organise the railways, and later the airlines, because there was a large number of people who were prepared to pay for carriage between a limited number of main points. The more diffuse markets served by taxis and messengers offer few advantages to large firms, and so few large firms are present.

Industries where the job is intricately intermingled with the holder's lifestyle tend to remain fragmented. Farming and long-haul trucking are industries with a continuing high proportion of small enterprises, because, in part, the benefits of the lifestyle compensate the operators for the uneconomically low returns they get for their time, trouble and capital.

Large and small firms coexist in the hospitality industries, because these markets can be segmented fairly easily into customers who want fast service with a consistent product at a predetermined price and customers who want a new pleasurable or exciting experience. The same person may be, at different times, a customer in either segment, grabbing a McDonald's takeaway when the kids are hungry and the larder empty, and going to a gourmet restaurant when the kids are safely parked with a minder or old enough to go off on their own. A business traveller stuck in a hotel overnight between meetings has one set of expectations; the same person, travelling on a family or a romantic holiday has others. The chains will always dominate the business travel market, but specialists will always find niches in the leisure markets.

Discussing growth involves analogies, and while the trees in a forest can be used quite effectively as an analogy, there are two critical ways in which such analogies fail to capture important aspects of a modern market economy. One is that trees have very little ability to take purposeful control over their own destiny; even if we should describe the top executives of a major corporation as being 'wood from the neck up' we would not expect to be taken literally. The second major weakness in the forest analogy is that it tempts us to think of the ground as constant, but in the commercial world firms live off the market and are part of it. The very success of one group of businesses creates the conditions that, sometimes, allow new large businesses to emerge. The ground upon which businesses rest is continually changing.

The core competence of the corporation

Prahalad and Hamel (1990) introduced the term 'core competence' in an article in the *Harvard Business Review*, and it was rapidly and widely adopted, and almost as rapidly, according to Hamel, distorted.

Hamel's later explanation of the term concentrated more on culture than technical skill, the shared vision of what the company is about. 3M has a dual focus: one point is its concentration on stakeholders, with customers first and shareholders last, a policy set by its founder in the 1920s; and the other is that 3M is about 'surfaces'. 3M make sandpaper, sticking abrasives to the surface of paper. They make Post-it Notes, lightly adhesive and easily parted. They also make fire-fighting additives, enabling water to stick to burning and threatened surfaces rather than falling off and soaking into the ground. They even make cough mixtures and asthma pumps, acting on the surfaces of human throats and lungs.

Honda Motor is about engines, Hamel suggests. Honda engines are lighter, more efficient, more powerful, quieter, less polluting — whatever the market wants in engines, Honda can supply it first, and just a little better, than any of its rivals. Honda employs stylists and operates a dealer network, it assembles complete cars and motor cycles, but at the end of the day Soichiro Honda built engines and wrapped cars and bikes about them, and that attitude, along with Honda's determination to look after customers, and let the profits, and the shareholders, look after themselves, continues to drive Honda Motor today.

It is easy to identify the core competencies of 3M and Honda Motor: their founders set them out and their current managers and staff still believe in them. Every corporation must be good at something, or they would never sell anything and would be driven out of business rapidly. Many corporations are, however, only good at addressing a well-defined subset of the current requirements of a closely defined group of customers. This enables them to survive, and grow with the economy, or if they are fortunate in their customers, a little faster than it, but they are not preparing for the day when their present customers stop growing, or start calling on an alternative supplier who can meet their needs even better. Such passive corporations do not lack core competencies, but they seem to lack the insight that they need to use their existing capabilities in order to establish a position in new and growing markets.

Corporations, however they are placed, seldom do well when they undertake initiatives in areas in which they are not competent. This reads like a truism, but in reality many firms do not know what their core competencies really are. IBM was founded by a dazzling salesman, and its core competence lay in the skill, education, and discipline of its sales force. This powerful sales team gave IBM a unique ability to present complex concepts to the managers of large corporations in a readily appreciated way. The Watsons, father and son, understood this perfectly, but by the early 1980s IBM's top managers came to believe that IBM had unique competencies in hardware design and manufacture and the production of complex software. They even believed that IBM's '360 architecture' constituted an advantage. The personal computer and open systems revolutions of the later 1980s and early 1990s took IBM by surprise: they failed to realise that the computer industry was no longer under their control, and they failed to find ways to leverage their one true competence into the future. In the thirty years from 1954, IBM grew at a compound average rate of 20 per cent per year; in the following ten years the rate was more like 1 per cent.

It is hard, perhaps impossible, to identify the core competence of a large corporation from the outside, by looking at its product range and examining its accounts. The keys are found in its people, the things they talk about informally and the subjects that dominate discussion in the various informal networks that develop in every large organisation. Corporate mission statements, apart from those dictated by a committed and active founder, are seldom a good place to look for indicators of the core competence.

Occasionally top management succeeds in creating a new core competence. British Airways, on the eve of its privatisation in 1987, was not very popular with its passengers, but kept them, in part, through political deals that limited competition on many routes. The complex and — some might say, devious — arrangements British Airways made with the travel departments of its major corporate customers kept more and the dogged patriotism of many British travellers accounted for most of the rest. 'Belated Arrival' was one of the nicest plays on the letters 'BA' used by its frustrated customers. Lord King and Sir Colin Marshall, the Chairman and Chief Executive, announced that British Airways was 'the world's favourite airline' (with a subtext focusing on high value business travellers) and shamed, shocked, and trained the staff into turning the slogan into reality.

Corporate predation

Some opportunities are exploited by new, fast growth businesses, even in relatively mature industries. During the early 1990s regional banks in Australia showed marked growth, winning significant shares of the retail market. The opportunity was created by the policies of the major banks, who raised charges and reduced their service levels in order to repair the holes in their balance sheets left by their reckless corporate lending in the 1980s. When large companies discover that they have lost valuable market share points through inattention, they seek ways of regaining it.

One way an established corporation can set about regaining market share is for it to update its products and to renew its marketing strategies, attracting new customers and reinforcing the loyalty of old ones. The other is to simply buy one of the upstart companies that have invaded its markets. The first approach strengthens the large corporation in the longer term, while the second directly affects its short term position. Companies that are managed so as to keep their share price high are only interested in the short term, and so the merger and acquisitions route will seem very attractive. The following factors favour mergers over organic development:

▲ New product development expenditure and marketing activities are usually treated as a current expense, and so when a large firm increases its spending in these areas its current-period profit will fall, often taking the share price with it. By contrast, money spent on takeovers is recorded in the accounts as a capital transaction, and so does not affect the current period's reported profit.

▲ Shares in smaller companies often trade at lower prices, relative to their assets, growth prospects and profits, than shares in larger ones. The major share-buying institutions tend to stick to larger companies: in Australia, the 50 Leaders; in the United States, the Fortune 500. This makes it relatively easy for a large company to make a takeover bid that offers the smaller company's shareholders a substantial profit.

▲ There are sometimes quite genuine synergies available and efficiency gains to be realised from a merger. The larger firm's staff and service functions may be able to absorb the demands from the smaller one at little extra cost, while the energy and entrepreneurship that made the smaller company an attractive takeover target may be applied to improving the performance of its new parent.

Many individual entrepreneurs have found that a sale to a large corporation provides a relatively straightforward, and remunerative, form of exit. The pressures on corporate managers, as described above, ensure that willing sellers of successful growth businesses seldom have much trouble finding eager buyers.

Large company entrepreneurship[2]

Many large companies pursue 'organic' development instead of, or in addition to, their mergers and acquisitions. This may be because their industry is so concentrated that there are no small companies left to be taken over, or it may be because the ownership structure is such that the company is managed for objectives more enduring than tomorrow's share price quotation.

The term 'organic' is often a poor one, because it suggests that a company can grow by doing 'more of the same'. Large firms are unlikely to find true organic growth rewarding unless they have gone through a period of neglect and under-investment. Simply building more factories, opening more outlets, or appointing more sales people in the firm's existing markets will, for firms that have previously been well-managed, increase their expenses faster than their income. Large firms can recover from an investment drought by simply raising the scale of their activities, but beyond that point they can only grow by innovation.

Innovation, as we have seen in earlier chapters, is not always or even often a matter of 'gee-whizz' technology. A successful entry into a new market is an innovation, as is the successful introduction of major new internal processes and the acquisition and forming of partnerships with firms that offer true synergy. Many attempts at corporate innovation are relatively safe, in the sense that a failure will be embarrassing but not fatal.

A few corporate innovations have involved the 'you bet your company' fervour, and risk, of IBM's System/360 project. Boeing teetered on the edge of insolvency when its launch of the first series of 707 passenger jet aircraft was disrupted by a recession in the United States airline industry, and the development cost of the RB211 triple-shaft jumbo jet engine caused the bankruptcy of Rolls–Royce. Most corporate innovation, however, involves less dramatic initiatives: serious enough for the people involved in them, but not carrying a short term risk to the survival of the organisation. Westpac Banking Corporation's CS90 initiative cost the bank over $120 million for very little benefit, and several hundred people lost their jobs when the project was terminated, but at no stage was the survival of Westpac as a bank in doubt.

Who is the corporate entrepreneur?

Corporations want to grow, if for no other reason than the impressive effect of prospective growth on their share price. To grow they must implement innovations, and to implement innovations they must encourage entrepreneurs. How?

One way to increase the number of corporate entrepreneurs is to widen the source of them: every employee of a corporation has a brain in which ideas ferment. Thinking is not the exclusive prerogative of the chief executive and his (or very occasionally in Australia, her) team of executive sycophants. The tendency, particularly noticeable in the United States, for chief executive salaries to rise without apparent limit tends to discourage innovation from outside the chief executive suite: if the chief executive is being paid 100 times as much as the average employee, he may be widely expected to contribute 100 times as many ideas.

Chief executives, however, are seldom appointed directly from the front office or the factory floor, and while they talk a lot to other chief executives, they have little recent experience with dealing directly with their firm's customers. If they do try to get involved with the details of innovations, they may see the problems in terms of the technology, markets and products of the period when they themselves worked in the front line. Such nostalgia-driven contributions assist some projects, but they are a hindrance to more. Chief executive officers, and a corporation's other senior managers, should be discouraged from getting involved in new project minutiae partly because their interventions may be less than perfectly helpful, but also because focusing on one project must lead to them neglecting many others, often with a collective value exceeding that of the favoured one.

A project manager

An Australian company ordered a large and complex item of industrial equipment from an English firm in the days when England still had trade unions and industrial firms. The supplier engaged a project manager to see to the completion of the equipment in the factory, its delivery to Australia, installation and commissioning.

The project manager chartered an aircraft to collect the equipment and booked his flight to Australia. These plans looked like being disrupted when a group of workers began picketing the factory gate, holding the Australian (and some other) shipments as bargaining chips for their negotiations.

The elegant ritual that passed for bargaining was rudely interrupted when the project manager turned up with a gang of construction workers armed with picks and hammers.

'What are you going to do?' asked the astounded factory manager.

'Just knock down that old shed,' the project manager replied, 'so as to clear a landing space for the Chinook helicopter I have hired to lift my shipment over the picket line.'

The factory manager and the leader of the pickets had a very quiet discussion. 'Leave the building alone,' the factory manager told the project manager, 'and bring your truck around at 5 am precisely. We have agreed to open the canteen to the pickets at 4:55 am for twenty minutes, because of the cold weather.'

The shipment got to Australia on time.

Project managers play a vital role in many large companies, controlling costs, keeping effort focused, and ensuring that their projects secure and retain the confidence of the parent corporation's senior management. Some project managers are footloose, leaving a firm as soon as one project ends to find an interesting project with someone else. Others are an organisation's 'young Turks', demonstrating their fitness for eventual promotion to the highest levels. Either way they are model cavalry commanders: they are given their objective, and will attain it or die in the attempt. Casualties among their own team, and a certain amount of collateral havoc in other parts of the organisation, are an inevitable result of their operations. Like real cavalry commanders, they are seldom noted for the depth of their introspection or the frequency with which they ponder the meaning or intent of their assignment. Project managers are seldom the initial innovators in a corporation.

Hsieh and Barton (1995), two McKinsey consultants, writing about leadership rather than pure project management, use the term 'young lions' to describe those rising young executives who accept project management and other change-making duties, and 'old warriors' for retired senior executives who can also be effective in project roles, both as executives and mentors. They also introduce the idea of the 'high priest', the senior (but not quite top level) executive at the apex of his or her career who is respected as a thinker and analyst by the top managers of a corporation, but is unlikely to be given much or any executive responsibility. Such high priests are often the most senior people on the informal networks that define the corporation's core competence.

Hsieh and Barton's idea can be developed into an image of the innovation pathway in a typical major corporation. An innovative idea occurs to someone whose job exposes them to problems, either internal to the firm or as experienced by its customers. This person, the 'initiator', or their appropriate middle manager 'the sponsor', approaches one of the high priests (or 'mentors') for blessings and advice. They may try to skip the blessing stage and make a direct approach up the management hierarchy: if they are lucky, they will be diverted to the high priest; otherwise they will simply be snubbed. The high priest will discuss the proposal, and either explain why the firm will not adopt it, or describe the informal project approval processes in use in the company, and give the would-be innovators the names of some likely supporters. The originator and proposer will be told to prepare a business case[3] for the formal approval process to grind through, and to lobby the potential supporters to secure informal approval.

The corporate innovator can only succeed when the new idea can be aligned with one or more core competencies. When it is, there are no limits on the extravagance of the ideas that can be entertained. The impossible will be massaged by the internal networks into the merely incredible; the practical will be embellished with sufficient relevant extensions to make it interesting to the informal network. The network can generate a wave of enthusiasm which top managers can ride or which they can let swamp them.

Innovations from the top do not succeed unless they enlist the informal network or create a new one. King and Marshall personally initiated very few of the many small innovations that made British Airways attractive to business passengers, but they successfully empowered those staff who did not want to be associated with a 'bloody awful' airline to get their ideas adopted. Well-run corporations are generous with praise, and photos of successful idea initiators and early sponsors will fill the house magazine. Corporations are less likely to trust people who have demonstrated the ability to think for themselves with a project management job. Once an idea is adopted and a project approved, a project manager will be appointed, usually neither the originator nor the first supporter being considered for this job. The project manager may, however, coopt one or both of them onto the project. In some highly innovative companies, including 3M, such cooptation is obligatory.

The entrepreneurial process in a corporation
The initiator

Innovations start with a person, someone who sees a need and a means of satisfying it. This can be a production problem, where some waste of time or materials can be eliminated: the Japanese use the word *kaizen* — the 'way of improvement' — to describe the way in which shop floor employees contribute to the improvements of their products through suggestions that are individually small but cumulatively significant. It may be a structural problem in an organisation, with some part of the operation being stifled by inappropriate controls or reporting lines. It may be an external opportunity, to form an alliance with or to acquire a complementary business. It may, of course, be a market opportunity, a chance to create increased customer value through introducing a new product or enhancing or extending the distribution of an old one.

An initiator must propose a solution as well as identifying a problem: people who merely highlight problems without offering solutions are whingers, not contributors to corporate innovation. The solution need not be definitive or even particularly cost-effective, but it must address the identified requirement without being impossibly complex, ridiculously expensive, or dependent on a radical revision of the laws of nature.

Initiators seem to be found at the ends of the organisational tree even more frequently than their statistical predominance would indicate. Ordinary research workers generate more good ideas than laboratory directors; production workers (in Japan at least) offer more ideas than production supervisors; shop assistants learn about customer problems faster than store managers; the list goes on. Some good concepts are injected into the top of an organisation, either when a new chief executive arrives from outside or while the members of the original entrepreneurial team are still in charge. Even then the top–down innovation is doomed unless the ordinary workers in an organisation get involved in the myriad of lesser innovations that make the concept a success: the concept of the Boeing 747 'jumbo' jet came from the top, but the aeroplane only flies today because of a vast number of lesser innovations, solutions to the long list of technical and operational problems presented by the decision to build a passenger aeroplane four times larger than those then in service.

The champion and the mentor

Except for some of the ideas that start with the chief executive, the simple fact that a problem exists and has a possible solution is no guarantee of action. The concept needs a 'champion' or 'intrapreneur'[4] who will get corporate resources allocated to it. This may be the initiator or it may be someone with more experience or standing in the corporation. When initiators from the lower ranks of a corporation set out to champion their own ideas they need a sponsor, someone with sufficient seniority and experience in the corporation to guide them in its ways.

The champion, with or without sponsor, will still need the services of a mentor, either the corporate 'high priest' or a certified acolyte, who will guide the reformulation of the proposal into a form that can be understood by others in the corporation and can eventually gain their support. Only founding chief executives can act as their own high priests; when a new chief executive wants to make an existing corporation embrace a particular set of innovative changes they must enlist the support of the informal network or their efforts will fail. A new chief executive can appoint a new technical or marketing director, but new high priests emerge from within.

The corporate prelude to a business plan: The business case

Preparation of a complete business plan for a major initiative inside a large corporation is itself a major task, and will involve securing commitment from a large number of people. A new product will need to be sold, and so the senior sales managers must endorse it; it may need to be manufactured, and if so the production staff must be involved; it will often affect the corporate information systems, and so the managers of the IS/IT function will need to endorse it; and people and functions that the champion has never heard of will need to be propitiated. Except in the most unusual corporations these people will not want to expose themselves more than necessary, and so they will not offer their support until they have seen the project authorised by people senior to them in the firm. They may still oppose it, overtly or tacitly, in spite of its formal approval, but they will not support it until this formal top management approval has been secured.

The mechanism for securing the formal blessing of senior management on an innovation is the business case, a relatively short document and a precursor to the full business plan and the creation of a project.

The basis of a business case

Successful projects inside corporations start with a business case, a document or process that is intended to help senior management choose the most appropriate projects to be given access to the corporation's executive and financial resources. Each business case sets out the costs (trivial) and the benefits (enormous) of financing a particular proposal, but when all the available requests are assembled they will, except in the most conservative firms, greatly exceed the total resources available. Large corporations generally have a formal planning and commitment cycle which culminates in the selection of those projects that will receive funding in the following year. Often the cycle culminates in an intensive planning session involving the chief executive and the rest of the senior managers of the corporation: such sessions may last a week or more, and are often held at exotic locations.

Very few of the proposals put up to an annual planning festival will be genuinely innovative. Some will be 'organic' proposals masquerading as innovations, seeking extravagant funding to apply cosmetic changes to something that is already being done. Many will be for organisational changes: contract out this part of the operation, bring this other one back in-house, make more staff fly economy, re-equip this plant, close that one. Many may be 'more of the same' requests for independent spending authority, made by various turbulent barons concerned only with the glory of their own fief.

Obviously it makes no sense for a proposal to be forced past the lowest level at which it is possible to get it accepted and financed, and where corporate practice involves a substantial devolvement of new product and process development funds the manager of the devolved funds is the first person whose support must be sought. Divisional managers, even in nominally devolved organisations, will often be more enthusiastic in their vocal support than their financial support for a new initiative, since very few of them are able to maintain a true discretionary fund and those funds that they have nominal control of will be largely committed to current projects. A good proposal will often be seen by a corporate baron as the basis of a case to increase the fief's total resource allocation, forcing the unpleasant decisions into other baronies.

Whoever actually rules on a business case, it has to be written so as to bear scrutiny at the highest levels of management.

The corporate objective

Corporations are controlled by their directors, who are elected by the shareholders. Unless the directors provide the shareholders with a satisfactory return on their investment the shareholders may elect an alternative management of a corporation or even wind it up. Shareholder returns come in the form of dividends and capital appreciation on their shares; both can be combined into a calculation of the value of their shares:

$$value = \frac{\Pi}{\rho - \mu}$$

In this value equation Π represents current profit after interest, preference share dividends, and tax; ρ represents the risk-weighted rate of return appropriate to an investment in the company and industry; and μ represents the expected growth rate of the corporation's profit.

Examining the value formula shows that the value of shares in a corporation can be increased in one of three general ways:

▲ the profit rate, Π, can be raised, either by raising prices or by reducing costs; neither process can be continued indefinitely without cutting volumes, which will eventually cut profits

▲ the risk-weighted rate of return ρ can be reduced, either from the outside, when the government lowers interest rates and therefore required rates of return generally, or by the firm itself reducing the variability of the profit stream and therefore the risk weighting

▲ the long term profit growth rate μ can be raised (or the current rate sustained further into the future).

Innovation may be applied to all three areas, and sometimes more than one of them. A process innovation may reduce costs; if part of the saving is applied to marketing and part to price reductions, the result may be an increased rate of growth as new customers enter the market and others are attracted from the firm's rivals. The increase in market share of itself reduces the variability of a firm's returns and increases firm value.

Product innovations, ranging from facelifts to new lines, generate revenue growth, and a consistent product innovation policy holds the promise of sustained revenue growth and a corresponding increase in firm value. Line replacements need a more carefully worked out justification, since part of their justification comes from the assertion that the line that is proposed to be replaced is entering a period of slow growth or actual decline. Such messages are not always welcome, particularly when one of the executives who has to approve the investment in the proposed innovation built his or her corporate career on the product that is to be superseded.

Table 13.1 shows a synthetic example intended to represent a rather boring large Australian company. The items in the table represent the least that someone should be able to promise in order to justify a continuing expense of $1 million per year in the first column and $10 million a year in the second. The 'obvious' case, where a single expense is requested and a permanent income stream promised is exactly the same case as for the individual entrepreneur and a start-up company, and should be evaluated in the same way. Corporate finance managers are, by the way, deeply suspicious of any proposal that requests a one-time capital allocation and promises to be self-supporting, with no impact on any other part of the corporation's business thereafter.

As presented in Table 13.1 the figures are pretty meaningless to either the innovator or to the reviewing managers, but they capture the essence of value-adding entrepreneurial activity inside a corporation. The proposed project must cost money, at least initially: if it didn't there would be no need to seek investment approval. If it is not a freestanding enterprise, an acquisition, an entry into an untapped market, or some other action with a minimum impact on the firm's current activities, it can only be justified by its overall impact on the value of the corporation.

Value and the share price

The commercial value of something is what people will pay for it, not the result of any calculation made by the seller. The value of a listed company is measured by its market capitalisation: the product of the number of shares issued and the current share price. The logic behind the financial arithmetic of present values and risk-weighted discount rates is that they reproduce the calculations a fully

Table 13.1   *Justifying a new project*

The first column represents the current state of the firm while the second and third show the minimum effect needed to justify a $1 million and a $10 million annual expense

| | Current data | Proposed annual expense ($million) and minimum result | |
		$1	$10
Earnings standard deviation	20.00%	19.66%	17.41%
		or	*or*
Earnings growth rate	7.00%	7.08%	7.86%

The firm is assumed to make $100 million profit per year and can earn 10% on 'riskless' cash investments

informed and perfectly rational investor would make before deciding to buy or sell shares.

Finance economists refer to the 'efficient market hypothesis', which comes in three strengths. The strong form says that the share price is the true value of a company, reflecting all the circumstances that are likely to affect the company's future earnings, even those that are not public knowledge. The strong form of the efficient market hypothesis is used by certain commentators to defend insider trading and share price manipulation: since the share price is an accurate reflection of value, they argue, it is impossible for insider trading or share price manipulation to yield a profit. Paul Craig Roberts, a conservative columnist with the American magazine *Business Week*, argues that Mike Milken, who confessed to and was convicted for stock market manipulation, was innocent. Roberts appears to argue that, since the efficient market hypothesis 'proves' that Milken could not have made money out of market manipulation, the $500 million found in Milken's accounts was his just reward for valuable services to American industry.[5]

The medium strength, or semi-strong form of the efficient market hypothesis says that the share price reflects all *publicly available* knowledge about the value of a firm; this form says that it is impossible to make a profit from share trading except by the use of inside knowledge or market manipulation. The weak form merely says that the share price, over time, will approximate the true value of a firm.

History tends to support the weak form of the efficient market hypothesis: there are just too many examples of share prices moving up on a speculative surge, only to collapse to much lower levels, over a period when no new information about the firm or its markets became available. Part of this can be explained by simple incompetence or ignorance; share analysts spend little time working on smaller companies and are likely to make sweeping statements on a limited basis. Even analysts looking at larger companies may lack the technical expertise to appreciate fully the data that they are given or even to ask the right questions. The sort of short cut made by analysts includes projecting earnings growth (or losses) into future years: if a company reports an above-trend profit increase some analysts may revalue the shares on the assumption that the higher trend is permanent. The downsizing frenzy was fuelled by this process: companies that downsize almost always get rid of staff faster than they lose customers, causing a sharp rise in their short term profits and their share price. Two years later 60 per cent of downsizing companies fall behind their old trend and their share prices fall lower than ever, but the initial rise in the share price delivers handsome profits to some.

The way superannuation funds operate also tells against anything but the weak form of the efficient market hypothesis. In general, superannuation contributions are deposited with trustees who arrange for the pool of funds for which they are responsible to be managed by professional funds managers on a commission basis. The funds managers have little to gain by bringing in an outstanding return, and a lot to lose by bringing in a poor one. A high return means that they get a small increase in their commission, while a poor one leads to funds being withdrawn from their management and the task, and the commission, being given to another firm. Under these circumstances the fund managers invest on the principle of being as close to the average as possible, a little better than average if the opportunity arises, but never putting their commission income at risk by investing in small firms (whose shares may be hard to sell in a hurry) or fast-growing ones (whose share price tends to be too volatile). One of the techniques that the fund managers use to ensure that their returns are close to the average is called 'index weighting': they buy sufficient shares in the largest fifty companies to ensure that their return closely follows the 50 Leaders Index. This is not the same thing as selecting shares on the basis of their actual, or their prospective, performance. The semi-strong form of the efficient market hypothesis is used by such managers to argue that, since it is impossible to beat the index systematically without breaking the law, they can be doing their clients no harm by following it.

A third feature of share markets that can cause price and value to diverge is the existence of some investors who are less than perfectly rational. In a market where there are some such investors, a perfectly rational investor may be tempted into paying a price higher than the underlying value for a share. If an irrational investor buys shares in a particular firm at an excessive price, rational investors may buy at just below that price intending to onsell their shares to the irrational buyers. The increased volume and rising prices will draw more investors, rational and irrational, each expecting to sell at a profit before the bubble bursts. All bubbles burst eventually, giving rational and irrational investors alike the chance to learn yet again that markets can have discontinuities: the price can fall from high to low without stopping long enough in between for speculators to unload their shares and cover their futures positions.[6]

Presenting a business case

Most large firms will have developed a preferred format for a business case presentation, and some of them even have manuals to follow, but the essence of all successful business case presentations is the same:

▲ be brief: senior managers often suspect that anyone who uses a lot of words is trying to hide something unpleasant

▲ be clear about the demands of the proposal: how much money, over what time scale, and how much call there will be on other key resources, whether people or facilities

▲ show a clear corporate benefit directly related to the proposed investment: claims of indirect effects will arouse suspicion unless they are clearly separated from the direct ones and are not required to complete the business case

▲ don't build a proposal around the supposed failure of other products or the adverse results of prior management decisions: at best this will shift the focus of discussion from your proposal to the product or project that you are criticising, and at worst you will arouse a pack of sleeping dogs, determined to tear your proposal apart, and possibly you with it

▲ avoid any technical jargon other than terms generally current in the relevant industry and, unless a specific technological breakthrough is critical to the proposal's success, avoid any discussion of technology at all except in the most general terms

▲ keep any written material short and readable, with all complex issues and long justifications dealt with in appendices or in supporting documentation

▲ if presenting in person, use charts and handouts with care, don't use any numbers that you cannot justify, and stick to the point when answering questions

▲ treat financial numbers with proper respect:
  ▶ don't use broad brush or obviously over-rounded numbers (like, two million)
  ▶ don't use excessive numerical refinement either (like $2 003 156.22)
  ▶ make sure that all numbers add up, that balance sheets balance, that tax and interest are allowed for correctly
  ▶ use approved numbers whenever possible, such as interest charges, head office overheads, depreciation rates and capitalisation policies
  ▶ don't surprise or challenge the controller or the finance director with a freelance policy critique.

Development costs, risks and limits

Top managers in most corporations have learned, from bitter experience, that most attempts at innovation fail to bring the promised, or any, rewards. It is very important to show, at the outset, the limits to the risks to which they are being asked to expose the corporation. This requires a phased expenditure budget, drawn up to align with the firm's normal accounting periods, and showing liabilities in the period in which they are incurred, even when they are used to buy assets which can be leased. Internal costs must be shown, no matter how arbitrary the process of determining them may appear to be.

The expenditure proposal should not be allowed to become unduly complex, and often it will be in a form dictated by corporate standards in any case, but the following items should usually be broken out into separate lines:

- ▲ wages and salaries and payments to contract staff
- ▲ wage related oncosts and provisions
- ▲ equipment purchases
- ▲ consumables
- ▲ rent of premises (not currently rented by corporation)
- ▲ rent of premises (currently rented or owned by corporation and due to be vacated or not currently occupied)
- ▲ other external payments
- ▲ other internal payments
- ▲ project closure costs (assuming it runs to completion)
- ▲ contingency allowance.

Inexperienced corporate innovators often forget the contingency allowance, even though (assuming the other budgetary figures are best estimates) the absence of a contingency budget means that the project has a 50 per cent chance of failing by exhausting its cash allocation. Items like 'consumables' and 'rent' may be hard to estimate, but the controller's department will usually provide standard ratios which can be used to generate these cost lines.

Implementation and marketing cost estimates

The implementation and marketing costs will not need to be as detailed as the development budget, since they will be the subject of a later review if the development project proceeds. They will also be comparatively predictable once the development project has progressed to the point that there is a clearly defined product, whether a service offering to be packaged and distributed or a manufactured item to be produced or contracted.

A fairly general approach to this part of the budget will be adequate for an initial proposal, as long as the various cost lines are not significantly out of line with the appropriate corporate experience. Since these costs will, in conjunction with the revenue forecast, determine the long term profitability projections, they should be set, for planning purposes, on the high side. The following lines are probably essential:

- ▲ capital amounts for premises, plant and equipment
- ▲ unit material and variable costs including standard overheads (unlikely to be zero, even for a service)
- ▲ warranty and service costs, if appropriate
- ▲ gross distribution allowances, including standard margins, co-promotion allowances, sales and promotional incentives and the like
- ▲ launch budget, including the preparation of promotional material, sales training, initial advertising costs
- ▲ continuing marketing and administration budget.

In practice several of these items may be shared with existing product lines, but this is not likely to be seen as an acceptable reason for trimming the estimates at the planning stage. A new initiative should be viable on its own; it should not be a way of locking in previous decisions. In any case the impact on existing product lines will need to be dealt with under the revenue forecasts, and considering them under the cost section as well smacks of double counting.

Revenue projections

Revenue may come from sales, licences, royalties and service charges: projections can be made for each of these. The existence of revenue projections implies that there is a sales and price forecast: this, at the top level of most corporations, will be taken as supporting evidence rather than as a primary part of the case.

A sales forecast is difficult enough; what is more difficult, and more important, is to project the impact of an innovation on the corporation's existing product lines. Even when the proposal is for a line extension it is not always easy to separate out the likely sales with and without the innovation. When the innovation is an obvious bit of 'creative destruction', and the sales of the new product will clearly be at the expense of some established line, the proposers of the innovation can expect to be met with quite passionate hostility.

The innovators may feel, equally passionately, that the established line is living on borrowed time and that if it is not replaced by their innovation, it will be by a similar product launched by someone else. There are plenty of recorded cases where the upholders of the established lines have won, only to see some other company, often an upstart, reap the rewards.

In 1977, IBM announced that they had abandoned their 'Future System' (FS) project because of the possible impact of the implied product changes on their current customers (a coded way of saying, because of opposition from the supporters of the current product line). It took six years before the impact of this decision was made apparent by the stagnation of IBM's sales revenue, and a further seven before IBM's profits collapsed as well and the company was forced into a massive reorganisation involving large scale redundancies. In 1977, IBM accounted, on its own, for well over half the total revenue of the computer industry; by 1995, IBM's market share was around 20 per cent. In 1977 Hewlett–Packard's computer operations brought in a few hundred million dollars of sales only. By 1995, Hewlett–Packard's computer sales had grown to over $25 billion per year; this is only part of the revenue that IBM sacrificed in order to defend the *status quo* in 1977.

When the success of an innovation is certain to destroy a significant part of the existing revenue base, the business case must be built around the combined sales of the old and new product. IBM's experience carries a slightly different message in this regard: their pre-1977 product line had considerable strength left in it, and a business case built upon its premature replacement would have been fatally flawed. IBM was wrong to cancel FS, but the supporters of FS were equally wrong to demand that FS should immediately displace IBM's then-current product line. Technicians are quite good at predicting the impact of an innovation, but poor at predicting the time over which that impact will be felt. Computers were sold and are sold because of what they can do, not because of the virtues or defects of their logical architecture. An inferior logical architecture, like any product attribute that fails to attain the best possible standards, will eventually impact users by imposing excessive costs or by restricting their flexibility. It often, particularly in industrial and commercial applications, takes several years before such impacts are widely felt.

If the receivers are in the outer office it may be hard to get a corporation's management to allocate large resources to strategic innovations; but if they are not, senior managers will generally resent attempts to panic them into action by over-blown predictions of the imminent failure of the current product line or of the major processes.

The net value statement

Some innovations are so dramatic that the only way to evaluate them properly is to construct a financial model of the corporation with and without the proposal. An aircraft manufacturer contemplating a new airframe design, a motor manufacturer considering a new marque, a retailer considering building a series of stores based upon a new concept, these are all innovations whose impact cannot be isolated to part of the corporation. The new model of aeroplane or marque of motor car will gain some new sales, but it will also divert sales from the existing models and marques; it will require new manufacturing facilities, but it will also enable better use to be made of existing facilities; it will require extra staff, but it will also represent a career path for existing staff. People proposing such innovations will need to read more books than this one.

For every innovation on a billion-dollar scale, there should be a hundred million-dollar ones, and these are often large enough to demand serious examination, but too small to justify building a special corporate model to evaluate each of them. The hundred projects pursued may be chosen from a thousand proposed, and since at least some of them will interact the evaluation, to be complete, should be carried out on every possible combination of them. Such a calculation would, however, last far longer than the universe, so corporate finance departments use one of three quick and easy ways of ranking proposals. A fourth, based on the work of Dixit and Pindyck (1994), is described in Chapter 8 but it is not, at present, widely used.

The three shorthand ways of ranking investment proposals are the *payback time*, the *net present value*, and the *hurdle rate of return*. Dixit and Pindyck have demonstrated that the risk-weighted rate of return can be formally calculated, leading to the calculation of a risk-weighted (or risk-adjusted) net present value. This, or some variant of it, is likely to become the method of choice in due course, but the others will be around for some time yet.

The payback time is calculated by calculating the rate at which the innovation will earn profits, or cut costs, and dividing this into the expense of developing and introducing it. The answer is some number of years or months: proposals where the payback period is less than some maximum time are given further consideration, while the rest are rejected immediately. Payback limits vary from eighteen months to three years depending on the firm and industry. The payback method is appropriate for cost-reducing innovations whose total value is not likely to affect the overall position of a firm dramatically. It is less appropriate for revenue-generating innovations, projects with long lead times, or cost reductions significant enough to give a firm new strategic options.

The net present value method of capital budgeting takes a firm's 'weighted average cost of capital', treating the earnings per share as the 'cost' of equity, and calculating the present value of the net income stream generated by the innovation. This method usually leads to far too many projects being considered; as Dixit and Pindyck showed, borderline projects chosen using this methodology are likely to perform poorly in reality. The main advantage of the approach is that it allows a large number of proposals to be sorted into the order of their net value: the highest value one is then selected, its capital cost is deducted from the funds available, and the next highest value proposal selected; the process continues until all the available funds are fully committed. When applied injudiciously this can, as with the Victorian Economic Development Corporation (liquidated in disgrace in 1990), lead to worthless projects being supported simply because the worthwhile proposals run out before the available investment funds do (see Ryan 1989).

Another disadvantage of selecting projects by the net present value method is that it does not necessarily lead to the most valuable combination of projects: it assumes, quite falsely in most cases, that there is no interaction between the projects selected. American manufacturing companies taken as a group use equipment that is on average eight years old; until recently Australian manufacturing companies used even older equipment. By contrast, Japanese manufacturing companies use equipment that is, on average, three to four years old. This may be because of the 'cultural differences' certain economists are so fond of alluding to; but it might equally be due to the prevalence of net present value-based planning in the Anglophone countries. An investment in a new machine will generate small increases in the value of many of the large number of product lines produced by a major corporation, but this extra profit, even if fully accounted, may not be large enough to force it into contention against riskier, but apparently more rewarding, alternatives.

Hurdle rates of return can be used instead of the weighted average cost of capital in the net present value method, or projects can be ranked on the basis of their internal rate of return and the internal rate of return tested against the hurdle rate. Internal rates of return cannot be determined by a formula, but all useful spreadsheet packages will have a function available to calculate them. Firms using the hurdle rate method will rank projects on the basis of their risk level, and then reject those where the internal rate of return fails to exceed the 'hurdle rate' appropriate to the project class. As discussed in Chapter 8, Dixit and Pindyck have provided a formula for calculating hurdle rates, but most of the firms using hurdle rates at the time of writing set them on the basis of experience.

These heuristic hurdle rates vary from four or so percentage points above the current before-tax return on government bonds to twenty percentage points higher, with most of them in the middle third of this range. Lower-end hurdle rates, around 15 per cent, are appropriate for very long-lived projects with secure returns, such as buying newly privatised public utility distribution systems. Hurdle rates of 25 per cent or more will be used to evaluate projects involving a significant amount of development expense and time, or for forcing an entry into an established market.

The hurdle rates used by any corporation will be fairly widely known inside that corporation, which means that would-be corporate entrepreneurs may be tempted to 'cook the books', padding the sales figures and understating the probable expenses and the development time. This is a self defeating strategy, partly because corporate finance officers are very good at spotting such attempts and substituting their own estimates, well-padded in the other direction. Faking business cases is also self defeating in the sense that it is like volunteering to be a target for ammunition testing by the firing squad: if the project is accepted, and the returns are no better than the unpadded original estimates, the corporate witch-hunters will not have to look very far to find someone to blame for the debacle.

The product description and marketing plan

A business case should be accompanied by an overview of the proposed innovation, but *not* a detailed description or a technical discussion of it. Top executives do not expect to be presented with hoaxes: they need some idea of what they are being asked to support, but their technical input, if any of them are qualified to provide it, should have been sought long before a formal business case was put together.

Glossy pictures and celebrity endorsements (by an appropriate celebrity) are properly included: this part of the business case is a sales document, and the top managers who are being asked to support the case need to feel that the innovation is something that they personally, as well as the corporation, should be happy to be associated with.

The marketing plan overview in the business case should be no longer than needed to prove that there is a marketing plan and that some faith can be put in the marketing expense lines in the financial statements. As with the product itself, top executive input to the marketing plan can be sought while the business case is being put together. Collecting this input should not be allowed to confuse the evaluation process.

The product description and the marketing plan should state clearly the degree of market novelty involved:

▲ Is it a new product entering a new market?

▲ Is it a product proven elsewhere entering a new market?

▲ Is it a new product entering an established market currently dominated by this firm's competitors?

▲ Is it a new product entering an established market to replace other products supplied by this corporation?

▲ Is it a line extension?

▲ Does this proposal concern process or sourcing issues only, with no market impact intended?

The development plan

The definitive development plan will have been presented in the first part of the financial proposal, and so it is important that the descriptive material supporting the development plan is consistent with the proposed expenditure budget.

Technical details of the development proposal are not usually required, but strategic issues should be set out clearly:

▲ Is any key technology being bought in? From whom? What special conditions, such as royalties or distribution limitations, will apply?

▲ Will there be any partners involved in the development? How will they be rewarded? How will the intellectual property rights in the innovation be divided? Who will have ultimate management authority?

▲ What are the firm's competitors doing in this area? Do they hold any key patents or other rights? Will we gain any such rights?

▲ What is the degree of technological novelty?

❱ Does the proposal depend on scaling up laboratory results?

❱ Does the proposal depend on scaling up results obtained from a pilot plant?

❱ Does the proposal require adapting technology proven in other industries?

❱ Does the proposal only use proven technology?

Relationships and agreements with outside people and corporations that extend beyond sales and purchases are corporate strategy issues, and are therefore the exclusive prerogative of the top management of a company. When the corporation is listed on a stock exchange, such matters can be deemed material that should be disclosed to the stock exchange or listed in the corporation's annual reports. Any employee who sets up such relationships without top management endorsement is almost certain to be guilty of conduct warranting instant dismissal and possibly a suit for damages or a criminal prosecution as well.

Senior managers are the 'receivers' of the product champion's plan and, as in most sales situations, matters that are blindingly obvious to the sender can be dark and obscure to the receiver. There is no doubt that senior corporate managers kill many good ideas, and load those that they do approve with cumbersome reporting requirements. Sometimes good ideas are stifled out of incompetence or jealousy, and sometimes for good reasons that are never clearly explained to the champions. Every senior manager aborts many projects for each one that gets approved; a manager who stopped every proposal would do a lot less harm than a manager who approved them all.

Some degree of conflict between senior managers and product champions is inevitable, but as we described in Chapter 3, strategy is the prerogative of senior managers and lies outside the boundaries of an entrepreneurial business plan. In initiating and carrying through the many small and medium innovations that keep a corporation profitable, the senior manager's role is indirect. When the subject concerns major investments, relations with other corporations, or the endorsement of strategic technological directions, the senior manager's role is central and their prerogatives absolute.

End notes

1 Productivity is not simply a matter of working faster, although that happens. A major factor in increased productivity is that experienced employees make fewer errors, necessitating less rework and less spoilt material.

2 Professor Dan Jennings of Baylor University is an acknowledged expert in the field of corporate entrepreneurship. For an excellent commentary and overview series of readings on the field see, in particular, Jennings (1994), chs 11 to 14; see also Jennings and Munn (1994), and Jennings and Lumkin (1989).

3 This chapter concludes with the authors' suggestions on the proper preparation and presentation of a business case.

4 See MacMillan (1983). Here, MacMillan distinguishes the intrapreneur (operating under some form of corporate accounting system) and not having to face the same degree of personal financial risk from the entrepreneur who 'stands alone'. The authors of this book believe that being a product champion in a hostile corporate environment can be both lonely and risky. We use the term intrapreneur with the meaning of 'product or project champion for a new venture initiative within an established organisation'.

5 The best telling of the Michael Milken story is Bruck (1989).

6 An old but excellent treatment of a rational approach to futures trading is Teweles, Harlow and Stone (1977).

Case study two

HIsmelt Corporation
RTZ-CRA

The Rio Tinto Company was formed in London in 1873 to operate copper mines in Spain. Over the following years its operations spread to Canada, South Africa and Australia. The Zinc Corporation was founded in Melbourne in 1905 to operate at Broken Hill, and it operated there and elsewhere until 1949, when the company, Consolidated Zinc, was formed by the merger of The Zinc Corporation and Imperial Smelting.

In 1962 the Rio Tinto Company purchased a major share of Consolidated Zinc, changing its name to Rio Tinto Zinc, and in due course to The RTZ Corporation plc, while the Australian company became known as Con Zinc Rio Tinto, and in due course CRA Limited. In 1995 CRA and RTZ merged to become RTZ-CRA, the world's largest mining group, with annual sales for 1995 just under US$10 billion.

The sales revenue in 1995 was sufficient to support over 50 000 employees around the world, mining and producing copper, gold, iron ore, aluminium, coal, borates, titanium dioxide, diamonds and other minerals and mineral-based commodities. In addition, the group spent US$317 million on exploration and proving deposits, and US$120 million on research and development. In a company statement setting out the aims of the merged group the company said:

> *A key objective of the merger between RTZ and CRA is to provide a platform to maximise opportunities for the Group. RTZ-CRA's strategy is to focus on the mining industry, where the Group has a long-term competitive advantage. The Group will concentrate primarily on large, low-cost unit operations and continue to seek both geographic and product diversity.*

One of RTZ-CRA's many subsidiaries is HIsmelt Corporation Pty Ltd. In 1995 HIsmelt was fifteen years into a twenty-year, $200 million dollar project to revolutionise the way iron is made. How does this fit in with a 'focus on the mining industry'? Why was RTZ-CRA supporting it?

HIsmelt Corporation: Background
Steel politics

For a hundred years or so from 1860, iron and steel provided the sinews of war. The Yankees won the American Civil War because they had the factories to make guns and the railways to take them to the battles. In 1870, French power withered at Sedan under the blasts from 500 steel cannon made by Krupp. The

Royal Navy moved from wood to steel as the nineteenth century ended, and the 'wooden walls of England' were replaced by a fleet of Dreadnought class battle-ships. Germany's attempt to match the Royal Navy was one of the many factors contributing to the start of the First World War. The world wars were wars of steel; Germany was doomed in both by a sheer lack of manufacturing capacity for which no amount of allied ineptitude could compensate. The failure of the allied offensives in Flanders in 1916 was due, if anything, to too much firepower: the artillery barrages destroyed the drainage systems in this ancient farming area and turned no man's land into a sea of impenetrable mud.

The American response to the start of unrestricted submarine warfare in the Second World War was the liberty ship; welded steel ships built faster than the Germans could sink them. The decisive battle on the eastern front, and arguably of the war, was at Kursk in July 1943, where the Russians deployed two tanks for every German tank, and five guns for every German gun. The Korean War of 1949–53 was a war of tanks, ships and artillery, probably the last. In the Gulf war of 1991 the Iraqi side was equipped to fight a war of guns and tanks, but the western allies chose to fight with missiles and aircraft; the allied tanks only entered the battle when the Iraqi armour was destroyed.

The significance of steel in warfare was not lost among politicians. Nineteenth century America and Germany levied tariffs on steel imports in order to encourage their local steel industry. Josif Vissarionovich Dzhugashvili adopted the name Stalin — Steel — when he joined the Russian revolution, and his brutal purges and collectivisation programs of 1929–35 were claimed to be justified by the need to create a steel industry before Germany launched its revenge for 1918. When Imperial Russia entered the First World War in 1914 it was unable to provide all its soldiers with rifles, much less ammunition. In spite of huge losses during the first eighteen months of the German invasion of Russia during the Second World War, the Russians were able to produce far more tanks and guns than the Germans.

Australian politicians were also aware of the importance of steel. The Australian Commonwealth was formed in 1901 by federating the former colonies. At that time Australian opinion leaders thought and talked of their country as a British outpost, supplying the mother country with wool and min-erals and receiving manufactured products in return. The First World War caused something of a shock, as Australia continued to supply Britain with raw materials, 250 000 fighting men as well, and got almost nothing back. Even with no enemies active in the Pacific, the Australian economy needed steel if it was not to collapse, and the government frantically encouraged the growth of the nascent Australian steel industry at Newcastle, Port Kembla and Whyalla. At the end of the First World War the 1000-tonne steam hammer that had forged propeller shafts for the German fleet was carried back to Newcastle in repara-tions, where it was sometimes used as often as twice in a month.

The post-war Australian government encouraged the continued develop-ment of the Australian steel industry by placing an export ban on iron ore. The

South Australian mines yielded some of the world's purest iron ore, and the export ban ensured that it stayed cheap; since subsidising BHP would not have been good politics, it was put about that Australia's limited supplies of iron ore had to be reserved for strategic purposes. The Second World War led to an even more rapid and complete suspension of British exports to Australia. BHP's Chief Executive, Essington Lewis, was coopted as Director of War Production, and under his tireless direction Australia became all but self-sufficient in military production by the time the war was over. The iron ore export ban stayed in place after the war.

By the mid 1960s circumstances had begun to change. It had been known for many years that there was iron ore in the Pilbara region of Western Australia; it was becoming known just how much of it there was. The strategic fig leaf that justified the iron ore export ban became quite transparent. At the same time Japan had completed its recovery from the Second World War and had decided that supplying the world's markets was preferable to trying to conquer the world's countries. Japan needed industry, industry needed steel, and steel plants needed iron ore. Since Aboriginal Australians were not counted in those days, the Pilbara appeared to be totally empty, and no one was heard to object when CRA and BHP were permitted to develop huge export-oriented iron ore mines. There was, if anything, a sense of renewed Australian national pride at the scale and ambition of the mines and their transport operations.

The political obsession with steel had one sting left: the mining companies were required, at some unspecified future time, to undertake the development of an iron and steel industry in Western Australia, 'subject to technical and commercial feasibility'.

Steel making

Steel is one of the fundamental products of modern industrial society: about 750 million tonnes of it is produced worldwide every year. Steel is a refined form of iron, with each different grade and quality of steel representing a precise mixture of iron and certain other elements. Neither steel nor pure iron is found in nature, and all the steel that modern industrial economies need entered the economy as iron ore, a mixture of iron oxides and other iron compounds, and dirt. Iron ore is extraordinarily common on earth: in the Pilbara region of Western Australia alone there is 6000 billion tonnes of ore containing over 30 per cent iron.

Iron ore is not turned into steel without some trouble, and the discovery of iron-making in Africa and Asia during the second millennium before Christ was one of the decisive events in the development of civilisation. The basic chemistry of reducing iron ore did not change between then and 1980: carbon (once charcoal, now usually coke) is mixed with the iron and the mixture heated in the presence of calcium carbonate, usually in the form of limestone. If the temperature is high enough the carbon pulls oxygen atoms off the iron oxide, producing iron and carbon monoxide but absorbing some of the heat. Burning the carbon monoxide, and excess coal or charcoal, replaces the lost heat. The calcium carbonate reacts with the dirt to turn into a glassy material called slag. The slag floats on the molten iron and so separates the dirt from it.

The earliest iron makers built a cone-shaped brick or stone furnace a couple of metres high, loading it with charcoal, iron ore and limestone as they built it, firing it, and demolishing it to recover a lump of re-solidified iron from it after the fire had burned out. Modern integrated steel mills now reduce iron ore in blast furnaces 40 metres or more high, with the charge going in more or less continuously at the top and iron and slag being drawn off at the bottom. A single blast furnace can produce 4 million tonnes or more of crude iron per year. Blast furnaces use coke instead of charcoal, and so are usually associated with huge batteries of coke ovens, in which 'coking' coal is heated producing gas, bitumen and coke. The gas is then used to provide heat to the rest of the steel mill and the bitumen and tar is sold.

The iron recovered from the ore in a blast furnace, whether modern or traditional, is brittle and full of impurities, and another stage is needed to turn it into steel. Until the late eighteenth century this was done by blacksmiths beating red-hot iron on an anvil, bending it double, and beating it again. The impurities were gradually worked out as the process was repeated and a strong, tough material was left, suitable to make swords, and armour for the rich, but the process was too labour intensive and the result too costly for steel to be a widely used industrial material. Early cannons fired stone balls; iron was so expensive that iron cannon balls would have been worth more to the recipients than the cost of any damage that their arrival could have caused.

Blast furnaces are not very flexible. They only work with iron ore of an appropriate shape and consistency, and they don't produce useful iron if there are too many impurities, or impurities of the wrong kind, in the ore. Geologists are aware of vast deposits of iron ore with a respectable iron content, but with the wrong physical structure, or the wrong contaminants, for use in a blast furnace. Crumbly or powdered iron ore 'fines' can be sintered into pellets for use in blast furnaces, an expensive step, but one that is increasingly necessary as the deposits of 'ground to furnace' ore are worked out. Many deposits can't be used in blast furnaces at all: some contain unsuitable contaminants, while in others the iron compounds can't be reduced in blast furnaces. The iron from such ores can be retrieved in a laboratory, but there are no commercial plants operating that make use of it.

During the nineteenth century several methods were developed to make steel in industrial quantities, all based upon using hot air to burn off the excess carbon. By the end of the century the leading method was the Siemens-Martin 'open hearth', a huge brick frying pan in which a hundred or more tonnes of molten crude iron, mixed with steel scrap, was cooked under a blast of hot gas for ten or so hours. From the late 1950s, open hearth technology was progressively superseded by the basic oxygen converter, in which 50 to 100 tonnes of molten crude iron is subjected to a blast of pure oxygen, converting the contents to steel in a matter of minutes. Significantly, only a small proportion of scrap is needed by the basic oxygen process, and so the price of scrap fell and quantities began to build up.

Scrap steel is generally contaminated with a certain amount of rust and rubbish, but it is much purer than iron ore, and so it can be remade into new steel in a relatively simple electric arc furnace. When an electric arc furnace is combined with a continuous casting machine, the result is a 'mini-mill', a steel plant producing a few hundred thousand tonnes of steel a year and, where cheap electricity and ample supplies of scrap are available, producing it much cheaper than the virgin steel coming out of integrated steel mills. An electric arc furnace cannot remove many of the possible contaminants, and so the quality of the steel from a mini-mill is constrained by the quality of the scrap. Early mini-mills were limited to the production of reinforcing rods and light structural members, but modern mini-mills, by careful attention to the quality of the scrap and by other means, can produce steel of practically any grade.

By the mid 1990s the scrap metal mountain created by the move from open hearth to basic oxygen in the integrated mills had been largely consumed, particularly the more desirable grades, and the price advantage of the mini-mills was eroding. There were, however, few new integrated steel mills being built, and some of the established ones, like BHP at Newcastle, were planned to be converted to mini-mills and their blast furnaces demolished. Integrated steel mills are enormous, hugely expensive and not very good neighbours; new proposals have to surmount formidable financial and environmental hurdles. In a world of mini-mills, however, there must still be some source of virgin iron.

CRA Group Executive, John Innes, the original champion of the HIsmelt project, saw three major marketing opportunities in the iron ore processing business:

▲ Economic nationalism is by no means limited to Western Australia, and many developing countries would take steps to establish their own steel industries, but most of them would not have a home market big enough to support a modern integrated mill. New technology might reduce the minimum efficient scale of a steel plant, bringing the cost and scale to levels appropriate to developing countries.

▲ The shortage of high grade scrap, and the lack of new integrated steel mill capacity planned or under construction, means that there will be increasing shortages of virgin iron and the price is expected to rise while much investment in mini-mills risks being stranded if a suitable alternative to scrap iron cannot be provided.

▲ RTZ-CRA, HIsmelt's parent corporation, has mining rights over large iron ore deposits which are currently worthless because the iron or the ore is unsuitable for blast furnace processing.

HIsmelt: Early moves

In 1969 many people thought that the agreement to 'establish a steel industry in Western Australia' was a dead letter even as it was signed. BHP established a small rolling mill, subsequently closed, while CRA made few open moves at all. The whole Australian market absorbed a little under 4 million tonnes of steel, and was amply supplied by BHP's integrated mills at Newcastle and Port Kembla. The minimum efficient scale for a new integrated steel mill was 3.5 million tonnes per year, and it was hard to imagine a new mill in Western Australia paying its direct operating costs, much less offering a return to its shareholders.

The mini-mill concept had been developed and the first plants were operating in Italy, but the Basic Oxygen Converter was only slowly displacing the open hearth, and no one foresaw the impending scrap crisis or the loss of profitability among the integrated steel makers. The long economic boom from the end of the Second World War was still running, Singapore was looking surprisingly affluent for a third world country, and petrol was under 10 cents per litre in Melbourne. China had barely survived the Great Leap Forward only to plunge into the Cultural Revolution; the north was clearly going to win the Vietnam War and institute a socialist economic model. Over all, the world did not look very different in 1969 from its appearance ten or even twenty years earlier.

J. A. Innes, who began work with BHP and became an executive of CRA Ltd, tried, in 1969, to describe his view of the future in a paper he delivered to the British Iron and Steel Institute. Innes looked at two aspects of the steel industry. One was technical: the blast furnace and coke oven were scaled up technology from two millennia before Christ: they required high grades of ore and much of that had to be pre-processed. The other was political: Innes did not think that the countries, mainly in the third world, where suitable ore bodies were being worked, would be satisfied forever with supplying raw materials for someone else to process: like Western Australia, they would want a steel industry of their own.

Innes suggested, some years ahead of his time, that 'small country' steel plants would use electric arc furnaces and process a mixture of scrap and '… metallised material of 90–95% Fe [iron] content …'.

CRA, having been involved during the 1960s in investigating the use of direct reduced iron in electric arc furnaces, kept a watching brief on iron reduction and steel making technology. In the late 1970s their interest was again aroused by the development of a new generation of steel-making processes in Germany. CRA formed an alliance with Klöckner Werke, a German steel producer, to build an experimental direct smelting plant, and a pilot plant of 10 000 tonnes per year capacity was commissioned in 1984 and operated for the next six years. By the end of the 1980s Klöckner Werke was faced with the need to undertake a major restructuring of its business activities. It indicated that it would not be participating actively in the HIsmelt project in the future.

By 1990 large deposits of natural gas were being tapped on the North West Shelf off Western Australia. Natural gas can be broken down by steam into hydrogen and carbon monoxide: hydrogen is an even more effective reductant than carbon. Ore processed by the hydrogen method is 'direct reduced' rather than 'direct smelted'; all the dirt is still there. If direct reduced material is to be used in quality steel making either a very high grade ore must be used or the ore must be pre-treated to remove impurities. Natural gas is also relatively expensive and its price fluctuates, tending to follow the price of oil. Most of the natural gas extracted from the North West Shelf is liquefied and sold to Japan and other countries at a relatively high price, and only the excess is available cheaply to iron ore reducing plants.

Coal is, however, abundant and cheap, and CRA control large deposits of it. The HIsmelt system uses coal, and so is a 'smelting' system. Clay, soil and many other contaminants are removed with the slag and no prior refining is needed for common sources of iron ore: for these and other reasons CRA believed that smelting could compete with direct reduction. In 1990 CRA was able to draw up a table of direct smelting technologies that were then under active development.

HIsmelt was, in 1990, clearly a potentially attractive form of direct smelting technology, using less coal than its rivals and requiring no oxygen plant; on the other hand, CRA's partner in HIsmelt was pulling out and the process had only been operated on a large laboratory scale and would have to be scaled up by a factor of fifty to be genuinely commercial. Perhaps ten years work, including

Method	Ore requirements	Coal requirements	Blast gas
COREX C2000	Lump or pelletised	Lump, 1000 kg/t	Oxygen
DIOS	Fines	Lump and fines, 900 kg/t	Oxygen
HIsmelt	Fines	Fines, 700 kg/t	Hot air

the building of a 100 000 tonne per year pilot plant and a 500 000 tonne per year commercial prototype would be needed to prove commercial feasibility and bring CRA and HIsmelt to the point that they could begin seeking commercial returns. BHP was showing every sign of going for a gas-based direct reduction plant (as they confirmed in 1995).

HIsmelt: Battling on

Midrex Corporation of the USA was invited to replace Klöckner Werke in 1989, and work commenced on a scaled up pilot project at Kwinana, WA. This scaled up pilot, or pre-commercial, plant was intended to be capable of producing direct smelted iron at a rate of 100 000 tonnes per year, about a fifth of the output of the ultimate commercial plant.

Numerous technical problems occurred and were duly solved, but in 1994, nature intervened in the form of the Kobe earthquake. Kobe Steel was Midrex's parent, and in September 1994 they reluctantly advised CRA that they could commit no further funds to the project. CRA picked up the difference, and as at the end of 1995 CRA was the sole source of funds for HIsmelt Corporation, although they had an impressive array of research institutions assisting with the scientific side of the project.

By October 1993 the Kwinana plant had been fired up and produced iron, but for the next year and a half progress was disappointingly slow. Things began to look up during 1995, and fourteen days of continuous operation were achieved. The refractory lining of the reaction vessel continued to erode, but not as rapidly as in the previous year, and the erosion was sufficiently localised to give hope of reducing it substantially by minor configuration changes.

HIsmelt Corporation set itself the following immediate goals:

▲ eliminate the remaining process problems in the pilot plant

▲ prove the commercial viability of the process by the end of 1997

▲ put the first commercial plant into service early in the following decade.

As at 1995, CRA and HIsmelt could look at the world's steel industry and make certain projections.

▲ World steel production in 1995 was 750 million tonnes, rising at less than 1 per cent per year:

  ▶ 60 per cent was virgin steel produced by the blast furnace/basic oxygen converter route

  ▶ 31 per cent was resmelted steel produced in electric arc furnaces

  ▶ 4 per cent was virgin steel produced from direct reduced iron in electric arc furnaces

- ▶ 5 per cent was virgin/resmelted steel produced by the blast furnace/open hearth route, mainly in obsolescent plants in Eastern Europe with a projected life of no more than five years.

- ▲ CRA was mining over 50 million tonnes per year of iron ore and exporting 27 million tonnes per year of coal, all sold at the world commodity price (fines US$15/tonne FOB Western Australia for iron ore 62.5 per cent Fe, US$40/tonne FOB Queensland for steaming coal).

- ▲ By 2005, Pacific Rim countries will be producing at least 30 million tonnes of high grade (flat) steel products in mini-mills per year (up from trivial today):
  - ▶ this will require 35 million tonnes of high-metallic input
  - ▶ at least 25 million tonnes of this must be high-grade scrap or other low-impurity iron source
  - ▶ high grade scrap will rise in price to over US$190/tonne where it can be obtained at all, as many of the developed countries will supply more of their requirements from mini-mills and decommission some of their blast furnaces
  - ▶ world production of direct reduced iron was 27.4 million tonnes in 1994 of which no more than 20 per cent was traded, and most of this was produced by gas-based processes with their vulnerability to the world oil and gas markets and their restricted ore grades.

- ▲ Projected details of a commercial HIsmelt plant are:
  - ▶ capital costs US$200 per tonne of annual capacity (compare a new blast furnace at US$400 per tonne with coke ovens extra)
  - ▶ coal consumed 700 kilogram per tonne of iron produced
  - ▶ the HIsmelt product can be cast and sold as cold pig iron, or fed liquid to an electric arc furnace or a basic oxygen converter for conversion into steel of practically any grade
  - ▶ a HIsmelt plant will be compact and environmentally friendly.

Late in 1995 CRA and HIsmelt were still looking for a steel-making partner, and it is not likely to be BHP. The merger of CRA with RTZ to form RTZ-CRA has reduced the urgency of the search somewhat, as the combined group has the resources to support HIsmelt for an extended period should it choose to do so. HIsmelt, with or without a partner, is looking at four further years development and construction work, a total additional expense of well over $100 million before any positive cash flow starts in the years after 2000.

Chapter 14

The entrepreneurial financial model

Overview[1]

The key word is 'vital'

When a potential investor or other likely stakeholder picks up a business plan and reads it, the final point of their examination, the 'bottom line', is almost always going to be the financial statements, where the future performance of the business is

> *Your financial model must live and move with the times ...*

projected. A useful business plan must include an integrated suite of projected financial statements — known as 'pro-forma' statements — which are generated by an entrepreneurial financial model. The central feature of a good model is its ability to live.

In the prehistoric days before the widespread availability of personal computers, before 1985 or so, the financial projections were merely a static typed table of figures that could not be adjusted without completely re-typing them. This was a great constraint when an investor or part of the venture's management team wanted to explore some alternative possibilities. Everything had to be re-forecast from scratch. Modern PC-based models, when properly constructed, have a living capacity to produce changed results almost immediately after the inputs are changed. A vital entrepreneurial financial model must be capable of predicting the financial consequences of an unlimited number of alternative assumptions and revisions of data.

A dead set of figures has no role to play in creating or managing an entrepreneurial venture. The entrepreneurial business plan and the financial section of it, in which the results from using the entrepreneurial financial model are summarised, is not a 'report' in the sense of being just a record of a particular point of view at a particular time. It is a dynamic tool of practical management and must have the capacity to answer all kinds of interrelated 'what if' and 'what now' questions from all manner of readers of the plan. For instance, what if the material costs used in the original business plan rose by 2 per cent? What affect would this have on profitability? What if we were able to double the level of sales? Could we finance the working capital to support the higher throughput? Would we need new capital investments to support higher output levels? If so, how should these investments be funded? Should we seek to sell some equity or should we seek to borrow the funds? If we did borrow the funds, would the interest payments upon them be so high that the new level of business reduced profits? And so it goes. One question leads to another.

The generation of integrated pro-forma statements

Every business plan must include what accountants call 'pro-forma financial statements'. When the venture moves from plan to reality real figures will progressively replace the projected ones, and the plan will serve to show the entrepreneurial team the financial consequences of any deviations from the plan and allow them to plan their responses. At a minimum, three financial statements must be produced. They are:

▲ the income statement

▲ the cash flow statement, and

▲ the balance sheet.

The number of such statements that should be produced and the time period that they cover will depend on the planning horizon of the particular venture and the degree of detail which it is appropriate to convey. Suppose that the planning horizon is five years. It would be usual to project an income statement, a cash flow statement and a balance sheet for each of the first twelve months, to consolidate those monthly statements into an annual income statement, cash flow statement and balance sheet projection and then to produce annual statements for each of the next four years. Altogether, this makes seventeen statements *times* three, which *equals* fifty-four statements: a great deal of financial information.

Chapter overview

The method outlined in this chapter is based largely on the consulting experience of one of the authors, and has served him and his clients well through many years. Other approaches by other people may be as good: someone with a methodology with which they are comfortable and which produces satisfactory results does not have to change to this one to be called an entrepreneur. The most important thing is to have a well ordered, logical and comprehensive system for creating the financial model and producing the pro-forma financial statements. For people with extensive experience, the precise methods will become a very personal matter. What can never disappear, however, is the need for a systematic approach. We suggest that the one contained in this text book is simple, forthright and comprehensive. It will serve you well until your own experience enables you to enhance it.

The major sections are organised as follows:

▲ First, we introduce the basis of all financial projections: a beginning balance sheet.

From then on we will move through each of the major sections of a complete financial statement, the balance sheet, the cash flow statement and the income (profit and loss, or P&L, in American-speak) statement. In each case we start with the result and show how it can be developed in a systematic way.

▲ Next, we will look at what is needed in a set of projected income statements. We will make some general points about projected statement building and produce two examples of completed income statements for a hypothetical company, *ExampleCo*.

▲ Then we will put and answer the questions: How do we get there? What are the key steps to income statement projection? And while following the steps by which ExampleCo's income statements were produced we will demonstrate a systematic route which readers can use to prepare their own income statements.

Two sections of the chapter will, in like manner, explain the cash flow statement and a further two sections will explain balance sheets. In each case the first step will be to state what is required of the set of statements and the second step will be to show how to meet those requirements: an outline of the key steps which culminate in production of the cash flow statement and balance sheet.

▲ Finally, we conclude the chapter by describing some of the many uses to which the financial model can be put once it has been built. An entrepreneur who can produce an integrated suite of pro-forma financial statements is in a position to apply the power of simulation to manage variance and change once the business is running; as well as investigating the financial implications of a host of alternative strategies and scenarios while developing the plan.

What the chapter will not do

This chapter is not an introductory text setting out fundamental accounting principles or spreadsheet construction skills. We will assume that those who intend to create an entrepreneurial financial model already possess a basic knowledge of double entry book keeping and the production, structure and uses of financial statements, as well as the capacity to use an electronic spreadsheet, such as Microsoft Excel, Lotus 123 or Multiplan, at a basic level of operation. It is unreasonable to expect anyone to be able to produce an integrated pro-forma suite of financial statements — the core of the financial model and the heart of an entrepreneurial business plan — if they do not have a basic understanding of spreadsheet construction and accountancy. These are fundamental business skills, whether one is dealing with new or established ventures.

Readers without a good grounding in the basic principles of accounting may find this chapter heavy going. It is impossible to prepare a successful business plan without a good set of accounts, so budding entrepreneurs can plough on or skip the chapter and ensure that they have a good, entrepreneurially oriented accountant on their team.[2]

Introducing everybody's business: ExampleCo

The first rule of business planning and plan evaluation is that every business is different. This is a truism, but it still creates problems for a writer setting out the general principles of financial model creation. As a compromise between simply stating general principles with no illustration and providing so many illustrations that they become overwhelming, we are going to use data and format designs of a stylised business — ExampleCo — for illustrative purposes. The exact values of the data contained in the subsidiary schedules and financial statements projected for ExampleCo obviously do not matter. What does matter is that the examples draw out the general principles of model design and statement creation which can then be applied in a wide variety of situations.

With this emphasis in mind, let's make the acquaintance of ExampleCo.

The importance of a value-adding perspective

ExampleCo is a deliberately stylised and artificial creation, chosen to illustrate the importance of a value-adding perspective when it comes to building the entrepreneurial financial model for any business. Very simply, value-adding is the process of taking something acquired from somebody else — which may be called raw materials, but in practice may be components, semi-finished or finished goods, or for a professional service company, nothing at all — performing some of the firm's own processing upon it, and then selling the result for more than the combined cost of the inputs and the processing.

ExampleCo is involved in three major areas of income-producing activity. It manufactures Widgets; it gets a royalty stream for an invention called the Fidget; and it also retails Gidgets. The traditional approach used in most accounting text books is to split the process of setting out fundamental accounting principles by first describing how to prepare accounts for a service business (the simplest form of organisation and trading), then describing how to prepare accounts for a retail business (more complicated), and finally, teaching how to prepare accounts for a manufacturing enterprise (the most complex). We believe that by thinking of all businesses as value-adders it is possible to approach the task of projecting the financial future of any business in the same way. There is no need for a three-way split.

ExampleCo will illustrate the flexibility that flows from a value-added approach to financial statement modelling. It is important that, despite its artificiality, readers take ExampleCo seriously.

A beginning balance sheet

Lots of design options – but simple is often best

We ask readers to take a careful look at Table 14.1. It is the balance sheet for ExampleCo Pty Ltd as at 30 June 1996. As with every other illustration in this chapter, the specific figure for any amount is relatively unimportant. What the reader should be looking for in this and all other ExampleCo statement illustrations are the important general points that apply to the creation and design of all entrepreneurial financial models.

There are many ways of setting out a balance sheet. One of the best is also the simplest. The basis of all company accounting is that shareholders' funds are equal to assets minus liabilities and that's the format that ExampleCo has chosen to use for its balance sheet prior to creating its financial projections.

Information design principles: Equity

Equity — also known as shareholders' funds — is comprised of three items. One is the capital subscribed, otherwise known as the issued capital. This is the amount of shares that are outstanding. It is the equity that shareholders have actually put in to the business. Next come reserves. When you see any account labelled reserve, or special reserve as part of shareholders' funds, what you are looking at is the fact that some capital or some retained earnings have been allocated to special purposes. The third element of shareholder's funds, retained earnings (which the British call 'profit and loss appropriations') are simply the bringing forward of periodic profit or losses onto the balance sheet. Quite clearly, with nearly $10 million of negative retained earnings, ExampleCo is a company which has been undergoing losses for quite some time. As we will see shortly, the only good thing pertaining to past losses is the fact that they can be used as present and future tax credits. The company will not be liable to pay any company income tax until such time as its retained earnings exceed zero.

Table 14.1   The beginning balance sheet

Projected balance sheet at June 30, 1996

SHAREHOLDERS' FUNDS	
Capital Subscribed	16 548 068
General Reserve	
Retained Earnings	(9 746 368)
TOTAL EQUITY	6 801 700
ASSETS	
Current Assets:	
Cash and Short Term Deposits	
Accounts Receivable	
Materials Inventory	90 375
Other Current Assets	
Total Current Assets	90 375
Fixed Assets:	
Plant at WDV	765 025
Non-Plant at WDV	65 576
Land and Buildings	5 804 582
Other Fixed Assets	76 142
Total Fixed Assets @ WDV	6 711 325
TOTAL ASSETS	6 801 700
LIABILITIES	
Current Liabilities:	
Accounts Payable	
Short Term Loans	
Accrued Income Tax	
Other Current Liabilities	
Total Current Liabilities	
Long Term Liabilities:	
Long Term Loans	
Other Long Term Liabilities	
Total Long Term Liabilities	
TOTAL LIABILITIES	
NET ASSETS	6 801 700

Information design principles: Assets

Moving to the way the balance sheet design arranges ExampleCo's assets, we see that there are two main divisions: into current assets and fixed assets. This is standard, basic accounting practice. The company's current assets are cash and short term deposits, accounts receivable, materials inventory and a general account called 'other current assets'. We note that the company will begin its trading year with no cash, no accounts receivable and no other current assets, but with just over $90 000 of materials on hand. The company lists four categories of fixed assets: plant at written down value (WDV); non-plant at written down value; land and buildings; and investments. The key general point is that in listing and recording the company's fixed assets one ought to distinguish plant, that is the productive equipment used in the fundamental value-adding processes of the company, from non-plant, such items as office equipment, furniture, motor vehicles used by administrative staff, etc, that is to say equipment that is a fixed cost of doing business, the expenses of which, particularly depreciation, will be recorded below the gross margin line.

Information design principles: Liabilities

ExampleCo's liabilities are divided into two major areas, current and long term. The company lists accounts payable, short term loans, income tax and a general 'other' category. Its long term liabilities are 'long term loans' and 'other long term liabilities'. In this case the initial balance sheet shows that the company has no liabilities.

So it balances? So what?

As a necessity, net assets are exactly equal to shareholders' funds. This balance is absolutely fundamental and springs from the core accounting equation. It gives the balance sheet its name. It gives the statement reader a lot of valuable information. It also serves as a check on the construction of the spreadsheet. If the balance sheet doesn't balance, there is an error in the accounts, and accounting errors are like snags in pantihose: they run if they are neglected. A $1 misbalance today can explode into an error involving the loss or misappropriation of thousands, or millions, of dollars in just one or two accounting periods if it is neglected.

The reader should pause a moment to look at Table 14.1 again and consider what position a company with this sort of balance sheet is in.

ExampleCo's balance sheet looks like that of a company that has just been acquired or that has moved into the hands of new management. The lack of liabilities suggests a company starting a new business period with a clean slate, but obviously it is a company with a trading history and a pretty poor trading history at that, judging by the negative retained earnings. ExampleCo may well be a case of a failed business acquired by new management in the hope of turning it around and trading successfully in future. Maybe that's why they're so keen to build the financial model which we will see emerge in subsequent sections of this chapter!

Not all entrepreneurial planning concerns brand new ventures. Entrepreneurial financial planning is important in turnarounds and indeed for every established venture with a vision for the future that requires the careful management of projected rapid growth. The major general point illustrated in ExampleCo's beginning balance sheet is that the basis of any projected proforma financial statements for any business must be the balance sheet of the company's affairs immediately prior to the projection period.

ExampleCo is about to project its financial affairs over the next five years. The pro-forma financial statements it is about to produce will form an integrated network of financial information, extremely useful to managers and of vital importance to potential investors in the company. So it is with all businesses contemplating an entrepreneurial future.

The first set of projected statements: Income statements

Some general points

There are so many ways of projecting income and the costs associated with earnings that to try to classify all possible approaches would be an impossible task. The classic technique for a well established business that is using past history as a guide to future performance is the so-called 'percentage of sales' method. This technique, about which there is plenty of information in almost all basic accounting and financial text books, relies on the establishment of gross income forecasts, usually based on past history, as the fundamental building block. Almost all other figures in the income statement are then projected as a percentage of sales. Thus direct labour might be x per cent of sales, materials might be y per cent of sales and so on. The main strength of this system is its simplicity. The many weaknesses are obvious. Most importantly for an entrepreneurial business planner, contemplating new and different activities, there may be no history of past sales and associated costs on which to base either the forecasts in the first place or the percentage of sales for other income statement items.

Chapter 8 of this book provided readers with a far better base for the important forecasts associated with an income statement than simple percentage projections. A new venture succeeds or fails in the market; the models described in Chapter 8 reflect this and the market is the only reasonable place to start developing a financial income model. To be credible, revenue forecasts have to be market-based, well documented and supported by evidence that will stand the scrutiny of a careful, critical reader of the business plan. The same holds true for every other line item in the income statement and all of the other schedules and statements that this chapter deals with. In this chapter we describe a system for the generation and presentation of figures useful to an entrepreneurial venture, not the derivation of those figures. Chapter 8 presents a thoroughly researched technique for generating sales forecasts, but there may be cases where that technique is not appropriate and in every case there are alternatives. In this chapter we assume that the sales forecasts are available, and present some sound general principles for arranging and presenting those estimates in formats useful to the planner.

Let's take a look at Table 14.2, one possible layout of ExampleCo's finished set of projected income statements for the next five years before stepping back to

Table 14.2   *Income statement pro-forma in value-adding format*

Projected income statements – Five year period in Australian dollars

Notes		Year one 1996/97	Year two 1997/98	Year three 1998/99	Year four 1999/00	Year five 2000/01
	REVENUE					
1	Widget Revenue	4 471 220	5 743 013	6 249 918	8 110 475	9 306 629
1	Fidget Revenue	360 000	360 000	360 000	360 000	360 000
1	Gidget Revenue	158 000	166 000	170 000	174 000	174 000
1	Extraordinary Income					
2	Less Sales Tax					
	REVENUE less sales tax	4 989 220	6 269 013	6 779 918	8 644 475	9 840 629
	DIRECT COSTS OF INCOME EARNED					
3	Materials Used	233 470	272 636	284 668	353 117	391 524
4	Direct Labour	1 057 789	984 412	862 378	871 489	734 931
4	Overheads	84 581	80 481	68 153	65 623	50 198
4	Freight & Assoc. Costs	1 100 641	1 384 906	1 490 474	1 908 480	2 157 903
5	Production Rentals	26 947	28 294	29 709	31 194	32 754
	Total Direct Costs	2 503 428	2 750 729	2 735 382	3 229 903	3 367 310
	GROSS MARGIN	2 485 792	3 518 284	4 044 536	5 414 572	6 473 319
	GENERAL EXPENSES					
6	Marketing	128 573	135 973	146 841	158 660	171 518
7	Administration	276 615	284 610	304 970	327 267	351 737
8	Research & Development	120 000	132 000	145 200	159 720	
9	Depreciation Plant	123 740	144 129	154 716	164 244	172 820
10	Depreciation Non Plant	11 315	15 339	13 788	12 470	11 350
1	Bad Debts	9 978	12 538	13 560	17 289	19 681
1	Extraordinary Expenses					
	TOTAL Non Int. Exp.	550 221	712 588	765 875	825 131	886 825
	EBIT	1 935 571	2 805 696	3 278 661	4 589 441	5 586 494
	INTEREST EFFECTS					
11	ADD Interest Earned	56 648	90 066	240 357	439 681	666 449
12	LESS S/T Interest	7 000				
13	LESS L/T Interest	60 000				
	TAXABLE INCOME	1 925 219	2 895 762	3 519 018	5 029 122	6 252 943
14	INCOME TAX				1 304 191	2 251 059
	PROFIT AFTER TAX	1 925 219	2 895 762	3 519 018	3 724 931	4 001 883

break down the process of producing the finished income statement into its several steps.

Table 14.2 presents the finished income statement projections for ExampleCo's first five years. Consider the general format and layout of the statement. First of all there is a section on revenue, then there is a section on the direct cost of income earned which takes a reader down to what is called the gross margin line. Next comes a statement of general expenses. Notice that they are non-interest expenses and that they are classified by functional area: marketing, administration, research and development, and so on. When all these expenses are subtracted from the gross margin, we have a line known by its initials as EBIT (earnings before interest and tax). Next comes a section dealing with interest effects: additions for the interest which the business is projected to earn on its cash and short term security deposits followed by two interest subtractions. One is for the payments of short term interest that the business is projecting and the second is for estimated payments of long term interest.

When these interest effects are netted and subtracted from EBIT, the statement has arrived at the business's taxable income. It remains to subtract income tax at the projected corporate tax rate, remembering that the business is not liable to pay any income tax until it has used up all its tax credits; that is, until all negative retained earnings (accumulated losses) have been eliminated.

Notice in Table 14.2 that every significant line of the projected income statements carries a note, in this case presented as a number on the left hand side. These notes will and ought to be found at the end of the entire suite of financial statements. They will add further detail and explanation to each line item occurring in the income statement suite. Of course, in the context of an entrepreneurial business plan, the notes may well refer a reader back to sections of the plan rather than merely providing additional numerical information. For instance, a business plan will have a significant section on marketing. The relevant note may well point readers back in the direction of the marketing chapters and sections of the business plan where fully costed schedules and estimates of various expense categories and the reasons for them, were presented. The administration, research and development and, indeed, potentially for every other item in the projected set of income statements may refer to other sections of the business plan as well as, or instead of, a reference to the Notes to the Proforma Accounts.

In addition — as the examples in following section of this chapter demonstrate — all the aggregate numbers which get to be line items in the final income statement projections are supported by detailed subsections of the planner's spreadsheet and in sub-statements, the subsidiary schedules, in the notes. The next section of this chapter will describe some of the major subsidiary schedules that go into making up aggregate figures and therefore completing the entire income statement projection suite.

Break-even analyses

We have called the income statement format used in Table 14.2 a 'value-adding' format, for a very good reason. The layout clearly distinguishes between the main

> *The great virtue of a 'value-adding' statement design is that it facilitates break-even analyses at the level of the total business …*

functions of value-added: that is the direct or variable costs of income earned, as distinct from the fixed costs which the business would incur, whether it produced at the planned level, at some other level, or produced nothing at all. It is also important to distinguish non-interest expenses from interest expenses because the strategy and cost of financing a venture is quite a distinct matter from the actual operation of the venture. When costs are set out in the way that we see in Table 14.2, many calculations are immediately possible, the most important of which is an easy to conduct break-even and margin analysis.

We explain in Chapter 17 why potential investors want to look very carefully at the break-even analysis. Briefly, a break-even analysis enables the investor or other plan reviewer to determine how robust the planned business will be to variances in the level of sales. A supermarket, for example, has low fixed costs and high variable ones, and the plan for a new supermarket would not be thrown into confusion by one lost customer. An advertising agency or architect's office, by contrast, has negligible variable costs and high fixed ones: it can be thrown from strong profit into heavy loss by losing just one account.

In ExampleCo's case, we can see that the direct or variable costs of income earned include materials, direct labour, and direct overheads. Direct overheads will include such things as heat, light, and power associated peculiarly with production. In a furniture business, for example, overheads might include small items such as screws and glue and other items associated with the production of the main revenue earning item which it was unproductive to count individually. Variable cost lines, in the main or subsidiary schedules, will cover freight and associated costs, production rentals, repair and maintenance of machinery, and in some cases even the depreciation of plant.

It is a more usual accounting procedure to put all depreciation below the gross margin line, that is to say, the depreciation of plant would be listed in an account together with the depreciation of non-plant such as office equipment, etc. There is a growing trend, however, in financial circles — and it is particularly important for new ventures — to directly relate the usage of equipment to the income which it generates. Otherwise, quite a false picture of the gross margin can sometimes develop. The extreme case is when very expensive machinery wears out rapidly in service and must then be replaced rather than simply repaired. Another trend worth watching is the location of labour costs. Labour is a direct cost of production when the workers are paid piece rates, or are casual staff whose rosters can be changed on short notice. A firm that has built up a team of skilled and specialised workers will not wish to break it up because of a short term dip in revenue, and it can't increase it overnight to take up an opportunity, and so the ordinary-time wages, at least, may get moved below the line to sit alongside staff salaries. The mining house CRA has had, since the early 1990s, an active policy of replacing all wage employment by staff employment, and by implication, making all labour a fixed cost, below the gross margin line.

Two major problems can follow errors in calculating the gross margin. One is that the resilience of the business to unexpected revenue changes will be misunderstood. The other is that pricing and discounting policies will be unsoundly based.

Looking at general expenses, the key general point to note is functionality. Standard accounting procedures usually distinguish between so-called financial accounts (those used for external audiences of the venture such as the Tax Commissioner, shareholders and potential investors) and management accounts (those used to provide operational information to internal audiences). An entrepreneurial financial model and the projected statements it produces should seek to do both jobs with a minimum of duplication. It should be simultaneously useful to management and to its external users. Laying out the income statement in the value-adding format achieves this objective.

The naming of the aggregate lines and the item grouping in the income statement is also done for functional reasons. Anyone reading the ExampleCo income projections can see immediately the relative proportions that the company spends on marketing with respect to administration. They can see that, in its first year, it is spending nothing on research and development. An entirely different basis rules the design of a cash flow statement. The key issue there will be timing rather than function. 'When does the firm pay for things' becomes more important than 'what does the firm get paid for' in the cash flow statement.

Once the EBIT has been calculated, our anticipated interest effects can be incorporated and the statement will show a taxable income. Notice that in ExampleCo's case, it is showing taxable income of nearly $2 million in the first year, nearly $3 million in the second year and over $3.2 million in the third year without paying a cent of tax. ExampleCo started with a backlog of negative retained earnings which can be thought of as tax credits with which the business started. In ExampleCo's case new owners may have bought the business including its accumulated losses. New ventures may buy an entrepreneur's or inventor's business before it has earned any trading income, also creating negative retained earnings. Until such time as retained earnings become positive no income tax will be due, and the projected accounts should reflect this. In ExampleCo's case, tax is not projected to be payable until the fourth year of operation. Income tax will then be projected at the prevailing rate applicable in the economy and the country in which the business operates. Once tax (zero or positive — never negative!) is deducted we have a profit after tax.

The basic principle: Un-cluttered information provision

There are a couple of features of the presentation of an income statement (that apply equally well to what we will have to say about cash flow statements and balance sheets) that have nothing what so ever to do with figures or the logic that goes into producing figures. They are simply matters of good design and logical thinking.

For instance, it is highly desirable when presenting any information to any reader of anything not to overcrowd a page, to clutter it up and make it messy. A good policy for pro-forma financial statements is to make sure that the accounts and relationships that appear on the statements do not extend over a single page, usually an A4 or American quarto-sized page. It is most disconcerting to the reader of financial information to get, for example, halfway to the EBIT line only to have to turn over the page to pick up the thread. It is much more desirable to see the whole impact of each of the statements on one page.

The marketing expenditure account, for example, as we explain later in this chapter, is made up of many items. They are all listed in a subsidiary schedule and linked to the income statement by reference from the notes, or included in the 'Notes' section of the pro-forma accounts. They don't all get crammed onto the yearly income statements. Using statement notes and references to relevant sections of the full business plan, a reader of the statements is able to look up relevant subsidiary schedules and see in detail just what it is that justifies the aggregate figure for marketing. Imagine how crowded things would soon get if every item in the marketing subsidiary schedule were put on to the main income statement and the same thing were done for administration and the other summary lines. Where would one stop? For instance, would we have the expenditure for office stationery appearing or should there be a separate line for paperclips? By putting functional aggregates at the final statement level each reader can follow the notes to investigate areas of special concern without being buried in trivia along the way. It is quite possible to present a column for notes, a column listing the account names, and up to six columns containing figures representing, say, the first six months in monthly reports or five columns representing the five years of the five year projection on A4 or American quarto paper.

Personal design and layout preferences then come into play. We dislike the unnecessary replication of dollar signs in front of every figure. Equally, we feel that it is undesirable, unless one is dealing in billions of dollars (and very few businesses do that) to summarise figures to the nearest thousand. Every dollar counts. It is quite possible, as Table 14.2 shows, for an accurate presentation down to the nearest dollar to be accommodated in a layout comprising five or six columns and involving figures which run into the millions. If they are neatly presented, well laid out, and the entire statement is covered in no more than one page, this is a neat, clean, and useful mode of presentation.

Design for a variety of information needs

We now move from general principles of good design in information presentation to describing the flexibility which good entrepreneurial financial planning should permit.

Table 14.2 showed the income statement projections of ExampleCo in what we call 'value-added' format, whose main advantage, we have observed, is the clear distinction between fixed and variable costs and between interest and operational payments. Of course, many other possible layouts for projecting

Table 14.3 Income statement in merchandising format

Projected income statements – Five year period in Australian dollars

Notes		Year one 1996/97	Year two 1997/98	Year three 1998/99	Year four 1999/00	Year five 2000/01
	REVENUE					
1	Widget Revenue	4 471 220	5 743 013	6 249 918	8 110 475	9 306 629
1	Fidget Revenue	360 000	360 000	360 000	360 000	360 000
1	Gidget Revenue	158 000	166 000	170 000	174 000	174 000
1	Extraordinary Income					
2	Less Sales Tax					
	Revenue less sales tax	4 989 220	6 269 013	6 779 918	8 644 475	9 840 629
	COST OF GOODS SOLD					
	GOODS COMPONENT OF SALES					
	Mat. Inv. (beg. period)	90 375	46 905	73 170	141 619	160 450
	Mat. Purchases	190 000	298 901	353 117	371 948	394 265
	Total Inv. Available	280 375	345 806	426 287	513 567	554 715
	Mat. Inv. (end period)	46 905	73 170	141 619	160 450	163 191
3	Total Materials Used	233 470	272 636	284 668	353 117	391 524
	OTHER DIRECT SELLING COSTS					
4	Direct Labour	1 057 789	984 412	862 378	871 489	734 931
4	Overheads	84 581	80 481	68 153	65 623	50 198
4	Freight & Assoc. Costs	1 100 641	1 384 906	1 490 474	1 908 480	2 157 903
5	Production Rentals	26 947	28 294	29 709	31 194	32 754
	Total Other Direct Costs	2 269 958	2 478 093	2 450 714	2 876 786	2 975 786
	TOTAL C.O.G.S.	2 503 428	2 750 729	2 735 382	3 229 903	3 367 310
	GROSS MARGIN	2 485 792	3 518 284	4 044 536	5 414 572	6 473 319
	GENERAL EXPENSES					
6	Marketing	128 573	135 973	146 841	158 660	171 518
7	Administration	276 615	284 610	304 970	327 267	351 737
8	Research & Development		120 000	132 000	145 200	159 720
9	Depreciation Plant	123 740	144 129	154 716	164 244	172 820
10	Depreciation Non Plant	11 315	15 339	13 788	12 470	11 350
1	Bad Debts	9 978	12 538	13 560	17 289	19 681
1	Extraordinary Expenses					
	Total Non Int. Exp.	550 221	712 588	765 875	825 131	886 825
	EBIT	1 935 571	2 805 696	3 278 661	4 589 441	5 586 494
	INTEREST EFFECTS					
11	ADD Interest Earned	56 648	90 066	240 357	439 681	666 449
12	LESS S/T Interest	7 000				
13	LESS L/T Interest	60 000				
	TAXABLE INCOME	1 925 219	2 895 762	3 519 018	5 029 122	6 252 943
14	INCOME TAX				1 304 191	2 251 059
	PROFIT AFTER TAX	1 925 219	2 895 762	3 519 018	3 724 931	4 001 883

income statements are possible. One such alternative information-presentation format is the very often used and well recognised form of income statement, which we display here as Table 14.3.

Table 14.3 is what might be called a 'traditional retail' income statement layout, although it is derived from the same spreadsheet that produced Table 14.2. All the revenue items appear as they did in the 'value-added' format but from then down things are different. Instead of laying out the 'direct costs of income earned', the conceptual framework moves to 'cost of goods sold' and we notice that in this format the reader of the statement becomes very aware of just what has happened with the inventory of products which the business is selling. Since resale of inventory is the heart of retailing, this focus has clear merits. This form of ExampleCo's income statement projections also makes it clear, though, that materials or the physical goods that we sell are not the only component of cost of goods sold.

There will be direct labour. If the business were a retailer, such as a super-market chain, 'direct labour' might include blue collar employees in the ware-house and storerooms as well as checkout staff. There are overheads. There are freight and associated costs and there are other items which might be more pertinent to a retailer than to a manufacturer. Once the cost of goods sold is subtracted from the revenues, we again have gross margin and the statement then continues in the order of the previous format. Good entrepreneurial financial modelling, built from the ground up and well reported in spreadsheet format, is capable of a great degree of variety and flexibility in presentation.

How do we get there?

The key steps to income statement projection

Having seen two examples of what one might call the 'finished product', two completed, neatly presented versions of the same income statement, we now set out the steps needed to get there.

Subsidiary schedules and the power of modern spreadsheets

At the risk of being facile, the short answer to the question, how do we build up a complex set of pro-forma financial statements? is, by easy stages. This involves creating many subsidiary schedules, one or more for each line item in the aggregate income statement. The three great virtues of modern spreadsheet packages are:

▲ their ability to link with and combine data from many sources
▲ their ability to handle high volumes of data with ease

▲ their ability to recalculate the statements at high speed so that the numerical answers to a host of 'what if' questions can be seen almost instantly.

These are the three key virtues that an entrepreneurial financial model needs to have. Using spreadsheets, it becomes a relatively simple matter to take the output of one set of calculations and use them as the input to another table. Let's see how this power was employed to create ExampleCo's aggregate income statement projections and, in so doing, observe some general principles useful to the financial modelling of any entrepreneurial venture.

Using subsidiary schedules
Gross revenue
Table 14.4 is an example of a gross revenue projection schedule.

ExampleCo obviously has three major areas of activity which earn it revenue. They are Widget Operations, Fidget Operations and Gidget Operations. So, very simply, what the gross revenue subsidiary schedule does is to capture the projections for each operation and to aggregate them. The actual creation of a gross revenue schedule is a simple matter. The hard part comes in estimating the market's response to a new product or firm and that is a function of how good one's marketing research and modelling has been.

Table 14.4 *Revenue schedule*

Projected income (5 yr period) in A$

	Year one 1996/97	Year two 1997/98	Year three 1998/99	Year four 1999/00	Year five 2000/01
WIDGET OPERATIONS					
Widget Sales	4 471 220	5 743 013	6 249 918	8 110 475	9 306 629
Other Income					
WIDGET Subtotal	4 471 220	5 743 013	6 249 918	8 110 475	9 306 629
FIDGET OPERATIONS					
Fidget Royalties	360 000	360 000	360 000	360 000	360 000
Other Income					
FIDGET Subtotal	360 000	360 000	360 000	360 000	360 000
GIDGET OPERATIONS					
Gidget Sales	158 000	166 000	170 000	174 000	174 000
Other Income					
GIDGET Subtotal	158 000	166 000	170 000	174 000	174 000
GROSS INCOME	4 989 220	6 269 013	6 779 918	8 644 475	9 840 629

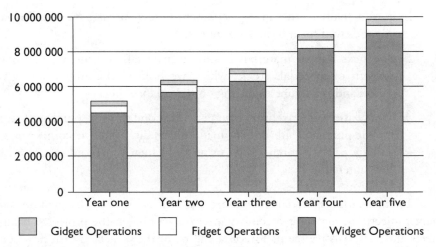

Figure 14.1 Gross revenue projection (graph)

Figure 14.1 shows a gross revenue projection graph. The golden rules for presenting financial information graphically are: keep it simple; and keep it clear. One can use bar charts, column charts, pie charts, line charts or any of the other alternatives in two or three dimensional presentations which are readily available and simple to use with modern spreadsheet packages. The main thing to avoid is confusing the reader of the financial information by overcrowding or over-complicating the chart. When in doubt, don't graph. Unless a graph clearly adds to the clarity of information presentation, you and — more importantly — your audience are better off without it.

The direct (or variable) costs of income earned

Materials

Materials can often be an area which causes confusion to the financial modeller. The key point to remember is that the financial treatment of materials has four distinct components:

> *The four faces of materials are usage, purchases, inventory and payments.*

▲ There is materials usage, that is, a dollar figure which records the volume of materials that goes into production to earn the revenue of the period. Materials usage is the figure that needs to be entered in the period's income statement.

▲ Then there are materials purchases. Purchases are the orders which the firm places with suppliers in a given period. Relatively few firms are able to purchase exactly the amount of materials they need when they need it;[3] purchases often support a safety stock. Usage is simply a function of the volume of activity. Materials purchases are very important but they don't actually feature in any statement unless one uses the retailing cost of goods sold form of income statement.

▲ The next face of materials is simply materials inventory. This is the amount of materials stocks which we hold at the end of any given period and is a figure appearing on the balance sheet.

▲ Finally, there are inventory payments. It is one thing to purchase materials but purchases are usually made on credit. When it comes time to actually pay for purchases by using cash, then we record this in a cash flow statement.

To summarise, materials usage forecasts will be used in the income statement projections, materials inventory forecasts will be on the projected balance sheets and materials payments forecasts will be in the projected cash flow statements. Materials purchases may never appear on any of these statements at all unless the cost of goods sold income statement format is used. The relationships between the 'four faces' of materials are illustrated in Table 14.5.

The schedule is straightforward. The first line lists the materials inventory at the beginning of the period, the next line is the estimate of materials purchases which will be made. Adding these two together gives the total inventory available. The next figure is the estimate for materials to be used. This is the figure that will appear in the income statement. We obtain the inventory at the end by simply subtracting usage from the total availability. Materials payments is a separate line altogether and is simply a function of company policy and the relative bargaining position of the firm and its suppliers. For example, if we were to pay all creditors on terms of thirty days, then the figure for materials payments in any month would be equivalent to the materials purchases figure for the previous month. Since these are annual statements, the estimates that have been used in the ExampleCo case are simply one-twelfth of the previous year's purchases plus eleven-twelfths of this year's purchases.

Table 14.5 *The four faces of materials*

Materials usage, purchases, inventory & payments schedule

	Year one 1996/97	Year two 1997/98	Year three 1998/99	Year four 1999/00	Year five 2000/01
Mat. Inv. (beg. period)	90 375	46 905	73 170	141 619	160 450
Mat. Purchases	190 000	298 901	353 117	371 948	394 265
Total Inv. Available	280 375	345 806	426 287	513 567	554 715
Materials Used	233 470	272 636	284 668	353 117	391 524
Mat. Inv. (end period)	46 905	73 170	141 619	160 450	163 191
Materials Payments	190 000	273 993	348 599	370 379	392 405

Table 14.6   Primary non-material costs projection

	Year one 1996/97	Year two 1997/98	Year three 1998/99	Year four 1999/00	Year five 2000/01
DIRECT LABOUR					
Widget Wages	900 092	833 087	723 978	731 049	610 073
Gidget Wages	37 000	39 000	40 000	41 000	41 000
Bonuses					
Fringe Benefits Tax					
Payroll Tax	47 511	44 215	38 734	39 143	33 009
Staff Training					
Superannuation	35 328	32 878	28 802	29 106	24 545
Workers Comp.	37 859	35 232	30 865	31 191	26 303
Other on Costs					
LABOUR Subtotal	1 057 789	984 412	862 378	871 489	734 931
DIRECT OVERHEADS					
Widget Overheads	80 581	76 481	64 153	61 623	46 198
Gidget Overheads	4 000	4 000	4 000	4 000	4 000
DIR O/H Subtotal	84 581	80 481	68 153	65 623	50 198
FREIGHT & ASSOCIATED COSTS					
Domestic Freight	37 845	47 143	50 778	65 019	73 516
Export Freight	1 062 796	1 337 763	1 439 696	1 843 461	2 084 387
F&C Subtotal	1 100 641	1 384 906	1 490 474	1 908 480	2 157 903
TOTAL (non Mat Dir. Costs)	2 243 011	2 449 799	2 421 005	2 845 592	2 943 032

Labour, overheads freight etc

Table 14.6 shows the subsidiary schedules for direct labour, direct overheads, and freight and associated costs for ExampleCo. Wages for the two major wage-requiring activities are listed, together with a schedule for all associated on costs. These include bonuses, fringe benefits tax, payroll tax, staff training, superannuation, workers' compensation and a general category for other oncosts. So, the labour subtotal in the final income statement is the total of the wages paid to staff plus all of these oncosts. In ExampleCo's case, the company doesn't currently pay any bonuses or fringe benefits tax, neither does it have an allowance for staff training with respect to its direct labour workforce. However, it has made preparation for the subsequent introduction of these items by including them in the schedule.

The schedule also provides the company's annual estimates for direct overheads with respect to both of its operating areas and estimates for domestic and export freight costs associated with distributing its products.

Progress report: The income statement to the gross margin line

We now look at the results of combining the calculations of all subsidiary schedules so far. Figures appearing in the emerging income statement projections are

The entrepreneurial financial model

Table 14.7 *The income statement down to the gross margin line*

Projected income statements – Five year period in Australian dollars

Notes		Year one 1996/97	Year two 1997/98	Year three 1998/99	Year four 1999/00	Year five 2000/01
	REVENUE					
1	Widget Revenue	4 471 220	5 743 013	6 249 918	8 110 475	9 306 629
1	Fidget Revenue	360 000	360 000	360 000	360 000	360 000
1	Gidget Revenue	158 000	166 000	170 000	174 000	174 000
1	Extraordinary Income					
2	Less Sales Tax					
	Revenue less sales tax	4 989 220	6 269 013	6 779 918	8 644 475	9 840 629
	DIRECT COSTS OF INCOME EARNED					
3	Materials Used	233 470	272 636	284 668	353 117	391 524
4	Direct Labour	1 057 789	984 412	862 378	871 489	734 931
4	Overheads	84 581	80 481	68 153	65 623	50 198
4	Freight & Assoc. Costs	1 100 641	1 384 906	1 490 474	1 908 480	2 157 903
5	Production Rentals	26 947	28 294	29 709	31 194	32 754
	Total Direct Costs	2 503 428	2 750 729	2 735 382	3 229 903	3 367 310
	GROSS MARGIN	2 485 792	3 518 284	4 044 536	5 414 572	6 473 319

aggregates of the greater detail which is contained in the subsidiary schedules we have just encountered. When combined, these figures take the business down to the 'gross margin line', that is, where the statements present an estimate of its earnings from operations — the fundamental picture of the company's value-adding activities.

You can now clearly see the importance of the notes attached to the income statement projections. For materials used a reader will go to the 'Notes' and find a reproduction of the materials schedule as well as any necessary explanations. The reader can do this for most of the other line items in the statement. Each of the notes should include the relevant subsidiary schedule(s).

Fixed non-interest costs

The one thing that all items used above the gross margin line had in common was that they varied with the volume of production. This is why they are called direct costs or variable costs. They vary with the volume of activity and are therefore in direct proportion to that volume of activity. From now on the remaining non-interest expenses with which we will be dealing are deemed to be fixed costs. That is, they are costs which do not vary in direct proportion to the volume of activity we undertake. They are a fixed function of the business's basic capacity to produce or are fixed by company policy.

A quite important point must be made here. In the ExampleCo case, all marketing expenses, administration and research and development expenses are listed as below the gross margin line; they are treated as though they are fixed costs. If there were some marketing costs, for argument's sake, which varied with volume, then those costs ought to be recorded above the gross margin line. A good example of this type of non-fixed marketing expense might be dealers' or sales people's commissions directly tied to the volume of production and expected sales. If that were a significant line item and it was a variable cost, then it would be proper to record it above the gross margin line. For simplicity's sake, we have picked an example where all the company's marketing costs are deemed to be fixed, as are all their administration and R&D costs.

Assigning costs for accounting convenience can develop into an extremely bad habit, and managers of many firms, large and small, who slashed the marketing budget because it was an 'overhead' and watched amazed as the sales plummeted have learned, painfully. Bonuses, sales and promotional incentives, and commissions are logically a variable cost, and it can be argued that promotional expense generally, since it is directly related to the volume of new name business, is also variable. It could be counter-argued that, since promotional expenditure is intended to win customers who will then provide an ongoing expenditure stream, promotion should appear as a capital expense. The accounts of a business are just a model: the best image of the real world that time, effort, and the rules of accounting permit; but an image for all that. Facts are discovered in the real world, not by staring at spreadsheets. The world is changed by people going and working in it, not by putting different numbers into boxes.

We re-state the importance of distinguishing salaries and non-salary components of functional cost areas. Any marketing costs, for instance, that we incur in a given period — be it projected year one or projected month one or whenever — are going to have two components when viewed from the point of view of timing of payments. Marketing salaries will be paid in the same period in which they are incurred, whereas the non-salary marketing expenses will ordinarily be bought on credit and if our terms of payment to suppliers are net thirty days, we will not pay for the non-salary marketing expenses until the next month.

Tables 14.8 to 14.12 contain ExampleCo's projected subsidiary schedules of fixed non-interest costs. They are virtually self explanatory, illustrating as they do the two general principles which should dominate the modelling of fixed non-interest costs.

▲ First, observe the key distinctions between income statements and cash flow statements. For income statements, the key concept is 'functionality': to what distinct category does the expenditure belong — marketing, administration, R&D etc? For the cash flow statement the key concept 'is timing of payments': when will this item be paid for?

▲ Second, flowing from this key distinction in approach, it is vital to provide separate schedules of the salaries and non salaries components of each category of expenditure before re-combining them as a total figure.

Table 14.8 *Projected salary expense*

Projected salaries expenses (5 yr period) (non-direct labour)

	Year one 1996/97	Year two 1997/98	Year three 1998/99	Year four 1999/00	Year five 2000/01
MKTG SALARIES					
Salaries	50 000	50 000	52 500	55 125	57 881
Allowances					
Commissions					
Bonuses					
Fringe Benefits Tax	766	766	804	844	886
Payroll tax	1 325	1 325	1 391	1 461	1 534
Staff Training	750	750	788	827	868
Superannuation	1 500	1 500	1 575	1 654	1 736
Workers Comp.	232	232	244	256	269
Other on Costs					
MKTG SAL subtotal	54 573	54 573	57 301	60 166	63 175
ADMIN SALARIES					
Salaries	205 000	205 000	215 250	226 013	237 313
Allowances					
Bonuses					
Fringe benefits tax	2 706	2 706	2 841	2 983	3 133
Payroll tax	5 433	5 433	5 704	5 989	6 289
Staff training	3 075	3 075	3 229	3 390	3 560
Superannuation	6 150	6 150	6 458	6 780	7 119
Workers comp.	951	951	999	1 049	1 101
Other on costs					
ADM SAL subtotal	223 315	223 315	234 481	246 205	258 515
R & D SALARIES					
Salaries					
Allowances					
Bonuses					
Fringe benefits tax					
Payroll tax					
Staff training					
Superannuation					
Workers comp.					
Other on costs					
R&D subtotal					
TOTAL SALARIES	277 887	277 887	291 782	306 371	321 689

Notice in Table 14.8 that there is a completely blank section for R&D salaries. This indicates that ExampleCo, while not projecting any research and development salary expenses, is keeping the possibility open that some might occur in the future and has made allowance in the financial modelling for that

Table 14.9 *Payroll summary*

Summary payroll schedule (yearly)

	Year one 1996/97	Year two 1997/98	Year three 1998/99	Year four 1999/00	Year five 2000/01
Wages (direct labour)	1 057 789	984 412	862 378	871 489	734 931
Salaries & on costs	277 887	277 887	291 782	306 371	321 689
TOTAL PAYROLL	1 335 677	1 262 299	1 154 160	1 177 860	1 056 621

possibility. ExampleCo does project some non-salary R&D expense in Table 14.12: this may be money intended to be paid to third parties under the line items shown.

Notice that for each of the three major functional fixed expenditure categories — marketing, administration and R&D — the schedule contains a detailed list of all of the items that go to make up the oncosts associated with the salary. One of the biggest mistakes made by prospective entrepreneurs when they use broad-brush financial modelling is to estimate the raw salary and wages figure for a particular activity and forget about the many, onerous oncosts that are associated with it.

Table 14.9 is a very short but important subsidiary schedule: the payroll schedule. It produces the total figure for wages: direct labour (variable human resources costs) which have been shown above in Table 14.4 and salaries (fixed human resources costs) which are presented in Table 14.8. All entrepreneurs should plan their payroll schedules with great care because one week's failure to meet the payroll effectively means the demise of any business as a going concern.

Tables 14.10, 14.11 and 14.12 are the aggregate subsidiary schedules for marketing, administration and R&D. They list the company's projections for all non-salaried components and then add the previously calculated salaried aggregates to come up with a total figure for the period. Look back at the income statement and observe that the figure listed for marketing in the income statement is the total figure shown in Table 14.10. The administrative figure shown for any projected year in administrative expenses is the total figure shown in Table 14.11. The R&D figure for any given projected year is the total figure shown in Table 14.12. Shortly we will see that the separate salaries figures are aggregated in the cash flow statement.

Before we move on one point needs to be made strongly. If you follow — and we strongly suggest that you do — the concept that functional area is the best way to list costs which occur below the gross margin line, the planner might have to split up the salaries of particular personnel into various components. For argument's sake, suppose that the chief executive officer of a company had a $100 000 salary and spent 60 per cent of her time in marketing and 40 per cent in administration. Then from the point of view of recording the expenses in the income statement in a functional manner, $60 000 should be listed in the

The entrepreneurial financial model

Table 14.10 Marketing expense projection

Projected marketing expenses (5 yr period) in A$

	Year one 1996/97	Year two 1997/98	Year three 1998/99	Year four 1999/00	Year five 2000/01
Export Mkt Development	25 000	27 500	30 250	33 275	36 603
Trade Shows	3 000	3 300	3 630	3 993	4 392
Consultants					
Advertising	14 000	15 400	16 940	18 634	20 497
Public Relations	5 000	5 500	6 050	6 655	7 321
Telephone & Fax	20 000	22 000	24 200	26 620	29 282
Local Travel	4 000	4 400	4 840	5 324	5 856
Vehicle Costs	3 000	3 300	3 630	3 993	4 392
Non Sal Mktg Sub Tot	74 000	81 400	89 540	98 494	108 343
MKTG SAL. & ON COSTS	54 573	54 573	57 301	60 166	63 175
TOTAL	128 573	135 973	146 841	158 660	171 518

Table 14.11 Projected administration expense

Projected administrative expenses (5 yr period) in A$

	Year one 1996/97	Year two 1997/98	Year three 1998/99	Year four 1999/00	Year five 2000/01
Heat, Light, Power	8 800	10 120	11 638	13 384	15 391
Stationery & Off. Supplies	7 000	8 050	9 258	10 646	12 243
Telephone & Fax	5 000	5 750	6 613	7 604	8 745
Vehicle Costs	15 000	17 250	19 838	22 813	26 235
Staff & Visitor Amenities	6 500	7 475	8 596	9 886	11 369
Cleaning & Maintenance	4 000	4 600	5 290	6 084	6 996
Sundry Admin Costs	7 000	8 050	9 258	10 646	12 243
Non Sal Admin subtotal	53 300	61 295	70 489	81 063	93 222
ADMIN SAL. & ON COSTS	223 315	223 315	234 481	246 205	258 515
TOTAL	276 615	284 610	304 970	327 267	351 737

subsidiary schedule for marketing salaries expense and $40 000 in the administration area. A bit of thought will soon enable a competent planner to allocate proportions of various people's salaries to their proper categories. Failure to do so simply means that your financial modelling is less potent than it could be because you lose the capacity to analyse cost areas in functional ways.

Plant costs and depreciation

Table 14.13 shows ExampleCo's plant acquisition and depreciation schedule. The layout is straightforward. The schedule begins with a beginning written

Table 14.12 *Projected R&D expense*

Projected R&D expenses (5 yr period) in A$

	Year one 1996/97	Year two 1997/98	Year three 1998/99	Year four 1999/00	Year five 2000/01
Technology Development		60 000	66 000	72 600	79 860
Field Trials		42 000	46 200	50 820	55 902
Animal Husbandry		18 000	19 800	21 780	23 958
Non Sal R&D subtotal		120 000	132 000	145 200	159 720
R&D SAL. & ON COSTS					
TOTAL		120 000	132 000	145 200	159 720

Table 14.13 *Proposed plant and equipment expense*

Plant acquisition & depreciation schedule (yearly figures)

	Year one 1996/97	Year two 1997/98	Year three 1998/99	Year four 1999/00	Year five 2000/01
Beginning WDV	765 025	1 191 285	1 297 157	1 392 441	1 478 197
Plant Acquisitions	550 000	250 000	250 000	250 000	250 000
Asset Sales					
Depreciable Total	1 315 025	1 441 285	1 547 157	1 642 441	1 728 197
Depreciation	123 740	144 129	154 716	164 244	172 820
Ending WDV	1 191 285	1 297 157	1 392 441	1 478 197	1 555 377

down value for the period, then any estimates of plant acquisitions are written in, any asset sales will be subtracted until the company arrives at a depreciable total for its plant. The depreciation calculation follows. When the depreciation is taken away from the depreciable total we reach an ending written down value. This is the figure which will go out to the balance sheet as the written down value (WDV) of plant and equipment. The depreciation figure will enter the income statement as a cost item.

Non plant costs and depreciation

Table 14.14 is a non-plant acquisition and depreciation schedule. It is similar in all ways to the plant depreciation schedule. A beginning written down value is augmented by our estimates of non-plant acquisitions, diminished by any assets of this type that we plan to sell. We wind up with a depreciable total. We estimate the depreciation according to whatever is the appropriate rate and method that pertains in the business and come to an ending written down value. Of course, in a large and complex business which may have several categories of assets, it may be worthwhile to produce several subsidiary depreciation schedules

Table 14.14   Non-plant expense

Non plant acquisition & depreciation schedule (yearly figures)

	Year one 30-Jun-97	Year two 30-Jun-98	Year three 30-Jun-99	Year four 30-Jun-00	Year five 30-Jun-01
Beginning WDV	65 576	72 261	86 922	78 133	70 663
N/plant Acquisitions	18 000	30 000	5 000	5 000	5 000
Asset Sales					
Depreciable Total	83 576	102 261	91 922	83 133	75 663
Depreciation	11 315	15 339	13 788	12 470	11 350
Ending WDV	72 261	86 922	78 133	70 663	64 314

and to list several different types of depreciation in the income statement. The ExampleCo schedule shows that this company is happy with a fairly broad level of non-plant planning. Whatever, the logic behind the schedule of projections for non-plant depreciation is the same as that driving the development of the schedule of depreciation for plant.

The really important thing to notice is that ExampleCo has chosen to distinguish its depreciation costs into two components: plant, the capital equipment used in directly adding value (such as machinery operated in a factory); and non-plant, items such as office equipment, furniture and motor vehicles for the permanent staff. This distinction provides valuable information to the statement reader. As we describe in Chapter 17, potential investors calculate various ratios as a check on the realism of the plan and the management competence of the entrepreneurial team: the accounts must make these ratios easy to compute, or venture fund managers and other investors will save themselves the trouble by setting the plan aside and investigating a better-presented one.

Interest effects

At a minimum, three projected average rates of interest need to be forecast and the forecasts shown: the interest that the firm will earn on its own cash and short term deposits; the average interest it will have to pay on all its short term borrowings; and the average interest it will have to pay on all its long term borrowings. The production of relevant subsidiary schedules based on these rates is then a simple matter. Table 14.15 shows ExampleCo's schedule of projected short term borrowing and interest payments.

Table 14.15 is typical of the schedules needed to calculate interest effects. We start with a beginning balance, list any extra borrowing, subtract any major payments and come up with a balance at the end for that particular loan category. It may be our overdraft, our fully drawn advance, or any one of a number of financial instruments. Every financial instrument that the company has, be it long or short term, ought to be planned in a similar way. There is then a line for

Table 14.15 *Short term loans and interest*

Short term loan schedule (yearly figures)

	Year one 1996/97	Year two 1997/98	Year three 1998/99	Year four 1999/00	Year five 2000/01
Balance (Beginning)					
Extra Borrowing	150 000				
Principal Repay.	150 000				
Balance (End)					
S.T. Interest Expenses	7 000				

the interest expenses and these are obviously calculated according to the contract struck with lenders. There is, of course, the additional matter of interest payments and, like wages and salaries, there is little or no room for late payment. Sometimes, interest expenses are accrued, in which case there will have to be a line providing for interest payable in the balance sheet. The more desirable situation and the more likely, because lenders want their interest payment promptly, is that interest expenses as they appear in the income statement are identical to interest payments as they appear in the cash flow statement because they are paid in the same period.

Generally speaking, the interest incurred for a period will have to be paid in that period. Obviously, there are differences. If those differences exist, then the financial model needs to take account of them. We notice in the specific example that ExampleCo is not heavily committed to any borrowing regime. During the first projected year, it is planning to borrow $150 000 at some stage and before the end of the year it intends to pay it back.

Taxation

The creation of a subsidiary schedule for taxation is very straightforward. Before a company has achieved positive retained earnings, it pays no tax because it is in the situation that trading has not, in the aggregate, been profitable. Once it has positive accumulated earnings, a company's taxable income will attract tax at the appropriate corporate rate. Any tax incurred but not paid in a given period will be listed on the balance sheet as an accrued tax liability. Table 14.16 shows ExampleCo's projected taxation schedules for the coming five financial years.

Table 14.16 is typical of a simple subsidiary schedule for taxation planning purposes. The layout shows the accrued income tax at the beginning of each period, augmented by the forecast tax applicable to the period to give the total amount of tax which accrues during the period. Any tax payments are then subtracted leaving a figure for the accrued income tax payable at the end of the period: a liability which must appear on the end-of-period balance sheet. ExampleCo, because of its accrued tax losses, does not have to pay any tax until

Table 14.16 *Income tax*

Income tax schedule (annual)

	Year one 1996/97	Year two 1997/98	Year three 1998/99	Year four 1999/00	Year five 2000/01
Accrued Inc. Tax (Beg.)					326 048
Inc. Tax Exp. This Period				1 304 191	2 251 059
Total Accruals				1 304 191	2 577 107
Inc. Tax Cash Payments				978 143	2 014 342
Accrued Inc. Tax (End.)				326 048	562 765

its fourth year of operation. It then only pays tax on the positive earnings which remain after netting the year's positive income with the previous period's negative retained earnings. From year five onwards the company will pay tax at the full rate on the full amount of profits it earns.

Cash flow statements

Some general points

Readers should spend some time examining Table 14.17. It is what one might call the long format for cash flow projections. The more you look at this statement the harder it becomes to conceive that anything of great significance has been left out.

Cash inflows have been divided into:

▲ trading receipts

▲ capital receipts, and

▲ financial receipts.

Of course, the major trading receipt is the net cash flow from sales and this will depend on the collection time taken between sales made on credit and their conversion to cash. This is a key time lag in any business cycle. Capital receipts are going to be the sum total of all capital asset sales that were made. They are quite distinct from trading. For instance, if a business manufactures injection mouldings, the sale of its production of injection mouldings constitutes normal trading receipts. If the business had to replace some of the means of production by selling some of the old equipment prior to buying new, the proceeds of that sale is a capital receipt and not income in the normal sense of the word. However, it is a cash flow, and a positive one, and must be recorded as such.

Financing receipts are very comprehensively set out in Table 14.17. There are, of course, interest receipts, that is to say, the monies that flow to the firm from any balances on its holdings of cash and short term securities (and indeed any holdings of long term investments and securities). In addition, there is space in the design of the 'long' form of the cash flow statement to project additions to the short term loans, additions to long term loans, additions to other short term

Table 14.17 *Long-form cash flow projections*

Projected cash flow statements (5 yr period) in A$

Notes		Year one 1996/97	Year two 1997/98	Year three 1998/99	Year four 1999/00	Year five 2000/01
	CASH INFLOWS					
	TRADING RECEIPTS					
15	Net Cashflow From Sales	4 929 600	6 133 828	6 717 396	8 448 499	9 706 316
	CAPITAL RECEIPTS					
16	Capital Asset Sales					
	FINANCING RECEIPTS					
11	Interest Receipts	56 648	90 066	240 357	439 681	666 449
12	Additions to S/T Loan	150 000				
13	Additions to L/T Loan	1 000 000				
17	Addit. to Other S/T Liab.					
18	Addit. to Other L/T Liab.					
19	Add. to Capital Subscribed					
1	Extraordinary Income					
	TOTAL CASH INFLOW	6 136 248	6 223 894	6 957 753	8 888 180	10 372 766
	CASH OUTFLOWS					
	TRADING PAYMENTS					
2	Sales Tax					
3	Materials Payments	190 000	273 993	348 599	370 379	392 405
4	Direct Labour Costs	1 057 789	984 412	862 378	871 489	734 931
4	Direct Overheads	84 581	80 481	68 153	65 623	50 198
4	Freight & Customs Costs	1 100 641	1 384 906	1 490 474	1 908 480	2 157 903
5	Production Rentals	26 947	28 294	29 709	31 194	32 754
20	Salaries Expenses	277 887	277 887	291 782	306 371	321 689
6	Non-Salaries Marketing	59 000	88 450	88 862	97 748	107 523
7	Non-Salaries Admin	53 300	60 629	69 723	80 182	92 209
8	Non-Salaries R & D		110 000	131 000	144 100	158 510
	Trading Subtotal	2 850 146	3 289 052	3 380 680	3 875 565	4 048 122
	CAPITAL INVESTMENT					
10	Cap. Expenditure Plant	550 000	250 000	250 000	250 000	250 000
11	Cap. Expend. Non Plant	18 000	30 000	5 000	5 000	5 000
21	Cap. Expend. Land & Bldgs		150 000			
22	Other S/T Asset Purchases					
23	Other L/T Asset Purchases					
	Capital Invest. Subtotal	568 000	430 000	255 000	255 000	255 000

The entrepreneurial financial model

Table 14.17   *Continued*

Projected cash flow statements (5 yr period) in A$

Notes		Year one 1996/97	Year two 1997/98	Year three 1998/99	Year four 1999/00	Year five 2000/01
	FINANCING OUTLAYS					
12	Repay S/T Loan Principal	150 000				
13	Repay L/T Loan Principal	1 000 000				
12	S/T Interest P/ments	7 000				
13	L/T Interest P/ments	60 000				
14	Income Tax				978 143	2 014 342
	Financing Subtotal	1 217 000			978 143	2 014 342
1	Extraordinary Expenses					
	TOT. OPERATING P/MENTS	4 635 146	3 719 052	3 635 680	5 108 708	6 317 464
	OPERATING CASHFLOW	1 501 102	2 504 842	3 322 073	3 779 472	4 055 301
	NON-OPERATING DISBURSEMENTS (EQUITY REDUCTIONS)					
24	Dividend					
24	Other Equity Reductions					
24	Other Non-trading disb.					
	TOTAL Non-Op Disburse.					
	TOTAL CASH OUTFLOW	4 635 146	3 719 052	3 635 680	5 108 708	6 317 464
	NET CASHFLOW	1 501 102	2 504 842	3 322 073	3 779 472	4 055 301
	BEG CASH BALANCE		1 501 102	4 005 945	7 328 018	11 107 490
	END CASH BALANCE	1 501 102	4 005 945	7 328 018	11 107 490	15 162 792

liabilities, additions to other long term liabilities, a section to record the cash received from the issue and sale of new shares, and finally, a place to record the cash flowing from any extraordinary income. Extraordinary income is income unlikely to be regularly received because it results from activities outside the mainstream of a business's normal activities. For example, if the business were a manufacturer but one of its officers had received some income by way of consulting for advising another manufacturing firm, but this was unlikely to be a regular source of income in future and had never occurred before, it would be best to call the income (and the ultimate resulting cash flow) 'extraordinary'.

Moving to the cash outflows section of Table 14.17, we notice that they exactly mirror the inflow section of the statement being divided into three major areas:

▲ trading payments

▲ capital investment, and

▲ financing outlays.

Trading payments are listed in the order in which they occur in the income statement with the exception that in the cash flow statement a distinction is made between aggregated salaries expenses and the non-salary components of marketing, administration and R&D. As has already been mentioned, the reason for this is that while subdivision into functional areas is the guiding concept for producing income statements, the key thing about cash flow statements is the timing of payments. And salaries will be paid in the period in which they incur whereas non-salary components will probably be purchases on credit and will be paid in a later period. The categories of capital investment are plant, non-plant, land and buildings, and general 'catch-all' categories for other short term purchases and other long term asset purchases. Financing outlays involve major repayments on short and long term loans, interest payments — short and long term — and income tax. Add them up and one has a financing subtotal. The final line item is, of course, the payments involved for extraordinary expenses.

At this stage of the cash flow statement, we can add up the operating payments, subtract them from the total operating receipts and come up with an operating cash flow.

The next section of the statement involves non-operating disbursements. This can be thought of as reductions of equity which have nothing what so ever to do with the day to day running of the business. They include dividends which may be paid from time to time to shareholders, any other equity reductions and any non-trading cash distributions that may be made.

When these items are subtracted from operating cash flow, we have a total cash outflow. We can now subtract to obtain a net cash flow for the entire 'ins' and 'outs' of the business for the period covered by the cash flow projection. When this net cash flow is added to the beginning cash balance, we arrive at an end cash balance for the business — the figure which will go to the balance sheet. Of course, the ending cash balance for one period is the beginning cash balance for the next and the whole process begins again for the new period.

Using the cash flow projection to explore financing options

The 'long' form of cash flow statement (Table 14.17) is very comprehensive. Virtually nothing has been left out that is needed for a detailed calculation of the company's cash situation. In this format, the cash flow statement is a very useful device for projecting alternative financing scenarios. One of the biggest tasks facing an entrepreneur is the need to work out exactly how much financing and in what form his or her venture or responsibility centre will need during those stages when its growth outstrips its ability to be self-funding. Using the financial model proactively enables the entrepreneur to project a whole range of different financing scenarios and the cash flow statement is the ideal place from which to control these explorations. Look back at the statement. See how easy it would be once a well balanced spreadsheet is built, to experiment with different combinations of additions to short term loans, additions to long term loans and additions to capital subscribed. Better still, readers can build their own spreadsheet model and try it!

Various combinations can be simulated and all of their effects can then be checked on the income statement to see which ones affect profitability in desirable or undesirable ways; they can be further checked on the balance sheet to see what equity consequences they have for the original shareholders of the venture. So, the cash flow statement is a very useful device in many ways. Cash is the lifeblood of any venture. A detailed and regularly maintained cash flow model is the monitor that tells the entrepreneur that the heart of the enterprise is healthy.

Meeting a variety of information needs

Of course, just as with the income statement, there are many other possible ways to arrange the presentation of a cash flow statement. Table 14.18 shows another possibility. In Table 14.18 the statement is divided into the key areas of trading, capital investment and financing — as in the previous design — but receipts and payments are netted by functional area to give first a trading cash flow, then a capital investment cash flow and then a financing cash flow. There is a section for netting extraordinary income and a section for netting non-operating disbursements. In this format of statement, which one might call the 'functional area' layout, it is very easy to distinguish the positive and negative contributions to cash flow being made by each separate area of business activity.

The key steps to cash flow statement projection

Whatever layout you ultimately choose for presenting your business's cash flow projections, there are three key things to keep in mind:

▲ ultimate output: it's one vital line in the balance sheet — the firm's cash position

▲ the heart of the matter is timing: keep asking (and showing) when the firm gets money in and when it has to pay it out

▲ never forget the essential simplicity of a cash flow statement's design: it is always cash in *minus* cash out *equals* cash held.

The ultimate output: One vital line in the balance sheet

Since cash flow is the lifeblood of any enterprise, it is possible for a business to go bankrupt while showing a profit: the nutrients (profits) have been ingested (net income earned) but they have not been digested and have not taken effect in the body of the business. If all sales were on credit but no purchasers ever actually paid for the goods a firm had sold them, that firm would have no cash, and would be unable to pay its suppliers. They would stop supplying the firm, which would also be unable to pay its workers who would stop working for it. The business would go bankrupt while showing a profit. This is why the cash flow statement for the entrepreneurial financial model is at the heart of the enterprise.

Table 14.18 *Cash flow projection in 'functional area' format*

Projected cash flow statements (5 yr period) in A$

Notes		Year one 1996/97	Year two 1997/98	Year three 1998/99	Year four 1999/00	Year five 2000/01
	TRADING					
	Trading Receipts	4 929 600	6 133 828	6 717 396	8 448 499	9 706 316
	Trading Payments	2 850 146	3 289 052	3 380 680	3 875 565	4 048 122
	Trading Cashflow	2 079 454	2 844 776	3 336 717	4 572 934	5 658 194
	CAPITAL INVESTMENT					
	Asset Divestments					
	Asset Outlays	568 000	430 000	255 000	255 000	255 000
	Capital Invest. Cashflow	(568 000)	(430 000)	(255 000)	(255 000)	(255 000)
	FINANCING					
	Financing Receipts	1 206 648	90 066	240 357	439 681	666 449
	Financing & Tax Outlays	1 217 000			978 143	2 014 342
	Financing Cashflow	(10 352)	90 066	240 357	(538 462)	(1 347 893)
	EXTRAORDINARIES					
	Extraordinary Income					
	Extraordinary Expenses					
	Extraordinary Cashflow					
	NON-OPERATING					
	Non-op. disbursements					
	Trading Cashflow	2 079 454	2 844 776	3 336 717	4 572 934	5 658 194
	Capital Cashflow	(568 000)	(430 000)	(255 000)	(255 000)	(255 000)
	Financing & Tax Cashflow	(10 352)	90 066	240 357	(538 462)	(1 347 893)
	Extraordinary Cashflow					
	OPERATING CASHFLOW	1 501 102	2 504 842	3 322 073	3 779 472	4 055 301
	Non-Op. Disbursements					
	NET CASHFLOW	1 501 102	2 504 842	3 322 073	3 779 472	4 055 301
	BEG CASH BALANCE		1 501 102	4 005 945	7 328 018	11 107 490
	END CASH BALANCE	1 501 102	4 005 945	7 328 018	11 107 490	15 162 792

But in one sense we ought never to forget that the cash flow statement, large though it is by subsidiary schedule standards, is simply that: a subsidiary schedule whose yield is one aggregate line item in the balance sheet, that is, the cash held by the business at the end of the period.

The heart of the matter: Timing

Table 14.19 is a schedule of the timing of the expected cash flow from sales. The calculations which go in to generating the initial expected cash flow is a matter

Table 14.19   Timing of cash flows

Schedule of timing of cash flow from yearly sales

	Year one 1996/97	Year two 1997/98	Year three 1998/99	Year four 1999/00	Year five 2000/01
Expected Cash From Sales	4 939 578	6 146 366	6 730 956	8 465 788	9 725 998
Bad Debts Expense	9 978	12 538	13 560	17 289	19 681
Net Cashflow From Sales	4 929 600	6 133 828	6 717 396	8 448 499	9 706 316

of timing. We model in our spreadsheet a time module for receipts. How much is going to be received in thirty days? How much is going to be received in sixty days? How much of a month's sales do we expect to receive in ninety days? And so on. These figures can be related back to the income statement projections and we arrive at an aggregate figure for the collections expected in any period. The schedule shows, however, that we must allow for bad debts to reduce this figure. There are many ways of projecting bad debts and they will vary so much from business to business that no single recommendation for handling them will be generally applicable. Usually the estimate is calculated as a percentage of all sales that lead to bad debts. When bad debts are subtracted from the otherwise-expected cash from sales, we come up with a projection for the net cash flow from sales and this is the figure that starts the cash flow statement.

The basic structure of a cash flow statement

Tables 14.17 and 14.18 presented the essential features of every cash flow statement in different formats, but these are not the only possible, or even the only useful, ones. In crude terms, any cash flow statement will have three major components: inflows, outflows and their difference.

Balance sheets

Some general points about building projected balance sheets

The first point to note is that the chart of accounts and the layout and design of the balance sheet are already known (refer back to Table 14.1). The basis of all our financial modelling began from a balance sheet immediately prior to the first projected period and we have already written, earlier in this chapter, about the design of that balance sheet and the presentation of the information in it. As we have been progressing through the production of income and cash flow statements, we have already built many of the subsidiary schedules which we need to produce figures for the balance sheet. For instance, retained earnings at the end of a period are simply going to be retained earnings at the beginning of the period (from last period's balance sheet) plus the after tax profit for this period (from the income statement). We already possess a materials' inventory figure: it is in the schedule we needed to calculate the materials purchases usages and payments (Table 14.5, above). The amounts of the written down value of plant and non-plant assets have already been calculated when we generated our schedules of depreciation (Tables 14.9 and 14.10, above). Cash, of course, is simply the net result of all the calculations on the cash flow statement.

There are really only two major subsidiary schedules left to generate and we will take a close look at them over the next few pages.

Design for variety of information presentation

Table 14.20 (see page 452) presents the projected balance sheets for the next five financial years for ExampleCo. The chart of accounts and the layout of those accounts is exactly the same as the beginning balance sheet on which the financial model is based.

Readers may experiment with different layouts for their balance sheets. One could, for example, set out the balance sheet in the form of a statement of all assets and then show how that balances with the total of all liabilities and shareholders' equity. Another possible design is to begin with working capital (a subtraction of current assets from current liabilities) and build up a treatment which adds net long term assets to working capital and shows how this figure balances with shareholders equity. In short, one can balance almost anything with anything else and this gives an unlimited number of possible presentations for a balance sheet.

Key steps to balance sheet projections

Given the amount of subsidiary schedule building which has already been conducted in order to generate aggregate income statements and aggregate cash flow statements, there is very little that needs to be done in order to proceed to the production of a balance sheet. The two remaining vital subsidiary schedules which must be built are the schedule of accounts receivable (debtors), and the schedule of accounts payable (creditors).

The schedule of accounts receivable (debtors)

Table 14.21 is an example of a satisfactory subsidiary schedule of accounts receivable.

The schedule of accounts receivable is simple to construct. It starts with accounts receivable at the beginning of the period, a figure brought in from the previous period's balance sheet. Next, sales for the period (we assume here that all sales are made on credit terms) are added. The figure is, of course, the gross

Table 14.20   *Projected balance sheets*

Projected balance sheets (5 yr period) in A$

Notes		Year one 30-Jun-97	Year two 30-Jun-98	Year three 30-Jun-99	Year four 30-Jun-00	Year five 30-Jun-01
	SHAREHOLDERS FUNDS					
19	Capital Subscribed	16 548 068	16 548 068	16 548 068	16 548 068	16 548 068
19	Reserves					
19	Retained Earnings	(7 821 149)	(4 925 386)	(1 406 369)	2 318 562	6 320 446
	TOTAL EQUITY	8 726 919	11 622 682	15 141 699	18 866 630	22 868 514
	ASSETS					
	Current Assets:					
	Cash & Sht Term Deposits	1 501 102	4 005 945	7 328 018	11 107 490	15 162 792
25	Accounts Receivable	49 642	172 288	221 250	399 937	514 568
3	Materials Inventory	46 905	73 170	141 619	160 450	163 191
22	Other Current Assets					
	Total Current Assets	1 597 649	4 251 404	7 690 888	11 667 877	15 840 551
	Fixed Assets:					
10	Plant at WDV	1 191 285	1 297 157	1 392 441	1 478 197	1 555 377
11	Non-Plant at WDV	72 261	86 922	78 133	70 663	64 314
12	Land and Buildings	5 804 582	5 954 582	5 954 582	5 954 582	5 954 582
23	Other Fixed Assets	76 142	76 142	76 142	76 142	76 142
	Total Fixed Assets @ WDV	7 144 270	7 414 803	7 501 299	7 579 585	7 650 415
	TOTAL ASSETS	8 741 919	11 666 206	15 192 186	19 247 462	23 490 966
	LIABILITIES					
	Current Liabilities:					
26	Accounts Payable	15 000	43 525	50 487	54 784	59 688
12	Short Term Loans					
14	Accrued Income Tax				326 048	562 765
17	Other Current Liabilities					
	Total Cur. Liabs	15 000	43 525	50 487	380 832	622 452
	Long Term Liabilities:					
13	Long Term Loans					
18	Other Long Term Liabs.					
	Total Long Term Liabs.					
	TOTAL LIABILITIES	15 000	43 525	50 487	380 832	622 452
	NET ASSETS	8 726 919	11 622 682	15 141 699	18 866 630	22 868 514

revenue figure from the income statement. From this gross estimate we must subtract bad debts calculated according to whatever formula seems appropriate to the business. And this brings us, by subtraction, to a total of all the accounts receivable during the period. From this we subtract the net cash flow from sales because, as accounts receivable are paid, they are obviously removed from our list of accounts

Table 14.21 *Accounts receivable schedule*

Schedule of accounts receivable (end of year)

	Year one 1996/97	Year two 1997/98	Year three 1998/99	Year four 1999/00	Year five 2000/01
A/C Rec. (Beginning)		49 642	172 288	221 250	399 937
Sales for Period	4 989 220	6 269 013	6 779 918	8 644 475	9 840 629
less Bad Debts	9 978	12 538	13 560	17 289	19 681
Total A/C rec.	4 979 242	6 306 117	6 938 647	8 848 436	10 220 885
Net Cashflow From Sales	4 929 600	6 133 828	6 717 396	8 448 499	9 706 316
A/C rec. (end)	49 642	172 288	221 250	399 937	514 568

to be paid. The subtraction brings us to a figure for accounts receivable at the end. The fundamental layout of this subsidiary schedule (which of course can be made more complicated and have several more line items injected to add depth and information content to it) never varies from business to business.

The schedule of accounts payable (creditors)

Just as we extend credit to people who buy from us, so do other suppliers extend credit to us and the balance sheet needs to show the schedule of the accounts that are payable to them at the end of any given period. There are many ways to build a schedule of accounts payable (creditors). One of the simplest and least likely to cause complications or error is demonstrated in Table 14.22.

This subsidiary schedule of accounts payable starts with a figure for accounts payable at the beginning of the period. Then, basically two things happen. All credit additions are totalled and added to the accounts payable at the beginning and all credit reductions are totalled and subtracted from that figure. The result is the accounts payable at the end of the period and that is the figure that we want for the balance sheet.

If you have been building your model according to the principles set out so far, all the figures that we want along the way already exist. The figures for credit additions are drawn from the income statement — our direct overheads, our non-salaries marketing and our non-salaries administration — are all figures that have appeared in the income statement. Our materials purchases are drawn from the appropriate subsidiary schedule. Our credit reductions are all figures that come from the cash flow statement: materials payments; direct overhead payments; non-salary marketing payments; and non-salary administration payments. Plant acquisitions and non-plant acquisitions come from the relevant subsidiary schedules. In this way, the accounts payable subsidiary schedule draws on all the work previously done in building the financial model and generates the last liability figure needed to produce the finished balance sheet projections shown as Table 14.20.

The entrepreneurial financial model

Table 14.22 *Accounts payable*

Schedule of accounts payable (end of year)

	Year one 30-Jun-97	Year two 30-Jun-98	Year three 30-Jun-99	Year four 30-Jun-00	Year five 30-Jun-01
A/C PAYABLE (Beg.)		15 000	43 525	50 487	54 784
CREDIT ADDITIONS					
Trade Credit Additions					
Materials Purchases	190 000	298 901	353 117	371 948	394 265
Direct Overheads	84 581	80 481	68 153	65 623	50 198
Non-Salaries Marketing	74 000	81 400	89 540	98 494	108 343
Non-Salaries Admin	53 300	61 295	70 489	81 063	93 222
Non-Salaries R&D		120 000	132 000	145 200	159 720
Other Expenses					
Total T.C. Additions	401 881	642 077	713 299	762 327	805 748
Capital Equip. Additions					
Plant Acquisitions	550 000	250 000	250 000	250 000	250 000
Non-Plant Acquisitions	18 000	30 000	5 000	5 000	5 000
Land & Bldg Acquisitions		150 000			
Total Capital Additions	568 000	430 000	255 000	255 000	255 000
TOT. CREDIT ADDITIONS	969 881	1 072 077	968 299	1 017 327	1 060 748
CREDIT REDUCTIONS					
Trade Credit Reductions					
Materials Payments	190 000	273 993	348 599	370 379	392 405
Direct Overheads	84 581	80 481	68 153	65 623	50 198
Non-Salaries Marketing	59 000	88 450	88 862	97 748	107 523
Non-Salaries Admin	53 300	60 629	69 723	80 182	92 209
Non-Salaries R&D		110 000	131 000	144 100	158 510
Other Expenses					
Total T.C. Reductions	386 881	613 553	706 337	758 031	800 844
Cap. Equip. Reductions					
Plant Acquisitions	550 000	250 000	250 000	250 000	250 000
Non-Plant Acquisitions	18 000	30 000	5 000	5 000	5 000
Land & Bldg Acquisitions		150 000			
Total Cap. Eq. Reductions	568 000	430 000	255 000	255 000	255 000
TOT CRED. REDUCTIONS	954 881	1 043 553	961 337	1 013 031	1 055 844
NET CHANGE	15 000	28 525	6 962	4 297	4 904
A/C PAYABLE (End)	15 000	43 525	50 487	54 784	59 688

Other bridging issues

The shareholders' funds section of the balance sheet is calculated by referring to the relevant figures in the cash flow statements and the income statements. Retained earnings for this period will simply be the retained earnings of the previous period plus the profit, after tax, on this year's income statement. Reserves are a matter of policy and will simply represent an allocation of retained earnings (reserve goes up, retained earnings goes down, a simple subtraction). Capital subscribed is going to be the capital with which the business began the period plus any equity additions (a line item in the cash flow statement).

Thus, the process of finalising a projected set of balance sheets is a matter of what one might call 'bridging'. It is building a bridge between the figures we have already projected in our previous statements and the figures that we need for the finished balance sheet layout. From time to time, there will be special bridging issues that might arise in a very complex or a very large business, but when such circumstances arise the entrepreneur will have the services of a corporate finance department, aided by the services of a major accounting firm if needs be, to decide what should be done in order to produce a sound set of projected balance sheets.

Using simulation to manage variance and change

The implications of a living model

The opening section of this chapter stressed that for each and every business there is and will always be an unlimited number of possible questions which prospective investors, whether lenders or potential equity participants, and practising managers involved in the day to day operation of the venture, will want to ask. The entrepreneurial financial model has to be a living thing capable of answering those questions in dollar terms. In general, a question will be put in the form: 'If we did this, what will be the financial consequences?'

The entrepreneurial financial model must be capable of coming up with the answers. That capability has several obvious technical implications, and some that are less obvious.

One of the most important uses of the financial model comes immediately after a new product is launched, and involves substituting actual sales and revenue for the projections. Month by month, or even week by week, a pattern of actual sales will develop that can be worked backwards into the market response model to refine it, and which will immediately show the effect of any changes from the plan on the business's cash balances and net assets. If sales are too slow, then promotional expenditure can be boosted, staff hiring and equipment purchasing deferred, and orders for materials and components cancelled. If sales are rising faster than the plan, the reverse set of actions can be put in train.

Keeping the financial plan updated has further benefits for a new enterprise; one is that the firm always has a mechanism for testing its ability to handle a large, unexpected order: not all orders are good news, particularly for a small and rapidly developing firm. Sometimes such orders must be declined, or only accepted if accompanied by a deposit.

Before the venture is launched the financial model can be used to test various scenarios, such as faster or slower sales, or higher or lower costs, or better or worse customer response to the product. A series of trials of this nature test the boundaries of stability for a firm; sometimes they show that a given iteration of a plan is vulnerable to a tiny change in circumstances, while a different approach can give the firm a margin of safety. Potential investors will want to know that this has been done, and may wish to suggest some trials themselves.

One of the most important tests is that of the effect of different levels of capital: entrepreneurs cannot always raise all the capital that they would like, and the financial model lets them rebuild the plan on a lower capital budget, rather than simply ploughing on with inadequate resources. If a new venture is very successful in its first few years, it will receive many offers of additional capital: the model, if kept updated, will enable the entrepreneurial team to decide whether they will accept any of these offers, and if so, for how much.

As readers will recall from Chapter 11, directors of a company who permit it to trade when it is unable to pay its debts as they fall due are committing an offence. Directors who don't want to draw the 'go to gaol' card will make sure that the numbers in the line 'total current assets' are always bigger than those in the line 'total current liabilities', and that projected cash holdings will be sufficient to meet the business's projected liabilities in every future period.

End notes

1 In this chapter, there is nothing concerning the technical aspects of accountancy that is not dealt with in far greater depth in any established text book on accountancy. The authors make the assumption that the reader either has studied, is studying, or will study both accounting fundamentals and the basic operation of an electronic spreadsheet package. What the chapter supplies is some 'value-added' for those who have a good grasp of accounting and spreadsheet basics. The philosophy, perspective and design principles result directly from the paradigm of entrepreneurial business planning presented in Chapter 3.

2 People on entrepreneurial and management teams who don't understand basic accounting tend to get bullied by those who do.

3 Firms using *kanban* or just-in-time purchasing are the main exception, and even there the main benefit is that materials are held, by suppliers at each level of the value chain, in the least-transformed and therefore lowest cost form possible.

15

Chapter

We're from the government ...

Firms buy goods and services, transform them, and sell the result. The revenue from sales normally exceeds the cost of the purchased goods and services: the difference is the value-added. The value-added is distributed in interest payments to lenders, rent and lease payments to providers of premises and equipment, dividends and augmented equity to shareholders, licences and royalties to intellectual property providers, wages and salaries to employees, and taxes to various governments. These are the internal returns to the firm's activities. There are, however, external returns as well: customers generally enjoy a value-in-use that exceeds the price; rivals can observe the firm and emulate its successful initiatives; and as long as the firm is growing it will be recruiting people who might otherwise need to be supported by social security.

The existence of these external returns, or 'externalities' motivates governments to encourage existing firms to expand and new firms to establish themselves. Some measures adopted by governments are essentially passive, including such measures as setting corporate taxes at a low level and eliminating vexatious regulations. Others are more active, and include tax concession schemes and direct assistance measures. Vast areas of government activity affect the prospects for new enterprises, without formally being described as industry policies. Governments build or facilitate infrastructure development to enable goods and services to be delivered to and from firms; they maintain education systems to provide firms with literate and numerate employees and customers; they support a public research infrastructure to expand the scientific basis of technology and to provide an environment in which future private sector scientists and engineers can learn advanced research techniques; they provide other services conducive to popular wellbeing and social harmony; they maintain police forces to enforce law and order; and they maintain defence forces to deter foreign enemies.

Both the magnitude of the externalities generated in normal commercial transactions, and the effect of government efforts to boost them, are matters of bitter political controversy. Neo-liberal and conservative commentators argue that the externalities are small and in any case that government employees are incapable of furthering any interests but their own. If a firm receives government assistance and is subsequently successful, these commentators argue that the firm would have succeeded anyway and the assistance represented nothing more than a transfer of taxpayer funds to the firm's employees and shareholders. If a firm receives government assistance and subsequently fails, neo-liberal and conservative commentators declare that this proves the inefficiency of public servants at 'picking winners'.

Until the 1970s, the neo-liberal argument was countered by socialists of various flavours, arguing that each successful firm's profits detracted from the externalities that trading operations normally generated, and the 'means of production, distribution and exchange' should be socialised. A person who supported a mixed economy with a limited amount of government intervention in the private sector was a moderate, subject to equally virulent attacks from left and right. To some extent these cancelled each other and permitted moderate politicians and public servants to pursue a considered path. The decay and ultimate collapse of the east European communist governments destroyed whatever credibility the socialist movement had enjoyed, while the death or retirement of everyone who had experienced the Great Depression first-hand removed an important source of scepticism about neo-liberal policy recommendations. Moderate people found themselves in an apparently extreme position; the voice of reason is easily drowned by the shouting of slogans.

The Australian population as a whole is, however, decisively moderate as the contrasting election results of 1993 and 1996 showed. The electorate supports a system of selective assistance to industry and governments of both parties have responded to this. Direct payments to firms carry too many political risks to be attractive to governments, and so there is a general theme running through government support programs, one of 'co-payment'. By and large the various Australian governments do not give money away unconditionally: they match payments made or committed by firms and entrepreneurs.

Neo-liberal doctrine can draw very little support from comparative studies of different national economies: with the somewhat dubious exception of Hong Kong, all the national economies which grew rapidly in the post-Second World War era had governments that had explicit industry policies and took explicit measures to implement them. Neo-liberals may cite neoclassical economic theory to support their position, but the work of economists such as Paul Romer (1986) and Brian Arthur (1994) has shown that sound economic theory cannot justify unequivocal opposition to state intervention in the economy. A careful study of the Australian economy has shown that, broadly speaking, government expenditure has had a positive effect on its long term performance.[1] Economists now realise that new enterprises, and proposals to expand existing ones, face formidable financial hurdles:[2] appropriate assistance may help promising firms over these; and in the absence of such assistance many opportunities may go begging for an extended period, people may be unemployed, and capital resources may be under utilised.

Government industry support programs in Australia can be divided into a number of broad groups:

▲ there are a number of industry-specific programs

▲ there are a number of programs aimed at encouraging the generation of new technology-based products

▲ there are a number of programs aimed at supporting exporting firms, and

▲ there are certain programs intended to encourage small and medium enterprises by helping them bring their products and processes up to 'world best' standards.

As befits a federation, every state in Australia has its own programs and puts its own spin on common ones. AusIndustry provides an umbrella organisation through which entrepreneurs and firms can obtain details about those government programs for which they may be eligible, and AusIndustry also provides a general brand name for the ensemble of programs. The balance of this chapter describes, in relatively general terms, the programs available at the beginning of 1996. Matters of policy and practice, to say nothing of the administrative consequences of maintaining 500 or more different programs, means that the details change fairly frequently. Enterprises and entrepreneurs should contact the sponsoring department, either directly or through AusIndustry, to get details of the applicable qualification standards and application requirements before assuming that any program described here still exists or is available to them.

This book is going to press before the 1996 Commonwealth budget is handed down, and rumour suggests that many of the programs listed below may be curtailed and some may be eliminated in that budget. Others may be the subject of action in the World Trade Organisation (WTO) leading to their modification or restriction. International experience, as well as the economic research referred to above, suggests that the consequences of eliminating government support for industry would be politically fatal as well as economically disastrous, and some schemes will continue and others will be introduced to achieve the same effects under different titles and rules. The year or two following the 1996 Australian budget may, however, be harder than usual for Australian entrepreneurs.

Industry specific programs

Motor parts duty rebate

When Australian-based firms export motor cars or components, they create a balancing import credit, and they may subsequently import vehicles or components duty-free up to the value of the exports. This scheme is generally used by motor vehicle manufacturers and importers who act as agents for Australian car parts manufacturers, representing them to the manufacturers' and importers' overseas principals and collecting the duty rebate on their imports of finished cars into Australia.

Many Australian-based motor vehicle components companies have been able to develop substantial export businesses. Some of these are: Henderson Ltd, which sells springs to Mercedes-Benz; Britax-Rainsford Ltd, which sells external mirrors to Japanese and American manufacturers as well as to the Australian industry; ROH Ltd, which sells aluminium wheels around the world; the Holden Engine Company Ltd, which sells car engines to Germany, South Korea and elsewhere; and Bishop–Bendix Ltd, which sells components and licences power steering technology worldwide.

The worldwide motor vehicle industry is acutely sensitive to quality and performance when sourcing components, looking to price only when these two factors are assured. Any Australian manufacturer who is capable of meeting world-best standards of quality and delivery performance can benefit from the duty rebate program: they will find that the major car manufacturers and importers are quite generous with their time (not their money) in identifying opportunities for Australian component manufacturers to supply their Australian and their overseas requirements.

From time to time the United States threatens action under the WTO treaty to force Australia to abandon this scheme. It is, in any case, under review and new arrangements will apply from January 2000 in any case.[3]

> *What's good for the USA is good for General Motors, and vice versa ... ('Engine Charlie' (Charles E.) Wilson, President of General Motors and later US Secretary for Defence, 1953)*

The Factor *f* scheme

The majority of therapeutic drugs sold in Australia are bought by the federal government under the Pharmaceutical Benefits Scheme: patients pay a common prescription charge to their pharmacist irrespective of the actual cost of the medicines. As the dominant buyer in a market for products with a very low variable cost, the government is able to force prices well below the free-market level.

Under the Factor *f* scheme, the federal government relaxes its price squeeze to a significant extent for therapeutic preparations supplied by firms who meet defined targets for production, export, and research and development in Australia. The Factor f scheme offers little direct benefit to a new enterprise, since only firms with an established share of the pharmaceutical preparation market can get any benefit from increased prices. New and small firms may benefit from forming alliances with established ones, allowing their research to be counted towards the established firm's research contribution.

The United States has signalled its unhappiness with the Factor f scheme, and threatened to raise it with the WTO.

Partnership for Development

The Australian government is the largest purchaser of information technology equipment and services in the country and is a significant buyer even on a world scale. The government's purchasing procedures for large contracts are complex, arbitrary, pedantic and largely irrelevant to the end use of the purchased equipment; securing such a contract can involve the expenditure of tens of millions of dollars over a period of several years, and even the winner does not start to turn a profit until its 'get well' measures begin to take effect two or more years after the contract is awarded. Few if any Australian companies, and no small or medium ones, could hope to secure their fair share of government business under these conditions.

The *Partnership for Development* scheme attempts to overcome this problem by persuading large, foreign-based companies to act as agents for small Australian ones in their deals with the government. In return for being allowed to contest the mega-orders, firms enrolled in the partnership scheme undertake to carry out nominated volumes of research and development, and to source software, components and equipment of an agreed value from Australia.

Small and medium enterprises wishing to benefit from the Partnership for Development scheme should note that the three things that major firms place the highest weight on when they source components and software from third parties are quality, marketability and complementarity. Quality means much more than freedom from egregious defects. It requires proper documentation at all levels as well as correct operation and ready maintainability; marketability means that the product addresses an identified market demand and has features and attributes that make it readily saleable; and complementarity means that the product addresses a gap or a weakness in the major firm's product range, as distinct from merely duplicating something that the firm already has and is selling strongly.

When small or medium firms are developing a proposal to a large one, the benefits that the large firm may gain

> We have no eternal allies and we have no perpetual enemies. Our interests are eternal and perpetual, and those interests it is our duty to follow. (Lord Palmerston, British Foreign Secretary, 1848)

from the Partnership for Development scheme should be cited, if at all, as an additional benefit the large firm may gain from the deal. The Partnership for Development scheme guarantees small and medium Australian firms the opportunity to approach the major information technology and telecommunication companies, but it doesn't guarantee any orders. The products offered should stand up on their own.

The United States has criticised the Partnership for Development scheme, and threatened to complain about it at the WTO.

Textile, clothing and footwear industries

Before the Australian government announced an accelerated series of unilateral tariff cuts in 1991, the textile, clothing and footwear (TCF) industries were among Australia's largest employers. The commodity end of the TCF industry did not wait for the tariff cuts to take effect, and relocated to low-cost Asian countries over the next two years, increasing unemployment in Australia by some 80 000. A series of government measures under the rubric 'TCF2000' were put into place, rather too late in many cases, in an attempt to retain the high value-added end of the industry in Australia.

TCF best practice program (expires mid 1997)

Dollar for dollar grants of up to $100 000 are available to firms that develop 'world best practice' programs and then permit themselves to be used as Australian benchmarks for other firms to emulate. Five specific areas may be addressed:

- ▲ people practices
- ▲ leadership development
- ▲ customer relations
- ▲ supplier relations
- ▲ benchmarking.

TCF quality program

Firms that successfully complete an introductory quality program with a firm on AusIndustry's register of endorsed TCF Quality Improvement Services may receive a dollar for dollar grant of up to $2500.

TCF quick response program

The AusIndustry TCF quick response (QR) program is designed to assist groups of TCF firms that together form a supply chain to undertake joint business activities in order to increase their market responsiveness. The adoption of QR is intended to give Australian manufacturers a clear advantage over importers in areas such as delivery times, the development of strategic relationships with retailers, and response to changing market conditions.

The program takes place in three stages using endorsed facilitators. The stages cover an audit to identify opportunities, a workshop to evaluate and set priorities on them, and an implementation stage.

The import credit scheme (expires 2000)

Australian TCF firms that export TCF goods, wholly or partly finished (except to New Zealand), may be eligible to claim an import credit equal to the duty that would have applied to an imported good at a price equivalent to the value-added in Australia by the exporter. These credits may be used to offset duty on the firm's imports, or can be sold to other firms for that purpose.

Firms must earn a minimum of $100 000 in two consecutive years from export sales to be eligible for this scheme.

Overseas assembly provisions (expires 2000)

The overseas assembly provisions (OAPs) enable participating firms to assemble or embroider clothing made from shapes that have been cut or knitted in Australia in overseas locations, and subsequently import the finished products at a concessional rate of duty. Duty will only be calculated on that proportion of the price that does not represent Australian value-added.

Firms must make application in proper form to join this scheme, and only firms and product lines meeting certain conditions will be accepted into it.

Technology programs

Economic growth is something of a mystery to the conventionally educated economists who give advice to Australian government ministers, but there is something approaching a consensus among them to the effect that the rate of development and adoption of technology is closely related to national economic growth. While the various programs described in this section are not without their critics, they still enjoy fairly widespread support in the bureaucracy and the community generally. The most strident criticism generally takes the form that the 'government is subsidising activities that firms would undertake anyway'. The broad econometric data does not support this conclusion.

The 150 per cent tax incentive for R&D

In the 1995–96 financial year, the revenue foregone because of the 150 per cent tax incentive represented the largest single government commitment in support for the development and exploitation of technology by the private sector in Australia. The scheme permits eligible expenditure on R&D to be set off against company tax at $150 for every $100 of actual expenditure; the effect is that each $100 of expenditure on R&D for a tax-paying Australian company reduces after-tax profit by only $46.

Research projects must be approved by the Industry Research and Development (IR&D) Board and must involve a minimum of $20 000 a year for individual companies and $500 000 a year for consortia. The board is expected to approve projects which:

▲ will be carried out by or on behalf of the company claiming the concession

▲ will have an adequate Australian content, and

▲ which will be exploited on normal commercial terms to the benefit of the Australian economy.

Once a project is approved, expenditure including salaries, wages and directly related overhead costs, and expenditure on research contracts, may be deducted in the current year; capital expenditure on R&D plant and equipment, including the building of pilot plants, must be deducted over at least three years. Expenditure on acquiring, or acquiring the right to use, technology for a company's R&D activities is fully deductible.

The rules for accessing this scheme were made more restrictive in the 'innovation' statement of 1995 and may be tightened further in 1996.

R&D syndication

Many young, technology-based companies have accumulated losses and are not liable to pay tax: the 150 per cent tax incentive offers them no direct benefits. Many such companies are distinctly short of cash and their products lack the two years of successful market exposure that venture capitalists (for reasons we explain in Chapter 17) demand before providing equity funding.

Such firms may be able to form a syndicate with a financial institution under which the financial institution effectively buys that young firm's accumulated tax losses, augmented by 150 per cent where they relate to eligible R&D expenditure. The firm gets access to low-cost loan capital with which to complete the development and market testing of its innovation, while the financial institution can offset its exposure to a firm which, in the normal course of business it would not lend a cent to, by the tax credit.

A syndicate

Multistack International Ltd (see Case studies one and three) currently uses the permitted refrigerant R22, but this must be phased out under the Montreal Agreement by the year 2030. The only currently available alternative is R134a, but this fluid degrades common lubricants and requires 20 per cent more energy when used with conventional compressors.

Laboratory testing has shown that a new compressor design could overcome these problems, but development for production will cost several million dollars and building a manufacturing facility will cost the same again or more.

Multistack led the formation of an R&D syndicate, which will complete the commercialisation of an efficient R134a compressor and grant Multistack a free licence to use the intellectual property in the resulting compressors for its own purposes. The syndicate will earn its return from licensing the technology and sales of the compressors to other manufacturers.

Multistack continues its policy of securing '40 per cent of a lot rather than 100 per cent of nothing'.

The 1995 'innovation' statement introduced additional rules into the establishment of such R&D syndicates which may make such finance harder to obtain and which will certainly increase the costs of setting such syndicates up. At the same time the Malaysian government introduced a scheme based on the original Australian one, with the additional twist that, so long as ultimate title to the resulting intellectual property passes to a Malaysian enterprise, the whole of the eligible expenditure need not be incurred in Malaysia.

Competitive grants for industry research and development

The IR&D Board may approve grants of up to 50 per cent of the projected costs of an R&D project over a period of up to three years. These grants are competitive, and will be awarded in order of merit until the budgetary provision is exhausted, should the number of applications in any one year exceed the allocated funds. Projects meeting one or more of the following conditions will be considered:

▲ market-driven R&D in dynamic firms in need of assistance but unable to take advantage of the 150 per cent tax incentive

▲ collaborative R&D activities which are high risk but could provide extensive benefit to Australia

▲ trial and demonstration projects involving technology developers and potential customers

▲ collaborative R&D activity between firms and research institutions involving the placement of a graduate within the firm.

Concessional loans for the commercialisation of technological innovation

The IR&D Board has a revolving fund from which to make concessional loans to firms with fewer than a hundred employees needing assistance to bring a completed development to market. Should there be more qualified firms applying to draw on this facility than there are funds available, loans will be made to the most meritorious proposals, as determined by the board.

Applicant firms will be expected to direct the loan funds to one or more of the following activities, including associated marketing research:

▲ design of the production process

▲ physical design of the relevant product(s)

▲ tooling and direct production costs associated with producing product for compliance and early market testing

▲ protection of core intellectual property

▲ trial and demonstration activities

▲ production of user and support documentation.

Cooperative research centres

A cooperative research centre (CRC) involves an alliance between one or more academic and research institutions on the one hand and one or more private sector companies on the other. The Commonwealth government provides partial funding for authorised centres, essentially matching the contribution to the centres made by the business partners. The Commonwealth is, of course, the chief source of funds for the CSIRO and university partners in each centre. Each CRC focuses on the needs of a specific industry, and carries out fundamental and applied research into the problems and opportunities facing firms in that industry. The CRC program is intended:

▲ to support long term, high quality scientific and technological research

▲ to strengthen the links between scientific researchers and the commercial users of their discoveries

▲ to create centres of excellence in both the conduct of research and the dissemination of its results

▲ to stimulate education and training, particularly at the post-graduate level.

Companies can seek involvement in existing or proposed CRCs on a longer term collaborative basis as a partner or an associate. Alternatively they may participate on a project basis, aiming to gain specific benefits from their involvement without making a longer term commitment to participation in the particular CRC's work. Money contributed to a CRC counts as eligible expenditure for the 150 per cent tax incentive: each after tax dollar contributed by businesses to a CRC generates over $6 expenditure on research. Businesses can gain additional benefits from access on a reciprocal basis, via their CRC participation, to research carried out by some of their competitors.

Programs supporting exporters

Standard economic theory declares that it is impossible for countries to have persistent balance of payments surpluses and deficits. When in the mid 1970s the United States began to demonstrate a persistent deficit, orthodox economists sought to explain it by saying that the problem was fixed exchange rates: the Nixon administration obligingly floated the United States dollar, and the United States trade deficit persisted. After twenty years of floating exchange rates the United States still had persistent, and growing, deficits: orthodox economists decided that the problem was the United States budget deficit, a proposition with little theoretical justification and no econometric one, but loudly proclaimed for all that.

Australia has trailed behind the United States in balance of payments problems as in many other areas: the Australian exchange rate was not floated until 1983, at which time the balance of payments deficit began to grow rather than shrink. In Australia, too, by 1995 the federal budget deficit was being blamed for the balance of payments one when twelve years of floating exchange rates had made no difference.

Non-economists have suggested other factors as contributing to the United States and Australian balance of payments deficits. A major part of the United States balance of payments deficit during the late 1970s and the 1980s was attributed to the large number of Japanese-made motor cars being exported to North America. Non-economists explained this by pointing to the superior fuel economy and higher reliability of Japanese cars. This explanation did not appeal to orthodox economists, since to them it was impossible for consumers to have demands which manufacturers did not automatically satisfy. Australian non-economists have also observed that much of the balance of payments deficit was made up by imported cars, particularly from South Korea, a country where tariff and administrative barriers all but ban motor car imports. Orthodox economists reject this argument with derision: according to the Law of Comparative Advantage, countries that tax or prohibit imports can only damage themselves.

Given the heavy influence of orthodox economists on Australian policy in the mid 1990s, it is surprising that any Australian schemes for the promotion of exports survived. The schemes did come under periodic attack from orthodox economists, usually on the grounds that any exporter who succeeded at all could have done so without government assistance. During the peak of the economists' ascendancy in the 1980s over the Australian government, several of the export facilitation services were moved to a user-pays basis, but since no users were prepared to pay, a number of subsidised schemes were retained and further ones developed.

Export market development grants

Austrade makes grants to exporters to partially reimburse them for certain of the costs incurred in seeking out, opening and expanding overseas markets. The overseas marketing activities must involve goods, services, industrial property rights and/or knowhow which is substantially of Australian origin. Any Australian resident — company, partnership or individual — may apply for a grant. Certain classes of organisations need special approval and may be subject to special conditions.

Grants can be up to a maximum of $200 000 towards eligible export marketing and sales promotional expenses. Eligibility is defined in the EMDG Act (Cwlth) 1974 and in general terms restricts grants to endeavours aimed at creating or increasing export sales. Exporters must spend a minimum of $30 000 to be eligible, and may receive grants equal to 50 per cent of their expense over $15 000. First-time users may elect to spread their eligible expenditure over two years. Firms may receive a maximum of four grants over an eight year period, with the proviso that each new grant must address a new market.

Economists 'got at' this scheme in 1995, reducing the maximum grant and introducing a requirement for firms to give advance notice of claims and applying additional screening criteria. It is, at the time of going to press, under threat of complete abolition.

Austrade loans

Firms with an appropriate history of successful operation and growth, including some success in export markets, may be eligible for concessional loans from Austrade. Applicants are required to present a comprehensive and soundly presented proposal leading to the generation of at least $3 million of new export revenue over five years. The minimum loan is $150 000; larger amounts may be advanced at Austrade's discretion.

Successful applicants may be offered low-cost loans, interest and repayment free for the first three years and repaid, with moderate interest, over the next three. Firms may be permitted to apply up to 30 per cent of the loan to the purchase of directly related capital equipment; the balance is expected to be applied to marketing activities including travel, promotion, advertising, salaries and office expenses directly related to the export program.

Preference will generally be given to small and medium sized firms who have developed an innovative approach to export marketing.

Asia business links

The Asia business links program provides a reimbursement of up to 50 per cent of the cost of flying a key contact to Australia, providing them with accommodation, and paying their fees on externally provided courses. Eligible visits last no less than two weeks and no more than six months and their program must be directly relevant to increasing Australian exports.

The grants must be approved in advance of the relevant visit, and applicants must show that they have the capacity and ability to capitalise on the opportunity created by such a visit, and to be able to make a quantified statement of the value of the likely benefits. In the event that more valid requests for assistance under this program than the budgetary provision can cover, proposals will be ranked in order of merit and the available funds allocated accordingly.

Export Finance and Insurance Corporation

The Export Finance and Development Corporation (EFIC) facilitates and encourages Australian exporters by providing them with insurance and support. As well as its direct measures, EFIC assists its clients in accessing conventional finance. EFIC operates a number of programs.

Credit insurance

EFIC offers exporters and their financiers insurance against the risk that payment may not be received for goods shipped on credit terms. The insurance available covers political and exchange transfer risk as well as commercial risks such as buyer insolvency, non-acceptance of conforming goods and contract repudiation.

Overseas investment insurance

EFIC offers insurance to Australian investors overseas against certain political causes of loss, including expropriation, damage or destruction of property as a result of war, riot or similar event and inability, for political reasons, to remit earnings or return capital to Australia. Insurance is only available to projects with a significant net benefit to Australia.

Export finance

EFIC may, to approved borrowers and projects, advance money on more favourable terms than are generally available on the finance markets. EFIC's terms are intended to match the subsidised export finance provided by certain other countries. EFIC may also collaborate with the Australian International Development Assistance Bureau to provide soft loans to support appropriate projects.

Bonding

EFIC operates 'unsecured' Performance Bond and Advance Payment Bond facilities to enable exporters of capital goods or related services to increase their drawings from their bankers beyond the point that the bankers, in the absence of such bonds, would be prepared to go.

Export working capital guarantees

EFIC offers guarantees to banks or other lending institutions to allow them to finance work in progress on an export contract where the exporter's own security is inadequate to support the funds required. Guarantees can be provided in support of all manufactured goods and services exports, but not the export of internationally traded commodities.

Access to export finance

Small, new exporters (defined as firms with less than thirty employees, who have been exporting for five years or less, and whose annual export sales are $5 million or less) may be reimbursed 50 per cent or $5000, whichever is the less, of their invoiced expenditure on consultants who assist them with the preparation of an application for export finance for a specific export proposal. It is not necessary for the firm to have actually received finance, but there must have been an application that was accepted for evaluation by a finance provider.

AusIndustry maintains a register of approved finance consultants, but applicants are not restricted to the consultants on this register.

Small and medium enterprise support

For most of the twentieth century large firms dominated the economies of developed nations, dominating both private sector output and employment. From the mid 1980s, however, following extensive deregulation of their national finance industries, many major firms in the English-speaking countries adopted strategies aimed at improving their profits without attempting to grow their revenue, and many of the staff who were required when these firms were expanding were 'outplaced' as their former employer 'downsized'. The new emphasis on profit rather than growth meant that many activities previously considered strategic, or at least an intrinsic part of the business and therefore reserved for employed staff, were reclassified as non-strategic and therefore eligible for outsourcing.

Much publicity has been given to the number of people retrenched as major corporations downsized. It came to be confidently asserted that the era of large firms was over and small and medium sized ones were going to be the new engine of employment and economic growth.[4] After ten years of this process there is no clear statistical evidence, in either Australia or the USA, for any decisive shift away from large firms as the major employers. Some large firms never downsized; many of the firms that outplaced functions did so to other large firms who, in consequence, grew even larger, and many successful small firms grew to become large ones, continuing to grow once they had left the small firm cohort.

One of the things that definitely has happened in the English speaking countries is a decisive shift away from the concept of large firms as 'good employers'. There is very little excitement to be had from working in a firm that has abandoned growth as a business strategy, and not much joy in belonging to a firm that will lay off staff for no better reason than to make the next quarterly earnings report look better. While highly qualified and well-motivated people still join large firms, they no longer do so with the intention of building a career: the large firm is a source of income, experience, and a set of contacts which build the employee's capacity for an independent career.

In the United States from 1995 on there was increasing concern among some large companies, such as Ford Motor Company, about the declining quality of applicants for their staff and technical positions and the fragile loyalty of those whom they did appoint. These companies stated their ambition to become 'employers of choice'. Ford has a share ownership structure that insulates it to some extent from the short term pressures of the share market; the example is unlikely to be widely followed until the share market accepts it as valid.

Excitement has not left the economy entirely: there are many very exciting small and medium enterprises, where employees share the excitement and the chance to participate in the growth of an enterprise and the development of new markets with entrepreneurs. The challenge and involvement offered by jobs in such firms may compensate their employees for the lower salaries and even greater insecurity when small-firm employment is contrasted with that offered by large ones. There are, however, a very great number of small and medium enterprises, and United States studies suggest that no more than one in two hundred of them are genuine fast growers, while 95 per cent of them aren't growing at all. Just getting a job in a small or medium enterprise, or even starting one, is no guarantee of challenge and excitement.

The disillusion with large firms as the drivers of economic growth, and the exaltation of small and medium ones, no matter how dubious the factual underpinning of either sentiment, has led to a pronounced effort by governments, in Australia and elsewhere, to encourage small and medium enterprises with targeted programs. Some of these are described below.

Enterprise improvement

AusIndustry has adopted and enhanced a set of programs originally developed by the National Industry Extensions Service (NIES). AusIndustry maintains a team of case officers who provide a client manager service for firms, advising them of suitable programs and, under certain circumstances, recommending a subsidy to assist with the costs of engaging an appropriate consultant.

The AusIndustry enterprise improvement program helps firms to:

▲ assess their business in terms of its overall cost-effectiveness and market positioning

▲ identify problem areas which may be preventing firms from running a cost-effective operation or providing the goods and services that the market really wants

▲ identify options for addressing problems and affect the cost of engaging specialist external advice, and

▲ develop a plan of action for improvement.

The suite of programs is very comprehensive, and firms taking advantage of it have the assurance of a defined program and a defined cost each time they elect to purchase a module.

Technology Access Program

The Technology Access Program aims to enhance the competitiveness of Australian firms, particularly small and medium enterprises by improving their ability to understand, evaluate and adapt appropriate technology to lift their capability and their performance. The program also aims to improve companies' access to the technical knowledge and expertise found in a range of institutions across the country, generally in the TAFE and university systems. The program does not support the purchase of capital equipment.

There is a system of competitive grants available to sponsoring institutions, in order to encourage the development of high quality centres for providing advice and establishing demonstration and training facilities in the various relevant technologies. AusIndustry deploys a number of technology counsellors, whose task it is to direct enterprises to the appropriate technology centre and to ensure that they receive appropriate advice.

While the program provides no capital subsidies, client firms may be able to obtain subsidies under the Enterprise Improvement Program for studies and consultancies leading to improved plans for the adoption and integration of new technology into their operations.

Business Networks Program

The Business Networks Program assists groups comprised of at least three separate businesses to undertake joint activities with the intention of increasing their competitiveness or their capabilities. Activities can include jointly targeting export or domestic markets, forming a consortium to win large contracts, undertaking joint product development, building joint production facilities or managing a common procurement scheme.

The program is designed in three stages.

Stage 1

In the first stage the program provides a network broker who will assist the prospective participants in a network to set out a basis for their future cooperation, identifying their common interests and objectives and suggesting an appropriate management framework. The broker's services are uncharged during this stage, but the prospective network members will have to pay for their own marketing research, and their legal and financial planning advice.

Stage 2

During Stage 2 the network participants, under the guidance and with the assistance of the broker, prepare a business plan for the operation of the network. The network members are required to meet 50 per cent of the broker's costs during this stage.

Stage 3

The third and final stage is the implementation of the business plan, supported by assistance with the network's operating costs for its first year. Support can be requested for a range of activities, including the salary of a network manager and the costs of rationalising production or distribution.

Support is limited to a maximum of $60 000 on a dollar for dollar basis for any one network, and if the members of the network require more than the trivial involvement of the broker during this stage, the broker's costs will be deducted from any grant ultimately made.

Eligibility

Admission to the program follows an assessment process and is not automatic. The primary criteria are:

▲ there must be at least three participants, two of which must be small or medium enterprises, defined as firms with less than 500 employees or an annual turnover of less than $100 million — the third core participant can be a small or medium enterprise but it can also be a research agency, a public enterprise, a TAFE or higher education institution, or a large private enterprise

▲ the network must intend to produce or market internationally traded goods and services

▲ the participants must be prepared to cooperate in a strategic business activity

▲ participants must be prepared to disclose confidential financial and other information about their firm to the broker, and eventually to each other

▲ the senior staff of each enterprise must be fully committed to the success of the network, and the staff designated as network contacts must have appropriately delegated authority.

Getting help
Form and substance

Public servants have a reasonably well-developed sense of self preservation, and one of their most important defence mechanisms is a concentration on procedural correctness. If the law and/or the current regulations state that an application for assistance under a given program must be made on a given form, it is extremely unlikely that applications made on a different form will be successful. Programs such as the 'access to export finance' program described above show that the government recognises that getting applications together in the proper form and to the proper people is not necessarily simple, but the proper form is still required.

Many public servants are disposed to be helpful, and if asked will tell an applicant what errors have been made in completing a form, or which program the applicant should have been applying for in the first place. Such helpfulness is not always maintained in the face of shouting or physical threats. The people with whom the public deals are seldom those who designed the forms and almost never those who devised the policy. Shouting at them will not change either.

Before an entrepreneur applies for assistance on any government program they should get a copy of the application forms and any guides or advice that may be available. If they think that they are qualified, but there seems to be a lot of detailed information needed, they should consider getting their accountant or their lawyer to complete and submit the application. This may increase the chances of success on the first application and it may reduce the peak level of the entrepreneur's blood pressure.

Life and death

All the programs described in this chapter have been put together on the assumption that the entrepreneurial enterprise applying for them is vigorous and successful. The programs are intended to make a successful firm more so, or to bring the date

> *These programs are not intended to rescue dying firms from the grave ...*

at which some major achievement can be celebrated forwards. They are not intended to rescue dying firms from the grave.

In general firms should base their applications for assistance upon the assumption that they are already successful and will continue to be so whatever the outcome of the application. While we do not encourage deceit, we feel that a robustly confident attitude is appropriate even when the facts do not fully support it. Problems should not be concealed, but they certainly should not be emphasised.

'Grant ready'

All the programs come with explanatory material, which we have only summarised here. Different programs are appropriate at different stages of an enterprise's development, and the entrepreneur should ensure that the enterprise has not only reached the appropriate stage but has documented its achievement before applying for a grant.

EFIC should not be approached by anyone without an order, or at least an unequivocal letter of intent, from an overseas buyer. Even when there is an order, the enterprise should have run the appropriate credit checks before approaching EFIC. If a firm wants something more complex than simple credit insurance from EFIC, or from any other agency, they will need to be able to state in considerable detail exactly what they propose to do with the money. Firms might like an export market development grant or three, but before approaching Austrade they should decide which countries they want to export to, what they want to sell them, in what quantities and over what timescales.

The questions granting agencies will ask are basically the same as those a potential investor would ask, and competent managers should generally know the answers: the effort, if any, will be in documenting the answers, not finding out what they are. Firms which develop and maintain an entrepreneurial business plan, as we describe in this book, should have little difficulty answering any questions they might get asked, and they may expect little more in moving from application to reception of their grant.

End notes

1 Otto and Voss (1994) demonstrated, by means of a long term longitudinal study, a positive, causal relationship between government investment and economic growth in Australia.

2 Dixit and Pindyck (1994) are not concerned (in this book) to make a case for or against intervention; if anything, their other publications show them to be against direct government intervention in private sector investment and pricing decisions. They do, however, demonstrate that the 'marginal' theory of investment is fatally flawed and so a country wishing to stimulate investment cannot rely solely on slightly lower taxes and/or wages than its established rivals to persuade firms to relocate from them to it.

3 The United States relentlessly deploys economic theory in the service of its political and economic interests. Australia, from time to time, confuses economic theory with its political and economic interests. The difference is significant.

4 Large firms are something of an embarrassment to orthodox economists, whose theories are based upon the assumption that all firms are infinitesimally small. This may have made some economists over-eager to celebrate the end of the large enterprise.

The entrepreneurial business plan

The entrepreneurial business plan paradigm

There are a very large number of books in print setting out rules for writing a successful business plan.[1] With so much advice, not all of it entirely consistent, which entrepreneurial business planning guide should you follow?

The best answer may be that most of these guides miss one of the central points: formal excellence in plan presentation is neither a necessary nor a sufficient condition for a plan to be successful. A business plan is a documentary record of certain analyses and the conclusions and recommendations drawn from them, and if the preparatory work has been done correctly, presenting the results in a different order will not detract from the validity of the conclusions and recommendations.

In Chapter 3 we presented a paradigm, a 'rule of rules', for entrepreneurial business planning. In Figure 3.2 we set out the paradigm in tabular form. This enhanced paradigm is a general template for the production of entrepreneurial business plans. A successful plan must cover four key areas:

▲ it must be a communication with a well-defined sender and receiver:

 ▶ the sender must be a competent entrepreneurial team inviting the receivers to join the project, as financial investors or participants in some other form

 ▶ the receiver(s) must be people who could reasonably respond positively to this invitation

▲ it must convey a clear proposal for an entrepreneurial act of venture creation with well-defined objectives

▲ it must be useful as a simulation device, to answer potential investors' questions about the likely outcome and possible tactical options under various changes in external circumstances or internal capabilities

▲ it must include two particular elements:

  ❱ a well written document as we describe in this chapter

  ❱ a fully functional financial model as we describe in Chapter 14.

We also set out six fundamental success rules:

▲ adapt the length of the plan and the depth of its detail to the interests and circumstances of the target audience

▲ empower the plan reader

▲ adapt the plan to meet the specific interests of particular investors

▲ anticipate and address the target audience's 'due diligence' requirements

▲ structure the 'deal' such that each investor receives a reward appropriate to the level of their investment and the degree of risk assumed[2]

▲ present a 'base case' scenario that is clearly:

  ❱ practical

  ❱ at least locally optimal (such that no single parameter or timing change can improve the outcome)

  ❱ soundly based.

Structuring the written plan

The rules set out in Chapter 3 and summarised above set out necessary and sufficient conditions for a plan to be successful. One of the two key elements is the written plan, and here we set out a proven set of recommendations for producing an intelligible and attractive plan document. This is not the only possible structure: many of the popular business planning guides include valid structures that differ in detail from this one; but it is a structure that we are comfortable with. Entrepreneurs and planners who invent their own plan structure as distinct from adapting one of the established ones may be, in our opinion, adding an unnecessary layer of complexity and risk to their task.

We have learned from long and sometimes bitter experience that, whatever the exact format, two constraints should be observed if the plan is ever to be read by someone important enough to authorise it:

▲ A plan must start with an executive summary which must be brief, readable and to the point. Plan writers whose executive summary exceeds two A4 sized pages or 700 words should examine it very carefully to make sure that they have not been verbose or included extraneous material.

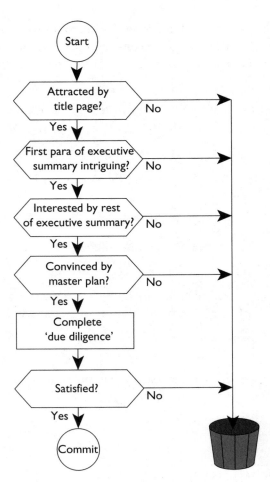

Figure 16.1 The evaluation route: 'Every post a losing post except the last one'

▲ The master plan, including the executive summary, should contain the *minimum* amount of material needed by a plan reviewer to make an initial judgement. Plans that exceed forty A4 sized pages of text and five A4 sized pages of red tape, headings, titles, indices etc, are extremely difficult to read as well as difficult to appreciate as a whole.

The second constraint will generally mean that much material a careful reviewer needs to examine will be left out of the master plan. This material should be prepared and either supplied with the master plan or provided on demand, according to the reviewer's wishes. It will generally be much more detailed than the equivalent section of the master plan and it need only be friendly to specialist readers. The master plan might, for example, state that a key invention was patented: an attachment might contain the full patent specification.

The reason for setting upper limits on the size of the plan and of the executive summary is found in the nature of the review process. Senior executives in major companies spend, according to Gary Hamel,[3] a little over an hour a week thinking about the future of their corporation; they recognise that this is too little, but it is all the time that they can spare from current pressing matters, and they are not going to waste it if they can help it. Professional venture capitalists spend more time considering the future, but they have more proposals to consider: a professional first stage review of a business plan can take two or more days, and every venture capitalist is likely to be asked to support twenty or more projects every week.

The first paragraph of the executive summary tells the reviewer whether he or she should read the rest of it, pass the plan to someone else, or forget it, and the rest of the executive summary tells the reader whether the rest of the plan is likely to repay the effort of reading it. The body of the plan must be flexibly bound and easy to handle because, among those plans and proposals piled into the 'to read' stack, those that can be read on an aeroplane or added to an overfull briefcase to be taken home are those that are actually likely to be read by the targeted receiver.

A: The executive summary

The executive summary must be structured, from its first paragraph, to capture the attention of the manager or venture capitalist for whom it has been prepared. At the same time, it must be an accurate overview of the plan as a whole. Certain points as listed below must be covered in the summary. The order given is not 'Holy Writ', but it makes a certain sort of sense.

▲ Who is the target reader (venture capitalist, banker, colleagues, superior manager in the same company, partners to a collaboration, partners to a new venture …)?

▲ What does the plan writer want the plan reader to do?

▲ What is the principal benefit that the reader can expect, if she takes the recommended action and the plan is then carried out successfully?

▲ What is the most significant and collateral (non-cash) benefit offered to the plan reader?

▲ What is the project described by the plan intended to achieve? What is the objective measure of success, and when will it be reached?

▲ What is the maximum cash exposure as far as the reader is concerned? What is the planned investment, over what period is it to be drawn down, and what is the internal rate of return (IRR)?

▲ If the aim of the project is to introduce a new product, describe it in one sentence. What, in one more sentence, is its state of development?

▲ If it is a new product (a good or a service), will it be pioneering a new market, an early entrant in a developing market, or a new product challenging for a share of an established market?

▲ What is the projected time to positive cash flow and to a positive cash balance?

Further material is optional: if the executive summary can be kept to a single page, so much the better. If additional material is going to be included up to the word limit, then it must be material that the reviewing manager or investor wants to hear. Such material might indicate who, if anybody, is going to be adversely affected by the new product. When a plan is being prepared for an existing business, an opportunity to punish a trade rival or put some pressure on an over-bearing supplier may be regarded more favourably than a less aggressive plan with a slightly higher IRR.

A number of boxes in this chapter will be based upon the hypothetical — and inconsistent — UMB. The imaginary facts are not always going to be the same.

This plan has been prepared for evaluation by professional venture investors. We are seeking a lead investor who will head a syndicate that will raise a total of $2.5 million to enable the early success of the Ultimate Metal Bashing Company (UMB Pty Ltd) to be built on.

UMB has just completed its second year of trading, turning over $2 million and showing a trading profit before abnormal items. We need extra capital to expand our facilities in order to fill a contract with a major multinational company. We hold a letter of intent covering sales to this customer of $8 million over the next three years. Other opportunities worth three times this are on hold until we are equipped to meet them.

Our plans show that UMB can be made ready for a stock market flotation, either on the ASX or NASDAQ, in no more than five years at which time it will have annual sales of over $35 million and still be growing strongly. EBIDT will be over $7 million.

UMB have designed and now manufacture a critical part of the catalytic converter used in motor vehicles. Cars incorporating our patented design weigh 750 g less and use 0.5 g less platinum than cars using older technology. These are important benefits for both fleet fuel economy and total manufacturing cost, and all the major motor manufacturers have shown a strong interest in our product.

We will look to the lead investor for advice on the most appropriate structure of the investment, but the example shown here suggests that the investing syndicate should receive an effective annual ROI of no less than 55 per cent.

B: The opportunity statement

B1: The value statement

Before describing the opportunity in any detail summarise it in general terms, first from the users' and then from the supplier's viewpoint. State whether the product is bought by consumers or by businesses, whether it is consumed, what the repurchase interval or frequency is, and what is the nature of the benefit the user anticipates. If the product is to be bought by businesses, state how it fits into these customer businesses' value chain. If the product is to be bought by consumers, state the key valuable properties.

By taking the purchaser's viewpoint it becomes possible to determine where the supplier is in the delivery chain, what proportion of the final value results from the supplier's activities, and what factors assure the supplier of a continuing business. A firm's managers are also better placed to consider strategic options, such as downstream integration or alternate channel strategies, when they lift their focus from the cash they receive for their products to look at what their customers are doing with these products.

This section might reasonably conclude with a summary of the basic value proposition. If the product is to be marketed to other businesses, include a short description of how the product is to be put into use and an indication as to whether the primary advantages are received as cost reductions or revenue increases. Some indication of the absolute value a typical user might receive from using the product could fit in here. Any assumption about the size of a typical business user or the demographic characteristics of a typical consumer should be stated and not left to the reader's imagination.

Motor vehicle suppliers in most countries are obliged to observe strict pollution standards, including limits on nitrogen oxide and carbon monoxide emission. In the United States they are also required to achieve certain fuel efficiency targets. Most petrol-engined vehicles are equipped with a catalytic converter in the exhaust system, which accelerates the conversion of nitrogen oxides and carbon monoxide to harmless nitrogen and carbon dioxide. The catalyst used is platinum or some other rare and precious metal.

UMB supply metal matrices to catalyst manufacturers, who add the platinum and sell converters to exhaust manufacturers, who build up complete exhaust systems which they deliver to motor manufacturers for assembly into complete vehicles and eventual sale to the public.

UMB matrices are lighter than those now generally used, which helps manufacturers to improve the fuel economy of their cars, and the superior airflow characteristics means that less platinum is required, reducing the cost of the completed converter.

There are thirty million cars produced annually, and nearly 400 million in service worldwide, and if all of them used the lighter weight catalytic converters incorporating UMB's patented design, annual oil demand would fall by about 1.5 million barrels, worth $30 million. The saving in platinum is worth, at current prices, approximately $90 million a year.

B2: The gap

An opportunity consists of the combination of a product and the existence of a latent or unsatisfied demand for that product. A cautious reviewing manager must ask the questions: Why this product? Why this time? Very few ideas are wholly original. Most have been thought of before, but either no venture was launched, or a venture was launched and failed. Very few opportunities go begging indefinitely, and so the circumstances that make the new opportunity feasible must be relatively recent.

If some apparent demand has been unsatisfied for a long time, then there is an automatic doubt going to be raised about its urgency. The most attractive conditions for launching a new venture are when some recent and continuing change in the physical, technological, economic or social environment is activating the latent demand. If there is some proprietary technology that makes the venturer uniquely positioned to satisfy this demand, so much the better.

The nature of the changes that are creating a new set of opportunities should be explained and quantified. If, for example, a new set of environmental standards is about to be adopted there will be a market in products that assist and test conformance. How long will it be before the demand for these products will become significant? How long will it take to be satisfied? What follow-on opportunities may there be?

Catalytic converters were first fitted to cars in the late 1970s in response to environmental concerns, and considerable effort was expended in optimising their design over the next few years. In recent years relatively little effort has gone into improving the performance or reducing the cost of these devices.

UMB have secured the services of Dr Olga Petropavlosk, whose previous credits include the design of the airspeed measuring assembly on the MiG 31 fighter aircraft. Dr Petropavlosk applied advanced mathematical methods to the fluid mechanics of catalytic converters, and was able to show that a revised design could achieve a significantly more uniform exposure of the exhaust gases to the catalyst. She was also able to develop a practical way of manufacturing the new core matrix.

B3: The industry, product and market

If the history of the market, or of previous products offered in it, or of previous versions of the product of which this plan is the subject, will assist the plan reviewer to understand the scale and urgency of the opportunity described, then a brief description of the history and current state of the relevant industries and markets should be included here. This may be vital if the project involves a resurrection of some previous failure, particularly if the failure was notorious. If the reviewer needs to know something about the industry, and probably doesn't know enough, then it should also be included in this subsection

If a reviewer needs some essential technical background information to make a proper judgement, this material should be provided here. This heading should not provide an excuse for the plan writer to show off, nor should it stray too far from the relevant products and markets. This is not the place to correct the shortcomings in the reviewer's education in economics, politics or modern history. If an employee of a computer company is directed to prepare a business case for a new software product, they may not enhance their career prospects by starting their plan with a twenty page dissertation on Babbage, Turing and Ada Lovelace. If a former employee of a computer company sets out to write a business plan for anyone else, they should make a conscious effort to avoid the liberal helpings of alphabet soup in which the computer industry is prone to float its output.

B4: Product definition

At the risk of being obvious, include a dispassionate and reasonably complete description of the actual product, including its name, its principal components, and how it is produced and used. Do not assume that the target readers have any technical knowledge whatsoever, or indeed, any specialist knowledge of any sort at this point.

If 'arch' phraseology is avoided, then a statement of the totally obvious should not cause offence, and it may save the plan from being rejected by someone who does not understand something which most people would find perfectly obvious. An English training establishment was thrown into confusion when a noble lord, enrolled on one of its courses, complained that there was something wrong with the water because his toothbrush would not foam. It was eventually discovered that this was the first occasion in the noble lord's life that he had not been attended by a nurse or valet and had therefore been expected to put tooth powder on the brush himself.

Do not assume that the readers of the plan can drive a car, cook, sew, sweep floors or explain the operation of a nuclear reactor.

The complete product definition includes all the associated services, whether being offered under this business plan or not, the physical delivery system, and the principle marketing messages. The relationship between the typical buyer, the user and the end-user must be stated, possibly in general terms.

> UMB manufacture catalyst matrices, fabricated metal objects about 250 millimetres long and 120 millimetres in diameter, which are then supplied to Johnson Mathey Ltd or to other catalyst suppliers for the addition of catalytic material before onselling to manufacturers of exhaust systems.

The catalytic converters are placed where the exhaust gases from the motor car's engine must pass through them. They are required to slow down and diffuse the exhaust gases so that at least 99 per cent of the nitrogen oxides and 80 per cent of the carbon monoxide is catalysed to harmless byproducts; at the same time, they are required to allow the exhaust gases to flow freely, so that back-pressure does not reduce the efficiency of the car's engine.

The exhaust gases are hot and somewhat corrosive as they arrive at the converter, and the matrix has to be able to function for at least the design life of the exhaust system without losing its structural integrity or efficiency.

B5: Pre-launch product development

There should be a clear and unambiguous statement of the state of development of the product (concept, prototype, ready for market, on market for x years with sales of y dollars) and if the product is not ready for market there should be a clear statement of the time and money expected to be involved in getting it ready for market. This must include any regulatory permission and certifications required.

If the product is not already on the market it is useful, at this point, to include a short summary of the track record and qualifications of the staff responsible for completing the development and for gaining the regulatory approvals and test certificates. Examiners and plan evaluators are aware that nearly-ready and nearly-approved products can easily become massive financial liabilities.

UMB have been shipping Petropavlosk-designed matrices for performance and accelerated life cycle testing for the past two years. No serious problems have been discovered, and the minor ones have been completely rectified. Once the needed production equipment is in place deliveries of the first model can start without further development.

Each different make and model of car will require a new design, but this is a routine process which Dr Petropavlosk has largely automated.

B6: Product security

What factors prevent or inhibit an imitator from replicating the product and initiating a price war? Outline the key patents, registered designs, copyrights, business names and trade marks that provide legal protection for the product. Describe other product security aspects if necessary: trade secrets, unique skills, pre-emptive marketing and/or production strategies, or any other means proposed to avoid excessive, or excessively early, competition.

Any given model of matrix can be reverse-engineered fairly easily, and we expect the after-market business to be substantially penetrated by such 'clones' in spite of our strong patents.

Each new geometry of matrix needs to be recalculated and without access to Dr Petropavlosk or the computer programs that she has written this will prove exceedingly difficult. There are only six other mathematicians of Dr Petropavlosk's eminence specialising in flow problems of this type in the world, and it is unlikely that any of them will give up their current positions to go into competition with her.

The circumstances that led to a world-class mathematician starting work at a small, Adelaide-based metal fabricator are not likely to be repeated. Dr Petropavlosk will leave us shortly to take up a senior position at a leading Australian university, but she has signed an agreement with us that ensures that she is very unlikely to become our competitor.

B7: Product risks

Without turning the prospective investor's hair white too rapidly, summarise the major risks to the successful exploitation of the opportunity, and the risks consequential on success. If the opportunity is to supply a safety-critical component for a range of passenger aircraft, product failure may have greater consequences and the possible legal liability may extend further than would be the case with a proposal for marketing pre-loved pet rocks.

This subsection of the plan should convey a justified confidence that the risks and possible liabilities have been properly analysed, and that the risks are minimised and the liabilities quarantined. In some cases a full failure-mode analysis will have been carried out and the results supplied as an appendix. Note that product liability is a developing area of the law and intuitive conclusions may lack legal support. It has been claimed, for example, that potatoes are only tolerated by long familiarity. A new product with the same level of oxalic acid and propensity to produce the poison solanine would be banned or supplied on prescription only.

B8: Development plans

A successful new product inevitably attracts imitators, and familiarity with the product almost equally inevitably reduces the perceived fair price of each unit of the product over time. If unchecked, these two factors will lead to the stunting or failure of the innovator's business.

A continued development plan is needed to anticipate and avert this cause of premature business failure. This plan will provide for the progressive addition of features to the product or introduction of complementary products. This in turn will maintain the innovator's market share and ensure that the innovator's business continues to grow, with the market when it is no longer possible to grow faster than it. While the forward plans need not be stated in detail they must be outlined and their probable cost set out. It will be useful to show what the development program will cost as a fraction of revenue, but some definite number, either of staff or of dollars, should also be shown.

If the plan is truly for a 'smash and grab' type opportunity with no intention of building an ongoing business, this should be stated clearly and early in the plan, since the absence of a long term revenue stream will have a significant effect on the present value of the opportunity. If the plan is for a continuing business, but no long term development plans are outlined, investors may evaluate it as if it was a simple market raid.

C: Marketing analysis

C1: Summary

A marketing statement must be included in the completed plan, covering the main points raised in Chapters 9 and 10 of this book. It is not always necessary to bind the complete marketing plan with the business plan, but a complete plan should normally be prepared and can then be referenced by the marketing statement.

The marketing statement should commence with a summary (which should normally fit on to a single page) in which the following points must be covered:

▲ the unit volume and the gross revenue for the product launch year and the last year of the business plan

▲ an indication of the early market research results and a consequent estimate of the marketing risk associated with the launch

▲ the geographic extent of marketing and distribution in the product launch year and the last year of the business plan

▲ the main and supplementary distribution channels that are to be used in the product launch year and the last year of the business plan

▲ the primary promotional messages (unique selling propositions) and vehicles to be used at product launch and at the end of the plan period.

In 1995 UMB shipped 110 000 standard model core matrices at an average price of $20, as well as 5000 Petropavlosk cores for testing at $22. Approximately 90 per cent of these cores were eventually fitted to Australian manufactured vehicles. In 1996 we expect to ship 70 000 Petropavlosk cores and 90 000 standard models, with 60 000 units exported. By 1999 we hope to ship 1 million cores, all Petropavlosk models, and approaching 90 per cent exported.

C2: State of the market

This subsection should provide an analysis of what state the market is currently in and in what direction or directions it is heading. If the current proposal involves creating a new market, explain how the relevant needs are currently being satisfied — or frustrated. Explain how the market would develop if this proposal did not proceed. Describe the established firms that are most likely to identify the opportunity and fill the gap.

If the new product is to be launched into an existing market, describe the state of development of the market with as much precision as possible: how long since the first product into this market was launched, the fraction of potential users who are now actual users, the growth in the market in each of the last three years if known. Name the largest supplier to the existing market and estimate their market share. Provide an estimate of how this share has been changing in recent years. Estimate the number of suppliers in total, and how many of them have a market share above 1 per cent.

> … the world market for cars, and therefore catalytic converter core matrices, is relatively stable at around thirty million per year. The demand for Petropavlosk cores is very new and the product very exciting to specialists, but adoption will be limited, partly by the rate at which new models are introduced, and partly by UMB's capacity. Motor vehicle manufacturers do not like cutting in a new part of the emission control system during a model's life, because of the large cost of re-certification, and UMB has made a strategic decision to be a manufacturer to avoid making life too easy for imitators …

C3: Volume and revenue projections

There should be a projection of sales to final purchasers for the whole of the plan period. The projections can be based on quarterly or annual periods; products with high margins sold in low volumes are best projected on an annual basis, while a quarterly projection suits faster-moving products. The projections should show the average price and the final purchaser revenue for each period. Depending on the proposed distribution arrangements these figures may need some manipulation in order to predict periodic cash receipts and periodic accounts payable for the new venture.

The methodology for developing the sales forecast should be stated, but not necessarily explained in detail in the main body of the plan. If a computer model has been used, the model should be made available to the examiners or reviewing managers, and the main parameters and assumptions set out in the plan. We generally recommend the use of a computable model along the lines described in Chapter 8, but other methods of projection, to the extent that they have been proved in practice, can be used if they are believed to be more suitable.

Not every business plan will be improved by the use of a computed adoption and sales model. This is particularly so in the case where the major product is an expensive item with a very small number of potential users. Model results, for plans involving less than four sales per period, are little better than guesses.[4]

C4: Distribution channels

The whole route from the planned venture to the end user should be mapped out, and where the venture is itself critically reliant on one or more suppliers, partners or distributors the relationship between these suppliers and the venture must be shown.

Note that there are a number of information and possibly material flows that may need to be described.

▲ Product information, both current and planned, must reach potential buyers and users. It may also be required by retailers, dealers, agents, franchisees etc. How is it going to get to them, how much is it going to cost, and who is going to pay?

▲ Orders must be taken from buyers and processed in some way. Who takes these orders at each stage in the distribution channel, and how are they motivated and paid?

▲ Who arranges physical delivery or service application? What are the quality controls, and how is customer satisfaction measured?

▲ What are the after-sales service requirements, and how are they satisfied? What are they projected to cost, and how are they to be paid for?

▲ Who collects the user's money, how does it find its way back to the supplier, what commissions and charges are taken off it in transit, and how long will the journey take?

▲ How does legal liability flow up and down the channel? Can this supplier be put in jeopardy by the actions of an indirect agent or retailer? How is this risk controlled?

C5: Promotional strategy

The business plan does not have to include the complete promotional plan, but it should include an overview of the proposed launch and follow-on promotional strategy. Matters that should be covered include answers to the following:

▲ What is the planned launch budget and what are the principal launch events?

▲ What are the key promotional messages that will be used? How do they relate to the value proposition set out in section C1?

▲ What is the total promotional budget in the first and last year of the plan, expressed both as a dollar amount and as a percentage of budgeted retail sales?

▲ What is the approximate division of the proposed expenditure between above the line (advertising) and below the line (focused promotion)? What sponsorships or other high-profile activities are planned?

▲ What media split is foreshadowed (trade press, general press, radio, television, billboards etc)?

▲ When the downstream distribution system involves retailers, dealers or other third party distributors, who pays for the advertising and point of sale promotion material? Who designs it? Who determines (or strongly recommends) the expenditure level?

▲ What are the metrics and targets of the promotional campaign, in particular, the target levels of name recognition and brand/product approval among potential purchasers?

C6: Price management

The proposed launch price or price structure should be set out, together with an indication of the post-launch pricing strategy. Where there are competitors already established in the market, their pricing policies should be summarised here, together with an account of these suppliers' reactions to previous attempts to break into their markets. Some indication should be given as to the scale of volume and *ad hoc* discounts that are likely to be encountered.

If the product and the market are both new, an account of the price setting process should be included here including a reasonably detailed account of the current costs borne by a typical user in satisfying or suppressing the needs that the new venture's products address. When the product is offered to business users, or confers some prestige or exclusivity benefits on early consumers, some account must be provided as to how the price structure will be managed after the early user benefits are exhausted and the perceived fair price falls.

> ... core matrices have been traditionally sold by weight, and we shall continue to do so, although our price per kilogram for Petropavlosk cores will be higher than that for standard cores, reflecting their increased sophistication and higher performance. The price to the catalyst manufacturers will typically be 5 per cent higher for a Petropavlosk core than for a standard one, while the catalyst manufacturers can sell the completed catalytic converter at 3 per cent less while increasing their own margins ...

D: Key actions and events

D1: Summary

For some plans, a complete project plan covering thousands of events and actions might be appropriate, and if such a plan exists, a one or two page summary could be included in the business plan at this point. In any case, a product launch will involve numerous events connected by time-consuming activities and a reviewing manager might like to see that these have been allowed for.

Similarly, when venture capitalists and reviewing managers permit projects to proceed, they have a natural curiosity about the results. This section of the plan tells them how long they will have to control themselves before demanding to see what has been done with their money. The primary purpose of the action plan is, however, a way of formalising the risks in terms of both time and function that run between 'time now' and the time that net cash becomes positive.

D2: Operations

A business plan is a plan for doing things, and this section of the plan is a suitable place to describe what is going to be done, and when. If the product(s) to be marketed have a tangible component or components, these must be manufactured, packed and distributed with a provision for handling returns, providing warranty service and the like. If the plan is primarily concerned with a service opportunity, there will be training and documentation requirements for the service delivery personnel and provision for quality control and performance feedback.

Premises will be needed: Are they to be built or are existing premises suitable? Are they to be bought or leased? What are the possibilities for expansion or contraction? There may be vehicles, plant or tools to be acquired: What will the terms be, and what contingent liabilities are going to be incurred?

D3: Milestones

Many venture capitalists and reviewing managers may be unfamiliar with fully developed PERT diagrams and Gantt charts, but they will generally understand a milestone list. A list suitable for inclusion in the main business plan should be no more than one or two pages long, and the number of levels of significance should be selected accordingly.

Care should be taken to include the milestones of particular interest to the reviewer, particularly those that should be achieved before major capital draw downs or the incurring of serious commitments. Events such as 'sign contract for new factory' should take place after events such as 'secure regulatory approval to market new gadget' unless the approval is known to be a formality.

Plans where the proposed product is at a prototype or earlier stage at the time the plan is being written must include a detailed account of the stages that the product must go through before it can be put into production or released to the service delivery staff and start generating cash. This must be synchronised with the pre-launch marketing activities. Very few new ventures are sufficiently well funded to recover from a launch aborted in mid-flight because the product was undeliverable.

E: The management team

E1: Summary

There is no project so divinely blessed that no one can screw it up, and there are few proposals beyond hope of rescue if the right combination of talent and determination can be found to manage them. Errors in the presentation of the rest of a business plan can often be corrected, but if the management team does not inspire confidence the plan, as a proposal, must fail.

In the particular case of plans seeking funding for new ventures, the initial entrepreneurial team is unlikely to be a wholly balanced management group, and a reasonable investor would not expect it to be. The team may lack anyone with manufacturing or sales experience, or be unfamiliar with the duties of company directors or accountants. This section of the plan should show that the entrepreneurial team has recognised their own limitations and made plans to recruit and reward a person or a small group of people to complement the team's talent.

Strong feedback applies at this point. The management team listed here will have, implicitly or explicitly, accepted responsibility for the construction of this plan. If the reviewing manager or prospective investor has any grounds to suspect the competence, accuracy, or dedication of the management team, then this suspicion will spread, like a dull grey cloud, over that manager's perception of the entire plan. If, on the other hand, the reviewing manager has great confidence in the management team proposed, then any minor doubts that the reviewer has about other aspects of the plan may be passed over in silence.

This, in turn, can become a serious threat to the project, particularly if the leading lights in the management team are believed to be unapproachable as well as infallible. To minimise this risk, the plan, and the management section in particular, must make it clear that the reviewing manager or venture capitalist or their trusted representative is being sincerely invited to become an essential, trusted, and respected member of their team.

E2: Individual résumés

A *curriculum vitae* (CV) is (literally) a life story, and while preparing such a document (or book) is a valuable activity, including it at this point of the business plan is not obligatory. A résumé, a focused précis of the full CV, is more appropriate. If a full CV exists, it may be referenced as an optional appendix. Each résumé should include the subject's major relevant educational and career highlights, a list of the most significant achievements, and the names of two or three suitable career referees if appropriate. One page, or about 350 words, is usually a reasonable target length: too much, particularly if some of the entries look like padding, is much worse than too little.

A short personal selling statement may also be appropriate. Such a statement should impress the reviewing manager or venture capitalist with the commitment of the member of the proposed management team to the new project and the ample alternative opportunities for less stressful or more pleasurable occupations that the team member is passing up.

E3: Descriptions of the missing people

Very few entrepreneurial teams will include in their number people with all the different varieties of experience and talent needed to staff an operating business: a project that was so blessed would be automatically suspected of either triviality or reckless indifference to resource consumption. It is more common to find an entrepreneurial team with some glaring holes: brilliant technicians with the sketchiest idea of accounting and no knowledge at all of sales or marketing; or a marketing genius with an incomplete prototype and no idea of how to get it ready for economical manufacturing; or a brilliant development, sales and marketing team with no idea at all of how to move into routine production.

Reviewers will be looking for the quality of self-knowledge that enables the entrepreneurial team to identify those necessary tasks for which they are not fitted, and then to identify, recruit, and reward the appropriate people. A new venture that needs a first rate sales executive, or a high profile chairman, must be prepared to make an attractive offer to get the right person even when the necessary enticement may appear to dilute the entrepreneurs' rewards significantly.

E4: Understudies and succession planning

It will be generally recognised that the members of the initial team will play a key and possibly a unique role in bringing the venture from birth to a successful growth business. This introduces two controllable risks. First, the growth of the business may place increasing and eventually impossible demands on the key person's time. Second, an accident (in the general sense of an unplanned event) may temporarily or permanently deprive the venture of the contribution of a key person.

The first of these circumstances leads to insidious damage to the venture as critical work is skimped or omitted. The second may prove catastrophic. 'Key person' insurance sounds like a good idea, but it is unlikely to provide enough cover to compensate the venturers for the complete failure of their business and the consequent loss of the opportunity that the business represented.

Dependence on a few key staff creates a further risk to the value of the business: if the investors wish to harvest the growth in their investment, or the venturers wish to take up a new opportunity, the market value of a business that depends on a key person is going to be considerably lower than that of a similar business where the loss of any single individual will not be crippling.

The succession planning section of the plan will illustrate how understudies will be developed, initially to secure the business against the loss of a key person, and eventually to facilitate his or her departure.

F: The organisation plan

F1: The organisation

We dealt with organisational issues in Chapters 7 and 12 and suggested there how certain information should be captured. That information should be presented in this section of the written plan. Plan reviewers will look to this section in order to assure themselves that the plan objectives are going to be achievable with the proposed staff numbers and organisational structure. The staff numbers will then give credibility to the cost lines in the financial operating plans. Most plans will describe a changing organisation as the venture grows towards its various objectives, and so the organisation and staff levels should be described at various key points in the projected development of the venture.

The numbers in this section will be compared to the phased revenue targets in order to arrive at a number of key indices, such as revenue and profit per head, sales per salesperson, and average number of positions reporting to each manager. When a plan proposes numbers that lead to unusual values for any of these indices, these numbers should be explicitly justified, either in this subsection or in later subsections of this section.

F2: Staffing requirements

As a new business grows, there will be more work to be done, which will generate a higher management and staff workload. Although a part time book keeper may suffice to get the project off the ground, the cash flow will hopefully grow rapidly to the point that a full time accountant is needed. Stores may once have been kept in a heap at the back of a garage: soon a storeman may be needed to keep track of what is in stock and where it is.

Many growing businesses fail to anticipate these needs, and get plunged into unnecessary cash or stock crises just at the point where the business appears to be about to take off. There is a double potential for error in this part of the plan: failure to recruit the necessary staff in time may cause an unpleasant glitch at a delicate time, and failure to put these heads into the operating plan will make it look suspiciously optimistic.

F3: Off-payroll staff

Some new ventures are proposed on the assumption that manufacture, distribution and delivery, as well as staff functions like accounting and marketing, can be delegated to contractors. This often makes the operating plan look better than it might otherwise be, but it is seldom a basis for long term viability.

If the project becomes a success, the various contractors and contract staff will be eager to reap where they have but lightly sown, and there may be little left over for the venturers. The extent to which it is proposed to use off-payroll staff for both line and staff functions should be stated, as is the mechanism proposed to keep their hands out of the till once the business prospers. A clear indication of how much value is going to be added by off-payroll workers will also suggest the level of risk that will be involved in continuing with them.

F4: Key skills and key personnel

It is a rare new venture where all the skills required in the first few years of its existence can be found among the founding entrepreneurs. Even if the requisite skill types and attainment levels were present at the founding of the venture, its success would soon stretch the founders to breaking point unless assistance was found for them.

Both time and money may need to be allocated in order to establish the venture staffing levels as required from time to time by other aspects of the plan. When the venture opportunity involves a new product and/or a new technology it may be impossible to recruit suitably skilled staff and provision must be made for staff training. The training provision may involve more than money: a trainer must be recruited or someone transferred to training duties.

This subsection may need to be cross referenced to the failure mode analysis referred to in section B7. Often the best or only way to control risks is to control the quality of the manufacturing, delivery and service processes. This in turn comes back to recruiting and motivating a suitable member or a suitable group of members of staff. The need for a training and succession plan follows as a logical consequence.

G: Financial projections

G1: Summary

We discussed the essential elements of the financial statements in Chapter 14, where we emphasised both the production of certain statements and a spreadsheet model. The statements are included in the master plan; when the reviewers get to the 'due diligence' stage of their examination they will almost certainly want a copy of the spreadsheet model on disk.

All the main revenue and expenditure headings must be present on the profit and loss forecast, and the balance sheet and cash flow statements must be complete. Some care is required in preparing the chart of accounts, in order to ensure that significant numbers are not lost in aggregates, while the clarity of the plan is not destroyed by trivia.

Spreadsheets should be allowed to talk: they should not drivel or shout. A well laid out plan should require no more than a single page, or at most a double page spread, for each of the main statements. This may require putting the complete quarterly or monthly spreadsheets into an appendix, and only reproducing annual summaries, or annual summaries after the first year, in the body of the plan. There should be plenty of explanatory notes: one for every line in the chart of accounts would not be excessive.

G2: Statements

A properly laid out set of pro-forma profit and loss statements, balance sheets and cash flow projections should be prepared covering the whole of the plan period. Attention should be paid to phasing of revenue and expenses, and the proper accrual of taxation reserves and utilisation of early tax losses. Interest should be shown whether earned on funds on deposit or due on overdrafts or other borrowing instruments. Care should be taken to ensure that interest is paid and credited in the correct periods.

Revenue should usually be shown as the recommended final purchaser price, and standard commissions and promotional offers should be shown as separate lines. (Recall that the 'final purchaser' is the last buyer who recognises a discrete product, and the term includes a purchaser who incorporates supplied components or materials into a product for subsequent sale.)

The balance sheets should balance and link the profit and loss and cash flow statements. Funds must be available to cover all payments, with a reasonable contingency to allow for slow sales or even slower creditors. Numerical accuracy is critical: this section of a business plan will frequently be reviewed by an accountant, and reviewing accountants are congenitally incapable of approving statements incorporating errors, no matter how trivial.

G3: Graphs

Well-prepared graphs can add significantly to a reviewer's understanding of the financial implications of a proposal, and at a minimum the value of various critical indicators such as the break-even points should be presented graphically. Further graphs are a matter for judgement, and to some extent the skill of the people preparing the plan. If extra graphs are prepared there must be a clear rationale for presenting them and the presentation must clarify rather than obscure the plan.

H: The investment opportunity

H1: Deal structure: The financial proposition

This part of the plan is going to be scrutinised with a great deal of care before senior managers or venture capital providers authorise the project or commit funds. At the same time, it is where senior managers and venture capital providers will look to decide whether the proposition that they are being offered is worth their further consideration.

Senior managers and venture capital providers are acutely aware of the tendency among innovators, particularly high technology ones, to regard the people who provide the money as intellectual inferiors whose only mission in life is to obstruct the advance of technology. It is a short step from this attitude to a deliberate attempt to secure the financial support needed by a promising project by trickery. It is extremely important that nothing in this section of the plan, and particularly the summary to this section of the plan, arouses the slightest suspicion. One technique that is often successfully used to allay suspicion is to be honest, lucid, and unambiguous in the presentation of the financial proposal.

A financial proposition for a new enterprise includes a statement of the equity and debt capital required, the security offered and the proposed repayment schedule in the case of debt capital, the internal rate of return (that is, the annual interest rate at which the net present value of the investment, on the day in which the investment is made, would be zero) and the proposed harvest method (public float, trade sale, capital return or dividend stream). When there are different classes of equity investors the returns each can expect should be shown separately. Where the founders propose to hold shares issued at a lower price than the first venture investor is being asked to pay, this should be justified by their prior contribution to the venture, and 'we had the idea in the first place' may not, from the investor's viewpoint, seem a sound argument.

A proposal from within an established enterprise should indicate the maximum cash expenditure required to complete the project and the cash exposure, the maximum loss the company could sustain if the project was abandoned. To the extent possible within the firm's accounting and overhead allocation system, the internal rate of return of the project or the net present value should be stated. When key staff or key facilities will be required by the proposed project, this should be stated here as well.

UMB currently has tangible assets worth approximately $1.5 million, which are sufficient to support its current standard model business which earns $230 000 before taxes and dividends — $2.5 million is needed to meet the orders now in hand and reasonably anticipated for the Petropavlosk cores. Of this $1.5 million will be spent on plant and equipment and $1 million will be needed to finance materials and debtors.

We suggest that the investor should subscribe $1.5 million in new equity and will then hold 40 per cent of the common stock on issue, and provide a further $1 million as a convertible note, to be converted not earlier than December 1999 for shares of an equivalent value, discounted 10 per cent.

Assuming no dividends are paid before a stock market flotation in June 2002, and the stock sells at a p/e of 6.5, the investor's return will be 57.5 per cent effective annual rate before personal tax but with all company taxes paid.

H2: The new asset

The ethical and financial justification of a new venture requires that the result of undertaking the proposed enterprise will be the creation of something that is worth more than the value of the resources (including people's time) consumed to create it. A venture can be a financial success without being ethical, as when the value in the resulting enterprise was not created, but simply transferred from a dupe — or the unsuspecting public. It is unlikely to be an ethical success without being a financial one: there is nothing particularly praiseworthy about failure and the dissipation of resources.

The pro-forma balance sheet for June 2002, at which time the market value of UMB is expected to be $85 million, shows tangible assets and cash worth $38 million. The major intangible asset will, at this stage, be our continued exclusive rights to the Petropavlosk designs, but we will also expect to have a very highly skilled and motivated workforce such that cash flows could be maintained even if other manufacturers started matching the technical performance of the Petropavlosk design ...

A firm's capacity to add value to the fixed assets that it controls can be measured by the market-to-book ratio (M/B) — the difference between the price of the assets and the value of the firm as a going concern. Firms where M/B is less than one are destroying value: the assets in these firms would be more valuable outside the firm than inside it. When M/B is greater than one, the firm contains 'something' that makes the whole worth more than the parts. One way to boost the apparent M/B is to understate B, the book value of the assets. After a period of inflation, as in the 1970s and 1980s, many firms had assets, particularly real estate, in their books at its original purchase price. Raiders bought many such firms and sold the assets at market price, sometimes recovering the whole purchase price in this way.

Successful entrepreneurial firms have a high M/B, but there are seldom any undervalued assets available to attract a corporate raider. The difference between the market and the book value of such firms represents invisible assets, assets that are only valuable as long as the firm is a going concern, and which would have little or no value if it was broken up. Some of these invisible and 'off balance sheet' assets are:

▲ the embodied 'know-how' of the firm, an ability to get things done when the task lies outside the capacity of any single employee or manager

▲ the human capital of the firm, its ability to attract and retain people with unique skills and knowledge

▲ the firm's 'brand equity', the revealed preference of consumers for products bearing that firm's brands and trade marks

▲ the firm's reputation, as revealed by the preference towards the firm shown by industrial buyers and the preferential treatment it receives from its suppliers and distributors.

It is well worth the effort to set out, in a few paragraphs, just what invisible assets will be created if this business plan is put into effect successfully. Such a statement will lay the basis of a defence against market raiders if the venture should be listed: it is said that an American wheeler-dealer made a successful hostile takeover bid for a software firm. As he moved into his new conquest the staff moved out, and he learned that he had paid many millions of dollars for a few old desks, some worn out computers, and a large amount of unfinished, and now worthless, computer code. An understanding of the true asset base of a firm can be a guide to the appropriate conduct of the firm under stress: if the basic invisible asset is brand equity, a firm might settle consumer complaints even when the law might not be on the consumer's side. Firms whose human capital is vital should be careful about enforcing punctuality rules or dress codes.

H3: Risks and opportunities

Real life seldom follows a plan exactly, but a clear discontinuity is relatively rare. Plans involving innovations are almost always based upon exploiting a change: numerically, an opportunity is often the difference between two very large numbers. Quite small changes in either of these numbers can cause a dramatic change in the scale of a particular opportunity. This is emphatically true when the opportunity is created by changes in the broader social and economic environment.

When the product is its own agent of change, as for example when the proposed new venture offers a product that is superior, but equivalent, to a product already on the market, there is a different but no less serious set of risks. The suppliers of the established products may launch their own improved versions, or respond to a new entrant with deep price cuts. Either action will have an effect on the eventual outcome of a new venture. Changes in this area affect the market assumptions underlying the plan.

H4: Environmental dependencies

This section of the plan should set out the assumptions made about the physical, political and economic environment by the plan writers. It must state clearly what both the base and trend assumptions were, and show what the effects of possible changes in these assumptions would be on the plan outcome. It is worth taking some trouble to explore the longer range causes and effects: examine the likely reaction of the new venture's customers to various environmental changes and explain how these reactions will translate into positive or negative influences on the plan outcome.

Where possible, there should be some attempt to derive a metric linking the scale and direction of environmental change to the revenue projections for the business, and to provide a probability scale. A new lawn watering system, for example, would be harder to sell if a drought resulted in a ban on lawn watering from the public supply. The probability of such a drought can be established: this is a risk which should be acknowledged in the plan. Purchases of such systems are likely to be tied to demographic and economic factors: an improvement in the economic growth rate, or a successful satellite city development, could both increase demand for lawn watering systems. Economics and politics are even more unpredictable than the weather, but they should still be listed as influences on the plan outcome. In particular, an opportunity for rapid growth may be inaccessible unless there is access to additional capital. If the possibility is foreshadowed in the plan, and the conditions demonstrably exist, the additional capital is likely to be made available promptly.

H5: Internal, or market factors

When the venture proposes to launch a new or redeveloped product into an established market, the launch of the new product will almost certainly lead to a response from the established suppliers. When the venture is launched from within a division of a company that already supplies the target market, there will be an effect on the firm's established products. The plan must have assumed a certain scale and direction of the competitors' responses and the cannibalistic impact. Variation in these effects will represent risks or create new opportunities.

Research, or even anecdotal evidence, of how these suppliers responded to previous challenges will help the plan reviewer in estimating the risks and opportunities.

I: Appendices

I1: Appendices and supporting material

This section should list each appendix and other supporting document together with between ten and fifty words of description. The information provided must be sufficient to enable the reviewing manager or venture capitalist to decide whether to call for it himself or herself, to have it sent for separate review (and in such cases, what class of professional should review it), or to pass up the opportunity of examining it.

12: Research sources and tools

The major research sources used should be listed and the information gained from them summarised. Often this will involve a cross-reference to an appendix. When there has been a significant amount of market research undertaken, the tools used to analyse it should be listed and the confidence in the research results indicated.

13: Reference books and papers

All published books and papers which were relied on in constructing the plan should be listed in a standard reference format. Where the significance or importance of the reference cited is not obvious, a ten to fifty word paragraph could be added to explain these points. An explanation should always be provided when the reference is apparently out of date, as is often the case when using census or yearbook data.

End notes

1 Professor Karl Vesper (1993), one of the pioneers of American entrepreneurship scholarship, called them 'countless'. See for example: Abrams (1991); Banfe (1991); Bangs (1989); Bell and McNamara (1991); Berle (1989); Blechman and Levinson (1991); Brandt (1982); Cohen (1990); Crego, Deaton and Schiffrin (1986); Day (1991); Eckert, Ryan and Ray (1985); Fry (1993); Golis (1991); Kuratko and Hodgetts (1989); Longenecker and Moore (1991); Lynn (1989); McLaughlin (1987); McQuown (1992); Nesheim (1992); Osgood and Curtin (1984); Osgood, Fletcher and Curtin (1986); Rice (1990); Rich and Peters (1989); Rich and Gumpert (1985); Richardson and Richardson (1992); Roberts (1983); Ronstadt (1989); Ryan (1985); Sahlman and Stevenson (1992); Samson (1988); Schillit (1990); Siegel, Schultz and Ford (1988); Stevenson, Roberts and Grousbeck (1989); Taylor (1986); Timmons (1990); Vesper (1993); Vogelaar (1991a); Vogelaar (1991b); Welsh and White (1983).
2 Stevenson, Roberts and Grousbeck (1994), pp. 242–47.
3 Based on remarks made by Hamel at a seminar in Melbourne in 1995.
4 For example, if a model based on essentially correct assumptions predicted 50 sales in a given year, the rules from Chapter 8 suggest that the annual sales will mostly likely fall between 45 and 55 units. In any one month, the expected value is 4.5 and any outcome between 2 and 7 is consistent with the model.

Part IV

17
Chapter
Investment and investors

Corporate entrepreneurs struggle round bureaucrats, dodge sniping from their rivals and shrug off carping from their critics, get stuck in an apparently endless cycle of proposal reworking to placate this or that department, and continually rebuild their spreadsheets to adjust to the latest edict from the controller's office. They must sometimes envy the individual, creating his or her own proposal, answering to nobody. The corporate entrepreneur enjoys one magic moment that the individual cannot hope for: when the memo from the controller's office arrives, saying:

> ... the Board has approved your proposal of ... date. Your account number is ... and your attention is drawn to the financial accountability section of the corporate manual. Freda Charisma is your project accountant responsible for preparing monthly progress reports on your project; she must countersign all orders and cheque requisitions in excess of $5000. Please note that the Board must approve all contracts involving more than $100 000 per month or capital sums in excess of $2 million ...

For the individual entrepreneur and the start-up team, there is no controller's office to play either the wicked or the good fairy. As soon as the team members' personal financial capacity is fully committed, the rest of the finance for venture must come from relative strangers, people who start with no particular reason to regard the venture or the entrepreneurial team in a favourable light. The business plan, completed as we described in Chapter 16, provides the essential information that investors will need to review before deciding to support a venture. However, merely preparing a plan does nothing: the right investors

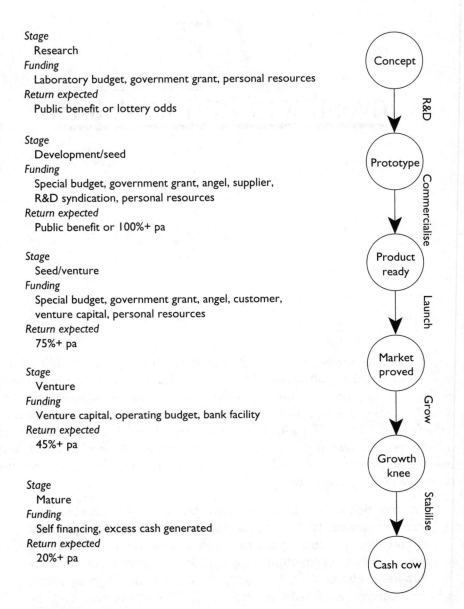

Stage
  Research
Funding
  Laboratory budget, government grant, personal resources
Return expected
  Public benefit or lottery odds

Stage
  Development/seed
Funding
  Special budget, government grant, angel, supplier,
  R&D syndication, personal resources
Return expected
  Public benefit or 100%+ pa

Stage
  Seed/venture
Funding
  Special budget, government grant, angel, customer,
  venture capital, personal resources
Return expected
  75%+ pa

Stage
  Venture
Funding
  Venture capital, operating budget, bank facility
Return expected
  45%+ pa

Stage
  Mature
Funding
  Self financing, excess cash generated
Return expected
  20%+ pa

Concept

R&D

Prototype

Commercialise

Product
ready

Launch

Market
proved

Grow

Growth
knee

Stabilise

Cash cow

Figure 17.1 Growth and finance

must be approached, and they must be made an offer which they will find worth considering. (If they accept it at once it is probably too generous!)

This chapter is organised into two main sections: we follow a venture through its product life cycle and discuss the funding requirements and suppliers of funds at each stage; and we discuss each of the different classes of investor separately.[1]

Figure 17.1 links these together and brings out the point that new venture financing is a continuous process, which parallels the product life cycle. At no stage is financing an action that is completed, banked and forgotten. Even within stages, there may be successive financing steps. In the early stages of a project the only finance sources for new ventures are informal ones supplemented by government schemes, while once the venture has become an established, profitable and cash positive business the successful entrepreneurs will have little trouble securing finance, although there will always be arguments about the terms. Venture capital funds service the gap between the exhaustion of the various informal sources and government subsidies and the arrival of conventional financiers.

Figure 17.1 has been drawn as an open loop, but obviously the cash needed to finance R&D and the early stages of commercialisation must come from somewhere, and most of it comes from the value-added in normal operations during the normal trading activities of established businesses. The value-added in business operations is partly paid out in salaries, and senior executives may earn enough to become 'business angels' upon their retirement; part of the value-added is paid as dividends, much of it to investment funds who must then re-invest most of what they get; some of it is paid as taxation, both as income and payroll taxes on employee salaries and as corporate income and other taxes, and this funds the government, which pays some of it out as various forms of R&D support; and some of it is retained within major corporations, where it could be, and sometimes is, spent on early stage development projects.

Listed corporations must keep their share price up, and this means, not only being profitable and paying dividends, but giving investors confidence that future profits and dividends will be higher than the current ones. Products that have reached the mature stage of their life cycle are no longer capable of generating increasing revenue, although a sufficiently ruthless attack on costs can make profits grow for a while. Corporations need a steady supply of products in the growth phase, generating growing revenue and 'new' profits, in order to support their share price.

Corporations can grow by acquisition, buying promising new companies whose products have passed the growth knee but have not yet matured into cash cows. Rapidly growing businesses need cash (which major corporations generally have plenty of) but also generate growing profits, a task which major corporations often find difficult. Alternatively, corporations can 'grow their own growth', providing funds for speculative research and concept development, and bringing the risk back to acceptable levels by spreading it over a sufficient number of projects.[2] Once a sufficient number of unrelated projects are started, even if the expectation of success for any one of them is low, the group as a whole has a defined variance and can be judged on normal financial criteria.

In general terms, single products in the stage labelled 'R&D' in Figure 17.1 are hard to justify on financial grounds for technology-based projects, because of what economists call 'spillovers' or 'externalities'. In economic terms, spillovers and externalities occur whenever the benefits of a transaction are, because of the nature of the transaction, shared with people who did not pay for it. Consider, for example, wheat production: the Australian crop is worth about $5 billion, and so research that produced a 1 per cent yield improvement would be worth

$50 million per year, a profit stream which would justify a considerable amount of research. If any one of the 10 000 wheat farmers in Australia undertook the necessary research, however, he or she would only gain an extra $5000 per year, far too little to justify even a nominal research project; the other $49 995 000 would 'spill over' to other farmers. Since there are obvious public benefits available from R&D in the wheat and many other industries, much pre-commercial research is publicly funded, in universities or CSIRO or other public research institutions, and most of the rest takes place in private sector laboratories that are maintained by corporations on a *pro bono* basis out of a sense of moral obligation or in the expectation of public relations benefits or a little of both.

Very early stage activities present less of a funding problem in consumer products companies and service businesses, since there is, in general, little technology risk and the concept can be elaborated on paper in spare or otherwise unallocated time and so it will appear, at least in the formal accounts of a business, costless. Consumer product and service companies do not face the long delays between prototype and launch that sap the returns of high technology and metal manufacturing industry companies, and often enjoy substantial first-mover advantages once their product is launched, restricting their spillover losses.

Intellectual property protection, such as patents, do not solve the spillover problem facing technology-based products at the concept stage, in part because scientific principles can't be patented, and an otherwise undeveloped concept does not contain much more than that, but also because a patent granted at the concept stage would often have expired before any cash could have been generated. These rights are not really strong enough to justify a socially desirable level of investment in development and it has been argued with considerable force that in industries, such as pharmaceuticals, where most development is commercially funded under patent protection, the outcomes are far from socially optimum.[3]

Finance and project stages
Research stage: Concept to prototype

A concept is an idea: 'wouldn't it be nice to have … I wonder why no one makes/does it …' Sometimes the idea is well-advanced, as when Ray Kroc saw the original McDonald's hamburger restaurant and wondered why people had to drive half way across America to get a properly prepared hamburger at a fair price in clean surroundings. Sometimes it is little more than a glint in the eye as when Fleming (later Sir Alexander) looked at a Petri dish and wondered why there were no bacteria inside a little ring around each of a few spots of penicillium mould. Fleming and Kroc lived to see their concepts become real products and realised their respective ambitions: Fleming died at a ripe old age, loaded with honours; while Kroc made a great deal of money and could, at the end of his life, reflect that it had been made honourably. To this day the McDonald's group returns something to the community beyond the consumer benefit provided by its products, including the relatively lavish provision and endowment of apartments near major children's hospitals to allow parents to stay near seriously ill children.

By contrast with the twentieth century work of Fleming and penicillin, the idea of powered flight is over 2000 years old, and although in 1903 the Wright Brothers built the first heavier-than-air machine to actually get a person off the ground and then safely back to it, very few of the concepts they employed were their own. Even being the successful constructors of the first prototype aircraft did not lead the Wrights into a major position in the aircraft business: it was not until the First World War was well advanced (or well bogged down) thirteen years after the Wright's first flight that aircraft came into serious use as weapons. It was not until fifty years after the Wright's first flight that civil air transport began to displace trains and ships as the dominant international and intercity passenger transport mode.

Finance

Broadly, a concept will not, in most industries, attract finance from even the most generous venture capitalist. The term 'concept' is used in the film and musical comedy industries to describe what in technology would be called a prototype, a plot outline together with the provisional agreement of key people to participate: such concepts do get financed, but by specialists, and the returns to any one project are usually poor to zero, just occasionally remarkable. Films are legally counted as artistic works, with the strong protection against direct imitation provided by copyright, and so the spillover or externality problem can be controlled.[4] Service and packaged consumer goods industries take concepts seriously, but don't generally pay outsiders for them; large companies in these fields employ staff whose job it is to think up new products and new ways to present and market established ones, and if they get suggestions from the public they may consider them, but they won't pay for them.

Firms with a technology based concept can apply for a grant under one of the various government R&D schemes, or form an alliance with a researcher in a university department or other research organisation, and try to prove the concept to prototype stage. There are a number of cooperative research centres (CRCs) in Australia, actively trying to turn science into practical ideas, and a firm that is a member of a CRC can suggest its concepts as valid areas for investigation. All members of the CRC will share in the results of such an investigation, and so not every person with a good idea will wish to propose it to a CRC.

People who want to be involved in advanced technology, but don't have a fully worked out concept, can approach a CRC, a university department or a CSIRO division working in their field of interest and ask if they have any research ready for commercialising. They will often be offered their choice of a large number of promising projects: one reason why it is hard to sell a concept is that there are so many of them around.

People and firms whose concept is essentially a service or software one should start building an informal team to elaborate it, at least to prototype and possibly to market testing stage before they make any attempt to approach any unrelated person for support. There are a number of government-aided centres in Australia such as the Victorian Innovation Centre in Melbourne and the Centre for Engineering Innovation in Sydney where firms and potential entrepreneurs can get introductions to potential partners.

Development stage: Prototype to product

A prototype is a realised concept, built to prove technical feasibility. It must work, although it does not have to work well, and it need not look exactly like a finished product. If it is a physical object, it may have been handcrafted at vast expense; if it is a piece of software, it might run incredibly slowly and be subject to various glitches; if it a new musical, the score may be sketched out on a piano and the author may stand in for the chorus line; but whatever it is, the prototype will be seen as proof that the concept 'works'.

A great deal of effort needs to be applied to turn a prototype into a marketable product: the mechanical prototype must become a smoothly operating and well-presented device suitable for volume production, and the production details such as bills of materials, operations plans and the like must all be complete; the software must work reasonably reliably and rapidly, be in a form suitable for installation, and have complete documentation ready for the printer or CD-ROM publisher; the musical must have a full score and complete choreography, actors, singers, and chorus fully rehearsed, the scenery built and every other detail of the production finished.

While it is rare for an unsurmountable problem to occur during the commercialisation process, the process is often subject to delay. Delays may be due to individuals: development of a musical show might have been started in the expectation that a particular star would be available to open it, and any number of things can delay this; or a product might have to meet stringent certification conditions, and minor issues force one or more sets of trials to be resubmitted. Plans for the development phase of a new product should not assume that 'it will all be right on the night'; such an attitude almost guarantees that it won't. Two useful proverbs that an entrepreneur undertaking product development should recite regularly are: 'more haste, less speed', and 'better late than never'. One of the worst things that can happen to a development project is that a sales person takes charge of it: enthusiasm and determination are great attributes in a sales person, but in a development manager they encourage short cuts and expedients that often lead to unnecessary delays in bringing the product to market. Short cuts almost inevitably insert hidden flaws which will cause trouble once the product has reached customers; if the managers in Exicom (liquidated in 1996) who decided to skip humidity testing in their telephone development project[5] could turn back the clock, a different decision would be taken the second time around.

The Boeing 777

The Boeing Commercial Aircraft Company abandoned many traditional practices when developing the B777. New aircraft development had traditionally been carried out in great secrecy, so as to keep the new ideas away from possible competitors; but this also kept them away from potential customers and the certification authorities.

Boeing, on the B777 project, gave several major airlines and the United States Civil Aviation Authority (CAA) general read access to its design data bases, so that they could make suggestions and start planning their tests long before anything capable of flying was built.

Previous Boeing aircraft had had to undergo up to two years of testing after the first aircraft was completed, while sales negotiations bogged down in trivia such as the location of lavatories and the size of the galleys. The B777 completed its CAA testing in months, rather than years, and the airlines had all their small requests catered for while it was a matter of changing a data base, not cutting aluminium, and so deliveries could start almost the day certification was complete.

Finance

Professional investors are extremely unlikely to agree to back the most promising development projects without some special encouragement, not only because the hurdle rates that they would apply would make it very difficult to come to an agreement with the entrepreneurs, but also because of the large amount of management time a development project requires. Most product development in technology and technology-dependent industries takes place within corporations or is organised by members of fairly tight groups of specialist financiers.

When corporations undertake product development they rely on their combined corporate competencies in applying the relevant technology, managing related development projects, and selling the result into a reasonably well defined group of markets. Corporate entrepreneurs are involved in the selection, management and marketing of these projects, and financial criteria are used to choose between them, but the finance is often treated as a normal expense of doing business in the relevant industry rather than a freestanding investment. When a 'paper entrepreneur' or asset-stripper gets hold of a company one of the first things to get slashed is the development budget: the result is a major boost to short term profits, and the share price, bought at the cost of long term corporate decline and ultimate failure.

Technology based development projects are often eligible for government grants or other forms of support.

Many entrepreneurs complete their development stage without any formal financing, running up bills on their credit cards, borrowing from friends or relatives, and drawing down their savings. Entrepreneurs may keep their day job, working on development part time or at weekends, or taking contract jobs to build up their finances between bursts of work on their project. Entrepreneurs with life partners may live off their partner's income while they work on product development.

Other entrepreneurs ignore the Companies Act or give it the minimum of legal deference and raise what they need in relatively small sums from their friends and acquaintances: with an average of 110 people in each person's 'chatter group' no single acquaintance need put up very much in order to get a tidy amount of money together. Such payments are more in the nature of gifts than investments: the people who subscribe should treat the money as spent, should be grateful if they ever get any of it back, and ecstatic if they get a positive return. Language fails to express the appropriate response if they find that they have backed the next *Crocodile Dundee*,[6] but astonishment is a good start.

The reason that professional investors avoid development projects is that the major risk to every venture, that of rejection by potential customers, is only tested once development is complete. Some entrepreneurs have been able to short-circuit both the risk and the professional investors by selling their concept, supported by a real or virtual[7] prototype, directly to its probable customers and taking deposits against future deliveries. Real estate developers do this when they sell 'off the plan' and home building firms do it when they demand a deposit and progress payments from their customers. There are, of course, plenty of opportunities for fraud in such arrangements, and both parties would be well advised to get their lawyers to check any related agreements, but the elements of a win–win coalition are still there: the customers get exactly what they want; and the entrepreneurs get access to the finance needed to give it to them.

Suppliers are sometimes willing to back a venture in its fairly early stages, not so much for the direct financial benefits from the investment, as much as the possibility that the venture, if successful, will attract many imitators and the final outcome will be a substantially increased demand for the supplier's product. Often such support is channelled through industry associations.

The term 'angels' came from Broadway, the centre of American commercial theatre. 'Angel' was the somewhat cynical term applied to investors who could be encouraged to finance new stage productions with very uncertain financial prospects; the investor's return came, in part, from the opportunity to associate with the stars and to participate in the general theatrical glamour. The modern business angel is a little more prosaic, providing a small financial injection in return for an opportunity for personal participation in a development or early stage marketing project. Business angels are often retired executives who want an opportunity to use the skills that they spent their working lifetime developing; they won't refuse a dividend if their investment pays off, but their real return comes from the pleasure that they get from being useful for a few hours per week without the stresses of personal entrepreneurship or full time employment.

Launch stage: Market proving

We use the term 'launch stage' to cover the period immediately following the first time a new product is offered for sale; others call it the 'early growth' phase. As we explain here, the reasons why there is a distinction between a launch/early growth phase and a growth/fast growth phase are financial, not market based. If a venture's or new product's marketing campaign is optimally funded on the day of the launch, *and the product is destined for success*, the growth/fast growth stage starts immediately and this stage is skipped.

A product can only be destined for success when a sufficiently large number of people want it badly enough to pay for it. There is only one real way to discover if potential purchasers really want a product: it is to offer the product to them at an economically viable price and see if they buy it. Even this immediate response does not guarantee the success of an enterprise: early customers must repurchase and/or recommend it if sales are to grow faster than marketing expenditure and the product is to deliver a satisfactory profit on its investment.

Some products have very high margins. Such products may only need market development finance during the months surrounding the launch, when marketing expenditure is going out and revenue from sales is yet to flow in, and growth beyond this stage can be financed directly from revenue. The only costs beyond marketing expenditure incurred by the producer of a successful film after opening night are the trivial ones of reproducing and transporting copies of the film to the many cinemas eager to show it. The same applies to a new computer software package. By contrast, a new manufactured product may earn gross margins of 20 to 30 per cent, and for each dollar of new sales in a month financing is required for 70 to 80 cents worth of inventory, work in progress and debtors for the three or more months between the time when suppliers must be paid and the time that the manufacturer's share of the retail or user dollar finally filters back.

The marketing expense can, of itself, be a major item, even for high margin products. The major film production companies limit the risk of wasting marketing expenditure on a flop by showing a film to preview audiences. They do not commit to the expense of a full launch until the response of the trial audiences convinces them that early audiences will recommend the film to the extent needed, at least, to comfortably cover their marketing expenditure.

A small scale film producer must bear the expense of early marketing and possibly even the rental costs of a few cinemas in order to carry out a market test, and only when the test is successful are they likely to get the money that they need for a full scale launch from a major distributor or production company. Independent film producers are just one example of an entrepreneur without the support of a major, cash-rich company. Such entrepreneurs need money to distribute and promote their product in order to prove that the market will accept it, but conventional financial sources are extremely reluctant to provide finance for a new enterprise until they can see proof that the market has, in fact, accepted its products.

Entrepreneurs with strictly limited ambitions may not find the absence of external finance a major problem. If they had set out to create a new small business, they need sufficient money to live, and to pay any fixed expenses of the business, for a couple of years but at the end of that time the business is likely to be capable of surviving and paying wages or a little more. It might be an idea with tremendous potential, but without sufficient finance to launch a major marketing effort the potential will not be realised. If the idea is a good one, and a more ambitious entrepreneur picks it up, the idea's original creators may or may not get something out of it. Ray Kroc paid the McDonald brothers for the use of their name and their concept as, for a while, the KFC company did when they paid Colonel Sanders for the use of his face in their advertising and his recipe in their kitchens.

Entrepreneurs with more general ambitions need to keep their business, and its business plan, alive while they prove that their product can, not only gain sales from new customers, but satisfy them to the point that they will return for more and tell their friends and acquaintances about the product. At some point they will find a venture capital supplier of some type ready to open negotiations with them, and they are ready to drive their business into its growth phase.

Corporate entrepreneurs should also prove that their product will be acceptable to the market before they call for a full scale launch. This may take the form of extensive research, or test marketing, or even a significant production and marketing effort: Sony Corporation made a million Walkman cassette player-radios for their market trial. If such a trial is successful, very few major corporations will be unwilling to finance a proper launch, at least in the corporation's domestic market. Many Australian corporations seem struck by paralysis at the thought of international marketing, either through fear of the unknown or because they realise the size of the financial effort needed and are unwilling to put it up.

Finance

There are very few grants available for market proving of new products, but there are export facilitation schemes available for taking products that are established in Australia to new markets; some entrepreneurs at least can look to the government for help.

Distributors, assemblers and major retailers can sometimes be approached successfully for assistance at the market proving stage; not usually with an equity investment; but a firm order, or even better, a firm order accompanied by a deposit, will have a marvellous effect on the willingness of venture capital funds to support the new enterprise. By and large venture capitalists avoid firms without a sales record, counting the market risk as too high, but an order from a major name in the appropriate industry can change their view of that. The major names are not, in general, looking for a specific return on an investment, but for products that leverage their entire product line. When Woolworths lists a new product, it will be one of the 200 000 or more in their computers; good, bad or indifferent, its performance won't perceptibly alter their bottom line. If, however, the product attracts more customers to their stores, who then add the product to a trolley-load of groceries that they might otherwise have bought at a rival store, Woolworths will find the listing decision more than justified.

A small suburban nursery near Melbourne developed a line of inexpensive, but attractive orchids and approached Woolworths Ltd (trading as Safeway in Victoria). Woolworths saw that the orchids were decorative anyway, and that they would attract customers with discretionary income who might go on to buy other relatively high-margin lines.

Woolworths waived all their listing, slotting and co-promotion fees and placed the orchids in a number of Melbourne supermarkets, where the sales did not disappoint Woolworths and were a major boost to the nursery. It applied the substantial margins it earned on sales through Woolworths to expanding its growing facilities and increasing its product range.

Many entrepreneurs look to their family and friends to continue supporting them into the market proving phase; it is important that entrepreneurs who rely on this support during the development phase do not exhaust it then, because it will still be needed when the development is completed and market proving has begun.

The growth stage

As we explained earlier, the period that we call the growth stage is called the fast growth stage by some writers, but growth is faster in this stage than the previous one because the marketing of the new product is better financed, not for any external reasons.

'New name' marketing involves a large expense for very little immediate net return; firms, as we explained in Chapter 8, should not plan on recovering more than $1 in contribution margin for each dollar spent on sales and marketing to first time users. The profits, if any, come from the early users' repurchasing and recommendations. If the major proportion of early users are extremely satisfied, practically all of them will repurchase the product in subsequent years and their recommendations will be so effective that one new user enters the market spontaneously every year for each two satisfied established users. The extent of repurchasing and recommendation can be estimated relatively accurately within two years after a product has been first put on the market by analysing the sales per period and the corresponding promotional expenditure statistically.

Packaged consumer goods companies don't wait two years: they send market researchers to the supermarkets a month after the launch and ask people with the new product in their trolley whether this their first or subsequent time of purchase. Some United States supermarket chains have introduced loyalty schemes where a customer presents a personalised card when checking out: these cards, combined with the scanner data and a certain amount of computer processing, enable the repurchase rate for new products to be estimated quite accurately.

If a sufficient number of relevant factors can be ignored, a once-off sales and marketing expenditure of a million dollars on introducing a new, frequently consumed and very attractive product will produce a negligible contribution in the year it is spent, but $1.5 million in the second year on the market, $2.25 million in the third year, $3.4 million in the third and so on to glory. All sorts of factors limit this picture: no product ever produced appeals to every consumer; the market for any given product has an upper limit; consumers die, or move, or switch their preference to rival products; these are the most significant. In practice, some consumers will like a new product, many of them will stay in the market for several years, and there are a lot of consumers in the world. An investor in a successful new consumer product cannot expect an infinite return, but such investors can get a very handsome one. The major consumer product companies know this, which is why they are prepared to launch new products with as little as a 10 per cent chance of surviving a year on the supermarket shelves.

Successful new consumer and intermediate durable products aren't as instantly lucrative as successful consumption products and so, with a few exceptions such as motor cars and advanced computing equipment, there are no giant corporations blazing away at the market with what resembles a bombardment[8] of new products. Even in the motor car and computing equipment industries the major companies control a relatively small fraction of the total value-added, and there are many openings for new entrants to supply components or complementary products. Occasionally, as with Microsoft, the component supply business may demonstrate extraordinary growth and profit. Even then there are opportunities: Microsoft Word version 6.0a included seven components from other vendors (as acknowledged in the product's copyright statement).

Venture capitalists are attracted by new, market proved products because of the relatively high returns for relatively moderate risk. They offer to manage the entrepreneur's capital raising and offer other management assistance in return for a share of the business. The venture capitalist's eyes are not on the profits made by the business during the growth phase as much as what happens when growth starts to slow down, the point at which approximately half of the potential customers have been reached. At this point the enterprise still has substantial growth prospects and is both profitable and cash positive: it is the sort of business that a major corporation would like to have as a division or it may be suitable for a stock market flotation. A successful sale to a corporation can be quite lucrative: Advent Corporation turned a $5 million investment in Cochlear to $20 million in three years when they sold the business to Pacific Dunlop (who floated it separately three years further down the track for double the purchase price). The stock market flotation is the prospect that every venture capitalist dreams about.

Finance

During the whole of the five- to seven-year growth phase, a growing business will require capital to finance its debtors ledger, to cover material and equipment costs, to throw a defensive ring of product variants around its core product, and to keep driving the market. As a very rough rule of thumb, each financing round needs to raise twice as much as the preceding one, and the financiers are allocated the same fraction of the shares. The founding entrepreneurs have no spare cash (if they had they would not have invited venture capitalists to their party) and the firm is not in a position to pay them substantial dividends. For this reason they won't be able to buy shares in the various new issues and they will rapidly find themselves minority investors in 'their' enterprise.

Table 17.1 shows how the equity financing process works in an idealised case: although the venture's founders become paper multi-millionaires, and real ones if they sell their interests after a successful stock market float or if their firm gets absorbed by a major corporation at a fair price, their degree of control of the venture falls quite dramatically. The way in which venture financing through equity extrudes the entrepreneur from control of the enterprise has led to the tag 'vulture capitalists' being applied to venture capital firms, and there are many examples of venture capitalists removing the founding entrepreneur from the chief executive's position once the firm starts to grow.

Such extruded entrepreneurs may denounce the venture capitalists as vultures; they may even (very misguidedly) demand to be bought out of the enterprise. The

Table 17.1 *Stylised venture investment pattern (observe the dilution of the founder's equity)*

Year (finance stage)	Nominal share price	Shares issued (000s)	Shares on issue (000s)	Founders' holding	Founders' value ($000s)
0			600	100%	
1	$2.50	400	1000	60%	$1 500
2	$5.00	400	1400	43%	$3 000
3	$10.00	400	1800	33%	$6 000
4	$20.00	400	2200	27%	$12 000
5	$40.00	400	2600	23%	$24 000
6	$80.00	400	3000	20%	$48 000

First venture capitalist pays $1 million for 40% of venture

supposed vultures have their own story to tell: phrases such as 'pig-headed', 'erratic' and 'no sense of running a business' will generally occur frequently.

Sometimes an entrepreneur retains full control in spite of the selling-down process; the two essential ingredients are managerial competence and a sound understanding of the financing process. In the mid 1990s the Toyota Company broke with a long tradition and appointed a chief executive who was not from the Toyoda family. At the time the last Toyoda was appointed, the family's entire share holding accounted for about 1 per cent of the voting capital; the financial institutions and individuals who owned the rest of the Toyota stock would not have wanted to hurt the feelings of the founder's family unnecessarily, but if the members of the Toyoda family had not been competent managers the shareholders would have overcome their sense of deference rapidly enough.

Founders who want to retain control do not always have to rely on the sensitivity of their major shareholders. Golis (1993) describes a meeting with an American entrepreneur who was in rock-solid control of his fully financed enterprise: this entrepreneur had taken charge of the capital raising from the beginning, and placed every tranche with a different syndicate, so successfully that the second largest holding on the register, after the entrepreneur's, was only 5 per cent of the voting stock. Where the founders are personally important to the ongoing success of the venture, they may be able to negotiate arrangements involving options and partly-paid shares that strengthen their control, but such arrangements must make the venture less attractive to other equity investors, and new investors may wish to pay less for shares where such arrangements exist than they otherwise would.

Exit and harvest

No market is infinite, and a stage will be reached when the only people to whom satisfied users can recommend the product will be each other. If there has been sufficient continuing expenditure on enhancing the product and maintaining its market position the strong preference its users have for it will not be challenged by the firm's competitors. Mature products can earn good margins; the revenue that they generate will not, however, be capable of being grown much faster than the economy. Fast growth typically ends well before the market is actually saturated, usually when the market has reached about half its ultimate penetration.

In a market, even one with several active competitors, it doesn't make financial sense for any one competitor to detach satisfied customers from the others: the cost, in sales effort and marketing expense, simply exceeds the value of the revenue stream that such detached customers provide. Two factors are at work to limit the financial rewards to competitive capture programs:

▲ among the people who switch suppliers in response to a special promotion there will be a high proportion of people who form weak product loyalties and are therefore likely to switch to yet another supplier if offered a promotional incentive

▲ many of the people who buy the attacking product while the incentives are on offer will return to their original choice as soon as the incentives are removed.

Firms operating in relatively mature markets cannot rely totally on the rationality of their competitors, and from time to time one firm may launch a major promotion aimed at gaining market share without any way to retain the customers gained. More dangerously for the complacent, an attack may be launched on the back of an innovation that does make the aggressor's product more desirable, and so a significant proportion of those users who trial the attacking product stay with it. Sporadic promotional wars and occasional innovations mean that the cash flow from products in a mature market is not perfectly stable, but it tends to be consistently positive and so the shares in companies marketing such products are attractive to those financial institutions whose own business involve paying out money as pensions or insurance claims.

Life assurance and superannuation funds need stable cash flows to meet their pension and annuity commitments, high liquidity so as to be able to pay insurance claims on demand, and steadily rising share prices in order to make their funds attractive to prospective policy buyers and superannuation contributors. New venture investments, no matter how socially desirable or valuable in the long term, fail on all three of the criteria used by life assurance and superannuation fund managers. By contrast, firms with a portfolio of products with substantial market shares in mature markets are very attractive to financial institutions.

Finance

Financial institutions are continually looking for suitable new investments; simply buying shares in established companies pushes the price up without increasing the dividends that the funds receive. Although the funds won't back new ventures, they rely on entrepreneurs to generate a steady supply of new enterprises that meet their particular requirements:

▲ most financial institutions have a small pot of 'funny money' which they will put into syndicates providing third or fourth round finance to growing ventures

▲ large corporations are placed under pressure by demands from their institutional shareholders for high dividends as well as steady growth — this discourages corporations from investing in their own new products and encourages them to buy firms whenever the cost of the cash flow is lower than their own average price/earnings ratio

▲ if a new enterprise has grown to noticeable size, the managers of some of the smaller and more specialised funds will be willing to participate in a syndicate that underwrites a public flotation of it.

Small is a relative term; a start-up entrepreneur would not consider a million dollars as trivial, but to the managers of major superannuation and life insurance funds, a million dollars is an irritation, a nuisance if it gets mislaid and the auditors complain, and nice if a few extra ones turn up as the result of some long-forgotten investment[9] but of no real significance to their business.

In America, but not, so far, in Australia, there is a high-volume market for corporate debt and so the major investment funds can secure the stable cash flow that they crave by buying interest-bearing corporate securities and corporations can, at least in theory, provide capital for their stable lines from debt and apply their shareholders' funds to product and market development. This may be one of the reasons why share prices in the United States rose steadily through the first half of the 1990s while those in many other countries, including Australia, grew slowly if at all.

Investors and their criteria

People who support a new enterprise with money or other assets are investors, but the term covers many different classes of people and firms, each of which will have its own special considerations, both for investing in the first place and for the type of returns that they expect. Below, we provide thumbnail sketches of the various classes of investor that an entrepreneur might deal with, what they expect for their participation, and the areas where they are likely to show particular concern.

Table 17.2 summarises the balance of this chapter.

Personal resources

Personal resources must be considered first, for the simple reason that an entrepreneur will have a great deal of trouble persuading people to invest in an enterprise that the entrepreneur is not personally prepared to support. In Table 17.2 we suggest that $10 000 is a reasonable level of personal commitment; even entrepreneurs who do not have that much cash in their purse or wallet can usually raise it from a bank as a personal loan or a credit card limit. The entrepreneur's home and any other personal assets will be pursued by a failed venture's creditors and so a decision to become an entrepreneur means putting these assets at risk.

Any competent accountant or lawyer can draw up a scheme of trusts and gifts which places an entrepreneur's personal assets far out of the reach of the entrepreneur's creditors, and any responsible bank manager or venture fund manager will look for such arrangements, and if they are

He that hath wife and children hath given hostages to fortune; for they are impediments to great enterprises, either of virtue or mischief. (Francis Bacon, first Baron Verulam and Viscount St Albans (1625), 'Of Marriage and the Single Life', Essays)

Table 17.2 *Venture investors summary*

Source	Amount	Will support if ...	Won't support if ...
Personal resources	$10 000 plus value of home less mortgages	Serious about venture	
Life partner	Living expenses	Trust in relationship	
Family and friends	$10 000–$100 000	Minimal belief in venture; some confidence in entrepreneur	No belief in venture
Government	Varies	Relevant conditions met (see Chapter 15 and individual scheme guidelines)	1 Proper forms not followed or procedural error 2 Budget allocation exhausted
Business angel	'Cherubs' to $25 000; 'seraphim' to $500 000	1 Reasonable prospects for venture 2 Opportunity for angel's involvement in management and planning	'You want my money but you don't want me'
Customers and suppliers	Orders, deposits, facilities etc	Strong possibility of leverage: new product may increase 'investor's' throughput and/or margins	No visible benefit for their business in new product
Venture capitalist	$1 million–$5 million	1 High confidence in market acceptance of product 2 High confidence in integrity and capability of venture team 3 Strong business plan 4 Clean exit and harvest probable 5 Reassuring break-even and cash flow analysis	1 Product not ready for market 2 Any doubt about integrity or commitment of venture team 3 Failure to come to agreement on KSFs and action if breach 4 Demands by entrepreneur(s) for permanent control 5 Mark of the 'living dead'
Lease finance	To $5 million	Credible promise to pay lease charges	Any doubt about recourse to the leased equipment
Bank	Varies with security	Credible promise to pay interest when due	Any doubt about recovery of loan in the event of a default
Corporate bond market	US$50 million (minimum)	[Market essentially US based]	
Private share investor	$2000–$50 000	1 Investor understands industry and/or product 2 Prospect of capital gain and/or secure income stream 3 Prospect of shareholder benefits	
Institutional investor	No limit	1 Secure stable or growing cash flows 2 Reasonable liquidity	1 Other institutions not willing to invest 2 Due diligence criteria not met

found, will treat any proposal from such an entrepreneur with deep suspicion. Australia's bankruptcy laws are far less severe than those of Elizabethan or even Victorian England, and bankrupts (and their families) are allowed to keep their tools of trade, their personal clothing, certain jewellery such as wedding rings, a sound second hand car, and retain enough of their income to provide food and rent a modest house.

Australian bankrupts are not generally able to retain their houses, pay private school fees or private health insurance, keep a fleet of luxury cars, or even take an overseas holiday without permission from their trustee. People for whom the prospect of enduring such privations for three years or more is intolerable should not set out to found a new venture.

Life partner

Many people are blessed with the loving companionship of another person, and many successful entrepreneurs have relied on their life partner to provide food and shelter during the early years of an enterprise. Before an entrepreneur with such a partner runs up any substantial debts, the two need to agree about a number of issues; they may even be well-advised to have a lawyer draw up an appropriate agreement.

There are upsides and downsides to look out for. If the enterprise fails, and ravenous creditors start hammering on the front door, the life partner may wish to say: 'Be off! This house is mine, as are all the cars in the garage, the jewels in the safe, and the shares in my thick portfolio. My unfortunate lover owns nothing but the clothes he stands up in.' If this statement is backed by a properly drawn up legal agreement, the baffled bailiffs must withdraw, snarling to their kennels.

Should unhappy differences arise between the parties, the supporting partner can of course pull the agreement out of the drawer, push the ex-lover out the front door, and declaim: 'Be off! This house is mine etc etc.' If the differences arise after the enterprise has become wildly successful the entrepreneurial partner may use the agreement as an excuse to leave the ex-lover in charge of the house, jewels etc while keeping sole ownership of the founder's share of the venture. If the dispute finds its way into the courts, the house, clothes, share portfolio and the founder's shares in the venture may all be sacrificed to keep a large number of lawyers employed.

Successful business partnerships are not based on lust or on a superior capacity for browbeating. An entrepreneur who relies on a life partner for support is morally and prudentially obliged to explain the risks and options to that partner, and if they can't agree on the appropriate sharing of risks and obligations, either to abandon the relationship or the enterprise. If a couple want to draw up a legal agreement during the period while a new venture is being founded, they also need to agree to update it regularly. They can, of course, dispense with the legal agreement altogether and take their chances together, as joint venturers, joint guarantors of the venture's debts, and joint participants in the eventual rewards for success.

Family and friends

A person's family and friends form a network of mutual obligation and respect, and friends who will not help each other out to the extent of a few hundred, or even a few thousand dollars are poor friends indeed. As long as such arrangements stay informal, with a verbal agreement to repay the money when it is possible, the friendship is not being abused.

The two deep traps are the *de facto* partnership and the loan guarantee. If the written or other understandings between the entrepreneur and the entrepreneur's friends and obliging relatives take certain forms, it may be possible, in law, to infer that a partnership agreement existed, and the friends, as partners, would in consequence become 'jointly and severally' liable for the venture's debts. This means that the creditors can pursue the friends on the basis of their ability to pay, not the size of their contribution: friends may legitimately be asked for a few hundred dollars to help a mate, but they should not be entrapped into pledging their house to the success of the mate's venture.

The loan guarantee is a harmless looking explosive device: a lender promises to cover the entrepreneur's financial needs if someone, usually a parent, affluent sibling or close friend, will guarantee it. The standard guarantee contract that the parent, sibling or friend will be asked to sign is unlimited. Although the loan may be for $5000 or $10 000 the guarantee document pledges the guarantor's entire wealth: house, car, savings — the lot. If the venture fails the guarantor may be pursued for sums far greater than the original loan, with the costs of the pursuit added like arsenic-green icing on a poisoned cake. The Australian courts have repeatedly upheld such guarantees, and their consequences.

Loan guarantees are superficially attractive, and slightly more so when the lender will agree to limit the guarantor's liability in default to the principal amount of the loan, but the entrepreneur is still obliged to pay interest at a time when the venture may have no sales at all, and is unlikely to be generating a positive cash flow. The interest simply compounds, eventually forcing the lender to seize the venture and/or the security so as to recover the principal and the accrued interest.

Government schemes

The various government schemes available at the time of writing are described in Chapter 15. The public servants and quasi-voluntary committees administering these schemes are almost all perfectly sincere in their desire to help new and growing ventures, and their duties include spending their budget allocation; they get no praise for spending too little. They are, however, tightly bound by the auditing rules of their respective public services, and shouting at them will not overcome the problems they will have in responding favourably to a partial, inconsistent or misdirected application.

Customers and suppliers

Potential customers and suppliers are often an important source of support for a new enterprise, but they are only rarely prepared to become formal investors. Requests for money do not always get a good reception however they are phrased. Customers and suppliers look for leverage possibilities, the chance that, if the venture is successful, their own throughput and/or margins will rise substantially. When they see such possibilities they will look for opportunities to support the venture by means short of direct investment.

Customers may give (implicitly conditional) orders; they may also assist with marketing research and may even provide introductions to the purchasing executives in their rivals' organisations. If they have technical facilities they may give the venture access to them or even lend expensive equipment to the venture. If the product is one that needs better testing a partner-customer may arrange it. Suppliers will often assist with materials; they too may offer help with marketing research and introductions.

Most of all, suppliers and customers offer credibility: not only every venture capital fund manager but every bank manager has heard of BHP and Ford. If firms as important as this take the new venture seriously, the bank or fund manager must do so too.

Business angels

The model business angel is a retired executive, 55 years or older, living on generous superannuation or other investment income, who does not want to return to full time employment but still wishes to make use of the skills developed over a working career. Angels are not usually expected to put up very large sums of money; $25 000 would be a lot; but they do expect to contribute their time and knowledge to the venture.

Because angels are private they are not always easy to identify, and such research as has been done casts some doubt on the model in the previous paragraph. Wenban, Hindle and Jennings (1996) reported on a research project which was completed in 1995. The project managed to find and get information from approximately forty Australian angels, and the results, in brief, are:

▲ they are very largely male — it appears that women prefer to be partners or proprietors than investors

▲ they can be divided into two distinct groups based on the size of their preferred investment tranche:

▶ part of the group, called in the paper the 'cherubs', invest in amounts around $25 000

▶ the 'seraphim' invest $500 000 or more in a single enterprise

▲ their backgrounds are also diverse:

▶ some are well educated professionals with undergraduate degrees and sometimes postgraduate qualifications, in the age group 35 to 45

▶ others are older 'battlers' who may not have even completed secondary education but have built a substantial asset base through operating their own business

▲ their main financial criteria for selecting investee firms were, first, the prospect of effective annual rates of return of 30 per cent or higher, and second, the strength of the prospective cash flows the investee firms could generate

▲ the dominating non-financial factor in choosing investee firms was the angel's evaluation of the management team, and they also placed significant weight on the market growth potential.

VECCI's business finance support program

In December 1994 the Commonwealth government announced, among other things, its intention to take steps leading to an improvement in access to finance for small and medium enterprises (SMEs).

The Victorian Chamber of Commerce and Industry (VECCI), was awarded a grant under this initiative to develop a pilot program. VECCI invited Bob Beaumont, who had had extensive experience in the non-bank finance sector, to suspend his retirement and launch the scheme.

Bob started a publicity campaign to make his operation known, and rapidly learned that there was no shortage of would-be business angels in Australia. Most of the people who approached Bob were retirees in their 50s or 60s with at least $500 000 that they could afford to place into a growth business. Once the scheme had captured data on the interests and preferences of 1200 potential angels the publicity was stopped to keep the scheme's growth under control.

Over the same period some 600 small and medium businesses approached Bob and his staff, a ratio of two angels per requester. This is the reverse of the ratio observed with established schemes in Britain and the United States, and Bob expected the Australian pattern to converge on the overseas one as the VECCI scheme, and similar schemes operated by other agencies, became more widely known.

Businesses are accepted into the program after a preliminary screening process: essentially, they must have a business plan, which the principals not only understand but are thoroughly familiar with, and they must be prepared to accept some loss of control over their business, either in the form of equity or a general charge over the business's assets.

When the scheme was first started, practically none of the business applicants were prepared to consider outside equity, but after the scheme had been operating for eighteen months about one applicant in six indicated that an equity investor would be acceptable, a sign of increasing maturity — or desperation — among Australia's small and medium business proprietors.

The scheme operates on 'dating agency' principles: name and address information is not released until both parties have agreed to a facilitated meeting. Investors can search the business data base using a number of keys, such as industry, amount requested, age and size of business and the like, but they can't trawl the data base for a list of targets. Typically an investor will be asked to refine his (they are practically all men) search until there are three to five candidate firms showing, after which a facilitated meeting can be arranged.

Matching services of this type have been operating in the United Kingdom since 1990 or so, and in mid-1996 there were thirty-six such services in the United Kingdom making about 300 matches per year each. The Australian target was to have ten to fifteen services directing $100 million per year into small and medium enterprises by the end of 1997.

Bob Beaumont believes that Australia's financial deregulation in 1985 created the need for schemes such as his. Before 1985 the banks operated arms-length business finance subsidiaries, whose executives acquired considerable skill in negotiating deals with small and medium enterprises. Post-deregulation the finance subsidiaries were absorbed into the banks, and the people with the particular skills needed to manage small and medium business finance were dispersed or offered early retirement.

Matching services are an effective way to deliver finance to small and medium enterprises while controlling investor risk and minimising the intermediary costs. Venture capital firms in Britain, and to some extent in Australia as well, often refer small applicants to matching services. British experience suggests that at least one in five business assisted by a matching service will grow to become attractive to venture capitalists, and a significant number will grow to the point that they can be floated successfully on the stock market.

In America, research has found that 'informal' finance plays a far greater role in new enterprise formation than does formal venture capital, and may retain its importance even into the growth phase. Angels may be approached by entrepreneurial teams with a proposal for a new venture or by the proprietors of established firms seeking growth finance. The respondents to the survey reported on by Wenban, Hindle and Jennings regarded both classes of business as entrepreneurial and there was no unambiguous indication that they preferred one to the other. The importance that they placed on the strength of the management team is a hint that an established firm seeking funds for a growth project might have an edge over a start-up team.

Angels can be found by trawling the entrepreneurial team's friends and acquaintances, by asking their lawyer and their accountant, and by participating in one or more of the match-making schemes operated by the Chambers of Commerce and Industry in the various Australian state capitals. The combination of rapid economic growth and light or variable taxation systems in Southeast Asia has built up a substantial population of potential angels prepared to put

$500 000 or more into an Australian venture; they are best approached through mutual friends and we do not suggest that entrepreneurs should buttonhole passers-by in Singapore or Kuala Lumpur.

Venture capitalists

There is a pervasive myth about venture capitalists, to the effect that they are a group of dedicated men and women roving the world looking for promising ideas to back with millions of dollars. George Doriot, an American venture capitalist, did a great deal to set the myth going when, in 1957, his venture capital firm backed the young Ken Olsen and with $77 000 to buy soldering irons and other toys. Olsen and friends founded Digital Equipment Corporation[10] and invented and then innovated the minicomputer. Digital Equipment went from negligible sales in 1957 to $11 billion in 1989, and George Doriot's ARD got fifty times its money back when Digital was floated on the New York Stock Exchange.

Doriot, in modern parlance, was a particularly blessed angel, not a venture capitalist at all, at least in his relationship with Ken Olsen. Modern venture capitalists do not enter the picture at the soldering iron stage, and very seldom as early as the launch: they want to see that the venture that they are being asked to back has a product with genuine, sales-proven, market appeal.

The managers of venture capital funds are intensely suspicious (those that were only moderately suspicious have all been fired) and besieged with proposals. Professional venture capitalists may fund as few as one in every hundred proposals that crosses their desks. Any suspicion about the integrity and commitment of the entrepreneurial team means sudden death to the proposal. If the actual and pro-forma accounts are not transparently clear and clearly honest the fund manager knows that she will have to rebuild the accounts in order to evaluate the proposal, and so she will almost always go straight to the next proposal

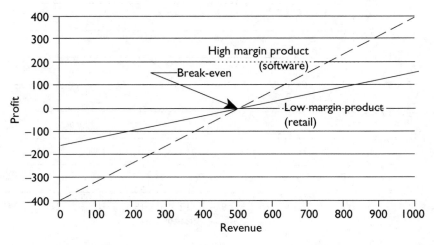

Figure 17.2 An enterprise level break-even chart

instead. Proposals from technical enthusiasts may get short shrift: at the point that the venture capital fund first invests the major problem the venture faces is building profitable market share for the products it has, not creating new ones. Proposals that are too long, or bound in stiff covers, or presented with spelling and grammatical errors are begging to be passed over; their wish is usually granted.

Most venture fund managers will look to find some fairly simple ratios and indices when they examine the historic and projected accounts. They will look for a break-even chart, as in Figure 17.2, and a cash balance projection, as for example Figure 17.3. When examining a break-even chart the venture fund manager will use the chart to estimate both the upside and downside potential of the business. Obviously if actual sales turn out to be somewhere to the left of the break-even point, the business will not be able to cover its fixed expenses. For businesses where the variable cost is a high fraction of the price (that is, low contribution margins, as in mass market retail), sales will have to be a long way to the right of the break-even point in order to generate a decent profit, but from there they are fairly safe from slipping all the way back to a loss. By contrast, with high-margin products such as software and professional services, a business can look very profitable with sales just above the break-even level, but only a relatively small fall in sales can leave the business making an equally large loss.

A cash balance or cumulative cash flow chart, such as Figure 17.3, gives the reviewing manager two vital pieces of information. The first is the low point: in the example shown, the business has a cumulative cash flow of –$500 000 at month three, and therefore the venture fund must find $500 000 to give the business a 50:50 chance of surviving into month four. The model business depicted in Figure 17.3 sharply curtailed its marketing expenditure from month

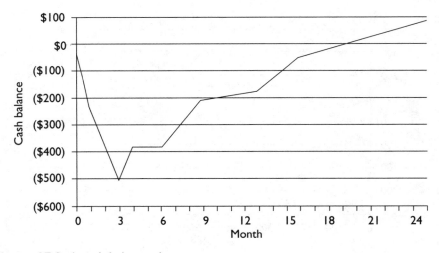

Figure 17.3 A cash balance chart

Table 17.3 *Golis's ratios*

Ratio	Calculation	Expected ranges
Net margin	Post tax profits divided by sales revenue (as received, not as at retail)	5%–10%
Gearing	Ratio of total debt to shareholders' funds	less than 100%
Stock, creditors and debtors	Value of stock, debtors and creditors respectively, multiplied by 365 and divided by annual sales gross revenue	Stock greater than 60 debtors greater than 50 creditors less than 40
Return on equity at maturity	Profits after tax and interest divided by shareholders funds	Greater than 15%
Interest cover	Pre-interest cash flow divided by interest payments	Greater than 2
Annual sales/ employee	Re-calculate monthly based on planned workforce growth but presented as an annualised figure	Less than $200 000 greater than $80 000
Contribution margin	Re-calculate monthly	Industry-dependent
Break-even sales	Re-calculate monthly	Less than forecast sales
Manufacturing cost analysis	Specialised figures	To survive examination by independent expert

Based on Golis 1993

seven onwards, pushing it into positive cash flow immediately and bringing the cumulative cash flow positive within two years.[11] This particular model business pays off its launch expenses fairly quickly, and when the cash balance does cross the zero line it does so relatively definitely, giving an analyst confidence that positive cumulative cash flow will be reached, if not in month twenty-one, certainly by month twenty-three.

Golis (1993) provides a list of indices that he checks when reviewing business plans: these are summarised here in Table 17.3.

Once the venture fund manager has found reasons to reject the majority of proposals in front of her, she will start looking for reasons to support some or all of the remainder. The principle behind hurdle rates was explained in Chapter 8: an example, intended to be typical, of a

> *The dominant question is not: How will the fund put money in? but: How can the fund get it out again?*

product with two years of sales history, suggested that the minimum risk-weighted rate of return acceptable to a venture fund should be about 31 per cent. Australian venture fund managers, probably suspecting that even the most conscientious entrepreneur cannot resist polishing the financial projections a little, tend to look for 35 per cent or even 40 per cent on the plan, in the hope that they will get at least the 31 per cent minimum in reality.

Since a new venture needs all its cash to grow, the venture fund cannot get any money out as dividends, and when the growth knee is reached, perhaps five years from the date the venture fund invests, and the firm stops growing rapidly, it will have only just started to produce a positive net cash flow. At this point, the venture fund, having put (say) $1 million in, wants between $3.9 million and $5.4 million out. The venture hasn't got it, the entrepreneur hasn't got it, so where is it coming from?

There are really only two possible sources:

▲ the business can be sold to the public through a float on the Australian Stock Exchange or possibly the United States 'over-the-counter' (actually, electronic) market NASDAQ

▲ the business can be sold to a larger company which sees the venture's products as complementary to its own, and where the venture's profit stream will assist its adoptive parent to report improved earnings.

Successful stock exchange floats are very rewarding for the venture capital funds and the founding entrepreneurs. To be sure of being successful, the float must be underwritten, and underwriters want 5 per cent of the subscriptions plus their considerable expenses, and they are not very interested in floats raising much under $40 million on the Australian stock exchange. To raise $40 million a new firm should be able to show a strong trend in profit growth and at least $6 million profit before tax and dividends at its most recent balance date. NASDAQ issues are not usually underwritten, and firms down to $20 million capitalisation can get traded, but they must show high margins and high growth to excite traders and buyers in that market.

A sale to a larger company does not need underwriters, but it does need a large company that wants to buy the venture. Consumer brands are usually easy to sell: new wine labels, new retail chains, new fast food concepts (once proven and franchised), but some very profitable ventures are not. High technology, particularly medical high technology, gives the boards of major Australian corporations palpitations. The major assets of some firms, including software companies, advertising agencies and many forms of brokerage are 'liveware'. A buyer may get nothing but a heap of resignations and some worn desks.

Australian venture capital fund managers have a rather unkind term, the 'living dead', for firms that don't get quite big enough to float and don't get fashionable enough to find a corporate buyer. Such firms can be vibrant and successful, as far as their employees, customers and founders are concerned, and yet with no buyer the venture fund is 'locked in', drawing dividends but unable to extract its capital.

Firms can become 'living dead' by not growing big enough, or by being in an unfashionable industry. They can also become so by executive action. If the entrepreneur(s) discover(s) the effect of second and later stage financing, as shown in Table 17.1, they may refuse to allow their share holding to be diluted any further.

Subsequent growth will be slowed or stifled by a lack of capital and, although the venture fund's money is safe, it will be stuck for an extended period of time.

Australian venture capital funds are listed in the *Venture Capital Guide*, issued regularly by the publishers of the *Venture Capital Journal* (Bivell (ed.) various dates).

Leasing

In general terms, when a new venture requires an item of equipment or access to premises, it will be possible to buy it, using up scarce capital, or arrange to lease it for a regular, usually monthly, payment. Leases come in a rich variety of shapes and sizes, but the basic premise in every case is the equipment is safe from the venture's creditors: if the venture fails, the lessor gets the equipment or the premises back. Since the value of the returned equipment or premises should be positive, the lease company may be able to work on a lower rate of return than the venture: if a venture's natural hurdle rate is 35 per cent, leasing, even at effective interest rates of up to 25 per cent, may be the correct decision.

Entrepreneurs should shop around for their lease finance, remembering that it is a crime in Australia under the Trade Practices Act to tie the sale of goods to a particular leasing company: a firm that sells them equipment cannot require them to use a particular finance provider. Huge differences in the effective interest rates charged by different leasing companies, and by the same leasing companies at different times, are common, and the other clauses, particularly those covering security deposits and penalties for early termination, will also vary dramatically between lease financiers.

Leasing deals will be killed stone dead by any suspicion concerning the lessor's security of title. If leased equipment is 'sold', either by a corrupt entrepreneur or by bailiffs on behalf of creditors, the lease company faces a long and tortuous legal route to recovering its property, while in the event of a venture's bankruptcy the lessors of the missing equipment are unsecured creditors without much hope of recovering their money.

Banks

Banks create money (see box) but the machine can run in reverse and destroy money as well. Banks are required to maintain certain prudential ratios, ensuring that depositors' money is not at serious risk. Banks usually stay a little bit on the safe side of the minimum level so as to be able to absorb minor write-offs without triggering a crisis.

If a bank does find its reserves close to the prudential minimum, the consequences of a further loan default are extremely serious. A major Australian bank 'on the limit' would, in the event of a $100 million bad debt:

▲ report a capital loss of $100 million, or about 1 per cent of shareholders' funds

▲ recall or sell to another bank $1.1 billion of loans

▲ report an earnings reduction of about $130 million until it can dislodge the excess deposits and reduce its recurrent expenses by $50 million or so.

Bankers' magic

Banks take deposits from investors and depositors, set a proportion aside as reserves, and then lend the rest. Borrowers use the advance to pay bills, and the people who get paid deposit their cheques in the bank, which then sets aside a fraction as reserves and lends the rest ...

Each bank's shareholders' funds act as an insurance for the depositors. If a borrower defaults, shareholders' funds are drawn down, which is bad enough, but the reduced shareholders' funds can now only insure a smaller deposit base, which is worse.

A bank's margin is the difference between the interest it pays depositors and receives from borrowers; the profit is the margin less expenses — $1 of shareholders funds can support about $12 of lending, and at a typical net margin of 1 per cent, generate 12 cents of profit, or a 12 per cent return on capital.

If a bad debt of $1 has to be written off, the bank must not only report a $1 loss but must contract its lending by a further $11. This will leave it over-deposited, with $12 of deposits that it can't lend but on which it must pay interest. The $1 loss then leads to a $1.20 annual reduction in margins until the bank can re-instate its capital or persuade $12 worth of depositors to take their money elsewhere.

Events such as these would knock the share price down by 10 per cent or more, causing outrage among the major shareholders. Several senior managers might join the 1000 employees who would be shown the door in an attempt to bring expenses back into line with the reduced level of business.

These facts of banking life make banks extremely unwilling to lend money where they might be forced to write it off, and they will go to considerable, sometimes ludicrous, lengths to protect themselves. They may ask for personal guarantees for sums that vastly exceed the guarantor's resources; they will try to extend their security over property worth far more than the amount of the loan, if they can get away with it; and they will reject, at least when in an insecure mood, propositions that ordinary people might regard as cast-iron. During the 1991–92 recession at least one medium size business's managers were astounded to be told that a signed, unconditional order from one of the world's richest non-finance companies could not be accepted as security at its face value.

When a bank does get into trouble, the process of cutting down the loan book can get ugly and extremely arbitrary. Profitable businesses with ample assets and a perfect payment record have been ordered to return half, or all, of their overdraft at one month's notice, and have been forced into receivership, involving a wipeout of the shareholders and substantial losses to the bank, if they could not comply. Other businesses have had their overdraft interest rates pushed to usurious levels on specious 'risk' grounds as a troubled bank desperately tries to rebuild its balance sheet.

Banks are fair-weather friends, and overdrafts, which may be the only finance offered to a small but growing business, are short term debt and can be recalled at any time. Even specific, secured term loans often have a clause allowing the bank to recall them or seize the security more or less at will. Listed companies are sometimes able to raise debt finance through fixed interest notes, often 'convertible' notes where the lender can, at its option, be repaid by the issue of a preset number of shares. New ventures may include convertible notes in a venture investment package organised by a venture capital fund, but they are unlikely to find banks among buyers of such securities.

Corporate bonds

In the United States there is a large and very active market in corporate bonds, usually fixed interest, fixed term securities. Each lender is graded and regularly re-rated by the ratings agencies, and so the buyers of these bonds can choose from a range with government-guaranteed debt at one end and 'junk bonds' at the other. Australian borrowers can tap this market with two provisos: the instruments are written in United States dollars, and so the enterprise carries an exchange risk; and the minimum issue unit on the bond market is US$50 million, putting United States-issued corporate bonds out of the reach of most Australian firms.

There are less active bond markets in other countries, and financial engineers of various degrees of integrity may offer to raise fixed interest capital for a new business, but in general terms the fixed interest markets are 'out of the new venture's league'.

Share market investors

New ventures in unfashionable industries cannot rely on being bought by a major corporation, and so they must look to the stock market to reward the venturers and supply additional capital once the fast growth phase is over. Investors are either institutional, representing superannuation and life insurance funds, or individuals of moderate to high net worth.

Institutional investors in the Anglophone countries have, since 1987, come to demand large and rising dividends as their price for supporting a firm's shares. Since the dividends come from money that would otherwise have been retained within the business, hopefully to develop it, large firms with institutions dominating their share registers have tended not to grow very rapidly. If a growing firm sees its ultimate owners as large, managed Australian funds it should plan to dress itself so as to appeal to them. This requires a solidly defensible market share, minimal exposure to either commodity prices or changes in fashion, and the ability to grow steadily, probably by mergers and acquisitions and line extensions rather than by developing radical new products.

Individual investors have a less calculating approach to their portfolio and they tend to take a longer term perspective than the institutions, looking to growth and to some extent emotional satisfaction as well as dividend flows. Small investors[12] cannot afford to be as fickle as large ones, simply because of the transaction costs involved in buying and selling their shares, and the small shareholders' habit of holding on to their shares has helped many managements threatened by a hostile takeover. While it is neither legal nor ethical to overstate the immediate prospects of a venture in order to entrap investors, large or small, a firm whose revenues are intrinsically volatile would do well to attract individual investors, who are much less likely than the institutions to dump their shares or accept an undervalued takeover bid on the basis of a single setback.

End notes

1 The treatment provided in this chapter is designed to provide a general overview of the types of funds and fund providers appropriate to various stages of financing a growing entrepreneurial venture. For greater detail on both the technicalities of finance provision and the specific availability of funds we suggest the following references:

Martin and Burrow (1991) — this is an Australian work of international relevance: a thorough treatise on the principles and applications of financial mathematics geared to both mathematically-oriented students and users of financial calculators. It contains many worked examples. McMahon, Holmes, Hutchinson and Forsaith (1993) — this is a useful work for the student of entrepreneurial finance. By exploring the small business and entrepreneurship finance literature, this work raises all the issues relevant to financial management of small and growing ventures. However, it presumes that the reader possesses the financial skills acquired after doing a university finance course. It is a suitable companion to Weston and Brigham. Weston and Brigham (1993) — this is a highly respected and frequently recommended finance text book. Van Horne, Davis, Nicol and Wright (1990) — this large work addresses the theoretical and technical areas covered by Weston and Brigham in the framework of the Australian financial system.

For a study of financial markets from an entrepreneurship perspective see: Phillips (1986). Golis (1993) — this very readable work explains the financial aspects of business planning and new venture management requirements in a practical and thorough way. Australian Academy of Technological Sciences (undated) — this report was the genesis of the Australian venture capital industry. Carew (1996) — this book provides greater depth on one of the several institutions covered in Hicks and Wheller. Hicks and Wheller (eds) (1990) — the book is an introductory text for students undertaking post secondary study in the banking and finance field. It provides an up to date grounding in the Australian financial system; its markets, institutions and securities.

Other interesting scholarly and reference works include: Bygrave and Timmons (1992) — an important work on the modern venture capital industry. Bivell (ed.) (various) — provides regular monthly reports on the Australian venture capital industry. Arthur Anderson (1996) — a survey of the Australian venture capital market.

Some popular accounts of recent history in the financial markets can provide insights not always found in text and reference works: Bruck (1989) — this is an excellent account of the Michael Milken story. Burroughs and Helyar (1990) — this book relates the story of the biggest leveraged buyout in history and presents an indictment of the 1980s philosophy that 'greed is good'. Lewis (1990) — called by Tom Wolfe: 'the funniest book about Wall Street I have ever read'. Marsh (1992) — this institution affects the life of everyone on the planet. Marsh tells its story well. Wilson (1988) — an account of the family that dominated European finance from 1560 to the 1980s.

2 The concept of variance is meaningless for a single project where the expectation of success is less than 50 per cent, and so the risk-weighted hurdle rate of return is undefined.

3 Many public health specialists believe that far too much money is spent on developing ethical preparations offering trivial advantages over those already on the market while the development of vaccines and treatments for infectious diseases is relatively neglected.

4 Governments in most countries of the world support 'non-commercial' theatre and other forms of artistic expression, suggesting that, as with pharmaceuticals, a commercial system supported by intellectual property protection does not fully satisfy community needs.

5 Exicom Ltd held a major contract to supply telephone handsets in Australia. Their early products failed in tropical conditions, and the cost of recalling and replacing several hundred thousand handsets crippled the company.

6 The actor-producer Paul Hogan raised most of the finance needed for the film *Crocodile Dundee* from private investors, many of them friends and many more fans of his TV persona. When the film became a major hit, the investors received several times their money back.

7 Architectural drawings supported by engineering calculations are a prototype in the sense used here, as was Boeing's B777 data base. Virtual reality preceded the computer industry, although technology promises to make virtual prototypes much more fun to examine.

8 The analogy is not very far-fetched: US consumer products companies launch twenty thousand or more new products a year; on an eight hour day/five day week basis this is a little more than a product every two minutes.

9 Long-forgotten equals three months or more since the investment.

10 Often referred to as 'DEC' (pronounced 'deck') by outsiders, but always Digital, or Digital Equipment, by the people who work for it.

11 The model firm is not well-managed from the point of view of long term market share or long term shareholder value; cutting marketing expenditure at this early stage means slower growth and conceding a greater market share to imitating rivals.

12 Compared to institutions like the AMP Number 1 Fund, every individual is a small investor, some smaller than others.

Case study three

Multistack: Refinancing

APR Ltd had been founded by two geologists with what may have been an optimistic view of the profits to be made from fostering Australian technology. By 1987 they were running distinctly short of cash, while the growth of Multistack and the needs of their other subsidiaries was placing a heavy demand on their resources. They decided on a partly underwritten flotation on the stock market, closing at the end of October 1987. To their, and many other people's, surprise the stock market fell 20 per cent in that month and new issues were not seen as attractive. None of the new APR shares were bought by the public, and half the shortfall wound up in the unwilling hands of their stock broker.

APR was extremely short of cash, and so when Graham Coningsby, an acquaintance of Conry, offered to buy part of Multistack his offer was accepted and he became the owner of 12.5 per cent of the Multistack equity. Shortly after this deal was completed, a property company called Crestwin took the unwanted APR shares off the underwriters' hands for a small consideration, and privatised the group with the intention of making a back door entry to the United States by rolling their shares into a shell listed on NASDAQ. In the middle of this intricate manoeuvre the industrial property market in Australia 'tanked' and Crestwin, like APR before it, was suddenly very short of cash. Coningsby assembled a consortium including Super Link and Dunn Air Ltd, Multistack's Australian distributor, and made an offer to APR for the remaining shares in Multistack.

APR/Crestwin came to an agreement in principle with the Coningsby group, but dithered about finalising it. They may have hoped for a better offer, either from Coningsby and Dunn or from the North American firm Trane. Westpac, the banker to Crestwin, did not like their exposure to the property market and when an interest payment date was missed, Westpac appointed receivers to Crestwin. While Multistack had been trading profitably and was nominally solvent, it was swept into Westpac's bag by a series of cross-guarantees, and the deal between the Coningsby group and APR was 'off'.

The Coningsby group turned its attention to Westpac, and so did Trane: after various 'alarums and excursions' the Coningsby group won and took possession of the assets of the former Multistack at the beginning of 1990. It was clear that Multistack needed cash to expand, and its growing sales to China looked, in 1990, to be attractive to stock market investors. The new management began preparing a prospectus for a stock market flotation — a task that was to occupy much of the next two years.

Crashes on Wall Street and the Australian Stock Exchange had little effect on China, where the industrial boom raged on. Super Link was writing business faster than the Panyu factory could assemble units or Multistack could supply heat exchangers. Multistack was enormously profitable and desperately short of cash. Multistack had licensed Super Link to start the manufacture of its unique heat exchangers in China alongside its assembly operations: $1 million would be required for Multistack's expenses in transferring the necessary technology.

The United States sales effort was still focused on renovations and replacements, where the unique modular design of Multistack systems offered dramatic cost advantages over conventional unitary systems. In 1992 the United States firm Multistack Inc. had earned a gross sales revenue of US$3.4 million. And 1992 was the first year in which Multistack Inc. had made a profit, after several years of start-up losses; the profit was small at US$59 000, but much better than losing money. In 1992 Multistack grossed $6.8 million from sales, of which $1.6 million consisted of exports to China, and a further $2.2 million in licence fees and royalties, of which $907 000 was associated with licences to Chinese factories.

Multistack was floated on the Australian Stock Exchange in 1992, offering seven million shares at $1, consisting of 20 cents par value and an 80 cent premium. Ron Conry held 1.2 million shares, and was therefore now a millionaire, on paper at least. The other investor-directors held a total of six million shares and the Hong Kong based principals of their Chinese distributor, Super Link, also held 1.2 million shares. For the time being, Multistack had enough cash on hand to continue its expansion. Things were going so well that a further $3 million was raised by a private placement at $2.15 per share a few months after the original float.

The giant is tranquillised – almost

The proceeds of the float and the subsequent placement covered Multistack's immediate Chinese obligations and allowed for a substantial expansion of its production facilities in Boronia, near Melbourne. This included a new press and furnace for manufacturing Multistack's unique heat exchangers. Sales, liberated from the production constraints, boomed to $16 million in 1993, with about half coming from exports to China. A further $4.3 million was earned in licence fees and royalties, all but $700 000 coming from China.

However, 1994 started ominously for Multistack, with new policies from the Chinese government intended to reduce inflation and to direct more investment to the relatively neglected north and north-west of China. When the financial year ended in June 1994, Multistack's sales to China were seen to have actually fallen by $1.9 million, and this was not fully offset by increases in sales in other markets and in licence and royalty fees. Net profit after tax was almost stagnant. One institutional shareholder dumped its holding at $1.60 per share, and the share price fell below $2 and settled around $1.60 to $1.70.

Australia's investment community had regarded the size of Multistack's Chinese operations as a source of great strength, but with China adopting a more stringent monetary policy the exposure to China suddenly became

	1991	1992	1993	1994
Revenue (RMB)	40 876	85 232	220 229	313 322
Operating profit (RMB)	8581	23 277	67 101	110 047
Attributed profit (RMB)	6076	15 156	47 498	84 492
Revenue (A$)	6488	13 529	34 957	49 734
Attributed profit (AUD)	964	2406	7539	13 411

regarded as an unacceptable risk. Multistack could no longer look to the Australian financial markets to fund its growth.

Super Link

Multistack had done well out if its Chinese operations over the years 1992–94, but its distributor, Super Link, had done better still. Over the years 1991–94 its figures (all numbers in thousands) were as shown in the table above.

Super Link distributed all the components of air conditioning systems, not just chillers, but Panyu Super Link, the factory that made Multistack-designed chillers in China, was not doing badly: its 1994 gross sales were RMB177 million (A$28 million) and its after tax profit was RMB60 million (A$9.5 million). Super Link were sufficiently optimistic to plan the production of more Multistack-designed equipment at another of its subsidiaries, Panyu Precision. Panyu Precision was, in 1994, an importer and licensed manufacturer of ancillary equipment, much of it sourced from or designed by The Airflow Company, an innovative United States designer and manufacturer of components of air conditioning systems, with a special reputation for military and demanding civilian applications, such as clean rooms for semiconductor manufacture.

Various North American suppliers of air conditioning plant let it be known that, if Super Link was having trouble obtaining all the equipment it needed from Multistack, they would be happy to step into the breach. At the same time Multistack became aware that R22 was unlikely to be an acceptable refrigerant for very much longer, and none of the offered alternatives would work in their current generation of sealed unit compressors. Multistack had to start developing a new compressor. Keeping up with the Chinese market meant adapting Multistack's modular systems to their needs, and their needs turned out to include air-cooled chillers and reverse cycle units, each of which had to be developed and tested before shipping.

Multistack: Into the future

During 1994 Multistack realised that it faced far more opportunities than it could pursue; worse, its strength in the Chinese market was threatened unless it could boost its output and its R&D effort so as to keep its products abreast of China's increasingly sophisticated demands, and the entire basis of its competitive advantage was threatened by its inability to use R134a in a low-maintenance, hermetically sealed compressor. Money was needed to address these problems, and so Multistack's executive team set about looking for it.

In December 1994 Multistack bought the entire issued capital of Super Link and Dunn Pty Ltd, its Australian distributor, and the 50 per cent of Multistack Inc. that it did not already own. At the same time it raised $33 million in an underwritten share placement at $1.75 per share. The Dunn and Multistack Inc. transactions were carried out for cash and a nominal share placement, costing $7.2 million, while the Super Link transaction involved the payment of $15 million and the issue of sixty-four million shares to the owners of Super Link, Messrs Leung and Yan. This would represent 62 per cent of the total shares on issue; in effect, Super Link had effected a reverse takeover of Multistack.

Part of the $10 million left in Multistack's coffers was used to support the continuing development programs, while the rest was used to acquire Airflow Inc., a North American manufacturer of precision control systems for air conditioning plant and another supplier and licensor to Super Link in China.

An R&D syndicate was arranged to assist with the financing of the new compressor development, and by the beginning of 1996 the work of the syndicate was complete and a prototype of the new compressor had been tested. Under test conditions, the new compressor required 20 per cent less power for a given volumetric performance than existing R134a compressors. A lubrication system suitable for lifetime use in an hermetically sealed motor-compressor unit had also passed stringent tests.

Ron Conry prepared an estimate of the remaining costs of bringing the new compressor to market. A further $4.5 million would be needed to develop from prototype to production; special tooling and test equipment would cost about $5 million; while premises, other production equipment, working capital and initial marketing expense were put at $14.5 million. The board of Multistack considered this estimate, and decided that Multistack would not go into compressor production on its own account. They would, however, insist that any purchaser of the technology embodied in the new compressor granted Multistack an exclusive, royalty-free licence to use the new compressor in 'modular chillers'.

18
Chapter

The product launch

What and why

The launch of any new product, whether it is a good or a service; whether it is absolutely new or just new to a market; whether it represents the first use of new technology or just a repackaging of familiar technology, is a singular event.[1] It is impossible to describe it even approximately using continuous mathematical functions, and so it is an event lying outside the orthodox economist's universe. It does not, however, lie outside the economy.

Every new product represents the result of a past investment. Maintaining the product in the market will require an ongoing expenditure, and in most circumstances there will be a period following the launch of the new product when the continuing expense exceeds receipts from sales. The money needed to create the product and to sustain it in the market during its early life may have been sourced directly from investors or from the cash flow of an established business, but in many cases part of the initial investment will have been by way of a bank or other loan, on which interest must be paid. Premises may have been rented and equipment leased. When there are such standing costs the investors' position will usually deteriorate until the surplus from trading rises sufficiently not only to cover operating costs but the standing expenses as well.

When the investment was initially made, it would have been in the expectation of a commensurate return, and waiting diminishes the value of this. If a long time elapses before there is a substantial trading surplus, the investors are bound to be disappointed, even if there is no interest default and seizure by a bank in the meantime. As we explained in Chapter 4 and showed how to model in Chapter 8, three distinct factors underpin the growth of sales of a new product:

▲ there are 'externally influenced' customers: those that the supplier has persuaded, with discounts, advertising, free samples and other legal means to try the new product

▲ there are 'internally influenced' customers, those that decide to try the new product after observing or receiving the recommendation of one or more established customers

▲ there are repeat customers, those who, having made satisfactory use of the product or a direct antecedent from the same supplier, return to that supplier when they need to purchase more of the product.

The very new business or radically new product starts with no customers, and therefore no repeat purchasers and no satisfied recommenders. The first customers it gets will be people whose trial has been secured at considerable expense, and it can only succeed as a business if a sufficient fraction of these early users become recommenders and/or repeat purchasers. When a product is a line extension or the direct successor to an established product the previous patterns of repurchasing and recommendation will continue, possibly somewhat attenuated. There will be some customers for such a product, and in due course, some recommendations, even without a planned launch. Even in this case a special launch promotion may well be vital if the product is to become a success: a change is bound to disturb the loyalty of some existing customers, and a launch helps a supplier recruit replacements.

The product launch should be seen as part of the investment needed to get the product to market: the sales directly generated by the launch activities may cover their direct costs, but they won't do better and they may do worse. Many consumer products include a free sampling program in their launch: the firm actually pays people to give its product away. Airline inaugural flights generally carry invited guests only; a publican taking over a license offers drinks 'on the house'; theatres 'paper the house' on opening night; the first 'sales' of industrial products are often more like indefinite free loans.

A launch is an investment made to accelerate the creation of a core of recommenders and repurchasers. To do this it must offer favours of some kind to early purchasers. Few people refuse an unconditional gift, and the special value offered to launch and early customers will be seen, in hindsight when they have become users, as such a gift. People who buy the product under launch conditions often assume a mild obligation to the giver: not enough to make them betray their friends by recommending a rotten product, but enough to cast a faint rosy glow over an average one. If the supplier has followed Soichiro Honda's maxim and the new product has amazed and astounded its customers by its excellence, early purchasers will wish to boast of their superior judgement or outstanding luck in buying the product before their colleagues and acquaintances did. Such boasts do the supplier nothing but good.

Launch economics

Launches, in the sense of a deliberate, planned introduction of a new product to the market, are generally a good idea (Gaylen & Hanks 1993). By stimulating the rapid development of a customer base, they bring forward cash flow from sales by recommendation and repurchase and therefore increase the return on the overall investment in the new product. There can, however, be too much of a good thing. In Chapter 5 we introduced the idea of the available annual gross margin, or AAGM, as a way of quantifying the value implicit in a market. We use the concept here as to make our description of launch planning as far as possible scale-independent.

> A computer company launched a new model, targeted at medium-sized businesses, in Australia. The marketing plan included an allowance for one customer in each Australian capital city to be given a 50 per cent discount in return for allowing their computer system to be used as a showcase.
>
> At the end of that year the company had made sales in all states of Australia, with Perth, relative to its market size, looking particularly good with six systems sold. A closer look showed that three of them were 'showcases' where the customer had received a 50 per cent discount. It took two more years before the books of the Perth branch were back in the black.

Since every market contains a finite number of people, the point will be reached where the number of subsidised sales will cut into the value of later full-price ones. This is less of a problem with packaged consumer goods and frequently used services, where those who rate their first trial as successful will start purchasing the product at its full price within a month or two, than it is with durable and infrequently purchased products. Model studies suggest that, as an upper limit, the launch year marketing budget for a durable product should not exceed about 25 per cent of the AAGM.

For frequently repurchased products the model study suggests that the optimal marketing spend is much more sensitive to the discount rate used to calculate the ultimate market value, and the discount rate is, of course, a surrogate for the market risk. If a firm uses a standard hurdle rate of 18 per cent, and expects one out of two of its new consumer varieties to be withdrawn after a year, the appropriate discount rate (using the principles explained in Chapter 8) is 58 per cent, and the upper limit on the launch budget is less than 7.5 per cent of the AAGM. In practice, marketers of fast moving consumer goods frequently carry out a test marketing exercise, and only proceed to a full launch once they are confident that the product will achieve a reasonable life on the market. Once they expect the line to last at least five years they can relaunch it with a one year marketing budget of up to a third of the AAGM.

Magazine publishers routinely test the market by printing and selling a first edition, which newsagents and other resellers will only take on a sale-or-return basis. Advertisers in such first issues give permission for their copy to be used, rather than actually paying to have it printed. The results of this exercise indicate whether the publisher should make a full scale launch, with a heavy drive for subscribers and genuine advertisements, or quietly fold the title with no second issue.

The market risk depresses the amount that durable product companies are generally willing to spend on their product launches. If the advertising doesn't work, or the users aren't as satisfied as expected, the high launch year expenditure will not look like such a good idea in retrospect. The launch budget may need to be controlled to avoid a conflict between the optimum marketing and the optimum manufacturing strategy for a new product. A large launch year market-ing budget, followed by a sharp reduction in the second year, a relaunch in the third and a slow tailing off of marketing expenditure thereafter gives the net marketing income (gross margin less marketing and sales expense) its highest possible present value. Such a marketing expenditure pattern makes the first year a sales peak, followed by a distinct contraction, followed by another jump before settling down to steady growth towards maturity. This is not the ideal pattern for a product needing extensive manufacturing investment.

Using the same model as before, but constraining year one sales to half of year two and avoiding any year-on-year falls, produced a recommended market-ing budget of 5 per cent in the launch year, 9 per cent in the second year, and 6 per cent in subsequent years, all against the hypothetical contribution base described above. This reduces the year one present value of the marketing con-tribution by some 20 per cent when compared to the unconstrained model, but this may be amply compensated by the more controlled investment pattern in manufacturing.

The model studies suggest the following three rules for setting the early year marketing budgets for a new product:

▲ For a frequently repurchased product, prepare but do not commit a launch costing up to 25 per cent of the hypothetical annual gross margin in the market and launch a test marketing or market research exercise to gain confidence in the market size projections and the expected warmth of buyer response. Commit to the full launch if and when the necessary confidence is gained.

▲ For an infrequently repurchased product where there are no production or distribution restrictions the year one launch budget can be as much as 25 per cent of the AAGM with a very much reduced second year budget. Expenditure should be raised in the third year if the second year sales demonstrate that an adequate level of recommendation is being achieved.

▲ For an infrequently repurchased product where there are production restrictions or production requires a significant product-specific investment, the year one launch budget can be as much as 5 per cent of the AAGM, the year two budget up to 9 per cent of it, and the year three 6 per cent of it. The year two results should be analysed before committing the year three marketing campaign, as if recommendations by early purchasers are not leading to a sufficient number of additional buyers, further marketing expense may not be justified.

Launch budget: Examples[2]

A consumer product: 1

A product manager is planning a line extension in a convenience food category, which she estimates to be generating $2 billion per year at an average gross margin of 17 per cent. Her firm's brands currently hold 22 per cent of this category, and the target for the line extension is to gain two further points, to bring the firm to 24 per cent. The AAGM available to her is therefore $2 billion *times* 17 per cent *times* 2 per cent *equals* $6.5 million. She prepares a budget showing a test marketing/market research program costing $325 000 and a roll-out support program, conditional upon the success of the test marketing, to cost $1.3 million.

A consumer product: 2

A product manager visiting the United States notices that the leading product in her category lacks a feature that has made her Australian product the category leader. In Australia her product is generating $120 million in sales annually at a gross margin of 22 per cent. She prepares a plan to launch her product in the United States. Noting that the United States economy is eighteen times larger than Australia's she calculates the AAGM as 18 *times* $120 million *times* 22 per cent *equals* $475 million and the launch budget needed to seize an appropriate share of the United States market would be $475 million *times* 25 per cent *equals* $115 million. She shows this to her managing director who turns purple in the face and utters some politically incorrect words. This provokes her to resign and travel to the United States. There she presents her idea to a leading consumer products company who instantly give her a job at five times her previous salary and allocate her a $150 million launch budget.

A high margin durable

A small team of computer programmers develop an educational PC game for secondary school students which they believe will raise its users' tertiary entrance ranking (TER) by an average of five points. Publishing and other costs are small in comparison to the $99 proposed price, and after distribution which they estimate will cost them 40 per cent of the retail price the gross margin will be $49 per copy. They estimate the total number of secondary students in English speaking countries with access to a PC at ten million and believe that they can reach 30 per cent of this market before imitators and pirate copies swamp it. The AAGM is $49 *times* 10 million *times* 30 per cent *equals* $147 million and the appropriate launch budget is therefore $147 million *times* 25 per cent *equals* $36 million. Since they haven't got this much money they compromise and spend $2000 on small advertisements in a computer magazine. This gains them fifty sales, all but two to pirates and imitators, and so they go back to maintaining networks while their idea goes on to gross a billion dollars.

A manufactured durable

An Australian manufacturer of gardening equipment designs a superior motor mower incorporating a patented feature which will make it considerably more attractive than currently available models (including their own model) without raising the manufacturing cost. The category is worth, in their estimate, $150 million per year in Australia at retail; the manufacturing gross margin is 18 per cent of the retail price or $27 million annually. The manufacturer currently holds a 40 per cent market share and believes that the new feature will raise its share to 50 per cent: the AAGM is therefore $27 million *times* (50 per cent *less* 40 per cent) *equals* $2.7 million and the appropriate launch budget is $2.7 million *times* 20 per cent *equals* $675 000 to be spent over three years with $135 000 in year one, $245 000 in year two and the balance in year three.

Allocating the budget[3]

Anyone with a budget will find plenty of people willing to help them spend it, and not all of these ways will support the project for which the budget was allocated. The point of a special launch budget is that it will persuade a sufficiently large number of people to give the new product a trial, and become repeat purchasers and satisfied recommenders as a result. The launch budget should not be stretched to cover expenses which are the normal part of a continuing business. By and large costs that would be incurred if the new customers had bought without the special launch incentives should be carried by the rest of the business. A special sales training event could be charged to the launch budget, but an annual sales conference, which would have been held in any case, should not be.

The following list covers most, but possibly not all, the activities that will be needed to make a launch successful:

▲ printed sales material must be available, including one or more of:

⏵ catalogue sheets

⏵ customer brochures

⏵ management information brochures

- ▶ point-of-sale material
- ▶ packaging or packaging add-ons
- ▶ sales presentation kits
- ▲ promotional material must be available, including one or more of:
  - ▶ press kits
  - ▶ press advertisements (general press) — in all relevant languages, and checked by a native speaker whenever the language is not the product/project manager's first language
  - ▶ press advertisements (specialist press) — in all relevant languages, and checked by a technical specialist and a native speaker whenever the language is not the product/project manager's first language
  - ▶ television and radio advertising must be prepared, as and when necessary
  - ▶ video and multi-media material must be prepared, as and when necessary, and adequate numbers of copies produced
- ▲ launch events must be planned, including:
  - ▶ a general staff briefing session, whenever the success of the new product will be of significance to the whole enterprise
  - ▶ a sales briefing event (possible extending into an extensive training program if the product or the marketing tactics are radically new)
  - ▶ a press briefing
  - ▶ an event for key customers and hot prospects
  - ▶ an event for other customers and warm prospects and suspects
- ▲ commercial terms must be set out, including:
  - ▶ standard trading price and discount schedule
  - ▶ special offer rules for key customers
- ▲ the sales and sales management team must be in place:
  - ▶ procedures for pre-disclosure and pre-selling must be agreed
  - ▶ the sales bonus scheme must be set up and approved
  - ▶ sales staff must be recruited or re-assigned
- ▲ the distribution channel must be set up and sufficient stock manufactured or service providers trained to meet the day one demand.

The launch [project] manager

Someone must take full executive responsibility for organising the project launch. When there is a product manager already appointed for the new product that person may be appropriate, but product managers may be too junior or lacking in management experience to control a major, particularly an international, launch program. In these cases a full time project manager should be appointed. The project manager can be someone already in the firm who can be relieved of all other duties for the required time, or it can be someone recruited explicitly for the job.

For a major 'you bet your company' launch there can be a considerable advantage in recruiting an outsider as launch manager, since the nature of the task makes it almost certain that great offence will be caused to many of the firm's employees, particularly the senior ones. Managing directors, chairpersons, and founding entrepreneurs seldom like working from scripts and have been known to respond quite badly to stage directions. Employees looking forward to a long future with a company are extremely reluctant to tell their chief executive that the lectern is more animated and convincing than he is. (Female chief executives are rare and in any case women are generally more aware of the need for presentation skills and so react less violently to coaching.)

The offence will continue as the launch plan ripples through the organisation: technical people will be outraged by the over-simplifications in the brochures and advertising; the sales staff and managers will scream that the price is too high, the launch discounts are too small, and the bonus scheme would have made Ebenezer Scrooge blush; manufacturing and supply will complain that the volumes are too low or too high or both; and the legal department will attempt to remove every adjective and neuter every positive statement in the copy for fear of the trade practices law and of litigious competitors and of both in combination.

If the product fails the launch manager will be blamed, while if it succeeds the launch manager will have demonstrated an organising and management ability that less creative senior managers may see as less of a corporate asset than a personal career threat.

Printed material
Catalogue sheets
A catalogue sheet is a single sheet, often double sided, which contains the essential specification of a product. One catalogue sheet should be prepared for each of the products to be launched. A catalogue sheet should be capable of being the first (and if possible) the only document setting out the 'description' of the product in the event of a subsequent dispute with a customer or the Australian Competition and Consumer Commission. Catalogue sheets should be dated with some form of serial number control so that there should be no dispute about which was the current one at any given point in time.

Companies marketing a substantial range of products to businesses often provide their customers and likely prospects with a binder in which to file the catalogue sheets: the issue of a new sheet, even if it is only a minor update of an existing one, is then an occasion justifying a sales call to update the binder and explain the benefits of the product range again.

Customer brochures
For many products, or product ranges, users and prospective customers may appreciate a friendlier and less legal document than the catalogue sheet, in which

the use and benefits of the product(s) are described. Such brochures are often printed in colour on quality paper, and can include photographs of satisfied users together with suitable testimonials, as well as a more extended description of the key features of the product. Care must be taken to ensure that the brochure does not damage the legal standing of the catalogue sheet or stray into claims of fitness for purpose.

Most customers for lower value and faster moving consumer products do not expect to be provided with a brochure routinely, but brochures are useful in responding to queries and complaints. If a customer rings up Lever–Rexona Ltd to complain that they used one of their washing powders in their new, front-loading washing machine and can no longer get into their laundry for the bubbles, the customer may be sent a brochure showing all the major Lever–Rexona household products with illustrations showing their application, and in particular, the need to use low-suds powder in front-loading machines. This is much less likely to cause offence than asking why they didn't read their washing machine's instruction manual, and may even lead to sales of other Lever–Rexona products to that household.

Because brochures must be attractive if they are to do their job, many people with no intention of buying or even considering a product will try to get their hands on the brochure, and this can prove expensive. Small boys of all ages are particularly fond of brochures for expensive cars and military aircraft, for example. It would be counter-productive to try to screen brochure applicants: the screening would be expensive, and it is worth giving dozens or even hundreds of brochures to small boys if one arouses he interest of a genuine buyer. Some consumer brochures are sold for a nominal price, not to cover their cost, but to make small boys think twice; others are only supplied on request, again a barrier sufficient to eliminate the totally unmotivated without deterring serious inquiries.

The management information brochure

Many sales are negotiated with people who have no intention of becoming users: industrial products may be bought by corporations where the actual users and operators have no contact at all with the directors who are required to approve the purchase. In many cases the directors will have a legal or accounting background, and technical specifications will mean nothing to them. Even directors with engineering degrees are often a long way from the shop floor or the working face and are likely to misinterpret technical data. Other products are sold through distribution channels such as supermarkets and department stores where the key decisions are made by people who may have no intention of using the product themselves.

A management information brochure helps to persuade such people that they are making a proper commercial decision in the interests of their business and not merely indulging the technological or other fantasies of their subordinates. Management information brochures need not be very long or contain a lot of words, but they must at least say:

▲ who the supplier is, and the most important things about them: 'XXY Ltd is the Australian division of the worldwide XXY Group, a $many billion corporation with offices and factories in …' or 'yyx Pty Ltd is a new enterprise led by the outstanding businessman Sir Madi T Big to bring the brilliant discoveries of Fred Smart to market …'

▲ what the major commercial benefit is, essentially more output, higher margins, lower costs or greater prestige (and where possible, all four) in terms that directors are likely to understand: a new fast food may have all sorts of interesting contents and be made by the most amazing processes, but retail executives will want to hear that the public will buy more at higher prices in smaller packets than they would for any competing line

▲ who are some key commercial references, more to the supplier than the product: setting out what the supplier's or its key employees' major, publicly recognised achievements are.

Point of sale material

If a new product is to be sold at retail, there should be appropriate posters, stickers, display racks or stands or whatever can get it to stand out from its surroundings. The unfamiliar can totally fail to register with shoppers, and the special display material can go some way to overcome this. When the product has had press, TV and catalogue support the point of sale material serves to trigger recall among the audience, increasing the number of trials.

Products that are not sold at retail still need some dressing in the form of front office displays, posters, desktop gadgets and the like. People in the supplier organisation need to be able to share in the sense of excitement that should accompany a new product. Getting a new product ready for market involves a lot of stress but also a lot of anticipation, and settling down to wait two or three years for the market's verdict can be an anti-climax. An event releases the tension and prepares the staff for the hard work ahead.

Packaging

Most product shipping packages are strictly utilitarian, and as far as members of the public and even the store staff handling them are concerned, the new product might as well be more of the old ones. A few bright, adhesive stickers on the first few weeks' shipments can make the product stand out, and give the people who see it some echo of the interest they may show in the first car of a new model, or the new season's clothes, or the first cuckoo of spring.

Even when the supplier's usual practice is to use colourful packaging, the launch manager should ensure that the new product is clearly different from anything in the established product line.

The product launch

The sales presentation kit

Sales people, and particularly male sales staff, tend to get excited by new products; sometimes too excited to learn very much about them before they start selling them. A sales kit becomes a script for their early sales calls. It often includes a desktop presenter, a sort of fold-up slide show, which the sales person can use to illustrate the story. Successful sales kits have included audio tapes, to be placed in the sales person's car and hammer home the key selling messages, videos, toys and gadgets. Several companies have given a Swiss Army knife to each of its sales persons in order to impress upon them the versatility of the product that they were selling.

Sales presentation kits are needed for products sold through distributors and retailers as well as for products sold directly to users, since the sales staff are responsible for securing listings for the new product and for getting it shelf or other space allocation.

Promotional material
The press opportunity

News programs are watched by a vast number of people, including public broadcasting system viewers, and newspapers, while not as popular as they once were, reach a significant fraction of the population. Print and broadcast journalists can be invited to a special launch event, and apart from opportunities to see, talk and drink they should be given a press kit. The press kit should include the user brochures, an explanation of the new product 'ready to print', and some human interest material about the product and/or the people associated with it. The catalogue sheets will normally be too technical and the management brochure may be too politically compromising to make good inclusions.

Press releases very seldom make it to the mainstream press, although the trade and specialist press will often run them. If there are any good stories, professional journalists like to discover them themselves, and so an invitation to a one-on-one session with a senior executive can be included in the kit given to selected journalists. TV journalists will appear to film a stunt, but unless it goes wrong, or the stunt is very telegenic, the clip won't make it to air.

TV may run a picture if an appropriate celebrity can be persuaded to attend the launch: the means of persuasion generally consist of large numbers written on small pieces of signed paper, and the bigger the cheque, the better known the personality and the more likely it is that a clip will get to air. There is of course no certainty that the clip will go to air no matter how famous the personality, and there is a fair chance that the sponsoring firm will get edited out of the story unless the firm's products and logo are inescapable. Under no circumstances should the personality be allowed to say anything about the product: it will inevitably sound insincere. They should be invited to say something about the firm, its executives and its staff; as long as everyone wears large name badges the celebrity may get their names right.

Celebrity guests should only be asked to do things that can be repeated several times for the cameras: this rules out eating and setting off explosives. If they are given a souvenir gift it should be chosen for its on-camera sparkle and the way the name of the firm or the product can be placed so as to be visible in every possible camera angle.

General press advertising

There seem to be two common mistakes made by people buying advertising space in the daily and Sunday newspapers:

▲ some firms are so convinced that they understand how to write copy that they do not engage an advertising agency or professional copywriter

▲ others are so impressed by the smooth young people at the advertising agency that they automatically approve every suggestion.

It is quite easy to go wrong either way by forgetting why the advertisement is being placed and what its placement is expected to achieve. An advertisement must say, in pictures and/or words, what the product is, who should buy it, and how they go about getting it. When the product is new its name should be set out particularly clearly. If it has famous antecedents or the right to use a famous trademark the trade mark may appear in lieu of the supplier's name. If the supplier is new and has no reputation or famous antecedents its name should only appear if it supports the purpose of the advertisement.

If the product is being launched in a new country the copy must be checked by a native speaker, even if the new language is nominally English. Idiom seldom crosses frontiers unchanged, spelling conventions can differ, and words in common use in one country can have a startlingly different significance in others. Even grammar can be important: the English avoid split infinitives with a determination bordering pedantry, while many North Americans choose as a matter of taste to boldly split infinitives that no man has split before. If a product is being translated to Chinese or Japanese or another ideographic language double and treble checking for double entendres is critical.

When the former United States President Jimmy Carter visited Poland he wished, in his reply to the welcome address, to express North America's fond regard for the noble Polish people. He had a phrase of Polish written out for the purpose.

The words he used, roughly retranslated, said: 'I want to have [consensual] sex with all the Polish people', a somewhat out-of-character statement for a chaste Baptist; even so, it drew thunderous applause from the welcoming crowd.

Specialist press advertising

Trade journals and special interest publications generally work on the basis that the amount of editorial space devoted to any one supplier or product will bear a simple relationship to the volume of advertising placed. When the general press runs special 'advertising supplements' similar rules apply, although they may be stated less bluntly. Copy written by advertisers for such journals and supplements to run is referred to as 'advertorial'.

An English chemical company wished to increase the sales of its polyphosphate compounds. Polyphosphate has the property of making food treated with it absorb a lot of water. The company ran a large advertisement on the cover of a specialist trade journal, with the headline: 'Why sell ham when you can sell water?'

The advertisement received prime-time TV exposure on a consumer affairs program, and led to an extensive set of regulations limiting the water content of ham and other packaged food products. It is not known whether polyphosphate sales rose, but it seems unlikely.

Advertisements for the trade and specialist press are often written and illustrated by relative amateurs and since they go on advertising they can't be suffering too badly. We suggest that a professional copywriter or an advertising agency should be considered for such work, but acknowledge that 'home made' advertisements, as long as they keep the message clear and simple, often work. Firms should not assume that advertisements written for the trade press, or statements reproduced in it, will never reach the general public.

The advertorial is a more complex matter. Those readers who identify it won't believe it, making its preparation, and possibly even the money spent on advertisements, a waste of time and money if the source is too obvious. Suggestions for successful advertorial writing include:

▲ don't run the advertorial on the same page, and if possible, not even in the same issue, that the corresponding advertising appears in

▲ don't use superlatives, or if they are essential, use very few

▲ don't (at least in Australia) employ a didactic tone

▲ do include a story, preferably one that shows the supplier overcoming difficulties, or helping a customer to overcome difficulties.

The former Australian footballer, professional rough diamond and fitness fanatic Mark Jackson, or 'Jacko', has been used for many years in Australian television advertising for Union Carbide's 'Energiser' batteries. Energiser has become one of Australia's leading brands.

Union Carbide experimented with Jackson in California: ads featuring him were put to air and the response measured by a survey, showing:

▲ the 'Jacko' ads had one of the highest audience recall levels ever recorded

▲ viewers who recalled the ads were less likely to buy 'Eveready' and 'Energiser' products than those who did not.

Getting the language right in foreign countries is just as important when dealing with the trade and specialist press as it is with the general press and the same comments apply, with the added proviso that do-it-yourself advertising of any sort is extraordinarily dangerous when the copy language is not the writer's first one, and still dangerous when the copywriter is not completely familiar with the local culture. Australian idiom does not work very well in the United States, for example, and North American idiom can sound jarring in Australia. The time and expense saved by not finding a local copywriter or advertising agency is likely to be lost three times over in a poor or even a negative response to the resulting advertisements.

Broadcast media advertising

Broadcast media, that is, TV and radio, is normally used for consumer products and only used for public relations purposes by industrial product suppliers. The general quality of TV advertising is extremely high: some TV commercials cost more to produce per second than the most expensive feature films. When an audience is new to TV advertising, even poorly made advertisements can be effective, but as the audience gets more familiar poorly shot and scripted advertisements start generating a negative reaction: if the advertisement is that bad, many potential buyers think, can the product be any better?

Cheap video cameras and PC-based editing systems mean that it does not take much money to make a TV commercial, but cheap pencils have not turned every western schoolchild into a new Leonardo da Vinci and cheap cameras don't turn every adult into a creator of effective advertising. Good TV commercials are always going to be expensive; not always on the scale of the British Airways relaunch advertising 1991–93 with its cast of thousands, but always far more than the cost of pointing a home video camera at the product and overlaying some computer graphics.

TV advertising should be used:

▲ if a significant fraction of the likely viewers are also possible customers

▲ if the product is one where a TV advertisement is likely to stimulate trial

▲ when the budget is sufficient to pay for professional creation and production.

A regular audience response measurement system should be put in place, either in the form of audience surveys, telephone numbers and/or addresses in the advertisements to stimulate inquiries, or an accurate sales reporting system (measuring daily sales). Whatever the method, advertisements that do not perform should be withdrawn, no matter how much that they may have cost to produce. If TV advertising is critical to the success of a new product, the budget should be large enough to allow more than one advertisement to be prepared if needed.

Radio is much cheaper than TV as an advertising medium, both in the cost of production and the cost of broadcasting. Radio also offers a more focused audience than broadcast TV, as each station tends to target a particular audience profile. The lower cost may be important in the early life of a product or concept with limited financial backing, but when money is short measurement is even more important. Daily sales tracking or hourly counts of telephone calls received will give some indication of the effectiveness of the advertising.

Video, multi-media and the Internet

When prospective users of a product are likely to require a substantial amount of information before deciding to buy it, a video showing the product's key features and applications lies between printed brochures and a visit to a satisfied user, both in the expense and the efficiency of information transfer. Video recordings are passive; an interactive CD-ROM or World Wide Web site allows potential users to absorb information at their own pace and focus on points of particular interest.

Before preparing videos or interactive promotional material, some questions must be asked:

▲ Do the target buyers have video cassette players, multi-media PCs, or Internet connections? And if they have Internet connections, are they high-bandwidth ones, sufficient to convey a useful amount of information between breakfast and bed time?

▲ Can the launch budget cover the preparation of material of an adequate quality?

Professional video production costs range from $1000 per minute and up and multimedia development costs are similar. The Web is too new, at the time of writing, for site development costs to be estimated, but they are unlikely to be much less, on an information content basis, than professional video and multimedia. The Web can, of course, be used simply as a publishing method, by loading brochures and other print material onto a Web site and stitching it all together with 'hot' words and buttons.

As at 1996, we recommend that the Web be considered as an auxiliary promotional medium, but, except in very special circumstances, it should not be the only or even the main one.

Launch events

Because the launch of a product is a singular event, marking the end of preparation and the start of active selling, production and delivery it is a natural time for celebration. One task has been completed, new tasks lie ahead, and the present moment is therefore unique and special. Planned launch events are built on the unique nature of the occasion, and they can be used to bring all the stakeholders in a new enterprise together to celebrate and reaffirm their association. For the team that has brought the new product to market the event is a kind of triumphal funeral: the project has been a success, and so now the team, as a team, must die, its members going off to different tasks and new associations. If this event is not properly celebrated the psychic mourning will continue: members of the team will go into their new tasks with part of their mind firmly fixed on the past; they may even resent, and in extreme cases sabotage, the new team that has taken over the active marketing and selling of 'their' product. Many members of such teams leave for new employment, taking their experience, and their secrets, with them.

On the most dispassionate economic criteria, an enterprise that loses its most committed staff is worse off than it could have been had it kept them: a launch celebration is therefore an investment in the enterprise's future, a necessary step in retaining and motivating the key staff who will lead the development of the next product. From the moment a product is launched it starts to become obsolete, and any firm that does not want to be a nine-day wonder should start planning its replacement on, or even before the day the original product first goes to market.

An established firm's customers are also stakeholders in its new products: the margins that they paid on their purchases of the established product line provided the cash which financed the development of its replacement. They, too deserve to be part of the launch celebration. Again, the economic motive supports the moral and emotional arguments: as established customers, they will need less convincing (and slimmer discounts) to become customers of the new product line; and they can be, even before they have bought the new product, recommenders of it.

The staff event(s)

A large company may decide to have two events: one for the staff most directly involved in the development of the new product, and a more general one for the rest of the staff. A new small enterprise might decide that the entire staff have been involved in the new product and that only one event is needed.

The event for the deeply involved staff should be a special one, sufficiently formal, and blessed with the presence of a sufficiently senior executive, to make it clear that the firm as a whole is providing the event, that it understands the significance of the effort that the new product team has made, and that it appreciates it. It should be sufficiently informal to allow the team members to relieve their feelings in whatever (reasonably legal) way suits them best. One successful format involves senior executives at the start, making appropriate speeches and then circulating for half an hour or so while refreshments are served, before discreetly withdrawing. In countries where alcohol is served at such occasions, staff should not be expected to drive their cars home and neither should they, from thirty minutes after the speeches end until they voluntarily leave, be expected to be perfectly sober or perfectly polite.

In a large company, where most of the staff will not have been sufficiently involved with the new product to get an invitation to the team celebration, there should still be a formal event at which the new product and its significance is explained and, culture permitting, some limited refreshment taken. On average, each member of staff will have 110 friends and acquaintances, and, when all these chatter groups are aggregated, they are bound to contain a number of potential buyers and recommenders for the new product. When it is a consumer product, a firm's staff can, by their attitude, make the difference between an ordinary first few months in the market and a spectacular one. If it is a supermarket product, they will, just by buying it themselves, help it to gain the stock movement rate that keeps a product displayed and listed.

The sales briefing

Good sales persons are not introspective or given to long periods of deep contemplation. They are, however, fiercely competitive and eagerly grasp new challenges. Really good sales people can see the difference between difficult and impossible objectives, and they will not put any effort into a cause that they perceive as hopeless. Sales persons are, inevitably, interested in money, as much for the status that earning a lot of it confers as for the things that they can buy with it. A good sales briefing event must take all these factors into account.

The event should not be seen as a way to convey general product information to the sales staff; they will either read the appropriate manuals and other documents themselves at their leisure, or never bother to learn. The only information about the product that they will be prepared to absorb will be the names of a small number of key features which they can turn into sales messages; the *unique selling propositions*. They will then expect to be told about the bonus scheme, including the high performance bonus system, and the rules for offering incentives, for churning established customers, and any other restrictions on their activities.

A sales event should conclude with the announcement of a list of competitions and prizes, such as:

▲ first sale to a 'new name'

▲ largest sale to a 'new name' in the launch year

▲ first sale on standard commercial terms without special incentives of any kind

▲ first sales person to book $1 million

▲ best sales performance (over a qualifying level) by area, state, country, region, world and so on, by month, quarter, year …

No refreshments are necessary at a sales launch: the sales staff should be expected to rush straight to their cars and go off in search of customers. They have their celebration when the prizes are handed out.

Key customers and hot prospects

Key customers and hot prospects can be invited to a cocktail party or even a dinner, in any case a fairly formal event, at which they can be thanked for their past contribution to the firms success and given a confidential briefing on the new product (not a 'hard sell'). They can be given a satchel as they leave containing the main brochures and any available self-sell material, such as videos and CD-ROMs, but the customers are not there to be sold to (they have been already) but to put peer pressure on the hot prospects to raise their status to that of 'customer' as soon as possible.

Commercial terms

Selling a new product means delivering some goods or a service to some person or firm in return for a valuable consideration. This may be cash on delivery; it can, for some lucky people, be cash, or at least a deposit, in advance. Other suppliers find that they must offer thirty or more days credit, or sale or return, or even, as mentioned in Chapter 10, counter trade, where payment is partly or wholly in goods. In some markets customers expect to pay the marked price, while in others the marked price is simply seen as the seller's opening gambit, awaiting a counter-offer.

Consumer goods and services are, as described in Chapter 11, sold subject to statutory warranties and guarantees in Australia and many other countries, but goods and services sold commercially will be subject to the common law in the absence of a written contract (and possibly, if the contract is challenged, in spite of one). Suppliers are well advised to have their legal advisers draw up their own contract rather than wait to be presented with one by the purchaser.

A new firm has to decide what forms of payment it will accept: cash and cheques are always desirable, but will it take credit cards? And, if so, which ones? Is it going to connect to an electronics fund transfer (EFT) or an electronic document interchange (EDI) system? Can it afford not to? What payment terms are its customers currently used to? Will they accept more stringent ones? Will more extended terms give a competitive advantage?

These issues all need to be sorted out before the first customer comes through the door. If a specific contract is going to be used, it must be drafted, proofread, and then printed. If the contract is immutable, the sales staff must be told this (they won't believe it, but if the point is made strongly enough they may not actually propose variations to customers), while if there is going to be some tolerance, an approval and checking process must be set up to ensure that any accepted contract variations do not expose the supplier to an unacceptable level of risk.

The price list needs to be established, and the prices entered onto the appropriate data bases: if there are features and options, each must be considered and either priced or its cost bundled into a parent product. A complete discount structure may need to be established, with an appropriate basis for discounts: this can be based upon the size of a single order, or the size of a single delivery, or the volume of sales in a period, either rolling or fixed. If the product includes a good or goods to be marketed in the United States, the discount schedule should be checked for compliance with the Robinson–Patman act covering price discrimination.

The launch manager is not necessarily responsible for preparing the commercial terms and the price list entries, but he or she is responsible for ensuring that this work is complete and the results distributed correctly before the day of the launch.

Sales and distribution

An appropriate number of sales staff and sales managers must be in place on the day of the launch. If the firm is new these will have been recruited especially, while if it is an established one there must either be sales staff specifically assigned to the new product or an appropriate arrangement made for including the new product in the existing sales persons' portfolios. If the product is to be sold through dealers or distributors, some dealers or distributors will have to be appointed before the day of the official product launch; further ones will be enlisted as sales grow.

Sales staff require sales managers; a relatively tight management structure is often needed in order to maintain sales performance and maintain discipline in the matter of discounts and contractual terms. If the right calibre of sales management has been recruited, the lowest level managers will not need to be managed quite as tightly as the front line sales staff, but this level of management may still be necessary. Sales staff are very outward-focused: the front line sales staff will be more interested in their particular customers and prospects than in the company as a whole, the low-level sales managers will focus on their sales people, and at some point a strong sales manager is needed to keep the interests of the sales staff and the company at least roughly aligned.

Sales staff, dealers and distributors all need some sort of reward or incentive: selling a new product, even a very attractive one, is hard and lonely work in the first few months or even the first two years; it is only once sales have started to accelerate, in the second or third year on the market for many products, that prospects are actually welcoming. Sales staff for a new firm will just have to put up with the problems, but sales people and dealers with a substantial portfolio including new and established products will tend to put less emphasis on the new products than the firm's broader interests demand.

Sales bonus and dealer incentive schemes need to be designed very carefully if they are to maximise the firm's sales rather than its sales persons' incomes. Badly designed bonus schemes can encourage 'bottom drawering'[4] or its opposite, raising phantom orders at the end of one period and putting through a cancellation at the start of the next one. Bonuses and incentives can easily become seen as a right rather than a reward, and good scheme design and strong sales management will be required to stop this happening. Writing a million dollars of orders in a year for a new product can take more sales creativity and effort than writing five million dollars for the same product in its third or fourth year on the market, when it is well established and customers have the example of their peers as well as the arguments of the sales staff persuading them.

If the product is to be sold to consumers at retail, supplies must be in the retailers' warehouses before the launch day and merchandisers must be told about the impending launch and told how it is to be displayed and promoted. Production and delivery arrangements must be in place for fast restocking: retailers loathe empty shelves, and if a new product 'walks out of the store' the supplier must be at the back shovelling more in. Once the shelves are bare adjacent products will move in to fill the gap, and the new product will have to fight for its display space all over again.

Starting again

The entrepreneurial journey started with a concept, an idea for change. While the idea was progressively refined a team was built to turn it into reality. For a period of months, or years, or even decades the entrepreneurial team enjoyed the fierce excitement of creation. Quite suddenly, it is all over: the product is on the market, and its success or failure is now out of the entrepreneurial team's hands. Some members of the team may stay with the product or the enterprise as managers; others will look for new challenges.

The new challenges may come from taking the new product into new markets: readers who have followed the entrepreneurial process in real life may want to re-read Chapter 10 now. Others will want to work on new products, or new variants on their original product. Successful entrepreneurs change the world; not always very much, and sometimes not for the better, but their passage is noticed. Like every activity, entrepreneurship is always easier the second time around.

Go for it!

End notes
1 It is no easy matter to try to stylise 'what one should do' to launch a new product because so many ingredients of a successful launch will, of necessity, be product and case specific. The key idea is of

course to maximise the likelihood of effective performance. A relevant study is Brush and Vanderwerf (1992). A study of the rationale for starting a business is Birley and Westhead (1994).

2 These examples are synthetic, based upon the authors' experience and do not represent any single real firm or person. They are included to stimulate discussion of business practice and are not, themselves, representative of either good or bad practice.

3 Since most of the launch budget concerns marketing communications — the promotional 'P' of the marketing mix — the principles presented in Chapter 9 above apply.

4 Bottom drawering — holding signed orders past the end of one period because they will earn a greater bonus at the start of the next period.

Bibliography

Our sources

In this book we have attempted to set out a minimum of theory, very little of that in the form of a standard scientific argument, and we have tried to provide an essentially practical view of the problems and opportunities presented to an entrepreneur. The book is our original work, but we do not claim to be the originators of all the ideas in it. We have, through the text, used notes and references to identify those authors whose work most influenced our thinking. Undoubtedly we have failed to acknowledge all the writers who deserved it: to those we have slighted in this way we sincerely and humbly apologise.

There are two main strands in the references that we have used in this book, and in particular the works that we discuss in this bibliography. There are works originating in the study of entrepreneurship and management, essentially pragmatic discussions of relevant aspects of the real world: in general terms, such works introduce very little pure theory and may be based more on experience than on formal field research or the rigorous development of the consequence of stated postulates. Other works come from people who use much more rigorous approaches to analysis and to the collection and reduction of data from field research: these people are often economists by training who have chosen to step beyond the boundaries of the pure *a priori* model of economics.

Occasionally (not nearly often enough) there are cross references: a management or entrepreneurship writer will quote an economist or (even more rarely) an economist will quote a management writer. Those economists who do deign to notice writers from outside their discipline often do so with a display of condescension straight from Jane Austen's Lady Catherine de Burgh. Non-economists, such as Kirchhoff (1991), reviewing the work of economists tend to remark on the poverty of their models and show very little sympathy for the rigour needed before a true scientist can make an unequivocal statement.

Economics

Some of our readers may wish to move beyond the practical scenario set out in this book, and conduct research into those individual and environmental factors and techniques that promote or retard successful entrepreneurship. Others may wish to participate in debates about public policy insofar as they affect entrepreneurship and innovation; some will, of course, do both. The language of the public policy debate is that of economics, the Queen, or Wicked Witch (depending on one's perspective), of the social sciences, and participants need to be familiar with the main concepts and terms, at least.

Economics covers a very broad field, and among economists there are many differences of perspective and opinion. Many economists seek to understand, explain, and make recommendations about the real world. There are others who argue *a priori*, or from 'self-evident' logical propositions and who, when the real world fails to respond in the way that their theories predict, blame reality (Jones 1992). It is not, in general terms, possible to have an argument with one of these *a priori* economists, because, since their concepts have no contact with reality they are protected from the possibility of refutation by counter-examples.

The '*a priorists*'

It is not possible to even discuss entrepreneurship with an *a priori* economist, because recognisable entrepreneurs do not exist in their models (Baumol 1968). To the extent that *a priori* economists discuss entrepreneurship at all, they do so in the context of principal-agent theory. This theory assumes that businesses are founded when a group of capitalists come together and engage an entrepreneur to carry out a precise plan that they have devised. The major object of concern to principal-agent theorists is the possibility that the entrepreneur might deviate from the instructions that he or she is given, reducing the returns to the capitalists. 'Corporate governance' is the study of how to make the managers of a firm devote themselves exclusively to the firm's shareholders' interests, whatever the law may say. It has become a major field of concern to economists (Fox 1995; Kay & Silberston 1995).

A priori economics is taught as the only form of 'real' economics in the first two years of undergraduate study in most Australian universities, and a firm belief in the infallibility of the *a priori* method is needed to gain appointment to a position of influence in the Australian Public Service (Pusey 1991). Even so, there are some embarrassing gaps in the explanatory power of the orthodox *a priori* theory. These are not simply problems which further research is expected to resolve, but come from the very nature of the *a priori* method. By assuming that there is perfect but unobservable reality underlying temporal phenomena, the *a priori* economists cut themselves off from even considering the possibility of beneficial innovation: if underlying reality is perfect, then it cannot change (Schumpeter 1942; Grossman & Helpman 1992; Hunt 1995).

An entrepreneur, in the eyes of the orthodox economist, is attempting an act of sacrilege,[1] denying the perfection of the world as it is. If the entrepreneur brings a new product to market, he or she becomes a monopolist, disrupting perfect competition. Paul Ormerod's *The Death of Economics* (1994) presents a critique of the orthodox economic model. Brian Toohey's *Tumbling Dice* (1994) provides a critique of the model and its application from an Australian perspective. Both Toohey's and Ormerod's books are essential reading for any entrepreneur or manager who may come into contact with policy making bureaucrats in Australia's state or federal governments, or who are tempted to believe the editorials in the *Economist*, the *Wall Street Journal* or the *Australian Financial Review*. Readers with a British perspective should read Will Hutton's *The State We're In* (1995) for an account of the triumph of financial capitalism over entrepreneurial capitalism in England and a description of the consequences.

Anyone who feels that they need to understand the basic appeal of *a priori* economics should read one of the many introductory texts where the list of authors starts with Paul Samuelson, such as Samuelson and others (1992). These books are beautifully written, illustrated and presented, and while no one with any business experience is likely to be fooled, the simple messages that these books present have a strong appeal to the young and inexperienced. Heilbroner and Thurow in their *Economics Explained* (1982) present a readable and much less ideological account of economic theory, and one we recommend to people who want to understand something about it, but their book is not intended to engender the ideological fervour to be seen in Canberra and it leaves the general reader thinking that economists are reasonable people. This is an impression that, unfortunately, is not universally supported by experience.

The Austrian school

A group of economists known originally as the 'Austrian' school, but now generally identified with the University of Chicago, suggest that the world is not really very close to the ideal equilibrium state portrayed by Samuelson, and such social and economic progress as occurs is due to the economy's slow approach towards it.

A prominent member of this school, Israel M. Kirzner, introduced the concept of 'entrepreneurial discovery' (1982). If, in Kirzner's view, the world is not in a perfect equilibrium state this must reflect some defect in public knowledge, as, for example, when the price of a product in some market did not accurately reflect its average price in all markets adjusted for transport costs. An entrepreneur would be able to buy in the market where the price was lower than it should have been, and sell, with a profit on top of all costs, in the market where it had been higher. These profits, suggested Kirzner, would attract the attention of other entrepreneurs whose competition would eventually eliminate the discrepancy. The profit earned by the initial entrepreneur, Kirzner argued, would be justified by the increased efficiency of the economy with the price discrepancies removed.

Kirzner's arguments have subsequently been used to justify every form of speculation and market manipulation, and provide a theoretical fig leaf for the use of the term 'entrepreneur' to describe the financial manipulators of the 1980s. On this logic the standover gangs and extortionists who dominated Russia in the years following the collapse of communism have been described as 'entrepreneurs' because of their assumed role in rectifying various information defects associated with the communist system.

Evolutionary economics

Evolutionary economists, if they seek an analogy with the physical sciences, look to biology and in particular Darwin's theory of natural selection. They discard the concept of equilibrium and look on the economy as a continually developing system, where every development in one part of the economy creates the opportunity for further developments elsewhere. They consider the economy to be 'path-dependent', meaning that the ultimate state of a market, an industry or an economy is affected by its history. The Australian economist John Nightingale (1993) provides an insight into one aspect of this variant of economics.

The existence of path dependence is a challenge to the extreme *laissez faire* school of economists and politicians, because if market forces can produce many different outcomes as a result of tiny, chance events they can't all be the best possible. As soon as it is recognised that market forces don't always produce an ideal outcome, it becomes possible that social intervention in an economy might, under some circumstances, improve it. This is enough to make true ideologues splutter in their soup.

Evolutionary economists draw support from the work of the complex system theorists; Waldrop's book *Complexity* (1992) and the book *Frontiers of Complexity: The search for order in a chaotic world* by Peter Coveney and Roger Highfield (1995) provide accessible accounts of the development of complex system theory. The book *Bionomics* by Michael Rothschild (1992) provides a very readable if somewhat idiosyncratic outline of evolutionary economics and provides some excellent historical material on innovation.

Innovation

Joseph Schumpeter was an economist whose work provides the bridge between economics and entrepreneurship. Karl Marx, the founder of communism, is widely acknowledged as one of the first economists to interpret capitalism as a dynamic rather than as an equilibrium system, but Marx held the view that capitalism must eventually grind to a halt as the rate of profit on investments fell. Schumpeter inherited from Marx the view that capitalism is an intrinsically dynamic system, but went beyond Marx with his insight that innovation could 'reset the clock'; that although the falling rate of profit (more often referred to as 'decreasing returns' by modern economists who don't wish to acknowledge any debt to Marx) would eventually stop economic growth in any industry, innovations would restart the process.

Schumpeter wrote (1933):

> Obviously the face of the earth would look very different if people, besides having their economic life changed by natural events and changing it themselves by extra-economic action, had done nothing else except multiply and save. If it looks as it does, this is just as obviously due to the unremitting efforts of people to

improve according to their lights upon their productive and com-
mercial methods, i.e., to the changes in technique of production,
the conquest of new markets, the insertion of new commodities,
and so on. This historic and irreversible change in the way of
doing things we call 'innovation' and we define: innovations are
changes in production functions which cannot be decomposed
into infinitesimal steps. Add as many mail-coaches as you like,
you will never get a railroad by so doing.

Serious students of entrepreneurship, sooner or later, get around to serious study of the works of Joseph Schumpeter because his theories on the role of innovation and entrepreneurship as engines of economic growth are at the heart of the matter. He is best read in the original; references to him in the orthodox economic literature are often deeply misleading. His *Capitalism, Socialism and Democracy* (first published 1942) is a deliberately popular account of his work: his *Business Cycles: A Theoretical, Historical, and Statistical Analysis of the Capitalist Process* (first published in English in 1939) is his major academic work.

Grossman and Helpman (1992) take Schumpeter's basic insight and shown how the orthodox economic model can be extended to accommodate it. They confirm one of Schumpeter's suggestions: one of the things that must be jettisoned from the orthodox model to accommodate long term growth is 'perfect' competition. Since an unconditional preference for 'perfect' competition lies at the heart of *a priori* economics, the clash between innovators and entrepreneurs on the one hand and the economically orthodox on the other is not resolvable without surrender by one side or the other. Any economist who is not familiar with Grossman and Helpman's *Innovation and Growth in the Global Economy* (1992) is not seriously interested in economic growth. The book is, however, somewhat difficult for anyone without a strong background in mathematics or mathematical economics.

Entrepreneurship

Ever since Newton's *Principia* set mathematical models at the pinnacle of a scientific paradigm, scientists of all disciplines — not just the physical sciences — have striven to express their theories mathematically. In the social sciences, mathematical models are more often than not a little more than a Laplacian[2] fantasy. Nevertheless, mathematics is being used more and more extensively by social scientists — none more so than economists and business researchers. William Bygrave (1992) focuses on one area of social science, entrepreneurship, and examines the difficulties of trying to use mathematics to model entrepreneurship processes.

The entrepreneurship process involves a discontinuous change of state. It involves numerous antecedent variables. It is extremely sensitive to the initial value of these variables. To build an algorithm for a physical system with these characteristics would be daunting to the most gifted applied mathematician. Bygrave suggests that each instance of the entrepreneurship process is initiated by the volition of a unique human being, and for this reason mathematical modelling may be impossible, because there is an 'essential non-algorithmic aspect to conscious human action'. He argues that today's most prominent mathematical representation of entrepreneurship, population ecology, falls far short of Penrose's specification for a 'useful theory'.

Some observers believe that the answer to entrepreneurship theory may be found in chaos theory — a relatively new science that was popularised by Gleick (1987). Bygrave (1992) explores the chaotic zones of several algorithms that provide alluringly simple representations for the entrepreneurial process. One of them is the fundamental equation of population ecology theory. It shows how under some conditions that equation exhibits some wild, chaotic behaviour that gives an observer the feel of entrepreneurship. But it is no more than a mathematical metaphor because the accuracy of measurements that are needed to observe true scientific chaos in the entrepreneurial process are unattainable in practice.

Dan Jennings' *Multiple Perspectives of Entrepreneurship: Text, Readings and Cases* (1994) provides an excellent treatment of the many ways that entrepreneurship can be — and is — perceived and explained. This book goes a little deeper into theoretical issues than is usual with entrepreneurship and management texts, and includes a short but lucid discussion of the relationship between economics and entrepreneurship. We can confidently recommend Jennings' book as a complementary text to this one, with some excellent cases and expositions.

Economic development

Freeman (1994) provides a survey of work by economists on growth and technological change, including a twenty-two page bibliography. In this section we discuss a few of the major contributions to the theory of innovation-driven economic development.

Each act of entrepreneurship takes place at a particular time in a particular place. It is the proper role of economists to look beyond such unique events in order to draw a picture of regional, national and global development. Paul Romer (see, for example, Romer 1986, 1993, 1994) has made a major contribution to our understanding of how a succession of innovations can generate self-sustaining economic growth. Romer develops a two-dimensional characterisation of property: there is the public/private axis, and the rival/non rival axis. Personal property is private and rival in this view: the money in my pocket is clearly mine, and as long as it stays in my pocket you can't use it. Fish in international waters are public and rival: no one person or firm owns them, but once one boat fishes up a shoal, there is nothing left for anyone else. The urban road network is public and non-rival: the community as a whole owns it, but (subject to congestion) the fact that I might be using it doesn't stop you doing so too. Romer looks at private commercial knowledge as private and non-rival: society recognises ownership, but a design for an artefact, a piece of music or a software program, can in principle be used by many people at once. Intellectual property protection helps the originator of a new item of knowledge to get some return on it, but there are inevitable 'spillovers' as people who made no contribution to the development of an idea are able to get a commercial benefit from it.

Microsoft Word and WordPerfect are alternative word processing programs, and from time to time one or the other is released with a new feature. Whenever this has happened the other one is shortly released with an equivalent new feature, not a literal copy for legal and practical reasons, but one that preserves the balance of user-perceived value between the two products. The follower in each case is spared the (significant) effort of conceiving and market testing the new feature: this is the spillover.

Romer showed that, under plausible circumstances, these spillovers from the commercialisation of new knowledge can lead to positive feedback, overcoming the normal presumption of diminishing returns and producing sustained economic growth.

Paul Geroski (1994) suggested that the apparent negative consequences of such spillovers might be overstated. The naive might think that the authors of Microsoft Word might be discouraged by the thought that some of the benefit of their ideas might be captured by the authors of WordPerfect, and vice versa. Geroski suggests that imitation is far from costless: Microsoft Word and WordPerfect must both maintain strong development teams if they want to understand how the other one achieved any particularly advantageous effect and so, on balance, each will gain about as much from imitating the other's innovations as they lose by having their own innovations imitated. Geroski's insight strengthens Romer's view by removing a major potential objection.

Tisdell's paper *Economic Justification for Government Support of Research and Development: A review of modern microeconomic literature and its policy implications* (1994) presents a comprehensive survey of growth theories in language that is accessible to lay persons.

Self organisation

The emergence of order is, quite reasonably, used to infer the existence of a plan. When a vacant plot of land turns into a building we assume that this represented the result of many deliberate, planned and sequential acts, planned by an architect and/or builder. We normally associate random, unplanned actions with disorder and decay, not the construction of complex structures and systems. Adam Smith's idea of the 'invisible hand' represents one of the best known assertions that complex systems, such as a modern economy, can arise without the existence of a controlling planner.

Smith imagined the interaction of many small enterprises, each itself directed by an intelligent human being, but Jaques Monod (1971) took this idea further with his suggestion that order could emerge in biological systems without any intelligent direction or lucky coincidence. Kauffman, in his book *The Origins of Order* (1992) develops a complete account of the emergence of complex systems from simple ones, quantifying and expanding Monod's concept in a *tour de force*, although one which may be rather difficult for readers without a strong mathematical background to appreciate fully.

Kauffman shows how, in an emerging system, some states are inaccessible, no matter how desirable: 'you can't get there from here'. Brian Arthur (1994) develops the concept of lock-in and path dependence in an economic context. Arthur is one of those economists whom other economists regard as dangerously radical, while practical managers and marketers come upon his work and express surprise that anyone should put so much effort into proving the blindingly obvious (see, for example, Dickson 1995).

Paul Krugman's *The Self-Organizing Economy* (1996) summarises his work on path dependence in urban development in a book based on a series of public lectures, and therefore accessible to people with very little mathematics in their background. Krugman won an award in 1991 as the best young economist in the United States, and while he is a fierce critic of various other economists for propounding opinions that he considers insupportable, he is an aggressive defender of economics as a discipline. Krugman, in this book and other works, demonstrates that a rigorous training in mathematical economics does not inevitably lead to separation from the real world.

The enterprise

As we mentioned before, the orthodox economists' view of the enterprise is ludicrously astray: the principal-agent model that they use is not even a legal way of managing a limited liability firm, much less an optimum one. Having made the assumption of 'perfect knowledge' for analytical convenience, many *a priori* economists then treat it as a reasonable approximation to the real world. Firms, particularly large firms, appear in the standard economics text books as the result of a successful conspiracy against the common good. Even the IO (industrial organisation) economists, who specialise in the study of 'imperfect' markets, are unable to provide a convincing explanation of large multi-product firms (Beath & Katsoulacos 1991).

Roger Kerin, Vijay Mahajan and P. Rajan Varadarajan in their book *Contemporary Perspectives on Strategic Market Planning* (1990) provide an excellent practical account of large modern firms and of many of the methodologies used to manage them: we can recommend this book to both practising managers and students. William Fruhan's *Financial Strategy: Studies in the creation, transfer and destruction of shareholder value* (1979), in a short, well-written and easily appreciated book introduced the concept of value creation: the idea that a firm could systematically create shadow assets that enabled it to earn an unusually high return on its physical plant and equipment.

Gary Hamel and C. K. Prahalad (Prahalad & Hamel 1990; Hamel & Prahalad 1994) created the term 'core competence of the corporation' to describe a corporation's shadow assets. Both their 1990 article in the *Harvard Business Review* and their 1994 book, *Competing for the Future*, are well worth the effort of locating and reading. John Kay (1991, 1993a, 1993b) makes the attempt to create a modern 'theory of the firm' which incorporates Fruhan's added value and Hamel and Prahalad's core competence in a framework that economists trained in the orthodox tradition should be able to appreciate. Kay's book received a somewhat dismissive review in the *Journal of Marketing* (Hulland 1995); his book may be rather less useful to practitioners than it should be to people trained in economics who want to understand business practice as a prelude to talking about it or participating in it.

However analysed and defined, the strength of a firm comes from the people inside it and their interactions with each other and with the people with whom they deal in the course of business. The foundation text in this area is Robert Axelrod and William Hamilton in their paper (1983) and Axelrod's book *The Evolution of Cooperation* (1984). A very readable brief treatment of the same subject can be found in the chapter 'Nice guys finish first' in Richard Dawkins' *The Selfish Gene* (1989: pp. 202–223). Avinash Dixit and Barry Nalebuff in their book *Thinking Strategically: the competitive edge in business, politics and everyday life* (1991) provide a learned yet readable commentary on business strategy and related issues.

Planning

Chris Golis' *Enterprise and Venture Capital: a business builders' and investors' handbook* (1993) is essential reading for anyone concerned in any way with new venture formation in Australia and may be useful to entrepreneurs and planners working in countries with similar legal and financial systems. This book is a guide for people looking to build new businesses around bright new ideas and investors awake to the opportunities offered by new business building. It sets out in a straightforward and practical way how to put venture capital to work. It goes on to explain the sources of venture capital available — from seed finance for new initiatives to the leveraged buyout of mature companies. It explains for the business builder the principles and steps involved in obtaining appropriate financing, including the preparation of a business plan, the choice of a venture capitalist and advice on negotiations with investors. The book concludes with advice to investors on how to invest venture capital wisely and how to manage a venture capital portfolio.

Day's *Market Driven Strategy: processes for creating value* (1990) provides a good overview of market-oriented planning with a distinct bias towards the needs of major corporations. Legge's *The Competitive Edge* (1992) is not entirely supplanted by the current book: it has been generously praised by both students and practitioners, and may prove useful to someone planning a new enterprise or a new product launch.

The theory behind new venture financial planning has been entirely revolutionised by Dixit and Pindyck in their *Investment under Uncertainty* (1994); this book is likely to be very heavy going for anyone without a background in mathematics or mathematical economics, but our treatment of the subject in Chapter 8 is very superficial. Until someone comes up with a popular presentation of Dixit and Pindyck's work, anyone involved in serious planning at a corporate level should grit their teeth and work through the book. Any economist who talks about investment without being thoroughly familiar with Dixit and Pindyck's work is either being professionally negligent or is an opportunist seeking an appointment to the Australian Treasury or some other citadel of ideological orthodoxy.

References

A.G. Nielsen & Co (1995), 'China's Emerging Middle Class', *Nielsen SRG News*, 79, September.

Abrams, Rhonda M. (1991), *The Successful Business Plan: Secrets & Strategies*, Oregon: The Oasis Press.

Adams, J.L. (1986), *Conceptual Blockbusting: A guide to better ideas*, Reading, Ma: Addison-Wesley Publishing Co.

Akaah, I.P. and Riordan, E.A. (1988), 'Applicability of Marketing Knowhow in the Third World', *International Marketing Review*, Spring, pp. 41–55.

Aldridge, D.N. (1987), 'Multi-country Research', in U. Bradley (ed.), *Applied Marketing and Social Research*, Chichester: Wiley, pp. 359–77.

Arthur Anderson (1996), *ADCAL 1995 Survey of Development Capital*, Sydney: The Australian Development Capital Association.

Arthur, W. Brian (1994), *Increasing Returns and Path Dependence in the Economy*, Ann Arbor: University of Michigan Press.

Asian Development Bank (1994), *Asian Development Outlook*, Economic Planning Agency, Japan.

Assael, Henry (1985), *Marketing Management: Strategy and Action*, Boston Ma: Kent Publishing, pp. 279–80.

Australian Academy of Technological Sciences (undated), *Australian Academy of Technological Sciences, Developing High Technology Enterprises for Australia* (popularly known as The 'Espie' Report), Melbourne.

Australian, the (1995), 'Malaysian consumers take to new shops', 19 May.

Axelrod, Robert (1984), *The Evolution of Cooperation*, New York: Basic Books.

Axelrod, Robert and Hamilton William D. (1983), 'The Evolution Of Cooperation', *Science*, 211, 1390–6.

Aydin, N. and Terpstra, V. (1981), 'Marketing Know-how Transfers by Multinationals: A Case Study in Turkey', *Journal of International Business Studies*, Winter, pp. 35–48.

Banfe, Charles (1991), *Entrepreneur: From Zero To Hero: How to be a blockbuster entrepreneur*, New York: Van Nostrand Reinhold.

Bangs, David H. Jr. (1989), *The Start Up Guide*, Upstart Publishing Company Inc.

Barker, Joel Arthur (1992), *Paradigms: The business of discovering the future*, New York: Harper Business.

Barnard, C.I. (1947), *The Functions of the Executive*, Boston MA: Harvard University Press.

Bass, Frank M. (1969) 'A New Product Growth Model for Consumer Durables', *Management Science*, 15(5), pp. 215–27.

Bass, Frank M. and Krishnan, Trichy V. (1992), 'A generalisation of the Bass Model: Decision variable considerations', Draft paper.

Baumol, William J. (1968), 'Entrepreneurship in Economic Theory', *American Economic Review*, Papers and Proceedings, 58.

Beamish, P.W., Craig, R. and McLellan, K. (1993), 'The Performance Characteristics of Canadian Versus UK Exporters in Small and Medium Sized Firms', *Management International Review*, 33(2), pp. 121–37.

Beath, John and Katsoulacos, Yannis (1991), *The Economic Theory of Product Differentiation*, Cambridge: Cambridge University Press.

Bell, C. Gordon and McNamara, John E. (1991), *High-Tech Ventures: The guide for entrepreneurial success*, Reading, MA: Addison-Wesley.

Bell, Daniel (1981), 'Models and Reality in Economic Discourse' in Daniel Bell and Irving Kristol (eds), *The Crisis in Economic Theory*, New York: Basic Books.

Berle, Gustave (1989), *The Do-It-Yourself Business Book*, New York: John Wiley & Sons.

Berry, L.L., Parasuramen, A. and Zeithami, V.A. (1990), *Delivering Quality Service*, New York: The Free Press.

Birley, Sue and Westhead, Paul (1994), 'A Taxonomy of Business Start-Up Reasons and Their Impact on Firm Growth and Size', *Journal of Business Venturing*, January, pp. 7–32.

BIS Shrapnel (1993), *International Competitiveness of Australian Service Industries*, Sydney: BIS Shrapnel.

Bivell, V. (ed.) (various), *Australian Venture Capital Journal*, Sydney: Pollitecon Publications.

Blechman, Bruce and Levinson, Conrad (1991), *Guerilla Financing: Alternative techniques to finance any small business*, Boston MA: Houghton Miflin.

Booz, Allen & Hamilton (1993), *Globalization: Implications for Australian Businesses*, (conference report), CEDA.

Bowman, Cliff (1990), *The Essence of Strategic Management*, New York: Prentice Hall.

Brandt, Steven C. (1982), *Entrepreneuring — The Ten Commandments for building a growth company*, New York: Nal Penguin Inc.

Braudel, Fernand (1981), *Civilisation and Capitalism 15th–18th Century* (3 vols) (tr. Miriam Kochan, rev. Sién Reynolds), London: Collins/Fontana, originally published Paris: Library Armand Colin, 1979.

Brogden, Stanley (1986), 'The Ansett Story', *Panorama* (February)

Bruck, Connie (1989), *The Predator's Ball: the junk-bond raiders and the man who staked them*, Melbourne: Information Australia Group.

Brush, C.G. and Vanderwerf, P.A. (1992), 'A Comparison of Methods and Sources for Obtaining Estimates of New Venture Performance', *Journal of Business Venturing*, March, pp. 157–70.

Burroughs, Bryan and Helyar, John (1990), *Barbarians at the Gate — the fall of RJR Nabisco*, London: Arrow Books.

Butler, B. (1987), *The Winners: An Analysis of the 1987 Australian Export Award Applications*, Canberra: Australian Trade Commission.

Bygrave, W.D. and Timmons, J.A. (1992), *Venture Capital at the Crossroads*, Boston MA: Harvard University Press.

Bygrave, William D. (1992), 'Theory building in the entrepreneurship paradigm', *Journal of Business Venturing*, 8, pp. 255–80.

Bygrave, William D. and Hofer, Charles W. (1991) 'Theorizing About Entrepreneurship', *Entrepreneurship Theory and Practice*, 16(2), Winter, pp. 13–22.

Carew, E. (1996), *Fast Money: the money market in Australia*, 5th edn, Sydney: Allen & Unwin.

Carlzon, J. (1989), *Moments of Truth*, New York: Harper & Row.

Carman, J.M. (1973), 'On the Universality of Marketing', *Journal of Contemporary Business*, Autumn, pp. 1–15.

Cateora, P.R. (1993), *International Marketing*, Homewood, II: Irwin.

CEDA (Committee for Economic Development of Australia) (1993) *Strategies for Venturing in Asia*, Melbourne: CEDA Strategic Issues Forum Publication.

Chalmers, A.F. (1984), *What Is This Thing Called Science?*, St Lucia Qld: University of Queensland Press.

Cohen, William A. (1990), *The Entrepreneur & Small Business Problem Solver: An encyclopaedic reference and guide*, 2nd edn, New York: John Wiley & Sons.

Cornford, F.M. (trans) (1966), *The Republic of Plato*, Oxford: Clarendon Press, (first published 1941)

Coveney, Peter V. and Highfield, Roger (1995), *Frontiers of Complexity: The search for order in a chaotic world*, New York: Fawcett Columbine.

Crego, Edwin T. Jr, Deaton, Brian and Schiffrin, Peter D. (1986), *How to Write a Business Plan*, Melbourne: Centre for Professional Development.

Dawkins, Richard (1989), *The Selfish Gene*, new edn, Oxford: Oxford University Press.

Day, George S. (1990), *Market Driven Strategy: processes for creating value*, New York: The Free Press.

Day, John (1991), *Small Business in Tough Times*, Melbourne: Lothian Publishing.

Department of Foreign Affairs and Trade (1992), *Australia's Business Challenge — South East Asia in the 1990s*, Canberra: East Asia Analytical Unit.

Dholakia, N. (1981), 'The Future of Marketing in the Third World', in D.F. Mulvihill (ed.) *Marketing and the Future*, Chicago: American Marketing Association Proceeding Series, pp. 63–72.

Dickson, Peter (1995), 'Review of Increasing Returns and Path Dependence in the Economy', *Journal of Marketing*, 59(3), July, pp. 97–9.

Dixit, Avinash (1992), 'Investment and Hysteresis', *Journal of Economic Perspectives*, 6(1), Winter, pp. 107–32.

Dixit, Avinash and Pindyck, Robert S. (1994), *Investment under Uncertainty*, Princeton NJ: Princeton University Press.

Dixit, Avinash K. and Nalebuff, Barry J. (1991), *Thinking Strategically: the competitive edge in business, politics and everyday life*, New York: W.W. Norton & Co.

Dobbs-Higginson, M.S. (1993), *Asia Pacific: A View on its Role in the New World Order*, Hong Kong: Longman Group Far East, p. xvii.

Dockner, Englebert and Jorgenson, Steffen (1988), 'Optimal Advertising Policies for Diffusion Models of New Product Innovation in Monopolistic Situations', *Management Science*, 34(1), January, pp. 119–30.

Dodson, Joe A. and Muller, Eitan (1978), 'Models of New Product Diffusion Through Advertising and Word-of-Mouth', *Management Science*, 24(15), November, pp. 1568–78.

Dowling, G.R. and Midgley D.F. (1988), 'Identifying the coarse and fine structures of market segments', *Decision Sciences*, 19(4), pp. 830–47.

Drucker, P.F. (1958), 'Marketing and Economic Development', *Journal of Marketing*, 22, January, pp. 252–9.

Eckert, Lee A., Ryan, J.D. and Ray, Robert J. (1985), *An Entrepreneur's Plan*, New York: Harcourt Brace Jovanovich.

Flood, Robert L. (1993), *Beyond TQM*, Chichester: John Wiley & Sons.

Foster, Richard N. (1987), *Innovation: The Attacker's Advantage*, London: Pan Books.

Fox, Mark (1995), 'Annotated Bibliography on Corporate Governance', http://www.wp.com/CORPGOV/cgbibliography.html

Foxall, Gordon R. (1988), 'Marketing New Technology: Markets, Hierarchies, and User-initiated Innovation', *Managerial and Decision Economics*, 9, pp. 237–50.

Freeman, Chris (1994), 'The economics of technical change (Critical survey)', *Cambridge Journal of Economics*, 18, pp. 463–514.

Freund, Y.P. (1988), 'Critical Success Factor', *Planning Review*, July–August, pp. 20–3.

Fruhan, William E. Jr (1979), *Financial Strategy: Studies in the creation, transfer and destruction of shareholder value*, Homewood II: Richard D. Irwin Inc.

Fry, Fred L. (1993), *Entrepreneurship: A Planning Approach*, Minneapolis: West Publishing.

Garnaut, R. (1990), *Australia and the Northeast Asian Ascendancy*, Canberra: AGPS.

Gartner, William B, Bird, Barbara and Starr, Jennifer (1992), 'Acting As If: Differentiating Entrepreneurial from Organisational Behavior', *Entrepreneurship Theory And Practice*, 16(3), pp. 13–32.

Gartner, William B. (1985), 'A Conceptual Framework for Describing the Phenomenon of New Venture Creation', *Academy of Management Review*, 10(4), pp. 696–706.

Gartner, William B. (1993), 'Words Lead to Deeds: Towards an Organisational Emergence Vocabulary', *Entrepreneurship Theory and Practice*, 8(3), pp. 231–240.

Gaylen, N.C. and Hanks, S (1993), 'Measuring the Performances of Emerging Businesses: a Validation Study', *Journal of Business Venturing*, September, pp. 391–408.

Geroski, Paul A. (1994), 'Do Spillovers Undermine the Incentive to Innovate?', Conference Presentation, London: London Business School.

Gill, Alec (1994), 'All at Sea? The Survival of Superstition', *History Today*, 44(12) December.

Ginn, Martin E. (1995), *The Creativity Challenge: Management of Innovation and Technology*, Greenwich CT: JAI Press.

Gleeson, Russ (1987), *The X Factor: Business winners reveal their success secrets*, Melbourne: Information Australia.

Gleick, James (1987), *Chaos: making a new science*, London: Heinemann.

Golis, G.C. (1993), *Enterprise and Venture Capital: a business builders' and investors' handbook*, 2nd edn, Sydney: Allen & Unwin.

Goodyear, M. (1982), 'Qualitative Research in Developing Countries', *Journal of the Market Research Society*, 24, pp. 86–96.

Greenhalgh, Christine A., Taylor, Paul and Wilson, Rob (1994), 'Innovation and Export Volume and Prices — A disaggregated study', *Oxford Economic Report*, 46(1994) pp. 102–34.

Grossman, Gene M. and Helpman, Elhanan (1992), *Innovation and Growth in the Global Economy*, Boston MA: MIT Press.

Haas, R.W. and Wotruba, T.R. (1983), *Marketing Management: concepts, practice and cases*, Plano TX: Business Publications Inc.

Hafsi, T. and Thomas, H. (1985), 'Planning under certain conditions: the case of Air France', Working Paper, Chicago: Graduate School of Business, University of Illinois.

Hamel, Gary and Prahalad, C.K. (1994), *Competing for the Future*, Boston MA: Harvard Business School Press.

Heilbroner, R. (1986), *The Worldly Philosophers: The lives times and ideas of the great economic thinkers*, New York: Simon & Schuster.

Heilbroner, Robert L. and Thurow, Lester C. (1982), *Economics Explained*, Englewood Cliffs NJ: Prentice-Hall.

Herzberg, F., Mausner, B. and Snyderman, B.B. (1959), *Motivation To Work*, London: Chapman & Hall.

Hicks, J.R. and Wheller, D. (eds) (1990), *Money & Capital Markets in Australia*, Sydney: Harcourt Brace Jovanovich.

Hindle, Kevin (1992), *How To Use Organisational Behaviour*, Melbourne: Learnfast Press.

Hindle, Kevin (1996), 'An Enhanced Paradigm of Entrepreneurial Business Planning: development, case applications and general implications', PhD dissertation, Melbourne: Swinburne University of Technology.

Hobbes, Thomas (1967) *Leviathan, reprinted from the edition of 1651*, Oxford: Clarendon Press (first reprinted in 1909).

Hodges, Andrew (1983), *The Enigma of Intelligence*, London: Unwin Paperbacks.

Hooley, G.J. and Newcomb, J.R. (1988), 'Ailing British Exports: Symptoms, Causes and Cures', in Thomas, M.J. and Waite, N.E. (eds) *The Marketing Digest*, London: Heinemann.

Hseih, Tsun-yan and Barton, Dominic (1995), 'Young Lions, High Priests and Old Warriors', *McKinsey Quarterly*, (2), pp. 62–74.

Hulland, John S. (1995), 'Review of Foundations of Corporate Success: How business strategies add value', *Journal of Marketing*, 58(1), January, pp. 109–10.

Hunt, Shelby D. and Morgan, Robert M. (1995), 'The Comparative Advantage Theory of Competition', *Journal of Marketing*, 59, April, pp. 1–15.

Hutton, Will (1995), *The State We're In*, London: Jonathon Cape.

Ishihara, Shintaro (1991), *The Japan that can say no*, New York: Simon & Schuster.

Jacobs, Jane (1993) *Systems of Survival: a dialogue on the moral foundations of commerce and politics*, London: Hodder & Stoughton.

James, J. (1983), *Consumer Choice in the Third World*, London: Macmillan.

Jennings, Daniel F. (1994), *Multiple Perspectives of Entrepreneurship: Text, Readings and Cases*, Cincinnati: South-Western Publishing Co.

Jennings, Daniel F. and Lumkin, J.L. (1989), 'Functionally Modelling Corporate Entrepreneurship: An Empirical Integrative Analysis', *Journal of Management* 15(3), pp. 485–503.

Jennings, Daniel F. and Munn, Joseph R. (1994), 'Firm Size and Entrepreneurial Activity: Schumpeter's Hypothesis Revisited', Conference Paper, Waco TX: Hankamer School of Management, Baylor University.

Jones, Archer (1987), *The Art of War in the Western World*, London: Harrap Ltd.

Jones, Evan (1992), 'The Long Tyranny of Apriorism in Economic Thought', 21st Conference of Economists, The Economic Society of Australia.

Josephson, Matthew (1962, first published 1934), *The Robber Barons*, New York: Harcourt Brace Jovanovich.

Katz, R.L. (1970), *Cases and Concepts in Corporate Strategy*, Englewood Cliffs NJ: Prentice-Hall.

Kauffman, Stuart A. (1993), *The Origins of Order: self-organisation and selection in evolution*, New York: Oxford University Press.

Kay, John A. (1991), 'Economics and Business', *The Economic Journal*, 101, January, pp. 57–63.

Kay, John A. (1993a), 'Economics in Business', *Bureau of Industry Economics Occasional Paper 14 — 1993 Conference of Industry Economics*, Canberra: AGPS.

Kay, John A. (1993b), *Foundations of Corporate Succcess: How business strategies add value*, Oxford: Oxford University Press.

Kay, John A. and Silberston, Aubrey (1995), 'Corporate Governance', *National Institute Economic Review*, 153, August, pp. 84–97.

Kaynak, E. (1984), 'The Use of Marketing Research To Facilitate International Marketing Within Developing Countries', in E. Kaynak (ed.), *International Marketing Management*, New York: Praeger, pp. 155–71.

Kedia, B.L. and Chhokar, J. (1986), 'Factors Inhibiting Export Performance of Firms: An Empirical Investigation', *Management International Review*, 26(4), pp. 38–49.

Kerin, Roger A., Mahajan Vijay and Varadarajan P. Rajan (1990), *Contemporary Perspectives on Strategic Market Planning*, Boston: Allyn & Bacon.

Keynes, J.M. (1936), *The General Theory of Employment, Interest and Money*, Cambridge: Cambridge University Press.

Kinsey, J. (1982), 'The Role of Marketing in Economic Development', *European Journal of Marketing*, 16(6), pp. 64–77.

Kirchhoff, Bruce A. (1991), 'Entrepreneurship's Contribution to Economics', *Entrepreneurship Theory and Practice*, Winter.

Kirzner, Israel M. (1982), 'Uncertainty, Discovery and Human Action: A Study of the Entrepreneurial Profile in the Misesian System', in I.M. Kirzner (ed.) *Method, Process and Austrian Economics: Essays in Honour of Ludwig van Mises*, Lexington MA: D.C. Heath.

Kotler, P. (1994), *Marketing Management: Analysis, planning, implementation and control*, Englewood Cliffs, NJ: Prentice Hall.

Kracmar, J.Z. (1971), *Marketing Research in the Developing Countries: A Handbook*, New York: Praeger.

Krugman, Paul (1996), *The Self-Organizing Economy*, Cambridge MA: Blackwell.

Kuhn, Robert S. (1970), *The Structure of Scientific Revolutions*, 2nd edn (enlarged), Chicago: The University of Chicago Press.

Kuratko, Donald F. and Hodgetts, Richard M. (1989), *Entrepreneurship: a contemporary approach*, Chicago IL: The Dryden Press.

Kushner, J.M. (1982), 'Market Research in a Non-Western Context: The Asian Example', *Journal of the Market Research Society*, 24(2), pp. 116–22.

Langlois, Richard N. and Robertson, Paul L. (1994), 'An Evolutionary Approach to the Theory of the Firm', Conference paper, Canberra: Australian National University.

Lee, J.A. (1966), 'Cultural Analysis in Overseas Operations', March–April, pp. 106–14.

Legge, John M. (1992), *The Competitive Edge: How innovation creates and sustains the competitive advantage of enterprises*, Sydney: Allen & Unwin.

Legge, John M. (1993), *Pricing Strategy and Profit*, Melbourne: Longman Professional.

Levitt, Theodore (1965), 'Exploit the Product Life Cycle', *Harvard Business Review*, November–December, pp. 81–94.

Lewis, Michael (1990), *Liar's Poker – two cities, true greed*, London: Coronet Books.

Longenecker, Justin G. and Moore, Carlos W. (1991), *Small Business Management: An entrepreneurial emphasis*, 8th edn, Cincinnati: South Western Publishing.

Longford, Elizabeth (1972), *Wellington, Pillar of State*, London: Weidenfeld & Nicholson.

Lund, Daultram, Monroe, Kent and Choudhury, Pravat K. (1982), *Pricing Policies and Strategies: An annotated bibliography*, Chicago: American Marketing Association.

Lynn, Gary S. (1989), *From Concept To Market*, New York: John Wiley & Sons.

MacMillan, I.C. (1983), 'The Politics of New Venture Management', *Harvard Business Review*, November–December, pp. 8–16.

Mahajan, Vijay, Muller, Eitan and Bass, Frank M. (1990), 'New Product Diffusion Models in Marketing: A Review and Directions for Research', *Journal of Marketing*, 54(1), January, pp. 1–26.

Marketing News (1995), 'Creative marketing a must to generate mass appeal', 29(17), August 14.

Marsh, David(1992), *The Bundesbank: the bank that rules Europe*, London: Heineman.

Martin, P. and Burrow, M. (1991), *Applied Financial Mathematics*, Sydney: Prentice-Hall.

Martin, Stephen (1993), *Advanced Industrial Economics*, Oxford: Blackwell Publishers.

McGregor D. (1960), *The Human Side of Enterprise*, New York: McGraw-Hill.

McIntosh Baring (1993), *The Kangaroo Hops North: An Analysis of Australian Business Opportunities in Asia*, Melbourne: McIntosh & Co. Ltd.

McKinsey & Company (1993), *Emerging Exporters – Australia's High Value-added Manufacturing Exporters*, Melbourne: The Australian Manufacturing Council.

McLaughlin, Harold J. (1987), *Building Your Business Plan*, New York: John Wiley & Sons.

McLean, R. (1986), *Exploiting Opportunities in the Pacific Basin*, Melbourne: CEDA Strategic Issues Forum Publication.

McMahon, G.P., Holmes, S., Hutchinson, P.J. and Forsaith, D.M. (1993), *Small Enterprise Financial Management Theory and Practice*, Sydney: Harcourt Brace.

McQuown, Judith H. (1992), *Inc Yourself*, New York: Harper Collins.

Mintzberg, H. and Waters, J.A. (1982), 'Tracking Strategy in an Entrepreneurial Firm', *Academy of Management Journal*, 25(3), pp. 469–99.

Mintzberg, Henry (1994), *The Rise and Fall of Strategic Planning: Reconceiving roles for planning, plans, planners*, New York: The Free Press.

Modis, Theodore (1992), *Predictions*, New York: Simon & Schuster.

Monash Asia Institute (1993), 'The new rich in Asia: mobile phones, McDonald's and middle-class revolution' (Conference), Melbourne: Monash Asia Institute.

Monod, Jacques (1971), *Chance and Necessity* (tran. A. Wainhouse), New York: Knopf.

Nesheim, John L. (1992), *High Tech Start Up*, Saratoga CA: Electronic Trend Publications.

NIES Magazine (1993–94), Issue 9, December/January.

Nightingale, John (1993), 'Solving Marshall's Problem with the Biological Analogy: Jack Downie's Competitive Process', *History of Economics Review*, 20, Summer.

Nonaka, Ikujiro (1991), 'The Knowledge Creating Company', *Harvard Business Review*, November–December 1991.

Ormerod, Paul (1994), *The Death of Economics*, London: Faber & Faber.

Osgood, William R. and Curtin, Dennis P. (1984), *Preparing Your Business Plan With Lotus 1-2-3*, Englewood Cliffs NJ: Prentice-Hall.

Osgood, William R., Fletcher, William and Curtin, Dennis P. (1986), *Preparing Your Business Plan with Excel*, Berkeley, CA: Osborne McGraw Hill.

Otto, Glenn and Voss, Graham (1994), 'Long and Short Run Interactions of Public Capital, Private Output, Capital and Hours', Conference Paper, Sydney: School of Economics, University of New South Wales.

Overseas Trading (1993), 'Traditional Gift-giving Emphasises the Wrap', September, pp. 19–21.

Peterson, R.A. (1982), *Marketing Research*, Plano TX: Business Publications Inc.

Phillips, A. (1986), 'Theory and the Analysis of Financial Markets', in G. Libecap (ed.), *Advances in the Study of Entrepreneurship, Innovation and Economic Growth*, Greenwich CT: JAI Press.

Piercy, N. (1988), 'Export Marketing Strategy: Can Firms Afford the Key Market Concentration Strategy?' in M.J. Thomas and N.E. Waite (eds) *The Marketing Digest*, London: Heinemann.

Porter, Michael E. (1980), *Competitive Strategy: Techniques for analysing industries and competitors*, New York: The Free Press.

Porter, Michael E. (1985), *Competitive Advantage: Creating and sustaining superior performance*, New York: The Free Press.

Porter, Michael E. (1990), *The Competitive Advantage of Nations*, New York: The Free Press.

Prahalad, C.K. and Hamel, Gary (1990), 'The Core Competence of the Corporation', *Harvard Business Review*, May–June 1990.

Pusey, Michael (1991), *Economic Rationalism in Canberra: a nation-building state changes its mind*, Sydney: Cambridge University Press.

Rand, Ayn (1985), *Atlas Shrugged*, New York: Signet.

Rice, Craig S. (1990), *Strategic Planning for the Small Business*, Holbrook MA: Bob Adams Inc.

Rich, Robert D. and Peters, Michael P. (1989), *Entrepreneurship – Starting, developing & managing a new enterprise*, Homewood IL: Richard D. Irwin.

Rich, Stanley R. and Gumpert, David E. (1985), *Business Plans That Win*, New York: Harper & Row.

Richardson, Bill and Richardson, Roy (1992), *Business Planning: An approach to strategic management*, London: Pitman.

Richardson, Michael (1995), 'Regional Building Boom Attracting CSR's Expansion', the *Australian*, April 7.

Ridley, Jasper (1970), *Lord Palmerston*, London: Constable.

Roberts, Edward B. (1983), 'Business Planning in the Start-Up High Technology Enterprise' in Hornaday and others, *Frontiers of Entrepreneurship Research*, Wellesley MA: Babson College.

Roberts, Peter (1996), 'NRMA finds lowering staff turnover pays off', *Australian Financial Review*, 1 May.

Roethlisberger, F.J. and Dixon, W. J. (1949), *Management and the Worker*, Cambridge MA: Harvard University Press.

Romer, Paul M. (1986), 'Increasing Returns and Long Run Growth', *Journal of Political Economy*, 94.

Romer, Paul M. (1993), 'Implementing a National Technology Strategy with Self-Organising Industry Investment Boards', *Brookings Papers: Microeconomics*, 2, pp. 345–99.

Romer, Paul M. (1994), 'The Origins of Endogenous Growth', *Journal of Economic Perspectives*, 8(1), Winter, pp. 3–22.

Ronstadt, Robert (1989), *Entrepreneurial Financials*, Natick MA: Lord Publishing Inc.

Ropp, Theodore (1959), *War in the Modern World*, Durham NC: Duke University Press.

Rothschild, Michael L. (1992), *Bionomics: the inevitability of capitalism*, London: Futura Publications.

Ryan, Fergus (1989), *Report Of Inquiry — Victorian Economic Development Corporation*, Melbourne: Government Printer.

Ryan, Graeme (1985), *Business Planning — How to kiss a princess*, Chatswood, NSW: G&S Ryan Pty Ltd.

Sa, J.V. and Hambrick, D.C. (1989), 'Key Success Factors: Test of a General Theory in the Mature Industrial-product Sector', *Strategic Management Journal*, 10, pp. 367–82.

Sahlman, William A. and Stevenson, Howard H. (1992), *The Entrepreneurial Venture*, Boston, MA: Harvard Business School Publications.

Samson, Danny (1988), *Preparing a Business Plan*, Canberra: AGPS.

Samuelson, Paul A. and others (1992), *Economics*, 3rd edn (Australia), Sydney: McGraw-Hill.

Schillit, W. Keith (1990), *Entrepreneur's Guide to Preparing a Winning Business Plan*, Englewood Cliffs NJ: Prentice-Hall.

Schumpeter, Joseph A. (1933), 'The Analysis of Economic Change', *The Review of Economic Statistics*, XVII(4), May, pp. 2–10.

Schumpeter, Joseph A. (1939), *Business Cycles: A Theoretical, Historical, and Statistical Analysis of the Capitalist Process*, New York: McGraw-Hill, reprinted 1982, Philadelphia: Porcupine Press.

Schumpeter, Joseph A. (1942), *Capitalism, Socialism and Democracy*, New York: Harper & Row.

Sculley, J. with Burne, J.A. (1988), *Odyssey: From Pepsi to Apple*, New York: Fontana/Collins.

Serle, Geoffrey (1982), *John Monash: A biography*, Melbourne: Melbourne University Press

Shell Australia (1993), *The Shell Report: The Essence of Leadership*, November.

Shewhart, W.A. (1931), *Economic Control of Quality of Manufactured Product*, New York: Van Nostrand.

Siegel, Eric S., Schultz, Lauren A. and Ford, Brian R. (1988), *The Arthur Young Business Plan Guide*, Chichester: John Wiley & Sons.

SRC News (1993), 'Retail revolution continues', No. 71, February.

Stanton, J.L., Chandran, R. and Hernandez, S.A. (1982), 'Marketing Research Problems in Latin America', *Journal of the Market Research Society*, 24(2), pp. 124–39.

Star newspaper (1991), 'Malaysia Countertrade Steadily Rises', December 4.

Stevenson, Howard H., Roberts, Michael J. and Grousbeck, H. Irving (1989), *New Business Ventures and the Entrepreneur*, 3rd edn, Homewood IL: Irwin.

Stevenson, Howard H., Roberts, Michael J. and Grousbeck, H. Irving (1994), *New Business Ventures and the Entrepreneur*, 4th edn, Burr Ridge IL: Irwin.

Stuckey, John and White, David (1993), 'When and when not to vertically integrate', *Sloan Management Review*, Spring, reprinted in 1993 in *The McKinsey Quarterly* (3).

Sultan, Fareena, Farley, John U. and Lehmann, Donald R. (1990), 'A Meta-Analysis of Applications of Diffusion Models', *Journal of Marketing Research*, XXVII, February, pp. 70–7.

Taguchi, C. (1985), *What is Total Quality Control? The Japanese Way*, Englewood Cliffs NJ: Prentice-Hall.

Taguchi, C. (1986), *Introduction to Quality Engineering: designing quality into products and processes*, New York: Kraus.

Tanzer, Andrew (1993), 'The students who rose up and ate their teacher', *Business Review Weekly*, 12 February.

Taylor, James W. (1986), *How to Create A Winning Business Plan*, New York: Modern Business Reports.

Tetsuo Sakiya (1982), *Honda Motor: The men, the management, the machines* (tran. Kiyoshi Ikemi), Tokyo: Kodansha: 1982.

Teweles, R.J., Harlow, C.V. and Stone, H.L. (1977), *The Commodity Futures Game. Who Wins? Who Loses? Why?*, New York: McGraw-Hill.

Timmons, J.A. (1982), 'New Venture Creation: Models and Methodologies' in C. Kent, D. Sexton and K. Vesper (eds), *Encyclopedia of Entrepreneurship*, Englewood Cliffs NJ: Prentice Hall, pp. 126–39.

Timmons, J.A. (1990), *New Venture Creation: Entrepreneurship in the 1990s*, 3rd edn, Homewood IL: Irwin.

Tisdell, Clem (1994), *Economic Justification for Government Support of Research and Development: A review of modern microeconomic literature and its policy implications*, Canberra: Industry Commission.

Tolkein, J.R.R. (1966), *The Lord of the Rings*, London: George Allen & Unwin.

Toohey, Brian (1994), *Tumbling Dice: the story of modern economic policy*, Melbourne: William Heinemann Australia.

Townsend, Robert (1970), *Up the Organisation*, London: Coronet.

Tugendhat, C. (1973), *The Multinationals*, Harmondsworth: Penguin Books Ltd.

Tuncalp, S. (1985), 'The Marketing Research Scene in Saudi Arabia', *European Journal of Marketing*, 22(5), pp. 15–21.

Van Horne, J., Davis, K., Nicol, R. and Wright, K. (1990), *Financial Management & Policy In Australia*, 3rd edn, New York: Prentice Hall.

Varadarajan, P. Rajan (1984), 'Marketing in Developing Countries: The New Frontier', *Long Range Planning* 17(6), pp. 118–26.

Vesper, Karl H. (1993), *New Venture Mechanics*, Englewood Cliffs NJ: Prentice-Hall.

Vogelaar, Donald H. (1991a), *How To Write a Business Plan*, Melbourne: Information Australia Group.

Vogelaar, Donald H. (1991b), *How To Write Your Business Plan — Workbook*, Sydney: Prentice-Hall.

Von Neuman, J. and Morgenstern O. (1964), *The Theory of Games and Economic Behaviour*, New York: Wiley.

Wade, R (1990), *Governing the Market: Economic Theory and the Role of Government in East Asian Industrialisation*, Princeton NJ: Princeton University Press.

Waldrop, M. Mitchell (1992), *Complexity: The Emerging Science at the Edge of Order and Chaos*, New York: Simon & Schuster.

Wall, James A. (1986), *Negotiation: Theory and Practice*, Glenview IL: Scott, Freeman & Co.

Ward, John, Griffiths, Pat and Whitmore, Paul (1990), *Strategic Planning for Information Systems*, Chichester: John Wiley & Sons.

Welsh, John A. and White, Jerry F. (1983), *The Entrepreneur's Master Planning Guide*, Englewood Cliffs NJ: Prentice-Hall.

Wenban, R., Hindle, K.G. and Jennings, D.F. (1996), 'How to Catch an Angel: a survey of profiles and perspectives in Australia's private equity market', *School of Management Working Papers*, Melbourne: Swinburne University of Technology.

Weston, J.F. and Brigham, E.F. (1993), *Essentials of Managerial Finance*, 11th edn, Fort Worth: The Dryden Press Harcourt Brace Jovanovich International edition.

Wilson, Derek (1988), *Rothschild: a story of wealth and power*, London: Mandarin Paperbacks.

World Bank, the (1991), *Global Economic Prospects and the Developing Countries*.

Wright, Rod (1993), 'Sub-groups are the key to markets,' *Ad News*, April 23, pp. 45–7.

Wrong, Dennis (ed.) (1970) *Max Weber*, Prentice Hall: Englewood Cliffs NJ.

Yetton, P., Davis, J. and Swan, P. (1992), *Going International: Export Myths and Strategic Realities*, Melbourne, The Australian Manufacturing Council.

Zhukov, Georgi K. (1969), *Marshal Zhukov's Greatest Battles* (ed. Harrison Salisbury), London: Macdonald

End notes

1 The term 'innovation' was used in the eighteenth and early nineteenth centuries as a pejorative reference to attempts to change the Order of Service of the Church of England. When contemporaries referred to John Wesley as an 'innovator' they were not intending to flatter him.

2 Pierre Simon, Marquis de Laplace (1749–1827) was a French mathematician and astronomer who completed Newton's work on the solar system. He came to believe that the universe could be completely explained by a system of equations to the point that, if some super-intelligent being knew the position and velocity of every particle in the universe at a particular time, that being would also know the entire history and future of the universe. Later mathematicians have proved that a Laplacian being, if it were to exist, must be infinitely more complex than the universe itself.

Index